This book comes with access to more content online.

Watch videos, take practice tests,
and study with flashcards!

Register your book or ebook at
www.dummies.com/go/getaccess.

Select your product, and then follow the prompts
to validate your purchase.

You'll receive an email with your PIN and instructions.

Real Estate License Exams

4th Edition

by John A. Yoegel, PhD
Certified New York real estate instructor

Real Estate License Exams For Dummies®, 4th Edition

Published by: **John Wiley & Sons, Inc.,** 111 River Street, Hoboken, NJ 07030-5774, www.wiley.com

Copyright © 2021 by John Wiley & Sons, Inc., Hoboken, New Jersey

Published simultaneously in Canada

For general information on our other products and services, please contact our Customer Care Department within the U.S. at 877-762-2974, outside the U.S. at 317-572-3993, or fax 317-572-4002. For technical support, please visit www.wiley.com/techsupport.

Wiley publishes in a variety of print and electronic formats and by print-on-demand. Some material included with standard print versions of this book may not be included in e-books or in print-on-demand. If this book refers to media such as a CD or DVD that is not included in the version you purchased, you may download this material at http://booksupport.wiley.com. For more information about Wiley products, visit www.wiley.com.

Library of Congress Control Number: 2020942792

ISBN: 978-1-119-72485-8

ISBN 978-1-119-72484-1 (ebk); ISBN 978-1-119-72486-5 (ebk)

Manufactured in the United States of America

SKY10021519_092920

Contents at a Glance

Table of Contents

Introduction

S o you want to become a real estate agent? Welcome to the book that's going to help you become one. Being a real estate agent is an extremely attractive career for many people. If you like looking at houses and other kinds of property and enjoy meeting and working with people, this job may be for you. Add to that having a flexible work schedule, essentially running your own business, and being rewarded for working hard and smart, and you've pretty much described a career in real estate sales.

Somewhere along the line, however, you discovered that real estate sales is a licensed occupation. Don't worry, though; I wrote this book specifically to help you get that license. Ready for the full scoop? Read on, you soon-to-be real estate agent.

About This Book

Every state requires real estate agents to have a license to practice their occupation. Every state, at a minimum, also requires that you take and pass a state examination to get that license. Most states require more than just an exam. After you've made up your mind to become a real estate salesperson or broker (brokers' licenses usually are obtained after you've spent time as a salesperson), you need to find out what the procedure is for getting your license in your particular state. Because most states have an educational requirement, I assume that you have to take a course before obtaining your real estate license.

So how does this book fit in with your education? I wrote it specifically with the idea of:

>> Giving you material that is focused on the exam rather than general real estate practice.

>> Providing you with an additional resource that contains explanations and examples of material that you may encounter in the classroom, in a textbook, or on the exam.

>> Preparing folks in states that have no education requirements for their state exam.

>> Providing practice exams with explanations of the answers to help you prepare for the exam.

>> Helping you study key terms with flashcards online.

As the title states, this book is designed to help you prepare for and pass the state exam. In it, I discuss a wide variety of topics, such as the basics of the job, different real estate laws, the details of owning and transferring property, and issues such as contracts, leasing, and environmental regulations. Think that's a lot? Well, I also cover everything you ever wanted to know about numbers stuff, from appraising property to calculating mortgages, taxes, and investments. And to pull it all together, each chapter contains review questions, and I provide four full-length practice exams (complete with answers and explanations) to help you get ready for the real thing.

If you're a regular *For Dummies* reader, you know that a *For Dummies* book takes a modular approach to giving you information. That means you can pretty much read a section or a chapter and get the information you need without necessarily reading the entire book. That's true of this book, too. Although you certainly don't have to read the entire book to get what you need from it, it's okay if you do. I also provide you with plenty of cross-references so you don't have to remember where related subjects are. And just like all *For Dummies* books, feel free to skip sidebars; they offer good reading material, but their content isn't covered on the exam. A few terms I've written about in this book are common to most chapters. Understanding them can help you get the most out of what you read and study and will prepare you for the exam because you'll run into some of them there, too.

>> I use the term "real estate agent" to mean anyone who holds some form of license to represent someone else for a fee in a real estate transaction. In most places, there are at least two levels of licensure: broker and salesperson. Some states have more than two. Unless I'm referring to a specific type of license, I use the term "real estate agent."

>> The terms "real estate" and "property" are used interchangeably. Even though real estate has a technical definition that I give you in Chapter 6, conversational convention is to use those two terms to mean the same thing. The term "property" can be modified as personal property, which is also defined in Chapter 6. It can also mean "vacant land," but that is made clear as necessary.

>> The term "land" usually means vacant land, or land without structures on it, but it may also be used as a reference to the land-only portion of a property that has a structure on it. For example, "He bought a piece of land on which to build a house." "Her house sits on very rocky land."

>> The word "transaction" as I use it in this book involves any real estate deal. It can and often does mean a change of ownership, but it can also mean negotiating and signing a lease or some other real estate agreement.

>> I use the words "convey" and "transfer" generally to mean a change in ownership. Real estate can be sold, given away, willed, and exchanged. All of these are conveyances or transfers of ownership.

>> You may want to go to a party after you pass your real estate exam, but until then, I use the word "party" simply to mean a person or a company, as in, "There were two parties to the deal, a buyer and a seller."

>> The terms "landlord" and "tenant" can often be substituted for the terms "buyer" and "seller" when discussing items such as a real estate agent's representation of someone. In other cases the references are a bit more specific, but you won't have any trouble figuring out what I'm talking about.

>> When discussing the relationship of a real estate agent to the person he represents, I use the terms "principal" and "client" interchangeably. The agent represents the principal, also known as the client.

Here's some general information about what this book is *not* about. Many real estate textbooks on the market are designed to teach you about real estate. Some of them are used as textbooks in prelicensing real estate courses. Without going into a long explanation about the different approaches that each of these books takes, I want to be clear that this is *not* a real estate textbook.

Don't base anything you do in your real estate practice only on what you read in this book. That doesn't mean that this book does not contain accurate information about general real estate concepts. It does. But as I wrote this book, I had to leave out pieces of information or finer details simply because I don't believe you'll be tested on them. I think this book not only fulfills the purpose of preparing you to take the state exam, but it also provides a general overview of real estate issues. In all cases, whether in your real estate practice or sitting for the exam, you need to defer to information provided by your state licensing authority and any local prelicensing courses you may be required to take if it conflicts with the information in this book.

This book also doesn't provide legal advice. I'm not an attorney. Real estate sales and related issues are full of topics that many people, including attorneys, believe are matters that require an attorney's advice or that are best left up to an attorney. I unequivocally advise you that in any issue involving a legal matter, first and foremost, consult an attorney.

One last thing I want to mention concerns the subject of construction — not of the sentences in this book but rather of houses and other buildings. A significant inconsistency exists between and among states regarding whether they require you to know anything about construction for a state-licensing exam. It's obviously a pretty detailed topic, and I do encourage you to learn something about construction techniques and materials as you start your real estate career. I even include some material about construction regulations in this book. (If you're curious, check out Chapter 8.) In the interest of space, however, because of this inconsistency I decided to leave out a detailed chapter on construction. You do, however, need to find out whether knowledge of construction techniques, systems, and materials is a requirement for your state exam and then study the appropriate material.

Foolish Assumptions

I hope I'm not being too foolish, but the following are my assumptions about you, dear reader:

>> You're going to take, are taking, or have taken a prelicensing course for the real estate license that you're seeking (salesperson or broker), or, if your state doesn't require a course, you've already checked to see what the state wants you to know for the exam.

>> You're an aspiring real estate agent who needs a tactical guide to improving your score on the real estate license exam.

>> You still have to work for a living because you haven't won the state lottery, and you know that real estate can be a great career.

>> You're wanting some general knowledge about how real estate works and what agents do. You won't be disappointed and maybe you'll decide to become a real agent after all.

>> You have a reasonably good command of the English language. Both state exam writers and I assume this. Don't get discouraged if English is your second language, though. You may want to read what I have to say about this topic in Chapter 2.

Icons Used in This Book

The following icons are designed to help you use this book quickly and easily. Be sure to keep an eye out for them.

EXAMPLE

This icon points out sample questions within chapter discussions.

STATE SPECIFIC

Items marked with this icon may vary from one state to the next. I usually give some general information about the subject, but when you see this icon, you need to check out the specifics in your own state. Where do you look for those specifics? In general, if you're not required to take a course or use a textbook to take your state exam, all the material you need to read probably is available from your state licensing agency. (I give you information about how to find your state agency in Chapter 1.) In states where you have to take a course, make sure you look for and study those items that I mention as state-specific in your textbook or course handouts, or ask your instructor about them. I talk about this more in Chapter 27.

REMEMBER

This icon points to information that's especially important to remember for exam purposes.

TIP

This icon presents information like a memory acronym or some other aid to understanding or remembering material.

WARNING

When you see this icon, pay special attention. The information that follows may be somewhat difficult, confusing, or harmful.

Beyond This Book

In addition to what you're reading right now, this book comes with a free access-anywhere Cheat Sheet that includes tips to help you prepare for the real estate licensing exam. To get this Cheat Sheet, simply go to www.dummies.com and type Real Estate Licensing Exam For Dummies Cheat Sheet in the Search box.

You also get access to four full-length online practice tests and approximately 500 flashcards. To gain access to the online practice, all you have to do is register. Just follow these simple steps:

1. Register your book or ebook at Dummies.com to get your PIN. Go to www.dummies.com/go/getaccess.

2. Select your product from the dropdown list on that page.

3. Follow the prompts to validate your product, and then check your email for a confirmation message that includes your PIN and instructions for logging in.

If you don't receive this email within two hours, please check your spam folder before contacting us through our Technical Support website at http://support.wiley.com or by phone at 877-762-2974.

Now you're ready to go! You can come back to the practice material as often as you want — simply log on with the username and password you created during your initial login. No need to enter the access code a second time.

Your registration is good for one year from the day you activate your PIN.

You can also check out the free Cheat Sheet at www.dummies.com for some helpful definitions of terms, explanation of ownership, and a reminder of the fiduciary responsibilities of an agent.

Where to Go from Here

First things first: Contact your state real estate licensing authority and get the information you need for the kind of license you'll be applying for, such as a salesperson's license or a broker's license. (You can get information on how to find your licensing agency in Chapter 1.) If you're still not sure or you're a little confused about where you're headed, you may want to start your reading in Chapter 3, which explains the different jobs real estate agents do.

The information you want from your state includes a copy of the license law, an application, information on the content of the exam (if available), and any other information available about obtaining your real estate license. You may be able to get this information online. (If you're already a broker, you probably are familiar with most of this. If you're new to the field, you want the package of information your state sends out for people who want to become a licensed salesperson.)

When you get it, read the information carefully and take the next step. That may be enrolling in a course. In a few cases, it may mean studying the license law and the other information the state sends you. You have to do this anyway, but in states with no education requirement, studying this information and the material in this book is your preparation for the state exam. In either case, check out the chapters in this book that correspond with the subjects required for the type of license you're getting (see the Table of Contents for help) and start studying. Before you actually take the exam, be sure to check out the information about the basics of the exam in Chapter 1 and my best studying and test-taking strategies in Chapter 2. After studying the different subjects areas for the exams, take the four practice exams in this book. You can download a fill-in-the-bubble answer sheet at www.dummies.com/go/relebubblesheets and use it as you take each practice exam. Download as many sheets as you need. (You also can use them for the ten sample questions at the end of chapters that discuss the subject areas.)

If I were your personal tutor as you embark on your real estate education, I'd instruct you to do the following:

>> Go to class, pay attention, do the homework, and keep up with the reading.

>> As you progress through your course, study the material in this book related to the material you're covering in class.

>> After completing a section or chapter, test yourself with the practice questions at the end of each chapter, and then diagnose your need for more study accordingly.

>> When you're ready to take the state exam, take the four practice exams. Use them to diagnose your need for more study in specific areas. I've constructed the exams to make it easy to diagnose where you may need more study.

>> Make sure you study your state real estate license law for state-specific information that you may need to know.

>> Take the state test, pass it, get your license, and start earning your first million.

1
Putting Real Estate License Exams into Perspective

IN THIS PART . . .

Understand the different real estate licenses and exams and what each type of license requires and allows you to do.

Incorporate some test-taking tips and tricks in your arsenal to help you pass your exam with as little stress as possible, including some advice for preparing to take the exam as well as hints to help you while you're in the middle of taking the exam.

Conquer your mathphobia with some solid advice and tips for getting through the math sections of the real estate license exam.

Figure out how the exams are scored, how the scores are determined, and how you can achieve a high score.

Chapter 1

Sold! Taking a Glance at Real Estate License Exams

A state exam is one of the steps you need to take on your journey to becoming a licensed real estate agent. You may think that it's the most intimidating step, but don't worry; that's where this book comes in. In this chapter, I provide you with information to make sure the exam process isn't a total surprise and show you a few specific details to check out in your state.

REMEMBER

Because individual states issue real estate licenses, the ultimate authority on the state exam is your own home state. You'll probably get a copy of the state license law and the state-specific information you need about the exam from the instructor of the prelicensing course you may have to take. (See "Figuring out licensing procedures" later in this chapter for more details.) If you don't get the information from your instructor or if you're in one of the few states that doesn't require a prelicensing course, you can write to your state-licensing agency or go online to find information. Different states have different agencies that handle real estate licensing, but using a search engine like Google can get you where you need to go. Just type in your state's name followed by the words "real estate license law," "real estate commission," "real estate board," or "real estate licensing agency," and see what websites are listed. If you don't have access to a computer, try calling information in your state capital and asking for the agency's phone number, using any of the names I listed.

Checking Out Licensing and Exam Basics

Most states have at least two license levels for their real estate agents: salesperson and broker. (Briefly, a *real estate broker* is someone authorized by the state to perform certain activities such as sales on behalf of another person for a fee. A *salesperson* is someone licensed to do those activities but only under a broker's supervision. See Chapter 3 for more.)

Some states may have other levels or types of licensing, such as a time-share agent, associate broker, or salesperson apprentice or trainee. In any case, a state agency administers real estate license exams in each state (different states may have different names for their licensing agencies). In the following sections, I give you the lowdown on licensing procedures, the differences between the licensing and exams for salespeople and brokers, and the format of the exams themselves.

Figuring out licensing procedures

STATE SPECIFIC

After you decide to pursue a career in real estate, the next thing you need to do is get as much information as you can about the procedure for obtaining your license. Every state has specific requirements regarding age, citizenship, criminal background, education, and so on. For specifics about all of these necessities, you need to consult your state's license law directly. Each state's real estate license law typically has provisions about how to become a real estate agent in that state. In addition, it often has specific requirements regarding procedures to follow in your actual real estate business. And by the way, state exams often contain a few questions about the requirements to get your license, such as how old you have to be or the citizenship requirements. You need to get a copy of your state's license law either from the state website or from your instructor.

STATE SPECIFIC

Your state licensing system may treat real estate licensing educational requirements and testing in a wide range of ways. Very few states have no educational requirements whatsoever and require only that you pass the state exam. Other states require that you take (and pass) a minimum number of classroom (or online) hours of education before you sit for the exam. And still other states require you to take not only a minimum number of classroom hours, an apprenticeship, and more educational courses, but also a state exam after one or both classroom experiences. You likely have to take more coursework and pass another exam to become a broker, so expect to become a salesperson first, and get some experience before you can move up to the broker level.

Assume that where education is required — and it is in most if not all states — you have to pass a course exam in addition to the state exam. Your state may have only an attendance requirement, but be prepared for a course exam nonetheless. Where there is a course exam, it's usually similar to the state exam. This book helps you do well on both exams.

WARNING

As for the state exam, some states allow you to walk in and take the state salesperson exam before you complete the required education. Not much point in doing so in my opinion, because the education always helps prepare you for the state exam. And the course exam is good practice for the state exam.

Knowing the difference between salesperson and broker licensing and exams

In most cases, you're probably pursuing the first or basic real estate license level — in some states it's a salesperson's license; in others it's some form of salesperson trainee. How you move up the real estate ladder varies among the different states. The following illustrates two of the many possibilities.

In one case, you complete all of the necessary requirements, including taking and passing a state exam, to become a licensed real estate salesperson. And that's it. You can stay a salesperson for the rest of your career. To become a broker in this situation, you probably have to gain some experience, take additional coursework, and pass yet another state exam.

In the second case, you begin your real estate career by getting a license at whatever level your state provides as an apprentice or trainee, which can involve taking a course and/or a state exam. After a prescribed period of experience, you're required to move up to the level of a full-fledged, licensed salesperson, which can mean more coursework and another licensing exam. You can remain a salesperson for your entire career in this case, too. Moving up the next rung on the ladder to the broker's level usually involves additional coursework, an exam, and additional experience.

I need to add here that some states may have a way for you to skip part of the salesperson licensing procedure. Although it rarely occurs, doing so usually requires previous real estate experience. The experience may not exempt you from taking all of the required courses, but it may enable you to skip the salesperson exam. You can find out whether your state allows this exemption by checking the license law and speaking with your state-licensing agency. The state has final say over what constitutes a qualifying equivalent but, for example, someone who has bought, sold, and leased a significant number of his own investment properties might have the necessary experience.

REMEMBER

Your job as it relates to this book is to identify the particular exam you have to pass at this stage of your real estate career. If you're taking your first-ever exam, you're at the salesperson level or the salesperson trainee level. If you're already a licensed salesperson, you're shooting for the broker level. Then you need to find out the subject matter on the exam. In the vast majority of states, you're required to take coursework to get your license. Figuring out what you're tested on and using this book to help you is relatively easy. Just match up the material in the course with the various subjects in this book. If you're not required to take coursework to get your license, you can find out your particular exam's subject matter by checking with your state licensing agency and still use this book to provide information and further explanation of the required material.

This book covers as many of the subject areas as are typical on a variety of state exams. In general, fewer topics are covered on the salesperson's exam than on the broker's exam. Broker's exams cover more subjects because more topics have been added to the list of subjects you learned at the salesperson's level. For example, a state might test you on property management, which I cover in Chapter 3, on the broker's exam but not on the salesperson's exam. So if you're taking the salesperson's exam in that state, you don't need to worry about property management; however, if you're taking the broker's exam, it's time to brush up on your property management knowledge.

WARNING

If you're using this book to prepare for a broker's exam, be aware that many brokers' exams presume that you learned and remembered everything you covered in your salesperson's course. Although the emphasis may be on broker subject matter, topics typically on a salesperson's exam are fair game on the broker's exam. So it's a good idea to review all the material from the salesperson's exam as well as the new broker's material you learned if you're taking the broker's exam.

The topics at the salesperson's level are usually covered at a more basic level than on the broker's exam. Definitions and terminology are most important on the salesperson's exam. The broker's exam doesn't cover just additional topics; it may require you to apply your knowledge to specific examples and questions.

Two other subjects that should be mentioned for special consideration and preparation are math and ethics. Where appropriate, math formulas and problems are covered in the individual chapters in this book. In addition, Chapter 18 covers a variety of typical real estate math problems. The amount of math on the state exam varies by state. You need to know real estate math to be an effective real estate agent, but especially for you math-phobics you need to find out how much math is on your state exam.

Ethics is another subject that varies by state. You need to find out if your state has its own code of ethics for real estate agents or if it expects adherence to the code of ethics and standards of the National Association of Realtors. Most importantly for passing the exam, you need to find out how much emphasis there is on ethics questions on the state exam.

Looking at the format and other exam details

At any point in time (for example, a week after this book comes out), a state may decide to change its exam content or structure; therefore, talking with any certainty about exam formats is pretty much impossible. Ultimately the format of the exam really shouldn't matter when compared with a mastery of the material you have to know. Different structures have different approaches to the same material. If you know the material, the structure won't matter.

Most (if not all) states currently use a multiple-choice question format. Most people feel more comfortable with this format, and students believe these exams are easier to pass because the choices already have been narrowed down for you. Because most states use this format, I've chosen to write all the practice questions in this book, including the four full-length practice exams, in a multiple-choice format. How's that for service?

Exams are either a single, undivided exam or broken into two parts: a general part that covers key concepts, such as forms of real estate ownership, fiduciary responsibilities, and fair housing law, and a state-specific part. In this book you see many state-specific icons directing you to information that may vary from state to state. This type of information may end up on the state-specific part of these exams. In addition, any questions about state license law are covered in the state-specific part of the exam. (For more about license law, see Chapter 3.)

STATE SPECIFIC

You should check with your course instructor or the state-licensing agency about the following exam details:

>> Number of questions on the exam you're taking. The salesperson's and broker's exams may have a different number of questions.

>> Whether the exam is a single exam or whether it's broken into general and state-specific parts. If the exam is divided into parts, find out how many questions are in each part. If the exam is given in two parts, must you pass both parts at the same time; if you don't pass one part but pass the other, can you retake the part you didn't pass or must you retake the entire exam.

>> Whether the questions are multiple-choice or whether any other question format is used.

>> The form of the exam (paper and pencil or computer).

>> The time available to complete the exam.

There are a few other questions you should ask about exam procedures, such as what to bring to the exam. I give you this information in the following sections, as well as offer some hints about successful test-taking strategies in Chapter 2.

Sign Me Up: Registering for the Exam

You've fulfilled all your state's requirements. You've taken a course, read the license laws, and so on. These procedures definitely vary by state. In general, though, you have to send an application to the state at some point so you can take the exam. You may have to send the state a completion certificate as evidence that you passed the required prelicensing coursework, and you probably have to submit a fee. Your state's exam regulations detail whether the fee needs to be paid with cash, check, credit card, or another method. In the case of the salesperson's exam, some states require you to have your application form signed by a sponsoring broker. (You can find out more about the relationship between a salesperson to a broker in Chapter 3.)

It's likely that you have to register online to get a date to take the exam. After completing and sending the appropriate materials to the state licensing agency, you receive an entry permit in the mail or a printable one online allowing you to take the exam. You also receive information on where and when to arrive for the exam, as well as a list of anything else you might need to bring with you (see the next section). Read all of the information carefully and follow the instructions exactly. If you have any questions, contact the state-licensing agency well before the exam.

Keep in mind that in some states they may allow you to take the test by simply showing up at the exam site with identification and the fee in hand. This is usually referred to as a walk-in exam.

STATE SPECIFIC

Whatever the procedure may be, find out what it is from your course instructor or the state-licensing agency, and follow it carefully. It's silly and completely unnecessary to have your application returned because you forgot to sign it or sent in the wrong amount for the fee.

Knowing What to Take to the Exam . . . and What to Leave at Home

The big day is almost here. You passed with flying colors whatever prelicensing course you had to take. You also filled out and sent in your application for the exam and got something back in the mail telling you where and when to show up. You reviewed everything in this book that applies to the test you're taking, and you're ready to go. Now start packing.

REMEMBER

In some places, the question of what to bring to the exam has produced an art unto itself. General security issues are in effect in many public buildings, and you also need to deal with security issues that are specifically pertinent to exam-taking. The key here is simple. Read all of the literature you can find from the state licensing agency or the testing company your state uses to find out about what you can and cannot bring to the exam. (Some states have contracted with private companies to administer exams; if this is the case in your state, you can get contact information about this from your state licensing agency.) If you have a specific question that isn't covered in the material, you can call or email the state agency or testing company and get an answer to your question. In general, the items you need to bring are:

>> **A calculator:** Pay attention to the requirements for a calculator. Calculators are usually required to be silent, battery-powered, and nonprogrammable. In general, anything that can carry text won't be permitted. Those of you who have a calculator feature built into your cell phones may not be permitted to use them. In some places, you have to sign a form indicating the kind of calculator you're using.

TIP

If you're using a battery-powered calculator, change the batteries a few days before the exam, or bring two calculators. If changing the batteries in your calculator is really easy (you don't need a screwdriver or some other tool), you can also bring new batteries with you, just in case.

>> **An entry permit:** Make sure that you bring the entry permit that you received in the mail after you sent in your application, because it and any other necessary paperwork may be the only documents that enable you to take the exam. Necessary paperwork varies from state to state, so it's pretty difficult to tell you exactly what you need to bring, but at a minimum you need

that entry permit. In states that permit walk-ins at exams, you may need the application itself, plus the fee and probably one or two forms of identification.

TIP

» **No. 2 pencils:** Some states have gone to a computerized testing format. If that's not the case in your state, then you probably need some of those famous No. 2 pencils. Bring more than two with erasers. If you buy new ones, sharpen them before you go to the exam; don't depend on there being a pencil sharpener at the exam site. Sharpened No. 2 pencils are a little hard to carry. I always put them in a standard-size (No.10) envelope. And remember that even if the exam is computerized, you may be able to use scrap paper for making notes or doing calculations.

» **A pen:** Bringing along a pen with blue or black ink is a good idea in case you have to fill out some form that's better completed in ink than in pencil.

» **A photo ID:** An ID of some sort is pretty standard, so bring a photo ID with you. Not all photo IDs are created equal; for example, your state may not count your new photo ID library card. You may even be required to present two forms of ID. And if you're not a citizen, have the appropriate documentation with you showing your status.

» **A certificate from your prelicensing course:** Your state may require you to bring the certificate you received that shows that you passed your prelicensing course. In some cases, you may have already sent it in with your application and don't need to bring it. In either case, when you get the certificate saying that you passed the course, make sure you make a copy of the certificate and keep it in a safe place before you ever send it or give it to anyone. States have been known to lose documents. Some states require that the real estate school you went to send documentation directly from the school to the state certifying that you successfully completed the course. Check to see if your real estate school does that.

WARNING

You probably won't be allowed to bring scrap paper, food, books, notes, and so on to the exam. In a worst case, you may be turned away from the exam site if you have any of these items with you. In a situation almost as bad, you may be asked to leave the unauthorized item(s) in the hallway outside the exam room. If you need to bring food or water because of a medical condition, make sure you get permission first before the day of the exam. In addition, if you need to make accommodations for a handicap, like the use of a wheelchair, make sure those arrangements are made before the day of the exam.

Scoring High: Figuring Out How Scores Are Determined

STATE SPECIFIC

Information about scores is available from your state licensing agency or the testing agency (if any) used by your state. Here are a few points you may want to consider:

» Check out whether all the questions have equal weight. For example, a state may give an exam with 100 questions, all worth one point. But another state may give a two-part exam, with the first part having 80 general real estate questions worth one point each and the second part having 40 state-specific questions worth half of a point each. I've found in my teaching that this kind of information seems to provide comfort to the students because they feel like they know what's going on. To some extent, knowing which questions have more weight may guide your studying, but in any case, you have to answer enough questions correctly to pass.

>> Scoring may vary from state to state; most places give you a percentage based on the number of correct answers given. Passing scores vary by state, as well. In addition, some states make you wait for the test results, sending them to you by mail, whereas some states may be able to give you the results on the same day you take the exam. Your state may just advise you if you passed or failed.

>> What about getting the big prize — the actual license? In some cases, you can receive a temporary license on the day you pass the exam. In other cases, you get your license in the mail. And in other cases, you have to apply for the license after you get your test results.

Having more than one testing center, a state may vary its procedures from one place to another. One center might be equipped to give you your score and even a temporary license right away; another testing center in the same state may not be able to do that. If getting your license right away is important to you, especially if you have a hot deal ready to go as soon as you have your license, it may be worthwhile to travel a little farther to get instant results.

Take Two: Retaking the Exam

STATE SPECIFIC

You need to know how many times you can retake the state license exam. Your state may allow unlimited retakes of the exam, or it may limit you to a certain number of retakes before requiring you to take the prelicensing course again. Whichever the case, if you do fail the exam and plan to retake it, don't wait too long. Try to retake it the next time it's offered. If you have to reapply to take the exam, do that right away. (But I know that you'll pass on the first try with the help of this book!)

The same applies if you have to take an exam to complete your real estate course. Find out how many times you can retake it and when and if you would have to retake the course itself.

REMEMBER

The exam itself is actually pretty good practice for a second try. Remember the areas with which you had difficulty, and concentrate on those areas first as you study for retaking the exam. If you're lucky and live in a state where you receive some idea of the areas in which you were weak, use the information to study that specific material. You also can use the review questions and practice exams in this book to diagnose your weak areas. Checking out the studying and test-taking tips in Chapter 2 for even more help won't hurt, either. Above all, don't grow discouraged. Anyone can fail an exam, but only you can have the stick-to-itiveness to go back and try it again.

Chapter **2**

Using Successful Study and Test-Taking Techniques

I want to share something with you that I tell all my students on the first day of class. If you read through Chapter 3 and then the rest of the book, you discover that real estate sales and brokerage is much more than just driving people around and showing them houses. As you read this book, you also find out that you have to know much more information than you originally thought. At that point, your head may explode. Just remember, however, that what you're tackling is real estate sales and brokerage, not rocket science or brain surgery. It's doable by anyone with reasonable intelligence and a decent command of the language. You've already established that you're intelligent, because you've already taken the most important step as far as I'm concerned: You bought this book. So now, all things being equal, with the right preparation, you should do just fine on the state exam.

This chapter is all about preparing to take the state real estate exam and then taking and passing the exam. In the first part of the chapter, I talk about ways to prepare for the exam. In the second part, I give you some hints for doing your best on the exam.

One Word to Get You Through: PREPARE

Every teacher with whom you've ever taken a class has told you that the way to successfully pass an examination is to prepare for it. Maybe that's all they said, leaving you hanging, or maybe they gave you a few hints. I try to do better than that by providing you with a detailed plan for getting ready to take the exam. The plan is based on steps characterized by the letters in the acronym PREPARE. Each of the letters represents a separate step in getting ready for the real estate exam. In some cases, each step is made up of several smaller steps.

I'm not in the habit of making guarantees, but what I can tell you is that if you follow these steps and put some reasonable time into mastering the material in this book, you give yourself an excellent chance at passing the state real estate license exam the first time you take it.

Provide

You need to provide yourself with every opportunity to pass the exam. But, I bet you're asking, "How do I do that?" Keep the following in mind for test success:

>> **Get information about the state exam.** I discuss exam information in detail in Chapter 1, but it's important enough to repeat some of it here. No matter whether you're planning to take the salesperson or the broker exam, you need to find out what subjects, both general and state-specific, are on the test. (Take special note of the State-Specific icons throughout this book and the items in Chapter 23 to help you out.) You also want to find out about the exam's format, the number of questions on it, and the amount of time you have to complete the test. It may be obvious, but find out where and when the exam is given and how to get there. Remember to check out what you need to bring to the exam (and what you may not bring). Whenever you require special arrangements (for example, if you are handicapped or need to bring food into the exam because of a medical condition), find out about that, too.

So where can you get all of this info? Try contacting your prelicensing course instructor, your state licensing agency, or the testing company that's been hired to administer the exam.

>> **Take enough time to study.** Regular study, instead of cramming at the last minute, consistently seems to be the best way to approach material like this. What's more, when you leave your studying to the last minute and some emergency develops (believe me, one usually does), you lose out on what little study time you have left. You don't have to be fanatical about keeping regular study times and hours. You may want to study half an hour or an hour every night and two or three hours on Saturday or Sunday. The point is, put in regular time during a longer time frame so you can grow more comfortable with the material, including this book, state-specific material, and the textbook for your prelicensing course.

>> **A quiet place to study.** Although having a quiet place to study may seem obvious, it's worth its own note. Do what you have to, including going to the library if necessary, to crack the books in peace and quiet so you can concentrate and get the most out of your study time.

Review

Reviewing means that you've already read the material, which is what I'm assuming here. After you identify specific subject areas on the state exam you plan to take (either the salesperson's exam or the broker's), you need to spend time studying those chapters in this book. Then it's time to review the information, and don't worry about what you need to review or how. I've got the scoop on vocabulary and terms, state license law, and state-specific items.

Vocabulary and terms

Vocabulary is critical on all real estate exams, especially the salesperson's exam. So the words I've placed in italics throughout this book are the first items to review. Do what works best for you to focus on these terms. Highlight the term and its definition with a highlighter, if you like. And I don't mind if you write in this book! Wherever possible, I try to define a term in one sentence so that it's easier for you to focus on the definition. You can also use the glossary and online flashcards for further review of vocabulary.

TIP

If you like copying information as a way of studying, you can make a list of terms and their definitions, or prepare a three-by-five file card for each term. Don't forget to put a little notation on the corner of each card to indicate what general subject the term relates to. Doing so helps you remember the material in context. Or you can carry the card idea one step further and prepare flashcards. Write a term on one side of the card and the definition on the other side. Then you can either have somebody quiz you or quiz yourself.

BREAKING THE LANGUAGE BARRIER

In recent years, real estate sales and brokerage have attracted large numbers of nonnative-born Americans: intelligent, sometimes highly educated people who often are quite accomplished in their own countries. Nevertheless, because these exams often concentrate heavily on understanding the terminology and the application of certain principles, language can become an issue for non-English speakers.

Depending on how serious the language issue is, you have these options for dealing with it:

- Though it's unlikely, find out whether your state offers the state license exam in another language. I don't know of any states in particular that do this, but you can always ask.

- If you need to, drop back for a while and take an English-as-a-second-language course. If the course allows you to use optional reading assignments, ask whether the teacher will allow you to use this book for a practice text.

- Offer your services as an interpreter in a real estate office not only to translate, but to learn many of the common terms and practices.

- Study the material in this book, paying particular attention to vocabulary and definitions, and take the exam. Most importantly, take it easy on yourself if you don't pass the exam the first time; don't get discouraged. Recognize that you're dealing with a language issue, and this has nothing to do with your intelligence. Keep studying, and take the exam again.

State license law

STATE SPECIFIC

All states have their own real estate license law material, which usually covers more than just how to get a real estate license. It often provides rules and regulations regarding certain business practices in the conduct of a real estate business. It will usually also cover enforcement of standards and disciplinary measures for real estate licensees. This material may be available in hard copy from the state licensing agency or downloadable from the state licensing agency's website (try an online search for your state's site), or it may be given to you if you're required to take a course before taking the exam. Read the material several times, noting those items like license requirements, fees, and business practices. For more on license law, check out Chapter 3.

State-specific items

STATE SPECIFIC

In addition to reviewing the general information in this book, make sure that you find out about and review information that you know is unique to your state. You get this information in whatever course you're required to take. For those of you in states that don't require a course, if the information is going to be on the exam, it's probably available in whatever booklet or other exam preparation material is provided by your state real estate licensing agency.

TIP

One way to get a good start is to check out Chapter 23. That's where I highlight ten state–specific issues to study and watch out for on the exam.

Evaluate

As you prepare for the state exam, you continually need to evaluate how well you're mastering the material. The best way to evaluate your progress as you study is to answer the review questions at the end of each chapter.

As you read through the chapters in this book for the first time, you can answer the questions as a review of your reading. Don't write your answers in the book; use a separate piece of paper. Go over the answers and then reread the sections of each chapter that may be giving you trouble.

After reviewing all the material in the book, particularly the vocabulary and terms, try sitting down with several sheets of paper and answering each chapter's review questions in order, as if each were a test. You can take whatever time you need, but keep a couple of nights or a weekend afternoon to finish. Just keep answering all the review-question tests one by one until you've completed all the chapter questions. Don't forget to score each test and make a list of your scores in the same order as the chapters. Then you can study the chapters in order of your lowest scores to your highest scores. Do the same with the required course textbook if it has chapter review questions.

REMEMBER

Most people have limited amounts of time to devote to studying. Reviewing the real estate exam information in the way I describe in this section enables you to focus your time on the material with which you're having the most trouble. Just to be safe, review the chapters you do well on, but if you don't get a chance to, at least you know where to focus your limited time. After reviewing the material in areas where you're weakest, you can take the review-question exams again, if you like.

Practice

After you review the material, evaluate your weak and strong points, and review the material again, it's time for a final run-through. Whenever you can schedule two hours or so, sit down with a piece of paper and the writing tool of your choice and take one of the 100-question practice exams toward the end of the book, such as the first one in Chapter 19. Score yourself, and go over the answers to the ones you get wrong (Chapter 20 has the answers). If something isn't clear, review that section of the book. And don't stop there. Do it again on another day with the second practice test in Chapter 21; the answers are in Chapter 22. Do this with all four practice exams. If you've done everything that I've asked you to do so far, in the order that I've suggested, I'd be surprised if you don't do well on the tests. But if your scores still are low, review the material again and then go back on another day and take the practice tests again. Keep doing this until you can pass them all.

TIP

You need to be able to find out the length (number of questions) of the state exam and the amount of time you're allowed to complete it. You can use that info to take a self-timed practice exam that simulates the conditions of the real thing.

Arrive

Someone once said that 80 percent of success is showing up. To ensure that you arrive safely to take your state exam, in good humor, on time, and in the right place, you need to find out where and when the exam is scheduled and how long it takes to get there. With that information in hand, you need to get directions to the exam site (no winging it) and find out if you're likely to encounter any long waits to getting into the exam and if people routinely are turned away because of overcrowding at the test site. (You can get this information by calling your state licensing agency.)

These factors may vary from one exam site to another, especially if your state offers the exam at more than one location. If your state administers the exam in several locations, pick one that's most convenient for you, which may mean a little farther away but easier to get to or with better parking. When I took my broker's exam, I chose to drive farther away to a suburban location instead of taking public transportation to the test site in the city. Do whatever makes you more comfortable and leaves plenty of time to be early. If you live far away from the exam site, consider arriving in the area the night before the exam and staying over.

Relax

Relaxation part one: Relax the night before the exam. Don't study. Go see an early movie, rent a video, eat a light supper, read a non-real-estate book, and get to bed early. If you regularly meditate, jog, or take long walks, the evening before the exam is a good time for enjoying that kind of activity. Prepare everything you need for the next day, and have it ready to go.

Relaxation part two: Try to stay relaxed on the day of the exam. Eat a light, nourishing breakfast. Get to the test site in plenty of time, and follow the instructions to get a seat. If you can, close your eyes for a few seconds, take a few deep breaths, and remember that no one knows this stuff better than you do. Now sit down and feel yourself relax into the moment of actually taking the exam.

Relaxation part three: Stay relaxed during the test. You may get caught up in the moment, starting to rush and feel pressured. Every 15 or 20 questions, sit up straight, close your eyes, and take one or two deep breaths. Flex your shoulders and hands, and then begin again.

Enjoy

I know what you're thinking: "How can anyone ever enjoy taking a test?" You've studied. You've reviewed. You're relaxed. In short, you're prepared. In your mind you've already passed the exam and are making money working in real estate, maybe even having your own brokerage business in time. I hope you're getting the picture. Taking and passing the test certainly is a challenge, but it's one that with the right preparation (which you now have), you can easily meet. You're ready, and your real estate career awaits you.

Trying Terrific Test-Taking Strategies

So the big day has arrived. You've made it to the test site in plenty of time. You're seated and have the exam in front of you. You've carefully followed all of the instructions about how to properly answer the questions. Now you're ready to go. In this section I give you some test-taking tips and hints to maximize your score. Nothing replaces hard work and preparation before the exam, and no strategy helps you pass if you haven't prepared well. But some of these hints should help you make the most of what you've learned as you answer the questions.

It's all in the timing

The first thing you need to do is something you should have already done during your exam preparation — a little math equation. Divide the total number of minutes you have to complete the exam by the total number of questions. This information is available either from the state licensing authority or from your course instructor. Now figure out some benchmarks for yourself. For example, say your exam has 100 questions, and you get two hours to take the exam. That gives you a little more than a minute per question. At the one-hour mark, you need to have at least 50 questions completed. After the first half-hour you need to have 25 questions finished. You may move faster in some sections and slower in others, but overall you need to maintain the right pace so you don't leave anything unfinished. Whatever the time frame for your exam, always be aware of how many questions you need to have completed at what point during the exam time. You never want to leave any questions unanswered.

Make sure that you finish the exam, because as an instructor, I can tell you that nothing is more heartbreaking than seeing someone fail an exam because he or she didn't finish. You see, I know that students usually know the answers to at least a few of those eight or ten questions they never got around to answering, and so they never get full credit for what they actually know.

So how can you avoid this dilemma? Go through the entire exam fairly quickly, question by question, answering only the ones you know right away. Read quickly, not carelessly. Make sure that you spend enough time with each question to understand what it's asking, and read through all the possible answers. If you get to a question you're not sure about, eliminating one or two wrong answers can save you time later on. If you're taking a test on a computer, carefully follow the instructions for skipping questions. After you've gone through all the questions once, go back and do all the questions that you skipped. If you're mathematically challenged, save the math questions for the end. Always remain conscious of the time so you're not spending too much time on any one question.

Quickly answering the questions you know gives you a couple of advantages. You're assured that you get to all the questions that you know how to answer correctly, including the ones at the end of the exam. When doing a quick pass over the test, you may find a question near the end that triggers a memory or gives you information that helps you go back and answer an earlier question. For test takers who have a phobia of math, a quick pass over the test enables you to skip the math questions without wasting a lot of time on them. And finally, you have an idea of how much time you have left to spend on the remaining unanswered questions, especially those darn math problems. (For tips on dealing with math questions, see "Number crunching: Tackling math questions" later in this chapter.)

Besides, you'll probably be pleasantly surprised at how many answers you know immediately. And that definitely is a great confidence booster.

The last thing you need to do is actually count all the marks you made on the answer sheet to find out whether that number matches the number of questions on the exam. (If you're taking the exam on a computer, you need to scan the questions and answers to make sure you've answered every one.) In addition, make sure that you don't fill in two answers for one question. You want to confirm that the answers you choose are aligned correctly with the questions; if you entered something incorrectly, you may have to spend precious minutes fixing everything.

Reading everything carefully

I shouldn't have to remind you about reading with care, but I'm going to. Read all the material about getting ready for the exam; read about what to bring to the exam; read the directions on the exam itself; and above all, read the exam. And I mean every word of every question and all the possible answers. Give yourself every chance to understand what each question is asking and what each answer is saying.

Remember that exam writers may give you a choice of (A) or (B) that looks really good, but choice (D) nevertheless is the best answer. You won't know that unless you read everything. Beware of the partially correct answer. An answer has to be completely correct to be the right answer, and only one of the choices is completely correct. On the flip side, you also need to remember that you may encounter questions in which all the answers seem wrong. Nevertheless, one of them *is* the correct choice. And that answer may very well be the best of a bad lot, so to speak. That's the one to pick.

Avoiding too much analyzing

Don't think too much. I know that sounds bizarre, but trust me, it's good advice especially for students who have some background in one or more of the exam subject areas. I've seen students overthink or overanalyze a question to the point of getting themselves tied in knots, selecting the wrong answer, and wasting valuable time. This scenario seems particularly true for people with specific technical backgrounds. Maybe you have a background in environmental science and in answering a question about environmental issues; you can probably come up with ten reasons why all the choices are wrong. Obviously one has to be correct. The level of knowledge provided in this book and in whatever real estate course you take is the level on which you're tested. So leave all that extra stuff you know at the door. If you've studied well for the exam, the answer that first comes to you is usually the best answer. When you start overanalyzing, you may be in trouble.

Guessing

Even with all of your stellar preparation, some questions are just going to throw you for a loop, and yes, you have to guess. When it comes to guessing, find out whether any penalties are assessed for wrong answers. Of course, you lose points for each wrong answer, but through the years exams have been constructed so that a percentage is added onto your wrong answers as a penalty for guessing. I'm guessing that you won't run into this anywhere on a real estate exam, but you need to check it out just in case. Assuming you won't be penalized for guessing a wrong answer, when in doubt, guess. Don't leave anything blank. In fact, the last step you need to take on the exam answer sheet is counting up your answers to make sure that you haven't left anything blank. (For more about budgeting your test time, see "It's all in the timing," earlier in this chapter.)

The key to guessing is to increase your odds of guessing correctly. If you're given four choices to a question and have no clue as to the correct answer, you have a one-in-four chance of guessing correctly. However, if you can eliminate one or two of the answers as being wrong, you've increased your odds of getting the right answer to one in three or one in two. Most Las Vegas gamblers would take those odds anytime.

TIP

So how do you eliminate the wrong answers? For starters, if you're as well prepared as I know you'll be, the odds are in your favor. You most likely can pick out at least one wrong answer right away. After that, it may get a little tough. Try the following tips:

>> Answers with words "always" and "never" often may be eliminated. But be careful: Some things are always true, such as always owing your fiduciary responsibilities to your client. (Check out Chapter 4 for more information.)

>> Look for categories of answers. For instance, a question might ask about a landlord's interest in property. You've studied enough to reduce the possibilities to leased fee and leasehold so you've increased the odds of getting the correct answer (leased fee) to one in two. (You can check to see whether I'm right in Chapter 12.)

>> A specific strategy may work for questions in which the last answer is "All of the above." If you're sure that two of the answers are correct, then choose "All of the above" because it's a good bet that the third answer is also correct.

REMEMBER

I've seen a number of hints that help people guess at answers. The problem is that in every case, I can write a question that proves the hint wrong. The best way for you to answer exam questions correctly is to study, study, and study some more.

Second-guessing

Never ever change an answer after you've written it down. It seems that if you're well prepared, your mind tends to recognize the correct answer in a multiple-choice question immediately. From my own experience with correcting exams, I can tell you that all too often, I see correct answers erased and changed to wrong ones. I don't see the opposite as often.

That said, here are two exceptions to the rule:

>> If a later question helps you answer an earlier one. Say in question 42 you find information that helps you select a better answer to question 23. By all means, go back and change your answer.

>> If you get a different answer when reviewing a problem in the math section of the exam. If you have time, go back and do all the math questions a second time. If any of your answers are different, consider changing them. (For more about math questions, see the next section.)

Number crunching: Tackling math questions

Many test takers find math problems to be the most intimidating of all the questions they have to answer, but keep in mind that the math we're talking about is stuff you pretty much learned between seventh grade and your freshman year of high school. Memorizing a few formulas and conversion factors and doing lots of practice problems are tremendously helpful in giving you the confidence and knowledge to handle any math question.

For more details about real estate math, check out Chapter 18. Here are a few specific strategies that I give my students for dealing with math questions:

>> **Don't waste a lot of time on the math.** If you're truly uncomfortable with math problems, save them until the end, and spend whatever time you have left working on them. Guess if you have to. (See the "Guessing" section earlier in this chapter for the scoop.)

>> **Do the problem first, and get an answer before you look at the answers.** After thinking through the problem, you very well could have the answer correct.

>> **Read the problem carefully to make sure you've done all the steps.** Exam writers frequently give you an answer that merely appears correct, but only because you didn't go far enough into the problem. For example, you may find an answer about area that is correct when written in square feet, but the problem calls for the answer in square yards. Or perhaps an answer needs to be in months, but one of the choices is the correct answer for a year. Don't forget to divide by 12!

>> **Go back over the math problems, if you have time.** Fingers are big; calculator keys are small. You may write down a number from a calculator, then key it back in incorrectly. You may simply make a mistake. Do each math problem again and try to come up with the same answer twice. It's a good bet that's the right answer.

2

So You Want to Sell Real Estate: The Job and Basic Laws

IN THIS PART . . .

Agent, salesperson, broker, associate broker . . . understand each of these terms so you can decide which test (and career path) to take.

Get a perspective on the different real estate career opportunities, from brokerages and franchises to appraisers and inspectors.

Successfully navigate your way though the different types of agency relationships, including agents, principals, and customers, as you also look at agency law.

Go to the bank with your new understanding of how real estate professionals get that all-important paycheck at the end of a sale.

IN THIS CHAPTER

» Figuring out what real estate agents really do and how they get paid

» Checking out different career opportunities (including property management)

» Discovering the details of managing a real estate office and working independently

» Looking at important job-related laws you need to know

Chapter **3**

The Job: It Isn't Just Driving People Around

Welcome to the wonderful world of real estate. I wish I had you here in my classroom so I could ask you, as I do of my students on the first day of class, why you want to get your real estate license. Sure, it's to make money, but what drew you to the field? Have you always been interested in houses? Do you want to become an investor or a property manager? Do the flexible hours and being your own boss appeal to you? Real estate is exciting, and it's constantly changing and growing. I'm going to give you some information in this chapter about careers in the real estate field. Some of the information is nothing more than background so that you have an understanding of what real estate agents actually do and where they do it. Although interesting, it's not likely to be on the exam.

The rest of the material in this chapter is fair game for state exam questions. Understanding the different responsibilities that brokers and salespeople have, how brokers and salespeople are paid, and the working relationship between brokers and salespeople is important material in some states for the broker's exam.

I also give you plenty of information about property management as a career within the real estate business. Depending on your state, you may get questions about this subject. A few job-related laws also are discussed. As a means of putting all this information into the right context, I also give you an overview of a typical real estate transaction.

Recognizing Those in the Real Estate Business and How They Got There

You'd think that simply knowing what the main players do in a real estate business is pretty obvious, but I think that because of the terminology they share, the distinctions between the players gets a little muddled. So I try to clear up those distinctions for you and talk a little about laws governing real estate licensing in this section.

REMEMBER

Here are quick descriptions of players in the real estate game.

>> **Real estate agent:** This generic term pretty much refers to anyone who has a real estate license.

>> **Real estate broker:** This person is the key player. Most states require you to have a broker's license to perform certain activities like sell houses for other people.

>> **Real estate salesperson:** Salespeople are allowed to perform all the activities that the state requires a real estate license for. However, a salesperson cannot work independently; he must work under a licensed broker.

>> **Associate broker:** This person has a broker's license but chooses to work under another broker rather than opening his own business.

Agency law covers the relationships of these folks to each other and to the public. For the full scoop, check out Chapter 4 as well as your state licensing law.

REMEMBER

Regardless of whether you take the exam for a broker's or salesperson's license, your state's exam writers expect you to know the following basics of who a broker is and what a broker does. So regardless of the exam, you should know the material that follows.

The buck stops here: Brokers

A *real estate broker* is the person in the real estate business who's primarily responsible for various activities on behalf of the public. I admit that sounds pretty vague, so let me explain.

Every state has a state real estate license law, usually just called the state license law. The state license law governs these two primary factors in the real estate business:

>> A general list of activities that can be performed only by someone holding a real estate license

>> The requirements for obtaining a real estate license

The state license law may specifically address what real estate agents must do during the course of their activities, which includes things like presenting all offers to a seller as soon as possible.

REMEMBER

A real estate broker is someone who is authorized by the state to perform a certain list of activities on behalf of someone else and collect a fee for doing so. A broker is often called a real estate agent, which is correct in the sense that the broker acts on behalf of someone else (a client).

The license law provides a list of activities that, if they're done for another person for a fee, can be performed only by someone having a broker's license. Although the specific activities may vary from one state to another, the list of activities requiring a broker's license generally includes negotiating any type of real estate transaction, including sales, leases, and exchanges. A licensed salesperson or associate broker may perform these activities but only under the supervision of a broker. (For more general info on state license law, see "Making it legal: Looking at license law," later in this chapter.)

WARNING

You usually can do any of the previously mentioned activities on your own behalf without having a real estate broker's license. In other words, you can sell your own house by yourself without being licensed. The implication is that you also can help someone else like a family member sell a house themselves without a license as long as you don't collect a fee, but remember the gift of a fancy restaurant meal can be considered a fee. You definitely need a real estate license if you want to collect fees for your work.

Movin' on up: Salespeople

A real estate salesperson is someone who either works as an employee for a real estate broker or more typically as an independent contractor paid by commission. (For more about the latter, see "Working as an Independent Contractor," later in this chapter.) Generally speaking, a real estate salesperson is someone who can do all of the activities that a broker can do on behalf of a client, but must do so under the authority and supervision of a broker. Referring to a real estate salesperson as a real estate agent is somewhat accurate. The salesperson sometimes is viewed as a subagent of the broker but, in fact, has the same obligations as the broker with respect to a client. (See Chapter 4 for more about representation in agency relationships.) In general you become a salesperson first, spend a number of years learning the business, and then become a broker. Of course, you can remain a salesperson for your entire career.

In between: Associate brokers

STATE SPECIFIC

Some states have an intermediate level of licensing that is called an associate broker. An *associate broker* has all the qualifications of a broker but doesn't want to operate his own real estate business. Associate brokers choose to work under the licenses of other brokers just like salespeople. Be sure to find out how your state refers to this level of licensing and what the qualifications are.

Making it legal: Looking at license law

STATE SPECIFIC

You need to go over your state's real estate licensing law in detail. Some questions about the law undoubtedly will be on your state exam. Although you need to become familiar with your state's law in its entirety, pay special attention to the following:

>> Qualifications for real estate licensees — broker, associate broker, and salesperson

>> Requirements for getting the various licenses

>> License fees and other fees associated with licensing

>> Continuing education requirements

>> Special requirements after you get your license, such as requiring a broker to maintain a place of business

>> Exemptions from licensing, such as for attorneys

>> Activities that require a real estate license

>> Standards of conduct and acceptable practice either with respect to the law and/or a code of ethics

>> Enforcement and disciplinary actions for license law and standards violations

Knowing What a Real Estate Broker/ Salesperson Does

STATE SPECIFIC

Real estate brokers and salespeople may do any or all of the things listed in your state's licensing law. Put another way, there is a list of activities in your state license law, and if you do these activities for another person for a fee, you need a real estate license. (See the previous section for more.) Although the list of activities is fairly universal across the United States, it may vary in detail from one state to the next. For exam purposes, you need to know the specific activities that require a real estate license in your state.

Perusing a list of common activities

Typical activities that require a real estate license are

>> Listing a property for sale

>> Finding buyers for property that is for sale

>> Negotiating the sale or purchase of a property

>> Negotiating a lease on behalf of a tenant or a landlord

>> Representing someone in the exchange of properties

>> Buying or selling options (the right to buy a piece of property at some time in the future) on real estate

>> Collecting rents for more than one building owner

This list of activities is at best only a partial one. Your state law probably requires a license to perform most, if not all, of these activities; however, license requirements can include more or fewer activities, depending on the state.

Checking out a typical real estate transaction

STATE SPECIFIC

Because buying and selling houses is the primary business of real estate brokers and salespeople, I want to give you a brief and somewhat generic overview of a typical house sale involving real estate agents. (By "agents" here, I mean either a broker or a salesperson. Remember, however, that the broker is primarily responsible in a transaction, with the salesperson working for her.) I use the word "generic," because although many elements are common to all simple real estate transactions, transactions can include state and even regional differences in some specific elements.

In the beginning, there was a house to sell

A couple decides to sell their house and enlist the services of a real estate agent. You're one of several brokers or salespeople the couple invites to their home to hear your listing presentation and explain what services you offer. In addition, you probably advise the couple on what price they are able to get for their house. After meeting with several agents, the couple chooses you, signing a listing agreement and agreeing to allow you to represent them as their agent in the transaction. (For more on listing agreements, see Chapter 4.)

As the couple's real estate agent, you begin marketing the property. In communities that have a multiple listing service (MLS), you enter their house information into a computer so that all other agents in the community can see what you've listed for sale. (See Chapter 4 for more about MLS.) In communities with no MLS, agents may spread the word around to other real estate agencies that they have a particular house for sale, and they may depend heavily on advertising. There may also be other formal or informal organizations or associations that permit sharing of listings so that a property gets the widest possible exposure to the market and to as many sellers as possible.

Eureka, a buyer!

An agent across town who's been working to find a house for another couple sees your house on the MLS and gets in touch with you, asking for more details and making sure the house still is for sale. The cross-town agent then contacts his buyers, and they agree to take a look at the house. After seeing the house, they agree to make an offer.

The way a buyer's offer is presented varies in different communities. Sometimes the offer is made in person with the buyer's agent present. The offer usually is made in writing with a small check from the prospective buyer that's called a *binder* or *earnest money*.

STATE SPECIFIC

After a deal is agreed to, often after some negotiation, a contract of sale is prepared. Exactly who prepares the contract varies by state and region. In many places, however, the seller's real estate agent prepares the contract, sometimes filling in the blanks of a preprinted contract form, but in other places, only attorneys prepare the contract. After the contract is signed, the conditions within the contract are triggered. (For more about sales contracts, see Chapter 11.)

WOULD YOU LIKE ANY HELP? REAL ESTATE CONSULTING

Real estate consulting is a relatively new phenomenon that is less about the services real estate agents provide than it is about how agents are paid. In a typical real estate transaction, the real estate agent gets paid when the property is sold. In a relatively new and not widely practiced arrangement called fee for services or real estate consulting, a broker can be paid for individual services leading up to the sale of a piece of property regardless of whether the sale is complete.

Take, for example, the seller who believes she can place her own advertisements in the paper and handle buyer inspections of the house but needs help pricing the house. She agrees to pay the broker (or the salesperson through the broker) a fee to provide a comparative or competitive market analysis of the property to come up with a listing (or asking) price. This arrangement sometimes is referred to as providing a menu of services.

You can find out more about consulting at the website of the International Association of Real Estate Consultants: www.iarec.com.

A typical real estate sales contract includes a provision for the buyer to obtain mortgage financing and may have provisions for the house to be inspected by a home inspector or engineer. The contract usually includes a provision that a *marketable title* must be conveyed. A *marketable title* means that a reasonable and proper search of the records has been conducted, showing that the title to the property has been documented from earlier owners to the current seller so that it can be conveyed (or transferred) without questions as to who the owner is. A records search that proves whether a title is marketable is called a title search. Title insurance also may be purchased (or even required) as part of the contract process to ensure that the title is legal. (For more on events before a closing, see Chapter 9.)

All's well that closes well

When all of the contract provisions are satisfactorily fulfilled, the buyer and seller may proceed to closing, taking the real estate agent one step closer to getting paid. Pinpointing the actual moment when a real estate agent earns a commission is a somewhat complex issue (see the next section). In general, it occurs when a ready, willing, and able buyer brings an acceptable offer to the seller. Sometimes contract provisions, such as financing, must be satisfied before for a commission can be earned. By general agreement, the commission usually is paid at the closing. When more than one broker is involved, the broker representing the seller distributes the preapproved share of the commission to the buyer's representative or co-broker. Each broker then splits a portion or percentage of the commission with the salesperson if any who worked the deal.

STATE SPECIFIC

In many places, real estate agents run the show and are joined at the closing by the buyer, the seller, a representative of the bank, and sometimes an attorney. In other places, lawyers do the bulk of the work, and sometimes a representative of the title company may actually conduct the closing. In some states, the closing is done *in escrow,* which means that as all the paperwork is completed, it is sent to an escrow agent. When the escrow agent gets everything in order, he or she sends checks, deeds, and any other important documents to the appropriate parties. (For more on the closing process, see Chapter 9.)

After the closing, any of those individuals involved in the closing may record the deed in the local office of public records and officially document the transaction. It's usually a matter of local custom as to who actually does the filing.

Understanding How a Real Estate Broker/Salesperson Gets Paid

A real estate agent gets paid for performing a service, which is usually bringing a buyer and a seller together to complete a property sale. Some confusion may exist as to when a commission actually is earned. In most cases, the commission is earned when a *meeting of the minds* is reached between a buyer and a seller — in other words, when a ready, willing, and able buyer is presented to the seller and all the terms of the contract of sale have been met. What sometimes is confusing to buyers and sellers is that the commission most often is paid at the closing, long after their meeting of the minds, when ownership of or title to the property actually changes hands. The payment of the fee at the closing is done as a convenience to the seller, who often has no money readily available except after the house is sold.

Commissions frequently are shared among two brokers and two salespeople. Here's what I mean: Salesperson A, who works for Broker A, lists a house for a potential seller. Salesperson B, who works for Broker B, represents a buyer who buys the house from the seller who listed a house with Broker A. Before the sale is complete, Brokers A and B agree how they'll split the commission.

After completing the sale, Broker *A* — the listing broker — receives a commission check from the seller and keeps his firm's part of the total amount and then gives the remaining portion of the total commission to Broker *B*. From their respective proceeds, Brokers *A* and *B* give prearranged portions of their commissions to their respective salespeople.

REMEMBER

As you can see, a real estate salesperson doesn't get paid directly by a client. The broker receives the fee for any services rendered and then pays the salesperson. This arrangement often is written into state law. In a typical situation, a salesperson may receive a check for the commission at the closing, but the check needs to be made out to the broker. The broker then pays the salesperson from the proceeds of that sale. The split between the broker and salesperson is entirely negotiable, varies from one brokerage to another, and may depend on the experience of the salesperson and the volume of business that salesperson generates.

WARNING

State law and federal law, specifically the Real Estate Settlement and Procedures Act which I discuss in Chapter 9, also cover prohibitions regarding nonlicensed persons receiving payment, finders' fees, commission, or kickbacks as part of a transaction — including any gifts, vacations, or other nonmonetary compensation received as part of a transaction. Suppose, for example, that in return for a percentage of the fee you earn, you arrange for a friend who runs a beauty salon to steer real estate buyers and sellers your way. Unless the beauty shop owner has a real estate license, you'd be violating any law that your state may have regarding kickbacks. (See why checking out your state laws is so important?)

In an arrangement where a buyer's agent represents the buyer, the buyer sometimes pays the buyer's agent. I know it seems a little odd that I use the word "may," because, after all, you'd think the person being represented *should* pay the fee. A peculiarity in the law nevertheless enables a broker to agree to represent one person but be paid by another. For instance, the seller may pay the buyer's agent. I discuss more about payment and representation in general in Chapter 4.

For more on myths regarding commission, check out "The price isn't right: Price fixing," later in this chapter. For the scoop on figuring a commission, see Chapter 18.

Working Hard: Career Opportunities

Real estate agents (either a broker or a salesperson) can work in a number of places. In some cases real estate training can provide good background for jobs that may not require a real estate license. In the following sections, I give you a little background on each of these possible areas of employment. It's unlikely that you'll get any exam questions on this material, but you may want to know what some of the employment possibilities are.

Considering independent brokerages and national franchises

The vast majority of real estate agents are employed as salespersons working for independent brokers. An independent broker may have more than one office and be affiliated with a multiple listing system, which enables brokers to share information about properties that are for sale. (For more on multiple listing systems, check out Chapter 4.) Many independent brokers have chosen to affiliate themselves with national franchises. These arrangements vary from a fair amount of control and standardization from the franchise's headquarters to an extremely independent operation in which the local broker pays a fee to maintain an affiliation with the national franchise. The benefits of franchise affiliations often are related to the nationwide exposure they provide through major advertising. Franchises frequently provide specialized training programs they require their salespeople to complete.

Of course, you definitely need a real estate license to work at a brokerage.

Checking out corporations (in and out of the real estate world)

STATE SPECIFIC

The sole purpose of some companies is to buy properties and then lease them out. These are real estate investment companies working for themselves. They may build on and then hold their properties or buy properties with existing structures. These companies may need people to locate properties to invest in (see Chapter 17), or they may need property managers (see "Taking care of business: The duties of a property manager," later in this chapter). As long as you're working for the company and managing properties it owns, you may not legally need a license to do the work; however, you need to find out whether any of your state's regulations require a license under those circumstances. On the other hand, if the company provides real estate property management services to other people or companies, a license is more likely to be required.

In addition, large corporations, particularly those with significant space or location needs, sometimes hire in-house real estate people. These jobs can involve leasing office or retail space for the company or buying land to locate company facilities. Depending on the company, you may find yourself leasing office space for a new company operation, buying a piece of property to locate a new gas station or fast-food restaurant, or negotiating with someone for an oil/gas lease. Although real estate training is good background for these jobs, a real estate license more than likely is unnecessary from a legal perspective. A company may, however, want you to have a license as part of your qualifications.

Building business with builders

When you're working with a builder, your job may range from finding land for the builder to build on to selling the houses or other buildings the builder may construct. The main distinction that determines whether you need a license when working with a builder is whether you're working for that one builder as an employee, in which case you most likely do not need a license. You most likely need a license when working for one or more builders for a fee as an independent contractor (not as an employee).

When working with a builder, you may find yourself as an on-site salesperson. You may be spending plenty of time at the building site, showing people new homes or helping them select a design and special features or options for the new home the builder will build for them.

Going into government

Local, county, and the federal government often employ people to perform real estate services including maintaining records, selling surplus property, buying property for various purposes, and obtaining easements. As a government employee, you would most likely be exempt from needing a real estate license. Governments can hire real estate agents from time to time. In this case a license would be required.

WARNING

Note that government jobs that deal with real estate are fairly specialized and not widely available.

Appreciating appraising

Appraising is a field that's related to but distinct from a career in real estate brokerage. Although the knowledge you gain in coursework and experience as a broker or salesperson is useful in appraising, a separate license and education are required to become an appraiser. An appraiser's job is to estimate the value of a piece of real estate in a variety of circumstances. The vast majority of appraisals are done for mortgage-loan purposes. Lenders hire appraisers to estimate the values of properties as a basis for the loans that the lenders extend to buyers.

You can get more information about the appraisal career field at www.appraisalfoundation.org. For more on appraising property in general, see Chapter 14.

Homing in on home inspections

STATE
SPECIFIC

Many buyers have the homes they're considering inspected by home inspectors before buying them. Although you don't need a real estate license to be a home inspector, some states provide for the licensing of home inspectors. You can get more information about this career field at the International Association of Certified Home Inspectors (U.S.) website at www.nachi.org.

Property Management: A Special Kind of Career Opportunity

Property management is a specialized job within the real estate field. Because most property managers have duties for which a real estate license is required, and they usually perform these activities for more than one client, real estate agents usually must have a real estate license to be a property manager. A license may not be required in some instances, though, such as when a property manager is an employee of a real estate investment company. If you're interested in this career field, you should check out your home state's requirements for property managers.

In this section I discuss the duties and responsibilities of a property manager and the basic details of a property management agreement. For more information, check out the latest edition of *Property Management For Dummies* by Robert S. Griswold (John Wiley & Sons, Inc.).

REMEMBER

Some state license exams have questions about property management.

Taking care of business: The duties of a property manager

The duties of a property manager generally are defined as maximizing income and maintaining or increasing the overall value of the property being managed. I tell you more specifically here about how a property manager is responsible for the financial and physical condition of the building and cover a manager's duties in actually renting out a property's units or floor space and handling insurance.

Financial responsibilities

Some of a property manager's duties include the following responsibilities:

>> **Creating an annual operating budget:** This task includes analyzing the building's income and expenses over time. The manager also examines ways to reduce building expenses. (For more about analyzing properties, see Chapter 17.)

>> **Collecting rents:** A manager usually creates some system of collecting and accounting for rents.

>> **Setting rents:** The manager examines the rents and vacancy rates for competing buildings in the area and either sets rental rates or recommends rates to the owner.

>> **Paying bills:** A manager is typically responsible for paying bills for operating expenses and repairs and maintenance.

>> **Preparing periodic financial reports:** These reports relate to the building's financial condition and its income and expenses.

Physical responsibilities

The building manager also is responsible for properly maintaining the property's value, by maintaining the physical condition of the property and buildings. These duties include the following:

>> **Physical analysis of the building:** The property manager analyzes the building with a view toward immediate and long-term repairs and improvements that might be made to enhance the desirability of the building and allow for higher rents.

>> **Preparation of capital and repairs budgets:** Using the property analysis as a basis, the property manager creates a capital budget that includes larger improvements and repairs to the building. Capital budget items typically include the replacement of major items, such as roofs, boilers, and air-conditioning units, while repair budget items deal more with making repairs and maintaining those same fixtures.

>> **Maintenance:** Part of the manager's responsibilities is arranging for routine cleaning and maintenance of the building and grounds, including scheduling janitorial services, preventive maintenance, and needed repairs on equipment like the boiler. The manager typically hires outside people to do these jobs, has his own employees for this work, or uses a combination of the two.

Rental responsibilities

A manager usually is responsible for renting the space in a building. I say "usually" because sometimes an owner takes care of this task directly or hires a real estate agent other than the manager to find tenants and negotiate leases. You can find out more about different types of leases and their provisions in Chapter 12.

Advertising for tenants is another rental responsibility. "For rent" signs on the building and print ads in appropriate media, such as newspapers for apartments and specialized publications for office or industrial space, can be useful. Billboard, direct mail, and Internet advertising also may be used. Radio and TV ads usually are less effective but may prove useful in some markets. One commonly held belief is that recommendations by satisfied tenants may be the most effective advertising for a building.

The manager is also responsible for providing necessary services to the tenants as agreed to in the lease, for trying to settle any disputes that may arise with tenants, and for engaging in eviction activities if necessary.

Insurance responsibilities

Property managers sometimes analyze the insurance needs of a building that they manage or call in insurance experts to do it. Unlike a single-family house, which usually has a single insurance policy that covers a number of things, large, complex buildings may require different types of insurance policies to cover specific items. Proper insurance coverage is part of an overall risk management plan that a property manager needs to consider.

TIP

In general, managing risk, or in some way dealing with potential liability issues, can be handled by a system known as CART, or controlling, avoiding, retaining, and transferring risk. These four general risk management options are described in the list that follows:

» *Controlling risk* means anticipating it and preparing for it. Emergency lighting systems are an example of controlling risk.

» *Avoiding risk* means removing the source of danger. Storage of paint or other flammable materials can be removed from the building and moved to another location.

» *Retaining risk* means accepting the liability. This step sometimes is taken when the risk of something happening is small; or, in essence, when you agree to pay whatever liability costs arise from the building's funds when a particular event does occur. *Self- insurance* is another way of describing this situation. An alternative to retaining risk is purchasing insurance coverage with a very high deductible (the payment made by the owner before insurance kicks in).

» *Transferring risk* means buying the appropriate type and amount of insurance to cover the payment whenever an insured incident occurs.

REMEMBER

The following are the more common types of insurance that are available to cover different types of risks:

» **Boiler and machinery insurance:** Because of the substantial cost of heating units and air-conditioning systems in large buildings, a separate type of insurance is available to cover the replacement and repair of this type of machinery.

» **Casualty insurance:** This type of insurance covers losses caused by theft, vandalism, and burglary.

» **Co-insurance:** This coverage essentially is for situations in which the owner takes on part of the risk by self-insuring for a portion of the risk. Incorporating a large deductible before the insurance policy starts to pay off is one example.

» **Errors and omissions insurance:** This type of insurance can cover property managers against any errors they make in the performance of their duties. This insurance doesn't cover losses caused by fraud or other dishonest or malfeasant activities.

» **Fire and hazard insurance:** Depending on what it covers, this type of policy sometimes is called an all-risk, all-peril policy. It basically covers loss of the property caused by fire, storms, and other types of damaging conditions. This type of policy usually does not cover flooding and earthquake damage.

» **Liability insurance:** This type of insurance covers losses caused by injuries that are the result of negligence on the part of the landlord. The classic case is the person who falls on an icy sidewalk that the landlord was supposed to have cleaned.

» **Rent loss insurance:** This insurance sometimes is called business interruption insurance or consequential loss insurance. It pays the owner of the building for the loss of rent from tenants if the building is destroyed by fire.

» **Surety bond:** Technically a surety bond provides payment whenever something is not done within an agreed-upon period of time. However, the coverage provided by surety bonds has come to mean making up for losses caused by dishonest acts of an employee. For example, this type of insurance covers a loss that is the result of rents being stolen by the rent collector.

CAN YOU MANAGE?

If you're interested in the field of property management, you can get more information from the following:

- The Institute of Real Estate Management (www.irem.org) is connected to the National Association of Realtors. You can get information and training from this organization. They award the Certified Property Manager (CPM) designation.

- The Building Owners and Managers Association International (www.boma.org) is another source of information particularly with regard to the management of commercial buildings.

  Information and sometimes training and professional designations also can be obtained from the International Council of Shopping Centers (www.icsc.org), the Urban Land Institute (www.uli.org), the National Apartment Association (www.naahq.org), and the International Real Estate Institute (www.iami.org/irei).

Saying yes: The property management agreement

The basis for the relationship between a property manager and a property owner is a contract called the property management agreement. Although every agreement is unique, particularly with respect to the details of duties, responsibilities, and payments, certain elements need to be specifically addressed in any property management agreement, including:

>> **Who:** The parties to the agreement (both the property owner and the property manager) need to be clearly identified. In any partnership situation, both partners need to sign. The appropriate corporate officer needs to sign for a corporation.

>> **Where:** The property to be managed needs to be clearly identified at least by its address and possibly by legal description. You can check out the specifics of legal description in Chapter 9. If any elements of the property are not to be managed by the property manager, they need to be identified. For example, if a building has a large empty piece of land next to it that is leased as a parking lot for use by an adjacent building, the owner may not want to have you manage that lot.

>> **How long:** The term or length of the agreement needs to be stated. Owners tend to want a short time frame; managers want a longer one. A minimum of one year is the general recommendation, because that gives managers a chance to show their skills and recoup some of their initial expenses in setting up a management program for the building.

>> **What — manager's duties:** The manager's duties need to be clearly defined and stated. All parties to the agreement need to know whether the manager will collect rents, pay bills, contract for maintenance, and so on. (For more, see "Taking care of business: The duties of a property manager," earlier in this chapter.)

>> **What — manager's authority as an agent:** A property manager usually is considered a *general agent*. As a general agent, the manager usually has authority over a range of activities on behalf of the owner. The extent of this authority needs to be spelled out in the agreement. For example, the agreement needs to flesh out whether the manager has the final word in setting rent rates or must first check with the owner for final approval.

>> **What information and when — reporting:** The principal form of communication between a property owner and a manager are the periodic reports prepared by the manager. The timing and content of these reports are negotiable and vary with the type and complexity of the

building being managed. Monthly reports are typical and can contain a variety of income, expense, vacancy, expiring leases, and maintenance information.

» **Who pays what — allocation of expenses:** This part of the agreement states which costs, if any, are paid out of the manager's fees rather than from the income of the building. For example the manager may be responsible for the costs of advertising, especially if the manager receives an extra bonus for new leases.

» **How much — the fee:** The fee for any management agreement is completely negotiable, but it's usually based on one or more of the following:

- Commission on new leases

- Fixed fees

- Percentage of the gross (before expenses are deducted) or net (after expenses are deducted) income from the building

- A combination of any two or three of the first three

» **What the landlord wants:** A clear statement of the owner's objectives for owning the building can be made part of the management agreement or addressed in some other written format, such as a letter of understanding between owner and property manager. Regardless of how the owner's objectives are handled, the manager must have a clear idea whether the owner is seeking long- or short-term profits or other financial objectives from his investment. Furthermore, it's equally as important for the manager to adequately meet the owner's objectives without compromising her honesty or ethics.

Managing a Real Estate Office: You're the Boss, Ms. or Mr. Broker

If you're taking the state examination for the salesperson's license, you probably can skip this section, but if you're taking the broker's exam, you need to read this section. Some states expect aspiring brokers to know something about the administrative duties and responsibilities of running a real estate brokerage, including supervising people who work for you, training those people, and setting office policies.

Keeping an eye out: Supervision

State laws may vary, but in general, a broker is required to supervise the people who work for her. This extremely specific requirement makes the broker responsible for the actions of salespeople who work for her. This responsibility extends to violations of the state licensing laws, fair housing laws, and illegal or fraudulent activities. The extent of liability and punishment is, of course, determined by state licensing officials, and in the case of criminal or civil actions, by the courts.

STATE SPECIFIC

The type of questions you're likely to get on this subject fall into these two categories:

» What your state law has to say about brokers' responsibilities with respect to supervising their salespeople.

» The expectation that you'll know most of the important points of the state licensing law with which you and your salespeople are expected to comply. (See "Making it legal: Looking at license law," earlier in this chapter.)

Although this material may be information you found out about when pursuing your salesperson's license, you still need to review the specific information that applies to your state's broker's exam.

Teach me! Training

Brokers are expected to provide training to their salespeople. Most states require prospective salespeople to receive formal training through prelicensing courses before they can get a salesperson's license. Even though this training gives you the basic background and the minimum amount of knowledge that the state requires you to have to work as a real estate agent, it often does not cover the day-to-day real world activities of an agent. Brokers are expected to provide that day-to-day type of training. After you get your salesperson's license, you can stay a salesperson forever. In most states, however, if you want to become a broker, you're required to gain some hands-on experience.

Setting office policy: Rules are rules

Formulating and periodically updating an office policies and procedures manual is a suggested means of at least partially fulfilling your training and supervision obligations as a broker. This manual is distributed to all employees along with training in the policies and procedures of the brokerage. Because most salespeople work as independent contractors (see the next section), the policy and procedures manual needs to rely on words like *suggested* and *recommended* rather than *must.* The subjects contained in an office policy manual can range from dealings with attorneys and other professionals to record keeping, using supplies, and attending sales meetings.

Working As an Independent Contractor

Most real estate salespeople work as independent contractors for their brokers. This typical working relationship between a salesperson and a broker affects everything from taxes to daily work. In this section I explain this relationship and some of the issues you need to understand for exam purposes.

The best way to understand work status as an independent contractor is to contrast it with a regular employee. A real estate salesperson can work as an employee for a broker, but doing so is not the norm. Although he is the boss, the broker doesn't have the same detailed authority over an independent contractor as with a regular employee. The two main differences are that

>> Employees must work the hours the employer tells them to work. The employer also must take out taxes from the employees' pay and pay Social Security on behalf of the employees.

>> Independent contractors are responsible for paying their own taxes and Social Security. They can deduct certain business expenses from their pretax pay that an employee can't deduct. Independent contractors can work their own hours and basically do the job in their own way. An employer cannot force an independent contractor to work certain hours or attend certain meetings, because that can jeopardize the independent contractor status of the salesperson. However, as part of the broker's duty to supervise and train salespeople, she can require attendance at certain training activities.

An employment agreement between the broker and the salesperson has become virtually mandatory to prove and maintain the independent contractor relationship.

Focusing on Job-Related Laws That You Need to Understand

A few common misunderstandings about the real estate business are pretty serious issues because they deal with federal antitrust laws. State exam writers expect you to be able to answer questions about them.

WARNING

Violations of the Sherman Antitrust Act can result in fines paid to the federal government of varying amounts and up to triple the damages paid to the injured party.

The price isn't right: Price fixing

First of all no rule says that a real estate agent must be paid on a commission basis. Just to be sure you're clear on this, a *commission* generally is a percentage of the final sale price of the property that usually is paid upon completion of the sale. (See "Understanding How a Real Estate Broker/Salesperson Gets Paid" earlier in this chapter for more.) Pay by commission is a common practice across the United States, but has never been established as a requirement by any government or private agency.

No such thing as a standard commission exists. No state that I know of sets commission rates. No local real estate board or other association of real estate agents has the authority to set commission rates or create any standardized fees for services. In fact, any attempt among real estate agents to create a standardized fee schedule is and has been viewed as violating federal antitrust laws. The fact that many brokerages in a particular area charge the same commission is a matter of competition and individual business decision.

The Sherman Antitrust Act, which is a federal law that prohibits activities that are considered to be in restraint of trade and therefore against consumer interest, forbids any type of price fixing in any industry. In simple terms, what that means is that if I own an appliance store and you own an appliance store, we can't get together once a month and decide that we're both going to charge the same price for a washing machine.

REMEMBER

In the real estate industry, antitrust laws essentially have been taken one step further as a result of a famous court decision in a case called *United States versus Foley.* The result of this case determined that even if no actual consultation occurred between individuals about price fixing, the mere discussion among competitors of prices for services is considered an invitation to fix prices and therefore violates antitrust law. As a result, the industry operates on the principle that discussing fees between brokers is illegal unless the brokers are cooperating on the same deal. Fees may be discussed in-house between brokers and salespeople and brokers, salespeople, and clients. In other cases, the courts determined that local boards of realtors can't dictate, recommend, or publish rate schedules.

Bad break: Market allocation

The Sherman Antitrust Act also has a provision against market allocation that affects real estate professionals. *Market allocation* is an agreement among competitors to divide the market in some way.

Consider two brokers, for example, who own their own brokerages and meet and agree that one of them will handle all the listings west of Main Street and the other will handle all the listings east of Main Street. Add to the mix two other brokers who meet and agree that one will handle only houses worth more than $300,000 and the other will handle only houses under that price. All four brokers have violated the Sherman Antitrust Act's provision against market allocation.

Feeling shunned: Group boycotts

Group boycotts — when competitors get together and agree not to do business with someone — violate the Sherman Antitrust Act.

Say *X* Brokerage and *Y* Brokerage don't like the way *Z* Brokerage does business. They meet and agree not to make any referrals to *Z* Brokerage. The *X* and *Y* brokerages have just violated the Sherman Antitrust Act prohibition against group boycotts. However, an individual broker can decide not to do business with another broker because he believes the other broker acts unethically. It's getting together as a group to boycott that's against the law.

What's your condition? Tie-in arrangements

Any requirement to buy one product or service on condition that you buy another product or service is called a *tie-in arrangement* or *tying agreement* and is an antitrust violation.

Say I am a broker who owns a property that a builder wants to buy. As part of the sale, I require that the builder relist the property with me (list back) when he sells it. Because I required the builder to list the property with me as a condition of my selling it to him, I broke the law.

Review Questions and Answers

For the most part questions in this section are aimed at people taking the broker's exam. In general, the exam may focus on broker responsibilities, license law issues, and the independent contractor status of salespeople. The antitrust questions may be on both the salesperson's and the broker's exams. You also need to check whether property management is a subject you're expected to know for the test at the license level you're going for in your state.

1. A salesperson paid an hourly wage and expected to be in the office from 8 a.m. until 2 p.m. to answer phones is probably a(n)

   (A) independent contractor.

   (B) employee.

   (C) contract agent.

   (D) associate broker.

   Correct answer: (B). A person required to work certain hours and paid an hourly wage is usually considered an employee. An independent contractor is allowed to work her own hours and is usually paid for her productivity by commission. An associate broker is not a status of employment but rather a licensing level. I made up the term "contract agent."

2. A division of a community along geographic lines for purposes of listing homes for sale by two salespeople working for the same broker is

   (A) market allocation in violation of antitrust laws.

   (B) legal.

   (C) a tie-in arrangement.

   (D) an in-house boycott that is illegal.

Correct answer: (B). The allocation prohibition is between two brokers not within one brokerage, which makes the situation in the question completely legal.

3. Broker Bob will not give any referrals to Broker Jane because he believes she acts unethically. He tells no one about this. He

   (A) is violating the antitrust law regarding group boycotting.

   (B) is entitled to his opinion but needs to have checked with his local Board of Realtors first.

   (C) is violating no antitrust law.

   (D) needs to refer business to her because he has no proof of her behavior.

   Correct answer: (C). No group is involved here. As long as no fair housing or civil rights laws are being violated, an individual generally is permitted to do business with whomever he or she wants.

4. Who sets the commission rate in a real estate brokerage office?

   (A) The state real estate commission in each state

   (B) The local Board of Realtors

   (C) No mandatory rates are in effect, but rates need to follow the published rate schedule.

   (D) The broker who owns the business

   Correct answer: (D). Antitrust laws state that no group of brokers can get together to set rates or publish fee schedules, and states don't set them, either. Answer (D) is the common and legal practice in the industry.

5. Broker Helen allows her dentist to use her vacation condominium for a week for free to thank him for sending her a person who listed a house with her. Helen

   (A) did nothing wrong.

   (B) violated license law.

   (C) violated the antitrust prohibition about tie-in arrangements.

   (D) should have checked with the state real estate commission first.

   Correct answer: (B). State license laws generally prohibit the payment of fees or gifts to non-licensed individuals as part of a real estate transaction. So Helen did something wrong, it's not an antitrust violation, and there's nothing to check because it is a license law violation.

6. A property manager is employed by the XYZ Real Estate Investment Company to manage its properties. The manager

   (A) most likely does not need a real estate license.

   (B) most likely needs a real estate license.

   (C) does not need a real estate license if the owner of the company has one.

   (D) needs a license only to collect the rents.

STATE
SPECIFIC

Correct answer: (A). Check your local state for the specific regulations, but generally an employee of a single company managing its own real estate need not have a license.

7. Property managers are usually considered

(A) special agents.

(B) general agents.

(C) universal agents.

(D) contractual agents.

Correct answer: (B). A general agent handles a range of activities on behalf of a client. Special agents handle only one activity like selling a piece of property, and universal agents act on behalf of a client in all real estate matters (I cover these two categories in Chapter 4). I made up contractual agents.

8. What type of insurance secures against employee theft of rent collected?

(A) Workers' compensation

(B) Surety bond

(C) Liability

(D) Business interruption

Correct answer: (B). Workers' compensation insures against employee injury. Liability insurance insures against injury to a member of the public injured on the property. Business interruption insurance (also called rent loss insurance) provides payments to the landlord when rents can't be collected due to some disaster like a fire. Surety bonds insure against an employee's dishonest acts (like the one in the question).

9. The amount of compensation received by a property manager is

(A) set by the local real estate board.

(B) set by the local property owner's association.

(C) a matter of individual negotiation.

(D) always based on a percentage of gross rents.

Correct answer: (C). This is the same as setting commission rates. It's all negotiable.

10. Because of the independent contractor status of most real estate salespeople, a broker

(A) should not bother with a policies and procedures manual.

(B) is not responsible for his salesperson's actions.

(C) is responsible for his salesperson's actions only with respect to fair housing law violations.

(D) need not withhold Social Security taxes unless they are employees.

Correct answer: (D). One of the distinguishing features of independent contractor status is that the broker doesn't have to withhold payroll taxes or Social Security payments. That doesn't relieve the broker of his responsibility for his salesperson's actions. All of the other answers are therefore wrong.

IN THIS CHAPTER

» **Choosing and establishing an agency relationship**

» **Looking at the duties of an agent to a principal and a customer**

» **Finding out who pays an agent and when**

» **Discovering how to end an agency relationship**

Chapter **4**

Understanding Agency Law

My guess is that the kind of agent you're most familiar with is the Hollywood agent. And that's as good a place as any to start talking about what the word *agent* means. Before and after the big parties and movie premieres, what does an agent do? An agent represents a client, and that means that agent always works for the client's best interest in any deal that the agent negotiates on behalf of the client. The agent tries to get the client the best role in the movie for the most money or may try to get the client a bigger dressing room at the studio.

Real estate agents are no different. They represent their clients and always work in their best interests. Except that the work isn't about better movie roles and bigger dressing rooms. It's probably about a better price for a house or a faster sale. Regardless of whether they're located in Hollywood or Topeka, or whether they're negotiating salaries or house sales, the relationship between agents and the people they represent comes with duties, responsibilities, and expectations.

In this chapter, I discuss the all-important agency relationship and its main players. I talk about how to establish such a relationship and define the elements of relationships between agents, principals (who are also called clients), and customers. I tell you about payday (who pays an agent and when), and I let you know how to end an agency relationship.

STATE SPECIFIC

Every chapter in this book is important and fair game for the questions on the real estate exam that you're going to take. That said, be sure to pay particular attention to the information in this chapter. People who buy and sell houses and other real estate continue to misunderstand the agency relationship. Although the situation has been getting better, various states are aggressive in making sure that their real estate agents understand the agency relationship, can act accordingly and appropriately, and can explain its nuances to the people who use their services. Specific types of agency relationships and laws governing agency vary a great deal from one state to the next, but the information I give you in this chapter is pretty much generic and therefore applicable in most (if not all) states. As such, you need to pay particularly close attention to the way your state deals with the entire subject of agency so that you know exactly what the agency rules are and how agency relationships are conducted. Through the years, the states have increased the number of hours they require in coursework on agency law, which, in turn, means that more emphasis is placed on this subject in the state's licensing exams. So be prepared for a bunch of questions about agency law on your state's exam.

Becoming Someone's Real Estate Agent: You're Hired

In this section, you find information about some important parts of agency law, who you represent, and how the agency relationship is established between you and that client.

Picking sides: Representation in agency relationships

You'd think that defining or establishing just who you represent is an easy question to answer. In fact, you're probably amazed that I'm telling you right now that many real estate agents, buyers, and sellers either are confused about what constitutes an agency relationship from the beginning or seem to forget about it along the way. I explain why this confusion exists at the same time that I give you information that clarifies who you represent in a real estate transaction.

Getting to know you: Agents, principals, and customers

Several people are involved in any given agency relationship, but first, I need to make sure that you understand who *you* are within that arrangement. An *agent* is someone who is authorized to represent the interests of another person. The three different types of agents, in the order of least to most authority, include

STATE SPECIFIC

>> **Special agents:** An agent who is hired by someone to represent that person in one transaction. A real estate agent who represents someone in the sale or purchase of a house is considered a special agent. In some states, this type of agent also is called a specific agent.

STATE SPECIFIC

>> **General agents:** An agent who represents someone in a range or group of activities. A property manager, who collects rent, pays bills, authorizes repairs, and negotiates leases, among other tasks, usually is considered a general agent (see Chapter 3 for more on property management). In some states the universal agent (see the next bullet point) is called a general agent, so make sure that you know the correct terminology for your state.

>> **Universal agents:** An agent who acts on a client's behalf in all matters and situations. Someone who has a power of attorney to act on someone's behalf in all real estate matters is an example of a universal agent.

STATE SPECIFIC

I talk about the relationship between brokers and salespersons in Chapter 3, but I want to say something more specific about brokers, salespeople, and the agency relationship. Licensed real estate salespersons work for and under the authority of a licensed broker. The agent in an agency relationship is the broker. The salesperson is considered an agent of the broker and a *subagent* of the seller or buyer (depends on who the broker is representing), forming one of the more common types of subagencies. However, enlisting the help of other brokers in the sale of a property is equally as common an idea. This can be done through a local multiple listing service (see "Looking at listing agreements" later in this chapter) or with individual brokers. These other brokers, who often are called cooperating brokers, also may become subagents of the seller. (It's not common to enlist the aid of other brokers when a broker is representing a buyer.) The point is you need to check out the specific responsibilities of subagents and characteristics of subagencies in your home state.

BUT I NEVER SAID THAT: VICARIOUS LIABILITY

There's a problem with the subagency relationship I describe earlier in this chapter. When using a cooperating broker or agent, the client can be held liable for the actions of the subagent. Let me give you an example. Say Client Jones wants to sell her house and hires Broker A to be her broker; that is, her agent. The client gives her broker permission to get the help of other agents to sell the house. Broker A puts the word out that this house is for sale, and Salesperson C who works for Broker B comes along and starts to show the house. In the course of showing the house Salesperson C makes a remark to a potential buyer that they might not be happy in the neighborhood because it's very ethnically uniform with many immigrants from one country. The buyer takes offense and considers this a violation of fair housing law. The buyer would be justified in filing a complaint against Salesperson C, Broker B, Broker A, and Seller Jones, because even though the seller has never even met Salesperson C, he is working for her as a subagent. The courts in these cases have often been reluctant to place blame on the unsuspecting seller/client. States have taken steps to eliminate this situation.

At least one state has created something called the Broker's Agent in an attempt to avoid the subagent dilemma. In this arrangement when the client's broker enlists the help of other agents, the other agents become subagents to the broker but not to the client. In other cases individual multiple listing systems no longer consider cooperating brokers to be subagents of the seller but rather subagents of the listing broker. Although subagencies with vicarious liability to the seller are gradually being eliminated, you should check to see if your state has dealt with the issue and how.

In addition to an agent, a few other key players in agency relationships are the following:

» **Principal:** A *principal* is the person you represent as an agent. This is the person you have the agency relationship with.

» **Client:** A *client* is another name for a principal.

» **Customer:** A *customer* is the other party to the transaction. In a typical real estate transaction, there's you (the agent or subagent), the principal or client (such as a seller), and the customer (such as a buyer). The customer is considered and sometimes referred to, particularly in exam questions, as the third party.

One or the other: Single agency with sellers or buyers

Most real estate agency relationships are *single agency relationships*, meaning you represent either the buyer or the seller. You know who these two people are, but which one is the principal (client) and which is the customer? The short answer is the principal (client) is the person with whom you have an agency agreement, that is, the person you've agreed to represent. The customer is the third party, that is, the person you do not represent. And this lineup is the same regardless of whether you represent a buyer or a seller.

This is important but not necessarily easy information to understand, so let me illustrate. Broker A is hired by Seller A to represent her in selling her house. Buyer B hires Broker B to represent him as a buyer's agent (don't worry; I cover buyer's agency in a little while). In these two relationships Seller A is the principal or client of Broker A. Buyer B is the principal or client of Broker B. Now let's say Buyer B wants to negotiate to buy Seller A's property. Seller A now becomes the customer to Broker B, while Buyer B becomes the customer of Broker A. There are other possible relationships; however, this is where it begins, in the single agency relationship between agent and client with the customer being the third party.

Remember that the reason for the confusion is pretty much because of the way the real estate business has worked for 10,000 years. (All right, maybe not 10,000 years, but who knows, a real estate agent may have been trying to sell someone a nice, cool tropical cave with an ocean view sometime back in the Stone Age.) The fact is that in most places, real estate agents traditionally represented the seller, yet spend most of their time with the buyer. If you've either bought or sold a house and used a real estate agent, you probably have a good idea of what I'm talking about. The real estate broker signs an agreement to act as an agent to sell someone's house, but the agent may not see the seller again except occasionally to bring people to the house to see it. Meanwhile, the agent spends every Saturday driving Mr. and Mrs. Buyer around looking at houses. Mr. and Mrs. Buyer are the customers. Nothing's wrong with this scenario; it's just that the agent, who's spending a lot of time with them, is so nice and helpful, and might even make a good match for their single cousin, actually represents the seller. But the Buyers begin thinking the agent represents them. And sometimes the agent begins to act like she does, too.

In an attempt to clarify things, particularly for buyers, something called buyer agency has been developed. *Buyer agency* is when the agent represents the buyer instead of the seller. In this case, the buyer is the principal or client and the seller is the customer. The rules and regulations covering buyer agency may vary from state to state, so you need to check out how buyer agency works in your state and any specific buyer agency laws that your state enforces.

A neat trick: Representing both sides in dual agency

Dual agency is a situation where both sides in a transaction, typically a buyer and a seller, are represented by the same real estate agent. Dual agency may actually be illegal in your state, but it's legal in enough states that I can give you some information that should get you through any test questions about the subject. You need to find out from your home state's specific laws whether dual agency is legal, and if so, under what circumstances.

Suppose you agree to represent Mr. and Mrs. Buyer as their buyer's agent to find a house. After working with them for several months with no success, you get a call from Mr. and Mr. Seller, who want you to represent them as their agent to sell their house. Just to be clear, you now have agency agreements with both Mr. and Mr. Seller and Mr. and Mrs. Buyer. At this point there's no dual agency or problem. However, you now show Mr. And Mr. Seller's house to Mr. And Mrs. Buyer, and the Buyers agree to make an offer. You are representing both sides in this transaction. That's dual agency. If your state allows it, the usual way to make this legal is to inform the Buyers and the Sellers of your dual agency status and get their consent to continue representing both parties. This is called obtaining informed consent. This is sometimes referred to as *limited agency* because each client doesn't receive the full range of your fiduciary duties. For example, neither party can receive your undivided loyalty. I discuss specific fiduciary duties later on in the chapter in "Keeping the Faith: The Relationship between an Agent and a Principal."

The man (or woman) in the middle: Transactional brokerage

In some states, the idea that a broker is really a kind of middleman in a transaction between two parties is being given serious consideration. Some states have passed laws creating what is called *transactional brokerage,* providing for a situation in which a broker represents neither buyer nor seller but yet can complete a transaction and be paid for it. In such an arrangement, the broker brings the buyer and the seller together, negotiates the deal, and handles some or all of the paperwork.

The major difference is that the transactional broker would not represent either side in the transaction. You need to check with your state's real estate law to find out whether this type of arrangement exists, and if it does, how your state has named the new arrangement, what brokers are called in this situation (because they may no longer be considered agents), and what the basic duties and responsibilities are, because they aren't fiduciaries. As you look for these laws in your state be aware that some states refer to this arrangement as non-agency and to the broker as a facilitator or intermediary as well as a transactional broker. (See "Keeping the Faith: The Relationship Between an Agent and a Principal," later in this chapter, for more on fiduciary responsibilities.)

Letting everyone know: Agency disclosure requirements

STATE
SPECIFIC

A famous study some years ago indicated that a majority of buyers thought they were being represented by the real estate agent who was driving them around town looking at houses. In almost all the cases, the real estate agent was representing the seller, but because the agent was spending so much time with and being so helpful to the buyer, the buyer thought he was their agent and not the seller's. As states began recognizing the confusion that exists regarding who represents whom in a real estate transaction, they've enacted laws requiring real estate agents to tell prospective clients and customers who they represent.

These laws, where they exist, are referred to as *agency disclosure laws.* Agency disclosure clears up any confusion for buyers and sellers as to who, if anybody, is representing them. It also gives them an opportunity to get an agent to work for them if they're not being represented. Disclosure typically is given in writing to both buyers and sellers. You need to find out what disclosure requirements, if any, exist in your state. (For more about the responsibility of disclosure, check out "You'd better tell: Disclosure," later in this chapter.)

Establishing the agency relationship (and doing it in writing)

STATE
SPECIFIC

Representing a party to a real estate transaction as an agent and (hopefully) getting paid for it are based on the agency relationship that you established with that party. The information in this section about how you can establish agency relationships is pretty universal, so it applies in most (if not all) states. Nevertheless, you need to check whether your state's licensing law recognizes or prohibits any of the following ways of establishing an agency relationship and whether your state perhaps recognizes other ways that I haven't covered.

An agency relationship can be established either by means of an agreement between the parties, an agent and a principal (client), or by means of the actions of the two individuals. The first of the bullet points that follow is the former, and all the rest are the latter. You should remember that although I give examples of agents selling houses to illustrate the following types of agencies, if the statute of frauds in your state requires that all real estate agency agreements be in writing, then it's unlikely that you can collect a commission by any of the non-written agencies. (For more on the statute of frauds, see Chapter 11.)

STATE
SPECIFIC

>> **Express agency:** *Express agency* is where the agency relationship is created through an agreement in which the agent and the principal state their intentions to enter into an agency relationship, that the agent will represent the principal. The parties state or express their intentions in words, either orally or in writing. Whether an oral agreement establishing an agency relationship is binding varies from state to state, so check it out. It may also be possible for an oral agreement to establish an agency relationship but not be enforceable by you, the agent, to collect a fee. The typical written agreement is a listing agreement or a buyer's agency agreement, both of which I discuss in the next two sections. The written agreement is the most appropriate and legally safe way to create an agency relationship.

>> **Implied agency:** *Implied agency* establishes an agency relationship through the actions of the two parties. Although nothing formal has been said or written down, the agent and the

principal *act* as if they have an agency relationship. Creating an implied agency may not have been what the two parties intended, but an agency relationship can be created anyway. If you find these circumstances hard to imagine, check out what happened to Ms. Seller.

Ms. Seller is selling her home by herself and puts up a for-sale sign on the lawn. You drive by, see the sign, and stop in. You identify yourself as a real estate agent and ask some questions about the house. Ms. Seller tells you she doesn't want to list the house for sale with any brokerage. She does tell you to feel free to bring any possible buyers around who might want to see the house. The next day you bring Mr. and Mrs. Buyer, who really like the house and want to make an offer. You tell Ms. Seller and begin negotiating a deal. If the matter comes down to commissions and lawsuits, only a court can finally decide, but you and Ms. Seller probably have established an implied agency relationship because of both your actions.

>> **Agency by estoppel:** An *agency by estoppel* is created when a principal doesn't stop an agent from going beyond the agent's normal duties, which thus gives the impression that an agency relationship has been established. Say you're the owner of a building and you tell your agent to show an apartment to a possible tenant. The agent goes ahead and negotiates a lease even though you didn't give the agent any direct authority to do so. The tenant assumes the agent has the authority and an agency by estoppel has been created.

>> **Agency by ratification:** An *agency by ratification* is created by accepting circumstances that created the agency after the fact. Suppose a real estate agent, without authorization and without ever speaking to the seller, negotiates a deal for a house that's for sale by the seller. One day the agent arrives with a completed contract simply awaiting the seller's signature and acceptance of the deal. An agency by ratification probably has been created when the seller ratified what the agent had been doing by accepting the deal. I say "probably," because the agent wants a fee for his services and may have to sue the seller to collect. When that's the case, the courts determine whether an agency relationship existed from the beginning of the negotiations — based on the fact that the seller accepted or ratified the agent's behavior by accepting the deal.

>> **Agency coupled with an interest:** An *agency coupled with an interest* is a situation in which an agent has some kind of interest in the property that's being sold. For example, suppose a part-time broker is also an architect. The broker/architect agrees to design some houses for a builder who's giving the broker/architect the listings for the sale of the finished houses. In essence the broker/architect made an investment in the project, so the builder can't cancel the agency agreement. If this sounds like a tie-in arrangement and an antitrust violation (see Chapter 3), remember that the broker/architect isn't making one activity conditional on the other. A tie-in arrangement would've been created if the broker had said that if the builder wanted him to sell the finished houses, the builder also had to hire him (as in pay him) to design the houses. In an agency coupled with an interest, it's as if the broker/architect was investing in the project.

Most agency relationships are established in writing with different agreements for buyer and seller agency relationships (see "One or the other: Single agency with sellers or buyers," earlier in this chapter). Listing agreements involve sellers, and buyer agency agreements involve buyers. (How did you guess?) Within the two categories are different kinds of agreements. Many details within various types of agreements are similar with respect to the duties to be performed. The differences usually deal with circumstances under which an agent will or won't get paid. The issue of payment of the broker's fee, which is covered in more detail in "Making Money (No, Not at the Copy Machine)," later in this chapter, usually is related to who is the procuring cause of the buyer or seller. The *procuring cause* means the person who found the buyer or seller and made the transaction happen. Often it's referred to as the person who brought about a meeting of the minds between a buyer and a seller. It also may be defined as the broker who brought a ready, willing, and able buyer to the deal in terms acceptable to the seller.

Looking at listing agreements

A *listing agreement* establishes an agency relationship between an agent and a property seller. The agent agrees to represent the seller in marketing the property. Here are the names and descriptions of the four types of listing agreements in the order that they are more commonly used:

>> **Exclusive right to sell listing:** In this type of listing agreement, a broker is given the exclusive right to market a property on behalf of the seller. The broker is paid regardless of who sells the property, an especially important point because it distinguishes this type of listing agreement from the others. I'll clarify: The owner always retains the right to sell his or her own real estate, even so, while the listing agreement is in effect, if the owner sells the property without any help from the broker, the owner still has to pay the agreed-upon fee to the broker.

>> **Exclusive agency listing:** In this type of listing agreement, a broker is hired to act as an exclusive agent, representing the owner in the marketing of the property. The broker, of course, earns a fee if the property sells. However, if the owner of the property sells the property without any help from the broker, the property owner won't have to pay the broker a fee.

>> **Open listing:** Notice anything missing from the name of this type of listing? The word "exclusive" is taken out because the property owner has the right to use as many brokers as are needed to sell the property. No broker has the exclusive right to represent the owner. This type of listing sometimes is called a nonexclusive or general listing. The owner who sells an open-listed property without any help from a broker is under no obligation to pay a fee to any broker. If a broker does bring a successful buyer to the property, the owner must pay the broker a pre-agreed to fee.

STATE
SPECIFIC

>> **Net listing:** A *net listing* is a listing for which a broker is hired to sell the property for a certain amount of money called the *net amount* or *net price*. The broker keeps any amount in excess of the net price. So if you take a net listing on a house for which the owner wants to net $200,000 from the sale, and you sell it for $225,000, you get to keep $25,000 as your fee. ***Note:*** Net listings are illegal in some states and discouraged in others. Some states allow it only if the maximum commission to be earned by the agent is made clear to the seller in writing in the original listing agreement. Check out your state law about this kind of listing. Questions about net listings tend to be favorites among test writers, especially if it's illegal in your state.

STATE
SPECIFIC

In addition to these four types of listings, you may encounter something called an option listing. An *option listing* is not as much a listing as it is a clause in any listing agreement that gives the broker the right to buy the property. Check out your local state law to find out whether option listings are allowed and what conditions or requirements may be imposed when using an option listing. You can see the danger of a conflict of interest here so states that do permit them tend to regulate them.

More people have probably heard about multiple listings than have heard about the listing agreements we just talked about. Don't get confused. A *multiple listing service* or *multiple listing system* (MLS) isn't really a type of listing as much as it is a marketing service that permits brokers to share listings with other brokers. A broker gets a listing to sell a house and then puts it on the local MLS. Tens, if not hundreds, of other brokers look at that listing, and one of them may have a buyer for the property. In an MLS arrangement, the broker who has the agreement with the principal is the one who earns a commission on the sale, although he often may split that commission with other brokers who helped bring about the sale.

TIP

Because multiple listing systems have more to do with marketing than anything else, rarely are there any questions about them on state exams. I mention the multiple listing systems briefly here just in case it happens to be used as an incorrect choice on a question or possibly as a correct choice for a question that has to do with which choice is not a type of listing agreement.

Examining buyer agency agreements

Traditional real estate brokerage continues to primarily represent sellers; however, as buyers became aware that they didn't have representation in real estate transactions, buyer agency agreements were developed to enable the buyer to become the principal and thus have all the advantages of being represented by a real estate agent. The several types of buyer agency agreements differ primarily in the circumstances under which the broker is paid. Here are typical agreements:

>> **Exclusive buyer agency agreement:** This agreement makes the broker the exclusive agent for the buyer, and no matter who finds the property that the buyer is seeking, a fee is owed to the broker, if and when the buyer buys the property. Even if the buyer buys property directly from an owner with no broker involved, the buyer still has to pay the exclusive agent a fee. This type of agreement is also called *an exclusive right to represent.*

>> **Exclusive agency buyer agency agreement:** This agreement makes the broker the exclusive agent of the buyer, but it requires the broker to be paid only if the broker finds the property that the buyer ultimately purchases. If the buyer finds property and buys it without help from the broker, the buyer owes no fee to the broker.

>> **Open buyer agency agreement:** This agreement enables the buyer to enter into agreements with any number of brokers and is therefore not an exclusive type of buyer agency agreement. The buyer pays only the broker who finds the property that the buyer buys. The buyer owes the broker nothing, if the buyer finds and purchases a property without help from the broker.

The buyer or the seller may pay the fee in a buyer's agency agreement. Fiduciary responsibility (see the next section) doesn't follow the money. A buyer's agent who owes complete fiduciary responsibility to the buyer can be paid from a portion of the commission paid by a seller to the seller's agent. This is no different from when a fee is split in a co-brokering arrangement in which both brokers represent the seller except for who is being represented. See "Making Money (No, Not at the Copy Machine)," later in this chapter, for more.

Keeping the Faith: The Relationship between an Agent and a Principal

The elements of an agent's responsibility to the principal are summed up in one word — fiduciary. *Fiduciary* means faithful servant, and an agent is the fiduciary of the principal. (In real estate transactions, the principal is also known as the client and can be either the seller or the buyer — see "Getting to know you: Agents, principals, and customers," earlier in this chapter.) The agent faithfully represents the interests of the principal above all other interests including the agent's own.

The specific fiduciary responsibilities of an agent have been handed down by practice and common law — what people have done and how the courts have interpreted those actions. Some states examined the fiduciary duties of real estate agents and incorporate them with their respective real estate license laws. Don't forget that the agent owes a fiduciary obligation to the principal or client. I discuss other duties and obligations that are due the customer in "Meeting Obligations: The Relationship Between an Agent and a Customer" later in this chapter.

STATE SPECIFIC

Although I discuss fiduciary responsibilities so that you have a good general understanding of the subject for exam purposes, you nevertheless need to check out your local state's interpretation of fiduciary duties so you're more in line with specific questions you may encounter on the state exam. Because fiduciary responsibilities are the basis of the agency relationship, exam writers want to make sure that you understand your obligations as an agent. Be prepared to answer several questions on this topic on the state exam.

Who has the money? Accounting

As a real estate agent, you handle money and sometimes large sums of it. Most often you'll handle the money that goes with the buyer's offer to purchase a property that is variously called the *binder* or *earnest money*. These funds are credited to the buyer and become part of the down payment. Eventually they belong to the seller but may be held by the broker for a considerable amount of time. The check may be written to the broker. Other funds from the buyer or the seller also may be entrusted to the broker.

The duty of accounting for all the funds that are given to you for safe keeping (yes, that don't belong to you) is part of your fiduciary responsibilities. Most states require that funds that belong to clients and customers be kept in a bank account that's separate from the broker's business account to avoid commingling or combining of client and customer funds with the broker's business or personal funds. *Commingling* is illegal even if you don't actually spend the money on yourself and can account for every penny. *Conversion,* or the act of using client or customer funds for the agent's personal or business expenses, also is illegal.

Better be careful: Care

Care is a broad and general word that best can be described as agents using their best efforts and skills on behalf of their clients' respective interests. Activities such as helping a seller client determine a fair asking price for a property and then making every reasonable effort to market the property are expectations of the client under the care provision of fiduciary duties. Advising a buyer to hire a home inspector and providing the buyer with information about pricing of other properties are normal parts of the care provision when the buyer is the client.

Shhhhh! It's a secret: Confidentiality

The agent is expected to keep all information that can harm the client's interest in the strictest confidence in addition to any personal information the client wants to be kept confidential, even if, in the agent's opinion, the information won't harm the client were it known. A seller client's desperate need to sell a property because of a financial situation needs to be kept confidential. A buyer client's equally desperate need to find a house before the school year starts needs to be kept confidential, and so does the buyer client's ability to pay more for a property than he or she is offering. Any client information that can be used to benefit the interest of the customer over the client must be kept confidential.

STATE SPECIFIC

In some places, the duty of confidentiality is considered to be part of the fiduciary duty of *loyalty.* (See "A friend to the end: Loyalty," later in this chapter, for more information.)

You'd better tell: Disclosure

The fiduciary duty of disclosure requires you, as an agent, to reveal any facts you're aware of that benefit your client. Disclosure applies to information that may benefit the client even if the client hasn't asked about it. As the agent, perhaps you know that the town is undergoing a tax reassessment that drastically may change the taxes on all the houses in town and that your buyer client wants to buy a home for the first time and doesn't have a clue what a reassessment is. (You, of course, can at least answer state exam questions about reassessment because you read Chapter 16 in this book, right?) As a buyer's agent, you're required to tell your client about the proposed reassessment, even though they didn't know enough to ask about it.

Disclosure also applies to information that can hurt your customer's interest and that your customer has asked you to keep confidential. Perhaps your buyer customer reveals to you some recent financial difficulty that may make getting a mortgage difficult. Regardless of whether your buyer customer asks you to keep the information secret, you need to tell your seller client about the possibility that the buyer may have difficulty getting a mortgage to buy the house. (See "Meeting Obligations: The Relationship Between an Agent and a Customer," later in this chapter, for more on an agent's responsibilities to a customer.)

REMEMBER

Disclosure is interpreted broadly. For example, the agent's duty to promptly give all offers to the seller client is considered part of disclosure. An agent who decides to buy his principal's property is something that must be disclosed. An agent buying a house that he has listed for sale is called *self-dealing.* Other people involved in the transaction, like a family member of the listing agent who is interested in buying the property, is information that has to be disclosed. If the information can help your client in any way or might harm him if he doesn't know it, it must be disclosed.

Keep in mind that the disclosure that is part of an agent's fiduciary responsibility isn't the same as a seller's obligation to disclose latent and material defects. In many states, a seller (whether or not she uses a real estate agent's services) must tell the buyer any bad news about the property that isn't readily visible by a normal inspection (rather than a special professionally done home inspection) and/or would have a material impact on the buyer's decision to buy the property. You should also remember that this type of disclosure isn't governed by the fiduciary duty of confidentially (see the previous section) or obedience (later in this chapter). See "Discovering defects," later in this chapter, for more.

One reason why states adopt agency disclosure rules, where agents must tell all those involved exactly who they represent and what that means, is the fiduciary requirement of disclosure to the principal. Too often, buyer customers begin to get so comfortable with the real estate agent that they reveal information that can hurt them in a negotiation and which the agent must reveal to his seller client. The customer either forgets that the agent represents the seller or never fully understands exactly what that means in terms of fiduciary duties. (For more, see "Letting everyone know: Agency disclosure requirements" earlier in this chapter.)

A friend to the end: Loyalty

Loyalty means always putting your client's interests above everyone else's, including your own. You may want to read that last phrase again — including your own. You must never profit by doing something against your client's interest.

EXAMPLE

You represent a buyer who wants to offer $200,000 for a house. You know the seller will take $180,000, and you're being paid a percentage of the total commission paid to the seller's broker based on the final sale price of the house. That means the higher the price of the house, the more money you make as the agent, right? I'm going to be blunt: Even though disclosing the seller's acceptable price is against your interest and you'll make less money, you nevertheless have to advise your buyer client to make the lower offer. If you don't, you're violating the fiduciary duty of loyalty and profiting at the expense of your client.

Yes ma'am: Obedience

Obedience, as a fiduciary duty, requires you as an agent to follow the instructions of your principal. Obedience is sometimes referred to as *faithful performance.* The only limitation on adhering to the duty of obedience is if the client's instructions are illegal or unethical. If your seller client gives you instructions that violate some provision of fair housing laws regarding marketing the property, your fiduciary duty of obedience doesn't require you to break the law and obey the client's order. I cover fair housing laws in Chapter 5.

The obedience requirement also doesn't extend to keeping things confidential regarding problems with the property itself. If your seller client instructs you not to tell potential buyers about a leaky roof, you wouldn't obey the client, because buyers have a right to have that kind of information.

Meeting Obligations: The Relationship Between an Agent and a Customer

Clients or principals clearly benefit from representation by an agent. Customers, who sometimes are thought of as the third party to a transaction, have rights, too. Remember that the customer can be either the buyer or the seller, depending on who the agent is representing as a principal. The agent is obligated to see that the customer gets whatever the customer is entitled to. Although not quite the same thing as a client-agent customer relationship, a seller working alone may also have obligations to the buyer. The agent's obligation to the customer is outlined in most places as providing

>> **Honest and fair dealing.** Agents must be honest and fair with their customers, including properly accounting for the funds left in their possession (see "Who has the money? Accounting," earlier in this chapter).

>> **Reasonable care.** Agents use their skills and expertise to help their customers, provided that doing so doesn't compromise their clients' interests.

>> **Disclosure of material facts.** Check out the sections that follow for more about the specifics of disclosure of information to the customer.

STATE SPECIFIC

Beyond the agent being trustworthy in handling the customer's funds, the customer mostly is entitled to information. I talk about several kinds of information that the agent is obligated to provide regardless of whether the customer is the buyer or the seller. The types of information principals and agents are obligated to reveal vary from one state to the next and frequently are interpreted by the courts. I only briefly mention the various things that you may have to reveal, so be sure to find out what your state expects an agent and a client to reveal to the customer. Just to be clear in case you didn't catch this, the seller acting alone, without representation, may have disclosure obligations to the buyer as governed by your state even though no real estate agent is involved. Expect there to be a question or two on the state test about this. Remember that disclosure of these facts applies to the customer, whether it's the buyer or the seller. In most cases real estate agents deal with seller clients and buyer customers, so most of my examples approach the issue from that perspective.

Discovering defects

Latent defects are problems with the property that the buyer customers or buyer agents wouldn't find out about through a normal inspection. Some states interpret latent defects to mean structural items and safety items. Structural items are things like problems with the foundation. On the other hand, the things that need to be revealed usually are called *material defects*. The word material, in this case, means important. A latent defect, such as a crack in the plaster in a closet, wouldn't necessarily be a material defect because it's not very important and probably wouldn't affect the decision of the average buyer to buy the house.

Disclosure of environmental risks, particularly the ones that pose health hazards, may also be information that you have to disclose. A leaking underground oil tank or the presence of a nearby nuclear power plant has to be disclosed to the buyer customer.

STATE SPECIFIC

The seller may also have an obligation to reveal material or latent defects. In some states real estate agent liability has been reduced by the adoption of specific forms that must be used as seller disclosure statements in which the seller is responsible for telling potential buyers about the condition of the property. Check this out in your state. These forms may more or less be mandatory or may carry financial obligations with them, as in money paid to the buyer if they're not completed by the seller. The agent often advises the seller of these obligations or tells them to check with their attorney. Get the details on what disclosure forms your state may have.

Looking at stigmatized properties

STATE SPECIFIC

Stigmatized properties are properties where events that make the property less desirable to some people have taken place. The event doesn't have to be documented as fact (actually happened) for the property to become stigmatized, but an agent may still have an obligation to tell a customer about it. A known murder or suicide can stigmatize a property, because some people don't want to live in a house where something like that occurred.

Reports of a house being haunted by ghosts can also stigmatize a property, even though no hard evidence proves the haunting. Stigmatized property is an extremely state-specific item of disclosure because of varying interpretations by different states and different court decisions regarding the requirement for disclosure. Be sure to check this out because you as an agent may have disclosure obligations and therefore may be tested on this on the exam.

Respecting Megan's Law

STATE SPECIFIC

The interpretation of Megan's Law, a federally enacted law that requires registration of sex offenders with the police and possible notification of neighbors regarding the location of a sexual offender, varies by state. Interpretations regarding the responsibility of real estate agents with respect to providing this information to prospective buyers also differ. Some states may require disclosure of the sex offender's whereabouts to prospective buyers. Some may require disclosure only in response to a direct question or providing a response that includes information about the sexual offender registry. Check out your local state's requirements to be sure. And remember you may have different obligations depending on whether you've got a buyer or seller client or customer.

Finding out about fraud and negligent misrepresentation

"This is the prettiest house on the street." When you, the seller's agent, say that to a prospective buyer, they realize you're giving them your opinion. They can also quite easily check it out for themselves. What you've just done is puff the property. *Puffing* is exaggerating the virtues or benefits of a property. It isn't illegal, and it's done all the time.

On the other hand, if you say property values are going to go up 10 percent a year for the next few years, you seem to be stating a fact, but the buyer has no way to check it out, because no one can predict the future. As the agent, you're perceived to be the expert and customers have every reason to believe you. However, if you're wrong, you could be in trouble. Worse yet is an outright false statement that you know is wrong: "No, sir, there are no plans to extend the six-lane road past your house." In court, which is where you may end up, your actions in either of these examples can be interpreted as *fraud* or an intentional misrepresentation done in order to sell the property.

Negligent misrepresentation is a little trickier than puffing and fraud. If you don't know something, you can't be expected to disclose it. Sounds right but it isn't. *Negligent misrepresentation* is when you don't disclose something, because you don't know it, *but you should have known it.* As a real estate agent, the public expects a certain expertise, knowledge, and level of care to be evident in your work regardless of whether you're dealing with a customer or client. The location of the new highway that will bring truck traffic down the residential street of the house you're trying to sell has been all over the local papers. Because you don't read the local paper, you neglect to mention this information to your buyer from out of town. By not telling your customer, however, you may have committed an act of negligent misrepresentation because the buyer expects you to know about such things.

Making Money (No, Not at the Copy Machine)

A discussion about how real estate agents are paid usually follows a discussion about agency relationships, because agents get paid if and when they fulfill their agency duties and complete the work of the agreement they've signed, helping someone sell or buy a property. Like any job, agents get paid when they accomplish what they were hired to do. The problem with the real estate business is how you define the phrase "accomplish what they were hired to do." And, because several people are involved in a typical real estate transaction, including a buyer and seller and possibly two brokers, who pays what to whom, why, and when isn't as straightforward as when you get your paycheck every week at the office. In this section I give you information about some of the issues that exam writers like to deal with regarding how agents earn their pay and how that relates to agency law. (For more information about agents' payment, see "Looking at listing agreements" and "Examining buyer agency agreements" earlier in this chapter.)

STATE SPECIFIC

I also give you some generally applicable information about fee arrangement in this section. But remember all of it is subject to your specific state's laws and regulations and to interpretations that your state courts may have made.

Pay up! Deciding who needs to pay an agent

In a normal business arrangement, the person who hires you pays you. But who said real estate is normal? In this section, I take a look at some possible fee arrangements.

In many, if not most, real estate transactions you're hired by sellers to be their agent. You owe them your fiduciary responsibilities and they pay you. So far, so good.

But what about when you're hired by the buyer as a buyer's agent? You owe your fiduciary responsibilities to the buyer. Yet, in many buyer agency arrangements, you'll still be paid by the seller. Feel free to read that sentence again; it's correct. You owe your loyalty and all your other fiduciary duties to the buyer but will be paid by the seller, because of a simple rule that you need to remember.

REMEMBER

Generally speaking fiduciary responsibility does not follow the source of the fee. This means that you can represent Person A and be paid by Person B even if your job is to represent Person A against Person B.

Looking at an example of a seller paying a buyer's agent may help you understand. Broker A is hired by Seller A as a seller's agent. Broker A will be paid a fee, usually in the form of a percentage commission based on the sale price of the house. To sell the house quickly and at the best price, Broker A puts the word out among other brokers in town that he has a house for sale, which is what usually is called a listing. Broker A may do this informally by phoning a few other brokers in the area or through a multiple listing service, which is a more formal arrangement for sharing listings (see "Looking at listing agreements," earlier in this chapter), and he offers to split the commission with any broker who brings someone to him who buys the house. Most likely he eventually executes a written agreement for sharing the commission with the other broker. Broker B is acting as a buyer's agent for Buyer B and brings Buyer B to Seller A's house. Buyer B likes the house and buys it. Broker B will be paid a share of the commission that Broker A offered. Remember, Broker A gets paid by the seller, and throughout the transaction, Broker B represented the buyer.

The seller doesn't always pay the buyer's agent's fee. The buyer can and sometimes does pay his broker's fee himself, an arrangement that is particularly true in the case of a buyer signing an *exclusive buyer agency agreement* in which the buyer must pay a fee no matter how he finds a property. So even if the buyer ends up buying a house directly from an owner with no broker involved, he still must pay his agent a fee.

Finally, where a buyer's agent and a seller's agent are involved in a transaction, it's always possible for the buyer and the seller each to pay their own agents. Just remember, your fiduciary responsibilities go to your principal, which is the person who hires you, even if you receive your fee from someone else.

Ready to go: Knowing when an agent should be paid

A question in the real world, and on state exams, is this: When, during the process do real estate agents earn their fees? The answer is when the broker produces a *ready, willing, and able buyer*. A ready, willing, and able buyer is someone who agrees with the seller to all the terms of the deal and is prepared to do whatever it takes to buy the property. For example, if the buyer doesn't have the full price in cash, he gets a mortgage. The broker in this case is considered the *procuring cause*, a fancy term for the person who brought the deal together.

TIP

An interesting factor that you notice about this answer is that it talks about the transaction from the seller agent's point of view, because most agents still represent sellers. Although a buyer's agency is growing, buyer agents' fees still are paid primarily by the seller (as the previous section mentions). So don't grow confused or worried about a question that deals with when the agent's fee is earned. The ready, willing, and able buyer answer should be fine.

Another factor to notice about the definition of when a fee is earned is that it says nothing about actually transferring ownership of the real estate from one person to another. A fee is earned when the minds of the seller and buyer meet in an agreement — a *meeting of the minds* — which simply is another way of saying that the buyer and the seller have agreed to the terms and are prepared to complete the transaction. A fee may well be owed to the broker, even if property ownership doesn't change hands.

If a seller agent produces a ready, willing, and able buyer who's ready to buy the property at the seller's price and has the money to do so, and for some reason, the seller changes his mind and refuses to sell the property, the broker still is entitled to a fee. Generally, whenever the broker is the procuring cause of the transaction, and the seller client does something to cause the sale not to happen, the broker is entitled to compensation.

Parting Is Such Sweet Sorrow: Ending an Agency Relationship

A real estate agency relationship can end in a number of different ways. Depending on the reason for the termination, the particular circumstances, and what is negotiated, the broker may or may not be entitled to compensation. You also need to remember that the fiduciary duty of confidentiality survives the ending of an agency relationship. A broker may not reveal information received from a client even after that client stops being the broker's client. Here are some of the ways an agency relationship can be ended:

>> **Completion of the terms of an agreement:** This method of ending a relationship sometimes gets forgotten. The relationship ends when you do what you agreed to do. Obviously, the agent receives payment in this situation.

>> **Expiration of the time period of the agency agreement:** Agency relationships are written for limited time periods, with six months being typical. If the agreement expires and no sale has been accomplished, the agency relationship ends with no payment to the broker.

>> **Destruction of the property:** If the property is destroyed by a natural or other disaster, such as a fire, a flood, a tornado, and so on, the property that was for sale no longer exists in its original form, so the agreement ends. No commission is paid. And yes, the owner can relist the now-destroyed house and semi-vacant land for sale.

>> **Taking of the property through an eminent domain proceeding (condemnation):** See Chapter 8 for more about eminent domain. Because the property doesn't belong to the seller anymore through no fault of his own, no commission is owed.

>> **Bankruptcy:** A bankruptcy filing by either of the parties (principal or agent) can end an agency relationship. It is unlikely that a commission is owed.

>> **Agreement by both parties:** Both parties agree to end the agency relationship before the terms of the agreement are met. In other words, no transfer of property takes place. An ending like this might result in some payment to the seller's broker for things like advertising costs.

>> **Death or declaration of incompetence:** When either party dies or is declared incompetent, the agency relationship is ended and no commission is due, but a broker may seek to collect some costs like advertising from the estate.

STATE SPECIFIC

>> **Renunciation or revocation:** *Renunciation* and *revocation* indicate the desire of one party but not the other to end the agency relationship. Permission to end the relationship this way varies from state to state, so be sure to check it out. The technical terms for this method of ending a relationship are *renunciation by the agent* and *revocation by the principal*. Depending on the particular circumstances, one of the parties may be able to collect money from the other.

STATE SPECIFIC

The information in this section on ending agency relationships is pretty general, but it covers the basic ways an agency relationship can end. However, you definitely need to check out whether any of these methods are permitted in your own state or if other ways of ending an agency relationship are acceptable.

Review Questions and Answers

Who you represent and your obligations are the essence of your work as an agent. And state test writers want to make sure you understand all of this. Expect a fair number of questions on this material on both the broker's and salesperson's exams. The salesperson's exam likely will ask more definition-type questions, and the broker's exam will expect more understanding and the ability to apply the law to short case studies. One other thing: You may want to re-read this chapter after you've completed the rest of the book. Agency is often taught near the beginning of a prelicense course and as you can see it appears early in this book. You need to know something about agency as you go through the rest of the material; however, it's been my experience as an instructor that students often have more questions about agency toward the end of the course than they did at the beginning because they have more context in which to understand agency obligations. And I often find the best of students can be confused about agency law even as they complete their prelicensing course. So be patient with yourselves, and ask lots of questions in class. Instructors don't know what you don't understand unless you ask.

1. A real estate broker generally acts as what type of agent?

   (A) Universal agent

   (B) General agent

   (C) Special agent

   (D) Ratified agent

TIP

Correct answer: (C). Remember the fact that as a real estate agent, you usually handle one special transaction rather than all (universal) or some (general) transactions for a client.

2. To whom does an agent always owe her fiduciary responsibility?

   (A) Buyer

   (B) Seller

   (C) Customer

   (D) Principal

Correct answer: (D). The principal is always the one with whom you have an agency relationship and therefore is the person to whom you owe your fiduciary responsibility. Either the buyer or seller, in given situations, can be the principal. So neither buyer nor seller can be answered as "always" being the object of fiduciary responsibility. In terms of customer and client, it's the client who's the principal, not the customer.

3. A real estate broker takes a listing to sell someone's house. What is the relationship between the broker and the seller?

   (A) Agent–principal

   (B) Client–customer

   (C) Agent–customer

   (D) Principal–principal

Correct answer: (A). Sorry folks, no fancy explanation here. The listing agreement is the usual way that an agency relationship is established between a broker and a seller. An agency relationship is between an agent and a principal. Remember that the principal is also called the client.

4. A broker will earn a commission on the sale of a property whether or not she was the procuring cause of the transaction under what type of listing agreement?

   (A) Open listing

   (B) Multiple listing

   (C) Exclusive agency listing

   (D) Exclusive right to sell listing

   Correct answer: (D). Multiple listing is not really a type of listing. In an open listing and the exclusive agency listing, the broker gets paid only if she finds a buyer and makes the sale happen.

5. An agent representing both a client and a customer would be practicing

   (A) single agency.

   (B) dual agency.

   (C) exclusive agency.

   (D) open agency.

   Correct answer: (B). Dual agency is the best answer. It can't be single agency, because even though the situation may have started out that way, something that shifted the customer to a client status occurred. Exclusive agency is too vague, although exclusive agency listings exist. It isn't open agency, because although open listings are a possibility, no such thing as an open agency exists.

6. What kind of relationship exists between an agent and a principal?

   (A) Exclusive

   (B) Special

   (C) Compensatory

   (D) Fiduciary

   Correct answer: (D). You'll have to remember this one. An exclusive relationship may or may not exist, depending on the type of listing agreement that is signed. Most agents in a single transaction are special agents, but you can also be a general or universal agent. No relationship called compensatory exists, although the word can confuse you, because you expect to be paid for being an agent. The question needs to be read in the broadest way possible. Any and all agents and principals have a fiduciary relationship.

7. What part of fiduciary duties requires the agent to use her skills and abilities in her client's best interest?

   (A) Obedience

   (B) Care

   (C) Disclosure

   (D) Confidentiality

   Correct answer: (B). All of the other choices are part of fiduciary duties. Obedience is following your client's orders. Disclosure is telling your client everything he needs to know for his benefit. Confidentiality is keeping your client's information secret. Reread "Keeping the Faith: The Relationship Between an Agent and a Principal" until you can distinguish among and between examples of each duty.

8. Accounting requires

    (A) a monthly expense statement provided to the client.

    (B) the conversion of funds to pay expenses.

    (C) commingling of funds.

    (D) no commingling of funds.

WARNING

Correct answer: (D). You may not see a lot of questions like this one, but I wanted to give you one anyway. It isn't a very good question in my opinion because the statement "Accounting requires" is too vague. Don't forget that you're taking a state real estate exam. Sometimes an assumption is made in the wording of a question such that you know that you're dealing with a question in a real estate context. So an accountant may think a client needs to get a monthly statement of expenses, but a real estate agent wouldn't think that unless he were a property manager and had specifically agreed to provide the statement to his client. Those circumstances are, however, too narrow for the monthly statement answer to be correct. Conversion is when a client's money is used for broker's expenses, and commingling is when the broker mixes a client's money and his own business or personal money in the same account. Both are illegal.

9. Your seller client needs to sell his property quickly to take a job in another city. What do you do with this information?

    (A) You tell buyers this so the house sells quickly.

    (B) You keep this information confidential.

    (C) You tell the buyers only if they ask.

    (D) You reveal this information only to a buyer's agent.

Correct answer: (B). Confidential it is. The confidentiality of this type of information is absolute. If the seller authorizes you to reveal the information to generate interest in the property, then you can reveal it only after explaining to the seller that he may end up with a lower price because of it. This information is personal to the seller's circumstances. Remember that if the information is about the property (like a leaky roof), it may have to be revealed to the buyer.

10. Which of the following types of information does not have to be disclosed to the seller client?

    (A) The buyer's financial condition

    (B) An offer that the agent feels is unacceptably low

    (C) The fact that the buyer owns a part interest in a sailboat with the agent

    (D) The occupation of the buyer

Correct answer: (D). You may have found accepting this answer tough. The buyer's financial ability to go through with the deal is important information. The agent doesn't have a duty to filter out offers. All offers need to be transmitted to the seller promptly. A partnership in a sailboat may not be a close relationship, but it nevertheless is a relationship that needs to be disclosed to the seller. The buyer's job is an important piece of information only if it affects his financial ability to complete the transaction.

Chapter 5

Knowing the Fair Housing Laws for Selling Real Estate

As a real estate agent, whether broker or salesperson, you're expected to know and abide by fair housing regulations. Real estate agents are key players in promoting fair housing and preventing discrimination in housing. State exam writers expect you to know about fair housing laws at the federal level, because those laws apply to all parts of the country. Many states, counties, and cities have enacted additional fair housing laws that supplement federal law. State examiners expect you to know about these local laws. As you study for the state licensing exam, you need to be sure to find out about fair housing laws that apply only to your state or local municipality.

In this chapter, I talk about laws the federal government has adopted to prevent discrimination in the sale and rental of land, houses, and apartments. These federal fair housing laws are a series of separate laws that were enacted at different times. I also talk about groups that are protected by these laws (called protected classes) and the specific discriminatory actions that are forbidden. And to top it all off, I also give you information about how the law is enforced as well as a few exceptions to the law.

Practicing Fair Housing: The Basics

The basic concept and goal of fair housing laws at the federal, state, and local levels is to prevent discrimination in housing and permit people to have an equal opportunity to live where they want to live. A student of mine once said that the only form of discrimination that's legal is monetary. An ad campaign promoting fair housing a while ago stated something to the effect that the only color you can discriminate against is green, as in the color of money.

In this section, I discuss specific federal laws that deal with housing discrimination, including some dates that you definitely want to remember. I also explain an interesting case that shows that a law is a law no matter how old it is. In addition, I talk about state and local laws, and the all-important fair housing poster.

STATE SPECIFIC

As a broker who hires people, you also need to be aware of and abide by nondiscrimination laws with respect to hiring practices. Generally speaking, equal employment laws aren't taught in real estate courses and are rarely tested. However, if you're a candidate for the broker's license, you need to find out whether your state's exam requires you to know anything about equal opportunity employment laws where hiring practices are concerned.

Understanding federal fair housing laws

Real estate agents primarily deal with and apply federal fair housing laws throughout the United States. In this section, I give you information on several federal laws, and I can pretty much guarantee that you'll see a few questions about these laws on the exam.

I discuss another set of laws related to fair housing in Chapter 15. That chapter is about financing real estate, and the laws I discuss there deal with providing equal opportunity and disclosure in the all-important mortgage loan process.

The 1866 Civil Rights Act

In 1866, right after the end of the Civil War, the United States Congress passed the Civil Rights Act of 1866. This law essentially prohibits discrimination in the purchase, sale, lease, or conveyance of real property (real estate and personal property) on the basis of race or color. The language of the act is clear insofar as it basically says that without any exception whatsoever, all citizens shall have the same rights regarding property regardless of race. The other unique thing about this act is that enforcement is accomplished by taking the case directly to federal court.

Although the act itself is important, an almost equally important 1968 court case that involved the act resulted in a landmark decision in fair housing law that you should remember. The case, *Jones versus Alfred H. Mayer Company*, essentially affirmed the fact that the 1866 act prohibited any discrimination on the basis of race by private individuals and the government *with no exceptions.* This case was filed shortly after the enactment of the Fair Housing Act of 1968 (see the next section).

REMEMBER

The lack of any exceptions to the 1866 Act is important, because more recent fair housing laws actually include exceptions. Because it was enacted first and still remains on the books, the 1866 act is deemed valid even today, having been affirmed in the *Jones versus Mayer* case as superseding later laws with respect to exceptions regarding discrimination on the basis of race. Because of that, no exceptions exist with respect to racial discrimination in housing. For more, see "Bending the Rules: Understanding Exceptions to the Law," later in this chapter.

The 1968 Fair Housing Act

The Fair Housing Act of 1968 is more technically known as Title VIII (read "Title Eight") of the Civil Rights Act of 1968. This act, the first in the 20th century, prohibited certain actions that were viewed as discriminatory with respect to housing and specifically defined groups, called protected classes, to which it applied. Unlike the 1866 Civil Rights Act (see the previous section), it included specific exceptions.

Together with the 1866 Civil Rights Act, the Housing and Community Development Act of 1974, and the Fair Housing Amendments Act of 1988, which added even more protected classes to the list, the 1968 act forms the basis of fair housing standards as they apply to real estate agents throughout the United States. The 1968 act is enforced by the Department of Housing and Urban Development (HUD).

These laws are best understood when they're broken down into what you can't do (prohibited acts), who you can't do it to (protected classes), and exceptions to the law. Presenting them this way enables me to cover this material within the context of what I discuss in the rest of this chapter. Check out "Don't Do It: Avoiding Discriminatory Actions," "Feeling Safe: Identifying Who's Protected," and "Bending the Rules: Understanding Exceptions to the Law" for more details.

Researching state and local laws

State and local governments like counties and cities have gradually adopted their own fair housing laws. These local laws need to be viewed and obeyed in addition to and not instead of federal law. The general rule regarding situations in which federal and local laws cover the same issues is that the more restrictive or stricter law applies. Local provisions usually don't add prohibited activities; federal law is pretty comprehensive with respect to prohibited discriminatory practices. Local provisions that are sometimes added include additional protected classes, or groups that require relief under the fair housing laws. For example, some cities and several states have added sexual orientation as a protected class to their fair housing laws. In addition, exceptions that the federal law permits sometimes are removed at the local level. (For more, see "Bending the Rules: Understanding Exceptions to the Law," later in this chapter.)

STATE SPECIFIC

Megan's Law is a federally enacted law that promotes registration of convicted sex offenders after they're released from prison and take up residence in a neighborhood. Megan's Law has raised issues of the civil rights and rights to privacy of offenders in local jurisdictions. So you need to check with your state to determine your obligations as an agent to provide information to prospective buyers regarding the presence of sex offenders in the neighborhood. (For more, see Chapter 4.)

STATE SPECIFIC

For exam purposes and, of course, for purposes of your future real estate practice, you need to research and find out as much as you can about any local, state, or municipal laws that supplement federal fair housing laws. Pay careful attention to any additional prohibited acts, additional protected classes, and exceptions to the exceptions.

Displaying the fair housing poster

The Department of Housing and Urban Development (HUD), which is responsible for the Federal Fair Housing Act, has created a fair housing poster that must be prominently displayed in all real estate offices. Failure to display the sign can be considered noncompliance with fair housing law and will be used as evidence of discrimination whenever a complaint is brought against the real estate office. HUD also requires that its fair housing logo or other such appropriate wording be used in all real estate advertising.

Don't Do It: Avoiding Discriminatory Actions

The basic provisions of the Federal Fair Housing Act of 1968 define certain actions that are considered discriminatory and prohibit them. I don't personally know the legislative background that went into writing this law, but it appears that Congress was trying to be specific enough to deal with people who may try to split hairs in attempts to circumvent a law that might simply have stated: "Do not discriminate." Specific activities, therefore, are listed in the act. I discuss and provide examples of each activity that's included. Remember these actions are considered discriminatory with respect to housing and are not permitted. For exam purposes, make sure you understand and remember prohibited activities and can identify them if they're presented in questions featuring short case studies. For more about groups that are protected, see "Feeling Safe: Identifying Who's Protected," later in this chapter.

No way: Refusing to sell or rent

This prohibited action is easy to pinpoint. Declarations like, "I won't rent you an apartment or sell you my house because you are (fill in the blank with a protected class: any race, color, religion, sex, ethnic background, familial status, or handicap)." Of course, a specific reason doesn't have to be mentioned for this kind of refusal to be considered discrimination.

On one condition . . . or a few: Changing terms for rental, sale, or services

A landlord or owner is prohibited from changing the terms or conditions of a rental or sale of a property for different tenants or buyers as a way to discriminate. Here's an example I use in my classes: You own an apartment building and have extensively researched damages commonly done by various types of individuals and developed a detailed schedule of security payments based on race, family status (with children, or not), and marital status. Is this activity legal or not? Emphatically, not! Even though you supposedly have objective data and probably claim that you're not using this activity to discriminate but rather only to protect yourself, it nevertheless is viewed as discrimination.

You need not apply: Discriminatory advertising

Discriminatory advertising is prohibited. Although discriminatory advertising is easy to understand, it may be a little confusing to apply. The obvious and outright discriminatory advertisement is, for example, "Apartment for rent, Latinos not welcome." You'd probably never be able to place such an ad in any reputable newspaper anyway, and even if you could, you'd be breaking the law. Suppose, however, that you place an ad in a suburban newspaper for a new housing subdivision that includes a picture of several White families sitting around the backyard barbecue. Such an ad also is considered discriminatory, because the ad can be viewed as welcoming only White people to the development. The reverse also would likely be considered discriminatory. For example, an ad showing only Latinos in the backyard might be viewed as an attempt to steer that ethnic group to that neighborhood. You can read about steering later in this chapter.

HUD issued guidelines that must be followed in real estate advertising. These guidelines cover primary areas of possible discrimination:

>> Advertising that uses certain words, phrases, pictures, or other visual representations that are discriminatory.

>> Using certain types of media as a means of discrimination. For example, advertising in media only available to or likely to be seen by targeted groups (protected classes) or in reverse not seen by those groups such as a local newspaper that is read by a White ethnic group.

REMEMBER

HUD provides fairly specific information about what language is and isn't acceptable in real estate advertising. For exam purposes and for real-world applications, remember that the use of certain words or phrases is prohibited even when your intent is not to discriminate. The categories of the prohibited language with some examples include the following:

>> **Code words, catchwords, or catchphrases:** These prohibited words may be a little more subtle or regional in nature. Obvious phrases like "integrated neighborhood" cannot be used. Words like "exclusive," although more subtle, may convey a racially exclusive or ethnically exclusive message and therefore are to be avoided.

>> **Color:** No use of words describing color as it relates to race or ethnicity is permitted. For example, "White" or "Black."

>> **Familial status:** The term *familial status* generally refers to the presence or absence of children in the family. Although marital status isn't a protected federal class, HUD guidelines prohibit advertising that states or implies "married couple only" or other similar language.

>> **Handicap:** "Property not suitable for a handicapped person" or any language that suggests an exclusion like that is forbidden. Inclusive words like "Apartment is handicapped accessible" are acceptable.

>> **National origin:** The use of words that describe national origin like Italian, Mexican, and so on are prohibited.

>> **Race:** No use of racially descriptive words, such as Asian or Caucasian, for example, is permitted.

>> **Religion:** Words describing religions, like Catholic, Christian, non-Christian, and so on, are prohibited.

>> **Sex or gender:** This category tends to be a problem more with rental housing than housing that's for sale. Any gender-preference words are prohibited. An exception is made for people who want to share an apartment or house with a roommate of the same sex. So you can advertise for a female roommate to share an apartment, but you can't advertise for only a male tenant for a rental apartment in an apartment house you own.

In addition any photos, drawings, or symbols that may imply preference with respect to any of the above categories are prohibited — for example, showing a picture of a church next to the house you're advertising for sale. Describing the location by using potentially biased references, such as "near the Catholic church," is prohibited. A reference to a known discriminatory facility must also be avoided. So you won't advertise a house for sale "near the XYZ Country Club" when the country club is known to discriminate in its membership policies.

Prohibited language, photos, symbols, and so on are considered discriminatory at their face value, or as they appear, meaning that good intentions don't count. Furthermore, discriminatory language can't be used to describe a tenant or buyer preference, the neighborhood, or the dwelling itself. So "Good Christian building" is just as bad and just as prohibited as "Apartment for rent: Only Christians need apply."

Avoid using welcoming and inclusive terms, such as advertising that states specific groups are welcome. The use of the HUD fair housing logo and words to the effect that fair housing guidelines apply are the proper ways to say that all groups are welcome to buy or rent.

One other factor that HUD addresses in its guidelines is the use of terms that have lost their original religious or exclusionary meaning. For example, an ad placed during December that reads "Give yourself a Christmas present with a new house" would not be prohibited.

All lies: Telling someone that property isn't available (when it really is)

If a house has been sold or an apartment already rented, so be it. But tell someone that an apartment is already rented when it isn't or that a house isn't available for sale when it is, and that's considered discrimination and therefore is prohibited. This form of discrimination may seem obvious and almost not worthy of its own rule. And although the background of this prohibition has faded into obscurity, I believe it had something to do with property owners saying that a dwelling unit was unavailable and then defending their action by indicating what they meant was that the unit was unavailable to a particular person.

Scaring people into selling: Blockbusting

Blockbusting generally is defined as encouraging people to sell their homes because of the entry or potential entry into the community or neighborhood of a particular group of people. The group usually tends to be different in some aspect, such as race, color, or country of origin. The fear that blockbusting generates is the possible loss of property value, and the idea behind it is to induce panic selling and generate listings of houses to sell or bargains for developers. The prohibition of blockbusting is particularly aimed at members of the real estate industry, because agents benefit from panic selling by getting new listings, but investors who use blockbusting techniques for profit may also be guilty of discrimination.

Telling people where to live: Steering

Steering is guiding, encouraging, or inducing people in some way to move to or stay away from a certain area or neighborhood, and it's illegal. Overt steering is easy to understand and avoid. Subtle forms of steering in the name of being helpful, like saying, "This is a good neighborhood," or "You wouldn't be happy here," also must be avoided. Participating in what I call self-steering is equally prohibited. What I mean, for example, is that a couple that asks to be shown houses "only in White neighborhoods" can't be accommodated. You must tell them that you can show them houses that meet their needs and financial situation in various neighborhoods, and then do so. And by the way, although avoiding discrimination is easy when someone says "White neighborhood" or something like that, it's sometimes a little more difficult to acknowledge the problem when someone asks for a neighborhood where a particular language is heavily spoken, because the family just came to this country.

Specifically accommodating a request like this is still considered steering, and it's illegal. Again, you can show the family a variety of houses that meet their financial and space needs and then let them decide. In some states offering opinions about the quality of the local schools is also considered steering and must be avoided. Though this probably isn't on the exam, real estate agents should provide the same information about a house to every prospective buyer. Providing different information to different buyers, especially when protected classes are involved, could be viewed as discrimination. You can read about protected classes in the section "Feeling Safe: Identifying Who's Protected" a little later on.

No money for you: Changing loan conditions

Once upon a time it was a common practice to not lend money to unmarried women regardless of their income or employment status. It was also common to not count a married woman's income in the mortgage loan calculation because she'd likely quit work to have children. Nowadays, any such actions, including discrimination on the basis of the other protected classes such as race or ethnic background, are forbidden. You can read about laws prohibiting discrimination in mortgage lending in Chapter 15.

Put away that crayon: Redlining

Redlining is discrimination in the lending of mortgage money based on location. This happens when a lending institution determines that for various reasons it will no longer make loans in a particular area. It figuratively or literally draws a red line around a particular neighborhood on a map and refuses to make loans on properties in that neighborhood regardless of the personal income qualifications of the borrower.

In 1977, as a result of past redlining activities, the federal government passed the Community Reinvestment Act, which requires certain financial institutions such as banks to develop and implement programs for reinvesting in their neighborhoods through mortgage, home improvement, and other types of loans. These financial institutions come under periodic review to determine whether they're in compliance with the act.

You can't join: Denying membership in real estate organizations

One of the more blatant forms of exclusionary discrimination is denial of membership in a multiple listing association to certain racial or ethnic groups. Because these associations share property listings of houses that are for sale, such a denial has a direct effect on keeping communities segregated. (For more on multiple listings, see Chapter 4.)

A more subtle form of this type of illegal activity is a club, group, or association that meets periodically to share property listings where a multiple listing system doesn't exist. Denial of membership in such a group is a prohibited action. The prohibition extends to any brokers' organization and includes professional real estate organizations.

Feeling Safe: Identifying Who's Protected

Federal fair housing laws protect essentially everyone. The government, however, has created *protected classes* — groups against which you can't discriminate. They're not so much groups of people as they are characteristics that can be used for the purposes of discrimination . . . and of course, should not be. In the sections that follow, I review federal, state, and local protected classes.

Knowing the federal protected classes

Since the adoption of the 1968 Federal Fair Housing Act, the history of federal fair housing legislation has been one of extending nondiscrimination protection to more and more groups. The following is a summary of the legislative actions, when they were added, and the classes they protect. You can expect questions on the state exam about the protected classes and when they were added, and you may see questions that are like case studies.

>> **1866 Civil Rights Act:** Protects against racial discrimination

>> **1968 Federal Fair Housing Act:** Protects race, color, religion, and national origin.

>> **1974 Housing and Community Development Act:** Protects against sex (gender) bias.

>> **1988 Fair Housing Amendments Act:** Protects the handicapped and familial status (presence of children). Take note that *handicaps* include persons with AIDS as well as alcoholics (but not drug addiction) in addition to conditions like visual, hearing, and physical handicaps and mental disability. (For more about laws related to the disabled, see "Extra Coverage: Protecting the Disabled from Discrimination," later in this chapter.)

Taken all together the current federal protected classes are as follows: Race, color, religion, national origin, gender, handicapping conditions, and familial status.

One relatively recent addition to the federal protected classes: In some instances, when the effect falls disproportionately on an existing protected class, criminal history may also fall into the category of a protected class. The guidelines for this class will probably become clearer in the coming years, but you should be aware of this change in the law.

Recognizing state and local protected classes

STATE SPECIFIC

Finding out whether the state or local governments (counties, towns, villages, or cities) within your state have added protected classes to fair housing laws is one of the most important steps you can take in preparing for the exam. Two of the more common classes these days are marital status and sexual orientation. In addition, mental disabilities may be more specially defined and protected in your state.

In addition, local exceptions to the exceptions may have been adopted, meaning that although federal law may permit an exception, local law may not. Questions based on state or local fair housing laws are fair game in state real estate exams. And remember that if a local fair housing law and a federal fair housing law are different, the stricter applies.

Bending the Rules: Understanding Exceptions to the Law

The 1968 Federal Fair Housing Act was written with certain exceptions, or cases in which people, in a sense, can discriminate in housing issues. In addition to remembering the exceptions themselves for test purposes, you need to remember these two important factors with respect to these exceptions:

>> Even if an exception is legal for an individual (such as the owner of a single-family home selling her house), a real estate agent is not permitted to participate in the exception. Real estate agents are held to a higher standard in fair housing matters.

>> Discriminatory advertising may not be used, even when the exception itself is legal. The owner of a single-family home can't use discriminatory advertising in selling her house, even though she could discriminate in the ultimate sale itself.

REMEMBER

Don't forget that regardless of exemptions permitted by the 1968 Federal Fair Housing Act, the 1866 Civil Rights Act permits no exceptions with respect to race. The exceptions in the 1988 Law are as follows:

>> **Age:** In order to accommodate age-oriented communities for older adults, an exception is made to the antidiscrimination laws involving age and familial (presence of children) status. Housing may be restricted to people 62 years of age or older or 55 years of age or older in cases where at least one occupant per unit is 55 and at least 80 percent of the units are occupied by people ages 55 or older. In these cases children may be excluded.

>> **Owner-occupied housing:** Multifamily housing of two to four units, where one of the units is owner-occupied, is exempt from fair housing laws.

>> **Private clubs:** An organization that restricts its membership may provide restricted housing to its members, as long as it doesn't offer housing to the general public.

>> **Public-law occupancy standards:** Local maximum occupancy standards aren't superseded in their application by the Fair Housing Act. For example, if a local law provides a maximum occupancy of two people per bedroom and you rent out a studio apartment in a building you own, you can't be forced to rent the apartment to a couple with a child.

>> **Religious organizations:** Housing sponsored by a religious organization may be restricted to members of that particular religious organization, provided the religion doesn't discriminate in its membership policies.

>> **Single-family housing:** The sale or rental of a single-family house is exempted from the rules of the Fair Housing Act if the owner doesn't own more than three units at one time, and neither a broker nor discriminatory advertising is used. If such a property is sold, no more than one house can be sold during every two-year period.

IT MAY HAVE HAPPENED TO YOU . . . OR YOUR GRANDFATHER

I want to share a true story with which I end my fair housing classes. Many years ago, my father was a plumber. His shop and many of his customers were located in a typical ethnic neighborhood of first- and second-generation immigrants. In this case, the immigrants were German. My father, born in the United States, was of German descent.

One day a customer called on him to provide an estimate on some bathroom repairs. The bathroom was old and located in an old three-unit apartment house. My father encouraged the owner to remodel and upgrade the entire bathroom with a new tub, toilet, sink, vanity, and tile work. Somewhat conspiratorially, the customer said that he didn't want to spend the money because the neighborhood was changing. When I was young, the word "changing," in that context, usually meant some "lower class of people," as perceived by the residents, was moving into the neighborhood. My father, knowing the neighborhood quite well, didn't know what the man meant and responded with a questioning look. The building owner answered the questioning look by saying, "Italians just bought the house down the block." But that's not the punch line. The Italians who bought the house down the block were my aunt and uncle, specifically my Italian American mother's sister. And that, as a famous radio commentator used to say, is the rest of the story. I include this story in class to remind my students that discrimination can happen to anyone for any reason and in fact may have happened to one of their parents or grandparents in the past.

Extra Coverage: Protecting the Disabled from Discrimination

The disabled are protected as a class with respect to fair housing law. Landlords must permit tenants to make reasonable changes to an apartment to accommodate their handicap. Tenants are responsible for returning the apartment to its original condition.

REMEMBER

However, another law relating to the protection of the disabled normally is covered on the test. Congress passed the American with Disabilities Act (ADA) in 1992 to ensure not only protection from discrimination but also to provide access to public spaces. This law, which affects public and commercial buildings, requires buildings to be accessible to handicapped persons. It also requires new multifamily housing of four or more units built after March 13, 1991, to be handicapped accessible. The rules vary slightly for buildings with and without elevators. Employers, including real estate brokers, must be aware of the necessity of their places of employment being accessible to handicapped employees and the handicapped public at large. Real estate agents also need to be aware of ADA regulations with respect to commercial or other public buildings with which they may be involved.

Staying Strong: Enforcing the Law

Complaints regarding violations of the Fair Housing Act must be made to HUD within a year of the event. HUD conducts an investigation and may attempt to remedy the situation by getting the property owner who violates the law to stop the action and take steps to prevent it from happening again. Those with complaints may also file a suit in federal court within two years of the violation.

If HUD finds a property owner guilty following an administrative hearing, it may impose fines of up to $10,000 for the first offense, up to $25,000 for the second offense if it happens within five years of the first, and up to $50,000 for a third offense, if it happens within seven years of the first event.

In addition, anyone who brings a HUD complaint can sue in federal civil court, where generally no limits are placed on monetary damages that can be awarded.

Remember that a violation of the 1866 Civil Rights Act prohibiting racial discrimination may be brought directly to federal court.

DON'T FORGET YOUR STATE AND LOCAL LAWS

State exam writers expect you to know both federal, state, and local laws. Any anti-discrimination law that a state passes, as long as it's stricter than the federal law, applies to situations and people in that state. Many states and even municipalities within the state have added protected classes. Some states or municipalities have minimized exceptions. In at least one state a disclosure of rights under the state human rights law must be provided to the client or customer, and a poster of the state human rights law must be displayed in the broker's office. State real estate commissions expect you, as a real estate agent, to obey your state laws going so far as to require periodic fair housing education as a condition of license renewal.

Review Questions and Answers

Questions on the state exam normally involve knowing which laws are which, what groups are protected, and what the exceptions are. At the salesperson's level you can expect the questions to be straightforward. At the broker's level the questions may require a bit more interpretation of the law. Remember to check your state law regarding state and local fair housing rules and additional protected classes.

1. Inducing people to panic sell by telling them that a "lower-class immigrant group" is moving into the neighborhood is called

   (A) steering.

   (B) redlining.

   (C) canvassing.

   (D) blockbusting.

   Correct answer: (D). Blockbusting is inducing people to panic sell in order for the real estate agent or a developer to make a profit. Redlining is discrimination in the lending of mortgage money based on location. Steering is directing people to or away from certain neighborhoods as a means of discrimination. Canvassing is sending out letters or knocking on doors to see if you can offer your real estate services to people. It is a fairly normal way of doing business.

2. "Sorry, we don't make any loans on houses in that neighborhood" is an example of

   (A) blockbusting.

   (B) steering.

   (C) redlining.

   (D) an acceptable business decision.

   Correct answer: (C). Redlining is a practice where banks and other lending institutions refuse to make loans in certain neighborhoods regardless of the qualifications of the borrower. Blockbusting is inducing people to panic sell to make a profit (for example, by getting listings to sell property). Steering is directing people to or away from certain neighborhoods as a means of discrimination. These actions are all illegal.

3. Which of the following would be unacceptable under the federal fair housing law?

   (A) The resident owner of a three-family house refusing to rent to an Asian man.

   (B) A senior residence for people over 62.

   (C) A private club of graduates of an exclusive prep school.

   (D) Baptist Church sponsored housing available only to Baptists.

   Correct answer: (A). Answers (B), (C), and (D) all fall under the exceptions to the law. There are no exceptions with respect to race. For more on exceptions, see "Bending the Rules: Understanding Exceptions to the Law," earlier in this chapter.

4. Mike the seller refuses to sell his house to a Black couple.

(A) He is breaking the law under the 1968 Federal Fair Housing Act.

(B) He is breaking the law under the 1866 Civil Rights Act.

(C) He is breaking no law as long as he doesn't use a real estate agent or discriminatory advertising.

(D) He is breaking no law as long as he owns fewer than three houses and this is the only one he sells in two years.

Correct answer: (B). Answer (B) is correct because race was eliminated as an allowable exception by a court case that upheld the 1866 law. Answer (A) is wrong because the 1968 law provides an exception to the owner of a single-family house. Answers (C) and (D) are wrong because there is no exception with respect to race, so Mike is indeed breaking a law.

5. The fine for a third violation of the federal Fair Housing Act can be as high as

(A) $10,000.

(B) $25,000.

(C) $50,000.

(D) unlimited.

Correct answer: (C). $10,000 is the maximum fine for a first offense, and $25,000 is the maximum fine for a second offense. There are no unlimited fines.

6. A deed restriction says that a property cannot be sold to a person of Native American ancestry. Which of the following is true?

(A) The deed restriction supersedes fair housing law.

(B) The fair housing laws do not apply to Native Americans because technically they are part of the Indian Nation.

(C) Fair housing law takes precedence over the deed restriction.

(D) This type of restriction was automatically removed by a treaty in 1888.

Correct answer: (C). A deed restriction must be legal to be valid (see Chapter 8 for more on deed restrictions). These restrictions, many involving race and some referencing ethnicity common in some areas, are illegal and therefore invalid because of the 1866 act or the 1968 Act. I made up Answers (B) and (D).

7. Which of the following advertisements for a house for sale would probably be acceptable?

(A) Quiet Christian neighborhood

(B) Fill your Easter basket with a new house

(C) Husband's dream workshop

(D) Two blocks from the local Episcopal Church

Correct answer: (B). In HUD's determination, holidays like Easter and Christmas have lost their uniquely religious context and are therefore acceptable to use in advertisements. "Quiet Christian neighborhood" targets a particular religious group. "Husband's dream workshop" can be viewed as being sexually discriminatory because wives can also enjoy a dream workshop. "Two blocks from the local Episcopal church" is incorrect because references to landmarks referring to a specific religion are deemed unacceptable by HUD.

8. Under federal fair housing laws, which of the following is legal?

(A) Refusing to rent an apartment to a man because he's gay

(B) Refusing to sell a house to someone because he's Buddhist

(C) Showing a White couple houses only in White neighborhoods because they asked you to

(D) Charging different security deposits based on the number of children in a family

Correct answer: (A). Sexual orientation is not a protected class in the federal law. It may be in your state, but that's not what this question says. Always make sure to read questions carefully, and be sure to check your state and local fair housing law to see if sexual orientation or other classes in addition to the federal ones are protected.

9. The Civil Rights Act of 1866 is not enforced by

(A) HUD.

(B) federal courts.

(C) state courts.

(D) the Federal Department of Justice

Correct answer: (C). The other answers may all be involved in enforcing the 1866 Act.

10. Which of the following is legal?

(A) A broker offering discounts to members of a certain ethnic group as a way of encouraging them to integrate an area

(B) Refusing to make a mortgage loan to a Black family with poor credit history

(C) A broker advertising property exclusively in Spanish-language newspapers

(D) A broker providing information on the demographics of a neighborhood including statistics on race and ethnic background

Correct answer: (B). Money is the only legal basis for discrimination. All the other answers are wrong because they are discriminatory on some other basis that is prohibited by law. Answer (D) might be confusing because the information is public. Real estate agents however must be careful not to imply in any way that they're steering people to or from certain neighborhoods.

3

It's All Mine: Owning and Transferring Real Estate

Get an overview of liens — their priorities, types, distinguishing traits, creations, and removal.

Add information about land-use regulations to your tool box — from making master plans to understanding zoning ordinances to construction regulations. Then you can check out eminent domain and what the government can and can't do.

Deeds are an important part of the job of the real estate agent. Uncover what's required to have a valid deed, discover about the various types, and understand why they are so important.

Examine the title closing process, and find out what you need before, during, and after to make closing on a property a success for you, the buyer, and the seller.

Understand the several different ways a property can be involuntarily lost, from the forces of nature to the government, and even due to death. As a real estate sales person in today's market, this is important information.

IN THIS CHAPTER

» Discovering different ownership terms

» Finding out about all types of estates

» Understanding the rights that go with owning real estate

Chapter **6**

Owning It: Estates and Interests

Owning real estate is different from owning almost anything else. For one thing, you can't move it anywhere. For another, you can do so many things with it. Real estate is literally the foundation on which people live their lives. It's exclusively yours and, subject to certain legal limitations, you can pretty much do what you want with it, on it, under it, and over it. When you drive across your neighbor's property to get to your land, it's because your neighbor has given you the right to do so. Real estate is a unique commodity, and owning it has its own unique laws and practices.

This chapter discusses the unique aspects of owning real estate and introduces you to the concepts that are specific to real estate ownership and the various rights that come with owning property. I talk about the specific terms that are used to describe real estate ownership and about a concept called the bundle of rights, which is about the rights you get when you own real estate. I also discuss some additional rights that go with owning real estate, specifically air and water rights.

STATE SPECIFIC

Although the concepts in this chapter are pretty much universal to all states, I nevertheless point out a few things that are specific to individual states. You need to find out about the concepts that apply specifically to your home state.

What Do You Own? Understanding Ownership Terms

You buy a car; you own a car. You buy a table; you own a table. Most of what is so different about owning a piece of real estate is about terminology that has evolved over time to precisely explain what people are talking about when describing real estate ownership. Remember, although I define the terms as they're properly used for exam purposes, you also need to be aware that in the real world, some of these terms are used interchangeably.

Looking at land

Land generally is thought of as the unimproved surface of the earth. It's the dirt, so to speak, with nothing built on it. Because of the complicated nature of ownership rights, when people say they own a piece of land, in reality, they also own the area under the surface down to the center of the earth and the air above the ground surface into outer space or infinity. (For details, see the "Eyeing Different Ownership Rights" section later in the chapter.) Although practical and legal matters make using all that space difficult at best, you don't have to stop dreaming about immense skyscrapers; the fact is, when you own a piece of land, the right to build that skyscraper is exactly what you own. Land ownership includes all the natural elements or features on the land like trees and rocks. Even if the rocks are gold. The related term *site* usually refers to land that has been improved in some way and is ready to be developed. In common usage, however, someone may refer to "the site of the new subdivision" but mean the unimproved land where the subdivision is supposed to go.

Recognizing real estate

The term *real estate* means the land and all natural and artificial improvements permanently attached to it. The term real estate refers to the physical thing that is owned as opposed to the rights of owning the land and its improvements (see the next section). The word *improvement* means something that is built on and permanently attached to the land. A house is an improvement, and so are detached garages, landscaping, walks, and driveways.

Defining real property

The term *real property* means land, natural and artificial improvements, and all the rights, benefits, and interests that go with owning a piece of land and the improvements. These rights include all surface, subsurface, and air rights that are automatically included with ownership of the land. (For the scoop, see "Eyeing Different Ownership Rights" later in this chapter.)

Checking out personal property

You're probably wondering why, if this book is about real estate, you need to learn about personal property. The answer: You need to know about personal property so you can tell the difference between it and real estate, and the difference almost always is covered on the test. *Personal property*, sometimes called *personalty*, is anything that is portable, movable, and not permanently attached to the real estate. *Personal property* sometimes is defined as anything of value that isn't real estate. Anything ranging from furniture to a car is considered personal property.

Personal property that becomes real estate is called a *fixture*. From a real estate perspective, the principal difference between personal property and a fixture is that personal property goes with the owner when a piece of real estate is sold, and a fixture stays with the property. Say you have lumber delivered to the house to build a deck. At the time of the delivery, the lumber is personal property that goes with you if you sell the house. However, if you build a deck with the lumber and attach it to the back of your house, the lumber now is considered a fixture that, of course, stays with the house when you sell it.

Ornamental trees and bushes are considered fixtures that remain with the real estate when it's sold. In cases where the seller wishes to take certain plants with her, like Grandma's prize rose-bushes, she would have to dig them up before listing the property for sale or specify in the contract that they are to be removed. Agricultural crops, however, are considered personal property. A farmer who leases some farm land has the right to his crops even when his lease ends before the end of the growing season. Crops grown on property just before it's sold generally are considered to be the personal property of the seller. A small technicality here is that although the farmer is entitled to crops he's planted, he would not be entitled to the apples on his apple trees after he sells the property.

When a question arises about whether a piece of personal property is a fixture, these four so-called legal tests commonly are used to make the determination:

» **Adaptation of an item to the real estate:** This factor occurs when an item of personal property is customized to fit in the house. A custom bar in a finished playroom is a good example.

» **Existence of an agreement:** An agreement made in advance between two parties — a landlord and tenant, for example — can define what is considered personal property and what is considered a fixture.

» **Method of attachment:** Sometimes this legal test is called the method of annexation and deals with how an item of personal property is attached to the building. A bookcase with a single screw to hold it against the wall, for example, would likely be considered personal property. A bookcase that has molding and a base built around it to attach it to the wall would be considered a fixture, because it is more firmly and permanently attached.

» **Relationship of the parties:** The best example of this test is a commercial tenant in a rental building who attaches fixtures to the structure, perhaps jewelry cases in a jewelry store. The tenant normally not only is able to take them when he leaves but probably is required to remove them. Such fixtures are known as *trade fixtures*. If the tenant left the fixtures and the landlord wanted to claim them, they would be considered permanent fixtures at that point.

Estates (Even Without the Castles)

The term *estate*, or *estate in land*, describes the extent and type of interest or rights that someone has in a piece of land. It essentially means the same thing as the bundle of rights theory (see the next section).

WARNING

You need to bear in mind that neither the term "estate" nor the term "interest" necessarily means ownership. For example, the right to use a property granted by an easement is an interest in land. (I talk about easements in Chapter 8.) A lease also is an interest in land that also happens to be an estate in land, because it designates possession of the land, unlike an easement, which designates only the right to use the land. (I talk about leases in Chapter 12.)

In the sections that follow, I talk about a general concept called the bundle of rights. I also discuss different types of estates in land and how they fall into two main categories: freehold and lease-hold. As you check out this material, concentrate most on terminology and on being able to remember the significant characteristics of each type of estate.

Pick and choose: The bundle of rights

A concept that long has been associated with real estate ownership is the *bundle of rights,* which sometimes is called the bundle of rights theory. By picturing a bundle of sticks or logs, each of which represents a specific right associated with real estate ownership, you begin to get an idea of what I'm talking about. One key element of the bundle of rights theory is that you can remove one of the rights (one of the sticks) and separate it from the rest of the bundle.

One obvious right of ownership of property, for example, is the right to actually possess or occupy it. However, if I own an office building, I can give that right of possession or occupancy to a tenant through a lease. I may still own the building, but I've separated a part of my right to occupy the building from my bundle of ownership rights. Doing so severely limits my right to occupy that part of the building that I leased to a tenant, even though I still own the building.

The bundle of rights includes the rights to use and occupy, mine, farm, develop the property, the rights to will, give, and restrict others from using the property, and the right not to do any of these things with the property.

Figuring out freehold estates

The essential characteristics of a *freehold estate* are that it must include ownership of real estate and that it lasts for an indefinite or indeterminate period of time that can be forever or for the lifetime of the person with the interest in the real estate. Fee estates and life estates are the two main types of freehold estates.

Fee estates

Several fee estates exist. Each of the ones you need to be aware of for exam purposes is described in the list that follows. The term *fee estate* is really a general umbrella term for unlimited owner-ship rights subject to different limitations (if any).

>> **Fee simple:** Also called *fee simple absolute* or *indefeasible fee,* this fee estate is the most complete form of ownership without limitations on rights of ownership, except for public and private restrictions on what can be done with the property. For example, zoning ordinances and deed restrictions are limitations on fee simple ownership. (See Chapter 8 for more.)

>> **Fee simple qualified estate:** Also called a *fee simple defeasible estate,* this fee simple estate has some limitations on it. The three types of qualified fee estates are

- **Fee simple condition precedent:** In this case, ownership, commonly referred to as title, won't pass from one person to another until a particular condition is met. An example is someone who donates property to the county for use as a park with the stipulation that nature trails must be built before the title passes to the county.

- **Fee simple condition subsequent:** This form of estate is a situation in which the grantor — that is, the original owner — can reclaim property if some condition isn't met after title has passed to the next owner. A grantor who donates property to the county for a park where nature trails are to be built, for example, may reclaim the property because the county built a park headquarters building on the land rather than the nature trails that the donor had required under the original agreement. The right to reclaim the property is known as the *right of reentry.* The grantor would have to take specific action to reclaim the property.

- **Fee simple determinable:** In this situation, title remains with the new owner as long as any conditions of ownership are being met. Say a property donated for a county park with nature trails stopped being used for that purpose. When that happens, ownership of the property automatically reverts back (is returned) to the original owner without the original owner having to take any action.

Life estates

A *life estate* grants possession and limited ownership of a property to a person for the duration of the recipient's life or the life of another person. The main difference between a fee estate and a life estate is that a fee estate has no time limit and a life estate does. The two types of life estates are

» **Ordinary life estate:** An ordinary life estate is a life estate in which the length of time of the estate interest is the lifetime of the person receiving the life estate. One situation where this form of estate comes in handy is when a husband wants to provide a place for his second wife to live until she dies but doesn't want to shortchange the children from his first marriage. In that case, the husband/father creates an ordinary life estate granting ownership rights to his second wife for the remainder of her life with the children named as *remaindermen* (even if they are women) who are entitled to the remainder interest in the stepmom's place after she dies.

» **Life estate pur autre vie:** The French words *pur autre vie* mean "for another life." As opposed to an ordinary life estate, the length of the life estate in this case is for the lifetime of a third party rather than the person actually receiving the life estate. The example I use in class is a chronically ill nephew for whom you want to provide care. You own a second house that is empty at the moment. You give your nephew's mother (that could be your sister or sister-in-law) a life estate pur autre vie to live in the house for as long as your nephew is alive. Upon his death the house reverts, that is, automatically comes back to you. You have a *reversionary interest* in the property. If you happen to die before your nephew does, the house would revert to your heirs upon your nephew's death. Here's another scenario: You're helping your sister take care of your nephew while you're alive but want to make provisions for his care after you die. You can create a life estate pur autre vie through your will. In that case, the house reverts to your estate or designated heirs upon your nephew's death.

STATE SPECIFIC

Some states have what are called *legal life estates*, which are life estates in one form or another that are created by state law. You need to check out whether your state has adopted any of these rights and find out details of how they work. General descriptions of four common examples of these legal life estates are

» **Community property,** which is a right of a spouse, entitling him or her to one-half interest in real property that was acquired during a marriage.

» **Curtesy,** which is the right of a husband to a portion of real property that is owned by his wife — after she dies and even if she leaves it to someone else in her will.

» **Dower,** which is the right of a wife to a portion of real property that is owned by her husband — after he dies and even if he leaves it to someone else in his will.

» **Homestead,** which grants the family home a certain level of protection from creditors during the owner's lifetime.

Understanding leasehold estates

Leasehold estates are considered interests in real estate because they give some rights to the tenant, such as a right to exclusive possession and use of all or some portion of the property, while the owner retains some rights, such as ownership, the right to collect rents, and the right to sell the property. Leases and the various leasehold-estate interests are covered in detail in Chapter 12. In looking at leases as estate interests, however, you need to remember two terms and whose interest they represent:

>> The *leasehold interest or estate* is the tenant's interest in the real property. Remember, the tenant holds the rights assigned by the lease.

>> The *leased fee interest or estate* is the owner's or landlord's interest in the real property. Remember, the landlord holds the fee or title to the property.

Eyeing Different Ownership Rights

A variety of rights come with real estate ownership. In this section I talk about the most important of these rights — water rights, air rights, surface rights, subsurface rights, and mineral rights. Whereas by no means the only rights contained in the bundle of rights (see the section earlier in this chapter), the rights I discuss here have particular features that are important to remember for exam purposes. Be prepared for a few definition-type questions and a case study or two that may require you to apply some of what you remember.

Going for a swim: Water rights

Land that's adjacent to a body of water normally carries with it certain rights relative to that body of water. A real estate agent is expected to know something about what these water rights involve. Although water rights may vary according to local law in specific situations — and a buyer should always consult an attorney to be sure of what their water rights are — several common rights of use exist. These common rights are explained in the sections that follow.

Littoral rights

Littoral rights are the rights commonly granted to owners of property that border a bay, a large lake, the ocean, or a sea. Owners of property abutting such bodies of water have an unrestricted right to use the water and have ownership of the land up to the average or mean high water mark. The government owns the land below that point. Littoral rights are *appurtenant to the land,* which means they go with the land when you sell it, so don't think that you can still go swimming after you sell the land.

Riparian rights

Riparian rights are the rights of property owners who own land abutting rivers and streams. The rights vary a little depending on whether the river or stream is considered navigable, or capable of supporting commercial water traffic.

When a river or steam is considered navigable, owners of property abutting the river own the land up to the edge of the water or the average or mean high water mark. The state owns the body of the water and the property under the water. On the other hand, when the river or stream isn't navigable, the rights of owners with property abutting the river or stream extend to the centerline of the river or stream.

In either case, owners of property that abuts a river or stream have a right to use the water, but they don't have any right to contaminate the water or interrupt or change the flow of the water.

Watering rights

In agricultural areas, rights to water may be controlled by special agreement between property owners. In addition, where water is scarce, the *doctrine of prior appropriation* may apply. The doctrine of prior appropriation is state-specific and may be used in states where water resources are limited. Although implementation of the doctrine can vary from state to state, it basically places the right to control water resources in the hands of the state rather than individual property owners. Water rights, or the rights to use water, then are granted by the state to individual property owners. You may want to check whether your state operates under this doctrine and find out about some of the details of how it is implemented.

Don't forget to look up and down: Other rights

Some of the rights associated with owning real estate have to do with what's going on over your head and under your feet. Ownership of land includes the ownership of the land down to the center of the earth and up to infinity. Although practical and legal limitations may inhibit your ability to actually use these rights, you nevertheless still have them.

Up there: Air rights

A property owner has an unlimited right of ownership of the airspace above her land up to infinity; however, these rights may not interfere with aircraft traffic. Air rights frequently are thought of in terms of selling or transferring them to someone else. Picture a 3-story building in a downtown urban area on property zoned such that its owner can build a 20-story building on it. Although the owner doesn't want to build those additional 17 stories, someone else does.

Assuming the construction, engineering, and legal aspects can be worked out, the owner of the property can sell the air rights of the property to someone else while retaining ownership of the land and the three-story building. The new owner of the air rights could then build up to 17 more stories of building space on top of the existing 3-story building.

Down there: Surface rights

The most obvious rights that you get when you own a piece of property are the *surface rights*, which are the rights to do whatever is legally permitted on the surface of the property. Surface rights generally include construction of structures and physical improvements of all kinds as well as things like planting crops.

Development rights, or the right to build on a piece of property, are rights that can be sold separate from the land. Conversely, a county can buy development rights from a farmer to preserve the property affected by those rights for environmental purposes. The farmer/property owner is able to stay and keep on farming, but he can never develop the land with houses or other structures. The farmer can even sell the property, but the right to develop the land stays with the county. The new property owner must be content being a farmer.

Surface rights also include the right to give your neighbor a driveway easement across the surface of your property. I discuss easements in Chapter 8.

Way down there: Subsurface and mineral rights

Because you own the property down to the center of the earth, you have the right to use the property beneath the surface or to permit others to use it. An example of subsurface rights is selling the city an underground or subsurface easement to install a sewer line across your property. Subsurface rights often are associated with mineral rights.

Mineral rights are the right to take minerals out of the ground. Today these rights are associated with oil and gas leases, which are agreements that landowners make with companies to take those specific resources or products out of the ground. These leases include the right to build structures necessary to extract oil and gas from the ground. In some places where valuable minerals were found many years ago, owners sold the property but retained the mineral rights. In areas where these transactions have occurred, seeing a deed that transfers ownership of the property excluding the mineral rights isn't uncommon.

Review Questions and Answers

Most material in this chapter is pretty standard regarding property ownership and rights associated with owning property. Although a few state-specific issues may be addressed on the exam, make sure you know the vocabulary well and can tell the differences among the terms; definitions are the most commonly questioned items on the exam.

1. Land, improvements, and all the rights of ownership is a good definition of

   (A) land ownership.

   (B) real estate.

   (C) real property.

   (D) property.

   Correct answer: (C). The statement in the question is the definition of real property. Land ownership and property are too vague relative to real property. The definition of real estate includes only land and structures, not rights.

2. Which of the following is not a fixture?

   (A) A fence

   (B) A dishwasher

   (C) A painting hanging on the wall

   (D) A dining room chandelier

   Correct answer: (C). You may think that fixtures can be only inside the house, but that isn't the case, so a fence is a fixture. The only other answer that may throw you a little is the chandelier, because many people take chandeliers with them when they move. When they do take a chandelier with them, they do so by prior agreement. The dishwasher is usually attached to the plumbing and electrical system in the kitchen and stays if no agreement exists to remove and replace it. Of course, if the dishwasher is your spouse, he or she will be going with you when you sell the house. The painting is correct because it is portable and not permanently attached to the structure, and unless an agreement exists to leave it, most people consider it to be personal property.

3. When a man wants to donate property to a conservation group, he agrees that the organization can take title to the property as soon as an education center is built on the property. What kind of estate is he creating?

(A) Fee simple absolute

(B) Fee simple condition precedent

(C) Fee simple condition subsequent

(D) Fee simple determinable

Correct answer: (B). The word *precedent* means "before," so the education center has to be built before property ownership passes to the conservation organization. Fee simple absolute is the most complete form of ownership and has no conditions. The word *subsequent* in fee simple condition subsequent means "after"; the conservation group in this case has to build the education center after it receives ownership of the property. Fee simple determinable would have been correct if the language in the question had talked about an ongoing condition, such as "so long as the property is used for an education center."

4. Sally owns a house that she will allow her sister Fran to live in for the rest of Fran's life. Upon Fran's death the house goes to Sally's children. Which of the following best describes the interest Sally has in the property?

(A) Ordinary life estate

(B) Life estate pur autre vie

(C) Fee simple condition subsequent

(D) Leasehold estate

Correct answer: (A). An ordinary life estate is an interest conveyed to a person that exists for as long as that person (the one who receives the interest) is alive. Life estate pur autre vie is a life estate that exists for the life of a third party — someone other than the person receiving the life estate. Fee simple condition subsequent is an actual transfer of ownership with a condition. Leasehold estate is the interest a tenant has in a rental situation. Don't be confused by the fact that the property goes to Sally's children upon Fran's death.

5. Joe rents office space from Fred. What type of interest does Joe have?

(A) Leasehold interest

(B) Leased fee interest

(C) Fee simple defeasible

(D) Fee simple absolute

Correct answer: (A). Remember the tenant holds the lease. The landlord has the leased fee interest. Fee simple defeasible and fee simple interest are ownership interests in the property. Theoretically the landlord could have one of these interests, but because the question asks about the tenant's interest, only leasehold interest is correct.

6. You own property on a river that has regular commercial boat traffic. What rights do you most likely have with respect to the water?

(A) You own to the centerline of the river.

(B) You have no rights to the water.

(C) You have rights to use the water and own to the edge of the river.

(D) You can use the water and own the land under the water to the midpoint of the river, but the state owns the water.

Correct answer: (C). Riparian rights, which is what you have on navigable rivers and streams, gives you rights only to the water's edge and use of the water. If the river weren't navigable, you would own to the centerline (A). Answer (B) is incorrect because properties bordering water generally have some type of rights with respect to the water. Answer (D) is a combination of statements that taken as a whole is incorrect.

7. What are the water rights called for oceanfront property owners?

   (A) Riparian rights

   (B) Littoral rights

   (C) Defeasible rights

   (D) Qualified rights

   Correct answer: (B). Littoral rights are those rights granted to owners whose land borders oceans, bays, and large lakes. Riparian rights are those rights granted to property owners of land next to rivers and streams. Defeasible rights have to do with a defeasible estate, which is an interest with certain conditions attached to it. A qualified estate is similar to qualified rights.

8. The right of the state to control water rights in some states is called

   (A) the bundle of rights theory.

   (B) littoral rights.

   (C) riparian rights.

   (D) the doctrine of prior appropriation.

   Correct answer: (D). The doctrine of prior appropriation exists in states where water rights are an issue and have to do with controlling the use of water. Littoral and riparian rights are rights auto-matically granted to land owners whose property abuts bodies of water. The bundle of rights theory is the overall theory of the rights property owners have.

9. The theory that best describes the rights that you get with a piece of real estate is

   (A) the doctrine of complete rights.

   (B) the bundle of rights.

   (C) the development rights theory.

   (D) fee simple absolute.

   Correct answer: (B). Fee simple absolute may have confused you here, but it isn't really a theory. Instead, it describes the highest form of ownership and may apply only in some cases. There is no such thing as the doctrine of complete rights or the development rights theory. The bundle of rights theory is the best answer.

10. Receiving back the property you gave in a life estate when that life estate ends is best described as

    (A) conveyance.

    (B) transfer.

    (C) reversion.

    (D) remaindering.

    Correct answer: (C). Reversion is the correct term when a property interest automatically returns to you, that is comes back, which is the way the question is worded. A remainder interest conveys the rights to a third party, such as your children if the life estate ends after you die. Conveyance and transfer are generally associated with straight changes in ownership from one party to another.

Chapter **7**

Understanding Forms of Real Estate Ownership

Real estate ownership comes in many forms. You can own real estate by yourself. You can own it with your spouse. You can own it with partners. You can be part of a corporation that owns real estate. You also may own real estate in the form of a condominium or cooperative. In each of these situations, ownership issues and forms are slightly different. Attorneys usually handle the form of ownership of a property. In some states, especially those where attorneys are less involved in real estate transactions, you may, as an agent, have to deal more directly with these issues. And speaking of states, there may be slight differences from state to state with respect to some of these forms of ownership. Pay attention in class and note anything that might be unique to your state.

Regardless of how much or how little you're involved in form-of-ownership issues in a real estate transaction, state examiners expect you to know something about the various types of ownership. In this chapter, I give you some basic terminology and key features of the various forms of real estate ownership, such as owning property by yourself, with others, with a spouse, in a trust, and in a business. I also cover special types of ownership, such as cooperatives and condominiums.

WARNING

Even in states where real estate agents do most of the work associated with buying and selling property, agents always need to be aware of the things with which they're not familiar. When ownership matters get the least bit complicated with regard to form, they need to and can refer clients and customers to attorneys skilled in real estate matters.

Real Estate Ownership: A Solo or Group Activity

That real estate can be owned by one person, two or more people, a married couple, or some type of business is obvious, because as real estate law evolved, it had to deal with these various forms of ownership with different terminology and sometimes different conditions.

REMEMBER

In this section, pay particular attention to the terminology and key differences among the various forms of ownership. Exam questions on this subject are likely to focus on recognizing these differences.

TIP

You see the word "tenancy" throughout this section. *Tenancy* means having an interest in a piece of real estate. Most of us associate the word with being a tenant, which essentially is what it means; however, it also means having an ownership interest in a property. On a state exam you see the word used in both of its meanings. By the way, the word tenancy comes from a Latin word that means "to hold."

One is the loneliest number: Owning real estate by yourself

Owning real estate by yourself is called *sole ownership* or *tenancy in severalty*. I know, the law has done it again. Right about now you're asking, "How can you use the word 'severalty' when you mean only one person?" The answer's actually pretty logical if you remember one thing. The word "severalty" doesn't come from "several" but rather from *"sever,"* meaning to cut off. Sole ownership cuts off all other interests in the property. In other words, no one has an ownership interest in the property except the one owner.

Join the crowd: Owning real estate with other people

Two or more people who aren't married can own property together in a form of ownership known as *concurrent ownership* or *co-ownership*. I describe two forms of co-ownership: tenancy in common and joint tenancy. Although these two similar forms of ownership are available to married couples, they may serve specific purposes of ownership for people who are not married but want to own property together.

Tenancy in common

Tenancy in common is a form of ownership in which two or more people own property together. The fact that two or more people are buying property together as tenants in common is stated in the deed. In some states, if the form of ownership isn't otherwise specifically stated in the deed, tenancy in common automatically is assumed when two or more people buy property together. (For general information about deeds, check out Chapter 9.) Probably the most common form of ownership where tenancy in common takes place is condominium ownership. See the section "More individuality: Condominium ownership," later in this chapter.

REMEMBER

The principal features of tenancy in common are

>> **Undivided ownership:** The land itself is not physically divided into or split between multiple owners, but rather percentages or shares of interest are granted in the property as a whole.

>> **Equal or unequal shares:** The percentage of ownership interest of each party need not be equal, so one person can have a 50 percent share, and two others can each have a 25 percent share in the same property, and so on.

>> **Sale without permission:** Any owner can sell his or her share without having to receive permission to do so from the other owners. The new owner is a tenant in common with the previous owners.

>> **No right of survivorship:** If one owner dies, she leaves her share to her heirs. The other owners don't have any right to her share of the property.

Tenancy in common might be the way two married sisters buy a vacation home to share. If one dies, her husband or children would inherit her part of the property. If one sister has more money invested than the other, there would be no problem because one would own, say, 60 percent of the property whereas the other owned 40 percent.

Joint tenancy

Joint tenancy is a form of ownership with special features for two or more people. Joint tenancy is said to be created with these four unities:

>> **Unity of interest:** Unity of interest means that each owner has the same interest in the property. If there are four owners, each has a 25 percent share in the whole property. If there are two owners, each has a 50 percent share. Some states now permit unequal shares in a joint tenancy. You should check out what the law is in your state.

>> **Unity of possession:** Like tenancy in common (see the previous section), each owner's interest is in an undivided property. Although interest in the property may be divided, the land and building, if any, may not be divided. In other words, no physical division of the property exists. Each owner essentially owns a share in the property as a whole.

>> **Unity of time:** Joint owners all take title (or ownership) to the property at the same time. A later owner can't be added to the joint tenancy as a joint tenant unless new documents are executed, effectively creating a new joint tenancy. If one of the joint tenants sells her interest without this happening, that new owner becomes a tenant in common. A joint tenant also may sell his individual interest without the permission of the other joint tenants.

>> **Unity of title:** Unity of title means that all the joint tenants names are on the deed together.

Any brother and sister who want to own a home together could buy a property as joint tenants. If one dies, the other automatically takes title (ownership) of the whole property.

REMEMBER

Perhaps the most important difference between joint tenancy and tenancy in common is the right of survivorship that you have as a joint tenant and that you don't have as a tenant in common. The *right of survivorship* in a joint tenancy means that if one of the joint tenants dies, the other tenant(s) automatically take title to the deceased tenant's interest in the property. For example, if four joint tenants each own a 25 percent share of a piece of property, and one joint tenant dies, the three remaining tenants each has a 33 1/3 percent share. That's why joint tenancy is a form of ownership that married couples sometimes use when they buy property. When one spouse dies, the other spouse automatically gets full title to the property.

STATE SPECIFIC

You may want to check whether your state still recognizes the right of survivorship in a joint tenancy. Some states are doing away with that aspect of this type of co-ownership unless it is specifically stated.

Getting hitched: Owning real estate when you're married

The law over time has developed special forms of real estate ownership for married couples. I describe the two common forms: tenancy by the entirety and community property, one or both of which may be available in your state.

Tenancy by the entirety

Tenancy by the entirety is a form of co-ownership specifically geared toward protecting the interests of married couples by providing a right of survivorship. A form of joint tenancy (see the previous section for the full scoop), the theory behind *tenancy by the entirety* is that a couple is treated as if it was one person owning property insofar as each spouse has an undivided and equal interest in the property. Upon the death of one spouse, the deceased spouse's interest automatically goes to the surviving spouse without having to go through the process of probating a will or other inheritance issues.

Another unique feature of tenancy by the entirety is that neither spouse can sell his or her share without doing so together. The entire property must be sold by the combined actions of both parties signing the deed. In the event of a divorce, a tenancy by the entirety is changed to a tenancy in common. (See "Tenancy in common," earlier in this chapter, for details.)

Community property

Some states operate under community property laws. Under these laws, all property that a couple acquires during their marriage is considered jointly owned and equally owned by both spouses, regardless of whose actual income was used to purchase the property. Property acquired by one or the other spouse before the marriage is called *separate property* and is not subject to community property requirements. Property inherited during the marriage by one or the other spouse is also considered separate property. The essential elements of community property law are

>> Community property may be sold or mortgaged only by joint action of both spouses.

>> Separate property may be sold or mortgaged by the person owning it (or bringing it to the marriage).

>> No right of survivorship exists. Upon the death of one spouse, the surviving spouse retains title to his or her half of the property. The deceased spouse's half interest can be willed to anyone else.

STATE
SPECIFIC

You need to check how real estate ownership of married couples is treated in your state. Laws may vary from one state to another, particularly with respect to the specific implementation of laws protecting the rights of married couples in real estate ownership and whether community property is a recognized concept. Some states, for example, may use joint tenancy with a right of survivorship for married couples.

Who do you trust? Ownership in trust

A third party can hold real estate for the benefit of someone else. The main players are the *trustor* (the person who owns the property and conveys it to the trustee); the *trustee* (the person who receives the property and administers it on behalf of the beneficiary); and the *beneficiary* (the person who receives the benefits of the property, like rent on an apartment house, as a result of the administration of the property by the trustee).

EXAMPLE

You leave your apartment buildings to your brother in trust for your favorite nephew. You are the trustor, because you created the trust. Your brother is the trustee, and he administers the buildings according to the terms of the trust, which in this case would likely be that the income from the buildings goes to your nephew because he is the beneficiary.

Ownership in trust requires a special type of deed called (you guessed it!) a *trust deed* or a *deed in trust*. For more, see Chapter 9.

All business: Ownership by a business

Ownership of real estate by business organizations is not so much about the forms of ownership as it is about the organizational structures of the businesses. You're not likely to be involved very often with this type of transaction in your everyday real estate practices, unless you work a great deal with commercial real estate and developers. State exam writers, however, expect you to know something about different business organizations and how they can own property.

You may hear the word "syndicate" in connection with business projects. A *syndicate* isn't a form of ownership. It's a term that generally describes two or more people or companies joining together to work on a project or form an ongoing relationship to own and manage buildings or other real estate.

Businesses (and syndicates) often purchase properties as investments. For more about investment properties and forms of investment ownership, see Chapter 17.

Corporations

A *corporation*, for legal purposes, is treated the same as an individual owner when it comes to real estate ownership. Generally speaking, unless a corporation is involved in co-ownership arrangements with other corporations, it owns property in sole ownership or tenancy in severalty. I discuss tenancy in severalty in "One is the loneliest number: Owning real estate by yourself," earlier in this chapter. A few key features of real estate ownership by a corporation follow:

>> People own shares in a corporation, but no direct ownership exists for individual shareholders in property owned by the corporation.

>> Shareholders have neither authority over nor responsibility for management of corporation property.

>> Shareholder liability generally is limited to the value of the shareholder's shares. For instance, if a shareholder owns $1,000 worth of stock in a real estate investment corporation, and the company loses a lawsuit for millions of dollars, regardless of whether the corporation has the money, the shareholder can lose only his $1,000 investment and no more than that. It should be noted that this protection is subject to court rulings in the event of a lawsuit.

>> Profits that the corporation receives from the property are taxed before they're distributed to shareholders, who then pay taxes again on amounts they receive. The so-called S corporation is a form of corporation with modified tax liabilities and is permitted by the government under strict rules.

Partnerships

A partnership is two or more people or companies combining to do business. A partnership may be short-term for one project like buying, renovating, and selling a building, or long-term for ongoing investment and management of real estate holdings. Many states have adopted the *Uniform Partnership Act* and the *Uniform Limited Partnership Act*, which allow real estate to be owned in general or limited partnerships.

REMEMBER

Partnerships are either general or limited. In a *general partnership,* all the partners share in the management and operational decisions over the business of the partnership. They also share in the liability for any actions the partnership takes without limit. The respective partners pay taxes according to their respective interests and liabilities, so that double taxation is avoided. On the other hand, in a *limited partnership,* one general partner usually manages the operations of the business, and a number of other limited partners have no management responsibilities. The liabilities of the limited partners are determined by and limited to the amounts of their respective investments in the company.

Limited liability corporations

The limited liability corporation (LLC), or limited liability company, as it's sometimes called, is a hybrid organizational structure that has elements of a partnership and a corporation. Similar to a corporation, the liability of the individual members within the corporation is limited. Meanwhile, they pay taxes as if they're part of a general partnership (see the previous section). Management by members of the LLC also may be along the more direct lines allowed in a general partnership.

Joint ventures

A *joint venture* is the joining together of two or more people or companies to do a single project like buy a house, renovate it, and sell it for a profit. A joint venture is somewhat like a syndicate in that it can own property in any of several forms, like tenancy in common, joint tenancy, or a corporation, among others (see the sections on these forms earlier in this chapter). However, ownership probably will include an ending date, because joint ventures aren't designed to be ongoing business relationships. A joint venture, like a syndicate, is really a name for two or more people or companies who want to cooperate in a real estate investment. The difference between a joint venture and a syndicate is that a joint venture brings people together for one real estate investment or project, whereas a syndicate usually does multiple real estate investments or projects at the same time or a series of individual projects over a period of time.

Special Types of Ownership: Cooperatives, Condominiums, and More

Cooperatives and condominiums are popular forms of ownership for a variety of reasons, but primarily because they

>> Usually are built to a higher density (more units per acre or in high-rise buildings), and they're often somewhat less expensive than a single-family house in the same area.

>> Provide some of the advantages of homeownership, such as building up equity by paying off a mortgage, and tax advantages like being able to deduct real estate taxes and mortgage interest. (I cover mortgages in Chapter 15 and taxes in Chapter 16.)

>> Provide the advantage of no outside maintenance, because the dwellings usually are maintained by a homeowners association in the case of condominiums or a board in the case of a cooperative.

These forms of ownership are unique because they involve ownership by more than one person, but the owners aren't known to each other nor are they in a business venture together. I cover cooperatives and condominiums, plus planned unit developments and time shares, in the following sections.

Share and share alike: Cooperative ownership

Strictly speaking, you don't own real estate when you're part of a cooperative. You own shares in a corporation that owns the real estate. As a shareholder, you receive a *proprietary lease* that enables you to occupy your apartment. For all intents and purposes, your ownership interest in a cooperative is treated like real estate, including the ability to finance your purchase just like a mortgage, except that your shares (and not the property itself) are pledged as collateral for the loan. In other words, if you can't pay off the loan, the bank can claim your cooperative shares in payment. (For more about mortgages, see Chapter 15.) Some of these expenses are deductible from annual personal income taxes, such as the cooperative owner's share of the property taxes.

A board of directors of the corporation makes rules and policies for the building, collects monthly fees from shareholders and maintains the building, and pays the taxes and any other expenses that may exist, like emergency repairs and a mortgage on the building itself. This mortgage on the building is generally referred to as the underlying mortgage and can sometimes make the monthly common charges a little more expensive than in a condominium because the share owners are responsible for payments on the underlying mortgage.

Two issues that frequently are considered disadvantages of cooperative ownership are

>> **Shared liability:** Whenever shareholders default on their common charges (the payments all shareholders make to maintain the building and pay taxes), the other (paying) shareholders are liable. This issue can become serious whenever too many shareholders default on their payments and the other shareholders have to pay the share of the money that wasn't paid by the defaulting shareholders.

>> **Cooperative board approval of newcomers:** This issue may be viewed as a negative or a positive, depending on your point of view. Requiring board approval of new cooperative buyers whenever someone sells shares in a cooperative is fairly common practice. The requirement allows new owners to be screened for financial ability to pay their loans and common charges, but it also may hold up the sale of a unit while a prospective buyer undergoes the board approval process.

Cooperative boards in many places may not be required to reveal the reasons they turn down a specific buyer. Insufficient financial ability is generally the best reason to turn a buyer down, but other reasons — including illegal ones such as fair housing violations — may exist despite the fact that cooperative boards are subject to these laws.

More individuality: Condominium ownership

Condominium ownership is a form of group ownership that involves actually getting a deed to your individual ownership interest. In general, the deed describes the airspace you own (in other words, the unit), which you own as a tenant in severalty, and your share as a tenant in common of the land under and around your unit. (See the "Tenancy in common" section earlier in this chapter for details.) A homeowners association usually collects set monthly fees, which pay for maintenance of the condominium building and complex.

Individual condo owners are responsible for paying their own property taxes, so defaulting on your tax obligations can result in a foreclosure on the unit but not on the entire complex. (For more about foreclosures, see Chapter 15.) *Condominiums* often are associated with complexes in the suburbs and are thought of as low-rise one- and two-story attached housing units. Condominiums, however, may also be found in high-rise buildings in urban areas.

STATE
SPECIFIC

You need to find out what the term "townhouse" means in your home state. Originally a term used to describe two- or three-story attached housing in urban areas, townhouses now are usually located in planned unit developments. Typically a townhouse owner owns the unit and the land under it and may even have ownership of small lawn or patio space. Because many early condos were built in a two-story townhouse style, in some areas common usage occasionally mixes the terms, calling condominiums townhouses regardless of the style.

Mix it up: Planned unit developments

STATE SPECIFIC

The *planned unit development (PUD)* is a somewhat hybrid form of ownership. In theory, a PUD is a large development often having mixed uses, such as different types of residential and commercial uses, and built by a single developer. In practice, a PUD may have only residential uses. Like a condominium, PUDs often are overseen by a homeowners association, and common charges paid by the homeowners go for outside maintenance.

How a PUD often differs from a condominium is that the owner of a PUD unit also owns land beneath it. In a condominium, you own the unit individually but the land under and around it as a tenant in common with others. (See the section on tenancy in common earlier in this chapter.) You generally don't own land individually in a condominium. You usually do in a PUD. You also usually own so-called common areas like recreation facilities, walking paths, and the internal roads as a tenant in common with others, just like a condominium. You should find out how the term PUD is used in your home state with respect to developments and property ownership.

Check your watch: Time shares

In a *time share,* a person has either a fractional ownership in a property or the right to use a property for a limited period of time each year or both.

Ownership in a time share may actually convey a fee simple ownership interest in the property. In other words, you have unlimited rights to the extent of your ownership interest, even if that ownership interest is the last two weeks in August every year. (For more about fee simple ownership, see Chapter 6.) A time share owner may only have a use interest, which is permission to use the unit on a periodic basis, such as the first week in June each year. A person with a time share use interest (in other words, the right to use a dwelling for a defined amount of time) leaves ownership of the property in the hands of a corporation or an individual.

Review Questions and Answers

Exam questions on the subjects in this chapter are about terminology and knowing the characteristics of the different kinds of ownership and their main characteristics. Concentrate on key words and characteristics, and you'll do fine.

1. Ownership by one person is called

    (A) tenancy by the entirety.

    (B) tenancy in severalty.

    (C) tenancy in common.

    (D) joint tenancy.

    Correct answer: (B). All the other answers involve two or more people owning a single property.

2. Joint tenancy requires unity of interest, unity of possession, unity of time, and unity of

    (A) ownership.

    (B) deed.

    (C) finance.

    (D) title.

Correct answer: (D). See the "Joint tenancy" section and remember the descriptions of the four unities. (I made up the other answers.)

3. The type of ownership available only to married couples that has the right of survivorship is

   (A) joint tenancy.

   (B) tenancy by the entirety.

   (C) tenancy in common.

   (D) community property.

   Correct answer: (B). Joint tenancy and tenancy in common aren't specific to married couples, and community property has no right of survivorship, leaving tenancy by the entirety as the correct answer.

4. In his will, Roger has his apartment house put in a trust to be managed by Alice on behalf of his son Jim. Which of the following is correct in this case?

   (A) Roger is the trustor, and Alice is the trustee.

   (B) Roger is the trustor, and Jim is the trustee.

   (C) Alice is the trustor, and Jim is the beneficiary.

   (D) Roger is the trustee, and Jim is the trustor.

   Correct answer: (A). The person giving the property or creating the trust is the trustor. The person managing the trust is the trustee. The person receiving the benefits of the trust is the beneficiary. Roger is the trustor; Alice is the trustee; Jim is the beneficiary.

5. In which of the following forms of co-ownership are all owners required to sign a deed of sale?

   (A) Tenancy in common

   (B) Joint tenancy

   (C) Tenancy by the entirety

   (D) Tenancy by survivorship

   Correct answer: (C). Tenants in common can always individually sell their interests in the property. Joint tenants, even though they receive their interest from the same deed, can break the joint tenancy by selling their individual interests; they're allowed to do this without the permission of the other joint tenants. Tenancy by the entirety is for married couples only and requires both parties to sign the deed of sale. I made up Answer (D).

6. In what form of ownership does the owner get shares in a corporation rather than a deed?

   (A) Condominium

   (B) Planned unit development

   (C) Townhouse

   (D) Cooperative

   Correct answer: (D). Condominiums, planned unit developments, and townhouses are all real estate ownership interests; no shares are involved since the owner gets a deed. A cooperative is ownership of shares in a corporation. Though not one of the choices, remember that a proprietary lease permits a cooperative shareholder to occupy her unit.

7. Liability is limited to the investment in what type of business ownership of real estate?

(A) General partnership

(B) Syndicate

(C) Joint venture

(D) Limited partnership

Correct answer: (D). In a general partnership, all partners are liable for their actions without limit. Remember that syndicates and joint ventures aren't really forms of ownership but rather general descriptions of two or more people or companies cooperating to do one or more projects. The limited partnership is the only one of the four answers that limits the liability of the limited partners to their investments.

8. In what form of co-ownership does a deceased owner's share go to her heirs?

(A) Tenancy in common

(B) Joint tenancy

(C) Tenancy by the entirety

(D) Tenancy in absolute

Correct answer: (A). In tenancy in common, you can leave your real estate interest to your heirs. In joint tenancy, the property may not be willed to anyone outside the joint tenancy. When one of the joint tenants dies, her share goes to the remaining joint tenants. Remember that this is called the right of survivorship and may vary in some states. In tenancy by the entirety, which is a form of ownership for married couples only, the share of the deceased spouse automatically goes to the surviving spouse. It may not be willed to anyone else. I made up tenancy in absolute.

9. You're married and own property with your spouse. When you die, she will keep her half of the property, and you will be able to leave your half to your sister. You probably live in what kind of state?

(A) Community property state

(B) Joint tenancy state

(C) Tenancy by the entirety state

(D) Tenancy in common state

Correct answer: (A). Community property is the only form of ownership specifically for married couples that permits what is described in the question to occur. Joint tenancy isn't specific to married couples. Tenancy by the entirety is a form of ownership for married people in which the deceased partner's share in the property automatically goes to the surviving spouse. And although you may be able to create a scenario in which you own property as a tenant in common with your wife that allows you to leave half to your sister, this is one of those questions where the word "probably" should lead you to the better answer, which is community property state. It demonstrates the importance of carefully reading every word in a question.

10. A corporation owns property in what form?

(A) Tenancy in severalty

(B) Tenancy in common

(C) Joint tenancy

(D) Tenancy by the entirety

Correct answer: (A). Remember, a corporation is considered an individual person for legal purposes. The other answers involve multiple owners, and because a corporation is considered a single individual, tenancy in severalty is the only answer that works.

Chapter **8**

Knowing the Limitations on Real Estate Ownership

Real estate ownership conveys many automatic rights, such as the right to sell it or build on it. But those rights usually aren't unlimited. Your right to use a piece of real estate that you own often is limited by or subject to the physical, financial, or legal rights of others, including other people or the government. Sometimes the limitations simply prevent you from doing something specific with your property, such as building a commercial building in a residential area because of government restrictions on land use. A private, as opposed to a government, limitation may give the right to another person, usually the person who sold you the property, to determine the style of house you can build.

This chapter provides information about private and government limitations that are likely to be on the real estate license exam. I specifically discuss topics such as voluntary and involuntary liens, regulations concerning new construction, and much more.

Carrying a Not-So-Heavy Encumbrance: Private Limitations on Property Use

An *encumbrance* is a right or interest in a piece of real estate that belongs to someone other than the property owner. Because someone else holds an interest in your property, that right is a limit or restriction on your use of the property. Encumbrances generally are considered private limitations; however, the government can make a claim on your property for unpaid taxes, which also is considered an encumbrance.

Encumbrances come in two flavors (no, not chocolate and vanilla):

>> **Financial claims against the real estate:** These claims are called liens.

>> **Limitations on the use of the property:** Included are easements, encroachments, and restrictions.

You can sample them in the sections that follow.

Looking at liens

Real estate *liens* are financial claims against someone's property. Depending on its purpose, a lien exists with certain characteristics. How and why you permit someone to place a lien on your property has to do with the type of lien to which you're subjected. I talk about all that in the following sections.

Abracadabra: Creating and removing liens

When you borrow or owe money, your real estate frequently becomes the security, called *collateral*, for that loan or debt. Collateral is an item of value you pledge in return for securing a loan. Okay so far? Even though you're actually borrowing the money, the lien attaches itself to the property like a leech. Thus the real beauty of a lien — not to you, of course, but to the person to whom you owe the money — is that it stays with the property, regardless of who owns it, until the debt is paid. Although you may think that attachment is unfair, it helps guarantee payment of the debt.

REMEMBER

When a lien is attached to real estate, it can limit ownership in a couple of ways. It can

>> Mean the property can be sold against your will to pay off the debt, such as for nonpayment of the mortgage or taxes.

>> Show up when you sell your property. Because the new owner doesn't want to pay your debts, you have to pay what you owe to clear the debt and remove the lien before the property sale can be finalized. If you don't have the money to pay the debt when you sell the property, the debt then is paid from what you get from the sale. Removing a lien really is just that simple unless you can prove the lien was a mistake.

Who gets paid first? Priority of liens

One characteristic of liens, the one that exam writers like to ask about, is called the *priority of liens*. A more appropriate term is *priority of payments* because it refers to who gets paid first when property is sold against the owner's wishes to satisfy a number of different debts. It also is referred to as the position of the person being paid, such as the "mortgage is in first position after taxes."

REMEMBER

The first person paid from a court-ordered sale of a piece of real estate is the government. Real estate taxes take first position in the payment of liens. If several liens are attached to the property and one is for unpaid real estate taxes, the real estate taxes are paid first, including any special assessments, or special taxes above and beyond the general real estate tax. Payment of general and special assessment taxes takes priority over all other liens, regardless of when the liens were attached. (For more on tax liens, see "One size doesn't fit all: Types of liens," later in the chapter, and Chapter 16.) Sometimes, because of too many liens, a property may not be able to be transferred or sold, primarily because not enough money can be gained from the proceeds to pay off the debt. Once in a while, some of the lien holders will take less money just so the property can sell. Quite often it is the second mortgage holder in a foreclosure sale who has to settle for less.

STATE SPECIFIC

Other than real estate tax liens, all other liens usually are paid off in the order that they were recorded in the appropriate local office of public records — the county clerk's office or some other office of public records. The particular state where you reside may have some variations on this general rule, but in most cases, the first-recorded, first-paid rule applies. If the real estate is sold to pay off one or more liens and money is left over after all liens are satisfied, the property owner receives the remaining money.

It's all in the name: Liens' distinguishing traits

All liens have two specific traits: They're either voluntary or involuntary, and they're specific or general. Here's what I mean:

» **Voluntary or involuntary:** You either agree to have a lien put on your property or it's put there against your will.

- A *voluntary lien* is where the property owner willingly takes some action that enables the placement of a lien against the property. A mortgage is the most common example of a voluntary lien.

- An *involuntary lien* is placed on the property against the owner's will. If the property owner owes money to someone, such as the tax collector, and the owner doesn't pay, a lien is placed on the property. Because this type of lien was placed on the property without the owner's agreement, it is considered an involuntary lien.

» **Specific or general:** One other characteristic of a lien is identifying how many separate pieces of real estate it can be attached to.

- A *specific lien* attaches to only one property.

- A *general lien* attaches to a number of properties.

EXAMPLE

If you own three properties and have a specific lien on one of them, no one can force you to sell either of the other two properties to pay off the lien. On the other hand, if someone places a general lien on the three properties you own, the lien applies to all the real estate that you own. In other words, all three properties are encumbered by that general lien.

Some general liens also can be placed against your personal property. For instance, income tax liens are general and can show up when you try to sell your yacht.

One size doesn't fit all: Types of liens

You may wonder what types of liens can be put on real estate. In this section, I point out what actions prompt someone to place a lien on a piece of real estate and some of their characteristics. Pay particular attention to whether the liens are general or specific, and voluntary or involuntary. For some reason, state test writers love asking at least a few questions about these four types of liens:

» **Tax lien:** A *tax lien* is placed on real estate for unpaid real estate taxes. Remember the government organization or agency placing the lien is paid first, if the property is sold. Different levels of government from cities, towns, and counties can place tax liens on property. School districts and water and sewer agencies also can place tax liens on property. Tax liens are involuntary and specific.

» **Mortgage lien:** A *mortgage lien* is a voluntary, specific lien. In fact, it's the most common type of voluntary real estate lien. When you borrow money to buy or refinance a piece of real estate, you give the lender a lien against the property. Some states call this a *deed of trust lien*. Mortgage lenders are careful about wanting to be paid the money they loaned you. They usually make sure that no other liens take priority over their lien and that they have what is called a *first mortgage lien*. Any other liens are called *junior liens.* If the mortgage lien is in first position, the only other lien that can take precedence over it for payment is a tax lien.

>> **Mechanic's lien:** A *mechanic's lien* is a lien placed on your property for nonpayment for work you had done on the property. For example, you didn't pay the plumber, so he puts a mechanic's lien on your property. A mechanic's lien is involuntary and specific.

STATE SPECIFIC

Your state may allow brokers to place liens on real estate for unpaid commissions. This practice varies by state and may vary by whether the commission was earned from a sale of property or a lease negotiation. You may also be able to put a lien on the property for an unpaid commission, if the listing contract or the purchase agreement contains a clause that enables you to do so. So check it out.

Instead of a lien, your state may permit brokers to place a lis pendens on the property. A *lis pendens* isn't a lien but instead is a notice of a potential lawsuit, which could result in a lien. It's recorded in the public records to give notice to future buyers of the real estate.

Some states permit brokers to place disputed commission funds in an escrow account while the disagreement is resolved. This is not a lien.

>> **Judgment lien:** *Judgment liens,* sometimes just called *judgments* or *money judgments,* usually are created as a result of a court action. Say someone sues you for a personal-injury claim, for example, and the court finds in favor of the person who sued you. If you can't pay immediately, the court may place a judgment lien against your property.

STATE SPECIFIC

Judgment liens are involuntary and general. They're certainly involuntary, because you didn't voluntarily put up your real estate as security the way you do for a mortgage. A judgment lien is general because it affects all your real estate; however, it usually applies only to property located in the county where the judgment is issued. Nevertheless, a judgment lien can be filed in other counties where you own property. In addition to real estate, judgment liens also can be attached to personal property, such as your car, boat, or antique furniture. Judgment liens, however, may vary from state to state, so you may want to check out specific laws in your state.

REMEMBER

When property is sold for nonpayment of mortgage debt, tax liens are paid first from the proceeds, usually followed by mortgage liens, and then by other liens (mechanic's and judgment liens, for example) in the order in which they are placed on the property being sold.

Easing into easements

An *easement* is the right of another person or entity to use someone else's property for his or her benefit. The other person or entity can be an adjacent property owner or another party such as a utility company. The easement can include the right to use the space beneath the ground, on the ground, or up in the air above the property.

The person or property receiving the benefit is called the *dominant tenement* or *dominant estate.* The property on which the easement was granted is called the *servient tenement* or *servient estate.* Don't worry so much about the words *estate* and *tenement*; the important words to remember are *dominant* and *servient.*

TIP

Think about the words *serve* and *dominate.* The property being used or serving the demands of the easement is servient. The property that benefits from the easement or dominates over the other is dominant.

You're probably thinking, "Why would you, as a property owner, actually let someone else use your property for his or her benefit? Or, for that matter, why would someone else let you use his property for your benefit?" But, the fact of the matter is that many times two people voluntarily create easements. On the other hand, easements also can be created in a couple of not-so-voluntary ways.

Categories of easements are pretty simple and often are part of the exam. You'll see information about gross and appurtenant easements, which involve the person who benefits from the easement. I also give you some information about how an easement can be created against your will.

Running with it: Appurtenant easements

Easements are defined by who benefits from them. An *appurtenant easement* benefits a neighboring property. By the way, don't get confused if your home state reverses these words and calls it an *easement appurtenant.* It's the same thing.

EXAMPLE

Your property can be landlocked, which means that it has no direct access to a public road. So to access your property from a public road, you must cross someone else's property. If that other property owner gives you a permanent right to drive or walk across his property so that you have access to yours, he's given you an easement appurtenant. Although as the property owner, you negotiated the easement for your use and benefit, the easement will continue after you and your neighbor sell your properties to other owners. So it is your property that actually benefits from the easement. Under the statute of frauds law, which exists in some fashion in every state, easements must be in writing to be valid.

Because an easement appurtenant attaches itself to a piece of property, it's said to *run with the land,* which means that whenever the property (dominant estate) that benefits from the easement is sold, the new owner has the same rights to use the easement that the old owner had. Just in case I've lost you here, let's put that in terms of the example in the previous paragraph where you were given an easement to cross someone else's property. When you sell your property, the buyer obtains the same right that you had to cross the neighboring property.

Several appurtenant easements covered on the test include

» A surface easement such as to build a driveway to get from a public road to your house

» An underground easement, for example to bring a water line from the city street main across your property to your neighbor

» An overhead or aerial easement to run an electric line to your house by crossing your neighbor's property

So gross! Easements in gross

Another type of easement is called an *easement in gross.* This type of easement benefits another person rather than a piece of property.

EXAMPLE

The gas company has a gas main running parallel to the street in front of your house and wants to connect it to another line in the street behind your backyard neighbor's house. The gas company needs an easement in gross from you and your backyard neighbor to install the connecting line across your respective properties.

Typical easements in gross that you may see on the exam are utility easements. For example, the city wants to connect two sewer lines by crossing your property with an underground pipe or the electric company wants to connect a line between two poles.

In need: Easements by necessity

A court order creates an *easement by necessity* to permit someone to gain access to a property. For example, say Property Owner *A* sells Buyer *B* a back portion of land but neglects to give Buyer *B* an easement for access. If *A* then refuses to give *B* the easement, *B* can go to court and get it by court order — an *easement appurtenant*.

Easement by necessity doesn't necessarily mean that you can buy a piece of property without any access and expect the court to order a neighboring property owner to give you an easement under all circumstances. Usually a seller's refusal to provide an easement is the circumstance under which the court gives you the easement.

The doctor didn't give you this: Easements by prescription

An *easement by prescription* is an easement that is created by the actions of one person against the interests of another person.

EXAMPLE

Every night when your neighbor Joe comes home, he drives his car across a corner of your property. The reason doesn't matter; he simply does it. You see him do it but never stop him, and he does it for a long time. Eventually you get tired of him driving across your property and tell him to stop, but he says, "No way, I've got an easement by prescription." Joe takes the matter to court, and the court agrees with him. Joe now has a permanent easement by prescription across your property. An easement by prescription is related to adverse possession, which is discussed in the "I thought I owned it: Encroachments and adverse possession" section later in this chapter. The principal difference is that a prescriptive easement gives you the right to use the property. Adverse possession gives you ownership of the property. Like adverse possession, easement by prescription is not automatic; it requires a court order as a result of a lawsuit.

STATE SPECIFIC

When looking at Joe's case for the details of how an easement by prescription is created, the fact that Joe's actions had persisted for a long period of time came into play. So how long is long enough? That length of time varies according to which state you're in. Ten years is the typical minimum time, but it can be longer or shorter.

You saw Joe cross your property. His use was open and what lawyers call *notorious*, meaning it wasn't hidden. In a sense, by not telling Joe to stop sooner, you gave him silent permission to use your property.

Joe crossed your property every night, so his use was continuous during the period prescribed by state law without interruption. This scenario brings up another issue. Suppose that in your state, the period of time required for a prescriptive easement to be created is ten years; Joe sells his property after five years, and the new owner picks up right where Joe left off, continuing to use your property in plain view for another five years. Do you think he'll be able to claim a prescriptive easement? Much to your annoyance, the answer is yes, because of something called tacking.

Tacking is a factor that allows for the addition of the times during which several different owners continuously engage in the same use. So if five different successive owners use your property for the prescribed period of time — for example, your state's ten-year requirement — the latest owner's request for an easement can be granted by the court.

Share and share alike: Party walls

In areas of the country where houses or other buildings are built side by side with no space in between, the outside wall that's shared by the two buildings is called a *party wall*. Each building owner owns half of the wall and has an easement for the other half. Fences on property lines and shared driveways work the same way. Agreements that deal with maintenance issues usually are in place for shared items like these. These party-wall easements are created at the time the buildings are built and sold. They're appurtenant easements because they benefit the adjacent property owner.

It was fun while it lasted: Ending easements

Now that you've let Joe and others walk all over you, so to speak, just how do you go about getting out of an easement? Easements can be terminated in several ways, including:

>> **An agreement or release:** The person who possesses the easement (dominant tenement) agrees to give it up or release the person across whose property the easement exists (servient tenement) from the obligation.

>> **By merger:** *Merger* is a fancy word for the joining of the two properties involved. For instance, *A* has an easement to cross *B*'s property. *B* buys *A*'s property. The easement disappears.

>> **By abandonment:** Use it or lose it. Say you had a driveway easement to some country property that you visit regularly, and for one reason or another, you stop going to the property. Eventually the easement may be considered abandoned and you can lose it.

>> **The need no longer exists:** The need for the easement may no longer exist. Perhaps, for example, a new road is being constructed that allows direct access to the property.

Terminating an easement is not automatic. Usually some form of court action is needed to terminate an easement, unless the two parties agree, in which case some form of legal document agreeing to the termination of the easement needs to be executed and recorded.

It won't let you drive, but it's still a license

A *license* is a temporary right to do something on someone else's property. A license usually is permission that's given for one-time specific use. Depending on the state law, the agreement can be either written or oral because it conveys no interest in the property but only short-term permission to use it.

Say, for example, your neighbor is building a house and construction vehicles need to have access to his property; however, until he installs his own driveway, the easiest way for them to get to his property is across your driveway. You give your neighbor a license to use your driveway for that purpose, but you retain the right to cancel the license at any time. This arrangement does not give your neighbor any permanent rights to your property.

No, you can't paint your house purple: Deed restrictions

A *deed restriction* is a limitation on the use of your property that appears in the deed to your property and is put there by another person. In fact, it's specifically called a *private land-use restriction*, distinguishing it from the public land-use restrictions that I talk about later in this chapter. A deed restriction is considered a private agreement, because no one forces you to buy the particular property governed by it and if you do buy it, you voluntarily agree to abide by the restrictions. Deed restrictions also are referred to as *covenants, conditions, and restriction* (CCRs), or sometimes *restrictive covenants*.

You're probably already asking yourself how someone can agree to a deed restriction and why? I'll answer those questions next and give you some other important information about how deed restrictions work. (For more on deeds in general, head to Chapter 9.)

What is it I can't do?

A deed restriction limits what you can do with your property. For instance, a deed restriction may limit you to building a house in only a certain architectural style or not allow you to build a house of less than a certain size.

Deed restrictions can limit almost anything you may want to do with your property. The only limit on the restriction is that it can't be something illegal. For example, a restriction that says you can't sell the property to a member of a particular ethnic or religious group is illegal and therefore invalid because it violates fair housing laws.

Deed restrictions bind not only the first person who buys the property after the restriction is put into effect but also all future owners, unless the restriction has a time limit.

REMEMBER

Sometimes a deed restriction and public law cover the same issue but have different degrees of limitation. In that case, the more restrictive or limiting of the two applies. Local zoning, which is discussed in the "You're in the zone: Understanding zoning ordinances" section later in this chapter, may require a minimum of one acre for each house you want to build. But say that the actual size of the property you're buying is three acres, and the developer of the subdivision has put a deed restriction in place that says individual properties may not be subdivided again. Even though the government, through the zoning ordinance, says you ought to be able to get three separate pieces of property out of your three-acre parcel, the deed restriction won't permit it. The deed restriction wins, because it's more limiting. Although not always the case, deed restrictions are often more limiting than local laws because they may be designed to do what local laws normally do not, for example, restrict the color you can paint your house.

Who says I can't do it?

Anyone can put a deed restriction on his property that binds all future owners. Typically, though, deed restrictions are placed on a group of individual properties that have been created as a result of a subdivision. The restrictions are placed in the deed by the person creating the subdivision as each property is sold. Subdivisions are discussed in the "Many from one: Subdivisions" section later in this chapter.

The term *restrictive covenants* is used to mean a set of restrictions that applies to an entire *subdivision*, which is a large piece of real estate that's been divided into smaller properties to be built on and sold individually. Restrictive covenants cover all the properties in the subdivision and may become part of the municipal subdivision approval itself.

REMEMBER

Every property owner has the right to seek enforcement of a deed restriction through the courts. So if you paint your house purple, when a restrictive covenant prohibits using that color, any of your neighbors can seek an *injunction* to force you to paint your house an other unrestricted color. However, if your neighbors ignore your new paint job for a certain length of time, they may lose the right to take you to court. The law of the state in which the property is located governs the time frame after which you can lose the right to seek enforcement of a deed restriction. The loss of a right that results from not using it is called *laches*.

I thought I owned it: Encroachments and adverse possession

The ultimate limitation on the use of your real estate is losing the use of it or, in some cases, actually losing ownership of it. Loss of use or ownership doesn't happen automatically. It requires a court's decision.

Crossing into the neutral zone: Encroachment

An *encroachment* is the unauthorized or illegal use of someone's property by another person. On one hand, an encroachment sometimes happens by mistake, as in the case of someone building a garden shed a few feet over the property boundary line onto your property. On the other, it can also be intentional. Someone, for example, may build a house on your country property. Yes, that really happens.

As is usually the case with unauthorized use and claims against someone's property, ownership or use is lost only as a result of court action. In a case involving a disagreement over a boundary line, court action may be necessary to resolve the dispute. Tell that to those feuders, especially when one of them claims they have the automatic right to that tomato garden because they've been using it for ten years.

Staking a claim: Adverse possession

Adverse possession is someone actually claiming ownership of your real estate because of how they're using it. Say your neighbor puts up a fence ten feet onto your property. It was a mistake. He knows it, and you know it, but neither of you does anything about it. Not a big deal you say. He'll just have more lawn to mow and you less. No problem, right? Maybe it is, or maybe it isn't. If the fence stays and your neighbor uses your ten feet of property as though it's his own for the required period of time set by the state, he can go to court and claim ownership of the property by adverse possession. And he may even win. (For more details about adverse possession and other ways of losing ownership of property, check out Chapter 10.)

One point to note about adverse possession if you're thinking of building a pool on the county property behind your house: Government land is usually protected from an individual claiming ownership or use because of adverse use of the government owned land.

Land-Use Regulation: A Major Public Limitation

A state's power to limit the use of your property is based on something called *police power*. You may think of police power in the usual way — traffic tickets — and you'd be partially right. The police power that every state possesses is a general power to pass laws for the health, safety, and welfare of the citizens of that state.

Although each state government may keep some of the power to regulate land use for itself, most of it is passed down to local governments like towns, cities, and counties. As a result the police power is passed down by the state through *enabling laws* or *enabling legislation* that it adopts.

Police power is pretty broad, and most of it has nothing to do with real estate. In this section, I talk about the part of police power that limits the use of real estate.

To the drawing board: Making master plans

Most municipalities (villages, towns, and cities) create what are called *master plans* or *comprehensive plans*. These are written documents, usually including many maps that are compilations of studies of current physical layouts of the municipalities, projections of how their governments want their municipalities to look in the future, and descriptions of what needs to be done to accomplish those projections. A municipality conducts a number of studies in completing its master plan. A partial list of these studies includes

>> **Capital facilities:** The municipality takes inventory and analyzes its publicly owned buildings and parks.

>> **Demographics:** Population characteristics of the municipality, such as age and level of education, are studied. These studies rely heavily on census data gathered by the federal government, which divides the entire country into *census tracts* from which it gathers population statistics as part of the federal census every ten years.

>> **Housing:** The municipality examines its current and future housing inventory and needs. This study includes public and privately owned housing.

>> **Infrastructure:** *Infrastructure* refers to roads, sewers, water lines, and other physical facilities that are important to the growth of a municipality. This study looks at current facilities and the need for new construction and improvements of these support facilities.

>> **Land use:** Areas of land within the municipality are examined, usually on a map, with respect to their primary use, such as housing, shopping, offices, industrial, and agricultural.

Based on these studies, and usually with citizen input, the municipality sets goals for its future and develops plans to achieve those goals. One of the primary ways by which a municipality implements its master plan is through the adoption of a zoning ordinance.

You're in the zone: Understanding zoning ordinances

A *zoning ordinance*, which in some municipalities is called the *zoning code*, is a set of rules that control what property in the municipality can be used for and regulates where on the land any buildings will be located, the maximum height of the building, and the amount of land it can cover. The zoning code essentially tells you what you can build, where you can build it, and how much you can build, all by designating zoning districts and establishing specific regulations for each district.

A *zoning district* is an area that's designated for a certain type of use — housing, shopping, and so on. Typically a zoning ordinance divides a community into different districts for residential use, commercial use, agricultural use, and industrial use. Several districts may be designated in each of these categories. For example, one residential district may permit high-rise apartment buildings while another may allow only single-family houses.

But I really want to build a skyscraper: Variances in zoning

Most zoning ordinances recognize unusual circumstances that require a certain degree of flexibility in applying zoning regulations. A one-property variation from the requirements of the zoning ordinance is called a *variance*. Variances can be granted whenever an owner can prove that a practical difficulty or hardship will result from an attempt to build on the land or show that existing zoning will deprive him or her of all economic use of the land.

For example, a zoning ordinance requires that a building must be set back 50 feet from the front property boundary line, but because of a rock outcropping that extends deep into the land from the back of the lot, the 50-foot setback would be impractical. A variance may be granted, permitting the building to be built ten feet from the front boundary line rather than the required 50 feet. This type of variance is called an *area variance*. A *use variance*, on the other hand, permits a different use of the land. One example of a use variance is where the owner of a single family house in an area zoned for single family houses receives permision to convert it into a home with two apartment units.

**STATE
SPECIFIC**

A state-specific item for you to look into is what board or agency grants variances in your state. Names like board of zoning appeals, planning and zoning board, or zoning hearing board are common, but be sure to check it out. Remember that a board in one locale may be a commission in another. You can probably get this information from your local building or planning department.

On one condition: Special-permit use

Another type of variation from the requirements of the zoning ordinance for an individual piece of property, in some places, is called a *special-permit use*; in other places, it's called a *conditional-use permit*, and in some places it may be called a *special-use variance*.

In any event, these variations are for uses listed in the zoning ordinance that are different enough from the permitted use within a zoning district that they require special review by municipal agencies. A nursery school in a residential neighborhood is an example of a use that may be appropriate in a residential zoning district but is different enough to make an additional review a good idea. The municipality may want to require the nursery school to observe specific hours of operation or install special safety features before issuing the special-use permit. These permits generally are issued to a property owner and either run for the length of ownership or for a specified period of time with the ability to renew them.

I was here first: Nonconforming uses

A *nonconforming use* refers to an established structure on or use of a piece of real estate that wouldn't otherwise be permitted under current zoning. Nonconforming uses generally are buildings or uses that existed either when no zoning ordinance was in effect at all or when an old zoning ordinance was in effect that allowed such buildings and uses.

Perhaps your grandfather built a factory at the edge of town at a time many years ago when the area had no zoning ordinance. The factory continues to operate, but in the meantime, the town grew, and a zoning ordinance was adopted that zoned the area around the factory for single-family houses. Speaking of your grandfather, it's not unusaul for this type of nonconforming use to be referred to as *granfathered* or a *granfathered use*.

Although the specific regulations dealing with nonconforming uses vary from one place to another, the factory probably would be allowed to continue to operate. Typical regulations require the removal of the factory if it's ever destroyed or closed for an extended period of time. The site of the factory probably wouldn't be allowed to expand or change into another nonconforming use.

Parking the car . . . and your family, too: Accessory buildings and uses

Zoning ordinances sometimes allow accessory buildings and accessory uses on a piece of property.

>> *Accessory buildings* are buildings separate from the main building on a property that support or are related to the main building. A detached garage and a pool house are examples.

>> *Accessory uses* are uses that are related to but a little different from the principal use of the property. A separate apartment for a family member in a district zoned for single-family houses is an example of an accessory use. Accessory uses can be in the principal structure or in an accessory building.

Many from one: Subdivisions

A *subdivision* is one piece of land that has been divided into two or more (sometimes many more) pieces of land. These individual pieces of property often are called *lots* or *parcels*. The purpose of subdividing is to allow for the sale of the smaller individual pieces of land. Most subdivisions are created for building homes, but commercial or industrial properties also may be subdivided.

STATE SPECIFIC

Most levels of government that have control over land use adopt subdivision regulations or land-development ordinances. These regulations are different from the zoning ordinance or master plan but may be adopted or periodically revised along with those two documents. You may want to find out in your state who adopts and enforces subdivision regulations. I give you some important information about particular aspects of subdivisions that may be on an exam.

Knowing the main players and plans in subdivisions

Subdividers create *subdivisions*. (And you thought this would be hard.) Subdividers generally never get their hands dirty. Most of their work deals with lawyers, engineers, surveyors, and sometimes developers. After a subdivision is approved, subdividers can sell the entire subdivision to a developer or builder. A subdivider can also sell individual lots with the promise to eventually put in roads, sewers, and water lines.

A *developer* actually, well, develops the subdivision, making physical improvements to it by putting in roads, utility lines, and other infrastructure elements. A developer sometimes builds houses for sale or sells individual lots to builders or people who want to build a house. A developer sometimes buys an approved subdivision from a subdivider or can act as the subdivider, too.

As you see there can be some overlap in these definitions, but it's good to understand that different people can be involved in the subdivision process, taking it from raw land to finished houses.

The specific legal requirements of a subdivision vary from place to place, but a typical subdivision proposal is based on a plat map. That's not a misspelling. A *plat map* shows how the entire property is to be subdivided, or broken down into the individual lots, by showing the precise boundaries of each lot. The area that's being subdivided often is broken down into blocks and lots, or sections and lots. For example, an entire subdivision may be divided into five blocks, with each block being divided into ten lots. The total subdivision would be 50 lots.

STATE SPECIFIC

Generally subdivision regulations are created and enforced at the local municipal level, but some places have additional regulations at the state level. Something that you need to check out in your state is whether it has a specific law dealing with subdivisions, what the requirements of the law are, and especially at what lot count the law takes effect. Some states, for example, may require that an offering plan with details about the subdivision be filed with the state government before any lots are sold. This requirement may be in effect only for subdivisions of more than a certain number of lots. This type of state requirement is in addition to any local subdivision rules and regulations.

Following the rules: Subdivisions and zoning laws

A subdivision must adhere to local zoning laws. Zoning is explained in the "You're in the zone: Understanding zoning ordinances" section earlier in this chapter. Here's an example of how zoning relates to subdivisions: You have a 50-acre piece of property that you want to subdivide. The local zoning code says that the minimum lot size for each new house is one acre. Knowing that 10 percent of the land typically is used for roads — in this case five acres — you're able to design the lots to take the most advantage of the land and can divide the remaining property into 45 lots. That's exactly what you'd do in a straightforward simple subdivision.

REMEMBER

To allow for more flexible design of subdivisions, some municipalities have adopted density-zoning and cluster-zoning ordinances.

>> A *density-zoning* ordinance permits the same overall density within the subdivision, which means the same total number of lots on the same overall size property as allowed by the zoning ordinance. The sizes of the individual lots, however, may be smaller or larger than the minimum required size. In the example I gave you, you still can get only 45 lots out of the whole 50-acre subdivision, but each lot can be bigger or smaller than one acre. As long as the average lot size is one acre the density zoning ordinance permits flexibility of design, lot layout, and road layout. It may also save money by reducing road length and utility (water and sewer line) costs.

>> *Cluster zoning* goes one step further than density zoning. It clusters or groups lots together in a relatively small area to preserve a certain portion of the property as open space. You may, for example, be able to cluster or group the lots in your subdivision into a total of only ten acres. That leaves 35 acres without any buildings. Once again, you won't be allowed to create more than 45 lots, but in addition to preserving open space, cluster zoning also makes for shorter roads and water and sewer lines, which, in turn, results in savings to the developer. In some places, cluster zoning also is known as *conservation zoning*.

Crossing state lines for real estate purposes

In this section, the subject of interstate land sales becomes part of the discussion; however, strictly speaking, it isn't a regulation about how land is developed but rather how it is marketed when subdivisions and land sales are discussed. And yet, it's important enough that state test writers want you to know something about it.

Land in one state has been offered for sale to people in another state probably for as long as people and land have been together in this country. Unfortunately buying land sight unseen is risky. Although many perfectly honest dealers do business in what are called interstate land sales, unfortunately many people have been victims of fraud in these types of deals.

The *Interstate Land Sales Full Disclosure Act* was enacted in 1968 to minimize fraud and dishonest dealings in the interstate land sales market. The act is administered by the Department of Housing and Urban Development (HUD).

The requirements of the act apply to interstate sales of vacant, or undeveloped, lots in subdivisions of 25 lots or more. The act doesn't apply if the lots are 20 acres or larger. However, the act requires developers to file information with HUD describing details of the project, including but not limited to utilities, recreation facilities, location of nearby communities, and soil conditions.

Building a house out of paper: Regulations for construction

You thought it took bricks and wood and nails and cement to build a house, right? It does, of course, but it also takes lots of paper. Building construction, residential (houses and apartments) and non-residential (pretty much everything else) alike, is regulated in most parts of the country. The regulations are in place to provide for safe and, in recent years, more energy-efficient construction.

A *building code* is a regulation that provides minimum standards relating to construction, electrical, plumbing, and safety materials and practices and energy-efficient items such as insulation. Building codes are adopted and administered at the local (village, town, city, and county) level.

STATE SPECIFIC

In some states, the state government adopts a building code and then requires each local government to use that code or one that is stricter. You need to find out whether your state has a state-wide code and how it applies to the local municipalities. In states that have an arrangement where the local government can adopt a stricter building code, this issue is a favorite question on the real estate exam.

The building code also provides details that govern the construction process, and that's where all the paper comes in.

Getting that house built

Although the process may vary from one place to another, you'd typically follow these steps to build a house:

1. Draft plans.

Plans are detailed drawings of the building that usually are prepared and completed by the licensed architect or professional engineer that you hire. They usually include *specifications or specs* that provide written details of certain features.

2. File an application.

You submit the plans along with an application to the proper government agency, typically the building commissioner or inspector or code enforcement department.

3. Review the plans.

The building department officials review your plans to make sure they comply with all the ordinances and regulations of the municipality.

4. Issue a building permit.

The building department then issues you a building permit, and you now can officially begin construction.

5. Conduct inspections.

An official from the building department inspects your project at various points during construction. Some typical items that are inspected include the foundation, framing, insulation, and electrical and plumbing work.

6. Undergo final inspection.

A building official inspects the project when construction is complete.

...ccupancy.

...rtment is satisfied that you've completed the project in accordance with ...ppropriate codes and regulations, it issues you a *certificate of occupancy,* ...*C of O,* which is important proof that you've properly completed the ...tion involves internal modification of the house rather than all new ...te of completion or compliance may be issued in some municipalities.

...Although not ...l part of the process, I can tell you that after having gone through it a ...ife, you definitely deserve a party.

...on construction regulations

...ions concerning development. Some states have more than others. In preparing for the exam, you're going to have to hunt around a bit in your home state to find out about your state's development regulations. Finding what state agencies play a part in controlling development, what the major laws are, and what issues both deal with, probably is enough; however, if you have to take a prelicensing course, pay special attention to the state agencies and laws ...may deal with. If you don't have to take a course, in addition to reading this book, just study the ...you to prepare for the exam.

Possible development issues that your state may deal with include the following:

>> **State roads:** Find out who controls whether you get permission to put in a new driveway off of a state road. Usually it will be your state department of transportation or highways.

>> **Fire and electrical concerns:** Your state may have a special agency or department that deals with regulations for electrical and fire safety issues.

>> **Environmental issues:** Some states have adopted regulations that require consideration of environmental issues in the development of land. Although adopted by the state, they may be administered at the local municipal level.

>> **Historic preservation:** Preserving area history is another factor where states have adopted regulations but delegated authority to administer them or adopt more stringent ones to the local municipality.

The Government Has Its Say: Other Public Limitations on Property Use

Government plays a major role in how land is used. I actually need to say *governments* because public limitations on land use exist at all levels of government: village, town, and city (usually referred to as municipalities), and county, state, and federal. Government regulations on land use can and do limit what you can do with your property.

However, other government limitations on real estate have to do with what you expect the government to do for you in terms of services and buildings. You expect the government to build roads, bridges, parks, schools, and many other infrastructure facilities. The government needs money and land to accomplish these things, so it places limitations on land use that include its rights to obtain the land and money that it needs to do these things.

Most local governments depend on property taxes to pay for their services like schools and road maintenance. Because land doesn't go anywhere, it is always there, is hard to hide, and unlike salaries, its value is fairly predictable from year to year. It provides a good, stable source of income for local governments.

STATE SPECIFIC

In this section, I talk about general concepts of public limitations on how you can use your real estate. With the exception of federal rules and regulations, all other specific limitations and how they are applied and enforced vary by state and even by municipality. Fortunately, most of the exam questions asked about this topic are about the general stuff. I point out some of the things that you need to check on for your particular state that may be on the exam.

The city wants to build a library: Eminent domain

Eminent domain is the right the government can exercise to obtain ownership of your real estate against your will. Before you get too upset, I need to clarify that the government always has the right, like any corporation or individual, to negotiate with you to buy your property. Conversely, you are free to turn down the government's offer the way you would in any sale of your real estate. In most cases the government prefers negotiating when it needs land for something as opposed to exercising its right of eminent domain.

The government uses its right of eminent domain when it must have your land, and you refuse to sell it voluntarily. It does this through a *suit of condemnation.* This process sometimes is called *taking.*

Because the government has the right to take ownership of your property through eminent domain, it also has the right to take less than full ownership or less than the entire property. So the government can take the front ten feet of your land to widen a highway but leave you the rest of the property, or it can take the right to install a sewer line under your backyard without actually obtaining the land itself. This type of limited right is called an easement, which I talk about in "Easing into easements" earlier in this chapter, and can be either an easement in gross or an easement appurtenant.

REMEMBER

The government must meet these three requirements to be able to obtain a property through eminent domain:

>> The ultimate use for the land must be for a legitimate public purpose. *Public purpose* may be to build a road or a park or install a sewer line, among other things.

>> A fair price must be paid to the owner. The price usually is determined by an appraisal and sometimes is challenged by the property owner obtaining his own appraisal.

>> The government must follow all required legal procedures, or in other words, exercise *due process.* The specific requirements of due process vary from state to state but may include certain mandatory notices to property owners, minimum time frames for owners to be notified, and environmental reviews before the eminent domain action can be taken.

People always can fight eminent domain proceedings in court either because they believe that the use is not a legitimate public purpose or because they believe due process was not followed. In addition, they can argue about the value of their property. In a related type of argument with the government, they also can pursue inverse condemnation. *Inverse condemnation* is where a landowner sues the government because of a loss in value that is the result of a government action. Building a sewage treatment plant can reduce the value of nearby properties, for example. Neighboring property owners may sue the government for payment of their property value losses or to force the government to buy their properties outright.

You didn't know the government was part of your family: Escheat

Escheat, which literally means transfer, is the process by which the state obtains property from people who die without heirs and without a will. The legal term for dying without a will is *intestate.* This state right prevents property from being without an owner.

WARNING

In case you're wondering, obtaining property by escheat isn't a significant way for the state to get the property it needs for various public works, and it has very little to do with your future real estate careers. The term, however, almost always is included in a list of government limitations on real estate use, and more important, often appears on state real estate exams.

Pay or lose: Taxation

Taxation of real estate is such an important subject that it has its own chapter: Chapter 16.

REMEMBER

Why it's mentioned here is because in most discussions of government limitations on the use of real estate, taxation is included. After all, it's the way most local governments (towns, villages, cities, and counties) raise money to provide public services and buildings, and if you don't pay your taxes, you lose your property through a process called *foreclosure,* the most limiting kind of restriction someone can put on your property.

Review Questions and Answers

Questions on the subjects in this chapter tend to be focused on general knowledge and definitions. State examiners don't expect you to become zoning experts, for instance, but they do want to know that you know the difference between a use variance and an area variance.

1. Which of the following is false?

   (A) Liens are encumbrances.

   (B) All encumbrances are liens.

   (C) Easements are encumbrances.

   (D) Deed restrictions are a type of encumbrance.

   Correct answer: (B). Among the several different types of encumbrances are easements and deed restrictions. Liens also are one type. So all liens are encumbrances, but not all encumbrances are liens. Remember — this question is asking you to select the answer that is not true.

2. Which statement is true about real estate tax liens?

   (A) They take priority over all other liens.

   (B) They are paid according to when they were recorded.

   (C) They take priority over all liens except the mortgage.

   (D) They are the only types of liens that do not attach to the property.

   Correct answer: (A). Real estate tax liens come first when property is sold for payment, regardless of when they are filed. There's no logic to this answer except that the government makes the rules, so you'll just have to remember that.

3. A judgment lien is

(A) voluntary and specific.

(B) voluntary and general.

(C) involuntary and specific.

(D) involuntary and general.

Correct answer: (D). It's involuntary, because you didn't want it, and it's general, because it covers all your real estate and can include your personal property. You agree to a voluntary lien. Specific liens only apply to one property.

4. Ann buys property that is landlocked. Betty agrees to let Ann drive across her property to get to the main road. Ann has

(A) an easement in gross.

(B) an easement by the entirety.

(C) an easement by necessity.

(D) an easement appurtenant.

Correct answer: (D). An easement appurtenant benefits a neighboring property — in this case, Ann's property. An easement in gross benefits an individual. No such thing as an easement by the entirety even exists. Under certain circumstances the court grants an easement by necessity when someone refuses to give an easement. In this case, Betty agreed to give Ann the easement.

TIP

Something else you need to notice in the question is the use of the term "landlocked." Test writers expect you to know that it means a property has no direct access to a road.

5. The loss of the right to enforce a deed restriction because of a failure to enforce that right within a specified time frame is called

(A) statute of limitations.

(B) laches.

(C) restrictive covenant.

(D) statute of frauds.

Correct answer: (B). Statute of limitations usually applies to criminal prosecution and civil suits. Restrictive covenants are the basis for filing for an injunction. Statute of frauds is something I cover in Chapter 11.

6. The right of the government to take your real estate against your will is known as

(A) escheat.

(B) negotiation.

(C) eminent domain.

(D) zoning.

Correct answer: (C). Eminent domain is the right of the government to take your property even if you don't want it to. Escheat is the government getting your property after you're dead. Negotiation is with your cooperation so it isn't against your will. Zoning limits the use of your property but does not give ownership to the government. The use of the word "take" in the question is typical when referring to eminent domain.

7. A detached garage on a house lot is an example of

   (A) an accessory use.

   (B) an accessory building.

   (C) a variance.

   (D) a special permit use.

Correct answer: (B). Remember an accessory use supports the primary use on the property. The key is that the question asks about a building.

8. The plan showing the individual lots in a subdivision is called

   (A) the master plan.

   (B) the plat map.

   (C) the zoning plan.

   (D) the lot-and-block plan.

Correct answer: (B). The possible confusing answer here is the lot-and-block plan, because you may remember that many subdivisions are divided into blocks and lots. But that isn't what the subdivision plan is called.

9. The term used to describe roads, sewers, water lines and other municipal service facilities is

   (A) utilities.

   (B) demographics.

   (C) accessory uses.

   (D) infrastructure.

Correct answer: (D). Go back and look at your definitions. And remember that test writers expect you to understand words like municipal, which means governmental unit (usually local), and facilities, which can be almost anything that's physical but isn't movable.

10. What document do you check to determine the amount of insulation needed in a new house?

   (A) Zoning ordinance

   (B) Deed restriction

   (C) Building code

   (D) Subdivision regulations

Correct answer: (C). Zoning ordinances tell you what you can build and where you can build it, but the building code tells you how it can be built. I imagine an energy-conscious person can put an insulation restriction in a deed but doing so is so unlikely that (B) wouldn't be the correct choice here. Subdivision regulations normally don't deal with building specifications.

Chapter **9**

Transferring Ownership: Deeds and Title Closing

Your job as a real estate agent all comes together when ownership of a piece of real estate goes from one person to another. You'll probably get paid only if ownership of the property is *transferred* as a result of a sale or an exchange. By the way, another term that means the same as transferred in real estate language is *conveyed*, and I use the two words interchangeably. From the real estate agent's perspective, after a deal has been reached, a few more steps still need to be taken by either or both the agent and attorneys to change ownership of the property from one person to another.

This chapter gives you important information about how ownership of property is transferred from one person to another. I talk about the documents that are needed, such as the deed, and how property is described so that no mistakes can be made about who owns what. And I discuss a process called title closing, where ownership of the property actually goes from one person to another.

REMEMBER

Title in real estate terms means ownership. So rather than use the word ownership, most people in real estate work say things like "The title was conveyed on Tuesday" to indicate when ownership was transferred. Unlike with automobiles, the title is not a document. And as already mentioned, the words *convey* and *transfer* apply to ownership of a property moving from one person to another, regardless of circumstances. Whether you're talking about a gift, sale, or exchange, title is conveyed or transferred.

Doing the Deed: Delving into Deed Basics

The *deed* is an extremely important piece of paper, a document that transfers title to a property from one person to another. It's important not only because it transfers title, but also because until you convey title to someone else, it serves as proof of your current ownership. It also serves as a permanent record of your ownership.

In this section, I give you information about what specific factors and terms must be included in a deed to make it valid, and I talk about some other language in the deed that can affect how you use the property and spell out some information about different types of deeds for you. This section also includes some information about how real estate is described so that no one can question who owns what.

Making it right: Requirements for a valid deed

STATE SPECIFIC

The requirements for a valid deed have been passed down through history by common practice and law so that no one can have any misunderstandings about

>> What is happening when the title to a property is conveyed.

>> Who owns the property now.

>> To whom the property is being conveyed.

>> What (exactly) is being conveyed in terms of the property boundaries.

>> What rights are being transferred.

STATE SPECIFIC

Because of the importance of establishing and proving property ownership, all states have adopted legislation called the statute of frauds. The *statute of frauds* requires that all real estate transfers of title be in writing. Depending on your state, and sometimes even where you happen to be within your state, attorneys are required to prepare deeds, the exact form of which may vary somewhat; however, the essential requirements for a deed, and therefore the conveyance, to be valid *are the same.* The requirements that follow are listed in the general order in which they appear in most deeds.

>> **Grantor:** The *grantor* is the current owner of the property who is conveying the title to someone else. The grantor must be legally competent and of legal age. In most places, the minimum legal age of competence is 18, but you may want to check what it is in your state, though it's unlikely to be a specific test question. Remember the grantor can be selling the property, exchanging it, or giving it away. The grantor can be a corporation or multiple parties if it's a co-ownership situation.

>> **Grantee:** The *grantee* is the person receiving title to the property. An important factor in naming the grantee in a deed is that the grantee be named in such a way as to avoid any confusion about who he or she is. So, if the grantee is John Smith III, then he better be named that way in the deed, especially if John Smith I and John Smith II are still around. Addresses for both grantor and grantee are also sometimes required. Grantees can also be corporations or multiple parties.

>> **Consideration clause:** The deed must contain words that indicate that the grantor is receiving something of value in exchange for the property. Generally, money is being received, and the *consideration clause* needs to state the amount. In some places, the phrase "ten dollars and other valuable consideration" or something similar is used for the consideration. No, the buyer did not get a super bargain as some people might think. The reference to ten dollars is used to

hide the actual amount paid for the property if someone wants to keep that information confidential. I show you how you may be able to find out what amount was actually paid in "Recording the right documents," later in this chapter. When the property is a gift, the words "for love and affection," or similar phrasing, are used.

>> **Granting clause:** A *granting clause* states that the grantor is conveying ownership of the property to the grantee. In fact, the *granting clause* also is known as the *words of conveyance*. (In Chapter 6, I tell you what it is you really own when you own a piece of real estate.) The granting clause includes words that describe exactly what rights the grantee is receiving in the deed and whether the grantee is taking title to the property with another person.

>> **Habendum clause:** The *habendum clause,* which contains the words "to have and to hold," further defines the rights being granted to the grantee. (For those of you who've already tied the knot, the habendum clause may sound a little like you're getting married again.) The words in the habendum clause must agree with the words in the granting clause.

STATE SPECIFIC

The inclusion of a habendum clause may vary from state to state.

>> **Legal description:** I provide detailed information about different ways a property can be described in "Painting the right picture: Property descriptions in deeds" later in this chapter. For now, though, just think of the legal description in this section as wording that's designed to leave no doubt about the exact boundaries of the property being conveyed.

>> **Exceptions and reservations:** In Chapter 8, I give you information about the limitations that can affect how the property is used through such things as deed restrictions and easements. This part of the deed is where those restrictions or limitations are described.

>> **Grantor's signature:** The grantor must sign the deed for it to be valid. Usually, if more than one person owns a property, all the owners must sign. In some states a husband or wife who owns property by himself or herself may have to have the spouse also sign the deed even though the spouse does not have title to the property. An attorney-in-fact can be permitted to sign the deed in most states. An *attorney-in-fact* is someone who is appointed by a power of attorney, which is a legal document signed by someone giving another person authority to act on his or her behalf, in this case to sign the deed. An attorney-in-fact doesn't necessarily have to be a lawyer. In some states, a third party must sign the deed stating that the grantor actually is the person who signed the deed.

If the grantor is a corporation, other rules may apply. A resolution by the corporate board of directors or the majority of the shareholders usually is necessary to convey property owned by a corporation. One or more duly authorized corporate officers must sign the deed. (See Chapter 7 for more about ownership by a business.)

>> **Acknowledgment:** An acknowledgment is a way of proving that the person who signs a deed signed it voluntarily and is, in fact, who he says he is (or who she says she is). An acknowledgment normally is witnessed and attested to by a notary public, before whom you produce evidence of your identity and indicate that you're signing the deed of your own free will.

STATE SPECIFIC

An acknowledgment technically is not required for a deed to be valid; however, in most states, a deed without an acknowledgment cannot be recorded in the official public records. You can find out more about recording a deed in "Recording the right documents," later in this chapter, but remember it is usually not necessary to record a deed for the transfer of title to be valid. It's an awfully good idea but not mandatory.

>> **Delivery and acceptance:** The *conveyance of title* to a piece of real estate has not officially taken place until the grantor delivers the deed and the grantee accepts it. The term passing title refers to the acts of giving and receiving the deed. The date of the transfer of ownership is the date the deed was delivered and accepted. An exception to this timing in some places occurs when closing in escrow, which is discussed later in the section "Closing in escrow." In that case, title passes when all requirements of the sales contract have been met, including the signing of the deed by the grantor and its delivery to the escrow agent.

The deeds of the many: Examining various kinds of deeds

STATE SPECIFIC

I'm sure you hope that only one kind of deed exists, but alas, I'm sorry, real estate grasshopper, you must deal with several different kinds, at least for the exam. Different deeds serve different purposes, and although all convey ownership, they differ in the kinds of warranties or guarantees they provide for the grantee. Although not required for a deed to be valid, many deeds provide for different warranties made by the grantor to the new owner. The various types of deeds also may differ because of who the grantor of the property is and why the property is being conveyed. Ultimately, these factors are mostly the stuff lawyers revel in, but most states want their real estate agents to have at least a basic knowledge of the different types of deeds.

STATE SPECIFIC

You should check out the most common types of deeds used in your state and find out whether they have names that are different than the ones I listed. You can get this information in your prelicense course, the textbook you use, and any handouts the instructor gives you. As you read this section for the exam, keep in mind that you usually can tell one type of deed from another by the different warranties provided and the different purposes for which the deeds are used. And state test writers expect you to know only the basic information. You may have plenty of questions that you need to ask your lawyer, but don't worry about them for the exam. I list the different types of deeds in the sections that follow.

REMEMBER

Title insurance usually is purchased regardless of the kind of deed that's conveyed. Even when the grantee receives a general warranty deed with all the guarantees back to the first owner, title insurance assures the new owner that if a title problem ever comes up, the grantee will be protected and compensated. In addition, title insurance usually is required by the bank or lender, whenever you borrow money through a mortgage loan to buy the property. (For more, see "Proving marketable title," later in this chapter.)

General warranty deed

General warranty deeds, which sometimes are called the full covenant and warranty deeds, provide the greatest protection and warranties by the grantor to the grantee. The warranties, which are usually called covenants, are listed here in the order in which they usually appear in the deed.

>> **Covenant of seisin:** Would you believe that some people can't even agree on the spelling of this? *Seisin* is the guarantee that the grantor is the owner of the property and has the right to transfer ownership.

>> **Covenant of quiet enjoyment:** No, this warranty doesn't mean that the grantor promises that your neighbor won't play the radio after 11 p.m. *Quiet enjoyment* means that the grantor guarantees that no one else can come along and claim ownership of the property. It also means that if a later party's title claim is found to be better than the owner's title, the grantor is liable and must compensate the grantee for any losses.

>> **Covenant against encumbrances:** The grantor guarantees that the title to the property has no encumbrances like an easement or lien. Easements are rights that enable someone else to use some of the property, and liens are financial claims against the property. You can find out more about encumbrances in Chapter 8. The only exceptions to this warranty are encumbrances that are specifically stated in the deed.

>> **Covenant of further assurance:** In this covenant, the grantor promises to obtain and provide documents necessary to clear up any problem that comes up with the title.

>> **Covenant of warranty forever:** This assurance sometimes is referred to simply as warranty forever. The grantor guarantees to pay all costs to clear up any title problems at any time in the future.

REMEMBER

A particular feature of a general warranty deed is that warranties cover any title problems that may have occurred during the ownerships of all past owners. The reason a general warranty deed provides the greatest title protection to the grantee is because this deed provides the most complete set of warranties and the grantor is responsible for all previous owners' actions with respect to title problems.

Special warranty deed

Special warranty deeds contain only two warranties. The first is that the grantor has title to the property. The second is a guarantee that nothing was done to affect the title during the grantor's ownership, and if a problem did exist, the grantor will correct it. The differences then between a special warranty deed and a general warranty deed are the number of warranties and the fact that the grantor takes responsibility for things that happened only during his ownership. In some states, the special warranty deed is known as a *bargain and sale deed with covenants against grantor's acts.*

Because of the limited warranties, people acting as third parties — that is, they don't actually own the property they are conveying — sometimes use special warranty deeds. The executor of an estate, for example, uses a special warranty deed to convey property belonging to an estate or trust.

Grant deed

STATE SPECIFIC

Grant deeds are used in a few states and provide limited warranties. The grantor guarantees that the property hasn't been conveyed to anyone else, that no encumbrances limit the use of the property except the ones specifically listed in the deed, and that if the grantor later obtains any other title to the property, it will be conveyed to the grantee. These guarantees are limited to the period of time the grantor owned the property. The grant deed is used in only a few states, but if yours is one, you need to remember this information.

Bargain and sale deed

The distinguishing feature of this type of deed is that it has no warranties. That the grantor has full title to the property is implied. Essentially it gives no protection to the grantee. This type of deed sometimes is used in foreclosure and tax sales. You can read about foreclosure in Chapter 15. Warranties can be put into the deed to make it similar to the special warranty deed, and in that case, it's referred to as a bargain and sale deed with covenant against grantor's acts.

Quitclaim deed

The *quitclaim deed* provides no warranties to the grantee and gives no implication of how much or how good the grantor's title to the property is. It conveys to the grantee only that much ownership interest that the grantor may have. Quitclaim deeds often are used to clear up a cloud on the title. A *cloud on the title* is something that makes the title less than complete, like someone appearing to occupy the property without the owner's permission, or indicates that some other ownership interest may exist, like two properties abutting a private road with both claiming ownership of the road. Quitclaim deeds sometimes are used for uncomplicated transfers of property ownership within a family.

Trust and reconveyance deeds

A *trust deed,* which sometimes is called a *deed of trust* or *deed in trust,* is used to convey ownership by a *trustor* to a *trustee* for the benefit of a *beneficiary* as security for a debt. Here's an example: Party *A,* the trustor, borrows money from Party *B,* the lender, and then signs a trust deed conveying ownership of the property for which he borrowed money to Party *C,* the trustee, a third party. The lender is the beneficiary. If Party *A* pays all the borrowed money back to the lender, Party *C* then reconveys the property back to Party *A.* If Party *A* fails to repay the debt, Party *C* sells the property and gives the money to the lender to pay off the debt.

On a related note, a *reconveyance deed* is used to reconvey title to property from a trustee back to a trustor after a debt for which the property is security has been paid off.

Trustee's deed

A *trustee's* deed is given by a trustee when ownership of property held by a trust is conveyed. Say, for example, that a young child owns property held in trust until he reaches legal age. The trustee of the trust can use a trustee's deed to convey that property to someone if the trust decides to sell the property.

Court-ordered deeds

STATE SPECIFIC

Deeds often are issued as a result of legal proceedings. An *executor's deed* in the case of a deceased person's estate and a *sheriff's deed* in the case of a sale of property seized by a local unit of government or the bank are two examples of such court-ordered deeds. State law establishes these deeds, and state law governs their form. You probably won't find many questions on your state exam about this topic, but you need to check it out just in case.

Painting the right picture: Property descriptions in deeds

Describing the boundary lines of a piece of land as accurately as possible in a deed is extremely important. Why this is so important is simple. When you get to the end of your land, you find yourself about to step onto someone else's land. Contrast that with owning a car. I know what my car looks like, and I know where I park it. No doubts exist about where the car begins and ends. Not so with real estate. (By the way, throughout this section I use the terms land, property, and real estate interchangeably.) Property descriptions of the kind we're talking about and the kind typically used in deeds are descriptions of the boundaries of the land but don't include any descriptions of the buildings on the land.

All property owners would want to know exactly what they own but it is especially important because many government land use regulations that govern what you can do with your property involve the size, shape, and boundary lines of the land. Read more about this in Chapter 8. Accurately describing your property is equally as important when transferring title from one person to another. The grantor needs to know exactly what he or she is selling, giving away, or exchanging, and the grantee needs to know exactly what he or she is getting. This property description usually is referred to as the *legal description of the property.* Legal descriptions are prepared in one of three standard ways that I describe in this section. A few math questions that relate to a property's description may be included on the exam. I also discuss the measurement of elevations for property descriptions and clue you in on two ways that you *can't* describe a property.

REMEMBER

Three systems of preparing a legal description can be used anywhere in the United States. Some parts of the country rely more heavily on one system than others. Exam writers like to ask about all three systems regardless of what state you're in, but they probably emphasize the system used in your state. So study all three systems and especially your local system of legal description. No one is trying to turn you in to a *land surveyor,* the professional who surveys the property, locating the property boundaries on the ground, and prepares these legal descriptions. Exam questions tend to be recognition type questions, the kind that require you to be able to tell the difference between the characteristics and key definitions of each system of legal description. But the questions can get a little more detailed. I go over this in the following sections.

Meeting your boundaries: The metes and bounds system

The *metes and bounds system* of legal description uses specific locations, distances, and compass directions to describe the boundaries of a piece of property. Starting at what is known as the place or point of beginning, the description follows a line or curve in a specific direction for a precise distance to another point. At that point the direction changes and the boundary line is then laid out again in a specific direction for a precise distance.

A simple metes and bounds description might then read:

> *From a place or point of beginning 100 feet North to a point then East 100 feet to a point then South 100 feet to a point then West 100 to the place or point of beginning.*

TIP

For fun, try drawing this description with pencil and paper. Remember that when laying out a property like this, as you face the paper, north is up, south is down, east is to the right, and west is to the left. What you end up drawing is a square. In reality, metes and bounds descriptions usually are not so simple. The directions often are broken down into degrees, minutes, and seconds, which all are precise points on a compass. The distances sometimes are measured down to inches.

Turning points especially in older descriptions of the boundary lines often refer to natural features like a rock or a stream. Sometimes the boundary of someone else's property is used as a reference. But property owners change, rocks move, and streams dry up. Over time natural and ownership references have been replaced by artificial markers placed permanently in the ground or simply by points known to the surveyor. Sometimes marking only the place or point of beginning is sufficient rather than marking every turning point. The term *monument* describes any point in the surveyed boundary that is noted on the survey. Monuments, which usually are turning points, can be man-made or natural. The term *monuments* may also refer to actual man-made physical markers placed on the land during a survey.

The metes-and-bounds description is clearly stated in the deed. On a large property, with a boundary that features many twists and turns, a metes-and-bounds description can be lengthy. The description also can be used to draw a map referred to as a survey map or simply survey. A *survey* is the actual determination of a property's boundaries on the ground. A *survey map* or *sketch* is a representation or drawing of the property's boundaries, sometimes showing structures that are situated on the property.

The metes and bounds system of describing property boundaries is the oldest property description system in the United States. It remains the primary way of describing property boundaries in the eastern part of the country, particularly in the states that formed the original 13 colonies.

You're so square . . . more or less: The rectangular survey system

The *rectangular survey system*, often referred to as the *government survey system*, is based on a system of lines that form rectangles and squares throughout the United States. The first sets of lines respectively are called *principal meridians*, which run north and south, and *baselines*, which run east and west. The principal meridians and baselines are based respectively on lines of longitude and latitude. Just in case you were out the same day I was in high school, longitude and latitude are imaginary lines that divide the earth through the north and south poles (longitude) and run parallel with the equator (latitude). Principal meridians, baselines, and where they intersect (cross each other) are used as the basis for formulating property descriptions in this system. They are the starting points for describing a property's boundaries. The following is a list of helpful terms:

>> **Quadrangles:** The basic squares of land of the rectangular survey system, *quadrangles* (also *government checks,* or just *checks*) are 24 miles square (that means each side is 24 miles long) and are delineated by a principal meridian and a baseline. Quadrangles have an area of 576 square miles, more or less, and are divided into 16 townships.

» **Townships:** The divisions of a quadrangle, *townships,* are six miles square (six miles on each side) and are delineated by township lines. Townships have an area of 36 square miles, more or less, and are each further divided into 36 sections.

» **Sections:** The divisions of a township, *sections,* are one mile square and have an area of one square mile, or 640 acres. Sections can be divided in several ways, but basically for purposes of the United States Geological Survey (USGS), they are divided in quarter sections.

» **Quarter sections:** The divisions of a section, *quarter sections* are formed by dividing a section into fourths that are delineated by their direction from the center of the section (northwest — NW, northeast — NE, southeast — SE, and southwest — SW). Quarter sections have an area of 160 acres.

» **Half sections:** *Half section* is a description of any two abutting quarter sections within a section, usually accompanied by a directional notation indicating the half of the section in which the two quarter sections are located. Half sections have an area of 320 acres. So there can be the north, south, east, or west half section.

Because of the curvature of the earth, the lines in the government survey system are only theoretically straight. Imagine trying to draw straight lines on a rubber ball. Although the lines start out the same distance apart, they get closer together as you get near one or the other end of the ball. *Correction lines* and *guide meridians* were established to correct this problem in the government survey system. Correction lines occur at every *fourth township line* or every 24 miles north and south of the baseline. The guide meridians occur every 24 miles east and west of the principal meridian. An area bounded on two sides by guide meridians and on the other two sides by correction lines is called a *government check, check,* or *quadrangle,* which is 24 miles square, meaning each of its boundaries is 24 miles long. A government check represents an area that measures 576 square miles. Remember that although these correction lines and guide meridians are the way the government deals with the issue of the earth's curvature, it isn't the way the government survey system describes land. In reality, because of this earth curvature issue, many sections and townships vary from their exact area measurements. A system of *fractional sections* and *government lots* are parts of standard practice to account for these discrepancies.

So how does the system describe land? Using principal meridians and baselines as points of reference, land areas are divided by two kinds of lines, township lines and range lines. *Township lines,* which run east and west, parallel to baselines, are horizontal parallel lines that form township tiers. Think about two lines running from left to right across this page about an inch apart. The *range lines* run north and south parallel to the principal meridians. These range lines form ranges. Think about two more lines running up and down the page on top of the first two lines, also about an inch apart. You got it: Tic tac toe. Where the two range lines and two township lines intersect, they form a township. Now the way it really works is for this page to be filled with the lines going up and down and right to left so that you have many townships. The township is the basic unit of measurement in the rectangular survey system. The area created by the intersection of a township line and a range line is a township. The townships are consecutively numbered by their location within the intersection of multiple range lines and township lines. The boundary of each township is six miles long, so a township contains 36 square miles and is described as being 6 miles square. These townships are not the same as political subdivisions.

REMEMBER

Each *township* is further divided into 36 sections of one square mile each, or 640 acres, by horizontal and vertical section lines. Sections also are numbered consecutively. Section one within any township is always located at the upper right or northeast corner of the township. The numbering then moves from right to left across that first upper tier. The numbering continues directly beneath the sixth section, except that it progresses from left to right on the second tier. The numbering changes directions in the third tier from right to left — see Figure 9-1. In other words, after section number 6, it drops down to 7 on the next tier then goes left to right to number 12. Then the numbering drops down to 13 and goes right to left again and so forth.

FIGURE 9-1:
Townships
are divided
into
36 sections
numbered
consecu-
tively.

6	5	4	3	2	1
7	8	9	10	11	12
18	17	16	15	14	13
19	20	21	22	23	24
30	29	28	27	26	25
31	32	33	34	35	36

© John Wiley & Sons, Inc.

Each section of 640 acres can be divided into halves and quarters called, get this, half sections and quarter sections. These divisions mean just that, for instance a quarter section always contains 160 acres, or a fourth of the total 640 acres in a section. See Figure 9-2. Specific directional references are needed in the actual description to locate a particular piece of property but for finding out how large a particular piece of property is, only the fractions matter.

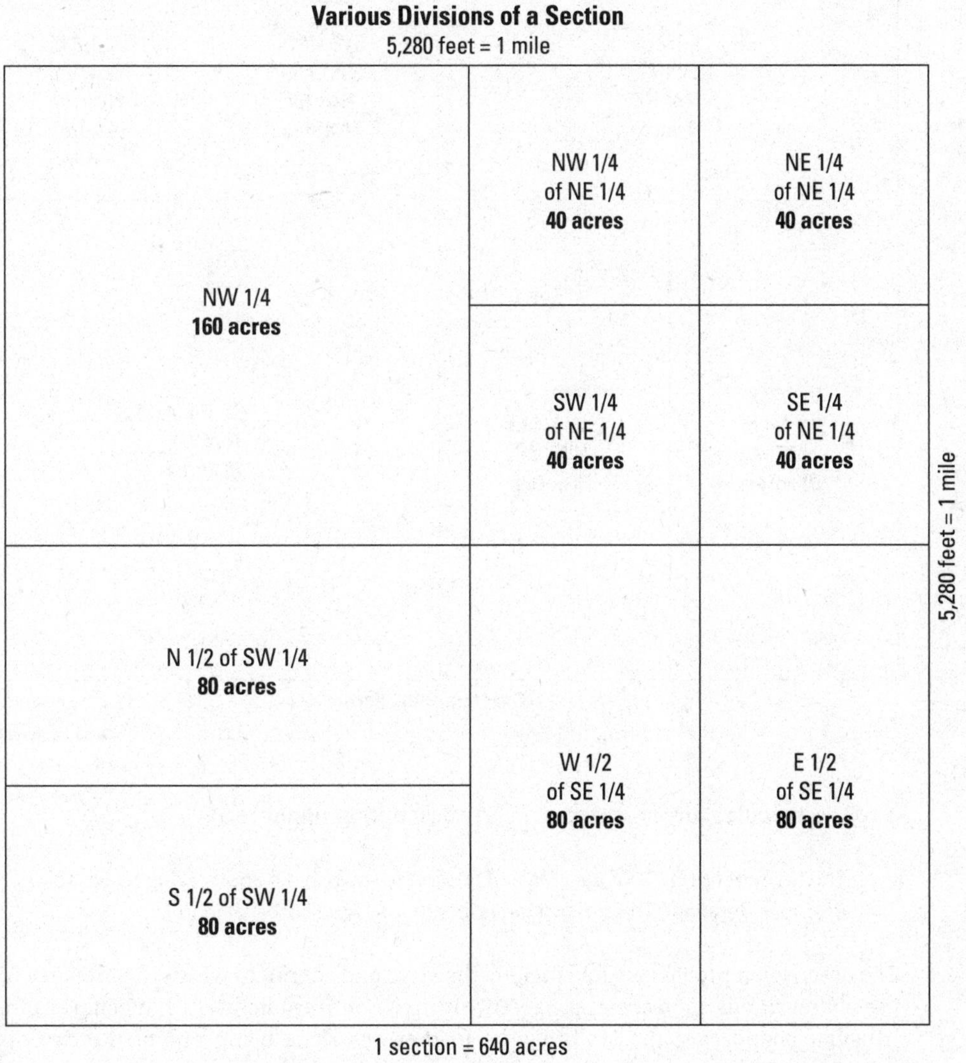

Various Divisions of a Section

5,280 feet = 1 mile

FIGURE 9-2: Sections can be divided in a variety of ways, including quarters and smaller sections.

TIP

Each half or quarter section can be further subdivided into halves and quarters. So you can refer to the south (S) ½ of the northwest (NW) ¼ of a section in a township, for example (see Figure 9-3 for a variety of divisions in a quarter section). Figuring out the size of that piece of property, which sometimes is called a parcel, is simple, if you keep in mind that you're always dealing with a section of 640 acres. Putting the above description into words is half of a quarter section. Doing the math, it's ½ × ¼ × 640 = 80 acres.

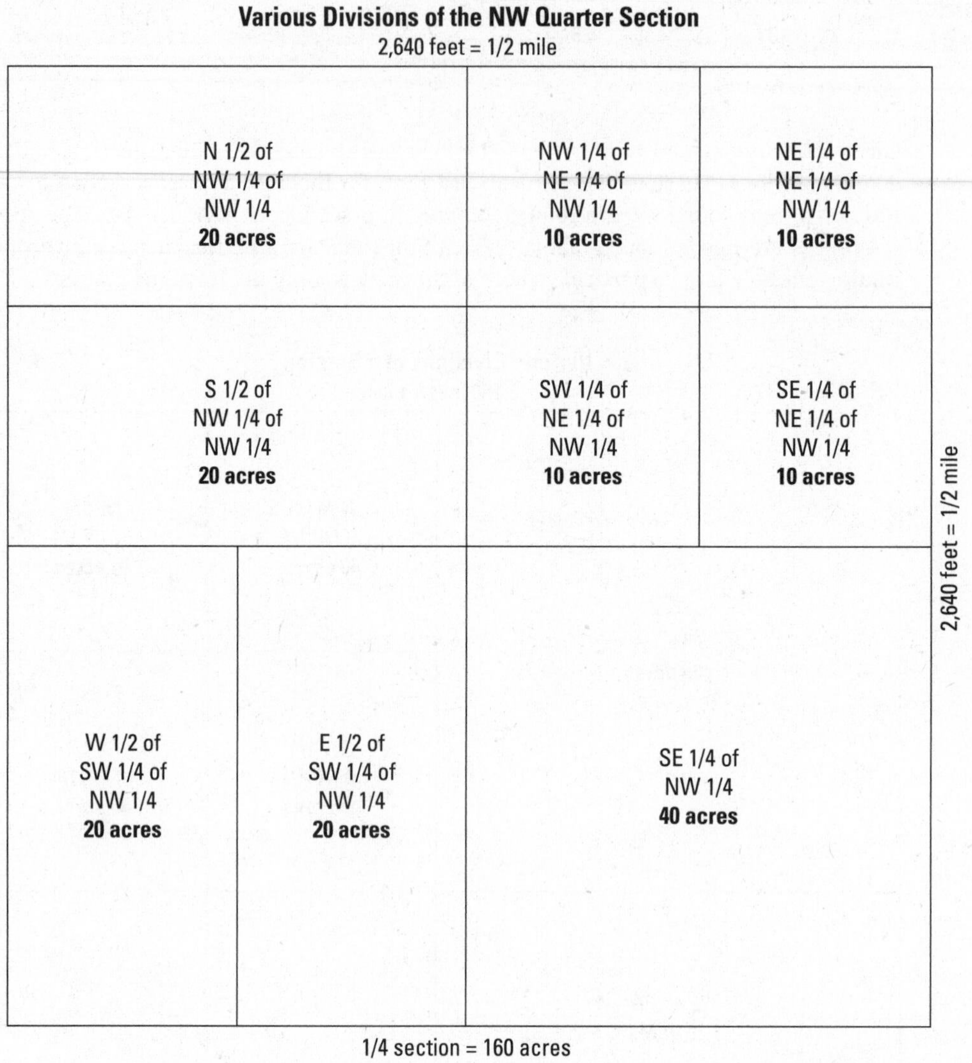

Various Divisions of the NW Quarter Section

2,640 feet = 1/2 mile

N 1/2 of NW 1/4 of NW 1/4 **20 acres**	NW 1/4 of NE 1/4 of NW 1/4 **10 acres**	NE 1/4 of NE 1/4 of NW 1/4 **10 acres**
S 1/2 of NW 1/4 of NW 1/4 **20 acres**	SW 1/4 of NE 1/4 of NW 1/4 **10 acres**	SE 1/4 of NE 1/4 of NW 1/4 **10 acres**
W 1/2 of SW 1/4 of NW 1/4 **20 acres** / E 1/2 of SW 1/4 of NW 1/4 **20 acres**		SE 1/4 of NW 1/4 **40 acres**

2,640 feet = 1/2 mile

1/4 section = 160 acres

FIGURE 9-3: A quarter section can be split into smaller parts.

© John Wiley & Sons, Inc.

A full rectangular survey system property description might read:

> The SW ¼ of the NE ¼ of the NW ¼ of Section 6, Township 4 South, Range 5 East of the Third Principal Meridian. (This description refers to a 10-acre parcel of land.)

The description probably would include the state and county in which the property is located and use abbreviations so in the example Township 4 South would be T4S. Whenever properties have irregular boundaries, the land may be further described using one of the two other systems described in this section.

REMEMBER

You're likely to see at least a few questions on calculating the area of part of a section, and you'll also see questions about terminology and some of the measurements that the rectangular survey system uses. You may even see a question or two about the numbering system used for sections. I've included samples of these types of questions in the review questions at the end of the chapter as well as in the practice exams at the end of the book. Because the rectangular or government survey system was instituted when the United States was a brand new country, it was used to describe most of the land west of the original 13 colonies, so most of you are likely to see some questions about this system.

Block party: The lot and block system

The last of the methods for preparing legal property descriptions is known by various names, including the *lot and block system, the recorded plat system, the recorded map system, the lot block tract system, the recorded survey system,* and the *filed map system.* You can find out the name commonly used in your area when you take your prelicensing course. Regardless of which name you use, the essentials are the same, and it's the system that's usually used in conjunction with a new subdivision, or a large piece of property that has been divided into smaller pieces usually to sell or develop separately.

A *map* or *plat* or sometimes *plat map* (they are all the same — don't you wish these guys could agree on what to call things?) of the subdivision is created, showing the boundaries of each (usually numbered) lot or parcel of land. If the subdivision is large, it may be divided into blocks or sections, each of which is then divided into lots. For example, you can have Lot 2 in Block 1 or Lot 5 in Section A. In a very large subdivision you might see all three terms used, with the subdivision first divided into sections; then the sections divided into blocks, and then the blocks divided into lots. Each lot has a metes and bounds description on it (see "Meeting your boundaries: The metes and bounds system," earlier in the chapter). This method is the only way a surveyor can look at the map and lay out the boundaries of the property on the actual property. So in reality, the lot and block system is a hybrid that makes use of another system.

After the surveyor draws the map, it must be filed in the local records office. The property owner, attorney, or surveyor usually files the map. If the map were of a new subdivision, then the local zoning, planning or other government officials would already have approved the subdivision. The records office goes by various names in different states and locales, but it generally is part of county or local government. The map is filed in the county (or municipality in at least one state) where the property is located and is kept on file as a public record. The filer is given a record of the filing that includes the filing date and may be marked with a specific reference number given to the map that refers to the document, what type of document it is, the book (sometimes called *liber,* which is Latin for book) in which it's kept, and the page number. This reference number helps anyone who wants to locate the map in the records office.

Now how does this work to provide a legal description, say to convey a property? Here's an example. Buyer A wants to buy Lot 3 in Block 2 of the subdivision I've been talking about, which by the way happens to be named Mary's Subdivision after the subdivision developer's daughter. (Don't laugh! That sort of thing goes on more than you'd think.) So now the developer has a deed prepared that includes a property description that reads something like "Lot 3, Block 2, on the final plat of Mary's Subdivision, filed in the Office of Land Records of Washington County (State), as plat map number 12345, filed on May 15, 2017." Slight variations may occur in these descriptions, but you get the idea. All deed descriptions always refer back to that recorded plat map.

REMEMBER

If you've been following this explanation, you may have figured something out. Because the lot and block system and the metes and bounds system are used all across the country, if the property you're describing is located in a part of the country that also uses the rectangular survey system, and the property is being subdivided into several lots, you can end up with a description that refers to the rectangular survey description and the filed map. And the filed map, which is prepared using the lot and block system, also includes metes and bounds descriptions of each lot in the subdivision written right on the map of the subdivision, even though the deed would use the lot and block number to describe the property.

Taking it up (or down) a notch: Measuring elevations

In surveying work and in preparing property descriptions, measuring or describing space as up in the air or describing an area below the ground surface for subsurface rights sometimes is necessary. As a property owner, you can sell or lease your *air rights*, or the airspace over your land or building. (For more about air and other ownership rights, see Chapter 6.)

Datum is a point, line, or surface from which elevations are measured. An *elevation* is a vertical measurement either up or down. Datum for the entire United States is defined by the USGS as the mean sea level in New York harbor. Individual cities, however, may establish their own datum.

Benchmarks are permanent markers established by the federal government to aid surveyors in their work. They exist throughout the United States. Benchmarks are known reference points from which surveyors can work to establish property boundary lines. They are used primarily for ground level locations of distances and directions for property lines, but they're also used together with a datum to measure elevations, for example, to do a condominium description.

Don't do that! Illegal ways to describe property

WARNING

Some of the things you can't use to describe real estate from a legal point of view are:

>> **The property's address:** The address is not considered an adequate description for a property from a legal perspective or for use in a deed. For one thing, it doesn't specify the boundaries of the land, and for another, in many areas, vacant parcels of land in particular, don't have addresses. Addresses are used and are acceptable for documents like leases, in which a precise description of the land is not necessary.

>> **The tax assessor's parcel number:** Because many assessors use a system of identifying properties that looks similar to the recorded plat map system, tax assessor's lot, block, section, and parcel numbers can be confusing. An assessor's parcel numbers, however, can change from time to time and therefore they don't provide consistency over time. The maps sometimes contain property sizes and general boundary measurements but don't usually have detailed boundary descriptions of the likes that a metes and bounds description provides. (For more about tax assessment, see Chapter 16.)

Getting Closure: Title Closing

Title closing is a point in time during a real estate transaction when all of the business of transferring ownership of a piece of property is finished and title to the property is conveyed by the grantor to the grantee. Title closing can be either a relatively simple process or extremely complicated. Complications often crop up because of problems with the title to the property. In the world of real estate brokerage, problems at closing can be the result of something so trivial as the owner of the property not mowing the lawn just before the closing. This section is not about those kinds of problems. Instead, it's about issues that can occur with the title to the property.

STATE SPECIFIC

This section deals with activities that take place before, during, and after the closing. Closings generally are similar from one state to the next, with the exception of places that close the title in escrow. Other subtle differences may exist regarding who pays for what in terms of various fees associated with the closing, so you need to look for any major differences between the typical closing process that I describe in this section and your particular state's practices. In addition I point out specific situations that are likely to be different from state to state.

Nearing the finish line: Before the closing

Let me give you a timeline here to put this section in perspective. Typically after all of the looking and talking and negotiation, when a buyer and seller agree on all the terms of the sale, especially price, they sign a sales contract. Essentially the seller (grantor) agrees to sell the property at a certain price to the buyer (grantee). (For more about sales contracts and other types of contracts, see Chapter 11.)

A number of things happen between the time the sales contract is signed and the day of closing title when transfer of ownership of the property actually takes place. Activities after the contract is signed but before closing usually have to do with satisfying the terms and conditions of the contract and any terms and conditions the lender may set, whenever a mortgage is involved in the transaction. One main thing that occurs during the period between contract signing and closing is the *title search*, which is a look at the records of title transfers between previous grantors and grantees to determine whether any prior claims are on the title to the property.

Proving marketable title

STATE SPECIFIC

A typical real estate sales contract requires the seller to convey *marketable title* to the buyer, which means that the title must be free from any reasonable doubts as to who the owner is and free from any defect in title itself. The objective of establishing a marketable title is to prove that no clouds are impeding clear title to the property. A *cloud* on the title is something that casts doubts on the grantor's ownership of the property. Although strictly speaking, it doesn't constitute a cloud on the title, clear title has been expanded to mean no problems such as illegal structures or unpermitted improvements to the property. The different ways the grantor may prove marketable title vary by state and may even vary by area within a state. Check out what your state's common practice is. In general, though, proof of good title can be accomplished in several different ways. Here are descriptions of the four most common ways:

>> **Abstract of title:** An *abstract of title* is a report of what was found in a title search, which is a search of essentially all public records related to the property's title, such as previous deeds and liens. (You can read about liens in Chapter 8.) These records are usually found in the county recorder's office or land records office of the county in which the property is located. Although anyone can search the public records, during a title search, an abstractor (someone who searches through title records) or attorney researches the chain or history of the title

from one owner to the next, looking for gaps in ownership or other factors that appear to cast doubt on the validity of the current owner's claim to the property.

The abstract of title then is given to the buyer's attorney to examine. When the buyer's attorney is satisfied that the seller has marketable title and issues an attorney's opinion of title, the closing can proceed. Although you won't be doing a title search, these are public records and as such can be examined by anyone. Some expertise is needed to look for title issues in the deeds and related filings — like liens — but you can look through previous ownership of the property simply by working backwards from the current owner. Smith, the current owner, is the grantee from Jones the grantor. But one deed back, Jones becomes the grantee from the previous owner, and backwards in time you go.

» **Certificate of title:** A *certificate of title* is similar to an attorney's opinion of title and may even be prepared by an attorney. It also can be prepared by a title company or an abstractor, the person who actually prepares the abstract. The certificate of title is an opinion about the validity of the title but not a guarantee of title. In this way, the certificate of title is similar to the abstract and attorney's opinion of title, because it doesn't protect against ownership claims that may not be in the public record. In issuing a certificate of title, an attorney examines the public records but no abstract of title is prepared.

» **Title insurance:** *Title insurance* can be purchased on its own or as a supplement to an attorney's opinion of title or a certificate of title. Normally issued after a title search, title insurance provides protection for the buyer, defending the new owner if any future claim is made against title to the property. In many cases where a mortgage loan is involved, the lender requires a title policy that at least covers the lender's portion of the purchase price. This coverage is called a *lender's* or *mortgagee's policy*. The owner may want to obtain an *owner's policy* to cover his or her interest in the property.

Title insurance covers various defects according to the laws of the state in which the company issues the policy. The American Land Title Association sets *standards for standard and extended coverage.* Standard coverage policies insure against things like forged documents, improperly delivered deeds, and incompetent grantors. The standard policy is based on what is found in the public record. The extended-coverage policy, in addition to the coverage in the standard policy, insures against defects that may be found by an inspection of the property, such as someone claiming ownership or rights in the property by virtue of their use. (For more about adverse possession, see Chapter 10.)

A title company may pay the owner of the property on a claim and then pursue action for damages against some other party. Through the right of *subrogation,* the title company is entitled to the same rights as the person it insures, which means that after it pays the owner, the title company can then pursue whoever may be responsible for the title problem, say a prior owner, collect, and keep the money it gets.

» **Torrens system:** *The Torrens system* is based on proper registration of the title. An abstract of title and a lawsuit to quiet title, which is where you can go to court to have the court declare that you have clear title to property, are filed with the appropriate authority or office, such as the county court clerk. If approved, a certificate of clear title, called a Torrens certificate or Torrens certificate of title is issued by the court, which unlike the attorney's opinion or an abstractor's certificate of title, is considered to be proof of ownership. The Torrens system gradually is falling out of use in the United States, but some states or areas within states may still use it. (Make sure to find out whether your state is one of them.)

Removing liens

The removal of liens is another activity that takes place before closing. As part of a title search, the title company determines whether the property is subject to any liens. Liens, which are discussed in Chapter 8, are financial claims against the property. The owner/seller customarily removes all liens from the property prior to sale but under some circumstances the buyer may pay off the lien. If a lien isn't removed or satisfied through payment before the closing date, liens usually must be paid off at closing with proceeds the seller receives from the buyer.

Examining encumbrances

Title searches also make note of any other encumbrances on the property. Encumbrances, which are discussed in Chapter 8, are limitations on the owner's use of property. They include liens but also can be an easement or a deed restriction (also covered in Chapter 8). Generally the buyer accepts ownership of the property subject to these encumbrances. They normally don't present a problem with the title to the property.

Meeting the conditions of the sales contract

This chapter is about transferring title and all the things that affect that transaction. Although most contract conditions (such as obtaining a mortgage or having a home inspection done) don't normally affect title, note that before closing, the buyer completes all the conditions that have been put into the sales contract. So, if a sales contract has been signed and indicates that a mortgage loan has to be obtained and a home inspection by a home inspector or other professional must be completed, the buyer is responsible for completing these activities prior to closing. By the way, neither of these things is mandatory nor must they be put in the contract. You can pay cash for a house (well, maybe you can but I can't) and you don't have to have it inspected. Immediately prior to closing — usually that day or the day before — the buyer personally inspects the property. The agent selling the property or the agent working with the buyer often conducts this walk-through.

The big day: At the closing

When the big day finally arrives, the buyer, seller, attorneys, and you, the agent, meet to close on the title to the property. By the end of the day, the seller has some money and the buyer owns some property. The people who come to a closing, the roles they play, and the specific activities and papers that are signed vary greatly from state to state and even from area to area within a state. I discuss the people, roles, activities, and documentation that are most important and common, because they are what exam writers like to ask questions about.

RESPA and TILA

The Real Estate Settlement and Procedures Act (*RESPA*) has to do with closing on the mortgage, which happens at the closing, and simply means signing all the paperwork necessary for the bank to give you, the borrower/buyer, the money that you don't have for very long because you give it to the seller, and for you to give them the mortgage. You can find out everything you need to know about mortgages in Chapter 15 where you can also read about the *Truth in Lending Act* (TILA), which governs certain aspects of consumer lending. Both of these acts are designed to protect consumers who borrow money

RESPA is a federal law designed to protect consumers who borrow money through a federally related mortgage loan (loans that are sold on the secondary mortgage market, which you can check out in Chapter 15) to buy residential properties, including condominiums and cooperative apartments. Some of the activities required by RESPA and TILA take place before the closing, specifically provision of the Loan Estimate form to the borrower. Combined actions under both laws also affect the closing itself, particularly the preparation of the closing statement, so

I include the discussion of RESPA and TILA here. The Federal Consumer Financial Protection Bureau administers the closing provisions of the integrated RESPA and TILA. It has four distinct requirements:

>> **Required reading:** The HUD booklet *Buying Your Home: Settlement Costs and Helpful Information* must be given to anyone applying for a mortgage loan.

>> **Estimated costs:** The lender must give the borrower a loan estimate of all costs associated with the mortgage loan no more than three days after receiving the application.

>> **Closing Disclosure Statement (closing/settlement statement):** At least three days before the mortgage closing, which is usually at the same time the title to the property is closed, a settlement statement or closing statement of costs must be prepared and given to the borrower. The settlement statement must be prepared on a form known as the Closing Disclosure Statement.

>> **Prohibited kickbacks:** RESPA prohibits kickbacks. A *kickback* is an undisclosed fee, usually secretly paid for referring business to someone. For example: A home inspector who pays a fee to a lender for recommending him to perform home inspections for one of the bank's customers is accepting a kickback. RESPA forbids such actions.

There are a few consumer protection regulations for the Truth in Lending Act (see more on this in Chapter 15) and RESPA that have been combined specifically with an eye toward protecting people who are obtaining loans to buy a house. The creditor or mortgage broker must do the following:

>> Deliver or mail a loan estimate to the consumer no less than three days after receiving the application.

>> Provide to the consumer a closing estimate no less than three days before the closing.

Allocating expenses with proration

Proration is the allocation of certain expenses between the buyer and the seller. A variety of costs are associated with buying and selling a piece of property. The principal cost is, of course, the purchase price paid by the buyer to the seller for the property. Part of the settlement at closing is accounting for all the costs and fees in addition to the purchase price, making sure they are paid, and allocating them appropriately to the buyer or seller. In some states the attorneys or a representative of the title company (sometimes called a *closer*) handle this accounting; in others, it falls to the real estate agent. No matter where you are, you need to know something about this.

REMEMBER

Two accounting words that you need to know when pondering the closing statement are credit and debit.

>> A *credit* is an amount owed to the buyer or seller or something for which they've already paid. For example, the purchase price of the property always is a credit to the seller, who is owed that money (and a debit to the buyer — see the next bullet point). The down payment, on the other hand, is a credit to the buyer (here, here), who already has paid it. Remember when the buyer paid a deposit (earnest money) at the contract signing, long before the closing. A credit essentially is a financial transaction that's in someone's favor.

>> A *debit,* on the other hand is a financial transaction that is not in your favor, in the case of a real estate transaction, something that the buyer or seller owes. So the purchase price of the house is a debit to the buyer, because he owes it to the seller. If encumbered by an existing mortgage loan on the property, the seller must pay off the mortgage at the closing. So it's a debit to the seller, but of course not a credit to the buyer because it's paid to a third party, that being the bank.

STATE SPECIFIC

Various fees and charges differ from state to state in several ways. Even local differences exist as far as what fees are owed, the amounts charged, whether the buyer or seller is responsible, and when the fee is actually paid. Although I can't guarantee it, you probably won't see any questions on specific fees or charges. But just in case, I give you this list of the most common ones so you have some points of reference for getting the additional information you need.

- » Attorney's fees
- » Appraisal fee
- » Broker's commission
- » Loan fees
- » Recording fees
- » Survey fees
- » Tax and insurance reserves
- » Title expenses
- » Transfer tax

Although this list is fairly complete, your state may have specific fees that are required or a particular type of transaction may involve additional fees. The fees and charges are accounted for within the closing statement as debits and credits according to who pays and who is owed.

REMEMBER

Two types of payments and costs that are allocated between the buyer and seller at closing are accrued items and prepaid items:

- » An *accrued item* is one that is owed by the seller but is paid by the buyer. Real estate taxes that are paid in arrears (after) is an example of an accrued item. The seller lives in a house where real estate taxes are due December 31 for the entire previous year, a situation in which the taxes are being paid in arrears. The seller transfers title to the house on June 30 but has paid no taxes yet for that year, even though the seller has the benefit of living in the house for six months. The buyer has to pay the full year's taxes on December 31, but has lived in the house for only six months. Not fair, you say. And you're right. The taxes are a prorated item at the closing, meaning the seller and the buyer have to share the costs and payments according to who paid and who used the property. In this case, the seller who used the house for six months owes the buyer money, because the buyer is going to pay the taxes for the entire year but only lived there six months.

- » A *prepaid* item is one that the seller has paid but from which the buyer benefits. I reverse the tax example that I just gave you. Suppose that taxes are paid in advance, such that the Seller pays a full year of taxes for the coming year on January 1 but sells the property on June 30. Having paid a full year's taxes, the seller nevertheless has enjoyed the benefit of living in the house for only six months. The buyer, on the other hand, has paid no taxes for that year, yet lives in the house for six months. Not fair, again; proration to the rescue. This time the buyer owes the seller money.

In many places, real estate agents either calculate prorations or help attorneys or title companies with the calculations. In other places, attorneys or title companies handle the whole thing. Whatever the particular practice in your area, you'll probably see some questions about proration on the state exam. I take you through examples of an accrued item and a prepaid item, starting with the simple tax example that I've been using with one slight change. (For more proration math practice, check out Chapter 18.)

The way costs are divided up varies from state to state. In the following problems, I use the most common method, a 12-month year and a 30-day month. In some cases, a calendar with the actual day count is used, so the annual tax would be divided by 365 and multiplied by the exact number of days. Ownership of the property on the day of closing is assumed to belong to the seller in many places, but it may vary according to local custom. You'll want to check that out in your state. Unless your state does something different, or unless you're given specific instructions in a problem, use the 12-month year, 30-day month method and assume the seller owns the property on the day of closing.

ACCRUED ITEM EXAMPLE

Note that I use complete dates (year included) in these examples so that there's no doubt about what I'm talking about. It's unlikely that test writers will do the same.

The annual real estate taxes on a property are due each year on December 31 in arrears (for the year just ending). In this case, the date is December 31, 2017. The property is sold on June 1 of that year (June 1, 2017). The taxes are $1,200. Who owes what to whom?

First of all, you know that the taxes are paid for the entire year, or annually, in one payment. Then you know that they're paid in arrears, which means use it first and pay after (at the end of the year). You also know that the seller owned the property during the first five months of the year and the buyer owns the property for the last seven months of the year. Aha! I may have caught you on that one. Look again at the closing date. The math is pretty straightforward.

> $1,200 ÷ 12 = $100 per month taxes
>
> $100 × 5 months that the seller owns the property = $500
>
> $100 × 7 months that the buyer owns the property = $700

Because the buyer owns the property on December 31, 2017, and therefore has to pay the full $1,200 in taxes for the entire year (all of 2017), the seller owes the buyer $500 for the period of time the seller lived in the house. Therefore, the $500 is a credit to the buyer and a debit to the seller. This appears in the closing statement. The $700 is not included in the closing statement, because it doesn't accrue until after the closing, when it becomes a debt of the buyer who of course has to pay it ($700) plus the $500 to the city for taxes for the whole year.

PREPAID ITEM EXAMPLE

Taxes on a property are paid in advance of the year for which they are effective, due on January 1 of that same year. In this case, the date is January 1, 2017. The property closes on August 17, 2017. Taxes are $3,600 a year. The seller will be charged for the day of closing. Who owes what to whom?

This problem tells you that the taxes are paid once a year at the beginning of the year for the whole year ahead. That year of use of the property is divided between the buyer and the seller, who share the tax payments, yet the seller (current owner — before closing) already has paid taxes for the full year.

> $3,600 ÷ 12 months = $300 per month taxes
>
> $300 ÷ 30 days = $10 per day taxes
>
> $300 × 4 months = $1,200
>
> $10 × 13 days = $130
>
> $1,200 + $130 = $1,330 due to the seller by the buyer

This amount is a seller credit and a buyer debit.

Look at a couple of the steps in this problem closely. The four months that you multiply the $300 by are the four months (September, October, November, December) that the buyer will own the house. The 13 days is likewise the part of the month of August that the buyer will own the house (remember that I used the 12-month year, 30-day month method). So the buyer owns the property for four months, 13 days and needs to pay the seller the share of the taxes for that period of time.

Not all prepaid items have to be divided up. For example, a home heated with oil often has fuel left in the tank when the house is sold. For example, suppose 300 gallons of oil were purchased and paid for by the seller sometime before the closing, and the seller has used some of the oil he paid for. The remaining oil is essentially sold to the buyer, who of course will use the rest of it after she moves in. In this example, the cost of the remaining oil in the tank will be calculated and will become a debit to the buyer. There is no credit to the seller because he already used a portion of what he paid for. Similarly, in rental properties, security deposits, which in reality belong to the tenants but are held by the landlord/seller in trust, are turned over to the buyer.

Passing title

At some point after the buyer and seller sign their names on a variety of documents, the seller (unless he's done it already) signs the deed, which is given to the buyer or more likely the buyer's attorney. Although some things have yet to happen after the closing, title, meaning ownership of the property, is conveyed when the buyer accepts the deed.

Closing in escrow

A process that's common in some states is called *closing in escrow,* and it involves using a third party, sometimes called an escrow agent, to gather all the documents necessary for the closing and then forward them and money (as is appropriate) to all the parties involved. Sellers provide, among other things, a deed, evidence of title, information necessary for either paying off or assuming an existing mortgage, and any other documents necessary to provide a marketable title clear of all defects, encumbrances, and liens. The buyer provides funds for the purchase, mortgage loan documents if any are required, and hazard or other necessary insurance policies.

Escrow agents may be attorneys or representatives of a title or an escrow company. Real estate brokers can offer escrow services but not in transactions in which they're directly involved.

State specific

You should find out if your state is one where closing in escrow is typical. If so, you may want to learn who can be an escrow agent, what the requirements might be, and any other information that might make for a test question or two.

A little paperwork: After the closing

A few things take place after the closing. Although ownership of the property changed from seller to buyer at the closing, the final closing statement needs to be prepared and a variety of documents need to be recorded.

Preparing the final closing statement

Although the Closing Disclosure Statement would have already been delivered to the buyer/borrower, until the closing is complete and final costs are allocated, the final settlement statement can't be prepared. The most common form of closing statement for residential properties is the Closing Disclosure Statement, required under the Combined TILA-RESPA Disclosure Rule, which is prepared at or just after closing. Copies of the statement are sent to the buyer and seller along with many other necessary documents. Closing statements can be prepared by anyone with all the appropriate information, but typically the buyer's or seller's attorneys or the title company prepares the closing statement. It's primarily a financial document stating who owes what to whom and who has already given over money that will be distributed (typically deposit money paid when the contract was signed and being held by an attorney or real estate broker).

Recording the right documents

STATE
SPECIFIC

The act of recording the transaction documents is the final step in the closing process. The documents are recorded at the appropriate government office that is designated for this purpose. Documentation of real estate transactions usually takes place at the county level, meaning you file documents in the county where the property is located. You need to find out the name of the office or department where deeds and other such documents are filed in your location. Typically, the title company files the documents but it could also be handled by one of the attorneys or anyone else connected with the transaction, for that matter.

All documents relating to an interest in real estate need to be filed. Deeds, mortgages, liens, long-term leases (usually more than a year), and easements are typical documents that are recorded. The act of recording provides what is called constructive notice to the public. *Constructive notice* provides an opportunity for anyone who's interested to research the records. These public records provide parties who have an interest in the property in some way — brokers, attorneys, abstractors, and the public — an opportunity to investigate the ownership of the property and possible encumbrances on the title.

Recording usually involves payment of a fee, or sometimes two, usually for the act of recording itself. Perhaps a dollar a page or some other amount is charged for actually processing the document. In addition, the recording office may also be the office to which the state and sometimes local transfer taxes are paid. This state transfer tax is mentioned in the list of possible closing costs in "Allocating expenses with proration," earlier in this chapter.

STATE
SPECIFIC

You definitely want to find out whether your state charges a transfer tax on real estate transfers and/or a mortgage recording tax and how much they are (particularly the real estate transfer tax). These taxes usually are based on the sale price of the property or the amount of the mortgage loan. In some cases, states have created surcharges for high-value property sales. Local municipalities, on occasion, also have created their own transfer tax.

REMEMBER

Be prepared for a math question or two on the subject of recording. I take you through a couple of samples.

EXAMPLE

Say, for example, the deed transfer tax in your state is $2 per $500 of the sale price, meaning that for every $500 increment of the sale price you pay a $2 tax on the transfer. So if the sale price of the property were $1,000, you'd pay $4 in transfer taxes. But if the sale price of the property were $255,000, how much is the transfer tax?

> **Answer:** $255,000 ÷ $500 = 510
>
> 510 × $2 = $1,020 transfer tax

Note: The number 510 is just that, a number and not a dollar amount. It's the number of times the unit of $500 is contained in $255,000.

Many deeds don't state the amount of consideration. They may state the price of the property as "$10 and other valuable consideration." No, you don't get to pay the transfer tax on the $10. You have to pay it on the total amount, and that leads to a neat trick you can use when you want to know what your brother-in-law paid for his house, but he won't tell you. Take a look at the next problem, which is the reverse of the earlier example. I'll do an obvious example first just to show you where I'm going.

If you look up the transfer tax paid on a piece of property and find out it was $2, then based on the transfer tax rate that I've been using ($2 per $500 of value), the value of the property is $500.

EXAMPLE

So you go to the county clerk's office and find the deed to your brother-in-law's property, and although it doesn't tell you how much he paid for it, you can find out that he paid $1,020 in transfer tax. The amount of transfer tax paid usually is a matter of public record and often is noted on either the deed or an attached document. Because you know the transfer tax rate is $2 per $500 of the sale price, you can calculate what he paid for the property.

$1,020 ÷ $2 = 510

510 × $500 = $255,000 sale price of the property

You see, all you did was find out how many units of $2 are contained in the $1,020 total transfer tax that was paid, and because each unit of $2 represents $500 of the sale price, the final step is to multiply.

If a mortgage is being assumed, that is, the buyer takes over the existing mortgage of the seller, the amount of the mortgage balance may be subtracted from the sale price of the property when calculating transfer taxes. So in the earlier examples, if you assumed a mortgage with a $100,000 balance, you'd only pay transfer taxes on the remaining $155,000 in some jurisdictions.

Review Questions and Answers

Most of the questions you'll see regarding this topic on an exam are definitional or fact-based. The examiners, at the very least, want to make sure you understand what various terms mean. This is especially true for the salesperson's exam. At the broker's level, you may have to wrestle with short cases that require an understanding and application of the material. However, even handling those types of questions starts with a basic understanding of what the terms mean.

1. Typical wording in the habendum clause would be

(A) "I hereby grant."

(B) "In witness whereof."

(C) "To have and to hold."

(D) "$10.00 and other valuable consideration."

Correct answer: (C). "I hereby grant," "In witness whereof," and "$10.00 and other valuable consideration" are other parts of a deed, but "to have and to hold" is typical language for the habendum clause.

2. The law that requires that a deed be in writing is called

   (A) the statute of frauds.

   (B) the tort reform act.

   (C) the acknowledgment law.

   (D) RESPA.

Correct answer: (A). The tort reform act has to do with civil suits. I made up the acknowledgment law. And RESPA has to do with federal requirements for closing title.

3. Whose signature is required for a deed to be valid?

   (A) Grantor

   (B) Grantee

   (C) Both grantor and grantee

   (D) Notary public

Correct answer: (A). The grantee must be named in the deed but does not have to sign. So that makes Answers (B) and (C) wrong. A notary public witnesses the acknowledgment. The acknowledgment is not required for a valid deed, only for the deed to be recorded.

4. What is the most likely explanation when you see the words "for love and affection" as the consideration in a deed?

   (A) The grantor and grantee are related.

   (B) The grantor and grantee want to keep the actual selling price of the property a secret.

   (C) The grantor and grantee were represented by the same real estate agent.

   (D) The grantor gave the grantee the property as a gift.

Correct answer: (D). The relationship of the grantor and grantee wouldn't matter because it still can be a sale. If they wanted to keep the price a secret, they probably would use "ten dollars and other valuable consideration." The nature of the representation in Answer (C) doesn't affect the deed.

5. The guarantee of the grantor's ownership of the property is called the covenant of

   (A) quiet enjoyment.

   (B) warranty forever.

   (C) further assurance.

   (D) seisin.

Correct answer: (D). You need to be able to describe each of the covenants in a sentence so that you can pick out the correct answer in a question like this. If it helps, remember that seize (the root of seisin) means to take hold of something.

6. A deed conveying title to property from a trust is called a

   (A) deed of trust.

   (B) deed in trust.

   (C) trust deed.

   (D) trustee's deed.

Correct answer: (D). The first three answers have to do with using a deed to convey an interest in the property as security for a debt. Tough question.

7. The area of a section is

(A) 43,560 square feet.

(B) 80 acres.

(C) 160 acres.

(D) 640 acres.

Correct answer: (D). 43,560 square feet is the area in square feet of one acre (a useful number to know). 80 acres and 160 acres are portions of a section.

8. Which section is bounded on four sides by sections 10, 14, 16, and 22?

(A) 9

(B) 15

(C) 17

(D) 13

Correct answer: (B). A pretty standard exam question is locating a section within a township. If you read this question and then looked at Figure 9-1 earlier in the chapter, you cheated, because you won't have that kind of crutch on an exam. Exam writers expect you to be able to lay out a township grid with all the sections properly numbered. Remember that every section within a given township is numbered the same way.

9. A title free from any defects is a good definition of

(A) equitable title.

(B) marketable title.

(C) certified title.

(D) insured title.

Correct answer: (B). You can find out about equitable title in Chapter 11. Certified title and insured title are close. A title usually is not certified or insured unless it's clear of defects. But the definition of title clear of defects is marketable title.

10. What type of notice is provided by the recording of a deed in the public records?

(A) Actual

(B) Inquiry

(C) Constructive

(D) Real

Correct answer: (C). Constructive notice is provided by recording the deed. Actual and inquiry are types of notice. Real is not.

Chapter **10**

Giving Up or Losing Property

I n addition to simply selling it to someone who wants to buy it, property can be conveyed or transferred voluntarily through a number of means. Property can also be lost involuntarily through the forces of nature, law, or the government. And finally, in fact very finally, property is transferred after you die.

In this chapter, I discuss a number of the more common ways that property can be conveyed and lost involuntarily. In your real estate practice, you may never encounter or be involved with most of these issues. They do, however, involve real estate, and, as a real estate agent, you need to know something about them. Equally as important, state exam writers expect you to know something about the various ways property can be transferred or lost.

Fine by Me: Giving Up Property Voluntarily

Most of the time, *title* to property, or the ownership of it, is conveyed or transferred voluntarily from one owner to another, which is a transaction formally known as *voluntary alienation*. Among the ways this kind of transfer can be accomplished are dedications, gifts, public grants, and sales. I explain these methods in the sections that follow. Exam questions tend to be definitional, using short cases to get the right answers out of you.

All for the government: Dedication

Dedication is a term used for a specific type of voluntary transfer of property from an individual to the government. You may well ask why anyone would want to voluntarily give their property to the government. Dedication typically refers to the process by which a developer transfers ownership of the lands that are needed for roads, sewers, waterlines, and other utilities to the government as part of a land development. A person who subdivides a large piece of property into smaller residential lots for sale may build the roads as the individual lots are sold. At some point, the developer turns over title to the government, creating a public street. Dedications may also include easements that the municipality may need, such as for getting to a drainage ditch for maintenance. (Check out Chapter 8 for more about easements.) Individual property owners (as opposed to developers) can also dedicate land to a municipality, such as land for a road to allow access to a town park.

Governments vary in the way they view and treat this type of dedication. They often decide how to deal with dedications on a project-by-project basis. A local government may require a subdivision street to be dedicated, but prefer the internal roads of a condominium development to remain privately owned so it (the government) is not responsible for maintenance.

Although not technically viewed as a gift (see the next section), generally no consideration, or thing of value, is given by the government in return for the dedicated land.

From me to you: Gifts

You know what a gift is, right? Think about Christmas and your birthday. Property can be conveyed simply by giving it to someone. A deed is executed to convey title, but the main difference in a gift situation (as opposed to a sale) is that no money or other thing of value, usually called the *consideration*, is exchanged for the property. In all other respects, the conveyance by deed is the same. I discuss deeds in Chapter 9.

A treat from Uncle Sam: Public grants

Public grants — sometimes simply called *grants* — are transfers of property in which the government gives a piece of property to someone. In years past, when the federal government wanted to settle a new part of the country, it simply gave grants of land to people who agreed to settle in that location. Some of your ancestors may have received grants, or else you may be living on a piece of property that once was part of a public grant.

The usual way: Sales

Representing someone in the sale or purchase of a property is, of course, where you make your money as a real estate agent. A sale typically involves a *grantor* (the person selling the property), a *grantee* (the person buying the property), and a *deed* (the document that transfers title). I discuss the requirements for a valid deed and different types of deeds in Chapter 9.

One important concept in a deed for a sale of property is the consideration. The exchange of money or something else of value in exchange for the property characterizes a conveyance of property as a sale rather than something else, such as a gift.

By Force: Losing Property Involuntarily

Sometimes your property can be taken against your wishes, or for some other reason it can be lost. These types of situations generally are known as *involuntary alienation*. I go over the principal forms of involuntary alienation — adverse possession, avulsion and erosion, eminent domain, foreclosure, forfeiture, and partition — in this section. Questions on involuntary alienation will most likely be definitional, so remember the chief characteristics of each of the forms.

It's really mine: Adverse possession

Adverse possession is the loss of your property or some rights to your property because of continued use by someone else. The original owner can lose complete title (ownership) to the property or only a right to use part of the property, such as an easement called a *prescriptive easement* or *easement by prescription*.

REMEMBER

The basic premise of adverse possession is that someone other than the owner uses a piece of property openly, publicly, and without the owner's consent for a specified period of time. The conditions necessary to claim ownership under adverse possession are

>> **Actual possession:** To gain possession, someone has to occupy the property.

>> **Adverse possession:** Someone usurps the real owner's rights of ownership.

>> **Claim of ownership:** Someone lays claim to the property.

>> **Continuous use:** Someone uses the property without interruption.

>> **Hostile:** Someone claims the property after using it without the owner's consent.

>> **Notorious:** Someone exerts possession that isn't in secret but rather is well known to other people.

>> **Open:** Someone's use of the property is visible and obvious to anyone viewing the property.

In addition, anyone who claims title by adverse possession must do everything required by law during a specified period of time, and laws governing adverse possession vary from one state to the next. When calculating the length of time someone other than the owner uses the property to claim adverse possession, a concept known as tacking comes into play. Tacking is the ability of a party claiming possession to count or accumulate the necessary amount of the time of possession during the ownerships of more than one owner. Say, for example, that three different people each occupy a property for six years each in an adverse possession situation. If the state in which the property is located requires a minimum of 15 years occupancy to claim title to the property, the adversary claiming ownership rights can rely on adverse use taking place during the previous occupants' ownerships to accumulate the required 15 years.

STATE SPECIFIC

Check out the length of time of continuous use that your state requires for someone to claim title by adverse possession. Although I don't claim to know the specific law in every state, among the ones I do know, the time requirements for adverse possession can range from as little as 3 years up to 30 years. Individual states may also have variations on the requirements for adverse possession that I listed. It's unlikely that you'll be tested on anything very specific other than the number of years required. But if you're ever involved in an adverse possession situation it would be useful to research your state laws.

Being awarded title through a claim of adverse possession is not automatic. The person claiming title must file a *lawsuit* or otherwise initiate *an action to quiet title* in court. If the quiet title action is successful, the person is awarded title to the property.

An easement by prescription may also be claimed through an adverse use of a property. For example, someone driving over a part of your property every day for the statutory period of time can eventually claim the right to drive across your property forever. If successful in a legal action, that person can be awarded an easement, which is the right to use the property in a specific way as opposed to complete ownership. See Chapter 8 for details on easements.

And just in case you have your eye on a few feet of that park behind your house, most states have rules exempting government lands from adverse possession.

You can't fight nature: Avulsion and erosion

Mother Nature definitely is a powerful force, even in the world of real estate. She can take away your land in a couple of different ways:

» *Avulsion,* or the sudden loss of land, can occur by natural processes. Earthquakes, landslides, and mudslides are examples of natural forces that can remove land involuntarily.

» *Erosion* is the loss of land through a gradual process. The wearing away of land by the action of a river or ocean is an example of erosion.

The opposite of losing land by natural processes is *accretion,* or gaining land by natural forces. One form of accretion describes gaining property by the natural action of water. Sand added to a beach or soil deposited by a river are examples otherwise known as *alluvium* or *alluvion* and is sometimes described as alluvial soils.

We need that, please: Eminent domain

Eminent domain is the taking of land against your wishes by the government or other public agency, such as a public water district, or certain private corporations, such as utility companies, for public purposes. In addition to the requirement that the land be used for a public purpose, the owner of the property must receive fair compensation, and the authority taking possession must follow due process, or the prescribed legal requirements necessary to take the property. I discuss eminent domain as a control on land use in Chapter 8.

Deep in debt: Foreclosures

Foreclosure is losing your property involuntarily to pay a debt. The most common types of foreclosure are the result of unpaid mortgage loans or unpaid property taxes. Failing to pay back borrowed money or taxes in a timely manner can result in a foreclosure. The lender or community to whom the debt is owed initiates foreclosure proceedings in court. These proceedings enable the lender or local unit of government to sell the property and collect the unpaid debt from the proceeds of the sale. In most places, homeowners' associations also have a right to foreclose on a property because of unpaid association dues or common charges. I discuss foreclosures that result from unpaid mortgage loans in Chapter 15. I cover the sale of property for unpaid taxes in Chapter 16.

Ignoring the rules: Forfeiture

You also can lose title to your property by disobeying some condition of the deed, such as using the property for something the deed forbids or not using it for the purpose required in the deed. For example, I've seen properties that were donated to municipalities for use as parks returned to their donors for failure to abide by the deed. Conditions limiting the use of the property can also be written into the deed. If the municipality ever uses the property for any other purpose, the person who donated the property (or that person's family or estate) can demand through a court action that the property be returned.

Making the split: Partitioning

Partitioning is a legal proceeding that is undertaken to divide a single piece of property that is owned in shares (in undivided ownership) by two or more people. (For more about the concept of undivided ownership, see Chapter 7.)

EXAMPLE

Two people who together own one piece of property with two vacation homes is a good example. One owner wants to rent out both units and the other wants to use the units. If the pair cannot agree on how to use the property or how to divide it, one can file a partition proceeding, asking the court to physically divide the property so that each party can own a piece of it. If for some reason the property can't be divided, the court may order the parties to sell the property and divide the proceeds from the sale proportionally according to the respective interests in the property of the two owners.

Losing Property Very Involuntarily: Passing Title After Passing Away

You may well wonder why the subject of wills and passing title to property after death is a subject that state examiners want you to know something about. After all, wills and estates are subjects better left to attorneys and the courts, right? Although that is true, real estate agents often are called in to help sell a property that's left in someone's estate. Familiarity with some of the terminology and issues that can arise is important. Exam questions focus on very basic information about wills, laws of descent or inheritance, and probate.

Where there's a will, there are heirs and relatives

A *will* is a document that determines how a deceased person's real property (real estate and the rights that go with it) and personal property (items not permanently attached to real estate) are to be distributed after death. The person for whom the will is drafted is called a *testator*. Up to the time of death, the testator can dispose of property even if it's mentioned in the will. A will takes effect only after death. Anyone who receives title to real estate through a will is known as a *devisee*; the gift of real property is called a *devise*. An addition or change to an existing will made by the person for whom the will was written is a *codicil*.

Where there's no will, there still may be heirs and relatives: Laws of descent

When someone dies without a will (*intestate*), he or she may still have *heirs*, or people who are entitled to inherit assets from the estate. Someone who dies with a will has died *testate*.

TIP

A good way to remember the difference between "testate" and "intestate" is that "with" is a shorter word than "without," and "testate" is a shorter word than "intestate." Someone who died with a will died testate, and someone who died without a will died intestate.

STATE SPECIFIC

Every state has *laws of descent, a statute of descent,* or sometimes a *law of descent and distribution* covering the distribution of the assets of estates when the deceased has no will. Spouses, children, and possibly other relatives are entitled to a portion of the assets of the estate by virtue of their relationship to the deceased. If your state exam requires you to know about the subject of involuntary loss of property, check out the laws of descent in your state. If your state specifically wants you to know something about the laws of descent, make sure you at least understand the basics of who would get what from an estate if there's no will.

When people die without a will and without heirs, the state can claim the assets of the estates by something called *escheat*. For more about escheat, check out Chapter 8.

The court has its say: Probate

Probate is the process of making sure that a will is legal and valid, the deceased's wishes are carried out, and the assets actually are in the estate. In the case of someone who dies intestate, the court determines who inherits the assets of the estate based on the laws of descent (see the previous section). Both processes take place in surrogate's court, which is sometimes referred to as *probate court*.

TIP

An analogy that may help you remember the name of surrogate's court is that of a surrogate mother, who simply is someone standing in for the real mother. Surrogate's court means the court stands in place of the deceased.

STATE SPECIFIC

During probate proceedings, the court appoints an *executor* of the estate to carry out the actual distribution of the assets. The executor usually is named in the will. The laws of individual states govern probate proceedings. Generally probate takes place in the county where the deceased person lived and may take place in the county where he or she owned property if different from the county of residence.

Review Questions and Answers

The language of involuntary loss of property is pretty universal and general from one state to the next, but the specific requirements may not be. For example, all states acknowledge the concept of adverse possession, or claiming the right of title to someone else's property because of continuous use, but each state uses different time frames for it to take effect.

The review questions in this section focus on the more general knowledge that is applicable in every state. So you need to check out the details in your own state before taking the exam.

1. The law governing how heirs inherit property when the deceased has no will is called the law of

    (A) descent.

    (B) devise.

    (C) testate.

    (D) escheat.

    Correct answer: (A). You may have wanted to choose escheat. Remember escheat applies only when the deceased dies with no will and no heirs. Devise is real property that's inherited, and testate is when someone dies with a will.

2. By which of the following can you not lose title to your property involuntarily?

    (A) Adverse possession

    (B) Foreclosure

    (C) Dedication

    (D) Avulsion

    Correct answer: (C). Dedication is voluntarily giving property to the government. The other answers are ways of losing your property involuntarily; you can brush up on those methods by reviewing

"By Force: Losing Property Involuntarily," earlier in this chapter. Be careful of questions like this that have a double negative. You might try restating the question to yourself, eliminating one of the negatives; in this case "By which of the following can you lose the title to your property involuntarily." Whichever answers fit that statement are all the wrong answers.

3. Mary crosses Joe's property for a number of years as she drives into her driveway. Mary sells to Alice, who continues to do the same thing. Alice sells to Barbara, who does it for a few more years and finally claims the right to do so by adverse possession. Barbara may have accumulated enough years to claim adverse possession by what concept?

   (A) Accretion

   (B) Encroachment

   (C) Notorious use

   (D) Tacking

   Correct answer: (D). Notorious use is one of the requirements for claiming adverse possession, but the accumulation of the required period of use by successive people is called tacking. Accretion is adding soil to your land by natural action. Encroachment is the unauthorized or illegal use of someone's property by another person (see Chapter 8).

4. Joe and Sam jointly own an apartment building. They can't agree on anything, including how to dissolve their partnership. Joe finally files a suit for

   (A) avulsion.

   (B) eviction.

   (C) escheat.

   (D) partition.

   Correct answer: (D). *Partition* is a court action to divide a single property that is owned by two or more people in shares. Avulsion is loss of land caused by a sudden act of nature like an earthquake. Eviction is the action of a landlord to remove a tenant (see Chapter 12). Escheat is when the state gets your property because you die without a will and without heirs.

5. The process by which a will is validated is called

   (A) surrogacy.

   (B) execution.

   (C) validation.

   (D) probate.

   Correct answer: (D). Surrogacy may confuse you because probate takes place in surrogates court. Validation is, of course, a real word but has no meaning in this context. Execution in real estate terms usually refers to signing a document like a contract.

6. You subdivide some land for a residential development. You want to give the streets to the town. You do so by

   (A) descent.

   (B) dedication.

   (C) avulsion.

   (D) divestiture.

   Correct answer: (B). Dedication is giving land voluntarily to the government. Descent refers to a state's laws of inheritance. Avulsion is the sudden loss of land caused by natural processes. Divestiture is a general business term meaning to get rid of in some way.

7. The right of the city to take private property for a public use is called

   (A) foreclosure.

   (B) dedication.

   (C) eminent domain.

   (D) escheat.

   Correct answer: (C). Eminent domain is the right of a municipality to take property against the wishes of the owner. Dedication is a when a person voluntarily gives property to a municipality. Foreclosure is when a bank or a municipality takes your property for nonpayment of a mortgage or taxes, respectively. Escheat is when the state gets your property because you die without a will and without heirs.

8. The person for whom a will is prepared is known as

   (A) the grantor.

   (B) the administrator.

   (C) the executor.

   (D) the testator.

   Correct answer: (D). The word "testator" is related to the word "testate," which means to die with a will. A grantor is a living person who conveys property to another. An administrator usually is appointed by a court to handle someone's property, as in the case of someone who may be declared mentally incompetent. An executor is appointed by the court to handle someone's estate after he dies.

9. The gradual wearing away of land by the forces of nature is called

   (A) avulsion.

   (B) accretion.

   (C) erosion.

   (D) alluvium.

   Correct answer: (C). Avulsion almost is the same thing as erosion, only it's a sudden loss of land, not a gradual one. Accretion and alluvium have to do with the accumulation of soil or sand by natural forces like a river.

10. Harry has a new grandson a year after he writes his will and wants to leave him a special gift. To make this change to the will, he most likely executes

   (A) a new will.

   (B) a codicil.

   (C) a devisement.

   (D) a descent.

   Correct answer: (B). There's a fine point here. Harry could execute a new will, but clearly the change to the existing will is a small one, which is exactly what a codicil is for. Devisement is related to devise, which is real property left to someone in a will. Laws of descent govern how property is distributed to heirs when there is no will.

4

A House Is Made of Lots of Paper: Legal and Physical Issues

Peruse the many different legal issues connected with the sale and purchase of a property, including some basics about the types of contracts you're likely to use, how a contract is discharged, and what happens when the terms of a contract aren't completed.

Examine how a contract is created and executed and the important role real estate agents play in this process.

Understand the requirements of a typical lease agreement, the different types of leases, and some ways people break leases. You may never handle a leased property, but the exam requires that you have a basic understanding of leasing.

Expand your knowledge with information about some of the environmental issues and government regulations involved in real estate work as well as the environmental effects of developing property from waste to water.

» Looking at different kinds of real estate contracts

» Discovering various ways of ending contracts

» Finding out what happens when someone breaks a contract

Chapter **11**

Contracts 101

When you agree to represent a buyer or seller as an agent, you and your client sign a contract for your services. After that, your hard work brings the buyer and seller together to sign a contract of sale. I said "signs" and "brings," not "might sign" or "could bring," because I know you're going to be a great success as a real estate agent.

A lease also is a contract, and in the real estate business you deal with a couple of other kinds of contractual agreements.

Negotiating, understanding, and in some cases, preparing contracts are important parts of your job as a real estate agent. State exam writers expect you to have some knowledge of contracts in general and specific knowledge about different types of real estate contracts.

In this chapter, I walk you through some basic information about contracts (including elements that make a contract valid). I also tell you about specific types of real estate contracts and give you some information about how a contract is discharged and what happens when the terms of a contract are not completed.

Agreeing to Do Something: The Basics of Making a Contract

People agree to do things all the time. I agree to pay the bill in a restaurant. Someone else agrees to pay the kids to shovel the snow off the driveway. You agree to represent someone as an agent. And, of course, a buyer agrees to buy a seller's house. All of these agreements are contracts.

REMEMBER

A *contract* is an agreement either to do or not to do something. The agreement must be made voluntarily by legally competent parties, have some form of legal payment (consideration) as part of the agreement, be about doing or not doing some legal act, and be enforceable.

In this section, I tell you about different ways that contracts can be created and give information on the elements of a valid contract. Although this section is about contracts in general, rather than real estate contracts in particular, remember that state real estate exam writers like to know that you know at least some basic information about contracts.

Exploring how a contract is created

A contract can be created in a number of ways, which usually are defined by the actions of each party to the contract. And a contract may fit into more than one of the following categories. Pay particular attention to the contract examples in the list that follows, so that you can distinguish among the different ways a contract may be created. There are usually at least a few questions on the exam that require you to distinguish among the different types of contracts.

>> An *express contract* is created when parties to the contract (the participants) clearly state in words what they agree to do or not do. The parties clearly *express* their intentions. An express contract may be either oral or in writing. Mr. Buyer agrees in writing to buy Mrs. Seller's house for $300,000. Mrs. Seller agrees to sell for that amount. This is an express written contract. Real estate sales contracts and (usually) leases for periods over a year must be in writing to be valid. On the other hand, you agree to represent a couple as the agent to sell their house, and they agree to pay you a percentage of the sale price when you sell the property. You have no written document of the arrangement, only your oral agreement. Foolish? Probably. After all, your money's on the line. And some states don't allow you to enforce an oral listing agreement when trying to collect the fee. But it's legal nonetheless — you have an express oral contract to act as the seller's agent.

>> *Implied contracts* are created by the actions of the parties. A classic example of an implied contract is someone who goes into a restaurant and orders a meal. That person never says to the server, "If you bring me the steak I'll pay you what it says on the menu." The fact that the person agrees to pay the bill for the meal is implied. In real estate work, an agent bringing a buyer to see a house that the owner is selling may create an implied contract. No agreement exists, but Agent Ambitious nonetheless brings a buyer to the house. The seller lets the agent show the house, and the agent takes it upon herself to negotiate a deal on behalf of the seller. And the seller lets her. Eventually a deal is made. The agent expects a commission from the seller by virtue of the fact that the agent brought together the buyer and the seller and both the buyer and the seller let her. Nothing is in writing, but the actions of everyone concerned may create an implied contract.

>> A *bilateral contract* is one in which two parties each agree to do something, in effect exchanging promises. For instance, I, the buyer, agree to buy your house for $300,000, and you, the seller, agree to accept my $300,000 and give me title to your house. This agreement is an express (the promises are stated) bilateral (both parties agree) contract typical of real estate sales contracts. In a bilateral contract each party can force the other to act. So I can force you to sell me your house, even if you become unwilling to do so, as long as I'm willing to pay you what I promised. A bilateral contract may be express, as in the case of a sales contract, or implied, as in the case of a tenant who has no lease and a landlord who keeps collecting the rent. Their actions imply an agreement that each can enforce.

>> A *unilateral contract* is a one-sided agreement in which only one party (Party A, for the sake of an example) is obligated to do what is promised. The obligation exists only if the other party (Party B) does what is stated in the contract. Party B, in this case, is free not to do what is stated in the contract. An example of a unilateral agreement in real estate is an option agreement. In this example, a seller agrees to not sell his property for a year while a buyer attempts to get financing and other approvals (such as building permits). The seller further agrees to sell the

property within a year's time to the buyer for $1 million if the buyer wants to buy it. The word "if" is key here. The buyer is free to buy or not to buy. But the seller must sell the property to the buyer at the stated price if the buyer wants to buy it within the year's time. The buyer is *exercising the option.*

STATE SPECIFIC

All states have passed some version of a law called the statute of frauds. The *statute of frauds* generally requires most real estate contracts to be in writing for them to be enforceable. You need to check out your state's specific real estate exceptions to the statute of frauds requirements for written real estate contracts. For example, at least one state exempts lease contracts of less than a year from having to be in writing.

STATE SPECIFIC

Most states also have adopted some form of the *Uniform Commercial Code* (UCC), which governs sales and contracts involving personal property like a car. For a sale of personal property to be enforceable, it must comply with the rules adopted by the state. A typical UCC rule is that all sales of personal property for more than $500 must be in writing. Although questions about the specific rules of the UCC probably won't be on the exam, you may nevertheless see a general question related to it. Cooperative apartments are considered personal property, so their sale is governed by part of the UCC. Check out in your state those portions of the UCC that deal with real estate issues.

What makes a contract valid?

For a contract to be *valid* (binding on all parties and legally enforceable), it must contain certain elements. State exam writers expect you to have an understanding of the following five elements that must be present for a valid contract to exist:

>> **Legally competent parties:** For a contract to be valid, the people making the agreement must be of legal age in the state in which the contract is executed. They must be sober, sane, and mentally competent to enter into the agreement. Parties to a contract need to be acting freely and voluntarily and be under no undue influence or duress.

STATE SPECIFIC

>> **Mutual agreement:** Sometimes referred as *mutual assent, mutual consent, meeting of the minds,* or *offer and acceptance,* mutual agreement means that all the terms of the contract must be clearly understood by all parties, who must also agree with and understand what they're agreeing to. Find out whether your state has any kind of law that requires contracts to be written in easily understandable language. These are commonly known as plain language laws. (Check out "Going back and forth with offer and acceptance" later in this chapter.)

>> **Lawful object:** Sometimes referred to as *legality of object* or *lawful objective,* lawful object means that what you're agreeing to do is, in fact, legal. In the movies, the classic mob contract to kill someone is not a valid contract because the object of the contract is illegal.

>> **Consideration:** Consideration is usually some clearly stated item of value that is exchanged for the promise made in the contract by the other party. The thing of value doesn't need to be money; it can be a promise to do or not to do something. In the case of a real estate transaction, it can be the exchange of one piece of property for another. You should remember that in a real estate sales contract, the consideration is the agreed-to selling price.

>> **Agreement in writing:** The agreement in writing rule applies to certain kinds of contracts, including most real estate contracts, as required by your state's particular statute of frauds. (See "Exploring how a contract is created," earlier in this chapter.) Likewise, be sure to check out how the parol evidence rule relates to oral contracts. Under certain circumstances, the *parol evidence rule* enables oral agreements to complete or clarify unclear written agreements, but it also presumes that in most cases, written agreements are more valid than oral agreements and more clearly state the intentions of the parties.

Here's an example: You contract to have a house built, and the contract says you're going to get Model A23 doorknobs. Later the builder agrees to install the more expensive Model B34 doorknobs at no additional cost. At the end of the project, he installs the Model A23 door-knobs. In attempting to get the better doorknobs by taking the builder to court, the court may presume that the written contract is the more valid indication of what was agreed and dismiss your case. On the other hand, if no doorknobs were specified, the court may view the oral agreement as the completion or specification for the contract, and you may get the doorknobs you want.

A *void contract* is one in which one or more of the required elements are missing. A contract to do something illegal is a void contract. A void contract, because it is missing one or more key elements, never really existed as a contract in the first place.

A couple of gray areas in the world of valid versus void contracts do exist, though:

» A *voidable contract* usually involves a situation in which one of the parties may not have the legal ability to enter into a contract but may confirm the contract at a later time. Suppose a minor who's younger than the legal age to enter into a contract signs an agreement to buy a house. The minor can either declare that agreement void within a reasonable time of reaching legal age or affirm it as a contract and move ahead with the purchase. Notice that, as is usually the case with voidable contracts, one party, in this instance the minor, can get out of the contract, but the other party is obligated to adhere to the agreement. If the contract were completely void, then neither party would have to act. The law generally views this example as a valid contract unless the minor decides to get out of it.

» An *unenforceable contract* is one that seems valid, and may, in fact, have all the elements of a valid contract, but for one reason or another can't be enforced by one party against another. Here's an example: You have a house custom-built for you. You believe that the builder didn't build the house according to the contract you signed. You sue the builder, but because the statute of limitations (the time limit set by law in which to sue somebody) has run its course for such lawsuits, you can't enforce the contract against the builder. The contract is unenforce-able. However, the builder can choose to honor his obligations and make good on the contract, a situation that is described as the contract being *valid as between the parties*.

The word "enforceable" means that the courts can, within the existing laws, make the parties to the contract do what they agreed to do. In this example, the court can't enforce the contract because the law says the time limit for enforcement has run out.

Two more words that are used to describe a contract are *executory* and *executed*. An *executory* con-tract is one in which one or more of the terms of the contract have not been completed. An *exe-cuted* contract is one in which everything is completed. For instance, after a real estate sales contract is signed it's considered executory. After title (ownership) passes from seller to buyer at the closing, the contract becomes executed.

So Many Choices: Examining Types of Real Estate Contracts

A number of different types of contracts are used in the real estate business. State exam writers expect you to understand what these contracts are, how they work, and what they're used for.

Finding out about agency agreements

I cover seller and buyer agency agreements in detail in Chapter 4, but you need to know a few specific details about agency agreements. Just remember that an agency agreement, signed by a real estate agent and a client, establishes the agent as the representative of the client.

Listing agreements

A *listing agreement* is between an agent and a property seller. Note when I use the word *agent* here, I'm using it in the sense of the person whose listing it is, and in all cases that is the principal broker. A salesperson working for that broker may be responsible for the listing, and it may be referred to as the salesperson's listing but in fact the agent the seller is hiring is the principal broker. The following are a few common listing agreements:

» The *exclusive right to sell listing agreement* requires that compensation be paid to the broker regardless of who sells the property, the broker or the property owner. This agreement is a bilateral contract because both parties exchanged promises and can be forced to act — the agent can be forced to do his duty and the seller can be forced to pay a commission. This type of listing agreement generally requires specific promises from both parties, it is *also* considered an express contract, which means that the promises have been spoken and agreed to (or more likely have been put in writing).

» The *exclusive agency agreement* is one in which a fee is owed to the broker only if the broker sells the property. If the owner sells the property, the broker is owed nothing. This contract is unilateral because nothing is owed unless the broker produces a buyer. This type of listing agreement becomes a bilateral agreement when and if the broker produces a buyer because at that point both parties have obligations that must be fulfilled and can be enforced. This type of agreement is usually express because the listing agreement contains the details to which both parties agree.

» In an *open listing agreement,* an owner agrees to pay a fee to any broker producing a successful buyer. An open listing is a unilateral contract because only one party (the seller) is obligated to act if and when an agent produces a buyer. Open listings can be express if, for example, a seller advertises his home for sale and the advertisement states that he will work with brokers.

Buyer agency agreements

Buyer agency agreements are formed between an agent and someone who wants to purchase a property.

» An *exclusive buyer agency agreement* requires that the buyer pay the agent whether or not the agent finds the buyer the house that the purchaser buys. So, if the buyer locates a property on his own and buys directly from a seller using no agent at all, the buyer still owes his agent a fee. This agreement is bilateral in that two parties exchange promises, and it's express because the promises are stated.

» With an *exclusive agency buyer agency agreement,* the buyer is obligated to pay the agent only if the agent produces a property that the buyer buys. It's a unilateral agreement because nothing is owed unless the buyer's agent produces a property for the buyer. It is usually express because the promises made are stated, usually in writing.

» In an *open buyer agency agreement,* a buyer essentially says he will pay any agent who finds him a property. It's a unilateral agreement because only one party is obligated to act, and it may be express if agents are notified in some way that the buyer is looking for a property and is willing to pay an agent who finds him one.

Examining sales contracts

Real estate sales contracts indicate a buyer's and a seller's agreement to exchange property for (usually) money. I discuss the elements necessary to make a sales agreement valid and enforceable. A sales contract is a bilateral (two people exchanging promises) express (each party states what they're agreeing to) agreement.

Making a sales contract valid (and knowing who prepares it)

STATE SPECIFIC

For a real estate sales contract to be valid, it must comply with the laws of the state where the property is located. Although they may vary slightly by state, the following elements generally are the minimum requirements:

>> Legally competent parties.

>> A contract that must be in writing.

>> A legal description of the property.

>> Words of mutual agreement to buy and sell the property.

>> Consideration, or what is being paid or exchanged and any other financial terms.

>> Signatures of both (or all) parties. The signing of a contract for the sale of a property gives the buyer *equitable title,* which isn't yet ownership and which can be conveyed only by a deed. Instead, it's a contract right that essentially gives the buyer the right to demand title (ownership) to the property when the agreed-upon price is paid.

>> Lawful object. This requirement is usually pretty easy to meet because the object of the real estate sales contract is to sell the real estate.

For exam purposes, you should remember what the elements for a valid contract are and what each of them means based on the list and definitions I provide above.

STATE SPECIFIC

A direct question about who prepares the sales contract isn't necessarily one you'll find on an exam, but you nevertheless need to check out your state's approach. Typical alternatives for testing you on documentation are situations in which preparation of the sales contract is done by the real estate agent, by an attorney, or by an agent subject to review by an attorney. Agents who prepare their own sales contracts often use a preprinted, fill-in-the-blank contract form. An additional piece of information that you need to check out is what, if any, role attorneys play in selling a piece of property in your state, a factor that varies widely throughout the United States. In no case can someone who is not an attorney practice law. In most cases, brokers protect themselves against the charge of illegally practicing law in these circumstances by stating on the form that the signer needs to consult with an attorney before signing the form or that the validity of the form is contingent on an attorney's approval.

Adding extras to sales contracts

In addition to the necessary items required for a valid contract, many sales contracts contain information about the type of deed that will be delivered to the buyer, encumbrances on the title, any money being deposited as part of the agreement, a statement of what constitutes evidence of good title, a date and place of closing, what happens in the event of destruction of the property before the closing, and other terms and conditions of the sale. (See Chapter 9 for more about deeds and title closing and Chapter 8 for the scoop on encumbrances.)

STATE SPECIFIC

You need to check out what, if any, laws exist in your state with respect to the consequences of destruction of the property. In many states, unless the contract says differently, the buyer bears the responsibility for any loss that results from destruction of the property. States that have adopted the *Uniform Vendor and Purchaser Risk Act* require the seller to bear any loss that occurs before title is passed to the buyer.

REMEMBER

One element that typically appears in a sales contract is a *contingency clause,* or a statement that requires that a specified condition (or conditions) must be met for the contract to be completed. Typical conditions in a real estate sales contract are a mortgage or financing contingency and an inspection contingency.

A *mortgage contingency* allows for the possibility that the buyer may not be able to afford to buy the house. Upon agreeing to purchase a house for $200,000 and coughing up $25,000 in cash for a down payment, the buyer plans to borrow the rest through a mortgage loan.

Because the sale can't go through unless the buyer can borrow the full $175,000, the buyer puts a clause in the contract that enables him or her the option of getting out of the deal if the lender refuses to approve an adequate mortgage loan amount. Without the mortgage contingency in the contract of sale, the buyer can lose the down payment, if the purchase doesn't go through as planned.

An *inspection contingency,* on the other hand, is an agreement that requires an inspection (or inspections) of the house by a home inspector. The house must pass the inspection. If this contingency clause is included in the contract, the buyer can get out of the deal if the inspector finds something wrong with the house and the seller refuses to repair it.

A third contingency that you may see is one in which the buyer must be permitted to sell his current home before being forced to buy the new home. This contingency protects the buyer from owning and having to pay mortgages on two homes at the same time.

Going back and forth with offer and acceptance

Because real estate deals often are the result of a process of negotiation, you need to understand a few of the concepts of the offer and acceptance process. Generally this process of negotiation follows the pattern of the seller listing the house for sale, the buyer making an offer to buy the house, the seller coming back with a counteroffer for the buyer, the buyer making a counteroffer to the seller's counteroffer, and acceptance by the seller with as many counteroffers proposed between offer and acceptance as are needed for the two parties to come to a *meeting of the minds,* which is also called *mutual assent.* An exam question on the offer and acceptance process may present a case of buyer and seller going back and forth and asking you if a particular offer is binding. Remember that as soon as a seller counteroffers to a buyer's offer, the buyer's offer no longer exists.

Suppose that I list my house for sale at $250,000. You offer to buy it from me for $200,000. I counteroffer that I'll sell the property to you for $240,000. You tell me you agree to that price. That's acceptance. For this process to lead to a meeting of the minds, the two parties must agree to all terms and conditions of the contract sale. For example, because of a hot real estate market, I advertise my house for sale for $250,000 and say that I want no mortgage contingency in the contract. You agree to pay the $250,000 but want a mortgage contingency in the contract. Your offer stands until I accept or reject it. If I stick to my original conditions, I counteroffer and tell you that I'll accept your price but not the mortgage contingency. When an offer or counteroffer is rejected, it ceases to exist, and all previous offers and counteroffers cease to exist.

Here's another one for you: You list your house for sale at $250,000. I offer you $180,000. You don't think I'm really serious, but you're willing to try and negotiate. You counteroffer $230,000, but I respond with a counteroffer of only $185,000. At that point, you get annoyed and issue a counteroffer back up to $250,000. After I counteroffered the $185,000, you effectively refused my offer and it disappeared. It was as if we were starting negotiations from scratch, so I can counteroffer anything I like.

STATE SPECIFIC

A *binder,* or *offer to purchase,* may be the first step toward solidifying a deal in some parts of the country, in different parts of the same state, and, in recent years, among different brokers in the same market area. A binder is used for residential real estate. A similar agreement, called a *letter of intent,* is used in commercial real estate transactions. A binder is used primarily to signify that a deal has been made and an agreement has been reached to go forward with more formal contract negotiations. At the point at which there's an accepted offer, both the buyer and seller sign the binder. A binder often is accompanied by an *earnest money deposit* or *down payment* to signal the buyer's seriousness in going forward with the purchase. In other parts of the country, binders are not used, but a sales contract is prepared immediately.

Discovering options

An *option* in real estate terms is an agreement in which a seller agrees to sell property to a buyer at an agreed-to price within a certain time frame if the buyer wants to buy it. The seller may not sell to anyone else during the option period. Unlike a regular real estate sales contract, the buyer doesn't have to buy the property, but if the buyer wants to buy, the seller must sell. Only one party, the seller, has to act. The buyer has the option of buying or not buying. Options are express unilateral contracts.

A real estate purchase option works like this. You're selling your property for $500,000. I want to buy it, but maybe I want to find out from the local government what I can build on the property and doing so will take some time. You agree to take the property off the market and give me an option to purchase the property at $500,000 within one year. I pay you something for the option that may or may not be credited toward the purchase price, depending on the terms of the agreement. The option gives me the right (but doesn't obligate me) to buy the property for $500,000 within one year. If I choose to exercise the option, you must sell me the property. If I choose not to exercise it, you can't force me to buy the property.

In addition to the basic elements of a valid contract, which you can find earlier in this chapter, the option normally has a time limit attached to it. It's unlikely that an option would run forever.

Looking at land contracts

A *land contract,* which may also be known as an *installment contract, conditional sales contract, contract for deed,* or *land sales contract,* may be used to purchase property without immediately paying the full price and without obtaining a mortgage. What happens is the buyer, or vendee, pays the seller, or vendor, so much money down and then pays the vendor a little at a time, usually in monthly payments over a period of years until the property is paid off. The buyer receives equitable title (the right to force the seller to give the buyer full title when the terms of the contract have been fulfilled) to the property, but the seller retains full title (complete ownership of the property). The buyer can use the property and must pay all of the bills on the property, but he or she doesn't receive a deed of ownership to the property until a certain number of payments are made to the seller (see Chapter 9 for more about deeds). A land contract is generally a bilateral express contract because the two parties are required to act and the promises are expressly made to each other. For the exam, remember that if you see the words "vendor" or "vendee," the question will likely be about a land contract.

Checking out leases

A *lease* is a form of real estate contract that gives someone exclusive use of a property for a period of time for a fee. Leases must contain all the elements of a valid contract. I talk about leases in detail in Chapter 12.

The End of the Line: Discharging a Contract

Discharging a contract means ending the contract in one of several appropriate ways. Test questions on this topic tend to focus on the definitions of these different ways of ending a contract. The most common and best way for a contract to be discharged is by performance, so I list that first, but I list the others here in alphabetical order:

>> **Performance:** *Performance* is the ideal way to end a contract, because all parties have fulfilled their obligations. "Time is of the essence" is a phrase that sometimes is used in contracts to mean that a breach of contract occurs if an obligation isn't completed within the specified time frame stated in the contract. (For more on breaches, see the next section.)

>> **Assignment and delegation:** Someone else takes over or is assigned the obligations of one of the parties to the contract. The party taking over the obligations is called the *assignee.* Say, for example, that I am a builder who agrees to build you a house. For some reason, I can't do the job, but I assign the contract to another builder who builds you a house under the same terms and conditions that you and I agreed to. This example is different from *delegation,* where I'd simply hire another builder to work for me to build you a house. In an assignment, my responsibilities and obligations are transferred. In a delegation, I remain primarily responsible.

>> **Death:** If you die, you definitely don't have to fulfill your obligations under a contract. However, that doesn't mean that someone else won't have to do what you agreed to do. For example, your estate may be required to go ahead and purchase a property that you contracted to buy before your death.

>> **Impossibility of performance:** In a situation where the action that was contracted cannot be performed legally, the possibility of performing the task can be declared impossible. For example, suppose you hire a builder to build an addition onto your house, and after you sign the contract, you find out the town won't let you build the addition. At this point you're no longer obligated to go through with the contract because performance is legally impossible.

>> **Mutual agreement:** In this situation, both parties to the contract agree to cancel it. They can agree with no penalty to either party, or they agree to some exchange of money to pay for any damage or loss to one or the other of the parties.

>> **Novation:** Novation is a situation in which a new contract with different terms replaces an old one. The new contract can be between the same parties or between one of the parties to the original contract and a new party. Writing a new contract when only minor changes need to be made is not the usual course of action. Each party usually just initials and dates the minor changes to signify their acceptance. Novation is reserved for major or more severe changes.

>> **Operation of law:** This type of situation can relate to some legal issue that arises that cancels the contract. For example a contract that is made on the basis of fraud is canceled when the fraud is discovered.

>> **Partial performance:** Discharging a contract for partial performance refers to an acceptance by one party of incomplete work by the other party and an agreement that the incomplete work will constitute fulfillment of the terms of the contract.

>> **Rescission:** A rescission of a contract sometimes is called a unilateral rescission. (Don't you wish these people could come up with normal names for this stuff?) Anyway, rescission is when one party decides not to fulfill its obligations under the contract and considers the situation to be as if the contract never existed. One party to a contract sometimes uses rescission when the other party doesn't appear to be fulfilling its obligations. For example, the painter who never shows up to paint your house may prompt you to rescind the contract.

>> **Substantial performance:** With the work under contract nearly completed, a substantial performance discharge of the contract may be in order. Under these circumstances, one party may force payment from the other party. Say, for example, you contract to build an addition onto your house. The builder finishes 95 percent of the work but you still owe him a third of the agreed upon amount for the project and refuse to pay until that last 5 percent of the work is complete. The builder can sue you for payment on the basis of substantial performance. The court may let you keep a small amount of money, not the 33 percent you're holding, to finish the job. The builder receives most of his payment and his obligations to you are declared over.

Breaching a Real Estate Contract

Sometimes people simply don't do what they promise to do, even after they sign a contract. These situations are the kind in which one of the parties but not the other refuses to do what he or she promised in the contract to do. A number of remedies and actions can be taken when a breach of contract occurs. I discuss these remedies from the buyer's side and the seller's side. (For remedies related to tenants and landlords in leases, see Chapter 12.) State exam writers expect you to know these different remedies and be able to identify them in a question.

When the buyer refuses to go ahead with the contract

When a buyer defaults and refuses to buy the house that she signed a contract to buy, even though the seller wants to go ahead with the sale, here's what the seller can do:

>> **Forfeit the contract:** In this case, the seller formally declares the contract forfeited. The seller typically is entitled to keep whatever money the buyer already has put into the deal. A liquidated damages provision in the contract deals with this.

>> **Rescind the contract:** After a buyer defaults, the seller declares the contract rescinded. This statement puts everyone back in the same position as when the contract never existed. Suppose the seller receives a higher offer a few days after signing a contract of sale. The buyer's money is returned, and the seller rescinds the contract.

>> **File suit for compensatory damages:** The seller brings a lawsuit against the buyer for monetary damages that the seller believes he has experienced because the buyer defaulted on the contract. An example is when the seller sues a buyer because he has lost a deposit on a house he was going to buy. The deposit was paid only after he had a signed contract to sell his own home.

>> **File suit for specific performance:** The purpose of this kind of lawsuit, which the seller brings against the buyer, is to force the buyer to buy the house. In a buyer's market — one in which there are more sellers than buyers and houses are selling slowly — the seller may use this remedy whenever finding another buyer is going to be difficult.

When the seller refuses to go ahead with the contract

The seller defaults when, even though the buyer is prepared to go ahead with the deal, the seller refuses to sell the house. Here are the remedies at the buyer's disposal:

>> **Rescind the contract:** The buyer can rescind the contract and basically let the seller off the hook. The buyer's money is returned and the contract no longer exists.

>> **File suit for compensatory damages:** In this case, the buyer sues the seller for monetary damages because the buyer believes she has suffered because of the seller's default. For example, a buyer sells her house and is living in a rented apartment with her furniture in storage because she'd signed a contract to buy another house, but the seller defaulted. The buyer can sue the seller for the cost of the rent and storage charges that she has to pay while looking for another house.

>> **File suit for specific performance:** This type of lawsuit is designed to force the seller to go ahead with the sale. Given the fact that no two properties are exactly alike, this remedy may be pursued when monetary damages won't satisfy the buyer, and the buyer really wants a particular house.

Review Questions and Answers

No one expects you to be an attorney, so the exam questions on contracts are going to be pretty basic. Definitions, the difference between two similar things (unilateral and bilateral, for example), and applicability (is this contract express or implied?) are the types of questions you can expect to see on the exam.

1. A real estate sales contract must be in writing because of what law?

    (A) Uniform Commercial Code

    (B) Statute of frauds

    (C) RESPA

    (D) SARA

    Correct answer: (B). The statute of frauds requires that real estate contracts be in writing. The Uniform Commercial Code deals with personal property.

2. A contract that depends on the actions of the parties as evidence of an agreement is referred to as

    (A) unilateral.

    (B) bilateral.

    (C) implied.

    (D) express.

    Correct answer: (C). A contract that depends on the actions of the parties can be unilateral or even bilateral. Express is the opposite of implied.

3. An option is an example of what kind of contract?

   (A) Implied and bilateral

   (B) Implied and unilateral

   (C) Express and bilateral

   (D) Express and unilateral

   Correct answer: (D). An option has to be expressed so that both parties understand their contractual obligations. Options are unilateral, because the obligation to act falls on only one party.

4. A contract to do something illegal is

   (A) voidable.

   (B) void.

   (C) valid.

   (D) executory.

   Correct answer: (B). A contract must have all required elements to be valid. One of those elements is that the thing you are contracting to do is legal.

5. What kind of title do buyers have when they sign an installment sales contract?

   (A) Executory

   (B) Implied

   (C) Full

   (D) Equitable

   Correct answer: (D). No such things as executory or implied titles exist. Full title also is not really a legal term. Equitable title is what you get in the executory stage of a contract.

6. The best word to describe a situation in which someone takes over the contractual obligations of another in a contract is

   (A) novation.

   (B) assignment.

   (C) voidable.

   (D) unenforceable.

   Correct answer: (B). If you missed it, the subtlety in this question is in the term "someone." A novation occurs when a new contract is written, which means both parties agree to a new contract. An assignment occurs when a third party takes over the obligations of one of the parties.

7. A buyer who will buy a house only if it passes inspection has what kind of clause placed in the contract?

   (A) An avoidance clause

   (B) An equitable title clause

   (C) A sale on demand clause

   (D) A contingency clause

   Correct answer: (D). Any specific action that is included in a contract and must be completed for the contract to be valid is called a contingency.

8. A minor change to a real estate contract generally is handled by

    (A) assignment.

    (B) novation.

    (C) initialing the change.

    (D) verbal agreement.

    Correct answer: (C). Minor changes generally can be accomplished by writing them into the contract and then having each party initial them. Novation is used when the changes are significant and require a new contract. Assignment means someone else is taking over the contract obligations. Changes must always be in writing.

9. You sign a contract to buy a house that the seller now refuses to sell to you. You still want the house. What do you do?

    (A) Sue for monetary damages.

    (B) Sue for rescission.

    (C) Sue for completion.

    (D) Sue for specific performance.

    Correct answer: (D). A successful suit for specific performance requires the seller to sell the house to you. Completion is not the correct term to force the sale. The other answers don't work because they don't get you the house.

10. If a buyer refuses to go ahead with a purchase of property for which he has signed a contract, what usually happens to the earnest money?

    (A) It is returned to the buyer.

    (B) It is kept by the seller.

    (C) It is kept by the seller less the broker's commission.

    (D) It is held by the title company.

    Correct answer: (B). The seller is usually entitled to keep the earnest money. This is considered forfeiture of the contract. No broker's commission is deducted, because the broker didn't produce a willing buyer.

Chapter **12**

Leasing Property

As a real estate agent, you may represent the owners of apartment buildings, office buildings, or retail buildings like shopping centers as a leasing agent. Leasing activity is an especially important part of property management and commercial real estate work if your real estate career goes in that direction. Just as you can represent a *buyer* in a sales transaction, you can also represent a *tenant*, who is someone seeking to rent an apartment or commercial space, in a leasing transaction. State real estate exam writers expect you to know the basics of leasing. You can answer most of these questions if you simply have a clear understanding of the different related definitions.

In this chapter, I talk about various kinds of estates (interests in real estate) in connection with leases. (For a more complete discussion of estates and interests, see Chapter 6.) I also give you some information about the requirements of a typical lease agreement, the different types of leases, and some ways people break leases. I also cover some unique details of commercial space leasing.

REMEMBER

In this chapter, I sometimes use the term *apartment,* which could mean a garden apartment, a duplex, or a single-family house as a rental. I also use *premises,* which is a common word used to describe a defined piece of land, building, apartment, or other space.

Identifying Who's Who and What's What

When you read this section, remember that I simply cover the basic definitions and terms connected with leasing. I also give you some information about the different *interests* (estates) that exist with respect to leases. State exam writers want you to be able to identify terms and apply them to pretty simple cases.

Owning property: Leased fee estates

A *lease* is an agreement between two parties for possession and use of a particular space, usually for a certain length of time. The person who owns the space, usually referred to as the landlord, is technically called the *lessor*. The landlord owns what's called the fee of the property. (For more in-depth information on fee simple interest and the various rights of ownership, see Chapter 6.)

REMEMBER

A lease separates two of the rights of ownership: ownership and possession. The owner still owns the property but has given possession to the tenant. The *lessor's* (owner's) interest in a property in a lease situation is called the *leased fee estate*. The lessor has a *reversionary right* to the possession of the premises when the lease expires, which simply means she gets possession of the property back. Sometimes the owner's interest is referred to as a *leased fee estate with reversionary right*.

Renting property: Leasehold estates

The tenant's interest in the property is called the *leasehold estate*. Another term for tenant is *lessee*. The tenant holds the lease, whereas the landlord gives the lease. In each of the following four types of leasehold estates, I use the term *estate*; however, note that the word *tenancy* can be substituted in each case.

Estate for years

An *estate for years* is a lease agreement with a definite starting and ending date. The tenant is required to leave when the lease expires, and the landlord isn't required to give the tenant notification to leave the premises. Neither is the tenant required to give notification to the landlord that she's leaving. Commercial property leases generally create an estate for years. No automatic renewal of an estate for years is available, but a new lease can be negotiated. Also, the agreement survives the landlord's death or the sale of the property. *Note:* In spite of the name, the lease could be for a term shorter than a year.

Periodic estate

A *periodic estate*, also called an *estate from period to period* or *periodic tenancy*, occurs when the original agreement doesn't contain any definite period of time. A month-to-month tenancy is an example of a periodic estate, though the period can be week to week or year to year. Essentially the agreement automatically renews itself from period to period with the original terms and conditions remaining in effect unless the landlord and the tenant renegotiate the agreement. In some parts of the United States, periodic estates are commonly used in residential leases. A periodic estate can be created when an estate for years (remember, a lease with an ending date) ends, the tenant doesn't move out, and the landlord continues to accept the rent. The tenant may be referred to as a *holdover tenant*.

STATE SPECIFIC

In the event of the death of the landlord or the sale of the property, the new landlord may be able to terminate the periodic estate by refusing to accept the rent. A typical notice for termination is usually one period, such as one month for a month-to-month lease. Periodic estates and their terminations are governed by state law, so check out how they're handled in your state.

Estate at will

An *estate at will* is when the landlord allows the tenant to occupy the premises, but there is no definite period of time when the arrangement will expire. An owner about to sell a building may allow a tenant to occupy an apartment under this type of arrangement. The estate at will can be terminated at any time with the proper legal notice (usually defined by state law), and it ends if the landlord or the tenant dies.

Estate at sufferance

An *estate at sufferance* occurs when a tenant who had a legal right to occupy the premises continues to occupy the space after the right of occupancy has expired, against the landlord's will. One example is a tenant who continues to stay in an apartment after the lease expires. The tenant is sometimes referred to as a *holdover.* No actual tenancy exists because the landlord is not accepting rent. In the event of the property's sale or the death of the landlord, the new owner has the same rights as the original owner to seek eviction (see "Breaking a Lease: Types of Eviction," later in this chapter).

An estate at sufferance can be converted to a periodic estate, which I describe earlier in this chapter, if the tenant pays the rent and the landlord agrees to accept it.

The Usual Suspects: Preparing a Typical Lease

Because a lease is a legal document, I recommend that a landlord have an attorney prepare a lease. On the flip side, when signing a lease, I recommend that a tenant's attorney reviews it. Even fill-in-the-blank lease forms should be reviewed by an attorney. In this section, I focus on the requirements for a valid lease, some of a lease's typical provisions, and laws related to leases.

Looking at laws governing leases

STATE SPECIFIC

The *statute of frauds,* which all states have adopted in some form, usually requires that a lease for a term longer than one year be in writing (see Chapter 11 for more). Some states have also adopted another law, the *Uniform Residential Landlord and Tenant Act,* which provides additional terms and conditions that should be addressed in the lease. In the following section, I give you some of the requirements that many states use as a minimum for a valid lease.

STATE SPECIFIC

The Uniform Residential Landlord and Tenant Act also provides protection for both landlord and tenant. Check out your state and local municipality's laws to determine if any provisions are applicable for specific tenant's rights.

STATE SPECIFIC

Laws also govern *rent control,* which is sometimes used as a generic term for any type of government control over what a landlord may charge a tenant. These laws generally govern residential units and vary from state to state and city to city. Check out if any type of rent control exists in your state.

Examining typical provisions of a lease

A lease is a form of a real estate contract. (For general information on contracts, see Chapter 11.) Like all contracts, a lease needs a few items to be considered valid. The main provisions of a valid lease are

>> **Legally competent parties:** Also referred to as having the capacity to contract, this provision means that everyone signing the lease has met all the legal requirements of age and competence.

>> **Mutual agreement:** The lease must include an offer and acceptance of the terms. All parties must clearly understand the terms of the lease.

>> **Legal objective:** This provision states that what is being contracted for is lawful.

>> **Consideration:** The exchange of space for money or other items of value must be enough to make the lease valid. The consideration could be in the form of services such as a janitor being given an apartment in exchange for working in the building.

>> **Agreement in writing:** Depending on the provisions in your state's version of the statute of frauds, the lease may have to be in writing. Typically leases for more than a year have to be written agreements.

STATE SPECIFIC

Your state may have additional, specific requirements for a valid lease, so be sure to check.

Although the minimum requirements technically create a valid lease, they really don't provide useful and specific details. Most leases also contain the following language to clarify certain details:

>> **A description of the leased premises:** This could be an apartment number or floor number and may include an actual survey description if a piece of land is leased. I cover property descriptions in detail in Chapter 9. In a nonresidential lease the description could include a drawing that shows the dimensions and location of the space within the building.

>> **The term of the lease:** The lease typically provides a beginning and ending date.

>> **The amount and date of rent payments:** This statement includes how much the rent is, when the rent is due, any grace periods that may be offered, penalties for late payment, and where the rent is to be sent.

STATE SPECIFIC

Check out when the default rent payment date is in your state. Lease provisions typically require rents to be paid in advance on the first of the month. The default position in some places is that rent is due at the end of the month for the previous month (in arrears).

>> **Provisions for rent increases:** Leases sometimes have provisions for automatic rent increases at certain intervals, which is sometimes called a *graduated lease*. Rent increases may be tied to the Consumer Price Index (an index that measures price increases and inflation), in which case the lease may be referred to as an *index lease*.

>> **The amount of security deposit:** Lease provisions provide for the deposit amount and clarify when the landlord must return it to the tenant at the end of the lease. State laws vary as to how security deposits may be used. For example, in some places (but not all) they may be used to cover defaults on the rent. State law or local ordinances may require that the security deposit be returned to the tenant within a specified period of time or an explanation be provided as to why all or a portion isn't being returned. Find out the relevant time frame, if any, in your state.

>> **How the premises can be used:** A landlord can limit how the tenant uses the leased space. For example, commercial space couldn't be used as living quarters.

>> **Whether and how improvements can be made:** Improvements to the space are often part of a commercial lease but also may be part of a residential lease. Whether the landlord or tenant does the improvements is a matter of negotiations. Typically, residential tenants are permitted to make improvements with the landlord's permission and are required to return the space to its original condition at the end of the lease.

>> **Provisions outlining maintenance responsibilities:** Landlords are generally required to maintain the premises in useable and what is called *habitable condition*. Certain commercial leases may require tenants to pay for or assume certain maintenance responsibilities.

>> **Details for destruction of the premises:** In cases where a tenant is leasing land or has built a building on leased land, the tenant may be responsible if the building or other structures are destroyed. Tenants aren't usually responsible for destruction of a building in which they lease only a part of the space. They would, however, always be responsible for their business equipment and personal items, just as the renter in a residential rental is responsible for their personal item insurance.

- » **Provisions for occupancy limits:** Depending on state or local law, a landlord may or may not be able to limit occupancy of the unit to the tenant who signed the lease.

- » **Provisions for (or against) subleasing:** The lease may provide for the renting of the space by the tenant to a subtenant through what is called a *sublease.* The sublease between the tenant and the subtenant is called a *sandwich lease.* Provisions may also be made for someone else taking over the lease. This is called *assignment.* In a sublease, the original tenant is still liable. An assignment to a new tenant usually needs the approval of the landlord even though the original tenant may remain liable.

- » **Termination on sale clause:** Under normal circumstances, if the landlord sells the building, the lease survives the sale and the new owner takes possession subject to the lease. If the lease contains a termination (or sale clause); however, the new owner can evict the tenant upon proper notice or renegotiate the lease with the tenant.

- » **The right of quiet enjoyment:** Whether stated or not, a lease generally conveys to the tenant the *right of quiet enjoyment,* a legal term that means the tenant has exclusive use of the leased premises without interference from the landlord. The landlord usually can't enter the premises without the tenant's permission except in an emergency.

- » **Any options:** A lease also may contain a renewal clause guaranteeing the tenant the right to renew the lease or a purchase option giving the tenant the right to purchase the property at or before the end of the lease term.

Distinguishing among Various Types of Leases

Though different types of leases have common features and have the same minimum legal requirements, they serve different purposes. The following sections can help you distinguish among the different types. Exam questions will likely focus on the major traits of various leases and may use short case studies to ask about types of leases used under certain circumstances.

Gross lease

A *gross lease* is where the tenant pays the same rent each month, and the landlord pays all the building's expenses, such as maintenance and taxes. The landlord may also pay some or all of the utilities, but in some gross leases, a tenant may pay his own utilities. The typical apartment lease is a gross lease.

Ground or land lease

The *ground lease* or *land lease* is a lease where someone rents an empty (vacant) piece of land specifically to erect a building on it. These leases tend to be long term and often exceed 50 years or longer. This lease term allows the tenant time to make his investment in the building worthwhile. In a ground lease, the tenant owns the building and the landlord owns the land. Ground leases usually require the tenant to pay all property expenses, such as taxes, utilities, and maintenance. In this respect, a ground or land lease is similar to a net lease.

Lease for oil or gas rights

Some leases give a company the right to search for and extract oil and gas from someone's property. The tenant usually pays a fee for the lease and then additional money is paid by the holder of the lease rights to the property owner according to how much gas or oil is removed. This type of lease is considered to be a limitation or cloud on the title to the property, which is anything that limits the rights you get when you buy a piece of property.

Net lease

A *net lease* is one where the tenant pays the building expenses on top of a base rent. Whether the tenant pays all or some of the expenses is negotiable. A *triple net lease* (sometimes referred to as a *net net net lease*) generally requires the tenant to pay all expenses such as taxes, utilities, maintenance, and insurance. The net or triple net lease is commonly used in renting commercial space.

STATE SPECIFIC

You may want to check whether a *double net lease* (or a *net net lease*) is common in your area. In some markets, the tenant pays two or three building expenses like taxes and maintenance or taxes and utilities but not all the other expenses.

Percentage lease

A *percentage lease* usually has a minimum monthly rental charge plus a percentage of the gross earned by the business. This arrangement is sometimes used in leases with retail stores, and the percentage is based on gross sales. The percentage lease may be either a gross or net lease, meaning that the tenant pays none, some, or all of the building expenses.

Proprietary lease

A *proprietary lease* is a lease that is given to the "owner" of a cooperative apartment. The owner doesn't actually own the apartment itself but rather shares in the corporation that owns the building. He receives a proprietary lease that allows him to occupy the apartment. (For more on cooperatives, check out Chapter 7.)

Variable lease

A *variable lease* allows for the rent to change over the life of the lease. The *graduated lease* is a variable lease in which pre-agreed to rent increases occur on specific dates. Another form of variable lease, the *index lease*, ties the rent increases or decreases to an index such as the Consumer Price Index at set intervals.

Breaking a Lease: Types of Eviction

When a lease expires, unless the tenant and owner renegotiate it, the tenant is required to leave the premises. However, under some circumstances, the tenant may be forced to leave either by the landlord or by conditions in the building before the lease term expires. The two main types of eviction are as follows.

>> **Actual eviction:** *Actual eviction* occurs when the landlord sues for possession of the premises. This usually occurs when a tenant violates the terms of the lease agreement or stays in the premises beyond the lease expiration date.

> » **Constructive eviction:** *Constructive eviction* occurs when a landlord's actions are such that the premises become uninhabitable. A landlord consistently over time not providing sufficient heat during the winter months may result in constructive eviction. In such a case, as soon as the leased premises are proved to be unusable, the lease is considered ended. Don't consider this a good way to get rid of a tenant; such actions by the landlord are illegal.

Getting What You Paid For

There is a somewhat unique situation that happens when you rent nonresidential space. It's a perfectly legal and accepted practice, but the fact is you may not actually get what you paid for. Read on to learn more about this concept.

Nonresidential building layouts

Think about the last office building you visited or the one you work in. Maybe it has a nice spacious lobby, some elevators, wide hallways, men's and ladies' rooms, and finally many separate offices housing doctors and lawyers and accountants and other businesses or professionals. The same goes for the last shopping mall you went to, only this time the space is divided up into stores instead of offices. It's logical that each of the tenants in the building pay for their individual office space. But they and their clients use the lobby, the hallways, the washrooms and the elevator. Who pays for that?

Commercial property landlords and tenants understand that the so-called *common spaces* in these buildings have value and are necessary for the building to function properly. It would be relatively easy for the landlord to simply recoup the costs as part of the rent, the way apartment landlords do, if the individual rented space was more or less the same size. But a tenant renting a 1,000-square-foot office would feel that it's unfair if he has to pay the same for the use of the common space as a tenant renting 5,000 square feet. What has developed to solve this problem is the concept of rentable and useable space.

Rentable space

Rentable space is the space that a tenant pays for when renting nonresidential space, say in an office building or shopping mall. It generally contains more square feet than the tenant is entitled to use exclusively and takes into account the common spaces used by the tenant and the tenant's visitors. The rent is generally stated as so many dollars per square foot annually (even though it might be paid monthly). In some cases it's stated as a monthly rent. In either case it is multiplied by the number of rentable square feet to arrive at the total annual or monthly base rent.

Useable space

Useable space is the square footage that the tenant is allowed to use exclusively. It's the space behind the door to the hallway. It's invariably less than the total square footage the tenant pays for.

Adding on and taking away

The difference between the rentable space and the useable space is called the *add-on factor* or the *loss factor*, depending on which way you do the calculations. It's pretty easy to remember. The add-on factor is added to the useable square footage to arrive at the rentable total square footage. The loss factor is subtracted for the rentable square footage to arrive at the useable total square footage. Both are usually stated as a percentage.

Following are a couple of simple examples that you probably won't have to do on an exam, but they help demonstrate the concept.

Loss factor

5,000 square feet (rentable space) × 10% (loss factor) = 500 square feet lost space

5,000 square feet (rentable space) – 500 square feet (lost space) = 4,500 square feet (useable space)

Add on factor

4,500 square feet (useable space) × 10% (add on factor) = 450 square feet (proportionate common space)

4,500 square feet (useable space) + 450 square feet (proportionate common space) = 4,950 square feet (rentable space)

Note that using the same numbers, the 10 percent has a different result depending on whether it's used as an add-on factor or a loss factor.

Review Questions and Answers

Expect a few exam questions that deal with recognizing different types of leases and some of the basic terminology.

1. A retail store tenant pays $3,000 a month rent plus a portion of gross sales. This rental arrangement is most likely

   (A) a term lease.

   (B) a net lease.

   (C) an index lease.

   (D) a percentage lease.

   Correct answer: (D). A percentage lease requires payment of a base rent plus some portion of the income of the business occupying the space.

2. Tenant A moves out of an apartment six months before the end of the lease. Tenant B moves in and pays rent to Tenant A for the remainder of the lease. Tenant B is

   (A) an assignee.

   (B) an assignor.

   (C) a sublessee.

   (D) a sublessor.

   Correct answer: (C). The key to this answer is that Tenant B pays rent to Tenant A and not to the landlord. When you assign a lease, the new tenant takes over the lease and pays rent to the landlord. This isn't the case in this question.

3. A landlord refuses to repair the broken furnace in an apartment building in the middle of winter. The situation may result in

(A) actual eviction.

(B) constructive eviction.

(C) abandonment.

(D) condemnation.

Correct answer: (B). Focus on the types of eviction here. When a tenant leaves as a result of the landlord creating circumstances by which the unit is uninhabitable, constructive eviction has occurred. Actual eviction is usually a result of the landlord taking action against the tenant for violating the terms of the lease.

4. Can a new owner force a tenant to renegotiate an existing lease when he takes ownership of the property?

(A) Yes, if the lease has a purchase option in it.

(B) Yes, if the lease has a sale clause.

(C) Yes, under any circumstances.

(D) No, under no circumstances.

Correct answer: (B). The only circumstance under which this situation occurs is the inclusion of a sale clause in the lease. Otherwise a lease survives the sale of a property.

5. A tenant refuses to leave an apartment after the expiration of the lease. The landlord continues to accept the tenant's rent. The tenant may be said to have

(A) a tenancy at law.

(B) a tenancy at sufferance.

(C) a tenancy by the entirety.

(D) a periodic tenancy.

Correct answer: (D). A tenancy at sufferance would have been created if the tenant stayed without the landlord's permission.

6. A net lease requires the tenant to pay

(A) all or some of the building expenses.

(B) all of the building expenses, including the mortgage payment.

(C) none of the building expenses.

(D) a percentage of income earned by the tenant's business.

Correct answer: (A). A tenant never has to make mortgage payments. Paying none of the building expenses is the opposite of the correct answer. A percentage payment is a trait of a percentage lease.

7. The principal difference between tenancy at will and tenancy at sufferance is

   (A) the term of the lease.

   (B) the expenses paid.

   (C) whether rent is paid in arrears or in advance.

   (D) the landlord's consent.

   Correct answer: (D). In tenancy at will, the landlord allows the tenant to stay in the premises, but there is no definite period of time when the arrangement will expire. In tenancy at sufferance, the tenant is staying against the landlord's will.

8. A typical apartment lease with a beginning and ending date is

   (A) an estate for years.

   (B) a periodic estate.

   (C) a net lease.

   (D) a percentage lease.

   Correct answer: (A). This is a definitional question. A typical apartment lease has a beginning and ending date, but it isn't automatically renewed from period to period, ruling out a periodic estate. It also tends to be gross (not net or percentage).

9. The landlord's interest in a lease is called

   (A) the leasehold interest.

   (B) the leased fee interest.

   (C) the gross lease interest.

   (D) the possessory interest.

   Correct answer: (B). The landlord owns the fee of the property and therefore has the leased fee interest. The tenant holds the lease and therefore has the leasehold interest.

10. A tenant remains in possession of a rented house after the bank has sold the property through foreclosure for nonpayment of the mortgage, and the bank wants to evict the tenant. The tenant has

    (A) a tenancy at will.

    (B) a tenancy at sufferance.

    (C) a lawful occupancy.

    (D) a periodic tenancy.

    Correct answer: (B). The key here is consent. If the landlord (the bank in this case) wants you out but you stay, it's a tenancy at sufferance.

IN THIS CHAPTER

» Finding out about environmental statements and assessments

» Identifying some major environmental problems

» Looking at water supply and disposal issues

Chapter 13

Dealing with Environmental Government Regulations and Issues

The public has been and continues to be concerned about the environment. This concern has gone in two directions: environmental preservation, and the study and elimination of environmental hazards. Environmental preservation also has evolved into the green, sometimes called ecofriendly, building concept of creating more energy-efficient homes and commercial buildings. Environmental hazards don't just come out of thin air — though of course they can affect the air. Environmental hazards also happen on the ground. And things that negatively affect the environment, like air and water pollution, often happen because of land development — vacant land that is bought and built on. Enter you, the real estate agent.

STATE SPECIFIC

As a result of the increasing concern about the environment, many states expect real estate agents to have some knowledge of environmental issues, government regulations, and the analysis of the environmental impacts of development. Although the information in this chapter crosses state lines, for exam purposes, check out whether your state requires you to know this information for the state licensing exam.

In this chapter I give you some basic information about environmental hazards, some of their health effects, government regulations about environmental issues, and a brief analysis of the impact of development on the environment.

REMEMBER

As you read this chapter, remember that no one is trying to turn you into an environmental scientist. In fact, most of the time in a real estate practice, you're going to recommend that buyers and sellers call in environmental scientists, engineers, planners, and attorneys who specialize in environmental issues when you or anyone involved suspects a problem. Your job is to recognize some basic laws and environmental hazards and their impacts. Liability for the real estate agent exists in these environmental issues but usually only to the extent that the agent should've known something or did know something and didn't reveal it to buyers or sellers.

Deciphering the Federal Government Alphabet Soup

As environmental concerns have grown across the United States, the federal government has passed a series of laws, regulations, and programs to deal with environmental issues. Many of them are known by the acronyms that their letters form. In studying this information for an exam, take time to discover not only the acronyms but also the full titles. You also need to have a pretty good idea of the type of issue that the program deals with and its important points. In a few cases just knowing what the letters stand for will be enough.

STATE SPECIFIC

In some cases, states have passed their own environmental laws to supplement or go further than federal laws. Be sure to check out these laws and find out whether you'll be tested on them. This information should be available in your prelicense course.

CERCLA

In 1980 the federal government adopted into law the *Comprehensive Environmental Response, Compensation, and Liability Act* (CERCLA). This law's purpose is to identify sites of environmental pollution and provide funds for cleanup. The act calls for the identification of people and/or businesses responsible or *potentially responsible parties (PRP)* for the creation of uncontrolled hazardous waste sites or hazardous waste spills. The act also created a $9 billion fund called the *Superfund* to pay for the cleanup of identified hazardous waste sites.

The act considers liability for such a site and its cleanup to be strict. *Strict liability* means that the property owner has no excuse with respect to his liability. The act also considers the liability to be *joint and several,* which means that if more than one person is responsible for the hazardous waste site, the law is enforceable on the group as well as on each individual. In fact, if, for example, one of two people had no funds available for cleanup, the other party could be held responsible for the total cost. The second party would have to try and get payment from the other person through a lawsuit.

Under CERCLA, a current landowner can be held liable for the cost of cleaning up a hazardous waste site even when he or she didn't create it. The current owner can then try to obtain reimbursement from the people who originally created the site or from the Superfund itself. The term *retroactive liability* also is used in connection with CERCLA and the Superfund. It means that previous owners also can be held accountable for the hazardous waste site.

EPA

The Environmental Protection Agency (EPA) is the federal agency responsible for dealing with environmental issues. The agency advises Congress and the president regarding laws to protect the environment. The agency writes regulations implementing laws that have been passed, and the agency enforces all federal environmental rules and regulations. The EPA administers, among other laws, the *Clean Water Act*, the *Toxic Substance Control Act*, and the *Resource Conservation and Recovery Act*.

HMTA

The important thing to remember for the exam here: The Hazardous Material Transportation Act (HMTA) is enforced by the United States Department of Transportation.

HUD

The United States Department of Housing and Urban Development (HUD) isn't a major player in the federal regulation of environmental issues. However, I mention it because the agency is relevant when concerned with lead paint disclosure, which I discuss in the "Lead" section later in this chapter.

LUST (It's not what you think)

The Leaking Underground Storage Tanks (LUST) program, sometimes referred to as the UST or Underground Storage Tank program, was created in 1984 as part of the Resource Conservation and Recovery Act administered by the EPA.

This program targets underground storage tanks used for the storage of hazardous substances such as chemicals or oil-based products like motor fuel. Such tanks must be registered with the EPA. There are a number of exceptions to the underground storage tank program, including tanks with a storage capacity of less than 110 gallons; tanks used for heating oil used on the property; and motor fuel storage tanks of less than 1,100 gallons on farms and residential properties. The program regulates such areas as tank installation and maintenance as well as spill prevention and monitoring.

STATE SPECIFIC

Individual states may have programs that supplement the federal underground storage tank program. Check out your state law to find out whether this issue is something that you need to know for your state test. Generally the state law may provide for additional registration of tanks, different minimum size tanks that have to be registered, and possibly different technical requirements.

OSHA

The Occupational Safety and Health Administration (OSHA), which is part of the United States Department of Labor, is responsible for providing and monitoring regulations regarding worker safety particularly in factories.

SARA

The *Superfund Amendments and Reauthorization Act of 1986 (SARA)* was passed when the original act, CERCLA, expired in 1985. (See the earlier section on CERCLA for more.) The three essential functions SARA performs are

>> Providing increased funding to the Superfund for environmental cleanup.

>> Creating stronger standards for cleanup of hazardous waste.

>> Creating something called *innocent landowner immunity*.

Where a property owner has been innocent of all involvement with a hazardous waste site, under certain circumstances, she may claim immunity from responsibility. In addition to having no involvement or knowledge of the situation, the property owner must have taken what is sometimes called *due care* or *due diligence* in having the property investigated for potential environmental contamination. This investigation usually takes the form of an environmental assessment. (For more on environmental assessments, see "Having suspicions: Environmental assessments," later in this chapter.) Before the innocent landowner immunity status was created, the current owner, regardless of guilt, could be held liable by the EPA to pay for cleanup of a hazardous waste site and then would have to seek reimbursement from a previous owner. SARA's immunity status can relieve a current innocent owner of this liability.

SDWA

The Safe Drinking Water Act (SDWA) established standards for the testing and quality of public water supplies. It requires that the public be notified if the drinking water contains contaminants above acceptable levels.

Assessing the Environmental Effects of Building Developments

Many land development projects, which include everything from building a single house to a major shopping center or multi-lot subdivision, impact the environment. The impacts are usually proportional to the size of the project, but a small project can have a large impact if it's built on environmentally sensitive land, such as a single-family house built near a wetland. (See the sidebar "Why would you want wet land?" later in this chapter.) In this section, I discuss the primary ways that environmental engineers, scientists, and planners examine the impacts of such projects.

Making a statement: Environmental impact statements

STATE SPECIFIC

Laws governing the examination of the environmental impacts of a proposed project vary from state to state. If environmental issues are part of your state exam, check out the particular rules and regulations that govern the review or impact study of environmental issues with respect to a proposed development project.

An environmental impact statement or study (they may be called something else in your state) examines the environmental impact a development project may have on the environment. Depending on the state requirements, such a statement may look at everything from the number of cars that will be put on the road to the animal life that will be disturbed. The study reviews both the impact of the project when it's completed and the impact it may have while it's being built.

An environmental impact statement or study sometimes requires that alternatives be presented and examined. For example, a developer may be required to examine various access roads into a new subdivision and then explain why the one selected is best. The study also usually requires a discussion of mitigation measures. *Mitigation measures* are those things that might be done to minimize or eliminate the environmental impact of the project. For example, a developer expects the shopping center he's building to generate a great deal of car traffic (car traffic equals air pollution). He may agree to provide room at the shopping center for a bus stop to encourage people to take public transportation, thus reducing the number of cars used.

Experts in environmental matters prepare these statements or studies. The public and key agencies may be invited to comment on the study. These studies can be expensive and time-consuming depending on the project's complexity.

Having suspicions: Environmental assessments

When someone involved in a real estate transaction suspects the presence of hazardous material on a piece of property, environmental engineers or scientists may be hired to perform an environmental assessment. An environmental assessment has four possible phases:

>> **Phase 1:** A Phase 1 environmental assessment is primarily a review of the records regarding the property in question. The records that are reviewed focus on any environmental complaints, violations, special permits, or other documentation that may indicate the current or previous presence of environmentally hazardous material. This phase also includes a visual inspection of the property. Phase 1 environmental assessments are commonly done before someone purchases an industrial or commercial property and are often required by mortgage lenders before approving a loan.

>> **Phase 2:** A Phase 2 environmental assessment involves actually testing and sampling to confirm the presence of any environmentally hazardous material or contamination.

>> **Phase 3:** A Phase 3 environmental assessment is done after the confirmation of contamination on the property. The Phase 3 assessment examines the extent of the hazard and develops a plan to remedy the condition. Remediation is done as a result of this phase and may include removal of the contaminated material and restoration of the property.

>> **Phase 4:** A Phase 4 environmental assessment is the development of a management plan for the contaminated site. Sometimes the contamination may be too large or extensive to be removed, and Phase 4 establishes a specific management plan to contain and manage the site so as to not affect surrounding properties.

This Stuff Can Make You Sick: Examining Environmental Pollutants and Situations

One of the primary functions of a real estate agent is to be aware of possible environmental issues with respect to a piece of property that the agent may be involved with as a seller's or buyer's agent. State test writers therefore expect a certain basic level of knowledge about what environmentally sensitive issues might show up in a real estate transaction.

Your job certainly isn't to become an environmental expert. However, as an agent, you do have a responsibility to make yourself as aware as possible of environmentally hazardous situations that may be present. You ask how? You perform this duty by a visual inspection of the property as well as asking the property owner. It also involves being aware of commonly known hazards in the area. The agent may further recommend the services of an environmental assessor or auditor who would conduct the appropriate environmental assessment.

In the following sections I provide some basic information about various environmentally hazardous substances and conditions.

Asbestos

Asbestos is a mineral that has been widely used in residential and commercial construction. Because of its resistance to the transfer of heat and its resistance to fire, builders have used it as insulation for pipes and heating ducts, roofing, siding, and flooring materials. The basic issue that exists with asbestos is related to its friability. *Friable* means the tendency to break down and give off dust and fibers that can be highly dangerous if inhaled. Exposure to asbestos fibers and dust can cause diseases that include lung cancer; *asbestosis*, a sometimes-fatal disease that makes breathing difficult; and mesothelioma, a cancer of the lining of the lungs.

In general, you can deal with asbestos in a building in three ways.

>> **Leave it alone.** Leaving it alone may be appropriate if the asbestos is in good shape and doesn't appear to be disintegrating or deteriorating in such a way that fibers and dust are escaping into the air.

>> **Remove it.** Removing it should be done only in accordance with experts who follow procedures established by the EPA and/or your state.

>> **Deal with it.** Dealing with asbestos is called encapsulation. *Encapsulation* is sealing the asbestos in place. Doing so prevents dust and fibers from getting into the air. Make sure that appropriate professionals do all evaluations and work in dealing with asbestos or removing it.

Brownfields

Brownfields are former industrial, factory, manufacturing, or storage sites that may have environmentally hazardous waste on or under them from their previous use. Federal legislation was passed in 2002 to help communities with the cost of cleaning up these areas. This legislation also protects owners of property from liability for hazardous wastes that were put there by a previous owner.

Building-related illness

Building-related illness, sometimes referred to as *BRI*, is a general term to describe various health issues related to the indoor air quality of buildings. The symptoms, which may include a variety of allergic reactions and respiratory illnesses, are present both while people are in the building and continue after they leave the building. The cause of BRI is related to chemical emissions from materials like paints and glues used in the building, as well as bacteria and dust in the air.

Electromagnetic fields

Electromagnetic fields are generated by so-called high-tension power lines and by power transfer or distribution stations and home appliances. Some research indicates that these electromagnetic fields can cause cancer as well as changes in behavior and hormone levels. This research is apparently somewhat controversial with other research indicating no health hazards. Real estate agents should familiarize themselves with the locations of the types of facilities that could generate electromagnetic fields so as to be able to advise property buyers of their presence.

Lead

Researchers recognized lead as a health hazard a number of years ago. It's particularly dangerous to children, negatively impacting mental and physical development. Lead particles can enter a person's system if he breathes lead dust in the air, drinks from a water supply that runs through lead pipes or copper tubing joined with lead solder, or actually eats lead-based paint flakes, as may happen with small children.

In 1992 the U.S. government passed the *Lead-Based Paint Hazard Reduction Act,* which requires that homeowners in homes built before 1978 fill out a lead paint disclosure form and give it to a buyer when they sign a sales contract. This form triggers a ten-day period of time during which the buyer can have the property tested for lead. This testing isn't mandatory but at the buyer's option.

The testing, done by appropriate professionals, can be done in two ways:

>> A *paint inspection* can be performed, which indicates the amount of lead present in all painted surfaces.

>> A *risk assessment* also can be performed, which goes further than the paint inspection. The risk assessment actually examines sources of lead paint risk such as peeling paint and suggests how to remedy it.

If the buyer decides to have the inspection done and a lead paint hazard is found, the seller has the option of correcting it or not. If the seller refuses, the buyer has the option of getting out of the deal and getting all his *earnest* (deposit) money back.

In addition to the disclosure form that the seller must complete, she must also provide a lead paint information booklet produced by HUD and the EPA (see "Deciphering the Federal Government Alphabet Soup," earlier in this chapter for more about these government agencies), as well as the United States Consumer Product Safety Commission. The disclosure rules also apply to the landlord's obligation to reveal to the tenant any known lead paint hazard. A real estate agent's responsibility with respect to lead paint disclosure is to advise the seller about his obligations to disclose possible lead paint hazards. An agent representing a buyer advises the buyer of the fact that he should receive the lead paint disclosure.

STATE SPECIFIC

Check whether your local state or municipality has any laws regarding lead paint hazard disclosure that supplement the federal regulations.

Radon

Radon is an odorless, colorless, tasteless, radioactive gas produced by the decay of natural materials such as rocks that are radioactive. It tends to accumulate in areas with poor outside air circulation such as basements. It may spread through a building by heating and air-conditioning systems, and it's believed to cause lung cancer. Tests can be done for radon, and a real estate agent representing a buyer may recommend that the buyer have the test performed before buying the property.

Professionals like private building inspectors can perform the test; do-it-yourself kits also are available for homeowners. If radon is found, the remedy generally is to introduce some kind of ventilation into the enclosed space to remove the gas. Although no safe levels of radon have been determined, the EPA recommends action to mitigate the gas be taken if a level of four picocuries per liter of air is found when tested.

Sick building syndrome

Sick building syndrome, sometimes called *SBS,* refers to symptoms that people sometimes experience when inside a building for a period of time, but which end when the person leaves the building. (Some people may call that BBS, also known as Bad Boss Syndrome.) The symptoms may include itchiness, breathing difficulty, dizziness, and runny nose.

The cause of SBS is believed to be poor indoor air quality as a result of chemical emissions from materials such as paints and glues used in the building, as well as bacteria and dust in the air.

Solid waste (radioactive and otherwise)

Various parts of the United States have radioactive waste sites. These sites store used fuel from nuclear power plants. The principal issue for real estate agents is to be aware of where these sites are located. People are generally aware of the potential health hazards associated with a leak of radioactive material and may choose not to live near such a site. Or if they do buy a home near a radioactive storage facility, they may expect to pay less than if the facility weren't there.

The storage of solid waste (I'm old enough to remember when it was called garbage) is more widespread. *Landfills,* which are areas that are excavated, filled with solid waste, and then covered, are located in many parts of the country. The environmental issue is primarily leakage from the landfill into nearby properties, as well as into nearby lakes, streams, and, wells. Older landfills, in particular, may cause problems because they may not have been constructed according to modern standards with appropriate liners, covering, and drainage control. Federal, state, and local governmental agencies all may be involved in monitoring landfills to prevent contamination of nearby properties and water bodies.

Underground tanks

Underground storage tanks range in size from relatively small tanks of a few hundred gallons for home heating oil to large tanks of thousands of gallons for industrial and agricultural gasoline, oil storage, and chemical storage. The issue for real estate, of course, is leakage from the tank into the ground and then into wells or nearby water supply systems of recreational streams and lakes.

In addition to the danger posed by tanks that are in current use, the issue of tank abandonment is significant. Usually local government agencies establish proper procedures for abandoning a tank. One of the most important ones is pumping out the material in the tank so that nothing is left to leak out. The tanks are then generally filled with material like sand.

STATE SPECIFIC

To read more about the federal Leaking Underground Storage Tank (LUST) program, check out "LUST (It's not what you think)," earlier in this chapter. Make sure you check to see whether your home state has any local programs that deal with tank registration, monitoring, or abandonment. As a real estate agent, you want to know about these specific procedures because they may affect your buyer or seller. If appropriate, you would need copies of the proper paperwork for your buyer, showing that the tanks were abandoned properly.

A few more quick definitions to keep in mind

Exam writers may expect you to know at least a little about the following issues, such as definitions and brief explanations. So that's what I'm giving you.

>> **Carbon monoxide:** This is a potentially deadly gas that occurs naturally in the burning of gas, oil, or other fuels. It can be lethal in the case of a faulty furnace or oil burner and where there is improper ventilation. Carbon monoxide detectors are mandatory in some building codes.

- » **Chlorofluorocarbons:** CFCs, as they are more commonly known, are gases that were once used in aerosol cans and in the freon of older air conditioners. CFCs are thought to be responsible for the depletion of the ozone layer around the earth. The *Federal Clean Air Act* banned their use. Replacing an older central air conditioning system often involves replacing equipment to handle the newer, less-environmentally hazardous gases.

- » **Mold:** This is usually caused by the presence of moisture. It can be present virtually anywhere in a building and can cause allergic reactions and respiratory problems.

- » **Urea formaldehyde:** This substance was used to create urea-formaldehyde foam insulation (UFFI), which the Consumer Product Safety Commission banned in 1982. Because of insufficient proof of adverse health risks associated with UFFI, the ban was changed to a warning. Gases related to UFFI are thought to cause respiratory problems and skin and eye irritations.

Go with the Flow: Water and Waste Issues

Water supply is a major environment issue in the United States. Without a sufficient supply of clean, drinkable water, development of real estate for homes and businesses is impossible. In this section, I discuss water sources and water pollution issues, and what happens to water after you use it and it becomes sewage. I also talk about storm water, a different kind of wastewater.

Water pollution

The term *domestic water* is used to describe the water you drink, cook with, and take a shower in. Domestic water comes from groundwater sources, which can be either reservoirs or underground water supplies, sometimes called *aquifers.* Groundwater supplies are subject to pollution from many sources ranging from the chemicals you put on your lawn to the oil on the highways.

In some places water is supplied to homes and businesses through the local government, a public water supply agency or commission, or a privately owned water supply company. The system of supply is generally from a reservoir or series of wells through a system of pipes to your home or business. Sometimes, in between the supply and the distribution pipes, the water may be treated or filtered in some way. The *Federal Safe Drinking Water Act* requires that public water supply systems be tested regularly.

WHY WOULD YOU WANT WET LAND?

Somewhere in your travels you may have heard the term *wetlands*. Wetlands are properties that because of their location and soil type have the ability to act as sponges soaking up volumes of water, sometimes at a greater capacity than other types of soils.

So why is this important? For example, say you owned a 40,000-square-foot piece of commercial property. You build a small store with a parking lot and cover half of the lot with building and pavement. The next time it rains, half the water that falls on your property runs off (and it's called *runoff*) the *impervious* (water can't get through) surface. So where does that rainwater go? Onto the part of the lot where there's still grass and the water then gets absorbed there. But suppose you paved over the whole lot to make a bigger parking area. And suppose the nearby property owners did the same thing. As more and more land is covered, the rainwater can cause street and house flooding. So wetlands in strategic places, which have the capacity to absorb more than their fair share of water, are preserved so all that rainwater running off your parking lot, driveway, or roof has someplace to go.

Those people who aren't served by a public or private water supply system get their water from individual on-site water supply systems called wells. Wells may (and sometimes are required to) be tested for the presence of pollutants and for adequacy of supply.

STATE SPECIFIC

Check your local state regulations regarding mandatory testing of wells. Many places require wells to be tested for pollution and adequate pressure when a new well is drilled and when the property is sold. Testing may be optional after that. Also find out what agency reviews the test results. Local health departments or environmental departments are typically the review agencies.

Sanitary waste disposal

Sanitary waste is what goes out the drain pipe of your house from the sinks, showers, toilets, and washing machines. Of course, it's not sanitary but must be treated in a sanitary manner to prevent pollution and illness.

Ideally when you flush, it becomes someone else's problem. The waste from your house travels through sewer pipes and eventually is treated at a sewage treatment plant, usually operated by the city, town, or county. If you live in a large residential complex or work in an office building that has no sewers, a small, nearby treatment plant may service your building or housing complex.

In many areas, sewage disposal is handled by individual on-site disposal systems called *septic systems.* In this case when you flush, it's still your problem because septic systems have to be maintained by periodically pumping them. The septic tank is one of two parts of a septic system. The other part is the *leach fields,* which are also called *absorption fields* or *septic fields.* The size of a septic system can vary and is generally sized according to the number of bedrooms in a house. The location of the leach fields as well as even the feasibility of using a septic system is determined by the capacity of the soil to absorb what is called leachate. *Leachate* is the liquid stuff that comes out of the septic tank after all the solids have settled to the bottom of the tank. The capacity of the soil to absorb leachate is tested by doing a *percolation* or *perc test.* Where there are wells and septic systems in the same area or on the same property, local authorities establish minimum distances that have to be maintained between the septic system and the well.

Storm water disposal

Storm water is rainwater that comes down into the streets that must be disposed of to avoid flooding of streets and houses. Generally storm drains in the streets that lead to storm sewers dispose the storm water and take it directly to lakes, rivers, or the ocean.

Review Questions and Answers

You'll find that most answers to questions about environmental issues come down to memorizing the facts. The other important tidbit to remember is to memorize the full terms of any abbreviations or acronyms.

1. A source of money to clean up major environmentally polluted properties was originally created by

(A) CERCLA.

(B) EPA.

(C) LUST.

(D) SARA.

Correct answer: (A). The trick is the word *originally.* SARA reauthorized the Superfund.

2. Immunity for a landowner innocent of creating the pollution on his property was created by

   (A) CERCLA.

   (B) OSHA.

   (C) SARA.

   (D) EPA.

   Correct answer: (C). Innocent landowner immunity didn't exist in the original CERCLA legislation.

3. Immunity for a landowner innocent of creating pollution on his property will most likely be dependent on

   (A) the type of pollution.

   (B) how long ago the pollution happened.

   (C) his due diligence in investigating the property.

   (D) how much money he has.

   Correct answer: (C). Due diligence is a key requirement of innocent landowner immunity. The landowner must have done some investigation to protect himself.

4. A review of records regarding environmental problems on a property would be part of

   (A) a Phase 1 environmental assessment.

   (B) a Phase 2 environmental assessment.

   (C) a Phase 3 environmental assessment.

   (D) a Phase 4 environmental assessment.

   Correct answer: (A). Review "Having suspicions: Environmental assessments," earlier in this chapter and make sure that you can clearly identify what occurs in each phase.

5. A management plan for an environmentally polluted site would be developed in which phase environmental assessment?

   (A) 1

   (B) 2

   (C) 3

   (D) 4

   Correct answer: (D). You need to be able to identify the four phases and what occurs in each phase. (Check out "Having suspicions: Environmental assessments," earlier in this chapter for the scoop.)

6. Friability is a term associated with

   (A) BRI.

   (B) SBS.

   (C) electromagnetic fields.

   (D) asbestos.

   Correct answer: (D). Friability is the tendency of asbestos to break down and give off dust and fibers that can be highly dangerous if inhaled. This question is a good example of how you have to remember information about various environmental hazards. For each one, you need to remember what it is, how and where it appears, associated key words (like friability and asbestos), illnesses it may cause, ways to handle it, and so on.

7. You get sick at work and the symptoms persist when you get home. You may be suffering from

    (A) BRI.

    (B) SBS.

    (C) EPA.

    (D) OSHA.

    Correct answer: (A). The symptoms of building-related illness are present both while people are in a building and continue after they leave the building. The symptoms of sick building syndrome (SBS) end when people leave the building.

8. The size of a residential septic system is usually based on

    (A) square footage.

    (B) number of occupants.

    (C) number of bathrooms.

    (D) number of bedrooms.

    Correct answer: (D). This can be a tricky question because square footage or the number of occupants seems logical. But the number of bedrooms it is. Check out the section "Sanitary waste disposal" earlier in this chapter if you need to refresh your memory.

9. Odorless, colorless, radioactive gas best describes

    (A) carbon monoxide.

    (B) carbon dioxide.

    (C) radon.

    (D) methane.

    Correct answer: (C). All of the answers are gases, but only one is radioactive: radon.

10. The test done to locate where to place a septic system is called

    (A) a depth test.

    (B) a soils test.

    (C) a percolation test.

    (D) an absorption analysis.

    Correct answer: (C). This is another one of those memorization questions; the term "percolation" is unique to septic system testing (and making coffee, in the world outside of real estate).

5

You Want How Much? Valuation and Financing of Real Estate

Find out the basics of the appraisal process so that you understand market factors that create value. As a real estate professional, you not only need to know the value of property, but you also need to know about the appraisal process to pass the real estate exam.

Know why taxes are collected, how tax rates are established, and how to calculate taxes on a specific piece of property. Get acquainted with the definitions of important tax terms and how tax deductions and credits are figured.

Examine the basics of the mortgage process and the sources of mortgage funding, including several considerations that lenders take into account when making the loans.

Discover different kinds of mortgages and repayment plans, do a little mortgage math, and find out about laws that require everyone to be treated fairly when they try to borrow mortgage money, even if they're 70 years old and want a 30-year mortgage.

Apply some simple math concepts to practical real estate problems. No one likes the math questions on the real estate license exam, but fear not — you learned most of the math on the test when you were in middle school.

Chapter **14**

Appraising Property

An important part of every real estate sale, or for that matter almost every real estate transaction, involves the value of the property. For example, you may need to know the value of a house you inherited for estate tax purposes. Real estate agents (brokers and salespersons) are expected to know something about why one piece of property is more valuable than another. Agents also are expected to know about the methods appraisers use to estimate property values.

This chapter helps you pass the exam by giving you information about market factors that create value. It also discusses different types of value and describes the principal methodologies that appraisers use in their work.

Figuring Out Appraisal Basics

A real estate agent is interested in a property's value for a number of reasons. An agent usually helps a seller set an asking price for a property when it's being offered for sale. An agent representing a buyer often advises his client on the values of properties that are being considered for purchase. Finally, a knowledgeable agent provides important information to the appraiser when she completes the mortgage appraisal.

Knowing what an appraisal is

An *appraisal* is an estimate or opinion of value usually undertaken by a trained individual licensed or certified to do this work based on research in the real estate market. The term *appraisal* refers to the work itself as well as the written product of that work. This definition often appears on state licensing exams and may sometimes be stated simply as an opinion of value.

ASSESSING OR APPRAISING

Many people commonly misuse the word *assessing* when they really mean *appraising*. Assessing and appraising are two different tasks. A real estate appraisal is an estimate of value. A real estate assessment is a certain type of value estimate done for the specific purpose of collecting property taxes. Because a whole chapter on property taxes explains assessments in detail (Chapter 16 if you're really curious), I don't go any further than that here. Just remember, an appraisal isn't an assessment, and the appraiser appraises property and doesn't assess it.

The words "estimate" and "opinion" are important in this definition. Notice, for example, that I don't define an appraisal as a calculation of value. Although appraisers use a variety of mathematical techniques in their work, the act of arriving at the value of a particular piece of property can never be that precise. So appraisers never say that they calculate value.

REMEMBER

An appraiser is a researcher, a private detective. To come up with an estimate, the appraiser investigates the following:

>> **Economic factors:** Employment and interest rates.

>> **Environmental factors:** The presence of pollutants in the area or on the land.

>> **Physical factors:** The real estate's location, size, and condition.

>> **Social factors:** Demand for a particular type of housing (such as demand by an aging population for a certain type of house).

REMEMBER

The property being appraised is called the *subject property*. Although the definition of the term subject property isn't critical for exam purposes, you need to understand the reference whenever you're asked a question that refers to the property being appraised.

Another important item to remember is that the client hires the appraiser to provide an objective opinion of the value of the subject property. Most appraisers work independently on a fee-for-service basis; therefore, they have no interest in what the property value is. Furthermore, the code of ethics and standards that licensed and certified appraisers must follow requires them to reveal any interest in the property they're appraising to the client. Say you find a property you want to buy, and you want to find out whether the asking price is fair. You look in the yellow pages, and hire Mary Appraiser, but it turns out that Mary's mother owns the property. Mary must tell you about her interest in the property or be in violation of the code of ethics and standards.

Seeking an appraisal: Why you need one

Hiring an appraiser for real estate transactions often is a big decision, and many reasons merit such a step. Anytime value is an issue, you may want to have an appraisal done. The following list includes reasons why people most often have appraisals done.

REMEMBER

I cover the details of some of the following subjects in other chapters. For exam purposes, however, what you need to remember from the following information is a general list of why appraisals may be done:

>> **Buying:** Buyers of real estate can hire an appraiser to determine the fairness of the asking price of the property.

>> **Eminent domain:** When the government seizes privately owned real estate for public use through eminent domain, it must pay for the property. The government determines the amount of payment with the help of an appraisal (see Chapter 8).

>> **Estate valuation:** When someone dies, federal or state taxes may have to be paid on the value of the estate. If the estate includes real estate, the property has to be appraised to establish the estate's value as of the date of death.

>> **Exchanges of ownership:** When owners exchange real estate, rather than selling it for money, the appraiser establishes the values of the properties to determine the fairness of the exchange (find information on property exchanges in Chapter 17).

>> **Mortgage approval:** Mortgage lenders, that is, banks, savings and loan associations, and other lenders order the vast majority of appraisals. When buying or refinancing a property, the borrower puts the property up as collateral. If the property owner defaults on the loan, the lender takes the property and sells it. The lender wants to be sure that if the owner defaults, the property value covers the loan. (For more information on mortgages, see Chapter 15.)

>> **Property taxes:** Real estate taxes are based on assessed values, which, in turn, are based on market values. Appraisals are sometimes done for clients who want to argue with municipal (city, town, and village) tax assessors for lower assessed values to obtain a reduction in taxes (I talk about taxes in Chapter 16).

>> **Selling:** People who want to sell their real estate can seek an appraisal to determine a fair and competitive asking price for their property. Most often a seller asks a real estate agent for his opinion of value when preparing to sell a house.

>> **Taxes other than property taxes:** Taxes often are due when someone gives a piece of real estate to someone as a gift. Alternatively, there may be a tax benefit in the form of a deduction if someone gives real estate to a charitable organization. In both cases, an appraiser comes in to determine the property's value.

>> **Various court proceedings:** Bankruptcy, divorce, and the dissolving of a partnership or corporation may all involve real estate holdings. Appraisals usually establish the value of the property in question.

BECOMING AN APPRAISER

Although this book focuses on you becoming a real estate broker or salesperson, people often are interested in what it takes to become an appraiser. Real estate appraising also is a licensed occupation governed by individual state laws, so if you're interested in the field, I encourage you to contact your state licensing authority to obtain the specific requirements in your home state. Some states have separate volunteer boards or commissions for brokers/salespersons and appraisers. Usually, however, the same state department or agency that handles real estate broker/salesperson licenses also governs appraisal licensing.

Prior to 1990, no widespread licensing of appraisers existed, but the savings and loan crisis of the late 1980s changed that after authorities discovered that a lack of honest and competent appraisals was part of the reason why banks loaned so much money on properties that were overvalued.

General information about appraisal licensing can be gotten from the Appraisal Foundation in Washington, D.C. (www.appraisalfoundation.org/). But you should check with your state to see what the local requirements are if you're interested.

Understanding the Importance of Location!

Many things ultimately affect the value of real estate. You've probably heard the classic real estate question: What are the three most important factors in determining real estate value? Answer: Location, location, location. Although not the only factor, location probably is the most important. I discuss this and other factors later in this chapter.

But what does location really mean? And why is it so important? And what about all the other factors affecting real estate value? This section discusses the whats and whys of the location issue and its importance to real estate values.

You can't move it

The most important characteristic of real estate and the reason location is such an important factor in its valuation is the fact that real estate is immobile. Exam questions in this area usually focus on the issue of immobility being the reason location is such an important value characteristic.

Unlike personal property, you can't move real estate. Think about this statement: It's what makes real estate so unique and the location issue so important. Say you own a piece of real estate in a low crime neighborhood. And over time that neighborhood begins to change and becomes somewhat unsafe. You just move the real estate, right? You can sell the real estate and move, but you can't move the real estate itself. What's more, because you can't move the real estate and the environment around it has changed, the value of the real estate probably has changed, too.

Not so with your brand new car. If you think it's unsafe to park on a street, you just park on a different block or in a parking garage.

You're not on Gilligan's Island

The fact that real estate can't be moved makes it particularly vulnerable to the effects of the surrounding area, which can be positive, such as a piece of residential real estate located in what is perceived to be a good school district. The influence on value can be negative if, for example, the real estate is located near a sewage treatment plant. My point is this: You're not on an island. Unless of course you are, in which case you have a 360-degree waterfront view — so who's better off than you?

REMEMBER

Real estate is immobile and highly affected by its surroundings; therefore, I provide the following list of some (but not all) of the environmental factors outside of the real estate itself that may affect value. And this is what is generally meant by real estate location:

>> **Access to employment:** Are there employment centers and therefore jobs available within a reasonable distance?

>> **Amenities and services:** Can you find shopping centers, libraries, restaurants, and so on?

>> **Hazards and nuisances:** Is the real estate too close to gas stations, waste processing plants, or other unsightly or hazardous land uses?

>> **Nearness to transportation:** Are you near highways or public transportation?

>> **Neighborhood compatibility:** The surrounding land uses are similar to your real estate.

>> **Safety:** Make sure the crime levels are as low as possible.

>> **Schools:** You may want to check with neighbors about the perceived quality of the schools. (See Chapter 5 for information about possible fair housing issues when discussing the quality of schools with a client or customer.)

>> **Traffic:** Are the surrounding roadways residential or commercial streets?

REMEMBER

Going into detail on each of these points isn't important, but if you want to pass the exam, remember that many of these factors are relative to the particular piece of property in question. For example, most people don't want their homes located on a heavily traveled street, but if you own a business property, then that is exactly where you want to be located.

You can't make any more of it

The amount of land available is limited. That may seem obvious, but think about it in the context of a car, a chair, or anything else that can be manufactured. You can make more of those products, but you can't make any more land. Only a limited amount of land is available anywhere. That of course doesn't make all land valuable, but it does say something about the value of property wherever people want to be.

If you look at the list in the previous section, I think you'll agree that most people want to live in safe neighborhoods with good schools and easy access to jobs and shopping. However, only so many of those properties are available at any point in time. Given that many people want to live in those neighborhoods, a competition ensues for those pieces of real estate and that competition raises prices.

Arriving at Different Types of Value

Value is value, you say. How could there be different types of value? In most cases you're correct. The type of value that appraisers usually deal with is called market value. But other kinds of value may be unique to a particular situation or a particular person. In addition to discussing market value in a fair amount of detail, this section briefly covers a few of the other types of value that you or an appraiser may encounter.

REMEMBER

Market value is the type of value most often covered in real estate exams. Being able to at least distinguish among the other types of value I cover is important for test purposes.

Going to market . . . value, that is

Market value is the value that appraisers deal with most often. It's the value we're most often concerned with in the typical real estate transaction. *Typical* is a key word here. A typical buyer and a typical seller will establish market value with the price the seller is willing to sell for and the buyer is willing to pay. Keep in mind that both seller and buyer typically know as much about the property as they can, have access to needed expertise like attorneys or home inspectors, act in response to typical motives like wanting a house to live in, and have sufficient time to look at a number of properties that have been on the open market. Anything that changes these typical motivations may change the sale price of the real estate but not its value.

For example, the old family homestead where your grandfather grew up is on the market and you just have to have it for sentimental reasons. Its market value is $150,000. But because you're so anxious to get it you offer and pay $200,000 for it. Its market value is still $150,000 even though the price paid is $200,000. Why? Because your motivation was personal, not typical. Typical buyers would have paid no more than $150,000, because they'd see it only as a normal place to live.

A sale meeting the market value criteria also presumes what is known as an arm's length transaction. An *arm's length transaction* implies that no relationship exists between the parties and that the buyer and seller each act in his or her own best interest. So buying your brother's house wouldn't be considered an arm's length transaction. Most exams ask for this definition, in relation to market value.

Value in use

Value in use is the value a property has to a specific person who may use it for a specific purpose that's generally unavailable to the typical buyer.

Suppose a doctor obtains special permission from the city to use two rooms in a house as a medical office. The typical buyer looks at such a house and puts a value on those rooms for family or personal use, such as a family room or den; however, another doctor looking at that property may be willing to pay a higher price because of his ability to use those rooms as a medical office. The typical buyer pays market value, while the doctor pays a higher price based on value in use.

Investment value

Investment value is the value to a specific investor with a specific plan for the property. Unlike value in use, which generally presupposes a use already in place, investment value assumes a use that may be proposed. Investor A may be willing to pay $3 million for a warehouse to be used as a warehouse. Investor B wants to convert the warehouse to a multiscreen movie theater. Investor B may want to pay only $2 million for the warehouse because of the additional expenses for the movie theater conversion project. Investor B probably would look for another piece of property that meets his investment criteria.

Assessed value

Assessed value is the value placed on a property for tax purposes. It is associated with the term *ad valorem*, which means according to the value. I cover assessed value in Chapter 16.

Creating, Changing, and Affecting Values: Some Economic Factors

Value doesn't just happen; people have to create it. Most of these personal actions, usually called *economic influences,* are nothing more than normal human behavior. In fact, as I go through these influences that affect real estate values, I expect you to say, "Oh! Sure! I knew that" or "Of course people want that." What you may not have known and unfortunately what the test writers want you to know are the technical names for these normal behaviors. The definitions in the following sections are usually covered on the exam, so be sure to remember them.

The test asks two kinds of questions about these economic principles or factors. You'll see questions about the definitions and questions asking you to identify the principle involved based on an example.

Anticipation

All property value is created by the anticipation of the future benefits the property will provide. You buy your house today (and set the price today) so you can enjoy a bigger house for years to come.

Balance

You find a balance between land value and building value in any given area. Overall property values and builders' profits on new homes are maximized when that balance is maintained. For example, in most cases you never want to build a house that costs $100,000 on a piece of vacant land that costs $500,000 (unless of course there was gold on the property; then who cares how much the house costs). No universal magic number exists for the proper balance between land and building value. But in general the balance needs to be similar to that which exists in the surrounding neighborhood.

Change

Change is closely related to anticipation. The idea of change is that nothing remains the same. Physical, governmental, economic, and social changes all affect property value. Physical factors can include environmental changes such as weather, pollution, and earthquakes. Governmental factors may include changes in development regulations like zoning or the construction of new roads. Economic issues may be a change in interest rates or employment levels in an area. Social factors are issues like the aging of the baby boomers. Any or all of these and others can have an impact on the values of properties.

Competition

Competition describes the fact that in real estate, the supply side (developers and builders) tries to meet the demand side (buyers and renters) until their demand is satisfied. A developer may see a need for a new office building in a particular location. If that building is a success, other builders are likely to follow with more office buildings until the last office building a builder erects remains partially vacant because the suppliers have created a surplus of office space.

Conformity

Value is created and sustained when real estate characteristics are similar. If you live in a neighborhood of single-family houses, you don't want an office building to be built across the street from your house. The price of your house probably will be negatively affected by that incompatible land use.

Contribution

In real estate terms, a building or a faucet is worth the value the market places on it, not its cost. You can spend a million dollars building a house, but if it's in the wrong location or has an extremely unusual design, it may not be worth a million dollars. On the other hand, a $1,000 paint job may increase the ultimate selling price of the house by $5,000.

Externalities

Real estate, because it stays in a fixed location, is affected by everything that happens around it. The gas station on the corner, the quality of the schools, the factory that closes in town, mortgage interest rates, and so on all have an impact on the property value.

Highest and best use

The principle of highest and best use states that every property has a single use that results in the highest value for that property. The use must meet four criteria. It must be

>> **Physically possible:** You can't build an airport on a two-acre piece of property. In fact, you can't build a regional shopping center either. But you can build a house or apartment building.

>> **Legally permitted:** You may physically be able to build any of the structures I listed previously, but if the zoning or deed restriction say that all you can build is a store or an office building, then your list of possibilities has just been narrowed considerably.

>> **Economically feasible:** Depending on the market conditions at the time, you may find that one or the other of the physically possible and legally permitted uses isn't economically feasible, which means that you won't make money on that use.

>> **Most (maximally) productive:** If you get to this point in the analysis and you still have at least two uses that meet the first three criteria then you need to determine which use will result in the most value. That becomes your highest and best use. If you get to the economic feasibility criteria and only one use emerges from that analysis, then that's your highest and best use.

Increasing and decreasing returns

Increasing and decreasing (sometimes called diminishing) returns relate to adding improvements to a piece of real estate. Increasing returns come in when an improvement adds more value to the real estate than its cost. A dollar spent gives you more than a dollar back. Decreasing returns occur when an improvement gives back less value than its cost. The principle of increasing and decreasing returns is based on the principle of contribution, which I discuss in the earlier "Contribution" section.

An example of this principle might be adding bathrooms in a new house (or adding them to an old house). My numbers here are for illustrative purposes only. Each bathroom may cost you $6,000, but the first one may net you back $10,000 in terms of value. The second one may net $8,000, and the third one only a break-even $6,000, the fourth one $3,000, and the fifth one nothing. The returns on each bathroom go from increasing the value to creating no additional value. It's obvious that the buyers are putting less and less value on what are essentially unneeded bathrooms.

Opportunity cost

For every investment opportunity you choose, you lose other investment opportunities. So when Auntie dies and leaves you $100,000, you can invest it in real estate. In doing so, you miss the opportunity to invest the money in certificates of deposit at the bank. And if you can get a 4 percent return on your money at the bank, you give up that return by investing in real estate. So you better make at least 4 percent and then some in your real estate investment.

Plottage

The *plottage principle* states that the whole is sometimes greater than the sum of its parts, particularly with respect to real estate. You can put together four individual 5-acre parcels of land, each worth $50,000, to create a single 20-acre piece of property. This larger piece may now enable you to do something with it that was impossible with the smaller pieces, such as building a regional-size shopping mall. It turns out the value of the whole property, or the *plottage value*, is now $300,000 rather than four times $50,000, or $200,000. The act of putting the individual properties together is called *assemblage*.

Regression and progression

You've heard the advice that you should always buy the smallest house in the neighborhood and not the biggest one. If you ever wondered why, it's because the principle of progression says that the higher values of larger homes tend to have a positive effect on the lesser value of the smaller home. Conversely, lower-priced homes have a negative effect on the value of the higher-priced home.

Substitution

This economic principle says that a buyer will try to pay as little as possible for the property that meets the buyer's needs. Given three houses, each of which satisfies the needs of the buyer, that buyer will buy the least expensive house.

Supply and demand

Because only so much land can be found in any particular location, and therefore only so much of anything — houses, stores, office buildings — can be built, the balance between supply and demand affects value. If demand goes up and supply goes down or remains the same, value increases. If demand goes down and supply increases or stays the same, value decreases. Sometimes on an exam the tester mentions only one of these factors, for example what happens to prices or values when housing demand goes up? The implication is that the other factor, in this case supply, stays the same. So don't get confused.

Surplus productivity

After the builder puts together the land, labor, materials, and coordination necessary to build a building and then sells it, the difference between the costs and the selling price is *surplus productivity*. Economists use this term to signify profit.

Finding Value by Analyzing Comparable Sales

The principal approach that appraisers use to estimate property value involves analyzing the sales of other similar properties, called *comparables*. This approach has several names, the most common of which is the *sales comparison approach*. Some people may refer to it as *the market analysis approach* or *the market comparison approach*.

The strength of the sales comparison approach lies in its reliance on the principle of *substitution*. This principle states that no one pays more than is necessary for a piece of real estate that meets that person's needs (see the section earlier in this chapter). The principle of substitution is what most people apply as they search for a house to buy, even if they don't call it that. Because this approach is based on previous sales of similar properties, it can provide an accurate estimate of real estate value. Appraisers use the approach most often when appraising single-family and two-to-four-unit residential real estate. The weakness of the approach is when the market is slow and it becomes difficult to find comparable sales.

Understanding the basics

The idea behind the sales comparison approach is to compare previous sales of real estate to the subject property being appraised to arrive at an estimate of the real estate's value.

EXAMPLE

You ask Joan the appraiser to appraise a three-bedroom, two-bath, 2,500-square-foot house in a typical suburban subdivision. Through her research into the sales in the area, Joan finds three sales of almost identical houses in the last four months. These previously sold houses are called *comparables* or *comps*. Each of the houses sold for $250,000. Joan, by the way, is a very lucky appraiser, because even similar houses don't often sell for the same price. Joan estimates that the value of the house she is appraising is $250,000 based on the fact that three similar homes recently sold for that price. And that is the sales comparison approach at its simplest.

An appraiser normally investigates as many as ten or more comparables, finally selecting a minimum of three to five to use in the sales comparison approach. After making all the appropriate adjustments to each of the comparables (see the next section), the appraiser examines the comparables and arrives at a value estimate for the property. It seldom occurs that the three adjusted sale prices are exactly the same. In this case, the problem is easy because the prices are all the same. Where the prices are different, the appraiser never averages the three prices but rather analyzes the comparables and the various adjustments made, and through experience and trained judgment arrives at the value estimate.

Adjusting the sales price

The situations that appraisers most often have to deal with in applying the sales comparison approach are comparables that aren't identical to the subject property. Appraisers go through an adjustment process to compensate for the differences in the properties.

The adjustment process is really quite simple and pretty intuitive. And the people who write the state tests expect you to understand it and be able to apply it.

EXAMPLE

The subject property is a three-bedroom, two-bath home. Joan the appraiser doesn't currently know the value of this house. A very similar house sold two months ago for $325,000. The comparable house, called Comparable A, is the same in all respects as the subject property except that it has four bedrooms. Comparable A is superior to the subject property. Joan's research indicates that the value of the fourth bedroom is $25,000. That means that the buyer of Comparable A paid $25,000 more for that house than he or she would have for a three-bedroom house.

Joan, when preparing her appraisal report, goes through the process of subtracting that $25,000 bedroom value from the $325,000 sales price of Comparable A. The resulting price of $300,000 is the *adjusted sales price*.

> $325,000 (sale price of Comparable A) – $25,000 (value of fourth bedroom) = $300,000 (adjusted sales price)

Using the principle of substitution, the adjusted sales price for Comparable A, or $300,000, is the estimated value of the three-bedroom house.

EXAMPLE

Now look at an opposite kind of adjustment. Joan is still appraising the three-bedroom, two-bath house. She finds another comparable, which she calls Comparable B. This comparable also is the same as the subject property except that it has only one bathroom. It is inferior to the subject and sold for $290,000. Her research indicates that the value of that second bathroom is $10,000. What does she have to do to make the comparable like the subject? She has to add a bathroom, or more specifically, the value of that second bathroom.

$290,000 (sale price of Comparable B) + $10,000 (value of second bathroom) = $300,000 (adjusted sales price)

The adjusted sales price for Comparable B, or $300,000, is the estimated value of the two-bathroom house.

WARNING

The adjustment process is a matter of adding or subtracting the value of the differences between the subject property and the comparable property to or from the comparable. Take a look at that again, because this part tends to confuse people. You make the adjustments to the comparable to make the comparable property like the subject property. So keep your hands off the subject. The adjusted comparables indicate to the appraiser the estimated value of the subject property.

It isn't old, it's mature: Making age adjustments

When I talk about age, I'm not talking about the age of the appraiser; I mean the age of a structure. The market (that is buyers and sellers) takes the age of a structure into account when deciding on what to pay.

Here's a little brain teaser: The subject property is 5 years old, and the comparable is 15 years old and sold for $190,000; otherwise, the houses are similar. The value of that ten-year difference in age is $5,000. Should you add or subtract that $5,000 from the sales price of the comparable? That's right, you need to add the $5,000 because the 15-year-old house is considered worse than or inferior to the 5-year-old house. For now, I made up the $5,000 figure but in another part of this chapter in the "Finding adjustment values" section, I discuss how you can find the value of an age or any other type of adjustment.

TIP

For some reason, when age numbers are introduced into the problem of making adjustments, the direction (plus or minus) of the adjustment becomes a little muddled. But if you apply the superior/inferior test, it becomes clear immediately. Older is considered worse; therefore, you add the adjustment value to the comparable sale. Newer is considered better; therefore, you subtract the adjustment value from the comparable sale.

Having time to adjust for time

The sales comparison approach is based on previous sales of similar houses (comparables) to indicate the current value of the property being appraised. The word "previous" can cause some difficulty, because real estate values tend to change over time. As recent history has shown real estate values can go up or down.

EXAMPLE

Take a look at an example of what is usually called a time or market adjustment. Once again, Joan the appraiser is appraising a house. She finds a comparable house that is almost identical in all respects to the subject property. The comparable house sold for $300,000 five months ago. Her research indicates that the real estate market has been quite strong in the area and property values have gone up approximately 1 percent per month during the past five months. To properly account for this rise in property values, Joan needs to ask the question, "What would the comparable have sold for if instead of selling five months ago, it sold today?" It would sell for 5 percent more. The adjustment calculation becomes

1 percent per month × 5 months = 5 percent

$300,000 (sale price of comparable) × 5 percent (increase in value for five months) = $15,000 (value of time adjustment)

$300,000 + $15,000 = $315,000 (adjusted sales price)

The adjusted sales price for the comparable, $315,000, is the indicated value of the subject property.

You calculate a downward trend in property values over time the same way, only the value of the time adjustment is subtracted from the sales price of the comparable to give you the value of the subject property.

TIP

And for you mathematical whizzes who are wondering about compounding the 1 percent per month, the common practice is to simply add the monthly increases in real estate value to get a total percentage increase for the period of time you're dealing with.

Figuring adjustment values

By now you're probably wondering where all these adjustment values come from. In fact many of my appraisal students think there's some kind of standardized set of numbers as to how much a bathroom or bedroom is worth. Although no such set of numbers exists, a method for getting those numbers does.

The main way appraisers find the value of an adjustment is by extensively analyzing the market and using a technique called paired sales analysis to find these adjustment values. *Paired sales analysis* is based on the idea that if two houses are similar in all respects except one, and the sales price of each home is different, the dollar amount of difference between the two houses is the likely to be value of the unique attribute or feature of one of the houses. Look at these two houses for an example. House A has four bedrooms. It sold for $400,000. House B, which sold for $360,000, has three bedrooms. In all other respects, House B is the same as House A. The only physical difference between the two houses is the fourth bedroom, along with a monetary difference of $40,000 between the two sale prices. The fourth bedroom, in this case, is worth $40,000

The appraiser can now take that $40,000 figure and use it wherever appropriate to make adjustments to comparables when applying the sales comparison approach to estimating value.

Finding Value by Analyzing Replacement Cost and Depreciation

Another method of estimating the value of real estate is called the cost approach. The *cost approach* is based on the idea that the components of a piece of real estate, or the land and buildings, can be added together to arrive at an estimate of value, if they're valued separately. The cost approach is particularly useful for unique properties that have few comparable sales and for new construction. If you were asked to appraise a church for example, you may use the cost approach because it would be rare to find many sales of churches.

A journey begins with the first step . . . or a formula

The formula for the cost approach is as follows:

Replacement or reproduction cost – depreciation + land value = value

A breakdown of the steps of this method follows:

1. **Estimate the replacement or reproduction cost of the improvement (structure).**

   Turn to the section "Estimating replacement and reproduction costs" for instruction.

2. **Estimate all the depreciation of the improvement (accrued depreciation).**

   See the section "Estimating depreciation" for more info.

3. **Subtract accrued depreciation from the reproduction/replacement cost.**

   Accrued depreciation is the total of all the estimated depreciation.

4. **Estimate the land value separately.**

   Flip to the section "Dirt costs money, too: Estimating land value" to discover the way.

5. **Add the depreciated cost of the structure to the land value.**

   The result is the estimate of value.

Reproduction/replacement cost	$300,000
– Accrued (total) depreciation	– $60,000
Depreciated value of improvements	$240,000
+ Land value	+ $75,000
Estimated value	$315,000

I devote the rest of this section to a discussion of each of these concepts.

TIP

The cost approach has a lot of terminology that may be unfamiliar. Remember, most salesperson's tests ask a lot of definition questions.

Estimating replacement and reproduction costs

Reproduction cost is the cost to construct an exact duplicate of the subject structure at today's costs. *Replacement cost* is the cost to construct a structure with the same usefulness (utility) as a comparable structure using today's materials and standards.

For example, you may use the cost approach to appraise a house with plaster walls. A reproduction cost estimate requires estimating the cost to construct plaster walls. A replacement cost estimate, however, estimates the cost to put up sheet rock walls according to the current standard.

Replacement cost is most often used in the cost approach. Reproduction cost would be used for say historically or architecturally significant structures.

REMEMBER

Two types of costs are included in every construction cost estimate: direct costs and indirect costs. *Direct costs*, also called *hard costs*, are those expenses directly associated with the actual construction of a building, including labor and building materials. *Indirect or soft costs* are expenses not directly related to the physical construction process, including permit fees, architectural costs, and builder's profit. Direct and indirect costs are part of the estimate of the costs.

REMEMBER

You should know the four methods for estimating reproduction or replacement cost. For exam purposes, your ability to distinguish among the four methods by their characteristics is sufficient. Generally, no calculations are required. The four methods include

>> **Square footage method:** Involves calculating the cost of construction by multiplying the square footage of the structure by the construction cost for that particular type of building. For example, you'd multiply a $100 per square foot cost to build the kind of house you're appraising by the 2,000 square foot total area of the house to arrive at a cost estimate of $200,000 to replace the structure. The square footage method is the one more commonly used by appraisers to estimate replacement or reproduction cost.

>> **Unit-in-place method:** Provides the cost to construct a building by estimating the installation costs, including materials, of the individual components of the structure. So if you know you need 1,000 square feet of sheet rock to cover the walls, you need to find out the cost of buying, installing, and finishing the sheet rock on a per-square-foot basis and then multiply by 1,000 square feet. Another approach to this method is to estimate the four main steps (units) to building a house. For instance, cost of foundation, cost of roof and framing, cost of mechanicals, and cost of walls and finish work. Each step is estimated separately and then all are added together.

>> **Quantity survey method:** More detailed than the previous method, it requires you to break down all the components of a building and estimate the cost of the material and installation separately. So in the sheet rock example, you estimate so many dollars each to buy the sheet rock, screws, and tape, and to pay for the installation.

>> **Index method:** Requires you to know the original construction cost (without land) of the subject building, the construction cost index number at the time, and the current index number. You then multiply that original cost by a number that takes into account the increase in construction costs since the building was built. National companies that do this kind of research publish these numbers. If a building cost $100,000 to build originally, the construction cost index at the time of construction was 125, and the current index in that area for this type of structure is 175, the calculation is $175 \div 125 = 1.40$. $100,000 (original construction cost) $\times 1.40 = \$140,000$ to construct the same building today.

Estimating depreciation

Now you've arrived at the second step in applying the cost approach to estimating the value of a piece of property. *Depreciation* is the loss in value to any structure due to a variety of factors, such as wear and tear, age, and poor location, each of which I discuss in this section. I generally view depreciation as the difference in value between the perfect new structure cost that you estimate and the actual value of the structure that's being appraised.

REMEMBER

The term *accrued depreciation* means the total depreciation of a building from all causes. You should also note that accrued depreciation isn't the kind of depreciation that concerns accountants when they depreciate a building or a piece of equipment for tax purposes. Licensing exams generally ask two types of questions about depreciation: A question asking for the definition of a particular type of depreciation and a question giving you an item of depreciation and asking you what type of depreciation that item represents. Occasionally you may get a question that asks you to calculate depreciation using a very simple technique known as the straight-line method. I review that technique in the section "Don't be a square: The straight-line method of calculating depreciation," later in this chapter.

Over the hill: Physical deterioration (curable and incurable)

Physical deterioration is the normal wear and tear that a building experiences as it ages, and it depends on the original quality of construction and the level of ongoing maintenance. The two categories of deterioration, curable and incurable, have more to do with economics than the actual physical possibility of correcting something. As part of applying the cost approach, the appraiser analyzes these items:

>> **Curable deterioration:** Refers to a form of deterioration that's economically feasible to repair. In other words, the increase in value exceeds the cost of repair. Painting is a good example of something that generally adds more value than it costs.

>> **Incurable deterioration:** If the cost of repairing an item surpasses the value it adds to the structure, the item is considered incurable even if you can fix it. Usually these forms of deterioration are physical items associated with the structure of a building — significant foundation repairs probably would be classified as incurable. They're incurable because you wouldn't benefit economically by fixing them

Functional obsolescence

Outmoded design in older structures or unacceptable design in newer structures usually points to a type of depreciation known as *functional obsolescence*. It too is separated into curable and incurable categories relating to economic feasibility. An older home that has four bedrooms but a single bathroom located off the kitchen suffers from functional obsolescence. This example shows incurability because the cost of constructing an entirely new bathroom probably exceeds any increase in value to the house it may generate.

A newer home built with only two bedrooms and a room for a home office would suffer from curable functional obsolescence. Most people want at least three bedrooms. Adding a closet to the home office space and converting it into a bedroom would be relatively easy. So the value of the house increases by an amount greater than what you spent to build the closet.

External obsolescence

External obsolescence is a form of depreciation caused by factors external to the land itself. It's always incurable because land can't be moved. Economically, no amount of money can correct the problem. This form of depreciation can be caused by economic or physical, usually called locational, features. A gas station adjacent to a single-family house is a source of external obsolescence. Unusually bad market conditions can also be considered external obsolescence.

Don't be a square: The straight-line method of calculating depreciation

The straight-line method of calculating depreciation is one of the few math questions you might be asked about the cost approach.

The *straight-line method* for estimating depreciation presumes that a structure deteriorates at the same rate each year. This method, which also is called the *economic age life method,* involves an estimate of what are called the total economic life of a building and its effective age. These numbers are somewhat subjective estimates that appraisers make when using the straight-line method. Don't worry about where the appraiser gets these numbers. For exam purposes, remember the definitions and how to do the calculations. The *economic life* of a building reflects the number of years it contributes to the value of the land. The *effective age* is an estimate of how old the building appears to be, given wear and tear, maintenance, and upgrades. For example, say you have two buildings built 40 years ago, and one has been completely upgraded and well maintained but the other has had little done to it. These two buildings will have different effective ages.

The calculation presumes that a building deteriorates at an equal rate during its economic life; therefore, if you estimate the economic life of a building to be 50 years, in one year it deteriorates 2 percent of its total value. In effect, it uses up 2 percent of its total economic life. The fraction 1/50 also is 2 percent. So the building depreciates at the rate of 2 percent per year because of physical deterioration. Just in case you get thrown a question with a different total economic life, say 40 years, the calculation would be 1/40. If you divide 1 by 40 you get 2.5 percent. Whatever the total economic life, if you divide the number one by the total economic life, you get the annual percentage that the building depreciates.

The next step is where the estimate of effective age comes in. Say the effective age of a building is ten years. That means it has used up ten years of its economic life. If the building's economic life is 50 years and from the previous calculation you know it depreciates at 2 percent per year, all you do is multiply the effective age by the annual percent of depreciation to get the total depreciation. In the example:

10 years effective age × 2 percent per year depreciation = 20 percent total depreciation

The final piece of the formula is multiplying the total percent of depreciation by the reproduction or replacement cost. To continue the example, say your reproduction cost was $100,000. The formula follows as:

$100,000 reproduction cost × 20 percent (0.20) = $20,000 total depreciation

$100,000 reproduction cost − $20,000 depreciation = $80,000 depreciated cost of improvements

For the test, you need to be able to do all these calculations when given the appropriate data.

Dirt costs money, too: Estimating land value

The final step in the cost approach is for the appraiser to develop an estimate of the land value and add it to the depreciated value of the reproduction or replacement cost. Appraisers use a variety of methods to calculate land value. The methods vary with the type of land being appraised and the information available.

The most commonly used method for estimating the value of a single piece of property on which you'd build a house is the sales comparison approach. (For more information, see "Finding Value by Analyzing Comparable Sales," earlier in this chapter.) Features like the land's location, topography, view, and size and shape are compared to arrive at an estimate of value. The intricacies of the various methods of site appraisal are beyond the scope of sales and brokers license exams, so you need not worry about that.

Finding Value by Analyzing a Property's Income

The third method for estimating the value of a piece of real estate involves analyzing the income that a property generates. The *income approach,* as it's called, analyzes the future financial benefits of a piece of real estate and converts it into an estimate of present value. As you may imagine, appraisers use this method to estimate value on properties that are purchased for their investment potential. Properties such as apartment houses, shopping centers, and office buildings usually are appraised using this method.

REMEMBER

The two methods within the income approach that I review are the gross rent multiplier method and the income capitalization method. I show you some calculations, but most exam questions are about definitions and methods. Math questions in this subject area are fair game; although you don't see many, you shouldn't be surprised to see one or two.

Grossing out the rent

The *Gross Rent Multiplier* (GRM) and *Gross Income Multiplier* (GIM) techniques for estimating value are based on the idea that a property value can be calculated as a multiple of the gross rent. These formulas state this succinctly:

> Gross monthly rent × GRM (factor) = value estimate
>
> Gross annual income × GIM (factor) = value estimate

The gross rent is the monthly income of the building with no deductions for expenses. Because single family and smaller residential apartment buildings of fewer than five units depend primarily on rental income, the GRM technique is used for these types of buildings. Larger apartment buildings and nonresidential commercial properties may have income in addition to rentals. In this case, the income used is gross annual income rather than monthly rent and the factor is known as the Gross Income Multiplier (GIM). Other than that, all the formulas are the same.

You're now correctly asking, "So where do I get the GRM or GIM factor?" As with all the data appraisers use, they calculate it based on the market. After getting all the information needed on the subject property, the appraiser researches the market for that type of property, which is usually the local market, to obtain a number of comparable sales. *Comparable sales* are recent sales of similar buildings. After locating a number of similar buildings, the appraiser needs to find the sales price and the gross income of each building. By dividing the sales price of the building by the gross rent, the appraiser obtains a GRM or GIM for each of the comparables. If the buildings are similar, which they should be if they're comparable, the gross rent multipliers also will be similar numbers. *Remember:* If you're dealing with a GRM, you're using monthly rent figures. If you're working with a GIM, the income figures are annual. Here I give you examples of each.

You may want to note that when you leave the classroom and are working on your first million dollars in real estate, buyers and sellers may use these terms interchangeably so you may find yourself talking about a GRM using annual rent numbers. You always need to be clear in your conversations with buyers and sellers in understanding what they and you are referring to. The distinctions I make in the previous section however should get you through the exam.

EXAMPLE

Say you're appraising a three-unit residential rental property. The gross monthly rent of this property is $1,000 per apartment or $3,000 per month for the whole building. You research similar buildings and find three comparable properties that are in the same location, approximately the same size, and that generate approximately the same gross monthly rent. The data is shown here:

Sale price	Gross monthly rent
$200,000	$2,000
$350,000	$3,500
$275,000	$2,750

You now apply the formula for finding the GRM to this data.

Sales price ÷ gross monthly rent = GRM

Applying the formula to the example data, you find that the GRM for each of the comparables would be 100, which means that the comparable buildings each sold for a price that was 100 times its gross monthly rent. The final step is to apply the value formula to the subject property:

Gross monthly rent × GRM = value estimate

$3,000 × 100 = $300,000

Now say you want to estimate the value of a small commercial building whose monthly income is $7,000. You find the following three comparables.

Sale price	Gross Annual Income
$1,000,000	$100,000
$900,000	$90,000
$950,000	$95,000

Using the formula — Sales price ÷ Gross annual income — you'd find that each building sold for ten times its annual income.

Then applying the formula — Gross annual income × GIM = Value — $84,000 × 10 = $840,000.

Note that in the problem I give you a monthly income figure of $7,000. You need to multiply this times 12 in order to arrive at the annual income of $84,000.

The GRM method is particularly useful for small-income-producing properties, such as one-to-four-unit residential properties. The GIM technique is more useful for larger residential properties as well as commercial and mixed-use properties. For more math related to the GRM, see Chapter 18.

Capitalizing the income

Another method for appraising real estate based on its income is known as the *income capitalization approach*. Like the GRM and GIM, this method converts the income of a property into an estimate of its value. Appraisers generally use this method for commercial buildings such as shopping centers, office buildings, and large apartment buildings. The basic formula for this approach, commonly referred to as IRV, is

Net operating income (I) ÷ capitalization rate (R) = value (V)

You can break this formula down into these three steps:

1. **Estimating the net operating income.**

2. **Determining the capitalization rate.**

3. **Applying the IRV formula to arrive at a value estimate.**

Keep in mind that I cover more math related to capitalization in Chapter 18.

Estimating net operating income

The appraiser needs to have access to income and expense statements for the subject building and for similar buildings in the area to estimate net operating income. Having that information on hand enables the appraiser to accurately estimate income and expenses for the building. Remember that all income and expenses in the income capitalization method always are annual figures. You can break down the actual process of estimating the net operating income (NOI) into four steps:

1. **Estimate the potential gross income.**

   Potential gross income is the income that the building generates when rented at 100 percent occupancy, at market rent or lease rent or a combination of both. *Market rent* is the rent that normally is charged for that kind of space in the market place. Lease rent is also known as *scheduled* or *contract rent.* Potential gross income includes adding in income from the principal sources of income for the building, such as rents in an apartment building.

2. **Subtract a vacancy and collection loss figure from potential gross income.**

   This number, which usually is expressed as a percentage, is the appraiser's estimate from the market for these kinds of buildings in the local area, and it reflects normal loss of income caused by nonpayment of rent and periodic vacancies.

3. **Add in other income.**

   Buildings sometimes generate income that is unrelated to or only moderately related to the primary source of income for the building. For instance, a utility company may rent space on the roof for a microwave antenna or the building may have parking spaces that it rents to the public. This is considered other income and is added in at this point. The result is called *effective gross income* or EGI.

4. **Estimate all building expenses and subtract them from the effective gross income.**

   Building expenses fall into three categories: fixed, variable (sometimes called operating), and reserves. *Fixed expenses* are expenses that don't change with the occupancy of the building, like property taxes and insurance. *Variable expenses* are pretty much all other expenses, some of which may vary with the occupancy of the building. These expenses include snow removal, utilities, management fees, and so on. *Reserves,* sometimes called reserves for replacements, are funds that landlords put aside for items that have to be periodically replaced but not on an annual basis. Cooking stoves in an apartment are an example of a reserve item. Note that the expenses don't include mortgage payments or building depreciation.

5. **Subtract the estimated expenses from the effective gross income.**

   The result is the net operating income.

You can put some numbers to these steps to see what the formula looks like:

Potential gross income	$200,000
– Vacancy and collection loss (5 percent of $200,000)	–10,000
+ Additional income	5,000
= Effective gross income	195,000
Expenses	
Fixed	$40,000
Variable	$95,000
Reserves	$10,000
– Total expenses	– 145,000
= Net operating income	50,000

Determining the capitalization rate

A *capitalization rate* is similar to a rate of return, that is, the percentage that the investors hope to get out of the building in income. There are a number of ways appraisers learn to calculate capitalization rates, most of which are beyond what you're required to know. The most straightforward method and the one I teach is pretty simple. All you need are some comparable sales — buildings similar to the subject property being appraised that have sold recently.

The formula you use is

Net operating income (I) ÷ sales price (V) = capitalization rate (R)

This formula is applied using the net operating income and sale price of each comparable that you're analyzing. Note in this formula, the reversal of the IRV formula for finding value (see "Capitalizing the income" earlier in this chapter).

A building sells for $600,000. Its net operating income is $60,000. Applying the formula, you divide $60,000 by $600,000, which looks like $60,000 ÷ $600,000 = 0.10 or 10 percent. Capitalization rates are expressed in percentages.

Although the results may look wrong because you're always dividing a smaller number by a bigger number, remember that you're trying to get a percentage, so the answer always is less than one.

After studying the various capitalization rates that you get after applying the IRV formulas, you select the one you think is the most applicable to the building you're appraising and apply it to the final step.

Applying the formula to estimate value

Now back to the basic income capitalization formula. You can use the numbers from the previous examples to calculate the value:

Net operating income (I) ÷ capitalization rate (R) = estimated value (V)

$50,000 ÷ 0.10 = $500,000

By dividing the net operating income of the subject property by the capitalization rate you have chosen, you arrive at an estimate of $500,000 as the value of the building.

Calculating income

Now don't panic. I didn't slip another step in here. But you may find one other part of the formula that test writers occasionally like to ask about: calculating net operating income. Notice that I said calculating and not estimating.

EXAMPLE

Suppose you have a commercial building that sells for $700,000 and its rate of return or capitalization rate is 8 percent. With that information, you can find out what the net operating income (NOI) is. In this case, you multiply the building sales price or value by the capitalization rate or rate of return.

Value (V) × capitalization rate (R) = net operating income (I)

$700,000 × 0.08 = $56,000

Reconciling a Property's Value

The final step in the appraisal process is coming up with a final estimate of value. When the appraiser uses as many of these approaches as possible, she estimates the final value using a process called *reconciliation*.

REMEMBER

Reconciliation is the process of analyzing and weighing the results of the various approaches as applied to an appraisal problem. It never involves averaging the values. The process first involves looking at each approach and relating it to the kind of property you're appraising. The appraiser relies most heavily on the approach (listed below) that's best suited to a particular kind of property.

>> **The sales comparison approach:** Single-family houses

>> **The cost approach:** Unique properties such as churches

>> **The income approach:** Investment properties such as office buildings

The appraiser uses the other approaches to support the resulting value estimate because the differences among the three individual value estimates usually is not that great.

Finally, the appraiser prepares the report in whatever format is appropriate for the project — usually either a form report, which is how most mortgage appraisals are done, or what is referred to as a narrative report. The form, which was created by federal agencies to provide a standardized way of preparing appraisal information, is known as the Uniform Residential Appraisal Report Form (URAR), or sometimes the Fannie Mae form, for the agency that was most responsible for its creation. A narrative report, which is used mostly for large commercial property appraisals, is like the term papers you did in school and contains more information than a form report.

Review Questions and Answers

The exam questions you're likely to get about appraising are definitional questions and some application questions. Memorizing the terminology and knowing the math will get you through the exam.

1. What approach to value would be most suitable to appraise a shopping center?

   (A) Income approach

   (B) Cost approach

   (C) Sales comparison approach

   (D) Reconstructed value approach

   Correct answer: (A). Real estate that is purchased for investment, such as a shopping center, generally is appraised using the income approach.

2. In the direct sales comparison approach, what type of adjustment should you make when the comparable is better than the subject?

   (A) Positive to subject

   (B) Negative to subject

   (C) Positive to comparable

   (D) Negative to comparable

   Correct answer: (D). Two things to remember here: First, you never adjust the subject, only the comparable. Second, when the comparable is better than the subject, the adjustment is negative.

3. A buyer who buys the least expensive house available to satisfy his needs is behaving according to what economic principle?

   (A) Supply and demand

   (B) Anticipation

   (C) Progression

   (D) Substitution

   Correct answer: (D). Note that this is a short case study question. The test also asks straight definition questions about these economic principles.

4. Reproductions cost is

   (A) used in the income approach to value.

   (B) the cost to construct a building using modern materials.

   (C) the cost to construct an exact duplicate of the building.

   (D) the same as market value.

   Correct answer: (C). Reproduction cost is the exact replacement of the structure. Replacement cost is a structure having the same utility (usefulness) but using modern materials.

5. The rent on a house is $500 per month. The gross rent multiplier is 180. What is the estimated value of the house?

(A) $270,000

(B) $1,080,000

(C) $36,000

(D) $90,000

Correct answer: (D). Gross monthly rent × gross rent multiplier = value.

$500 × 180 = $90,000

Don't multiply the rent by 12. This formula is based on monthly rent.

6. If a building's net operating income is $1,000 a month and an appraiser uses a rate of return of 10 percent, what is the estimated value of the building using the income capitalization approach?

(A) $100,000

(B) $1,000,000

(C) $120,000

(D) $1,200,000

Correct answer: (C). I ÷ R = V

$12,000 ÷ 10 percent (expressed as 0.10) = $120,000

Remember that with the income capitalization approach, you always use the annual income. So the first step is multiplying the monthly income by 12 months. Test writers also sometimes use the term *property* to mean any type of real estate. They also use the term *rate of return* to mean a capitalization rate. Don't be thrown by these references.

7. The reproduction cost of a house is estimated at $120,000. Its economic life is 50 years. Its effective age is 20 years. What is the depreciated value of the house?

(A) $72,000

(B) $48,000

(C) $60,000

(D) $96,000

Correct answer: (A). Read the question carefully (that goes for all questions) and make sure you do every step.

1 ÷ economic life = rate of depreciation per year

$\frac{1}{50}$ = 2 percent per year

Rate of depreciation per year × effective age = total rate of depreciation

2 percent × 20 = 40 percent

Reproduction or replacement cost × total rate of depreciation = total amount of depreciation

$120,000 × 40 percent (expressed as 0.40) = $48,000

Reproduction or replacement cost − total amount of depreciation = depreciated value

$120,000 − $48,000 = $72,000

8. A subject property has four bedrooms. A comparable has three bedrooms and sold for $160,000. In all other respects the properties are alike. The value of the fourth bedroom is estimated to be $20,000. What is the indicated value of the subject?

(A) $180,000

(B) $160,000

(C) $80,000

(D) $140,000

Correct answer: (A). If the comparable is worse than the subject, you add the adjustment amount to the comparable. The comparable has one less bedroom than the subject. So you add the $20,000 value of the bedroom to the comparable.

9. A comparable sold for $110,000 five months ago. You estimate that real estate values have been rising at 1 percent per month during that period of time. How much is an identical house worth today?

(A) $5,500

(B) $116,600

(C) $104,500

(D) $115,500

Correct answer: (D). 5 months × 1 percent per month = 5 percent

$110,000 × 5 percent (expressed as 0.05) = $5,500

$110,000 + $5,500 = $115,500

10. What appraisal approach would an appraiser most likely use to appraise a sports arena?

(A) Cost approach

(B) Income capitalization approach

(C) Gross rent multiplier approach

(D) Sales comparison approach

Correct answer: (A). Sports arenas are fairly unique, and you can seldom find comparable sales. Stadiums also are built as service-type buildings rather than investment properties. The cost approach most often is used for unique real estate.

Chapter **15**

Finding the Money: Mortgages

t's no secret that most people don't buy property for cash. They borrow money from banks, savings and loan associations, and other lending institutions so they can buy a home or investment property now rather than waiting to save up the money. Even the governmnet helps by allowing a certain amount of the interest on a real estate loan to be deducted when filing your income taxes. Part of a real estate agent's work deals with advising buyers where they may be able to borrow money to buy property. Because of all the various types of mortgages and repayment plans, real estate agents also need to be familiar with the idea that when it comes to mortgage money, one size does not fit all. Although in most cases, real estate agents ultimately refer buyers to banks and other lending institutions or mortgage brokers to get the financing they need to purchase a house, familiarity with many of the details of real estate financing is important to provide sound advice to buyers.

This chapter takes a look at the basics of the mortgage process and the sources of mortgage funding. I cover several considerations that lenders take into account when making the loans. You discover different kinds of mortgages and repayment plans, do a little mortgage math, and find out about laws that require everyone be treated fairly when they try to borrow mortgage money, even if they're 70 years old and want a 30-year mortgage.

The Way Things Work: Mortgage Basics

The place to start a discussion about real estate financing is with some basic concepts and terminology. In this section, I cover the basic mortgage process, review some important terms, discuss several mortgage theories, and give you the scoop on conditions included in a mortgage. After you understand how real estate financing works and get used to some of the terms, specific mortgage concepts will fit in pretty nicely. All of this information probably will be covered on the exam, especially the definitions and maybe a little math.

The nuts and bolts of the mortgage process

A buyer and a seller agree on a price and the other terms involved in the sale of a house. The buyer has some of the money in cash, say about 20 percent of the total price, for a down payment but needs to borrow the rest. The buyer goes to a bank or other lending institution to apply for a loan for the rest of the purchase price of the house. The lender considers these two things when examining the buyer's application:

>> The ability of the buyer to repay the loan, which includes factors like the buyer's credit and employment history.

>> The value of the real estate being purchased, which is usually determined by an appraisal, a topic that I discuss in Chapter 14. Most work in the appraisal industry involves estimating property values for mortgage purposes. Because property is considered security for the loan, lenders want to be sure that the property can be sold to pay off the loan if necessary. (See "Considerations for Lenders Accepting Mortgages," later in this chapter, for more.)

The lender issues what is known as a mortgage commitment, and on the day of closing (that's when title to the property changes hands — see Chapter 9), the buyer also closes on the mortgage loan. Closing on the mortgage simply means entering into the final and formal agreement to accept the money and pay it back. The check from the bank is given to the seller, and a short time later, the buyer begins paying off the loan under the terms of the mortgage agreement.

Liens, notes, and a mistake most people make

Although you may sign a whole bunch of papers at the closing, the two important documents you'll sign as part of the mortgage process are the note and the mortgage. I explain these and some other terms associated with mortgage loans in this section. Definitions are important here for test purposes, and basic definitions will guide you to an understanding of each term and choosing the right answers on the exam.

The process of using property as security for a loan is called *hypothecation.* In real estate circles, that process is accomplished through a *mortgage,* which is a document prepared by a lender and signed by the borrower (at the closing) that essentially serves as a *voluntary lien* on a piece of real estate. Liens are financial obligations that are attached to real estate. Remember, through hypothecation the owner of the property voluntarily places a specific (meaning that property only) lien on the property in favor of the lender without giving up possession of the property. When the mortgage is signed by the borrower, the property is committed as security for the loan. A mortgage lien enables the lender to sell the property after a foreclosure process, to pay off the debt, if the borrower *defaults,* or does not pay off the debt. For more about what's included in a mortgage agreement, see "Common conditions of a mortgage loan" later in this chapter. For more about liens, see Chapter 8.

The second document that the borrower signs as part of the mortgage loan process is called a promissory note (or sometimes just *the note*). A *promissory note* is an agreement to repay a loan according to certain terms and conditions.

STATE SPECIFIC

A *trust deed* is used in some locales to secure a mortgage loan. A trust deed also is called a deed of trust. For a deed of trust to work, a third party must be involved. The *trustor* (or borrower) gives a deed to a *trustee* (the third party). The deed gives title to the property, without the right of possession. This type of title sometimes is referred to as bare or naked title. The trustee holds the deed until the loan is paid off. The property then is reconveyed back to the trustor. If the trustor doesn't complete the terms of the loan, the trustee conveys title to the property to the *beneficiary* (the lender) for sale to satisfy the debt. (For more about trust deeds, see Chapter 9.) Now that you know about mortgages and notes allow me to clear up a common misuse of the word you just learned about — mortgage. In fact, the misuse is so common that I even hear real estate agents using it the wrong way. And in the meantime, you'll discover two other important words related to mortgages that can get you in trouble on the exam.

So, you're thinking, the buyer goes to the bank and applies for a mortgage. Wrong! Well, then, you say, "The bank gives the buyer a mortgage." Wrong! "So," you simply say, "I'm going to get a mortgage to buy my new house." Wrong, again!

Yes, wrong on all three accounts, and yet those are the things most people say, including virtually everyone in the real estate business. Why these commonly used phrases are wrong and the right way to describe the process are the focus of two words that you absolutely need to remember — mortgagor and mortgagee.

REMEMBER

You go to the bank to borrow money. In return for that money, you agree to give the bank a mortgage on your property. Remember, the mortgage is a voluntary lien that enables the bank to take the property and sell it, if you don't pay back what you borrowed. Thus, because you're giving the mortgage to the bank, you are the *mortgagor,* and because the bank accepts the mortgage in return for lending you the money, it is considered the *mortgagee.*

Compare mortgagor and mortgagee with the words lessor and lessee in a lease situation. The lessor is the landlord. The landlord provides the lease to the tenant, or the lessee. The thing to remember about the words mortgagor and mortgagee is that *borrowers are mortgagors because they give the mortgages to the banks, which accept them and therefore are the mortgagees.* And I tell my students that if they get that one wrong on the exam, I'm coming to their houses and telling their neighbors on them.

I have a theory . . . on mortgage loans

STATE SPECIFIC

The differences in how mortgage loans affect property ownership are more theoretical than practical, and so they've been boiled down into the three theories in the list that follows. You need to be sure to find out which of the theories your state follows.

>> **The lien theory:** Under the *lien theory,* the mortgagor (borrower) retains both the legal title and equitable title to the property. The mortgagee (lender) is granted a lien on the property. *Legal title* is the title or ownership that normally transfers in a property sale. *Equitable title,* which is fully explained in Chapter 11, gives the holder of the equitable title the right to force the transfer of title when all the conditions of a contract are met. Under the lien theory, the mortgagee must go through the legal process of foreclosure to get legal title to the property to be able to sell it for nonpayment of the debt. (For more about foreclosure, see "Shut down: Foreclosures" later in this chapter.)

>> **The title theory:** In the *title theory,* the mortgagor gives legal title to the mortgagee but keeps equitable title. Because the mortgagee already has title, gaining possession of the property for sale to repay the debt is more direct than under the lien theory.

>> **The intermediate theory:** Based on title theory, the borrower retains title to the property and the mortgage is a lien. If the borrower defaults on the loan, title is conveyed to the lender. *Intermediate theory* makes the mortgagee go through the foreclosure process before the property can be sold to repay the debt.

Common conditions of a mortgage loan

Like any business arrangement, the terms and conditions of a particular mortgage loan can differ from those of any other mortgage loan. But most mortgage loan arrangements have a number of terms and conditions in common and some of them may show up on the exam, so I give you some definitions and explanations in this section that you may want to remember.

A job (or a few) to do: Duties of the borrower

In a typical mortgage loan, the borrower commits to a number of obligations that are written into the mortgage or note documents. These include:

>> Paying off the debt under the conditions as specified in the note, which includes the interest rate and payment schedule.

>> Indicating the property that the mortgagor (borrower) is using as security.

>> Paying all real estate taxes on the property.

>> Getting permission from the lender before doing any major repairs, alterations, or demolition.

>> Protecting the lender's interest by maintaining a property hazard insurance policy on the property in case unforeseen damages occur.

>> Adequately maintaining the property.

You didn't do your duty: The acceleration clause

Mortgage loan agreements frequently include stipulations that are known as *acceleration clauses*, which effectively protect the lender from a loan for which the borrower is in default. *Default* is a situation in which borrowers don't fulfill the obligations of their mortgage loan agreements (see the previous section). An acceleration clause takes effect when the buyer is declared in default. The *acceleration clause* enables the lender to require the entire debt to be repaid immediately. Yep, you read that right. So, if you defaulted on the $100,000 loan that you were going to pay off over 30 years, it may be due in full — tomorrow, that is, if your mortgage agreement includes an acceleration clause. Remember the word *acceleration* means to speed up, and that's what happens to the loan. The payments are sped up so that the entire amount is due immediately. Moral of the story: Don't default. But just in case you do, you can read about foreclosures in "Endings You Didn't Anticipate: Foreclosures, Assumptions, and Assignments," later in this chapter.

Point taken: Points on mortgage loans

The normal interest on most home mortgage loans is paid out over the life of the loan, but sometimes lenders charge additional interest at the beginning of the loan that is based on the amount of the loan. This additional interest is called *points* or sometimes *discount points*. A point equals 1 percent of the loan amount, and that's something you don't want to forget, because it's a common math question. And remember, a point is not 1 percent of the sale price of the house, but 1 percent of the loan amount — unless, of course, the borrower is in the unusual position of being allowed to borrow the entire price of the property.

EXAMPLE

A bank agrees to make a mortgage loan of $100,000 to a property buyer. The bank agrees to a lower-than-normal annual interest rate on the condition that the buyer pay 2 points to the bank at closing. How much does the buyer have to pay in points?

$100,000 × 0.02 = $2,000

This additional prepaid interest usually results in a lower interest rate for the loan as it is paid up. For example, a lender may charge you a 7 percent interest rate with no points but give you a 6.75 percent interest rate, if you pay 1 point at the beginning of the loan. Throughout the loan's life, the lower rate means you pay about the same total amount of interest, but your monthly payments are slightly lower, and the *yield*, or overall profitability of the mortgage as an investment, stays appealing to private investors. Lenders often sell mortgages to investors to raise more money to make more mortgage loans.

The combination of the interest that is paid along the way plus the points charged in prepaid interest combine to form the *annual percentage rate* (APR), which is the real interest rate you're paying.

When points are paid to lower the interest rate, it's called a *buydown*. The buydown can be applied to lower the interest rate over the life of the loan or for a specific period of time, like the first year or two. Borrowers who use their buydowns to lower the interest rate during the short term usually are anticipating larger incomes later on during their loan repayment schedules. Builders of new homes may pay points to lower the interest rate for a few years to attract buyers to their development. When a seller pays this, it's usually referred to as a *seller incentive*.

Points sometimes are used to calculate loan *origination fees*. A borrower may pay one or two points — 1 percent or 2 percent of the loan amount — to the lender for administrative charges associated with the loan. This payment, however, won't reduce the interest rate on the loan. Origination fees sometimes are paid to mortgage brokers, who are individuals who don't lend their own money but rather arrange loans between borrowers and lenders.

Points are sometimes paid to *lock in* the interest rate for a period of time. Say interest rates look like they're going up. A borrower may want to assure himself that the interest rate in effect at the time he applies for the loan is the same rate in effect at closing. The bank usually charges a fee for this, sometimes using points to calculate how much to charge for the *rate lock*.

A long account: Escrow

An *escrow account*, which is required by most lenders, is an account held by the bank on behalf of the borrower that is used by the lender to pay the taxes and insurance on the property. The lender normally calculates a monthly payment that includes the mortgage payment and a portion of the annual taxes and insurance costs. This is the payment the borrower makes each month to the bank. The bank pays itself with the mortgage payment and accumulates the tax and insurance portion in the escrow account, making the appropriate payments as they come due. You can check out some mortgage payment calculations in "Comprehending Mortgage Repayment Plans" later in this chapter.

Tax liens are first in priority ahead of all other liens (see Chapter 8). That means if the property is sold for nonpayment of the mortgage loan, and taxes are due on the property, the taxes get paid first. If not enough money is left over from the sale to pay the mortgage loan, the lender can be stuck with the loss. To avoid this situation, the lender handles the payment of taxes, and because the lender also wants to make sure that its interests are protected in the event of damage to the property, it also collects escrow money from the property owner and sees to it that the borrower's homeowner's and mortgage insurance premiums are paid. When someone buys a piece of property with a mortgage loan, the lender may collect a substantial sum of money at closing to establish the escrow fund. You may see other terms on an exam that mean the same thing as escrow account, including *reserves, impounds,* and *trust accounts.*

Examining Sources of (and Insurance for) Funding

One of the important pieces of information that a real estate agent can provide a buyer is where to go for a mortgage loan, but oddly enough, it isn't something that exam writers ask questions about beyond distinguishing between the primary and secondary mortgage markets, which is what I'm going to tell you about right here. The *primary market* is composed of the lenders who lend money to people who want to buy property. The primary market is where you go to get a mortgage loan. The *secondary market* is composed of financial institutions to which the banks sell the mortgages to get more money to lend to you. You can find out more about the primary and secondary mortgage markets in the two sections that follow this one. So, I'll just define some terms related to the primary and the secondary markets so you can make some sense of the topics in the rest of this chapter, which exam writers do ask questions about. On a related note, I also cover different federal loan insurance programs and private mortgage insurance in this section.

As you get into who provides the money for mortgage loans, you need to understand a few terms because they relate as much to where you get the money as they do to the terms of the loan itself. The terms I discuss relative to mortgage loans — conventional, conforming, and nonconforming — relate to the down payment, which is the cash you put into the purchase of the property, and the qualifying ratios the banks use, which are the amounts of money they think you can afford to pay for a mortgage loan. These terms further relate to whether the lender (primary market) can sell the mortgage to the secondary market. One note as you read this section: The lender and the primary mortgage market is the same thing.

>> **Conventional loan:** These loans meet certain guidelines that can be set by the lender but often comply with standards set by Fannie Mae in the secondary mortgage market. You can read about Fannie Mae in "Number two: The secondary mortgage market" later in this chapter. The general terms are that the total amount of the loan won't exceed certain limits and typically that the borrower can borrow no more than 80 percent of the value of the property involved — although higher limits are possible. Conventional loans essentially are loans made within normal guidelines by lenders in the primary mortgage market. By the way, as far as I know, no such thing as an unconventional loan exists.

>> **Conforming loan:** This loan meets the criteria necessary for it to be sold in the secondary mortgage market. The way conforming loans are set has to do with the amount of money the borrower can spend on monthly payments. I help you do a little math in "Comprehending Mortgage Repayment Plans" later in this chapter so you can see how the numbers work with this concept.

>> **Nonconforming loan:** Here's a loan that doesn't meet the criteria of the secondary mortgage market. These loans may be made by lenders under specific circumstances and may include extra requirements that the borrower must meet, but they cannot be sold on the secondary mortgage market. How this works is that Fannie Mae, for example, sets a guideline that says a borrower can spend no more than 28 percent of his or her monthly income on the mortgage payment, taxes, and insurance. If the lender (primary market) chooses to lend an amount of money that requires the borrower to use 30 percent of his or her monthly income for those payments, the lender has just made a nonconforming loan that cannot be sold to Fannie Mae (secondary market); however, it may be sold to private investors who buy mortgages for the income from the interest payments that they generate.

Number one: The primary mortgage market

The *primary mortgage market*, which sometimes is referred to as primary lenders, is where consumers — you and I — go to borrow money to buy real estate. Although all of these institutions make loans directly to the public, some specialize in large projects, commercial properties, or residential properties. The list of typical primary lenders includes the following:

>> **Commercial banks and savings and loan associations:** These lenders are sometimes collectively referred to as institutional lenders. These institutions lend money for anything from the purchase of a single-family house to a regional shopping center. These institutions are one of the principal places the average consumer goes to borrow money to buy a house.

>> **Credit unions:** These institutions primarily are oriented toward lending money to the average homebuyer — consumers. Credit unions can be very popular for these types of loans, depending on the amount of assets upon which they can rely and the interest rates they charge.

>> **Insurance companies:** These lenders tend to specialize in lending for large projects, such as the construction or purchase of large office buildings or shopping centers. The average homebuyer wouldn't borrow money from an insurance company to finance the purchase of the property.

>> **Investment groups:** These groups of individuals or companies pool their money to make mortgage loans. They lend money for large real estate projects rather than to individual homebuyers.

>> **Mortgage banking companies:** These companies are set up by investors specifically to make mortgage loans. Unlike banks or credit unions, they don't generally offer other banking services.

>> **Pension funds:** Pension fund managers may lend money from their fund's assets for the construction of large real estate projects or purchases. Pension fund loans tend not to be made to individual home purchasers.

STATE SPECIFIC

Mortgage brokers usually are considered to be part of the primary mortgage market, even though they don't lend money directly for mortgages. A mortgage broker is similar to a real estate broker, except that instead of bringing a buyer and seller together, a mortgage broker brings a borrower and lender together. Be sure to check out the basic requirements for becoming a mortgage broker in your state. The key elements you're looking for are whether licensing or registration is required with some state agency, the state agency involved, and whether you must meet any financial, educational, or experience requirements under state law. In the wake of the financial downturn in the housing market in 2008, states have tightened up their policies regarding mortgage brokers. Exam writers like to ask a question about the criteria to be a mortgage broker and what mortgage brokers do.

Number two: The secondary mortgage market

The *Federal Reserve System* (the Fed) is a key player in financial markets that affect the availability of money for real estate mortgage loans. The system is regulated by two factors that have direct effects on the money that's available for mortgage loans. They are

>> The *reserve requirement* for banks, which is the requirement that the Fed imposes on banks to maintain a specified amount of their assets as reserve funds in cash. The reserve funds may not be used for loans. By increasing or decreasing the amount of money needed for reserves, the Fed can control the levels of money that are made available for mortgage loans.

>> The discount rate, which is how the Fed controls the flow of money. It sets and adjusts the *discount rate,* which is the rate of interest that member banks charge each other for loans between banks. Whenever the discount rate is high, interest rates on consumer loans increase and vice versa. The rate charged to the consumer impacts the way many people choose to borrow money for real estate purchases or refinancing and how much they can afford to borrow.

Banks and savings and loan associations get their money from you and me, their depositors, insurance companies get it from the premiums consumers pay, and investments groups get it from investors. Although that probably sounds pretty obvious, think about what happens when banks run out of money, or to be more precise, when their loans exceed their deposits. The *secondary mortgage market,* which buys loans from banks and other primary lending institutions, was created to prevent such a problem from happening. Although details of these transactions are fairly complicated, the essence really is pretty simple. A primary lending institution collects, packages, or pools (they all mean the same thing) its mortgage loans. These loans have value because the notes on which they're based are promises to repay specific amounts of principal and interest, plus they're backed up by a mortgage that enables the lenders to sell the properties if the debts are not repaid. The secondary market lenders pay the primary market lenders for these mortgage loans, which provide new money for the bank to lend to yet another group of home buyers. After the loans are acquired by the secondary market, the payments of the borrowers go to the secondary market institutions; however, the primary mortgage market institutions frequently retain a fee for servicing the loan, or collecting the monthly payments and sending them on to the secondary institutions.

REMEMBER

The three major (and one minor) players in the secondary mortgage market are organizations that either are directly or indirectly associated with the federal government. The following list explains some of the major characteristics with which you need to be familiar when being tested on information about the secondary mortgage market:

>> **Fannie Mae:** The Federal National Mortgage Association, or Fannie Mae, is a privately owned corporation chartered by Congress. Fannie Mae sells stocks and bonds to raise money to buy conventional bank mortgage loans. Although Veterans' Administration (VA) and Federal Housing Administration (FHA) loan programs are mortgage insurance programs (rather than direct loan programs) that insure mortgage loans made by lenders, Fannie Mae does deal in these types of mortgages in the secondary market. Fannie Mae is the leading purchaser of mortgages in the secondary market. It generally sets limits on the specific amounts of the mortgage loans that it buys. Any loan above those limits is referred to as a *jumbo loan.*

>> **Ginnie Mae:** The Government National Mortgage Association, or Ginnie Mae, is a government agency administered by the U.S. Department of Housing and Urban Development. Ginnie Mae provides investors with an opportunity to invest in mortgages by selling pass-through certificates to investors. With these certificates, principal and interest payments are paid to investors as a return on their investments in the program. Ginnie Mae works primarily with Fannie Mae in secondary mortgage market activities. Don't be thrown on an exam if you see the words "tandem" or "piggyback" associated with these two agencies. It means they're working together.

>> **Freddie Mac:** The Federal Home Loan Mortgage Corporation, or Freddie Mac, is a privately owned corporation that also provides a secondary market for mortgages. It sells bonds to raise funds to purchase mostly conventional mortgages.

>> **Farmer Mac:** The Federal Agricultural Mortgage Corporation, or Farmer Mac, serves as a secondary mortgage market for farm loans.

TIP

You may want to remember the names of the agencies in the previous list by associating female names, Fannie and Ginnie, mostly with FHA and VA loans, and male names, Freddie and Mac, with conventional loans.

See your uncle . . . Sam, that is: Federal loan insurance programs

The federal government sponsors a few programs that offer insurance coverage for mortgage loans. The real estate exam may include a question or two about these programs starting with the fact that they are loan insurance programs and not direct loan programs.

A conventional loan usually must be accompanied by a down payment, frequently as much as 20 percent of the value of the property that's being purchased. The two reasons for requiring a down payment are that it provides for:

>> A financial commitment on the part of the borrower. Buying property isn't all about using the bank's money; some of it has to be from you, the borrower, too.

>> A cushion between the bank and possible declines in property values. When the value of a property declines, if the lender can't sell that property for its original appraised value in a foreclosure, the lender loses.

Suppose, however, that a lender is assured of getting back all of the money that it loans out for a property, even if it lends 100 percent of the value of that property. Wouldn't the lender be inclined to lend more money on the property, relative to its value? Enter the federal government with insurance programs that guarantee that the bank will get back its money from the loan. So when borrowers don't have enough money to make down payments required by their lenders, they may seek a loan insured by the FHA or VA.

STATE SPECIFIC

Some state-run government direct-loan programs or loan guarantee programs may be operating in your state. If so, they may be fair game for questions on your state's real estate license exam. At the very least, those questions may refer to a state program as one of the potential answers to a multiple-choice question, so check out your state's programs.

The Federal Housing Administration

The Federal Housing Administration (FHA) is an agency under the supervision of the U.S. Department of Housing and Urban Development that insures loans made by primary lenders. Even though you may hear it referred to as an FHA loan, the FHA never directly makes any loans. The most commonly used FHA program is called a 203(b) loan. The numbering refers to the section of the law that governs such loans. Here are a number of the rules for this program (some of which you may see on a real estate exam):

>> FHA loans are limited to owner-occupied, one-to-four-family houses.

>> The buyer at closing pays a fee called a *mortgage insurance premium* (MIP). The MIP is based on a percentage of the loan.

>> An FHA-approved appraiser must make an estimate of the property's value. Standards govern whether the condition of the property and the neighborhood qualify for FHA assurances.

>> FHA-backed loans have high loan to value (LTV) ratios. Down payments may be as low as 1.25 percent for lower-priced homes. (For more about LTV, check out the section "Considerations for Lender Accepting Mortgages" later in this chapter.)

>> Upper-end limits on property value are in effect, and they vary from one state to the next and from one area to the next within the states.

>> Other borrowers may assume some FHA loans. The rules vary with the original date of the loan.

>> Lenders may not charge a prepayment penalty. Prepayment penalties are explained in the "Open mortgage" section later in this chapter.

>> Lenders may charge discount points, or additional fees, for the loan. The payment of these fees may be negotiated between buyer and seller.

The Department of Veterans Affairs

The Department of Veterans Affairs (VA) provides a loan guarantee program to eligible veterans and their spouses. Eligible primary lenders make the loans, and the VA guarantees all or part of the loan if the borrower defaults. Some of the important features of a VA guarantee are as follows:

>> The VA sets the rules for eligibility. Generally those eligible are veterans of military service who served during specific periods of time and their eligible widows.

>> The loans may require little or no down payment.

>> The loan guarantees cover owner-occupied, one-to-four-family homes, including mobile homes.

>> A Certificate of Reasonable Value (CRV) is required from an approved appraiser. The amount of the VA guarantee is based on the CRV. Although no dollar limits are set on the price of the home being purchased, the VA limits the amount of the loan that the VA will guarantee. The borrower may pay the difference in cash.

>> No prepayment penalty is permitted.

>> VA-backed mortgages are assumable under certain conditions.

>> A funding or origination fee is charged to the borrower to be paid to the VA.

The Farm Service Agency (FSA)

The Farm Service Agency (formerly the Farmers Home Administration) is an agency of the U.S. Department of Agriculture that sponsors programs targeted at agricultural and rural areas. It guarantees loans made by primary lenders and lends money directly to borrowers.

A private matter: Private mortgage insurance

When making a mortgage loan that has a high loan to value ratio (LTV) (for more about LTV, refer to the "Checking out the property value" section later in this chapter), the lender is lending a large percentage of the value of the property, and the borrower is making only a small down payment. In these circumstances, for its protection, the lender may require *private mortgage insurance* (PMI), which is insurance coverage that the borrower purchases that protects the lender, if the borrower defaults on paying the loan. PMI usually can be dropped when the borrower's equity in the property has increased to acceptable levels. *Equity* is the difference between the value of the property and all debt attributable to the property. Terms for PMI vary from lender to lender, and some states even established laws regarding PMI. The federal government enacted a law for loans made after July 29, 1999, that requires that lenders must drop PMI, if the borrower requests it when the borrower's equity has risen to 20 percent or more. The law further requires that PMI be automatically dropped when borrower equity reaches 22 percent. Private mortgage insurance is obtained from private mortgage insurance companies.

Considerations for Lenders Accepting Mortgages

A primary lender has two considerations when it is making a loan for the purchase or refinancing of real estate: the value of the property and the borrower's ability to pay off the debt. In checking out the value of the property, lenders want to be assured that if their borrowers can't pay off their mortgages (default), they (the lenders) can sell the properties and get back the money they loaned to the borrowers. Assuming the property value is sufficient to guarantee the loan, a lender wants to make sure that the borrower can make the monthly payment, including taxes and insurance, for the life of the loan.

Checking out the property value

The value of the property has a direct effect on the amount of money the lender will lend you, and you need to be prepared to do a math problem about this topic on the state exam. The percentage of value of the property that can be borrowed is called the *loan to value ratio* (LTV), an amount that is set by the bank and the secondary mortgage market. (See "Number two: The secondary mortgage market" earlier in this chapter.) The value of the property is based on an appraisal (see Chapter 14). In the event that an appraised value and selling price are different, the amount of money that can be borrowed is based on the lower of the two numbers. And yes, that means that if you're paying more than the appraised value for the house, your down payment will be higher than expected. Because you may encounter a problem about LTV calculations, here are some examples.

A property sells for $400,000. Its appraised value is $400,000. The LTV ratio for the mortgage is 80 percent. How much money will the bank lend? What down payment is required?

$400,000 (appraised value) × 0.80 (80 percent) = $320,000 mortgage amount

$400,000 – 320,000 = $80,000 down payment

Notice that after the $400,000 in the calculation, I used the term appraised value and not sale price. The reason I did this becomes evident in the next problem, which shows what happens when the sale price and the appraised value are different.

The sale price of the house is $315,000. The appraised value is $300,000. If the bank offers an 80 percent LTV ratio, what down payment will be needed?

$300,000 (appraised value) × 0.80 = $240,000 mortgage amount

$315,000 – $240,000 = $75,000

A final problem shows you how to calculate the LTV, if you're given value and loan information. Say the bank will lend you $240,000 on a property valued at $300,000. What is the LTV ratio?

$240,000 ÷ $300,000 = 0.80, or 80 percent

Note that in these problems I use the appraised value to calculate the amount of the mortgage, and then I subtract the mortgage amount from the selling price to find out the down payment that's needed. In doing a problem like this, just take the numbers for what they are. Don't get hung up thinking about things like whether you'd try to renegotiate the price or maybe not buy the property at all. These types of questions are about understanding the LTV concept and the use of value rather than sale price to calculate the mortgage amount. And don't worry if the values of the properties on the state exam don't seem realistic to you. Remember these are statewide exams. I've lived in two states where the prices of real estate vary wildly from one part of the state to another.

Examining the borrower's ability to pay

The second type of calculation involves determining how much a buyer can afford to pay for a mortgage loan. You need to understand some of the terminology and how it works.

REMEMBER

The lender uses a qualifying ratio to determine what a borrower can afford to pay for a mortgage loan. When using a *qualifying ratio*, you work backward from the buyer's gross income, usually using monthly numbers for principal, interest, tax, and insurance expenses to arrive at what the buyer can afford to spend on housing every month. You need to note that the acronym used for the payment of *principal, interest, taxes, and insurance* is *PITI*. When lenders do affordability calculations, they use PITI as the total monthly expense for mortgage loan payment calculations.

For example, a lender may say that a buyer can afford to pay 28 percent of total gross income in monthly payments (principal, interest, taxes, and insurance expenses). This percentage is called the *front-end ratio.* The lender also establishes that the borrower's total monthly debt payments, including PITI, can't be greater than 36 percent of the borrower's total gross income. This percentage is called the *back-end ratio.*

You may or may not find a qualifying ratio calculation question on the exam, but calculating them is a service that real estate agents routinely provide for their customers and clients. And just in case you'd like to do your own calculations, here's an example.

EXAMPLE

Say you make $96,000 a year. Using the fairly standard qualifying ratios of 28 percent for principal, interest, taxes, and insurance (PITI) and 36 percent for total debt, how much can you afford to pay for PITI per month?

$96,000 × 0.28 = $26,880

$26,880 ÷ 12 (months) = $2,240 maximum monthly PITI

Alternatively, you can do the calculation this way:

$96,000 ÷ 12 (months) = $8,000

$8,000 × 0.28 = $2,240

Now where, you ask, does the 36 percent back-end ratio come in?

$96,000 × 0.36 = $34,560

$34,560 ÷ 12 (months) = $2,880 maximum total monthly debt payments including PITI

Together, the front-end and back-end ratios work in such a way that the borrower's PITI and total debts have to fall below both criteria. So, if in the example, the borrower's total monthly long-term (usually 12 months or more like credit cards and car payments) debt payments without PITI were $2,000 a month, the lender would allow the borrower to spend $880 or less on PITI. On the other hand, if the borrower has no other debt, the lender still wouldn't allow the borrower to spend more than $2,240 on PITI.

Whatever amount of money is available for PITI, the lender uses that amount to calculate how much of a mortgage the borrower can afford to pay off.

Grasping the Different Types of Mortgages

Although a specific mortgage loan may not be available for every possible situation, enough variations are around to cover most people's real estate needs. And although mortgage professionals can and will help your clients and customers, real estate agents nevertheless are expected to know about the types of loans that are available for particular situations. That expectation translates into exam questions, so pay attention to the purposes and characteristics of the types of mortgage loans that I describe in the following sections so you can pick out the one that answers your exam question correctly. As a practical matter, knowing this information can help you make recommendations to a buyer who may not realize there is a mortgage product out there that can help her buy the property. And get you a commission.

Blanket mortgage

A *blanket mortgage* is a loan that covers more than one piece of property. It sometimes is used to finance a subdivision development. (See Chapter 8 for more about subdivisions.) Say, for example, that a builder buys six lots on which he plans to build houses and sell them. The lots are in an already-approved subdivision. The builder may want to use a blanket mortgage to finance the purchase, because it usually comes with a *partial release provision*. Remember that a mortgage is a lien on the property. (I also discuss liens in Chapter 8.) A *partial release* is a provision that allows the lien to be removed separately from each parcel as it is sold to a buyer and the bank is paid a portion of the loan amount.

Construction loan

A *construction loan* is made to finance a construction project. A typical case is when someone who owns property hires a builder to build a house. Money from the loan is released to the builder at certain points as the project progresses. At the end of the project, the loan generally is converted to a conventional mortgage.

Home equity loan

A *home equity loan* seeks to use the equity that a mortgagor has built up in a property either for improving the property or for some other use. *Home equity* is the difference between the value of the property and the debt attributed to the property. For example, say someone paid $200,000 for a house. Ten years later, the house was appraised at $300,000, and the mortgagor has $100,000 left to pay on the mortgage.

$$\$300,000 - \$100,000 = \$200,000 \text{ equity}$$

Home equity loans are granted with various terms and conditions. The most common types provide for either a flat amount of money to be taken out or for a line of credit to be created. The borrower can withdraw money from the line of credit as needed. Sometimes the borrowed funds can be paid back and withdrawn again like a revolving fund. Home equity loans have become popular as an alternative to the second mortgages to which they are related.

Open mortgage

An *open mortgage* is a mortgage loan that can be paid back at any time without a prepayment penalty.

STATE SPECIFIC

A *prepayment penalty* is a fee that is charged by a lender whenever a mortgage is paid off earlier than its normal schedule. This fee can vary from one mortgage to another and from one state to the next. You need to determine what, if any, laws your state has adopted regarding prepayment penalties in conventional (non-federally guaranteed) mortgages. Some states have limited the use of prepayment penalties, so check it out.

Open-end mortgage

An *open-end mortgage* is a loan that can be reopened and borrowed against after some of it has been paid down. For example, you can borrow $150,000 via a mortgage loan with an agreement in place that after you pay some of it down, you can borrow back up to the $150,000 limit again.

Package mortgage

A *package mortgage* is a loan that covers real estate and personal property being sold with the real estate. The buyer of a house in which furniture is being included in the sale may want to apply for a package loan. For example, this loan can be used to purchase a furnished vacation home.

Purchase money mortgage

The *purchase money mortgage* is the mortgage loan used to buy real estate. The term sometimes is used to mean the mortgage that a seller takes back as part of the sale price of a property. When a seller sells his property for $300,000, and the buyer has $50,000 cash, is approved for a $150,000 mortgage loan, but still falls $100,000 short, the seller can agree to take back a mortgage worth $100,000 to make the deal happen. In effect, the seller is extending $100,000 worth of credit to the buyer, which will be paid according to the terms of a promissory note the buyer signs with the seller. The mortgage is called a second mortgage and will be in second position to be paid off if the property has to be foreclosed and sold for nonpayment of the debt. Sometimes this second mortgage is referred to as a *purchase money mortgage*.

STATE SPECIFIC

State governments set rates for interest that cannot be exceeded — called the usury rate. These seller second mortgages may not be subject to the usury limits that are set by state law, so you need to verify that information in your state. Mortgages made by lenders (not sellers) are subject to these limits. However, if the interest rate is artificially low, the Internal Revenue Service (IRS) may calculate imputed interest. The *imputed interest rate* is the interest rate that the IRS says should have been charged based on market conditions. The IRS will increase the tax owed by the seller/lender accordingly, as though the seller had been charging the higher interest.

Reverse mortgage

Reverse mortgages sometimes are called *reverse annuity loans*. These loans enable a property owner to use the equity in the property (see "Home equity loan," earlier in this chapter, for more) without selling the property. Money may be paid out in periodic payments, a lump sum, or a line of credit up to a certain amount of the owner's equity in the home. No payment is due on the loan while the owner still lives in the house. These loans often are used for income by senior citizens on fixed incomes with large amounts of equity in their homes. They're usually paid off by the sale of the property after the homeowner dies or moves out.

Sale leaseback

A *sale leaseback* isn't actually a mortgage, but can be a source of project financing and a means of obtaining the equity in a property. It traditionally is mentioned in any discussions about real estate financing. Usually used in commercial property situations, an owner-occupant uses a sale leaseback to sell the building but agrees to remain in the building under a lease. The new owner has a tenant and the old owner has gotten his money out of the building to use.

Shared equity mortgage

The *shared equity mortgage* allows for a share of the profit on the property to be given to someone else in return for help purchasing the property. A relative, investor, or lending institution may agree to provide funds for a down payment or help with the mortgage payment. In return, when the property is sold, a predetermined share of the profit is given to the person who provided the financial help.

Temporary loan

A *temporary loan*, also called *interim financing, bridge loan, swing loan,* or *gap loan,* is used when funds are needed for short periods of time to complete a real estate transaction. A typical situation where a temporary loan may be used is when a seller is selling one house and plans to use the proceeds from the sale to buy another house. If that individual has to complete the purchase of the new house before the sale of the old house is complete, a temporary loan can come to the rescue. Money is borrowed just long enough to buy the new house and then paid off with the proceeds of the sale from the old house.

Wraparound mortgage

A *wraparound mortgage* is a new mortgage that literally wraps around an old mortgage. A seller sells a property to a buyer, but the seller doesn't pay off an existing mortgage. The buyer gives a new, larger mortgage to the seller. This new mortgage includes the amount due on the original mortgage. The buyer makes payments on the new mortgage to the seller. The seller, in turn, makes payments on the old mortgage to the lender. This mortgage is used when the old mortgage won't be paid off at the time of the sale of the property.

Comprehending Mortgage Repayment Plans

One key way that loans vary is in how they are paid back. Before I explain, I need to tell you about fixed and adjustable interest rates, which will make describing several different repayment plans and doing the math the exam writers want you to know a little easier. Pay careful attention to the terminology and definitions as you go through this material, and remember that what I'm telling you about here are the terms of the note that the borrower signs, even though most people refer to it as the mortgage.

Putting the various payment plans into perspective means that I need to give you the quick version of Banking 101. A bank (any lender really) has no money of its own. People invest their money in savings accounts and other interest-bearing instruments like certificates of deposit, and they expect to receive a return on or yield from those investments. The bank, on the other hand, lends that same money out and charges interest on the loans. Part of the interest payments go to the depositors and part of them are used to operate the bank. Your former economics teacher may have made it sound more complicated because many rules, regulations, and economic conditions obviously affect banking more than I'm letting on. But the essence of the loan process is just that — the bank acting as a middleman between depositors and borrowers.

REMEMBER

When people borrow money through mortgage loans, they must pay back the *principal*, which is the amount they borrowed, and the *interest*, which is what the bank charges you to use its depositors' money. The interest rates charged for mortgage loans vary with economic conditions, but they're often less than the interest rates on other types of loans. Mortgage loans, however, frequently are made for large sums for long periods of time. Because of the length of time the money is used, the total interest paid can be substantial. Depending on the interest rate and the length of the mortgage term, they can be even larger than the principal amount itself. As you go through the types of repayment plans, keep this in mind: The mortgage loan and the terms of the note aren't satisfied until the principal and interest are paid back to the lender.

It's in your interest: Fixed and adjustable rates

For a long time the only type of payment plan available to a borrower was a fixed interest that never changed throughout the life of the loan. As economic times changed, it became apparent that a more flexible approach would better serve both the borrower's and the lender's needs. The particular terms and conditions of any mortgage loan are, of course, fixed by the lender within the parameters of applicable law, but some general descriptions apply to both types of payment plans. And that's what I give you here — some basics that the exam writers want you to know.

Fixed-rate mortgages

A fixed rate of interest means that throughout the lifetime of the loan, the interest rate and the amount of the monthly mortgage payments do not change. What does change, however, in an amortized loan (see the next section) is the amount of principal and interest in each monthly payment. On a mortgage loan, interest is charged on the unpaid balance of the principal. So as you pay off the principal each month, the amount of interest being charged actually declines. And because the payments remain the same, the amount of principal you pay off each month increases.

For illustration purposes only, say you borrowed $200,000 in a 30-year mortgage loan. The amount of the interest rate is moot for purposes of this example. Your monthly payment on the loan turns out to be $1,330 for 360 months (that's 30 years × 12 months). The first payment may consist of $1,170 in interest payment and $160 in principal payment. The amount of interest is so high at this point, because you're being charged interest on the entire $200,000 loan. What that also means is that after you make that first payment, you still owe the bank $199,840 ($200,000 − $160 principal payment). Because the principal has been slightly reduced, the amount of interest owed that second month is slightly less than the first month. And because the monthly payment remains the same, the amount of principal paid off is slightly more than the first month. By the time the last payment rolls around, 30 years later, the situation essentially will be (almost) reversed, with $1,170 applied to payment of the principal and $160 applied toward the interest.

Adjustable-rate mortgages

An *adjustable-rate mortgage* (ARM) is a mortgage for which the interest rate is subject to change during the life of the loan. An ARM can be an amortized, straight, or partially amortized loan (see the next sections for these definitions). Although the specific terms of an ARM are contained in the note, you need to be familiar with its general features.

The interest rate for the loan is tied to the *index*, a rate over which the lender has no control. A federal treasury bond rate or other federal rate of some sort frequently is used as the index. The borrower's interest rate then is calculated by adding a predetermined rate called a *margin* to the index. For example, if the index rate is 4 percent and the margin is 3 percent, the borrower's rate is 7 percent. As the index changes, so does the borrower's rate.

The borrower's rate at any point in time for an ARM loan usually is subject to two limits that are called *caps* or *ceilings*, including:

>> The *annual cap*, which limits the amount that an ARM's interest rate can be adjusted upward in any given year. For example, if you start with a total rate of 4 percent (1 percent index plus 3 percent margin) with an annual cap of 2 percent and the index goes up by 3 percentage points, the resulting interest rate would total 7 percent (3 percent margin plus 4 percent index); however, because the 2 percent ceiling (the annual cap) is in place, the interest rate can increase by only 2 percent per year to a maximum total rate of 6 percent for that year. If the index increases beyond the annual cap in any given year, the additional increase usually can be carried over to the next year.

>> The *lifetime cap* or *ceiling*, which limits the total upward adjustment that the lender can make to the interest rate during the life of the loan, regardless of how high the index goes. Say, for example, you start out at a total rate of 4 percent and the lifetime cap is 5 percent. That means the highest the rate can ever be is 9 percent.

Another condition of the loan to be aware of is when the loan adjusts. Some loans adjust every year, others less often. Also some adjustable loans can be or are automatically converted to fixed rate loans after a specific period of time, for example five years.

A *payment cap* also can be put in place in an ARM, meaning that even if the rate adjustments reach their maximum each year, if the resulting monthly payment increases to more than a specified amount, that payment cap keeps the payment within reasonable limits. In some cases, however, exercising the payment cap can lead to *negative amortization*, which means the loan balance increases by the amount owed but not paid. So if the adjustment in a particular year brings your payment up to $1,500 a month but you have a payment cap of $1,400, you won't have to pay the higher payment; however, that extra $100 a month you're not paying may be added on to the total balance you owe, in effect increasing your loan amount.

Doing the math: Amortized loan

The most popular type of loan that buyers use to purchase homes is an *amortized loan*, or *direct reduction loan*. The primary feature of an amortized loan is that at the end of the *loan term* (the period during which the bank has loaned you the money), the loan is completely paid off. In other words, the borrower has completely paid the interest and principal of the loan. Each payment you make, usually monthly, is made up of principal and interest (see the earlier section "Fixed-rate mortgages"), so that you owe the bank nothing at the end of the loan term. When you have an amortized loan, making additional principal payments or converting the loan into bi-weekly payments rather than monthly payments usually is possible. In both cases, by reducing the principal at a more rapid rate, although the future payments remain the same, the interest rate component decreases and the principal component increases, thus reducing the total amount of interest being paid over the life of the loan. Remember you're always paying interest on the unpaid principal balance. Prepaying principal also reduces the length of time you'll be paying the mortgage.

STATE SPECIFIC

State laws may also allow the bank to impose a prepayment penalty on you for making early payments. You need to check out what your state allows in terms of prepayment penalties.

The monthly payments can be looked up in mortgage tables, which show you amortization (or payoff) rates for various percentage interest rates over a variety of loan terms in increments of $1,000 of loan amounts. (You can also do this through various online mortgage payment calculators; just do a search for *mortgage calculators* and take your pick!) But if you want to know the amortization rate for $1,000 at 6 percent interest for a 25-year mortgage, you can look it up in the table, and you'll discover that the factor is $6.44 per month. That factor is the amount of money it takes per month to pay off principal and interest on a $1,000 loan over a period of 25 years. So if you're borrowing $150,000, you simply drop three zeroes (the same as dividing by $1,000), and you get 150. Multiply that times the factor you looked up and see what you get.

$$150 \times 6.44 = \$966$$

The $966 from the equation is the monthly payment it takes to amortize a fixed-rate loan (pay off principal and interest at the same time) of $150,000 at 6 percent for 25 years.

REMEMBER

One other thing that you definitely need to note is that mortgage loan interest rates always are quoted on an annual basis. So the interest is a certain percent a year. In the event that an exam question wants to know the monthly rate all you do is divide the annual rate by 12.

Exam writers rely on a series of math problems to test your skills calculating different aspects of an amortized mortgage. Here are examples of the more typical of these kinds of problems. (Check out Chapter 18 for more mortgage math, including ways to figure out annual and monthly interest payments.)

Finding the monthly payment when you're given a mortgage factor

EXAMPLE

You borrow $200,000 for 30 years at an interest rate of 5 percent. The mortgage factor is $5.37. What is the monthly payment necessary to amortize this loan?

$$\$200,000 \div \$1,000 = 200$$

$$125 \times \$5.37 = \$1074$$

Remember that the mortgage factor is the amount of money needed on a monthly basis to amortize (pay off principal and interest) on a $1,000 loan at a given interest rate over a given period of time. In this example, 5.37 (it's often written without the dollar sign) is the amount needed to pay off a $1,000 loan at 5 percent for 30 years. But because you're borrowing $200,000, you have to divide by 1,000 to find out how many units of $1,000 are in the loan amount. Multiplying this amount by the factor gives you the answer.

Seeing how much the first month's interest is

You borrow $150,000 for 25 years at 4 percent interest in an amortized loan. How much interest do you pay in the first month of the loan?

1. $150,000 × 0.04 (4 percent) = $6,000 first year's interest

2. $6,000 ÷ 12 months = $500 first month's interest

Remember that you're always paying interest on the unpaid balance of the loan and interest rates always are quoted on an annual basis. So in the first month, you're paying interest on the entire unpaid balance of $150,000 at 4 percent interest. The first calculation gives you the total interest for the year. The second one gives you the first month's interest. Note that this calculation works only for the first month, because after that, you've already paid off a portion of the principal, so now you're paying interest on a lower principal.

Finding the principal balance owed after the first payment

EXAMPLE

I used the same numbers as I did in the last example so you can see how that problem can have an added component, if you're given some additional information.

You borrow $150,000 for 25 years at 4 percent interest in an amortized loan. The monthly payment is $792. How much of the principal do you owe after you've made the first payment?

1. $150,000 × 0.04 (4 percent) = $6,000 first year's interest

2. $6,000 ÷ 12 months = $500 first month's interest

3. $792 (principal and interest payment) − $500 (interest) = $292 principal

4. $150,000 (original principal) − $292 (first month's principal) = $149.708 principal owed after the first month's payment

In Step 1, you find the total interest due for one year. Remember the mortgage interest rate is an annual rate. In Step 2, you find out the first month's interest by dividing by 12. In case you're wondering, this step works only for the first month in any 12-month period. In Step 3, you find out how much principal is contained in that first month's payment. You're given the total monthly payment, which is made up of principal and interest. If you take away the interest, you're left with the amount of principal you're paying that month. In Step 4, you subtract the first month's principal payment from the original amount of the loan, and you're left with the remaining balance of the principal.

Finding the total interest on the loan

Another type of exam problem that sometimes gives people a hard time is the calculation of total interest paid over the life of the loan.

You borrow $200,000 for 30 years at 4 percent interest. It's an amortized loan, and your monthly payments are $954.83. How much interest will you pay over the life of the loan?

1. $954.83 × 360 (12 months × 30 years) = $ 343,738.80 total payments of principal and interest over the life of the loan.

2. $343,738.80 (total principal and interest) − $200,000 (loan principal) = $143,738.80 interest over the life of the loan.

If you took a minute and tried to do this problem before you looked at the answer, I'll bet you tried somehow to use the 4 percent interest rate. Almost everybody does, but it's useless information in this problem, because I already gave you the monthly payment amount.

In Step 1, you calculate everything you pay over the life of the loan. In Step 2, you subtract the principal from the total of what you pay. Remember that the payment you make each month, and therefore the total of the payments you make, are both principal and interest, so if you subtract the principal, what you have left is the interest.

On the straight and narrow: Straight loan

A *straight loan* (also called a *term loan*) calls for the payment of interest only during the term of the loan. At the end of the period of the loan, a single payment of the principal is required.

Say you borrow $300,000 to buy a commercial property on a straight loan at 5 percent interest with a term of 20 years. You'd pay $15,000 ($300,000 × 0.05) in interest each year for 20 years. At the end of the 20 years, you'd have to make a single payment to the bank of $300,000, which repays the principal. These loans are used more often for commercial properties than they are for residential properties and may be fixed rate or adjustable rate. See "Comprehending Mortgage Repayment Plans" earlier in this chapter for more about repayment plans. Commercial property owners who sometimes sell their property after five or ten years may want this type of mortgage, because unlike the homeowner, they're not necessarily interested in paying off the property.

A good mix: Partially amortized loan

Partially amortized loans are combinations of amortized loans and straight loans (see the two previous sections). Unlike the straight loan, a portion of each monthly payment of a partially amortized loan goes toward reducing the principal and toward paying interest. However, at the end of the loan term, unlike the fully amortized loan, some unpaid principal remains. This amount is paid off in a single payment called a *balloon payment*. These loans may have interest rates that are either fixed or adjustable and are more typically used for nonresidential purchases but nonetheless can be used to buy a house.

Fast times: Growing equity mortgage

A *growing equity mortgage* (GEM) uses a fixed interest rate but payment of principal increases (more than normal amortization) over time. As such, this type of repayment plan enables the borrower to pay off the loan faster. The GEM loan sometimes is called the rapid payoff mortgage, which you shouldn't confuse with a bi-weekly payment plan or making extra principal payments. I discussed both of those in the section "Doing the math: Amortized loan," earlier in this chapter. The GEM has a scheduled increase in principal payments that may, for example, be tied to the borrower's expectation of increasing income during the life of the loan.

Endings You Didn't Anticipate: Foreclosures, Assumptions, and Assignments

There's lots of good news in owning real estate. Unfortunately there can be some bad news, too; it's usually associated with what happens when you can't pay and the lender takes your property in a foreclosure. In addition, assumption and assignment involve new parties in the mortgage. The main things to remember about these three things for the exam are the differences among them and a few of the main characteristics of each.

Shut down: Foreclosures

When a borrower defaults on a loan, the lender may have to institute foreclosure proceedings. *Foreclosure* is the process by which the lender takes over ownership of the property and sells it for nonpayment of the debt. Mortgages may contain an *acceleration* clause that enables the lender to declare the entire balance due after the borrower is declared in default (the number of missed payments that result in default is set by the bank). Declaring the loan due in full makes the foreclosure process easier, because the entire debt is due right away and must be satisfied by sale of the property unless of course the borrower wins the lottery and pays off the loan. Any funds left after all the debts associated with the property are paid go to the borrower.

STATE SPECIFIC

If your state has a homestead act in place, the borrower may be entitled to a certain amount of money, the rest going to pay unsecured debts like credit card bills. See if your state has a homestead act in place and what the provisions are.

Foreclosure can occur in one of several ways:

>> **Judicial foreclosure,** which is where the court orders property to be sold as a result of a foreclosure action brought by the lender. This type of foreclosure is the most common. And you can remember it by relating the word judge as in judicial.

>> **Nonjudicial foreclosure,** which only some states permit, can apply to both deed of trust situations and mortgage loans. (You can read about deeds of trust earlier in this chapter in "Liens, notes, and a mistake most people make.") Nonjudicial foreclosure involves filing a notice of default in the county recorder's office and providing appropriate public notice, usually through the newspapers. After that, the property is sold to pay off the debt.

>> **Strict foreclosure,** which is an action that is permitted in some states, and requires that appropriate notice be given to the borrower and a period of time established by the courts during which the borrower may pay off the debt. If the borrower fails to meet the deadline, title to the property transfers to the lender. In this case, the sale of the property isn't specifically required by the court.

Many people mistakenly believe that whenever the lender forecloses on a property for nonpayment of the loan, the borrower automatically is off the hook. If, however, the lender cannot sell the property at a price that covers the entire debt, the lender can go to court and sue the borrower for the remainder of the debt. If the lender's suit is successful, the court enters a *deficiency judgment* against the borrower, who must then cover the portion of the mortgage loan debt that the property sale didn't cover. In the case of VA and FHA insured loans, this may not be true because insurance is in place to pay off the loan.

In the event of a default for nonpayment of the debt, depending on the state, the borrower may have a right of *equitable redemption,* a right that exists after foreclosure but before the sale of the property. During a specified time frame, the borrower may pay off the debt and reclaim the property. In other states, another similar time frame is effective just after the sale. During that time, the borrower can pay the debt and reclaim ownership of the property. This right to redeem the property after the sale is called a *statutory right of redemption.*

Sometimes a buyer voluntarily signs the property over to the lender by executing a deed to avoid a foreclosure action. This *deed in lieu of foreclosure,* or *a friendly foreclosure,* has a major downside from the lender's point of view. In a regular foreclosure action, all *junior* or *subordinate liens,* or liens on the property that are paid after the mortgage lien, effectively disappear. However, in a deed in lieu of foreclosure, junior liens remain in place and can become the responsibility of the next buyer. To make matters worse, the lender usually also loses any rights to FHA, VA, or private mortgage insurance. (See the section "See your uncle . . . Sam, that is: Federal loan insurance programs" earlier in this chapter for more about VA and FHA loan guarantees and private mortgage insurance.) The deed in lieu of foreclosure is not a particular type of deed (see Chapter 9 for more about deeds) but rather is whatever type of deed to which the borrower and the lender agree.

When an existing mortgage loan on a property is not being paid off and a lender is making a new loan on the property, that lender will require the first mortgage (the first lender) to execute a *subordination agreement* to protect itself from all other mortgage lien holders. This allows the new loan to move into first position for payment if a foreclosure becomes necessary. For example, real estate agents sometimes refer to the Bank of Mom (that's your mother) lending you $100,000 to buy a house, and you giving her a mortgage to secure the loan. Later on, the value of your house increases to $200,000, and you want to borrow $100,000 from the bank to do some work on the house. The bank probably will make you get your mother to sign a subordination agreement, so that if you default on your payments and the bank forecloses on the property and sells it, the bank will get paid first and then your mother. Sometimes the bank simply increases the total loan amount to cover the new loan plus pay off the old loan, so that once again the bank is in first position to be paid in the event of a foreclosure.

Who owes whom? Assumption and assignment

A *mortgage assumption* takes place when a new party takes over the obligations of another person's mortgage debt, and it usually requires the approval of the lender. A typical situation in which someone may assume a mortgage is when a buyer buys a house from a seller who has a mortgage loan at a much lower interest rate than is currently available to the buyer. The buyer pays the seller the difference between the sale price and the outstanding balance of the seller's mortgage (which the buyer is assuming) either in cash or with a new mortgage. By assuming the old mortgage, the buyer also agrees to take over the payments on the remaining balance due.

REMEMBER

When buying a property, you need to recognize the important distinction between taking over someone else's mortgage loan obligations by *assuming a mortgage* and by purchasing the property *subject to the mortgage*. This distinction makes a difference if during a foreclosure, not enough money is raised from the sale of the property to cover the debt.

>> If a property is purchased with the buyer *assuming the mortgage,* the buyer becomes personally liable for the portion of the debt not covered by the foreclosure sale. Say I buy a house for $200,000 paying the seller $100,000 cash and assuming a mortgage on which there is $100,000 left to pay. I lose my job, can't pay my mortgage, and to make matters worse, real estate values have plummeted. The lender forecloses and can sell the house only for $90,000. The lender holds me personally responsible for the remaining $10,000 of the mortgage debt that the sale of the house did not cover.

>> If the property has been bought *subject to the mortgage,* then the buyer is not personally responsible for the remainder of the debt owed by the seller. In some cases the original owner may be liable. Say I buy a house for $200,000 with $100,000 cash to the seller subject to the seller's mortgage, which has an unpaid balance of $100,000. I lose my job and on top of that real estate values take a nosedive. The lender forecloses, and because of lower real estate values, can sell the property for only $90,000. The lender can't hold me responsible for the $10,000 not paid by the foreclosure sale.

When someone is assuming a mortgage or paying off a mortgage early, the borrower (mortgagor) asks for a certificate from the mortgagee stating the amount that currently is due on the loan so that they know exactly how much is due on the loan. This statement is called an *estoppel certificate* or *reduction certificate.*

An alienation clause in the mortgage loan agreement helps lenders prevent or control future assumptions of a mortgage loan by a new borrower. The *alienation clause,* which also is known as a *due on sale clause, call clause,* or *resale clause,* requires the borrower to pay off the loan in full immediately upon sale of the property. Instead of requiring immediate payment in full, the lender can permit the new buyer to assume the mortgage. If the original mortgage loan's interest rate is lower than the current market rate for the type of loan being sought, the lender may grant permission to assume the loan only at a rate closer to or at market levels.

An *assignment* of a mortgage is the change in the person or institution to whom the debt is owed on a mortgage without changing the terms of the loan. The *assignee,* the new debt holder, is entitled to payment of the debt just as the original lender was. If this is confusing remember that assignment involves a change in the mortgage, that is, the lender. Assumption involves a change in the mortgagor, the borrower.

Being Fair: Consumer Protection Laws

As the government passed laws eliminating discrimination in housing, it also looked at discrimination in financing real estate purchases. Likewise, it also passed consumer protection laws designed to inform consumers just what they're getting into when borrowing money. In this section I explain these fair lending and consumer protection laws. Get to know the names of these laws and what they cover to get you through any exam questions.

Also don't forget to check out Chapter 9 for information about the Real Estate Settlement and Procedures Act (RESPA).

The Community Reinvestment Act

In 1977, the federal government passed the *Community Reinvestment Act* (CRA). This legislation required banks to address the financial needs of the communities where they are located, by making funds available for mortgages and other types of consumer loans to people within their service areas and to make periodic reports indicating activities that were undertaken with respect to providing loan opportunities to residents of the area.

The Equal Credit Opportunity Act

The *Equal Credit Opportunity Act* (ECOA), enacted in 1975, prohibits discrimination in the granting or arranging (for example a mortgage broker) of credit. Lenders are prohibited from discriminating on the basis of age (must be of legal age), color, dependence on public assistance, marital status, national origin, race, religion, and sex. The act further requires that people who are not granted a loan must be given the reason why they were turned down. It also prohibits discrimination against an applicant who may have used some right under the Consumer Credit Protection Act, usually the Truth in Lending Act, which you can read about a little later in this section.

The National Affordable Housing Act

The *National Affordable Housing Act* requires that borrowers must be notified whenever the servicing of their loans is transferred to another institution. Borrowers must be notified of the transfer at least 15 days before it becomes effective.

The Truth in Lending Act

The *Truth in Lending Act* is the popular name for the federal *Consumer Credit Protection Act.* This act was implemented by *Regulation Z* of the Federal Reserve Board. In practice, these three names are used interchangeably when referring to this piece of consumer protection legislation. The regulation applies to all real estate credit transactions for personal (home) or agricultural purposes but not for commercial properties. The primary purpose of the act is to require that creditors provide information to consumers so they can make informed decisions about the use of credit in real estate transactions. Creditors are defined in the act as people or institutions that make more than 25 loans per year or provide credit more than five times a year, if the loans use real estate as security.

The act provides for what is referred to as a *three-day right of rescission* in most consumer credit transactions. This right enables consumers to change their minds within three days after closing on the loan. This right does not, however, apply to purchase money mortgages, first mortgages, or deed of trust loans. You can read about these types of loans in detail in the earlier section "Grasping the Different Types of Mortgages," but these are loans that are used to buy property. Refinancing loans, such as home equity loans, are covered by the rescission provision of Regulation Z.

Advertising of real estate financing is heavily regulated by this act. If details about financing are presented in an ad, then the annual percentage rate (APR) must be stated. You can read more about APR in the section "Point taken: Points on mortgage loans," earlier in this chapter.

In addition, if the advertisement mentions any *trigger terms*, then additional regulations kick in that require more detailed information to be included in the ad. The trigger terms are the following:

» Amount of any payment, such as the monthly mortgage payment.

» Dollar amount of the finance charge, that is, the interest rate.

» Down payment.

» Number of payments.

» Term of the loan, that is, how long the loan is for.

If any trigger terms are mentioned in an ad, then it must also contain the following information:

» Annual percentage rate (APR)

» Cash price (amount of the loan)

» Down payment necessary

» Number, amount, and due dates of all payments

» Total of all payments to be made

The penalties for violating Regulation Z range from penalties paid to the consumer based on the finance charge to fines of up to $10,000 per day and jail time of up to a year.

A few of the provisions of the Truth in Lending Act have been combined with provisions of the Real Estate Settlement and Procedures act to further protect consumers who obtain mortgages. Chapter 9 discusses it in greater depth.

Review Questions and Answers

Questions about mortgages include definitions and terms, distinguishing between types of mortgage and how different mortgages are used, different payment plans, and mortgage math calculations. I give you questions that use key words involving definitions as well as short case studies.

1. Borrower Sam gets a loan from a bank to buy a piece of property and offers the property as security for the loan. Which of the following is true?

   (A) Sam is the mortgagee and gives a mortgage to the bank.

   (B) Sam is the mortgagor and gives a mortgage to the bank.

   (C) Sam is the mortgagee and gets a mortgage from the bank.

   (D) Sam is the mortgagor and gets a mortgage from the bank.

   Correct answer: (B). Look through all these answers very carefully. The lender gives the money and receives the mortgage, so the lender is the mortgagee. The borrower who received the money gives the mortgage to the bank as security. The borrower is the mortgagor. I'm afraid you'll just have to remember this.

2. What type of lien is a mortgage?

   (A) Judgment

   (B) General

   (C) Voluntary

   (D) Involuntary

   Correct answer: (C). The other answers are types of liens, but voluntary is the correct answer. For definitions of the other answers, see Chapter 8.

3. Which one of the following is not a participant in the secondary mortgage market?

   (A) Freddie Mac

   (B) Fannie Mae

   (C) Ginnie Mae

   (D) Banker Mac

   Correct answer: (D). Just remember the three that are participants.

4. How do a mortgage broker and a mortgage banker differ?

   (A) A mortgage banker arranges loans, a mortgage broker lends money.

   (B) A mortgage banker lends money, a mortgage broker arranges loans.

   (C) A mortgage banker works for the secondary mortgage market, a mortgage broker is a primary lender.

   (D) There is no difference between them.

   Correct answer: (B). Other differences may be evident in how they're regulated (locally and federally), but the essential difference is that the banker makes mortgage loans directly, and the broker arranges loans between borrowers and lenders.

5. What is the down payment on a property that's selling for $300,000, is appraised at $285,000, and the loan to value ratio is 90 percent?

   (A) $28,500

   (B) $30,000

   (C) $43,500

   (D) $256,500

   Correct answer: (C). The down payment and mortgage amounts are calculated against the appraised value not the selling price unless by some chance the selling price is lower than the appraised value in which case the lower number is used. Remember that the selling price has to be taken into account to determine the down payment.

6. The front-end qualifying ratio is a percentage of what to what?

   (A) PITI to gross income

   (B) PITI to net income

   (C) Total debt to gross income

   (D) Total debt to net income

   Correct answer: (A). First of all, qualifying ratios are calculated against gross income, so PITI to net income and total debt to net income are wrong. The front-end ratio is the PITI divided by gross income. The total debt divided by gross income is the back-end ratio.

7. One point is charged on a mortgage loan. It has no effect on the interest rate. It's very likely

(A) a buydown.

(B) a discount point.

(C) an origination fee.

(D) an APR.

Correct answer: (C). Origination fees, which have no impact on the interest rate, are sometimes calculated as points against the loan amount. A buydown is the other instance in which points are paid but it would have the effect of lowering the interest rate.

8. The amount of money a borrower can pay for a mortgage loan is determined by

(A) the LTV.

(B) the APR.

(C) the points.

(D) the qualifying ratio.

Correct answer: (D). The LTV is the percentage of the property's value that the lender will lend. You may argue with this question, because the APR and points definitely will determine what the buyer *has* to pay. But the qualifying ratio is what the buyer *can* pay under any given set of circumstances — and that is what the question asked for.

9. Lenders can get protection when making a low down payment mortgage loan from all of the following except

(A) LTV.

(B) PMI.

(C) VA.

(D) FHA.

Correct answer: (A). LTV is the calculation of the down payment. The question already presumes a low down payment. The VA and FHA provide guarantees for nonpayment of a loan so lenders are more receptive to low down payments. PMI is private mortgage insurance, which serves the same purpose.

10. A mortgage loan in which payments include principal and interest is generally referred to as

(A) an amortized loan.

(B) a term loan.

(C) a conventional loan.

(D) a conforming loan.

Correct answer: (A). The answer definitely isn't a term loan, because a term loan requires a payment of principal at the end of the term. The terms conventional and conforming have to do with amount of down payment made and the qualifying ratios used for the borrower.

Chapter **16**

It's So Taxing: Real Estate Assessment and Taxes

The only sure things in life are death and taxes. I don't know who said that, but it's true. If you own real estate, you'll pay taxes on it. You may pay more or less than someone who owns the same house in a different neighborhood, town, or city. You may have an exemption that reduces your payments or relieves you of payments for a while. Or you may not be able to pay your taxes and end up losing your property.

People who buy property are concerned about the taxes they pay and will ask you (if they ask nothing else) what the taxes are on the property. Buyers expect agents to know what amount of taxes is due each year on a piece of property. State exam writers expect you to know much more, like why taxes are collected, how tax rates are established, how to calculate the taxes on a particular piece of property, and how to protest tax assessments that may be unfair.

I cover these things and more in this chapter. I define some terms for you and show you a little math, but I hope this chapter doesn't get too taxing for you. (Sorry, I couldn't resist.)

Who Wants Your Money, and What Do They Want with It? Collecting Taxes

This morning you probably drove your car on a street to get to work, right? Call me George Jetson, but personally I'm still waiting for those flying cars they predicted everyone would be using by now. But assuming you don't have one, you drove your car. And if you're reading this during a school year, your kids probably went to school this morning. Now think about where your water comes from and where your sewage goes. Who gave you that parking ticket last week? Who put out the fire down the street? You and I expect the government to provide these services and facilities, don't we? And it takes money to give everyone what they want, doesn't it?

The kinds of services that I'm talking about generally are referred to as municipal services, and they're provided by the town, village, or city (or *municipality*) and sometimes the county. The primary way the municipalities pay for these services is by collecting taxes on real estate.

Why tax property instead of something like income? Real estate is hard to hide. The value is somewhat predictable. It provides a relatively stable way to collect the money needed for all those services we want.

A word that you need to know in connection with taxes is the word *levy*. It just means charged against, as in, "A tax of $1,000 is levied on that property."

REMEMBER

Taxes on real estate are called ad valorem taxes. *Ad valorem* means based on the value, and it refers to the fact that the taxes charged to a property are based on the value of the property. Ad valorem taxes sometimes are called a general tax or general real estate tax. In some communities a single, or general, tax is levied, and it pays for all municipal services. In other communities where individual taxing districts are set up, a property owner may also pay separate school district taxes as well as taxes for specific services like sewers. These individual taxing districts are generally called *assessing units*. In some cases a property owner may pay taxes to several different assessing units either directly or through the municipality they live in.

In some communities, a property owner may have to pay four or five different taxes on the same piece of property, with each tax designated to pay for a different municipal service.

STATE SPECIFIC

Although it's probably not crucial for exam purposes, you may want to see whether your state uses real estate tax revenues to pay for its operations. Most states use sales and income taxes. Some states have passed laws to limit the amount of taxes a local municipality can collect or the amount tax rates can be increased from year to year. You should check to see if your state has any laws like this.

Recognizing What's So Special about Assessments

Another kind of tax that's levied against real estate is called a special assessment. *Special assessments* are taxes that are collected against a particular group of properties, rather than against all the properties in a municipality. They are used to pay for infrastructure improvements like sidewalks, drainage projects, and other types of improvements in a particular area of the community. The area of designated properties is called a *special assessment district.* The town, city, or county passes an ordinance or law that creates the special assessment district and designates the purpose for which the tax money will be collected.

Go Figure! Calculating Taxes Step by Step

As a tax-assessor friend of mine observes, "If you think you're paying too much in taxes, go down the hall and complain to the mayor. But if you think the assessment on your property is too high, go see your tax assessor." The key elements in calculating the property taxes owed on an individual piece of property are its assessed value and the tax rates. In this section, I explain terms like assessed value and assessment ratio and show you how to do the calculations that you need to be able to do for the exam. (For extra practice on tax math, see Chapter 18.) I also discuss equalization rates for figuring county taxes (a good thing to know for the exam).

Oh so valuable: Assessing property for taxes

The word *assessed* really means to assign or give a value to something. The assessed value is not necessarily the actual dollar value of the property. A municipality may, for example, assess property at 50 percent of its market value. *Market value* is the price the property would bring in a fair and open sale on the real estate market (find more about market value and appraising property in Chapter 14). The *assessed value* is the value of the property that is used for real estate tax purposes. The percentage that is used to calculate the assessed value is called an *assessment ratio*.

To find the assessed value of any given property, you simply use this formula:

Market value × assessment ratio (expressed as a decimal) = assessed value

EXAMPLE

Say that the market value of a property is $200,000. In the community that assesses at 50 percent of market value, the assessed value is $100,000.

$200,000 (market value) × 0.50 (50 percent assessment ratio) = $100,000 (assessed value)

If you take the same property in a community that assesses at 70 percent of market value, the assessed value is $140,000. And if you go to a community that assesses at 100 percent of market value, the assessed value obviously is $200,000.

To apply this fairly on a purely mechanical or mathematical basis, the key is that each municipality uses the same assessment ratio for all the properties within its jurisdiction. To fully appreciate how this works, you need to understand that the taxation of property is about equity and not objective value.

REMEMBER

If you and I own property that has the same market value, we should be paying the same amount of taxes. And because taxes are based on assessed value, the assessed values of each of our properties should be the same. And if our properties have different market values, then the assessed values should be proportionally different, and so should our taxes. I put some numbers to this definition for you in Table 16-1, because calculating the assessed value of a property based on its market value and the assessment ratio is one of the types of calculations you may have to do on your state's real estate exam.

In Table 16-1, Properties A and B are being assessed fairly, because each of them is being assessed at the same assessment ratio of 50 percent. Remember the assessment ratio is calculated by dividing the assessed value by the market value. For Property C to be fairly assessed, you multiply the assessment ratio times the market value.

$400,000 × 0.50 (50 percent) = $200,000 assessed value

As you see, for the assessed values to be proportionally fair, it doesn't matter what the market values are for properties in a given municipality as long as the assessed value is calculated using the same percentage. Going one step further, as you look at the assessed values in the example, because taxes are based on assessed value, Property C will pay twice as much in taxes as Property A. And that's fair because Property C is worth twice as much as Property A.

TABLE 16-1 Figuring Assessed Values

Property	Market Value	Assessed Value
A	$200,000	$100,000
B	$300,000	$150,000
C	$400,000	?

STATE SPECIFIC

There are a few places, which you'll read about in your real estate courses, where the assessment ratios vary for different classes of property. A class of property for example, would be residential or commercial. These varying assessment ratios are more likely to be found in larger cities. Find out if any municipalities in your state use varying assessment ratios for different types or classes of property.

The numbers game: Understanding tax rates

Although calculating tax rates probably isn't something you specifically need to know how to do for an exam, it is something you need to understand in general to answer non-math questions about the process. Knowing how to calculate taxes also isn't a bad thing, because you probably pay property taxes and may want to know how these guys at city hall come up with their numbers.

REMEMBER

Tax rates in a municipality are based on a calculation involving the budget needs of the community and the total assessed valuation of the community. The municipality must first arrive at a dollar amount for its annual budget, and after that figure is adopted, the municipality looks at its *tax base*, which is the total assessed valuation of taxable property within the community.

So how do you figure out a basic tax rate? Easy! Just remember this formula:

Municipality budget ÷ total assessed valuation = tax rate

For example, say a city has adopted a budget of $2.5 million. Its total tax base is $50.0 million. You divide the budget number by the total assessed value to come up with the tax rate. In this case

$2,500,000 ÷ $50,000,000 = $0.05

This formula translates the fact that the municipality must collect five cents for every dollar of its total assessed value. However, tax rates never are expressed in cents but rather in one of the three ways I discuss next.

STATE SPECIFIC

Throughout the United States tax rates are reported in one of three different ways that vary by state and by municipality within the state. Using the basic tax rate that I calculated in the last paragraph, $0.05 of tax for every $1 of assessed valuation as an example, the three ways are

» Mills of tax per one dollar of assessed value — 50 mills/$1.

   One mill is one one-tenth of one penny, so 50 mills is $.050, which you get by dividing the number of mills, usually referred to as the mill rate or millage, by 1,000.

» Dollars of tax per hundred dollars of assessed value — $5/$100.

» Dollars of tax per thousand dollars of assessed value — $50/$1,000.

Each of these calculations is a different way of expressing the original calculation of $.05/$1.00.

Doing the decimal diddle: Calculating the taxes due

Although you may see a few questions on the exam about how taxes work, the math question you're most likely to see on your state licensing exam is one in which you must calculate the taxes on a piece of property. The basic mathematical procedure is to multiply the assessed value by the tax rate.

Assessed value of the property × tax rate = taxes due

Because different municipalities in your state may use the three different methods, I show you three problems using mills per dollar of assessed value, dollars of tax per hundred dollars of assessed value, and dollars of tax per thousand dollars of assessed value. You need to be able to calculate taxes using all three methods.

Take note that the tax rate in the examples that follow stays the same.

When the tax rate is expressed in mills

Tax rates frequently are expressed in mills, or as a millage (a tax rate expressed in mills per dollar of valuation). As already mentioned, a *mill* is one-tenth of one cent ($0.001). A tax rate of five cents of taxes per dollar of value is equal to a millage of 50 mills per dollar. Conversely, and this is the more likely conversion you'll have to make, a tax rate of 65 mills is $0.065 per dollar of assessed value.

REMEMBER

A typical question would be to calculate taxes on a property if you're given an assessed value and a tax rate expressed in mills. To convert the millage rate (sometimes called the mill rate) into something you can use in a calculation, just use the following formula:

Millage ÷ 1,000 = Mill rate expressed in dollars or cents of tax per dollar of assessed valuation

EXAMPLE

Suppose a property has an assessed value of $60,000 and a tax rate of 40 mills. The first step is to convert the millage into dollars. There are a couple of ways you can do this.

40 mills ÷ 1,000 = $0.040

TIP

Or convert the mills to dollars by moving the decimal point three places to the left, remembering that a decimal is always at the right end of a whole number even if it isn't actually there.

40 mills = $0.040

Now that you've done the conversion, you multiply the assessed value and the millage rate (expressed in dollars).

$60,000 (assessed value) × $0.040 = $2,400 taxes

When the tax rate is expressed in dollars per hundred

EXAMPLE

Again, say that the assessed value of a property is $60,000, and the tax rate is $4 per $100. The tax rate, in other words is $4 for each $100 of assessed value (or $0.040). How much are the taxes?

Remember that you find the taxes due by multiplying the assessed value and the tax rate. The calculation is

$60,000 (assessed value) × ($4 ÷ $100) (tax rate)

$4 (tax rate) ÷ $100 (ratio of assessed valuation) = $0.04 tax rate (per $100 of assessed valuation)

$60,000 assessed valuation × $0.04 tax rate = $2,400

The other way to do this by hand or by calculator is

$60,000 (assessed value) ÷ $100 = 600

600 × $4 = $2,400

When the tax rate is expressed in dollars per thousand

EXAMPLE

Say the assessed value of a property is $60,000 and the tax rate is $40 per $1,000 of assessed value. What are the taxes on this property?

Again, you multiply the assessed value and the tax rate, like so:

$60,000 (assessed value) × ($40 ÷ $1,000) (tax rate)

$40 (tax rate) ÷ $1,000 (ratio of assessed valuation) = $0.04 tax rate (per $1.00 of assessed valuation)

$60,000 assessed valuation × $0.04 tax rate = $2,400

Doing this problem with a calculator, you'd enter the following equations:

$60,000 ÷ $1,000 = 60

60 × $40 = $2,400 taxes

A nice balance: Using equalization rates

You may have to do a problem using equalization rates, sometimes called *equalization factors*, to figure out a county or school district property tax (as opposed to a city, town, or village property tax), so I'll explain what they are and how to use them. In a simple situation, several towns, cities, and villages within one county all levy their own taxes to pay for their own services, but the county also needs to collect taxes from all the residents in the county, and it may use the tax assessments from each town, village, and city. Equalization factors are needed in situations where county property taxes are being collected from several different towns, cities, and villages (municipalities) that are using different assessment ratios within that county. For example, House A in Town A has a market value of $200,000 and House B in Town B has a market value of $200,000, but Town A uses a 50 percent assessment ratio (for more about assessment ratios, see "Oh so valuable: Assessing property for taxes" earlier in this chapter), which results in an assessed value of $100,000, and Town B uses an assessment ratio of 40 percent, which results in an assessed value of $80,000. If you applied the same county tax rate to these two assessed values, House A would pay more county taxes than House B, even though they had the same market value. The equalization rate to the rescue.

The equalization rate is used to eliminate these differences and make sure people are paying their fair share of county taxes regardless of the assessment ratios their local municipalities use. Different counties may handle the math slightly differently, but the easiest way to look at this is that the equalization rate compensates for the individual municipal assessment ratios so that each property in the county is brought back up to its full market value. That value is then used for county tax calculation purposes. You need to note that although equalization rates are commonly used by counties — and that's the example I use — they can be used by any unit of government that collects taxes from different lower level taxing units, like a regional water authority that taxes multiple counties or municipalities. In the case of a centralized school district that encompasses several municipalities, the equalization rate compensates for the different municipal assessment ratios.

REMEMBER

To figure out the county taxes on any given piece of property, you take its assessed value and multiply it by a designated equalization rate to come up with its equalized value. (Don't worry — you won't be asked to calculate an equalization rate on the test.) You then multiply the property's equalized value and the tax rate (expressed in one of the three ways discussed in "Doing the decimal diddle: Calculating the taxes due," earlier in this chapter), and presto! You have the county taxes due. Here are two handy formulas:

> Total assessed valuation (in the municipality) × equalization rate for the county or other taxing unit = equalized value (total assessed valuation for the county or other taxing unit)

> Equalized value × tax rate for the county or other taxing unit = taxes due to the county or taxing unit

Want to see equalization rates in action? Say that Town A assesses its property at 25 percent of market value, Town B at 50 percent of market value and Town C at 80 percent of market value. (You can read about assessment ratios in "Oh so valuable: Assessing property for taxes" earlier in this chapter.) When the county applies its tax rate to all the properties in the county, properties of the same value would unfairly pay different amounts of taxes, because each house is assessed at a different percentage of market value. (*Remember:* Taxes are calculated against assessed value, not market value.) A $100,000 house in each of the three example towns respectively is assessed at $25,000 (Town A), $50,000 (Town B), and $80,000 (Town C). The simplest thing to do is to raise all the properties back up to their full market value and use that to calculate the taxes.

The equalization rate is based on the different assessment ratios in each town, so that taxpayers pay their fair share relative to each other. In the example that follows, all three taxpayers pay the same amount of county taxes, because all three houses have the same market value. I've calculated equalization rates for the assessment ratios I'm using in this example to show you how and why it works out.

> Assessed value × equalization rate = equalized value

> $25,000 × 4 = $100,000

> $50,000 × 2 = $100,000

> $80,000 × 1.25 = $100,000

REMEMBER

Notice a few factors here:

>> I've equalized the value up to 100 percent of market value. It doesn't have to be 100 percent; it can be equalized to any level of value as long as all the individual assessments are equalized in the same manner.

>> A different equalization rate is in effect for each property because each municipality assesses properties at a different percentage of market value.

EXAMPLE

You probably won't have to calculate an equalization rate, but you may have to calculate taxes using an equalization rate. Here's a sample problem. A property is assessed at $40,000. Its equalization rate for county taxes is 1.5. The county tax rate is 10 mills. What are the county taxes on the property?

$40,000 (assessed value) × 1.5 (equalization rate) = $60,000 (equalized value)

10 mills (tax rate) ÷ 1,000 = $0.01 (tax rate in dollars)

$60,000 (equalized value) × $0.01 (county tax rate) = $600 (county taxes due)

WARNING

Unfortunately, I've seen cases in which questions about equalization rates seem to indicate a lack of understanding of equalization rates on the part of the question writer. Just in case you get a question that mentions equalization rates and doesn't specify that it's for a county or school district, your best bet is to use the sample calculation that I used in this section and use the equalization rate to calculate the taxes due.

Home Free (Sort of): Eyeing Property Tax Exemptions

STATE SPECIFIC

Some properties are exempted from paying real estate taxes, and other property owners may actually pay reduced taxes for one reason or another. In this section, I tell you about the most common situations in which tax exemptions and reduced taxes are in effect. All information in this section is subject to state and local law, so you need to check to see what kinds of properties are fully or partially tax exempt in your state and what exemptions are available for certain groups of people.

A free ride: Fully tax-exempt properties

Government-owned properties, or properties owned by federal, state, county, town, city, village, township, borough, and any other level of government, are tax exempt to the extent that governments don't pay taxes to themselves nor do they generally pay taxes to a higher or lower level of government within which the property is located, provided that the property is also located within the borders of the government that owns it. So a town not only won't usually pay taxes to itself for a town park, but it also won't pay real estate taxes to the county for that park. The opposite also is true. The county won't pay taxes to the town for a county park within the town's borders. Federal government-owned and state-owned lands likewise are exempt from paying local real estate taxes. The one exception to this exemption is where property is owned by one government and is located in a completely different governmental jurisdiction. For example, Town A owns a reservoir in Town B. Town A may very likely pay taxes to Town B. But if Towns A and B are located in the same county, neither pays county taxes on the reservoir. Likewise, if County A owns property in County B, it probably will pay taxes to County B. This may vary by state, so check it out.

Other properties that are fully tax exempt, in general, include the following:

» School districts, water districts, sewer districts, and similar public service organizations that own property

» Property owned by private educational institutions, religious organizations, hospitals, and charitable groups

Just a small piece: Partial tax exemptions

STATE
SPECIFIC

Different states have different rules and programs that may exempt a portion of property taxes. You probably won't get a question on an exam about specific exemptions in your state, but you nevertheless need to check them out just in case.

A partial exemption may work in one of several ways: It can apply to the taxes directly by reducing the amount owed, it can apply to the assessment by reducing the assessment for an individual, or it can apply by reducing the assessment for a particular class or type of property. Here are a few examples:

>> Partial relief of total taxes that have to be paid may be granted. This partial exemption usually is a percentage of the taxes due and may be offered to senior citizens or the disabled. Income qualifications may also be attached to the exemption. So a person may have to be 65 years old and making less than a certain amount of money to qualify for an exemption.

>> Another type of partial tax exemption is a reduction in the assessment on the property. This type of exemption typically is offered to veterans. The exemption may be either a fixed dollar amount or a percentage of the assessment and may vary according to whether the veteran was in combat and/or is disabled. Special programs may also provide relief in the form of reduced assessments from various specific taxes such as for schools.

>> Some states also provide different assessment ratios for different types of properties. I discuss assessment ratios in "Oh so valuable: Assessing property for taxes," earlier in this chapter. For example, commercial properties may be assessed at higher assessment ratios than residential properties. What that means is that if you have a residential and a commercial property that have the same market value, the commercial property pays a higher amount of property taxes than the residential property of equal value.

Remember, when you're an agent selling a property, you need to find out the taxes on the property as if no exemptions were applicable. Your buyer may not qualify for the same exemptions as the seller. You can find out the taxes on the property by consulting the municipal or county assessor to get the assessment information and the receiver of taxes (treasurer or department of finance) to get the tax rate. Then using the methods described earlier in "Doing the decimal diddle: Calculating the taxes due," you can figure out the taxes.

That's Not Right: Protesting Assessments

Remember that tax assessments are about fairness, not necessarily objective reality. If your community assesses everyone at 100 percent of their property value, then you need to be on the lookout for your property being valued at a higher value than it actually is. You can argue that your property is being over-assessed, because it isn't really worth what the assessor says it is. (This situation is one of the few in which you ever try to make that argument.)

The other way assessments can be unfair is when properties in the same community are assessed at different percentages of their market value (also known as the assessment ratio — see "Oh so valuable: Assessing property for taxes," earlier in this chapter). For instance, if most of the properties in town are being assessed at 50 percent of market value and yours is being assessed at 70 percent of market value, you may have a case.

All states have some method or process in place for protesting the assessment on your property. Each state may have a slightly different process. Typically, each community has some sort of review board before which you can protest your assessment, usually during a designated time of the year. If you're still unsatisfied with the review board decision, court action usually is necessary. You may be asked a question about this process on the exam, so you may want to find out just how your state handles tax assessment reviews. At the very least, you need to find out what the local tax assessment review board, if one exists, is called in your state, county, or municipality.

Before you take your first official step toward protesting your assessment, you first need to check whatever records your local tax assessor has on your property, making sure that the description of the property upon which the assessment is based is accurate. Assessors are reasonable people, and you may find that you're being assessed for the back porch that the last owner tore down but never reported.

Pay or Lose: Tax Liens and Sales

You can read all about liens, including tax liens, in Chapter 8. But here are a couple of points you specifically must know about tax liens.

Individual state laws dictate the details of what happens when real estate taxes go unpaid. You're unlikely to get questions that deal with that level of detail. A number of practices are commonplace, however, and I discuss the ones that you need to be familiar with here. But just in case, you still should check out the details in your home state.

If you don't pay your taxes, eventually the taxing authority (call it the city) can take legal action to collect them from you. The first action taken generally is the placement of a lien against the property for the unpaid taxes. A *lien* is a financial obligation attached to a piece of property. After that, other legal action may take place that can take one of two forms.

>> **Tax sale:** One way for the city to collect the money you owe in taxes is to conduct a *tax sale*. The city sells your tax debt to someone. That person pays the city what you owe. If you don't pay that person back, usually including some kind of interest or penalty, that person can claim ownership of the property. Before and during this action, the property owner has a right to redeem the property by paying the taxes plus any penalties or interest that apply. The right to do this before the tax sale is known as the *equitable right of redemption*. The right to do this after the tax sale is called the *statutory right of redemption*. The time frames and details of how these redemptions work are governed by individual state law. You can remember these two terms by the fact that "*e*" for equitable is near the front of the alphabet and the equitable right of redemption is before the sale, and that "*s*" for statutory is near the end of the alphabet and the statutory right of redemption is after the sale.

>> **Foreclosure:** Another way the city can collect unpaid taxes is by *foreclosing* on the property, which means taking ownership of it and selling it to pay for the unpaid taxes. (For more about foreclosures, check out Chapter 15.) A term associated with foreclosure for unpaid taxes is in rem. *In rem* means the city takes action against the property rather than against you.

Banks that lend money for mortgages are particularly concerned about tax liens, because a tax lien takes first priority, which means it must be paid before any other liens, including the mortgage. The mortgage lender therefore is concerned that if a property must be sold for unpaid taxes, not enough money will be left from the sale to pay the balance owed on the mortgage loan. That's the reason many banks require the homeowner to pay into a tax escrow account from which the bank pays the taxes, just to be sure they get paid. You can read more about mortgages in Chapter 15.

Review Questions and Answers

In addition to a calculation question or two, you can expect questions through which you can demonstrate your knowledge of terminology associated with taxes. Memorize all the key words and know how to calculate taxes with and without equalization rates, and you'll do great.

1. A property is assessed at 50 percent of its market value. What is the 50 percent called?

   (A) The property value ratio

   (B) The assessment ratio

   (C) The assessment

   (D) The ad valorem tax ratio

   Correct answer: (B). This is something you'll have to memorize. With this group of choices you can at least eliminate assessment, because you know that the word *percent* in the question is the same as *ratio* in one of the answers.

2. A foreclosure for unpaid taxes against the property is called

   (A) a judgment.

   (B) a due on sale clause.

   (C) in rem.

   (D) a general lien.

   Correct answer: (C). A judgment has to do with unsatisfied liens. A due on sale clause is often part of a mortgage loan agreement. A general lien is put against several properties. In rem refers to the foreclosure action against the property specifically instead of against the person.

3. While representing an owner in selling his property, you find a partial exemption of 10 percent against the assessment because the owner is a veteran. Assuming the successful buyer is not a veteran and the tax rate doesn't change, what would the new owner's taxes be relative to the previous owner's tax assessment?

   (A) Higher

   (B) Lower

   (C) The same

   (D) Not enough information given to determine

   Correct answer: (A). The key to answering this question is to remember that an exemption against the assessment always means a reduced assessment and therefore lower taxes. Without the exemption, the new owner's taxes would be higher.

4. The period of time after a tax sale during which a property may be redeemed is called

   (A) the statutory period of redemption.

   (B) the equitable period of redemption.

   (C) the in rem redemption period.

   (D) the lien payment period.

   Correct answer: (A). The equitable period of redemption is before the tax sale. Remember that "*e*" for equitable comes before "*s*" for statutory in the alphabet, just like equitable right of redemption comes before the tax sale and the statutory right of redemption period comes after the tax sale. The in rem redemption period and the lien payment period are made up.

5. Public improvements in a specific neighborhood often are paid for by

   (A) ad valorem taxes.

   (B) special assessment district taxes.

   (C) a public improvement lien.

   (D) the general tax.

   Correct answer: (B). Don't overthink a question like this. If you see key words like neighborhood improvements, the exam writers probably are trying to find out whether you know about special assessment districts. Although I made up the term, I imagine that some kind of lien could be placed against a specific property for an improvement benefiting only that property. The general tax essentially is the same as the ad valorem tax and wouldn't commonly be used to improve one neighborhood.

6. A property has an assessed value of $60,000 and an equalization rate of 1.25. What is the equalized value of the property?

   (A) $40,000

   (B) $48,000

   (C) $60,000

   (D) $75,000

   Correct answer: (D). This question really is pretty simple. Just multiply the assessed value by the equalization rate.

   $$\$60,000 \times 1.25 = \$75,000$$

7. A property is assessed at $50,000. The tax rate is 8 mills. What are the taxes due?

   (A) $40,000

   (B) $4,000

   (C) $400

   (D) $40

   Correct answer: (C). The thing to remember when you're working with mills is to back up the decimal by three places to the left (in other words, you divide by 1,000), and then multiply the assessed value by the millage rate.

8. A property is assessed at $76,000 and the tax rate is $5 per $100. What are the taxes?

   (A) $380

   (B) $3,800

   (C) $1,520

   (D) $152

   Correct answer: (B). If you had trouble with this question, check out "Go Figure! Calculating Taxes Step by Step," earlier in this chapter.

   $$\$5 \text{ (tax rate per \$100)} \div \$100 \text{ (of assessed valuation)} = \$0.05 \text{ (tax rate per dollar)}$$

   $$\$76,000 \text{ (assessed value)} \times \$0.05 = \$3,800 \text{ taxes owed}$$

Alternatively, you can do it this way:

$76,000 ÷ $100 = 760

760 × $5 = $3,800

TIP

One other thing: Don't let the size of the numbers throw you. You may think $3,800 is an outrageous amount of property taxes to pay and therefore incorrect, so you pick another answer that seems to make more sense. I think $3,800 in taxes is outrageous, too. And I think so every time I pay my property tax bill, which is more than that. So learn the math and trust your skills in doing these problems.

9. A property is assessed at $44,000. The tax rate is $11 per $1,000. What are the taxes?

(A) $400

(B) $4,000

(C) $4,840

(D) $484

Correct answer: (D). This question is the same as question number eight but with a different tax rate expressed against $1,000 in assessed value.

$11 (tax rate per $1,000) ÷ $1,000 (of assessed valuation) = $0.011 (tax rate per dollar)

$44,000 (assessed value) × $0.011 = $484 Taxes

Alternatively, you can do it this way:

$44,000 ÷ $1,000 = 44

44 × $11 = $484

10. A property's market value is $250,000. The assessment ratio is 40 percent. The tax rate is 23 mills. What are the taxes on the property?

(A) $2,300

(B) $230

(C) $5,759

(D) $575

Correct answer: (A). This problem ties together an assessment ratio and a tax rate calculation. If you can do this one, you can probably handle any tax math problem thrown at you.

$250,000 (market value) × 0.40 (assessment ratio) = $100,000 (assessed value)

23 mills (tax rate) ÷ 1,000 = 0.023

$100,000 (assessed value) × 0.023 = $2,300

IN THIS CHAPTER

» **Getting in gear with investment basics**

» **Recognizing investment organizational structures**

» **Checking out ways to acquire investments**

» **Raking in cash with investments**

» **Understanding the government's relationship with investing**

» **Finding out how to analyze a real estate investment**

Chapter **17**

Investing in Real Estate

Real estate long has been considered one of the best ways to build wealth. A real estate agent who provides services to people who are buying and selling investment properties needs to be knowledgeable about different types of investment properties, various ways you can make money by investing in real estate, and some of the tax issues that affect real estate as an investment. Although they don't expect you to become an investment analyst or financial advisor, state exam writers do expect you to know the basics of real estate investing. In this chapter, I tell you about the basics of real estate investments (including types of investment properties), how money is made in real estate investments, and how the government helps real estate investors through its tax policies. I also take you through a brief investment analysis and talk a little about how you can invest in real estate without actually owning any real estate.

TIP

The info I'm giving you here is only what you need to help you pass the exam. If you decide that you want to find out even more about investing in real estate, check out the most recent edition of *Real Estate Investing For Dummies* by Eric Tyson and Robert S. Griswold (John Wiley & Sons, Inc.).

Focusing on Property Investment

Many people think that real estate investments must involve large and complicated properties, and that isn't necessarily true. Real estate investors often start small with residential properties close to home. I briefly discuss different types of properties, management issues, particular advantages and disadvantages, and getting help with your client's investments. With the exception of the list of investment properties, you can expect some state exam questions on all the material in this section.

So many choices: Examining different investment properties

An *investment property* can be almost any property for which people are willing to pay rent to use. I'm sure I may have left something out (lighthouses leased to the Coast Guard, maybe), but here's a pretty complete list of the different categories of investment properties.

>> **One- to four-family houses:** These are sometimes called duplexes, triplexes, and quadriplexes in some parts of the country. Essentially, they're small houses with one to four apartments. New investors often purchase them, and sometimes the owner occupies one apartment and rents the others.

>> **Apartment buildings:** These are distinguished from the one- to four-family house by the number of units, which can be anywhere from five units to hundreds of units in a single building.

>> **Large residential complexes:** This term is used to describe residential developments of several buildings, each of which contains multiple apartments. These complexes can consist of several high-rise buildings or low-rise, one- to three-story buildings called garden apartments in some parts of the country.

>> **Individual retail (store) buildings:** These buildings house department stores or smaller stores that usually have products and goods for sale.

>> **Strip malls/shopping centers:** Open-air complexes of retail stores known by either of these two names often depending on whether they're a small (strip mall) or large (shopping center) group of stores. This type of retail complex is known for accommodating automobile traffic with sufficient parking areas.

>> **Enclosed retail malls:** This term refers to large complexes of retail stores, usually all joined together in an indoor, climate-controlled configuration. They're also characterized by extensive parking.

>> **Office buildings:** These buildings are used for all kinds of offices, ranging from medical to business offices.

>> **Warehouses:** Refers to large buildings usually used for storage.

>> **Motels and hotels:** Buildings that can be configured in low-rise, one- and two-story structures along the highway, or high-rise buildings in a city center location are known as motels and hotels, respectively.

>> **Industrial properties:** This term refers to factory buildings.

>> **Vacant land:** This term applies to land with no buildings on it, purchased either to build something or for speculative purposes (simply waiting for the price to rise). They can also be leased to adjacent property owners for various purposes.

REMEMBER

Land generally isn't considered a good investment unless it's being purchased to build on. For more about vacant land, check out the section "Empty promise: Considering vacant land," later in this chapter.

Although you're not likely to get many (if any) questions about the real estate agent's role in advising clients about buying properties, it's important to know something about how investors think so you can help them achieve their investment goals. Generally, your role is to search out the type of property they want (see the previous list) and obtain relevant financial information so the client's accountants can check out the numbers to see if they'll get the return they want. You can find out more about how investors expect to make money later in this chapter in the section titled "Making Money by Investing in Real Estate."

For investors who don't know that much about investing, you may have to provide some advice on financial returns and management issues. You can read more about management issues in the next section.

In charge: Looking at management issues

One of the biggest decisions you first must make is whether to invest in real estate at all. Secondly, you have to select the kind of property in which you plan to invest. How you plan to manage your property is an important issue in making this decision. The two basic choices are managing a building yourself or hiring a manager. This decision usually is based on the investor's competence and experience with the kind of building, the building's location, the amount of time you have available for management duties, and whether the investment produces enough income to make hiring a manager possible.

Many investors start by investing in small residential properties (such as one- or two-family houses) close to home. They're usually familiar with residential properties, and the close proximity enables them to keep an eye on the property so self-management may be feasible. Moreover, these kinds of investments usually don't provide enough income (at least initially) to pay for outside management services.

On the other hand, someone who never has owned an office building before and has no familiarity with the needs of people who rent office space probably will hire a professional manager. Because an office building is used primarily during the day, providing on-site management or at least service people during business hours may be necessary. An office building is also more likely to generate enough income to support a property manager's salary.

A real estate agent may be asked to advise a client about property management issues and possibly recommend a property management company. The agent should try to understand his client's need and experience as well as possible, make recommendations with the understanding that any decisions lie with the client, and always recommend at least three reputable companies. See "The rule of three" sidebar in this chapter. For more about property management and the duties of a property manager, see Chapter 3.

THE RULE OF THREE

When recommending another professional's or tradesperson's services, a real estate agent should always recommend at least three people. Doing so minimizes the chance that you could be held liable in courts for other professionals' incompetent actions or advice. (In an era when people successfully sue for damages because they spilled hot coffee on themselves, I suggest you don't even think about this possibility too much, because it will give you a headache.) What the lawyers tell me is that by recommending at least three people, the person to whom you're making the recommendations has the chance to use his or her own judgment in the final selection and, therefore, bears at least some of the responsibility for the final choice made. So if you do recommend an attorney, accountant, or other professional or tradesperson, always recommend three. And I must add, make sure that these people you recommend are professionals you'd rely on yourself. Remember, every time you recommend someone else's services to your real estate client or customer, you're putting your reputation on the line.

Ask the experts: Knowing when to get help

Investing in real estate is an important decision. Locating the right property for investors and selling investment properties is something you'll be doing as a real estate agent. Knowing what you don't know is as important as knowing what you know. Good advice is crucial to making the right investment decision and maintaining that investment.

REMEMBER

The three people who need to be consulted in making real estate investment decisions are a real estate agent (that's you), an attorney, and an accountant. These professionals need to be consulted as early in the process as possible. I cover the agent's role in finding property and handling management issues in the previous two sections, but you also need to check out the roles of an attorney and an accountant. Make sure that you always refer your clients to these professionals as soon as possible.

Consulting an attorney is important any time you buy property, and doing so becomes even more important whenever you're buying property with a partner or several other people (see "Partnering Up: Real Estate Investment Organization Structures," later in this chapter). An attorney can help set up the proper organizational structure for an investment. You may also want an attorney to review any leases that exist in the building you buy.

The use of a good accountant likewise is crucial because of the tax implications of owning investment property. I talk about tax benefits in "Getting Uncle Sam's Help: The Government's Role in Investing," later in this chapter. The point to remember is that the value of the tax benefits derived from the same building sometimes varies from one owner to the next.

Oh no: Some not-so-good news about investing in real estate

WARNING

Investing in real estate is a great idea for several reasons: Over time real estate values tend to at least keep pace with inflation if not exceed it; properties often generate annual returns (income) on the investment; and investors can take advantage of tax benefits that may not be available in other investments. However, investing in real estate also has a few disadvantages. Here are four of them:

>> Real estate isn't considered a *liquid* investment. Unlike stocks or bonds, it takes time to get your money out of a real estate investment.

>> Real estate investments usually require substantial amounts of cash as a down payment, despite what the no-money-down gurus say. Reserve cash is also needed for unexpected repairs and vacancies.

>> Real estate investments usually require some level of management and involvement in property management decisions, too.

>> Real estate investments don't always turn out to be profitable. All investments carry risk; real estate is no different.

Although an agent wants to present the investment property in the best possible light, the important thing is to provide the potential buyer with factual data on current income, local vacancy rates for that type of property, and the physical condition, if known, of the property. You can guarantee very little about an investment unless you happen to have a really good crystal ball.

Partnering Up: Real Estate Investment Organization Structures

People invest in real estate as individuals or sometimes together with another person or several other people. Different organizational structures are used to accomplish different investment goals. Does it surprise you to find out that you also can invest in real estate without actually owning property or having ownership responsibilities? You don't have to become an expert in this area, but in this section I talk about each of these types of ownership and investment situations in enough detail to enable you to distinguish one form from the other, which is what state exam writers expect of you.

Real estate investment syndicates

A *real estate investment syndicate* is an ownership structure in which a number of people join together to invest in a single project or property. The term *syndicate* or *syndication* is more a descriptive than it is a legal term or an actual form of ownership. The actual legal structure of the syndicate also can take a number of different forms; you can find out more in Chapter 7. The key point to remember about syndicates is that they are created to invest in one piece of property.

Private syndication usually involves a small group of people, sometimes already known to each other. *Public syndication* involves a larger group of people, which may offer investments to the public in the form of securities or shares. Depending on factors such as the total number of investors and the value of the investment, the syndicate may be subject to federal and state securities laws designed to protect the public, which commonly are referred to as *blue sky laws*.

Two forms of syndicates used for real estate investments are general and limited partnerships. The principal difference between the two forms is the extent of management control and liability.

In the *general partnership*, all partners share management responsibility, profits and losses, and liability. If, for example, the partners are successfully sued and insurance can't cover the judgment, each partner can be held personally liable for the judgment.

In a *limited partnership*, one partner usually is known as the *general partner* and is ultimately responsible for any losses or liabilities on the project. Limited partners are entitled to certain profits (and losses, if they're beneficial to their tax situations), but the partners have no management responsibility, and their losses are limited to the amounts of their individual invest-ments. For more about partnerships and other forms of real estate ownership, see Chapter 7.

Real estate investment trusts

Real estate investment trusts (REITs) are trusts designed to pool the money of multiple investors in real estate projects. Real estate investment trusts are like stock investments or mutual funds that usually invest in a series of projects, real estate investments, or mortgages. The REIT can con-tinue as old investments are sold and new ones bought. REITs are available in these three differ-ent types:

>> **Equity trust:** A REIT that invests in a number of different kinds of real estate and sells shares to investors.

>> **Mortgage trust:** A REIT that uses shareholders' money to buy and sell real estate mortgage loans rather than properties.

>> **Combination trust:** A REIT that invests shareholders' money in property equities and mortgage loans.

Real estate mortgage investment conduits

WARNING

A *real estate mortgage investment conduit* (REMIC) is a type of investment tool that uses shareholders' funds to invest in mortgage loans. A REMIC may sound like a mortgage trust, but they're two different beasts. A number of complex rules govern REMICs regarding the types of mortgages and interest payments to investors. None of these details is likely to be on an exam. In fact, REMIC may be one of the *wrong* choices in a question about real estate investments, so keep your eyes peeled.

Spending Spree: Acquiring and Building Investments

An investor may buy one investment property and leave it at that. But great empires of wealth have been built by buying, selling, and holding multiple properties for investment. In this section, I talk about using borrowed money to increase profits in real estate investments. I also give you some information about buying one property, then another, and another. I also talk about one of the riskiest investments, land. For exam purposes, absorb the terminology, and wherever you see math, make sure you understand the basic idea.

Getting more for less: The joys of leverage

Leveraging is using borrowed money to increase the return on your investment. One reason real estate is such an attractive investment is that other people's money is available for you to invest. The beauty of leveraging is that the less of your own money you use, the higher the rate of return on your investment. You most likely use borrowed money to buy your home, which is also lever-aging. But the fact is that you buy your home for one reason and an investment property for a different reason, and the advantages of leveraging a real estate investment have a direct bearing on the profit you make on the property.

The formula to calculate the percentage profit based on using borrowed money, namely using leverage to increase your profit, is a two-part equation.

Part 1: Selling price − purchase price = profit (in dollars)

The second part of the equation presumes of course that there is a profit. Leveraging doesn't really matter if there's a loss.

Part 2: Profit ÷ cash investment = percentage of profit

EXAMPLE

Here are two examples of leveraging at play. You buy an investment property for $500,000 with $100,000 of your own cash and the rest financed with a mortgage loan. After several years, you sell the property for $600,000. You made a profit of $100,000. Now here's the good part. You made that profit of $100,000 on only a $100,000 investment, because that's all the cash you put up. If you do the math:

Part 1: $600,000 (selling price) − $500,000 (purchase price) = $100,000 (profit)

Part 2: $100,000 (profit) ÷ $100,000 (cash investment) = 1 (or 100 percent of profit)

EXAMPLE

You buy the same $500,000 property, only this time you pay all cash. You again sell it after a few years for $600,000. You made the same $100,000 profit. But the math this time is:

Part 1: $600,000 (selling price) − $500,000 (purchase price) = $100,000 (profit)

Part 2: $100,000 (profit) ÷ $500,000 (cash investment) = 0.2 (or 20 percent of profit)

Comparing the first example with the second example shows how you can make the same amount of money, $100,000, with only a $100,000 investment, instead of tying up $500,000, all by using other people's money — namely the mortgage loan. (For more about mortgages, see Chapter 15.)

Now that you've seen how basic leveraging works, think about the investor who has $500,000 cash. Instead of paying cash for one $500,000 building, he puts $100,000 cash into five $500,000 buildings. Using the first example above, he would reap 100 percent profit on each of the buildings and make a total of $500,000. Investors generally want to invest as little of their own money as possible and, of course, make the most profit in the shortest time.

Make sure you can handle a math question calculating basic leverage (as shown in this section's examples) and understand that leveraging is the concept of using borrowed money to extend the impact of your own cash investment. You may ask, what about the mortgage payments I'm making along the way until I sell the property? Don't those payments change the leveraging equation? The answer is yes and no. Refer to the later section, "Letting someone else pay off the mortgage: Equity buildup," where I discuss *equity buildup*, which is paying off the mortgage principal through the rents that are collected. The interest payments, as you also see, are accounted for in cash flow calculations. And an investor may want to account for all of this in evaluating the profitability of the investment. A simple leverage calculation should be enough to get you through any questions the test may ask.

Pyramiding: Not just for the pharaohs

Pyramiding is building multiple investments from one investment. You really need to think in terms of an upside down pyramid or triangle for this to make sense. Essentially, you start with one investment property and use the profits from it to buy two. Then, in turn, you buy four. So, the upside-down pyramid has the pointy end down — that's the one property you start with — and from there the pyramid expands up and out — that's the result of your addition of more and more investment properties. You can either sell each property and buy more properties, or refinance a property and use the resulting cash to buy another or even two more. In pyramiding, you're always aiming to increase the total number of properties, rental units or square footage that you own.

The down side of pyramiding, of course, is your increasing debt load, which can be very sensitive to economic conditions. And, of course, investing in more and more buildings presumes an adequate profit greater than expenses. But pyramiding is one way that people build a real estate investment portfolio over time and end up controlling a number of properties.

Empty promise: Considering vacant land

WARNING

Traditional real estate investment advice says to avoid investing in *vacant land,* meaning land that's undeveloped. I'm talking about buying a piece of empty land and waiting for it to grow (appreciate) in value. Sometimes people wait for time to take its effect, hoping that property values will rise. Sometimes people are simply waiting for development to reach the property or a new highway to be built. In these cases, investors aren't doing anything to add value to the property. Some people have made money with this investment strategy, but in general, vacant land is not recommended as a good real estate investment.

Vacant land produces no income while you own it. The only profit to be made is when you sell it. And that profit usually depends on factors over which you have no control, such as where a new road is built. Meanwhile, you have to pay taxes on the land and possibly maintain it in some way depending on where it's located.

On the other hand, if you do something to increase the value of the property, it may become a good investment opportunity. You may be able to build on it or get the local government to permit commercial development, which usually is more highly valued than residential development. Vacant land also can be rented (leased) on a long-term basis to someone who wants to build something on it. I talk about land leases in Chapter 12. Exam questions on this subject, if any appear, are pretty simple. Just remember that vacant land is not considered a good investment because it costs you money without generating an income.

Making Money by Investing in Real Estate

You can make money in several different ways, such as capital appreciation, renting, and equity buildup, by investing in real estate. As an agent (and as a test taker), you need to be familiar with all the moneymaking methods and the appropriate terminology. In this section, I cover the basics.

REMEMBER

The most important thing to keep in mind when it comes to making money on investments is that an investor expects these two kinds of returns:

>> **Return of the investment:** You expect to get back your capital, the cash you invested in the first place.

>> **Return on the investment:** You expect to receive something more than what you invested. The expected return on the investment is related to the risk of the investment. The risk in any investment is the possibility of losing all or part of your original cash investment. The higher the risk, the greater the expected return on the investment.

The several ways by which investors expect to accomplish the return *of* their investments and the return *on* their investments are covered in the following sections.

YOU'RE A REAL ESTATE AGENT, NOT A FORTUNETELLER

After you get your real estate license, you're officially an expert in real estate matters. You may not feel like much of an expert, but the state that just gave you your license says you are. More importantly, that license tells the people that you'll be helping that they can trust your expertise because you've studied, taken a real estate course, and passed a state exam. You and I both know that it takes more than completing a course, reading a book (even this one), and passing an exam to become an expert in anything. Mastering the many aspects of real estate will take time and focus. Investing in real estate is just one of those areas. So what does this have to do with fortunetelling?

People who buy a piece of property, whether it's a house to live in, a store for their business, or an apartment building as an investment, want to be as certain as possible that they're making a good investment, which means not losing any money down the road and probably making some. Because buyers of investment properties are specifically buying the property to make money, new investors especially will want reassurances that they're making a good, profitable investment.

Here's where the crystal ball comes in. Unless you have one that they didn't give me when I got my real estate license, you really can't say much about the future of any property. In fact, I tell my students in every investment class I teach that they can talk about a particular property or the market in general in the past and in the present but never in the future. Remember the state says you're an expert and clients have every right to expect that you know your business and that they can rely on your advice. But nobody can predict the future.

Focus your discussion with clients on current vacancy rates, market trends of the last six months or a year, competing rental rates, and even published economic reports, but avoid telling that new investor how she can be assured that her vacancy rate will go down, her rents will go up, and the sun will always be shining. You can't predict any of those things. And save your crystal ball for picking numbers when you by a lottery ticket.

Up and down: Buying low and selling high — capital appreciation

One of the ways investors make money in real estate is by selling property at a higher price than that which they bought it for in the first place. In this case, the value of the real estate *appreciates*, or increases, creating *capital appreciation*, or growth. The profit made from selling property for a price higher than what you paid is called *capital gain* for tax purposes. When you sell property for more than you paid for it, you get the return of your capital; that is, you get your original down payment back, along with the profit or capital appreciation, which is the return on your capital. So, if I buy a property that costs $500,000 with $100,000 cash (see "Getting more for less: The joys of leverage" earlier in this chapter) and a few years later sell that property for $600,000, then I get my original cash investment of $100,000 back (return of my investment) and an additional $100,000 in capital appreciation (return on my investment). For more about capital gains, see "More than your money's worth: Capital gains," later in this chapter.

Plenty of room: Rentals on property

Most investors get returns on their investments by means of rents paid on the property. All expenses, including the mortgage loan payment, are paid from the rent and whatever else (such as quarters from laundry machines) factors into the *building income.* Investors call the mortgage payment *debt service*. The money left over after all expenses are paid, except debt service, is called the *net operating income*. After debt service is subtracted from net operating income, what's left is called *cash flow*, or the money the investment has earned before taxes. Check out the following two-part equation:

Part 1: Building income – operating expenses = net operating income

Part 2: Net operating income – debt service = cash flow

Cash flow ideally is positive, meaning that you take money out of the investment each year. But cash flow also can be negative, meaning that the building's expenses are greater than the building's income. Three reasons why someone buys an investment with negative annual cash flow are

» The investor may believe that the shortfall is only temporary. Maybe the building isn't fully rented. Or the investor believes rents will go up faster than expenses or that expenses can be managed better and reduced.

» The investor may believe that when selling the building it will make enough profit to make up for the negative cash flow each year.

» The investor may be making a lot of money in another investment and wants to keep his income tax bracket lower by balancing a positive cash flow investment against a negative one.

Letting someone else pay off the mortgage: Equity buildup

The mortgage payment, or debt service, always is included in the expenses of any investment property. If the borrower borrows money with an amortized mortgage, every payment made on that loan is part interest and part principal. (That's what *amortized* means.) So every time the building's income (in the form of rents and other income) is used to make a mortgage payment, usually monthly, the overall mortgage debt is reduced.

By paying off some or all of the mortgage loan, when the owner sells the property, he owes the bank less money on the balance of the mortgage loan than when he first bought the investment. The owner (investor) gets to keep more of what he sells the investment for. Equity is the difference between the value of the property and all debts attributable to the property. Obviously any increase in the overall value of the property also increases the equity, but investors usually use the term equity buildup to specifically refer to the increase in equity that comes from the mortgage loan being paid off by the rents from an investment property.

For example, suppose you borrow $200,000 to buy an investment property that costs $250,000. You keep the property for 10 years, and through the monthly loan payments, which are coming out of the rents, you pay off $50,000 of the mortgage. Assuming the property doesn't appreciate in value when you sell the property, you owe the bank only $150,000. That $50,000 you paid off of the mortgage is yours, courtesy of your tenants' rent. I discuss mortgage loans in Chapter 15.

Getting Uncle Sam's Help: The Government's Role in Investing

The federal tax code isn't just about the government figuring out new and exciting ways to take away your money. Much of the code is devoted to encouraging different kinds of business activities. Real estate investments benefit from several programs that help investors retain more of their profits. This section tells you about the most common programs, some of which involve a little math that exam writers want you to know how to do. I give you the basics here, but don't forget the importance of hiring a good accountant when actually owning a real estate investment.

More than your money's worth: Capital gains

When you sell a property for more than you paid for it, you have made what, for tax purposes, is called a *capital gain.* That gain is taxable, but because the government wants to encourage people to make long-term (usually more than a year) investments over time, it treats capital gains more favorably than regular income for tax purposes.

Calculating the amount of capital gain that a property has earned starts with the *basis* of the property. The *basis* is the initial price you paid for the real estate, not just the cash you put in. The basis can change over time, because the costs of capital improvements are added to it. A *capital improvement* is a permanent improvement that adds value to the property, such as a new roof on the building or new kitchens in the rental units. This new number (original cost plus capital improvements) is usually still referred to as the *basis.* Depreciation, which is the government's way of enabling you to claim a loss on your property and which I discuss in the next section, is then subtracted from the total of the original cost of the property (the basis). The resulting number is called the *adjusted basis.*

Next, you subtract selling expenses, such as commission expenses and closing costs, from the selling price of the property. That total is called the *net selling price.*

Finally, the adjusted basis is subtracted from the net selling price, and the result is the capital gain. The calculations that follow show the amount of capital gain for a property initially purchased for $50,000.

> $50,000 (purchase price, or basis) + $8,000 (capital improvements) – $4,000 (depreciation) = $54,000 (adjusted basis)

> $90,000 (selling price to the new buyer) – $5,000 (commission expense) – $1,000 (closing costs) = $84,000 (net selling price)

> $84,000 (net selling price) – $54,000 (adjusted basis) = $30,000 (capital gain)

REMEMBER

Tax laws change from time to time, particularly with respect to the tax rate on capital gains. Expect a question or two requiring you to calculate a capital gain or to describe the basis or adjusted basis. You might even have to calculate the tax paid, but either the exam writers give you the tax rate to use or you use the one you learned in your prelicense class.

Feeling worn-out: Depreciation

Depreciation is the recovery of the cost of an asset that wears out. Another term for depreciation is *cost recovery.* Allowing you to deduct a dollar amount of depreciation from your annual tax obligation is the government's way of acknowledging that the asset, a thing of value, wears out and that if you didn't have the asset, you couldn't earn any money on which to pay taxes. With depreciation, you wind up paying less in annual taxes on any given piece of property (and keeping more of your profits).

The government wants you to pay taxes. No surprise there. For people who need physical objects like buildings, machinery, or automobiles (as you soon see) to earn their incomes and therefore to pay taxes, the government understands that no physical object lasts forever, and without that object you have no business and pay no taxes. Depreciation is the government's way of acknowledging that these things wear out and helping investors replace these items so that they can continue earning income and — you guessed it — continue paying taxes.

EXAMPLE

Here's a non-real estate example, including the tax impact, that I use in the classroom. Suppose that you have the smallest car rental company in the world with only one car. That car cost $40,000, and you rent it out and make $16,000 in what usually is referred to as gross income (income before taxes and expenses). After gas, oil, maintenance, and insurance expenses of $4,000 are deducted, you end up with $12,000 left as your *net income.* You're in the 20 percent tax bracket, so your tax calculation is

$12,000 (net income) × 0.20 = $2,400 (taxes)

At least that's how much your taxes would be if the government didn't recognize the fact that cars wear out and without a car you have no business and the government gets no taxes. So, the government lets you deduct depreciation, enabling you to do so during what is called a *cost recovery period,* say five years on the car.

$40,000 (cost of car) ÷ 5 (cost recovery period in years) = $8,000 (depreciation per year)

So now, instead of deducting only $4,000 in expenses from your income, you get to deduct another $8,000.

$16,000 (gross income) − $4,000 (operating expenses) − $8,000 (depreciation) = $4,000 (net income)

$4,000 (net income) × 0.20 (tax rate) = $800 (taxes)

A tax bill of $800 versus $2,400, courtesy of depreciation, sounds pretty good. And you thought those guys at the IRS were only after your money.

For more depreciation math, check out Chapter 18.

REMEMBER

Investment properties benefit from the same depreciation calculation; however, the cost recovery period for buildings is longer than for motor vehicles, and vacant land can't be depreciated at all, because land doesn't get old and worn out like a building. And a private home can't be depreciated because it isn't considered an income-generating asset. The type of depreciation that is used for investment properties is called *straight-line depreciation,* because an equal amount of the value of the building is deducted each year. The government periodically changes the rules governing the cost recovery period, the required ownership time, and the tax rate at which capital gains generated from depreciation are taxed. I suspect because state exam writers don't want to have to change exam questions every time the federal government changes the tax law, you probably won't get any questions on the specifics. But you may get a question about deprecation in general, how it works, and how it affects the basis.

The beauty of depreciation is that it's subtracted from annual income thereby reducing your annual tax burden, as the example shows. Of course you've most likely figured out that because depreciation reduces the adjusted basis of the property, it increases the capital gains on which you'll have to pay taxes. But capital gains are traditionally given favorable treatment by the tax code, so ultimately you're paying less tax on the capital gain than you would have on the annual income.

EXAMPLE

Check out this example for a cost-recovery period.

You purchase an investment property for $1,000,000. Typically the land value may be 20 percent, leaving a building value of $800,000.

$1,000,000 (total property cost) × 20 percent (land value portion) = $200,000 (land portion)

$1,000,000 – $200,000 = $800,000 (building cost)

If you use a cost-recovery period of 25 years, the calculation is as follows:

$800,000 (building cost) ÷ 25 (cost recovery period) = $32,000 per year in depreciation. This means that each year for 25 years, you could deduct $32,000 form the building's income before having to pay taxes.

Just remember that the rules regarding depreciation including the cost-recovery periods are complicated, can change from time to time, and can have a different benefit to different investors depending on their particular financial situation. Time to get that accountant.

On the way down: Tax deductions and tax credits

A *tax deduction* is something you can deduct from an investment property's income to reduce your taxes. A *tax credit* is something you can deduct from the taxes you owe. The federal and sometimes state governments create programs that permit tax credits or deductions to encourage certain activities with respect to investment properties. Historic preservation and energy efficiency are the kinds of things the government periodically tries to encourage. Within certain limits, property owners are permitted to deduct the interest payments on their mortgage loans and local property taxes.

REMEMBER

All things being equal, a tax credit is worth more in tax savings than a tax deduction. The credit is subtracted from taxes owed, and the deduction is subtracted from the net taxable income (your gross income after expenses). Most likely, the test will ask that question: Which is more valuable?

I doubt you'll have to do this kind of calculation, but here's an example anyway. The facts and numbers are made up.

EXAMPLE

Last year the government said you could deduct $3,000 for any work you did that increased the energy efficiency of your property. This year the government said you could take a $3,000 tax credit if you did the same kind of work. If the net income (gross income after expenses) of your building is $30,000 in each of those years, and you're in the 20 percent tax bracket, in which year are you better off?

Last year's tax deduction:

$30,000 (net income) – $3,000 (energy tax deduction) = $27,000 (net taxable income)

$27,000 (net taxable income) × 0.20 (tax rate) = $5,400 (taxes owed)

This year's tax credit:

$30,000 (net income) × 0.20 (tax rate) = $6,000 (taxes)

$6,000 (taxes) – $3,000 (energy tax credit) = $3,000 (taxes owed)

For more about real estate taxes, check out Chapter 16.

Real estate exchanges

You don't always have to pay cash for a piece of property. You can trade, just like you did with baseball cards (well, not quite). Under certain circumstances, the government allows you to exchange one piece of property for another. These exchanges are known as *1031 exchanges*, after the section of the law that governs them, or *tax deferred exchanges*, because one of the advantages is the deferral of capital gains tax. I discuss capital gains in "More than your money's worth: Capital gains," earlier in this chapter. You don't have to get too technical in terms of what to remember about exchanges, but here are a few facts and terms you need to remember for the exam.

» **Like kind:** To qualify for an exchange, the two properties must be of *like kind* according to IRS definitions, and they must be investment properties.

» **Time limits:** Exchanges generally have time limits during which the exchanged properties must be identified, and then the exchange itself, completed.

» **Boot:** If properties are exchanged and they don't have equal value, even if one of the properties has increased in value, capital gains tax is deferred, but it eventually must be paid when the property is sold. If the properties are not equal in value, cash or personal property may be included in the deal. This is called *boot*. The person receiving it owes taxes on the boot.

By the Numbers: Analyzing Investment Properties

As a real estate agent, you'll be called upon to provide information to investors about investment properties. Building condition, maintenance issues, and location issues are important in any real estate purchase, but much of the information in a real estate investment is about income and expenses for the property. Although you probably won't conduct an investment analysis yourself, you're still expected to know something about the numbers and how they're analyzed by investors. The agent's role is to provide the necessary information to the potential investor so that the investor or the investor's accountant can perform the analysis.

The beginning of a real estate investment analysis is the *operating statement*, which also is called the *income and expense statement*. This statement, which usually is prepared to keep track of finances for the building and for income tax purposes, tracks the actual annual income and expenses for a building. The income tracked on the operating statement is called the *contract* or *scheduled rent*, which is the actual rent paid by the tenants. Because the operating statement is used for income tax purposes, it usually contains information about depreciation and debt service (mortgage payments). I discuss depreciation in "Feeling worn-out: Depreciation," earlier in this chapter.

The second piece of information in a real estate investment analysis is the current rent roll. The rent roll is information about the leases that exist, the rents for each lease, and the term or length of time remaining on each lease. (For more about leases, flip to Chapter 12.)

A third piece of information in the analysis is the market rents, which are what the market would pay for the kind of space or apartment in the building. Market rents may be different from contract rents for that particular building.

REMEMBER

The final piece of information in an investment analysis is one that's created by the investor or the person doing the analysis on the investor's behalf. Called the *pro forma*, it's a financial statement of the building's potential income and expenses. By looking at the market rents for the kind of space being leased rather than the scheduled rents, a projection is made of the investment's future. The pro forma is a look at what can be. A few noteworthy characteristics of the pro forma are

>> Market rents, rather than actual or contract rents, are generally used, but actual rents for existing leases may also be used under certain circumstances.

>> Income figures are based on the building being 100 percent occupied, even if it currently isn't, and the figures may include other building income such as that from laundry machines.

>> Other income, such as income to the building for something other than the regular rents (for example a microwave antenna rental on the roof) is usually added after the vacancy and collection loss calculation is applied.

>> A vacancy and collection allowance is used, even if the space in the building is 100 percent rented or in a new building, 100 percent vacant.

>> Expenses generally are rounded off.

>> All figures are annual.

>> Debt service isn't accounted for in order to arrive at the net operating income, but it's used to determine cash flow. The mortgage is more about the owner's financial position than the value of the building.

>> Depreciation is accounted for only after before tax cash flow is calculated in order to determine tax consequences for the investment. The value of the depreciation may vary with the owner's financial position.

The basic numbers that you're looking for in a pro forma are the *net operating income* and *cash flow*. The basic formula for finding net operating income on a pro forma follows, but it will help you understand the formula if you first know the details behind some of the numbers called for in the formula.

>> **Potential gross income:** Market rent at 100 percent occupancy. On occasion, where the building has long-term leases in place, you may use the lease rent (also called the scheduled or contract rent).

Minus

>> **Vacancy and collection loss:** Used to account for periods of rent loss due to vacancies or bad debts; determined by examining other pro formas for the number they use, consulting investment analysts and commercial lenders. It's always expressed as a percentage. Note that this isn't a vacancy rate.

Plus

>> **Other income:** Income that isn't usually the principal source of revenue for the building such as a roof antenna rental or public parking garage.

Equals

>> **Effective gross income:** Also called *effective rental income,* these are the funds that should be available to pay the building's expenses.

Minus

>> **Operating expenses:** These are all the expenses that an investor will have to pay to maintain and operate the building. Don't include depreciation or debt service.

Equals

>> **Net Operating Income (NOI):** This the amount left after all the expenses except the debt service and depreciation are subtracted from the building's income. Calculating the NOI is a key step in estimating the value of an investment property using the Income Capitalization Method, something you should be familiar with, not only as a real estate student but as a real estate investor. Refer to Chapter 14 to see how the NOI is used to determine value.

Minus

>> **Debt service:** Refers to the mortgage payment.

Equals

>> **Before tax cash flow:** This is the money an investor theoretically has left for the year after all the building's expenses including the mortgage have been paid. I say theoretical because you'll have to pay off your uncle, that is Uncle Sam, by way of taxes before you can really walk away with your annual after tax cash flow.

Here is a simpler view of these formulas:

Potential gross income – vacancy and collection loss + other income = effective gross income

Effective gross income – operating expenses = net operating income

Net operating income – debt service = before tax cash flow

If you calculate the taxes owed on this cash flow and subtract it, you can get an approximate idea of the money you'll have after paying your taxes or what's called *after-tax cash flow.* I say approximate because not every expense that you deduct in the pro forma is an allowable deduction for income tax purposes. For example, you can deduct the interest portion of your mortgage payment but not the principal. Also you can't deduct the reserves because you haven't actually spent them.

In analyzing a building for investment, the return (the money you're going to make on your investment as well as the money you'll get back that you invested — return of investment) is calculated for a one-year period and for the project *holding period,* which is the length of time the investment will be owned.

Review Questions and Answers

Actual math calculations on this information may or may not appear on the exam, but the exam writers expect you to be able to explain in words what each investment term means and, if relevant, how it's calculated.

1. Real estate is considered

   (A) a no-risk investment.

   (B) a liquid investment.

   (C) an investment that requires little management.

   (D) an investment that requires good professional advice.

Correct answer: (D). Real estate isn't considered a no-risk investment especially because of its dependence on unpredictable future market conditions. It's definitely not liquid, meaning that you can't get your money out of it quickly. It's nonliquidity is generally considered to be one of the major disadvantages of real estate investment. It does require some kind of management even if you hire a professional to handle day-to-day operations.

2. The act of using borrowed money to extend the profitability of your investment is called

   (A) a REIT.

   (B) a capital gain.

   (C) leveraging.

   (D) pyramiding.

Correct answer: (C). The tricky answer here is pyramiding. Pyramiding is using the appreciation from one investment to make more investments. Leveraging is what makes an investment more profitable, because you're using less of your own money. A Real Estate Investment Trust (REIT) is a type of stock investment (like a mutual fund) that invests in real estate. A capital gain is the profit made by buying a piece of real estate at one price and selling it at a higher price.

3. I put a down payment of $50,000 on a $200,000 investment property. In five years, I sell it for $225,000. The fact that my profit is 50 percent is a result of

   (A) return of investment.

   (B) leverage.

   (C) tax benefits.

   (D) depreciation.

Correct answer: (B). This question puts some numbers to the leverage issue without you having to do the calculation. In case you're lost here, you divide the profit of $25,000 ($225,000 – $200,000) by the $50,000 down payment to get the 50 percent profit. Return of investment is incorrect because the example talks about the money I made above and beyond my original cash investment. Nothing in the example deals with taxes or depreciation; these items are present in most real estate investments, but the example doesn't give you any information about them. So tax benefits and depreciation are also incorrect.

4. Making money by selling a property for more than you paid for it is called

   (A) capital appreciation.

   (B) return of investment.

   (C) cash flow.

   (D) tax credit.

Correct answer: (A). Don't get confused here with the term capital gains. Essentially, capital gains and capital appreciation refer to the same thing; however, capital appreciation describes what the question is asking and capital gains usually describes the same thing for income tax purposes. Return of investment is the return of your original investment money (capital), not any additional money you make, which would be return on the investment. Cash flow is the general term used for the annual return on the investment after all expenses, including debt service, are paid. Nothing in this question refers to taxes, so you can eliminate tax credit right away.

5. When calculating capital gains, what is subtracted from the selling price?

(A) Depreciation

(B) Capital investment

(C) Operating expenses

(D) Adjusted basis

Correct answer: (D). The adjusted basis is the original purchase price of the property plus any capital improvements minus depreciation, and it's what's used to calculate capital gains.

6. The pro forma for a vacant building would use

(A) scheduled rent.

(B) debt service.

(C) market rents.

(D) you cannot do a pro forma for a vacant building.

Correct answer: (C). You need to remember this. Debt service isn't used because it's more specific to the property owner than the property itself. Remember that scheduled rents are used as part of the overall investment analysis but are not usually used in the pro forma unless long-term leases are in place. In the case of a vacant building, there are no leases.

7. A few years ago you bought an investment property for $100,000. You made $10,000 worth of improvements and took $6,000 in depreciation. You sell the property for $120,000. What is the capital gain?

(A) $20,000

(B) $16,000

(C) $10,000

(D) $4,000

Correct answer: (B). Here are the calculations:

$100,000 (purchase price) + $10,000 (capital improvements) – $6,000 (depreciation) = $104,000 (adjusted basis)

$120,000 (selling price) – $104,000 (adjusted basis) = $16,000 (capital gains)

8. You exchange properties with another person. Your property is worth $200,000. Her property is worth $250,000. You give the other party $50,000 in cash. This cash is

(A) boot and is taxable to her.

(B) boot and is taxable to you.

(C) capital gains and the tax is deferred until you sell your property.

(D) capital gains and the tax is deferred until she sells her property.

Correct answer: (A). The boot is money or personal property given in an exchange when the properties are not equal in value. The person receiving the boot pays the taxes on it.

9. You own an apartment house. The potential annual gross income is $40,000. The allowance for vacancies is 5 percent. The annual operating expenses are $10,000. The debt service is $12,000 per year. What is the net operating income?

(A) $16,000

(B) $18,000

(C) $20,000

(D) $28,000

Correct answer: (D) You have to remember the order of how to calculate a net operating income on a pro forma. You also have to remember that you don't use debt service in the calculation. Exam writers sometimes give you information you don't need. Remember to be careful whenever you get monthly numbers because all these calculations have to be in annual figures. The calculation is as follows:

$40,000 (potential gross income) × 0.05 (vacancy allowance) = $2,000 (vacancy and collection loss)

$40,000 (potential gross income) – $2,000 (vacancy and collection loss) = $38,000 (effective gross income)

$38,000 (effective gross income) – $10,000 (operating expenses) = $28,000 NOI (net operating income)

10. An amount of money that the government allows you to deduct from taxes owed on a building's income is called

(A) depreciation.

(B) cost recovery.

(C) a tax credit.

(D) a tax deduction.

Correct answer: (C). You have to read this question carefully. Depreciation is deducted from income, not from taxes owed. Cost recovery is another term that sometimes is used to mean depreciation. A tax deduction is deducted from income.

IN THIS CHAPTER

» **Measuring buildings and land**

» **Calculating percentages and commissions**

» **Finding out about mortgage numbers**

» **Seeing tax calculations in action**

» **Wading through proration problems**

» **Clarifying appreciation and depreciation**

» **Assessing appraised value**

Chapter **18**

All in the Numbers: Real Estate Mathematics

Working in the real estate field is more than just selling real estate. It involves many skills and a thorough knowledge of many subjects, including math. As an agent you may have to measure a room or a house, or calculate the taxes on a piece of property. And most important of all, you need to know how to calculate your commission.

A quick note to all you math phobics (you know who you are!): Those of you who suffer from math-itis, or whatever you call it, should relax. Work through the material in this chapter, and do your best. Above all, though, don't worry: The exam typically has few math problems. You'll do fine without necessarily getting the math questions right. Later on, as a friend likes to tell all her mathematically challenged students, by the time they're in the business a few months, they'll be able to calculate their commissions down to the last penny, in their heads, while waiting at a stop light.

In this chapter, I review some common math concepts and calculations. Notice I say *review*. You've already seen most of what is in this chapter in middle school and high school. You simply may not have seen it in a real estate context. I show you how to apply some fairly simple math concepts to practical real estate problems. I'm sure as you go through this chapter that it all will come back to you.

WARNING

Many students ask about rounding. Test writers are interested in you knowing basic formulas and techniques. They won't give you questions where the difference between a right and wrong answer is a tenth of a number that you might get wrong due to rounding.

REMEMBER

Exam writers expect you to know the formulas involved in math calculations as well as how to actually do the calculations. You may run into questions that I call *non-number math questions* where you may be asked to identify the correct formula to solve a problem without actually being asked to doing the calculations. Be sure and memorize the formulas and get comfortable with your calculators.

Don't Lose the Faith, but You May Have to Convert

Before you start doing most of the math problems in this chapter, you need to remember that test writers often throw problems at you that contain different units of measurements in the same problem. Before you can solve the problems, you need to convert those measurements to make sure you multiply feet by feet, yards by yards, and so on. Also, you may have to calculate the area of a room in square feet but later convert it to square yards. If any conversions are required to solve the problem, the exam writers won't give you the conversion factors. They expect you to know them.

REMEMBER

Memorize the following conversion factors to ease your problem solving.

1 foot = 12 inches

1 yard = 3 feet

1 mile = 5,280 feet

1 square yard = 9 square feet (3 feet × 3 feet)

1 acre = 43,560 square feet

A section = 1 square mile or 640 acres

A section = 5,280 feet (1 mile) on each side

1 cubic yard = 27 cubic feet (3 feet × 3 feet × 3 feet)

Land and Buildings: Measuring Area and Volume

Because you'll be selling land and buildings, knowing something about figuring out what size they are is important. For exam purposes, all you really need to know is how to calculate the area and volume of land and buildings after you have the measurements.

REMEMBER

Area is the amount of space on a flat surface. Calculating the *area* means figuring out how large a flat space is. It may be determining the square footage of a house, the amount of carpeting or tile needed to cover the floor of a room, or the amount of wallpaper needed to cover a wall. (Remember a wall still is a flat surface.)

HOW BIG IS IT REALLY?

Usually, land isn't something that you as a real estate agent measure. You may occasionally walk the boundaries of a piece of property and estimate its length and width. In general, however, if someone asks you the size of a piece of land, you'll look it up in the public records like the deed, tax records, or public map filings, or you'll calculate it from information on a map drawn by a surveyor. Unless a piece of land is perfectly rectangular, square, or triangular, calculating the exact area of the property is difficult and best left to surveyors.

As an agent, you may have to measure a house or individual rooms. In general, overall house size starts with a measurement of the outside walls of the house. If you need an individual room size, measure the actual room; however, due to discrepancies in measurement over which buyers can get cranky, many agents now rely on public records when they advise the buyers of the size of the house.

REMEMBER

Volume is the measurement of what it takes to fill up something. In real estate terms, calculating the volume of a warehouse, rather than just its floor area, is important when you're informing a potential buyer how much stackable space the property has.

In this section, I take you through a series of examples that cover all the standard area and volume calculations that you may encounter on a state real estate exam.

Calculating the area of a square or a rectangle

A *square* is a four-sided figure on which each side is the same length. A *rectangle* is a four-sided figure where two sides opposite each other are equal. For example, a rectangle may have two sides opposite each other that are 150 feet long, and the two other sides opposite each other are 80 feet long. See Figures 18-1 and 18-2 for examples of a square and a rectangle.

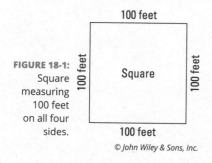

FIGURE 18-1: Square measuring 100 feet on all four sides.

© John Wiley & Sons, Inc.

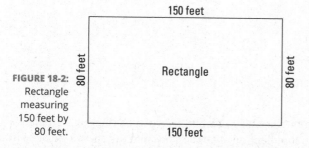

FIGURE 18-2: Rectangle measuring 150 feet by 80 feet.

The formula for calculating the area of a square and a rectangle is the same.

Length (L) × Width (W) = Area (A)

REMEMBER

Like most other calculations in this chapter, when calculating area, the units of measure must be the same. You have to multiply feet by feet, yards by yards, and so on. Furthermore, the answer to any area problem is always in square units. If you're multiplying feet by feet, your answer is in square feet.

EXAMPLE

You have a square piece of property that measures 100 feet by 100 feet. How big is the property?

100 feet × 100 feet = 10,000 square feet

Or, say you have a rectangular piece of property that measures 80 feet by 150 feet. What is the area?

150 feet × 80 feet = 12,000 square feet

REMEMBER

Notice in this second question where I put the longer figure for length. It really doesn't matter in a problem like this what you call each number. On a piece of land, the distance across the front of the property generally is referred to as the width, while the distance going from the street back is the length or depth. Sometimes a problem may refer to a front foot or *front footage, or frontage,* which usually is the same as the width of the property along the street. If you get a problem that simply states two measurements of a lot, say 100 feet by 200 feet, assume that the first number is the measurement across the front of the lot, namely the frontage or width.

Figuring out the area of a triangle

A triangle is a three-sided figure where all the sides join together. Look up at the end of a peaked roofed house and you'll see a triangle. That triangle is called the *gable end,* and you may have to calculate the area to determine how much paint or siding is needed to cover it.

The formula for the area of a triangle is

½ Base (B) × Height (H) = Area (A)

Some of you may have learned this equation as

Base (B) × Height (H) ÷ 2 = Area (A)

Figure 18-3 shows a sample triangle.

FIGURE 18-3:
Triangle with a base of 30 feet and a height of 12 feet.

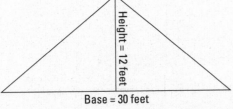

© *John Wiley & Sons, Inc.*

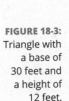

REMEMBER

Similar to the way you calculate the area of a square or rectangle, when calculating a triangle's area, don't forget that all the units of measurement must be the same and the answer must be in square units. The *height* is a line that is *perpendicular,* or at a right (90-degree) angle, to the base.

EXAMPLE

Say you want to paint your roof's gable end. The width of the house at that point is 30 feet. The height of the gable is 12 feet. How many square feet are you going to have to paint?

0.5×30 feet $\times 12$ feet $= 180$ square feet

Calculating the area of a circle

A *circle* essentially is a single line that curves around and meets itself. Pick up that quarter in your pocket, and you've got a circle. The *diameter* is a straight line drawn through the center from one side of the circle to the other, and the *radius* is half of the diameter.

The formula to find the area of a circle is

$\pi \times$ radius squared (r^2) (To *square* the radius, you multiply the radius by itself.)

π is the constant number 3.1416.

Check out Figure 18-4 for an example of a circle.

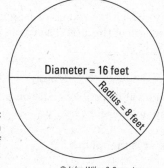

FIGURE 18-4:
Circle with a diameter of 16 feet.

Diameter = 16 feet

Radius = 8 feet

© John Wiley & Sons, Inc.

Maybe you're going to build a round patio. Or, if you live in farm country, you may have to rely on some of these calculations when determining the volume of a silo.

EXAMPLE

You're building a circular patio that's 16 feet in diameter. How many square feet of patio block will you use?

3.1416×8 (squared) $= A$ (area)

$3.1416 \times (8 \times 8) = 201.06$ square feet

Figuring out the area of an irregular shape

Unfortunately many houses aren't single squares or rectangles but rather are combinations of several squares and rectangles. A rectangular house with a small breezeway and attached garage is a good example of what I'm talking about. And the key to calculating the area of a house like this is that you have to divide the figure into squares and rectangles and occasionally even triangles, calculate the area of each individual figure, and then add them together. You can also come pretty close by using this technique to calculate the area of an irregular piece of land.

Determining the volume of almost anything

The formula for calculating the volume of any six-sided, three dimensional figure involves calculating the area and multiplying it by the height. Why six sided? Most shapes that you may encounter in your real estate work will have six sides with opposite sides of equal dimensions. Think of a warehouse (the example that follows) or a nice concrete patio in your backyard. The first part of the formula looks like you're finding the area of a flat surface. In the case of volume however you also want to account for the depth or height of the structure so the formula looks like this:

Length (L) × Width (W) × Height (H) = Volume (V)

EXAMPLE

Say you want to calculate the volume of a rectangular warehouse that measures 100 feet by 200 feet by 15 feet high. The equation would look something like:

200 feet × 100 feet × 15 feet = 300,000 cubic feet

REMEMBER

Length × width is the formula for calculating the area, but by multiplying that answer (called the *product*) by the third dimension, the height, you get the volume. Just like when you calculate area, the measurements must always be in the same units. With volume, the answer is always in cubic units. So if all three measurements are in feet, the answer will be in cubic feet.

In the case of a triangular-shaped object like an attic, in which the triangle's height already is used to calculate the area, you multiply the area by the length of the attic. The whole formula is

½ Base (B) × Height (H) × Length (L) = Volume (V)

Finally, suppose you need to find the volume of a cylindrical object like a silo on a farm. Once again, you just have to multiply the area of the silo's base by the silo's height.

EXAMPLE

If you had a silo 20 feet in diameter and 30 feet high, what is the volume?

π × radius squared (r²) × Height (H) = Volume (V)

3.1416 × (10 feet × 10 feet) × 30 feet = 9,424.8 cubic feet

Remember, the area of a circle involves the radius, which is half of the diameter. (That's why this example uses 10 feet instead of 20 feet.)

In case you're wondering about other shape figures, you'll probably not likely have to deal with the volume of an *octahedron* (eight sides) or a *tetrahedron* (ten sides) or some other unusual shape building. The preceding formula should get you through the exam, your real estate career, and that patio you may want to build in your backyard.

Percentages: Pinpointing What You Really Need to Know

Using percentages is another type of real estate math problem. Commissions usually are figured on a percentage basis. Shared ownership of a property may be on a percentage basis. Vacancy rates usually are expressed as a percent. You'll work with percents to figure out the selling price of a property. Property tax calculations may also involve percentages. So I think you can see the importance of understanding and being able to answer exam questions about percentages.

In this section, I provide the basics that you can apply to any problems asking you to use or calculate percentages. And by the way, I explain them to you as if you're doing these calculations by hand. Some calculators have percentage keys that you can use. Feel free to use them, if you know how, or ignore them.

A *percent* — which is expressed as a number like 4 percent, 8 percent, 7.5 percent, or 0.8 percent — essentially describes what part of a hundred you're talking about. The word "percent" comes from the Latin word *centum*, meaning a hundred. So 4 percent means four parts per hundred of whatever you're taking about. If 4 percent of the eggs in a truckload are bad, then four out of every hundred eggs are bad. And if you're allowed to build on 4 percent of your land area, it means you can cover 4 square feet out of every 100 square feet with a building. The calculations you do with percentages usually are most often multiplication and occasionally division, depending on the problem.

REMEMBER

You have two choices for turning a percentage into a number you can work with. You can either divide the percent number by 100 or move the decimal point two places to the left.

Say, for example, that you have to use 7 percent in a problem. If you divide 7 by 100, you get a number you can use in a calculator or by hand.

$$7 \div 100 = 0.07$$

That isn't 0.07 percent. It's simply 0.07, which is the same as 7 percent.

Another way to remember is that if a decimal point doesn't actually appear in the number, then it's assumed to be at the end. From there (the right side of a whole number), move the decimal to the left two spaces, even if you have to add one or more zeroes. Seven percent becomes 0.07. Check out a few more of these:

800%	8
80%	0.80
8%	0.08
.8%	0.008
.08%	0.0008
8.5%	0.085

Note: You probably won't be working too much with small percentages, such as 0.08 percent or 0.8 percent, either on an exam or in real life.

Don't forget the reverse of this concept so you can solve a problem like this.

EXAMPLE

You make a $20,000 commission on the sale of a $400,000 house. What is your commission rate? Keep in mind that the word *rate* usually means *percent.* The calculation is

$$\$20,000 \div \$400,000 = 0.05$$

Move the decimal point two places to the right to get the answer of 5 percent. Remember, to get from a decimal to a percentage, move the decimal two places to the right, or multiply by a hundred.

REMEMBER

One other thing you need to know how to do is to convert a fraction to a decimal and, in turn, a percentage. Don't worry. If you don't remember your sixth-grade math class, this step isn't too difficult. Just divide the upper number (numerator) by the lower number (denominator). Doing so gives you a decimal. Now move the decimal point two places to the right (don't forget to add zeroes as needed) and you have a percentage. Check out the following examples:

½ = 1 ÷ 2 = 0.5 = 50 percent

3⁄8 = 3 ÷ 8 = 0.375 = 37.5 percent

9/16 = 9 ÷ 16 = 0.5625 = 56.25 percent

Commissions: Tracking Your Moolah

You probably were wondering when I'd finally get to this all-important section — the amount you get paid. Discussing percentages is foremost, because most commissions are based on a percentage of the sale price of a property. If you haven't read "Percentages: Pinpointing What You Really Need to Know," earlier in this chapter, take a few minutes to scan it before reading this section.

In this section, I take you through a few variations on commission problems, including splitting the commission with other brokers and agents. I also have you look at how to get to a selling price working backward from a commission. Because of antitrust laws, which say that all commissions are negotiable and that brokers cannot agree among themselves (price fixing) to set certain commission rates, I make up all the figures that I use for commissions and commission splits in the examples that follow. (For more about commissions and antitrust laws, check out Chapter 3.)

Figuring out how much you and everyone else earns

Here I start you out with a couple of basic commission problems and then move on to commission splits.

Figuring your commission

EXAMPLE

You're a broker who sells a house. The owner has agreed to pay you a 5 percent commission. How much will you earn on the sale, if the house sells for $400,000?

Sale price × commission rate = commission earned

$400,000 × 0.05 = $20,000

Remember to turn 5 percent into a number you can use (in this case, 0.05) before you proceed with the rest of the problem.

Figuring out your commission rate

A variation on the commission problem has you figuring out your commission rate if you know the selling price of the property and the commission earned. I use the same numbers that I did in the last problem.

EXAMPLE

You sell a listed house for $400,000. You earn a $20,000 commission on the sale. What was your commission rate?

Commission earned ÷ sale price = commission rate

$20,000 ÷ $400,000 = .05 or 5 percent

Sharing the rewards: Commission splits

As a salesperson, your broker will pay you a share of the total commission earned for the sale. Remember that a salesperson works under the authority of a broker (see Chapter 3 for the full scoop).

All commissions and commission splits are negotiable between the salesperson and the broker. In a math problem, this split may be expressed different ways. For example, a problem may have a 60/40 split, which is 60 percent going to one party and 40 percent going to the other party. Whenever the commission shares are unequal, the problem will be clear as to what percentage each party gets. Examples of these types of problems follow.

EXAMPLE

Your firm receives a $20,000 commission that is to be split 60/40 between you and your broker. How much will you receive?

Commission amount × percentage share = commission amount share

$20,000 × 0.60 = $12,000

TIP

Why did I use the 60 percent and not 40 percent? If you read the question carefully, the 60/40 split is in the same order as the "you and your broker." If the problem doesn't give you any more information, you have to interpret what test writers mean. Scan the following problem, which contains more than one split.

EXAMPLE

Suppose a $30,000 commission is earned on the sale of a house. The listing broker and the buyer's broker agree to split the commission evenly. The listing salesperson receives 40 percent of the listing side. How much will the listing salesperson receive?

Where two brokers cooperate on a sale, they're often referred to as the listing side (the broker who originally got the listing agreement to represent the seller) and the buyer's side (the broker who finds the buyer). In this particular question, you also have to know that "split" evenly means that each of the sides gets half of the total commission.

$30,000 × 0.50 = $15,000 listing and buyer's side because the commission is split evenly

$15,000 (listing side commission) × 0.40 (listing salesperson's share) = $6,000 (listing salesperson's commission)

EXAMPLE

A variation of this question uses the same information but asks you what the listing broker's share was.

100 percent (total percentage of listing side commission) – 40 percent (listing salesperson's percentage) = 60 percent listing broker's percentage

$15,000 (total listing side commission) × .60 (listing broker's percentage share) = $9,000 (listing broker's share)

Determining how much a house should sell for based on a commission rate

Establishing how much a house should sell for is an interesting calculation that has many uses, primarily because it enables you to work backward from a percentage to a number. But first I have a problem that I want you to try.

EXAMPLE

Your seller wants to *net* (take away from the closing table) $300,000 after paying your 6 percent commission. How much does the house have to sell for to do this?

WARNING

This problem actually has two answers, $318,000 and $319,149 (rounded), but one of the answers, $318,000, happens to be wrong. Now before you start yelling or arguing or feeling bad that you got it wrong, allow me to explain. In virtually every math class that I teach, more than half the class comes up with the wrong answer. But by the time they do a few problems like the one that follows, nobody gets it wrong. Before I explain how you do this problem, I want to show you how to prove to yourself that the $318,000 is wrong. This proof may come in handy on an exam to check your answer.

Selling price × commission rate = commission paid

$318,000 × 0.06 = $19,080

Selling price − commission paid = net to seller

$318,000 − $19,080 = $298,920

The number $298,920 obviously isn't the $300,000 net the seller wants. If you got $318,000 for your answer, it's because you added the 6 percent commission to the net that the seller wanted, but that isn't how you calculate selling prices and commissions. You get a commission by taking it away from the selling price, not adding onto the net to the owner figure. If you did the same proof using the $319,149 and took 6 percent from that number, the owner gets the requested $300,000.

REMEMBER

Check out the following example if you want more clarification:

What it is	Percentage	Dollar amount
Selling price	100 percent	X (That's what you're looking for.)
Commission	6 percent	You don't know this and don't need to know.
Net to seller	94 percent	$300,000

See how the commission percentage and the seller's net percentage always equal 100 percent, which is the selling price.

REMEMBER

If you know a dollar amount and that is part of a larger dollar amount that you want to find, and you know the percentage of the total (100 percent) that it represents, you can always find the larger dollar amount by dividing the partial dollar amount by the percentage of the total that it represents. I'll say that again with numbers:

$300,000 is the dollar amount that is part of a larger dollar amount that you want to find — that is, the selling price. $300,000 is 94 percent of the larger dollar amount, which is 100 percent. By dividing $300,000 by 94 percent, you get the larger amount, which is 100 percent of the total.

$300,000 ÷ 0.94 = $319,149

In other words, if $300,000 is 94 percent of some number that you want to find (the selling price, in this case), all you have to do is divide $300,000 by 94 percent (0.94). You get $319,149.

In this particular problem, you had to subtract 6 percent from 100 percent to get the 94 percent, which is the seller's share. But the test writers may write the problem a little differently, trying to trick you.

EXAMPLE

You earn an $18,000 commission, which is 6 percent of the selling price. How much did the house sell for?

Using the logic for this kind of problem, you can restate it like this: $18,000 is 6 percent of some number. In this case, that number is the selling price. And if you know the dollar amount and the percentage of the whole number it represents, all you have to do is divide by the matching percentage.

> $18,000 (commission amount) ÷ 0.06 (commission rate) = $300,000 (selling price)

REMEMBER

So what's the moral of the story? When figuring commissions in relation to how much a house should sell for, memorize these two formulas:

> Net to seller ÷ (100 percent – commission rate) = selling price
>
> Commission amount in dollars ÷ commission rate = selling price

Making Mortgage Calculations without a Fancy Calculator

In this section, I do a few problems to review some of the math associated with mortgages. (Chapter 15 has the scoop on mortgages and additional math, such as problems involving loan to value ratios.) In these calculations, one important term to know is *amortized loan,* which means that each payment on the mortgage is a combination of principal and interest so that at the end of the mortgage term you have nothing left to pay.

TIP

One of the questions I'm often asked is how necessary having a financial calculator is either for real estate work or for the state exam. A financial calculator is helpful and makes life easier if you know how to use it. As for the state exams, a simple inexpensive calculator does just fine. In fact, you can probably do most of the problems on your fingers and toes (if you have enough of them).

Calculating interest

A few standard problems that you may find on an exam deal with mortgage interest and principal payments. Here are the likely possibilities.

Annual and monthly interest

All interest on mortgage loans is expressed as an annual interest amount, so if your mortgage interest rate is 8 percent, that's the annual rate. But most mortgages are paid on a monthly basis, so you sometimes need to calculate how much interest you actually paid in one month based on that annual rate.

First, look at an annual interest problem.

EXAMPLE

You borrow $200,000 at 5 percent for 30 years in an amortized mortgage loan. How much interest will you pay the first year?

Remember that in a mortgage loan, the interest rate is always quoted annually and is always based on the loan's unpaid balance.

Loan amount × interest rate = first year's interest

$200,000 × 0.05 = $10,000

WARNING

The 30 years doesn't matter. It's extra information to confuse you.

Now here's a monthly problem with different numbers:

EXAMPLE

You borrow $300,000 at 4 percent interest for 30 years in an amortized loan. What is the first month's interest on the loan?

Loan amount × interest rate = first year's interest

$300,000 × 0.04 = $12,000 annual interest

You wind up with $12,000 for the first year's interest. To figure out the first month's interest, all you have to do is divide the first year's interest by 12.

First year's interest ÷ 12 months = first month's interest

$12,000 ÷ 12 = $1,000 first month's interest

Note that this monthly interest calculation works this way only for the first month's interest.

Test writers may go further and ask you to calculate the second month's interest. To answer the question, you need to know what the total monthly payment is, and the test writers will tell you. I'll continue using the numbers from the previous problem. In this case, the monthly payment, which includes principal and interest, is $1,432 (rounded), information they have to give you. The question is how much is the second month's interest payment.

$1,432 (rounded) (monthly payment) – $1,000 (first month's interest) = $432 (principal payment)

$300,000 (loan amount) – $432 (first month's principal payment) = $299,568 (loan balance after first month's payment)

$299,568 (loan balance after first payment) × 0.04 (annual interest rate) = $11,982.72 (interest owed for the next 12 months)

$11,982.72 (rounded) (interest owed for the next 12 months) ÷ 12 months = $998,56 (interest paid for the first month of that next 12-month period, which is, in fact, the second month of the loan term of the loan)

What you need to remember here is that in an amortized loan, you're only reducing the amount you owe by the amount of principal you pay each month and not by the amount of the total payment, because each payment includes interest and principal.

Total interest

A type of interest problem that seems to confuse people is the calculation of total interest. Total interest is the amount of interest you pay during the entire life of the loan, assuming that you pay off the loan by making the payments within the required time frame. In general, banks provide these numbers to people, but you need to be familiar with this calculation because it is fair game on an exam.

EXAMPLE

Say you borrow $300,000 at 5 percent for 30 years in an amortized mortgage loan. Your monthly payments are $1,610 (rounded) What is the total interest on the loan?

WARNING

Most people fool around with the 5 percent for a while, but you don't need the percentage rate of the mortgage loan to work this problem. Watch this, because you're not going to believe how easy it is.

$1,610 (monthly payment) × 12 months × 30 years = $579,600 total payments during the loan's 30-year term.

$579,600 – $300,000 (original loan amount) = $279,600 interest paid during the course of the loan.

REMEMBER

Don't forget that every amortized loan payment contains part principal and part interest. In this example in 30 years, you pay a total of $579,600 in principal and interest. So if you subtract the principal, or the amount you borrowed, what you have left is interest. It's also a good demonstration of why you may want to pay that mortgage off as soon as possible.

Figuring out monthly payments

Unless you use a financial calculator, you're going to calculate mortgage payments using a mortgage table. These tables, which are arranged according to the percentage of interest and years of the mortgage term, provide the monthly payment to *amortize*, or pay off interest and principal, for a $1,000 mortgage loan. After you get that monthly payoff number, which sometimes is called the *payment factor*, you multiply it by the number of thousands of dollars of the mortgage loan (which you get by dividing the loan amount by $1,000).

EXAMPLE

The factor for a 20-year loan at 6 percent is $7.16. What is the monthly payment for a $150,000 loan?

$150,000 ÷ $1,000 = 150 (units of a $1,000)

150 × $7.16 (factor to pay off $1,000) = $1,074 per month

If you run into a problem like this on the exam, you'll either get a sample of a mortgage table or be given the payment factor you need to solve the problem. You'll have to remember the formula in the example. In the real world, that is, when you have your license and are working on your first million, printed mortgage tables, many online mortgage calculation sites, and financial calculators can make all this relatively simple.

Oh, the Pain: Calculating Taxes

If you want the lowdown on real estate taxes, check out Chapter 16, where you also find a bit of math on equalization rates. In this section, I solve a few sample problems that you may encounter about taxes. You need to know this information not only for the test, but also because every listing of a property for sale generally requires the agent to find out what the taxes are.

Calculating the assessed value of a property

Many municipalities use assessment ratios to assess properties. An *assessment ratio* is the percentage relationship between the market value of a property, which is the amount the property will sell for in a normal market sale, and the assessed value, which is a value tax assessors use to calculate taxes and is usually related to market value. (I discuss the details of market value in Chapter 14 and assessment ratios in Chapter 16.) The use of an assessment ratio creates the possibility of three kinds of exam problems.

EXAMPLE

A property has a market value of $200,000. The assessment ratio is 60 percent. What is the assessed value?

Market value × assessment ratio = assessed value

$200,000 × 0.60 = $120,000

EXAMPLE

What is the assessment ratio of a property whose market value is $200,000 and whose assessed value is $120,000?

Assessed value ÷ market value = assessment ratio

$120,000 ÷ $200,000 = 0.60 or 60 percent

EXAMPLE

What is the market value of a property assessed at a 60 percent assessment ratio whose assessed value is $120,000?

Assessed value ÷ assessment ratio = market value

$120,000 ÷ 0.60 = $200,000

Calculating taxes due

You can calculate taxes due using one of the following three methods, depending on how the municipality calculates taxes or how the exam question is asked.

> **Mills:** This method bases the tax rate on so many tenths of a penny (or mills) in taxes for each dollar of assessed value.

> **Dollars per hundred:** This method bases the tax rate on so many dollars of tax for each $100 of assessed value.

> **Dollars per thousand:** This method bases the tax rate on so many dollars of tax per $1,000 of assessed value.

You need to be familiar with all three methods for exam purposes.

Mills

EXAMPLE

The tax rate in town is 24 mills. The assessed value of the property is $30,000. What are the taxes on the property?

Assessed value × millage = taxes owed

$30,000 × $0.024 = $720

Remember, when working with a millage, move the decimal three places to the left, because millages are tax rates expressed in mills, or tenths of a cent.

Taxes per hundred

EXAMPLE

The tax rate is $2.40 per $100 assessed value. What are the taxes on a property assessed at $30,000?

Assessed value × tax rate = taxes owed

$30,000 × ($2.40 ÷ $100) = taxes owed

$2.40 (tax rate) ÷ $100 (ratio of assessed value) = $0.024 tax rate (per dollar of assessed valuation)

$30,000 × $0.024 = $720

Taxes per thousand

EXAMPLE

The tax rate on a property assessed at $30,000 is $24 per thousand. What are the taxes?

Assessed value × tax rate = taxes owed

$30,000 × ($24 ÷ $1,000) = taxes owed

$24 (tax rate) ÷ $1,000 (ratio of assessed value) = $0.024 tax rate (per dollar of assessed valuation)

$30,000 × $0.024 = $720

If it's easier for you to see, you can also divide the assessed value by the unit in which the tax is stated, in this case, you could do the following:

$30,000 ÷ $1,000 = 30 units of $1,000

30 × $24 (tax rate per unit of $1,000) = $720.

If the tax rate is stated per hundred dollars, then divide by $100 instead of $1,000.

Putting Proration into Perspective

Proration is the allocation or dividing of certain money items at the closing. (I discuss proration and closings in more detail in Chapter 9.) An attorney, a real estate salesperson, a broker, or a representative of the title company does the proration calculations at the closing. In any case, most test writers expect you to know the basics of proration math. The key to remember about prorations is that the person who uses it needs to pay for it. Here's an example that illustrates the point of proration.

EXAMPLE

The seller has paid taxes of $3,000 for the entire year ahead on January 1 and sells his property and closes title on June 1. Who owes what to whom?

The seller paid the full year's taxes, but used the property only for the five months (January through May). Read the problem carefully. The buyer needs to pay the seller for the taxes already paid for the months the seller won't own the property during the year. The rest is just the math of dividing up who paid and who pays.

$3,000 ÷ 12 months = $250 per month

$250 per month × 5 months (the time the seller owned the property) = $1,250

This is the amount of the taxes that the seller used from January through May.

$250 per month × 7 months (the new buyer's time in the house) = $1,750

This is the amount of the taxes the buyer will use, because he bought the house on June 1.

Because the seller had already paid the taxes for the whole year, the buyer owes the seller $1,750 for the taxes the buyer will be using but didn't pay for. In the terminology of proration, the buyer gets a debit and the seller gets a credit.

Here's another problem that has the buyer paying in *arrears* (or after the fact).

EXAMPLE

A buyer pays $2,400 in taxes in arrears for the entire year on December 31. He bought the house on September 1. Who owes what to whom?

$2,400 ÷ 12 months = $200 per month

$200 per month × 8 months (the time the seller owned the house) = $1,600

The seller used $1,600 of the paid taxes. Now to determine how much the seller didn't use:

$200 per month × 4 months (the time the buyer owned the property) = $800

Because the buyer paid the full $2,400 for the previous year, during which he owned the house for only four months, the seller owes the buyer $1,600. The buyer gets a credit and the seller gets a debit.

STATE SPECIFIC

When you get out into the real world, find out what the local practice is for dividing up the year for prorations. Some areas and attorneys use the exact day, rather than the month. So in the previous examples, divide by 365 days to get the amount of taxes paid per day. Some people use the 12-month annual calculation and then divide by the exact number of days in a month when the closing date occurs midmonth. As far as I know, no state law governs this practice, but rather, it's a matter of local practice. On the exam, test writers usually specify "actual days" if they want you to calculate it that way. If the time frame isn't specified or you're instructed otherwise on an exam, you need to use the third method, which is to divide a yearly cost or payment by 12 and the monthly number by 30, unless your real estate course or textbook specifies that one of the other methods is the only method used in your state. The other state-specific item that can affect proration is who owns the property on the day of closing. Unless your state says otherwise, assume that the buyer owns the house on the closing date. I'll do a problem with a midmonth closing date to illustrate the 12-month/ 30-day method.

EXAMPLE

An owner sells a house, closes on May 17, but paid a full year's taxes of $3,600 in advance on January 1. What is the proration of taxes?

$3,600 ÷ 12 months = $300 per month

$300 ÷ 30 days = $10 per day

The seller/owner owned the house for four full months (January through April) and 16 days in May. (Remember, the buyer is considered to own the house on the day of closing.)

4 months × $300 per month = $1,200

16 days × $10 per day = $160

$1,200 + $160 = $1,360 taxes used by the seller

$3,600 (total taxes for the year paid by the seller) – $1,360 (taxes used by the seller) = $2,240 (taxes used by the buyer)

The buyer owes the seller $2,240. The buyer gets a debit of $2,240, and the seller gets a credit of $2,240.

Appreciating Appreciation and Depreciation

As if you weren't confused enough already, you'll find there's only one kind of appreciation but there are two kinds of depreciation. Stay with me, though, because this stuff really is pretty easy.

Appreciation is an increase in a property's value caused by factors like inflation, increasing demand, and improvements to the property. *Depreciation* is a decrease in the value of a property caused by lower demand, deflation in the economy, deterioration, or the influences of other undesirable factors like a new sewage treatment plant going in next door. Another type of depreciation, which I discuss in Chapter 17, is a tax benefit the government gives people on real estate investments.

Real estate salespeople and brokers, buyers, and sellers always are interested in how much a property's value has increased or decreased. Investors, real estate brokers, and salespeople may want to know what tax benefits of a property are attributed to depreciation, although more often than not, an accountant needs to be doing these calculations for an investor. Test writers expect you to know the basics of how to calculate appreciation and depreciation.

Getting more or less: Appreciation and depreciation of a property's value

People always are interested in how much more they can sell their property for than what they paid for it. They may not want to consider a loss to their property's value, but that can happen, too. A real estate agent is expected to be able to track increases and decreases in a property's value and to apply market increases to specific properties. So if the overall real estate market values in an area have increased by 10 percent during the last year according to government or other statistics, you need to be able to apply this increase in value to a specific property. By the way, not only market values can increase. Any of the types of values that I discuss in Chapter 14 can increase or decrease. I show you some math on how to handle these problems in the real world and on the exam.

EXAMPLE

You bought a house for $200,000 and five years later sold it for $250,000. What is the rate at which the house appreciated?

The formula for this type of problem has two parts:

New value – old value = change in value

Change in value ÷ old value = percent of change in value

$250,000 – $200,000 = $50,000

$50,000 ÷ $200,000 = 0.25 or 25 percent

EXAMPLE

A different type of problem deals with a decrease in value. You bought a house for $200,000 and five years later sold it for $150,000. By what percentage did it depreciate?

The formula for this type of problem also has two parts:

Old value – new value = change in value

Change in value ÷ old value = percent of change in value

$200,000 – $150,000 = $50,000

$50,000 ÷ $200,000 = 0.25 or 25 percent

In either of these problems, you divide the change by the older value.

TIP

Keep an eye open for whether test writers ask you either of the preceding questions using the word "change" rather than "appreciate" or "depreciate." For example: "By what percentage did the value of the house change?" In that case, your answers will have either a plus or a minus sign in front of them. The appreciation answer would be +25 percent, and the depreciation answer would be −25 percent.

Now for a reverse problem:

EXAMPLE

A house sold for $260,000, which is 130 percent of what you paid for it. How much did you pay or it?

The formula for this type of problem is

Current price (or value) ÷ percent of original price = price (or value) sought

Notice in this formula that I say "percent of original price," which is always 100 percent plus the change, which is +30 percent. Now how did I know this, since the numbers were not given that way? Read the wording of the question carefully. It said that the house sold for 130 percent **of** the original price, not 130 percent *more* than the original price. Another way to look at this is to say, "$260,000 is 130 percent of some number" — in this case, the original price. If you can say it that way, you know to divide the dollar amount you're given by the percentage number.

With numbers the problem looks like this:

$260,000 ÷ 1.30 = $200,000

1.30 is the decimal equivalent of 130 percent.

Another problem similar to this reverses the question:

EXAMPLE

You bought a house for $300,000, which is 75 percent of what you sell it for five years later. What price did you sell it for?

Original price (or value) ÷ the percent of selling price = price (or value) sought

$300,000 ÷ 0.75 = $400,000

Once again, you can say, "$300,000 is 75 percent of some number."

In these types of problems, you can usually get the number you're looking for by dividing the number you're given by the percent that it represents. You can find similar problems in the section on "Determining how much a house should sell for based on a commission rate" earlier in this chapter.

Depreciation: The government kind

In Chapter 17, I explain the concept of depreciation that sometime is called cost recovery. Although in the real world accountants working for real estate investors usually do these calculations, test writers expect you to understand and be able to apply the basics. This type of depreciation has nothing to do with a property going down in value but rather is based on government regulations that are designed to help real estate investors reduce their tax burdens.

EXAMPLE

You have a building worth $250,000. You are allowed to depreciate it over a period of 27.5 years (also called the *cost recovery period*). What is the annual amount of depreciation?

> Cost of property ÷ cost recovery period = annual amount of depreciation
>
> $250,000 ÷ 27.5 = $9,090.91

TIP

Now suppose you were asked what the annual rate of depreciation is. You don't need the dollar amounts to figure that one out. You need only the cost recovery period.

EXAMPLE

You are allowed to depreciate a building over a period of 39 years. What is the annual rate of depreciation?

> 1 ÷ 39 = .0256, which equals 2.56 percent per year
>
> or you can also divide 100 by 39
>
> 100 ÷ 39 = 2.56 percent per year

Try it both ways on your calculator to get a little practice in decimals and percentages.

Estimating Appraised Value

If you want the lowdown on appraising property, check out Chapter 14. As a real estate agent, you won't actually be doing appraisals, but you can use these formulas to roughly estimate property values, particularly if you deal in investment properties. You can read about real estate investing in Chapter 17, but in the meantime, state test writers expect you to understand and be able to apply these formulas. In this section, the only real math-driven formulas for appraising, at least at the level that you're expected to know it, are formulas for finding value using the income approach. Two different methods are used in that approach to value. I give you formulas and examples for both.

The capitalization method

The capitalization method uses one formula for finding a property's value, and with a couple of variations you can find the property's income and the capitalization rate. *Capitalization* is a technique for estimating a property's value based on its income. You can read all about it in Chapter 14.

The formulas use the following symbols:

>> I = Income or net operating income

>> R = Rate of return or capitalization rate

>> V = Value or sale price

TIP

Don't be confused by the possibility that any one of these letters can mean two different things (such as income versus net operating income). Memorize these terms and the problem will be clear as to what is being asked. Also remember that in these problems, all the numbers are based on annual figures. So if, for example, you're given a monthly income number, you need to multiply by 12.

The formulas are as follows:

>> $V = I \div R$

>> $I = V \times R$

>> $R = I \div V$

In the following three examples, I use the same numbers to illustrate how these formulas work.

EXAMPLE

Find the value of a building that has a net operating income of $30,000 where the capitalization rate is 10 percent.

$V = \$30,000 \div 0.10$

$V = \$300,000$

EXAMPLE

Find the income of a building that was sold $300,000 where the rate of return is 10 percent.

$I = \$300,000 \times 0.10$

$I = \$30,000$

EXAMPLE

Find the capitalization rate of a building that sold for $300,000 and has a net operating income of $30,000.

$R = \$30,000 \div \$300,000$

$R = 0.10$ or 10 percent

The gross rent multiplier method

The method for finding the value of a property using the gross rent is an easy matter of multiplication. The *gross rent multiplier* is used to estimate the value of small investment-type properties like small multifamily houses. You can find out more about it in Chapter 14. The formula is

Value = Gross monthly rent × gross rent multiplier (GRM)

The variations of this equation are

GRM = sale price (or value) ÷ rent

Rent = sales price (or value) ÷ GRM

The following examples show you how to use these formulas with numbers.

EXAMPLE

You're appraising a building that generates a gross monthly rent of $3,000. You've calculated a GRM of 100. What is the value of the building?

Value = $3,000 × 100

Value = $300,000

EXAMPLE

You're trying to calculate GRM using information on a building that recently sold for $300,000 with a gross monthly rent of $3,000. Find the GRM.

GRM = $300,000 ÷ $3,000

GRM = 100

You would rarely have to calculate the rent using the GRM formula, but just in case, here's one last example.

Say you were looking at a building to invest in that was selling for $300,000 with a GRM of 100. What is the annual gross rent income?

Rent = $300,000 ÷ 100

Rent = $3,000

REMEMBER

Don't forget to note whether the numbers you're given are based on monthly rent or annual rent and whether the question involves a Gross Rent Multiplier (GRM) or Gross Income Multiplier (GIM). GRMs use monthly rent numbers and GIMs use annual rent numbers. You may have to convert one to the other or use the number given. And just to make your life more interesting (and confusing) I have seen GRMs sometimes calculated on an annual basis and GIMs involve deduction of expenses. I doubt your course or the exam will get this deeply into the whole subject, but you should clarify and make sure you understand the terminology used for your exam.

Review Questions and Answers

It would be great to get 100 percent on the state exam, but if math really sends you into a spin, don't worry. Not many math questions are on the salesperson's or broker's exam. In either case, if you really do well on the other questions, math won't make or break you.

1. Find the volume of concrete needed to pour a patio slab 30 feet by 20 feet by 6 inches thick.

   (A) 600 cubic feet

   (B) 600 square feet

   (C) 3,600 cubic feet

   (D) 11 cubic yards

   Correct answer: (D). Length × Width × Height = Volume

   30 feet × 20 feet × 6 inches

   30 feet × 20 feet × (6 inches ÷ 12 inches — remember you have to convert inches to feet if the other numbers are in feet)

30 feet × 20 feet × 0.5 feet = 300 cubic feet

300 cubic feet ÷ 27 cubic feet = 11.11 cubic yards. (Make sure that you read the problem carefully to complete all the steps. In this case, you had to convert cubic feet to cubic yards.)

2. You're selling a rectangular piece of property that measures 99 feet by 110 feet. What part of an acre is this property?

(A) .75

(B) .50

(C) .25

(D) .10

Correct answer: (C). Length × Width = Area

110 feet × 99 feet = 10,890 square feet

10,890 square feet ÷ 43,560 square feet = 0.25 acres

The answers are all in acres so you must convert by dividing the square feet by 43,560 square feet, which is the number of square feet in an acre. Watch out when one of the answer choices is the correct number of square feet but the question asks for acres.

3. A warehouse rents for $0.60 per cubic foot per year and measures 200 feet by 300 feet by 15 feet high. What is the monthly rent?

(A) $36,000

(B) $45,000

(C) $540,000

(D) $900,000

Correct answer: (B). Length × Width × Height = Volume

300 feet × 200 feet × 15 feet = 900,000 cubic feet

900,000 cubic feet × $0.60 per cubic foot = $540,000 annual rent

$540,000 ÷ 12 months = $45,000 monthly rent

WARNING

Note in this problem that $540,000 is a correct answer to a part of the problem. Be sure to read questions carefully or you may pick the right answer to the wrong question.

4. You sold 40 houses this year and 30 houses last year. What percent fewer houses did you sell last year?

(A) 133 percent

(B) 75 percent

(C) 66 percent

(D) 25 percent

Correct answer: (D). 40 (houses this year) − 30 (houses last year) = 10 fewer houses last year than this year

10 ÷ 40 = 0.25 or 25 percent

TIP

In this problem, you divide by 40 because you want to find out what percentage less than this year. If the question were how much more than last year, then you would have divided by 30.

5. How much is owed after the first month's payment on an amortized mortgage loan of $150,000 at 7 percent interest for 25 years, if the monthly payment is $1,059?

(A) $148,941

(B) $149,816

(C) $149,125

(D) $139,500

Correct answer: (B). See the following math.

$150,000 × 0.07 = $10,500 (first year's interest)

$10,500 ÷ 12 months = $875 (first month's interest)

$1,059 (monthly payment of principal and interest) – $875 (interest) = $184 (principal paid off in first month)

$150,000 (original loan balance) – $184 (first month's principal payment) = $149,816 (mortgage balance after first month's payment)

Take a look at "Making Mortgage Calculations without a Fancy Calculator," earlier in the chapter to find out how to go to the second month for this type of problem. Don't get thrown by what may appear to be an odd number in a question, like the 7 percent in this question (which I purposely put in) that at the writing of this edition of this book was much higher than market rates. Prices of homes vary around the country. Interest rates do fluctuate. And exams are sometimes out of date with respect to these kinds of things. Just use what the exam writers give you and don't worry if the information seems a little unrealistic.

6. If a house has depreciated 30 percent since you bought it, and it's worth $200,000 now, what did you buy it for?

(A) $285,714

(B) $240,000

(C) $230,000

(D) $160,000

Correct answer: (A). $200,000 is 70 percent of some number, the original purchase price of the house.

100 percent – 30 percent = 70 percent

$200,000 ÷ 0.70 = $285,714

7. The seller pays $1,200 in taxes for six months in advance on April 1. She sells her house on May 1. What is the proration on the taxes?

(A) Seller gets a credit of $1,000; buyer gets a debit of $200.

(B) Seller gets a credit of $200; buyer gets debit of $1,000.

(C) Seller gets a credit of $1,000; buyer gets a debit of $1,000.

(D) Buyer gets a credit of $1,000; seller gets a debit of $1,000.

Correct answer: (C). The seller owned the property for one month of the period for which the taxes had been paid, so she used $200 worth of the taxes but had paid $1,200. She gets a credit of $1,000. The buyer will be in the house for five months of the tax period but paid none of the taxes and will use $1,000 worth. He gets a debit of $1,000. The buyer owes the seller $1,000 at the closing.

$1,200 (taxes) ÷ 6 months = $200 per month

8. A broker receives a commission check for $13,000 based on a 4 percent commission rate. How much did the house sell for?

(A) $52,000

(B) $300,000

(C) $325,000

(D) $336,960

Correct answer: (C). Commission earned ÷ commission rate = sale price

$13,000 ÷ 0.04 = $325,000

9. A room 14 feet by 18 feet is to be carpeted at a cost of $23 a square yard. What will be the cost to carpet the room?

(A) $214

(B) $579

(C) $644

(D) $5,796

Correct answer: (C). Length × Width = Area

18 feet × 14 feet = 252 square feet

252 square feet ÷ 9 square feet = 28 square yards

28 square yards × $23 per square yard = $644

10. What is the area in acres of a piece of property that is one mile square?

(A) 640

(B) 320

(C) 160

(D) 80

Correct answer: (A). One square mile is 640 acres. You can memorize this fact, because it's also the size of a section in the Government or Rectangular Survey System. Or using the Length × Width = Area formula:

5,280 feet × 5,280 feet = 27,878,400 square feet

27,878,400 square feet ÷ 43,560 square feet per acre = 640 acres

TIP

You may also want to remember that the phrase "one mile square" means a length of one mile on each side. Test writers also like to ask the area of a figure where the side is some portion of a mile, say ½ mile on each side. Remember that a mile is 5,280 feet.

6 You're Ready: Taking Practice Exams

IN THIS PART . . .

Get a leg up on the test with four practice exams. You examine the types of questions that you'll see on the actual real estate license exam.

Check out the answers to the four practice exams and discover what chapters you need to go back to and review.

Understand more about the state-specific information you need to know for the actual exam.

Retake the practice exams as many times as necessary to strengthen your core knowledge. Each time you retake the tests, your score will improve, and you'll soon feel comfortable enough to take the real exam.

Chapter **19**

Practice Exam One

This exam has 100 questions, and I've laid it out to group similar subjects together. I group them for ease of reviewing the material in any one chapter. However, different subjects probably will be randomly distributed throughout the actual exam. And don't forget that a number of state-specific questions on the actual exam will deal with particular laws and practices unique to your state. Review the items marked with the State-Specific icon throughout this book, and study both the materials that you get in your prelicensing course (such as a textbook) and your state's license law.

Download a fill-in-the-bubble answer sheet from www.dummies.com/go/relebubblesheets and use it as you take the practice exam. Try doing the entire test in less than two hours. Chapter 20 features the correct answers to this exam, plus explanations and cross-references to chapters for review. (Don't peek at the answers until you finish the test, though.) If you discover that you need to brush up on your studying and test-taking skills, be sure to head to Chapter 2 before taking the second practice exam in Chapter 21. Good luck!

1. Which type of insurance is used to insure against rent being stolen by an employee of a property management company?

   (A) Rent loss insurance

   (B) Surety bond

   (C) Business interruption insurance

   (D) Liability insurance

2. Which of the following is not a typical way that property management fees are set?

   (A) Fixed fee

   (B) Commission on new leases

   (C) Percentage of gross income

   (D) Percentage of operating costs

3. For what activity does a person generally not need a real estate license?

   (A) Collecting rents as an employee of a building owner

   (B) Representing people in the exchange of properties

   (C) Selling properties on behalf of several owners

   (D) Negotiating leases on behalf of several commercial building owners

4. Roof replacement is considered what type of expense in a building's budget?

   (A) Capital

   (B) Operating

   (C) Maintenance

   (D) Fixed

5. Which of the following is true for an independent contractor working for a broker?

   (A) The broker is required to pay the contractor's Social Security taxes.

   (B) The broker is required to withhold income taxes from the contractor's commission checks.

   (C) The broker must give workman's compensation to the contractor.

   (D) The broker is required to supervise the contractor.

6. The primary duty of a property manager is to

   (A) ensure that income is generated by the building.

   (B) maintain the building.

   (C) protect the owner's investment in the building.

   (D) maximize income while maintaining the building's value.

7. A real estate broker hired to represent someone who wants to sell his house is

   (A) a special agent.

   (B) a general agent.

   (C) a universal agent.

   (D) a representative agent.

8. Fiduciary responsibilities are always owed to

   (A) the client.

   (B) the customer.

   (C) the buyer.

   (D) the seller.

9. Fiduciary duties do not include

   (A) care.

   (B) control.

   (C) accounting.

   (D) confidentiality.

10. The client is always

    (A) the seller.

    (B) the buyer.

    (C) the principal.

    (D) the customer.

11. Which of the following would not end an agency relationship?

    (A) The property was sold.

    (B) The house was burned in a fire.

    (C) The principal got married.

    (D) The broker declared bankruptcy.

12. When does a seller's agent earn a fee?

(A) She accomplishes what she was hired to do.

(B) She is the procuring cause.

(C) She finds a ready, willing, and able buyer.

(D) All of the above.

13. A homeowner refuses to sell his home to a family because of its race. The homeowner claims that because this is an owner-occupied home, he is exempt from all fair housing laws. The owner has violated

(A) the 1968 Fair Housing Act.

(B) the 1968 Fair Housing Act as amended in 1988.

(C) the 1866 Civil Rights Act.

(D) no law. He is correct.

14. A person who owns a 15-unit apartment building has established different security deposit amounts for different tenants based on their ethnic group and whether or not they have children. He has ten years of statistical research to back up the validity of this approach. Which of the following is true?

(A) What he is doing is illegal.

(B) What he is doing is legal under any circumstances.

(C) What he is doing would be illegal if he didn't have the factual research to back it up.

(D) What he is doing would be legal only if the owner himself lives in the building.

15. A real estate agent attempts to generate listings by contacting people in a particular neighborhood and suggesting to them that their property values might be going down soon because a particular immigrant group is coming into the neighborhood. This practice is called

(A) soliciting.

(B) farming.

(C) prospecting.

(D) blockbusting.

16. A church group decides to build housing for its members only. The church does not permit African Americans to join its congregation. Which of the following is true?

(A) The housing can be restricted to members of the church.

(B) The housing cannot be restricted to members of the church.

(C) The housing can be restricted as long as they do not advertise or use a real estate agent.

(D) The housing could be restricted if the prohibition for joining the church was not against African Americans but against some other racial or ethnic group.

17. Complaints under the Civil Rights Act of 1866 are handled by

(A) HUD.

(B) federal courts.

(C) state courts.

(D) state human rights commissions.

18. A homeowner gives a listing to the real estate broker to sell his one-family house with the warning that he does not want to sell to non-Christians. What should the broker do?

(A) Take the listing, but ignore the homeowner's wishes.

(B) Take the listing and follow the homeowner's wishes because of the owner occupancy exception.

(C) Explain to the homeowner that he's violating the federal fair housing laws and refuse the listing unless he removes the request.

(D) Take the listing, but only if the homeowner agrees to put the request in writing for the broker's protection.

GO ON TO NEXT PAGE

19. The First Bank of Main Street refuses to grant loans within a ten-block area of its offices because of declining property values. This practice is

(A) redlining and illegal.

(B) redlining and legal.

(C) redlining and usually illegal except where values are declining.

(D) legal in any other part of the town except in the immediate area of the bank.

20. A term used to describe land, improvements, and all the rights associated with ownership is

(A) land.

(B) personal property.

(C) real estate.

(D) real property.

21. A built-in microwave oven is an example of

(A) personal property.

(B) a fixture.

(C) a trade fixture.

(D) an attachment.

22. You want to donate a piece of land to a religious organization. The title will pass when they complete building a church on the property. The estate is

(A) fee simple.

(B) fee simple condition precedent.

(C) fee simple condition subsequent.

(D) fee simple determinable.

23. The estate that grants the most complete form of ownership is

(A) fee simple.

(B) fee simple condition precedent.

(C) fee simple condition subsequent.

(D) fee simple determinable.

24. An owner of a rental building is said to have what type of interest?

(A) Leasehold

(B) Leased fee

(C) Fee simple

(D) Fee on condition

25. Someone who has riparian rights on a navigable river owns

(A) nothing.

(B) to the centerline of the water.

(C) to the high water mark on the land.

(D) no water but to the centerline of the land under the water.

26. The term generally used to describe the rights a property owner gets when she buys a piece of property is

(A) fee simple rights.

(B) real estate rights.

(C) freehold rights.

(D) bundle of rights.

27. Unity of possession means that

(A) each owner has an undivided interest in the property.

(B) each owner took title at the same time.

(C) each owner took title with the same deed.

(D) each owner has the same interest in the property.

28. What form of ownership has no right of survivorship?

(A) Joint tenancy

(B) Tenancy in common

(C) Tenancy by the entirety

(D) All forms of ownership have a right of survivorship.

29. Joe, Sam, and Fred are joint tenants in a piece of property. Joe sells his interest to Bob. Bob now has what relationship to Sam and Fred?

(A) Joint tenant

(B) Tenant by the entirety

(C) Tenant in common

(D) Tenant in severalty

30. Condominium owners generally own their land as

(A) tenants by the entirety.

(B) tenants in severalty.

(C) joint tenants.

(D) tenants in common.

31. Which type of co-ownership requires the signature of all owners to sell the property interest?

   (A) Tenancy in severalty

   (B) Tenancy in common

   (C) Joint tenancy

   (D) Tenancy by the entirety

32. Who owns the apartment in a cooperative building?

   (A) The individual apartment owner

   (B) The corporation that owns the building

   (C) The bank that financed the purchase

   (D) The individual owner owns the apartment, but the corporation owns the common areas.

33. Which statement is true?

   (A) All encumbrances are liens.

   (B) All liens are encumbrances.

   (C) All encumbrances are financial in nature.

   (D) All financial claims against property are voluntary liens.

34. Homeowner Bob's house has been foreclosed and sold. He has unpaid local real estate taxes from last year. He owes on the mortgage he took out five years ago. And he owes the plumber for work that was done two years ago. Who gets paid first?

   (A) They each will receive a proportionate share.

   (B) The bank

   (C) The town

   (D) The plumber

35. A judgment lien is placed against you after you lose a court case for an accident that occurred at your home. This means that the lien is placed against

   (A) all your real property.

   (B) the one piece of property where the accident happened.

   (C) all your real and personal property.

   (D) your salary only.

36. The electric company needs to put a permanent electric cable across your property to get to a nearby street. The company obtains

   (A) an easement appurtenant.

   (B) an easement in gross.

   (C) an easement by necessity.

   (D) an easement by prescription.

37. The city needs your property for a road widening, but you don't want to sell it. The city probably will take it through its power of

   (A) escheat.

   (B) encroachment.

   (C) prescriptive rights.

   (D) eminent domain.

38. The study of population characteristics is called

   (A) economic base study.

   (B) demographics.

   (C) infrastructure study.

   (D) feasibility study.

39. Which of the following is not necessary for a valid deed?

   (A) Signature of grantor

   (B) Signature of grantee

   (C) Description

   (D) Granting clause

40. On what date does a deed become valid?

   (A) Signing date

   (B) Delivery and acceptance date

   (C) Recording date

   (D) Mortgage approval date

41. The one requirement that is not technically necessary for a deed to be valid but, in most cases, is required for recordation is

   (A) signature of grantee.

   (B) consideration.

   (C) granting clause.

   (D) acknowledgment.

GO ON TO NEXT PAGE

42. The type of property descriptions that use directions and distances is called

   (A) metes and bounds.

   (B) rectangular survey.

   (C) government survey.

   (D) plat map.

43. If the section you're buying is bound by section 16 on the north, section 22 on the east, section 20 on the west, and section 28 on the south, what section are you buying?

   (A) 21

   (B) 15

   (C) 27

   (D) 29

44. Elevations are measured from

   (A) a benchmark.

   (B) a monument.

   (C) a meridian.

   (D) a datum.

45. A developer wants to give the new streets in the subdivision she just built to the city. She does this by

   (A) dedication.

   (B) grant.

   (C) avulsion.

   (D) sale.

46. Which of the following is not a form of involuntary alienation?

   (A) Adverse possession

   (B) Avulsion

   (C) Grant

   (D) Eminent domain

47. You and your brother own a campground together. You and he have very different ideas about how to run it. Neither of you wants to buy the other out, but you can no longer operate the campground together. To resolve the problem, you file a suit for

   (A) adverse possession.

   (B) a grant.

   (C) partition.

   (D) prescriptive rights.

48. The process by which a will is processed is called

   (A) surrogacy.

   (B) a trust.

   (C) execution.

   (D) probate.

49. The government is giving lands away in Alaska. It does so by

   (A) public sale.

   (B) public grant.

   (C) public possessory interest.

   (D) escheat.

50. Actual title may be granted in an adverse possession situation after a successful suit

   (A) for adverse possession.

   (B) for partition.

   (C) to quiet title.

   (D) for prescriptive rights.

51. The rule that real estate contracts must be in writing is a function of

   (A) contract law.

   (B) the statute of contracts.

   (C) RESPA.

   (D) the statute of frauds.

52. As a real estate agent, you bring a buyer to a house being sold by the owner. The owner is aware that you are a real estate agent and eventually sells the house to the buyer you brought. Even though you never actually talked about it, you expect a commission because you feel you have

   (A) an express contract.

   (B) an implied contract.

   (C) a unilateral contract.

   (D) an executed contract.

53. Joey, a 17-year-old, is big for his age. Because he wants to begin his real estate investment career, he signs a contract to buy a house a few weeks before his 18th birthday. After he turns 18, he decides he doesn't want to buy the house. He can probably get out of the contract because it is

    (A) void.

    (B) voidable.

    (C) implied.

    (D) unenforceable.

54. Which of the following is an element unique to a real estate sales contract?

    (A) Consideration

    (B) Description of property

    (C) Legally competent parties

    (D) Mutual agreement

55. Joe lists his house for sale at $300,000. Alice offers Joe $200,000. Joe counteroffers with $280,000. Alice offers Joe $205,000. Joe gets mad and raises his counteroffer to Alice back up to $300,000. Can he do this?

    (A) Yes.

    (B) No.

    (C) Yes, but he owes a commission on the $280,000.

    (D) Yes, but only if he counteroffers within 24 hours.

56. Jim finds a piece of property on which to build a shopping center. It's going to take about a year to get the necessary permits, and there's no guarantee that he'll get permission to build. Meanwhile, he doesn't want to lose the property to another buyer. His best bet is to sign

    (A) a contract of sale.

    (B) an option agreement.

    (C) an easement.

    (D) an executory contract.

57. Harry's House of Hats can no longer pay its landlord, Jim. Nancy's House of Shoes agrees to take over the space and executes a new lease with Jim. This situation is

    (A) a sublease.

    (B) an assignment.

    (C) a novation.

    (D) a graduated lease.

58. A landlord does not keep a building in good repair, including not fixing a broken boiler in the middle of winter. The tenants want to move out and go to court to prove

    (A) constructive eviction.

    (B) actual eviction.

    (C) invalid possession.

    (D) lease violation.

59. Georgia's House of Mirrors agrees to pay its landlord a flat rental fee plus a portion of its gross sales each month. This situation is best described as

    (A) a gross lease.

    (B) a net lease.

    (C) a percentage lease.

    (D) a proprietary lease.

60. A person in a cooperative apartment gets what kind of lease?

    (A) Gross lease

    (B) Net lease

    (C) Ground lease

    (D) Proprietary lease

61. Alice refuses to move out of her apartment after her lease expires. The landlord refuses to accept the rent she offers to pay. This is

    (A) an estate at will.

    (B) an estate at sufferance.

    (C) an estate for years.

    (D) a periodic estate.

GO ON TO NEXT PAGE

62. A typical commercial lease is

   (A) a tenancy for years.

   (B) a tenancy at will.

   (C) a tenancy at sufferance.

   (D) a periodic tenancy.

63. The agency primarily responsible for dealing with environmental issues is

   (A) CERCLA.

   (B) HUD.

   (C) LUST.

   (D) EPA.

64. Under CERCLA, liability is considered to be

   (A) joint and several.

   (B) joint and strict.

   (C) strict and several.

   (D) joint, strict, and several.

65. The possibility of claiming innocence of responsibility for prior hazardous waste dumping on land you bought was made available by

   (A) SARA.

   (B) CERCLA.

   (C) OSHA.

   (D) HMTA.

66. Which phase of environmental assessment would confirm the presence of hazardous material?

   (A) 1

   (B) 2

   (C) 3

   (D) 4

67. You get sick every day at work but the symptoms disappear on your drive home. You may have

   (A) building related illness.

   (B) sick building syndrome.

   (C) asbestosis.

   (D) building radon illness.

68. Which program requires registering various types of underground storage tanks?

   (A) LUST

   (B) OSHA

   (C) SARA

   (D) CERCLA

69. An appraisal is

   (A) an estimate of value.

   (B) a calculation of value.

   (C) an educated guess of value.

   (D) an analysis of value.

70. The most important reason that location is such an important factor in the value of real estate is its

   (A) neighborhood compatibility.

   (B) amenities and services.

   (C) safety.

   (D) immobility.

71. In the sales comparison approach, if a comparable is better than the subject, what do you do?

   (A) Make a positive adjustment to the subject.

   (B) Make a negative adjustment to the subject.

   (C) Make a negative adjustment to the comparable.

   (D) Make a positive adjustment to the comparable.

72. Which of the following is not a type of depreciation used in the cost approach?

   (A) Functional obsolescence

   (B) Physical deterioration

   (C) Straight line deterioration

   (D) External obsolescence

73. You buy the smallest house in a neighborhood of larger, more expensive homes. What economic principle will most likely affect the value of your house?

   (A) Regression

   (B) Progression

   (C) Increasing returns

   (D) Opportunity costs

74. The gross rent multiplier is a factor that relates

(A) expenses to net income.

(B) net income to value.

(C) rent to value.

(D) expenses to value.

75. Effective gross income is potential gross income minus

(A) operating expenses.

(B) debt service.

(C) vacancy and collection loss.

(D) vacancy and collection loss, and operating expenses.

76. Al borrows money from the First Bank of Main Street. He is

(A) the mortgagor.

(B) the mortgagee.

(C) the lien holder.

(D) the note holder.

77. The Annual Percentage Rate could not be described as

(A) points plus interest rate.

(B) the actual interest rate.

(C) the discount rate.

(D) the yield.

78. Equity is best defined as

(A) the down payment.

(B) the amount owed on the mortgage.

(C) the difference between the value and the debt attributable to the property.

(D) the amount of cash taken out after the house is sold.

79. The VA requires what in order to secure a loan?

(A) LTV

(B) CRV

(C) PMI

(D) FSA

80. Which of the following is not a part of the secondary mortgage market?

(A) Fannie Mae

(B) Ginnie Mae

(C) Freddie Mae

(D) Farmer Mac

81. A single word to describe a loan where nothing is left to pay at the end of the term is

(A) a term loan.

(B) a balloon loan.

(C) a variable loan.

(D) an amortized loan.

82. Mom and Dad help you buy a house by lending you some money. They don't want any payments right away but tell you that when you sell, if you make a profit, they'll take a portion of the profit as payment of the loan. You have

(A) a growing equity mortgage.

(B) an open-end mortgage.

(C) a shared equity mortgage.

(D) a reverse annuity mortgage.

83. The rate that is used to adjust taxes among several towns in the same county is called

(A) the equalization rate.

(B) the capitalization rate.

(C) the mill rate.

(D) the assessment rate.

84. A town's property tax rate is typically determined by

(A) dividing the total assessed value of taxable property by the town budget.

(B) dividing the town budget by the total assessed value of taxable property.

(C) multiplying the total assessed value of taxable property by the town's budget.

(D) dividing the total assessed value of taxable property by the assessment ratio.

GO ON TO NEXT PAGE

85. The right to redeem foreclosed property by paying the taxes after a tax sale is called

(A) equitable right of redemption.

(B) statutory right of redemption.

(C) in rem right of redemption.

(D) post foreclosure right of redemption.

86. A combination REIT can invest in

(A) mortgages and bonds.

(B) equity real estate investments and bonds.

(C) mortgages and stocks.

(D) equity real estate investments and mortgages.

87. The tax deferred in a real estate exchange is tax on

(A) income.

(B) capital gains.

(C) corporate profits.

(D) net operating income.

88. Another term for depreciation is

(A) recapture.

(B) capital loss.

(C) adjusted basis.

(D) cost recovery.

89. All other things being equal, which of the following is worth more in tax savings?

(A) Deduction

(B) Credit

(C) Adjusted basis

(D) Capital gains

90. A building whose expenses are higher than its income is described as having

(A) positive cash flow.

(B) negative cash flow.

(C) negative amortization.

(D) excessive depreciation.

91. In general, in a real estate investment, the higher the risk,

(A) the higher the expected return.

(B) the lower the expected return.

(C) the greater likelihood that the return remains unchanged.

(D) the harder a property is to manage.

92. A seller wants to net $200,000 after she pays the real estate agent a 6 percent commission. What must the house sell for?

(A) $200,000

(B) $206,000

(C) $212,000

(D) $212,765

93. A buyer wants to know the size of a square piece of property that measures 264 feet by 264 feet. What do you tell him?

(A) 1 acre

(B) 1.3 acres

(C) 1.6 acres

(D) 2 acres

94. A peaked roof barn is used to store hay. The width of the barn is 40 feet. The height of the ridge beam above the second floor is 15 feet, and the barn is 60 feet long. If hay is stored only in the upper peaked roof portion of the barn, how much hay can be stored?

(A) 36,000 cubic feet

(B) 24,000 cubic feet

(C) 18,000 cubic feet

(D) 6,000 cubic feet

95. Five hundred houses were sold in your county this year. Four hundred were sold last year. What percentage of more houses were sold this year than last year?

(A) 100 percent

(B) 50 percent

(C) 25 percent

(D) 20 percent

96. If the cost recovery period on a property is 25 years, at what percentage does the property depreciate each year?

(A) 25 percent

(B) 10 percent

(C) 5 percent

(D) 4 percent

97. If the annual gross rent on a building is $20,000 and the gross rent multiplier for this type of building is 16, what is the estimated value of the building?

(A) $320,000

(B) $150,375

(C) $125,000

(D) $118,750

98. How much interest do you owe for the first year on an amortized mortgage loan of $250,000 at a 7 percent interest rate?

(A) $1,458

(B) $1,750

(C) $14,580

(D) $17,500

99. A property is assessed at $42,000. The mill rate is 22. What are the taxes on the property?

(A) $9,240

(B) $924

(C) $1,900

(D) $190

100. You bought a house for $200,000, which is 80 percent of what you sell it for six years later. At what price did you sell the house?

(A) $160,000

(B) $240,000

(C) $250,000

(D) $260,000

DO NOT TURN THE PAGE UNTIL TOLD TO DO SO **STOP** DO NOT RETURN TO A PREVIOUS TEST

Chapter 20

Answers and Explanations to Practice Exam One

All right! You're just minutes away from finding out how well you did on the practice exam in Chapter 19. Give yourself one point for each correct answer, and add up your total score.

Find the range that corresponds to your score in the following list:

» **Between 90 and 100:** Congratulations! You're on your way to your first million as a real estate agent.

» **Between 80 and 90:** Take a breath, pat yourself on the back, and keep reviewing the material so you don't forget what you've already picked up.

» **Between 75 and 80:** Too close for comfort. Check out your weakest areas, section by section, and review the corresponding chapters again, using the review questions at the end of each chapter for practice. If you got more than half of the questions wrong in any one section, that's a good indication you need more work with that chapter.

» **Below 75:** Don't be discouraged. The difference between this score and a higher one is time, and that time needs to be spent with this book. Check out your weakest areas in the exam, review the corresponding chapters, do the review questions at the end of each chapter, and try this exam again and the next three. By the way, I've chosen 75 percent as the passing grade, though your state may use a different one.

STATE SPECIFIC

Don't forget that no matter how well you did on this exam, the information here is general to most states. You still need to study the information unique to your state. Review the material noted with the State-Specific icon throughout this book as well as the list of subjects in Chapter 27. You can get state-specific information from your prelicensing course's materials, textbook, and instructor, too.

1. (B) Chapter 3

A surety bond insures against employee misdeeds like theft. Rent loss insurance (also known as business interruption insurance) insures against the landlord losing rent because of a disaster like a fire, and liability insurance covers losses caused by injuries that are the result of negligence on the part of the landlord.

2. (D) Chapter 3

TIP

Did the "not" in the question throw you off? A good way to handle this question is to repeat each answer in a positive way and ask yourself whether it's true or false. For instance, you say, "Fixed fees are a way to set a property management fee." True or false? Well, that's true, so it can't be the right answer. Percentage of operating costs is the only answer that doesn't fit.

3. (A) Chapter 3

Real estate license laws generally require a person to hold a real estate license when performing any number of particular duties for another person for a fee. You don't have to have a real estate license to do any of these things for your own property. An employee of a person who owns and rents out buildings is effectively acting directly on behalf of the owner, as if, in a sense, the employee were the owner. This could vary slightly by state, so check yours out just in case.

4. (A) Chapter 3

A capital expense is usually a major expense to improve or repair something that does not last as long as the life of a building, like a roof. An operating expense is an annual expense to keep the building running, like the gas or oil bill. A maintenance item is usually a repair that may happen occasionally and sometimes unpredictably like a furnace repair. A fixed expense is a term used to describe insurance and tax payments.

5. (D) Chapter 3

The first three answers are characteristics of being an employee, not an independent contractor. However, even when you're an independent contractor, the broker is responsible for your work and must supervise you.

6. (D) Chapter 3

WARNING

The keys to this question are the word "primary" and avoiding confusion when partially correct answers are among the choices. Maximizing income while maintaining the building's value encompasses the first three answers and is considered the primary duty of a property manager. Looked at another way, the first three answers are each a part of the more correct total Answer (D).

7. (A) Chapter 4

A special agent represents a client for one real estate transaction. A general agent represents a client in a range of activities, and a universal agent represents a client in all or almost all activities. I made up "representative agent."

8. (A) Chapter 4

Fiduciary responsibilities are defined as being owed to the client. A seller or a buyer can be your client. A customer is the third party in a transaction. The only thing that is always true in this question is Answer (A), the client.

9. **(B)** Chapter 4

The duties are accounting, care, confidentiality, disclosure, loyalty, and obedience. A question about these duties is so fundamental to being a real estate agent that I can almost guarantee you will see a question about this on the exam.

10. **(C)** Chapter 4

WARNING

Watch out for the word "always." The buyer or seller *could* be the client but not *always*. The principal is always the client; the two terms are interchangeable.

11. **(C)** Chapter 4

If an individual property owner contracts with a real estate agent to sell his property, that arrangement isn't affected by his getting married because the property ownership hasn't changed.

12. **(D)** Chapter 4

The first three choices all are essentially the same thing.

13. **(C)** Chapter 5

There are no exemptions for race to the 1866 law, plain and simple.

14. **(A)** Chapter 5

Changing the terms of rentals for any group in a protected class is illegal, no matter how many supporting facts one may have.

15. **(D)** Chapter 5

Blockbusting is the deliberate attempt to generate profits by scaring people into selling their houses under the circumstances stated in the question. The other answers are all legitimate ways to get listings of houses to sell, provided blockbusting isn't used.

16. **(B)** Chapter 5

The church housing exception, which is part of the 1968 Fair Housing Law, applies only if membership in the church or religion itself isn't restricted. Because the church in question discriminates in its membership policies against African Americans, the housing exception does not apply; therefore, the housing can't be restricted to only church members.

17. **(B)** Chapter 5

HUD enforces the 1968 Fair Housing Act, but the federal courts enforce the 1866 law.

18. **(C)** Chapter 5

Even if a homeowner has the exemption (in this case, the owner of a single-family home who doesn't own more than three units), a real estate agent may not be used. Real estate agents are always held to higher standards when it comes to fair housing issues.

19. **(A)** Chapter 5

Redlining, which is discrimination in the lending of mortgage money based on location, is always illegal.

20. (D) Chapter 6

Land is the physical "dirt." Real estate is the dirt and the structures attached to it. Real property is the land, everything attached to it, and the rights associated with owning it. Personal property includes tangible, movable, portable things that aren't real estate.

21. (B) Chapter 6

A fixture is personal property that becomes permanently attached to the real estate and is expected to stay with it when it is sold. Personal property is something tangible, moveable, and not attached to the real estate. A trade fixture is used to conduct a business and usually expected to be removed at the end of a lease period or when the property is sold. An attachment can mean anything attached to real estate.

22. (B) Chapter 6

Fee simple condition precedent is ownership subject to a condition that must be satisfied before title is actually conveyed. Fee simple is ownership without condition. Fee simple subsequent is ownership in which the grantor has the right to reclaim the property through court action if a condition isn't met after title is conveyed. In fee simple determinable, if a condition isn't met, the property automatically reverts to the grantor without the necessity of court action.

23. (A) Chapter 6

Fee simple is ownership without condition and is the most complete form of ownership. The other choices all have limitations.

24. (B) Chapter 6

TIP

Leased fee is the most correct answer. The owner may have a fee simple interest or a fee on condition interest, but when a question involves leases, the most correct answer involves either leasehold or leased fee interests. (The tenant has the leasehold interest.)

25. (C) Chapter 6

If the river is navigable, the property owner owns to the edge of the river or to the mean high water mark. If the river isn't navigable, the property owner owns to the centerline of the water. You just have to remember this difference.

26. (D) Chapter 6

The bundle of rights refers to *all* the rights a property owner generally gets when she receives ownership of a piece of property and is the most complete answer. The terms "fee simple" and "freehold" refer to estates or interests that a person may have in a piece of property. There really is no such thing as real estate rights in the context of this question.

27. (A) Chapter 7

Each owner taking title at the same time refers to unity of time, each owner taking title with the same deed refers to unity of title, and each owner having the same interest in the property refers to unity of interest.

28. (B) Chapter 7

STATE
SPECIFIC

This question can have a state-specific variation if your state does not recognize the right of survivorship in joint tenancy. But tenancy in common never has a right of survivorship.

29. (C) Chapter 7

A joint tenant can sell his share to another person. That new owner becomes a tenant in common to the other joint tenants, unless everyone executes new documents to create a new joint tenancy.

30. (D) Chapter 7

Condominium owners generally own the airspace encompassing their units in fee simple ownership. The land under and around the units is owned by all of the owners as tenants in common. A good way to jog your memory is to remember that condominium owners would want to leave their condo to their heirs, which is a feature of tenancy in common rather than joint tenancy.

31. (D) Chapter 7

Of course, tenancy in severalty needs "all" the signatures because there's only one owner, but it is not a form of co-ownership. Tenants in common and joint tenants can sell their individual interests with only their signatures. This action does not convey ownership to the whole property, so the word "interest" is crucial in this question. Tenancy by the entirety views the interest of the husband and wife as a single interest that can't be sold separately, so both spouses have to sign the deed to sell their interest.

32. (B) Chapter 7

The corporation owns the entire building. The individual tenant owns shares in the corporation and has a proprietary lease that enables him to occupy his apartment.

33. (B) Chapter 8

The statement that all liens are encumbrances is true. Liens (which can be voluntary or involuntary) are just one type of encumbrance, and encumbrances in general can be financial in nature or can limit the use of property.

34. (C) Chapter 8

Real estate taxes take first priority in all liens. After taxes are paid, liens generally are settled in the order in which they were recorded in the public record.

35. (C) Chapter 8

A judgment lien is involuntary and general. That means that it's placed without your consent and against all your real and personal property. There may be state-specific laws that limit the judgment being placed to property in the county where the lawsuit took place. Check this out in your state, but in the way this question was asked this answer is generally correct.

36. (B) Chapter 8

An easement in gross benefits a person. In this case the "person" that benefits is the electric company. An easement appurtenant attaches itself to the land. An easement by necessity is one that must be given to another person by a court order. An easement by prescription occurs against your will by someone continuously using your property.

37. (D) Chapter 8

The right of a municipality to take your property against your will for a public purpose is called eminent domain. In escheat, the state gets your land if you die without a will and without heirs. The other answers don't involve the state or local government taking your land.

38. **(B)** Chapter 8

Studies of demographics are used for planning purposes in a municipality.

39. **(B)** Chapter 9

The person getting the property (the grantee) doesn't have to sign (though he or she does have to be clearly named), but the person selling the property (the grantor) does.

40. **(B)** Chapter 9

Delivery and acceptance is the handing of the deed by the grantor to the grantee, though it is not generally done in any formal manner.

41. **(D)** Chapter 9

STATE SPECIFIC

An *acknowledgment* proves that the person who signs a deed (the grantor) signed it voluntarily and is, in fact, who he says he is (or who she says she is). This question may be state-specific in a few places. Consideration and a granting clause are always required, and the signature of the grantee is never required.

42. **(A)** Chapter 9

The metes and bounds method of description uses locations, distances, and compass directions to define property boundaries. The rectangular and government survey systems, which are two names for the same thing, describe property boundaries using squares and rectangles determined by longitude and latitude. The plat map system uses a map of a property, usually a subdivision, which is filed in the local recording office. The map divides properties into blocks and lots for description purposes.

43. **(A)** Chapter 9

If you check Figure 9-1 of a township divided into sections (part of the rectangular survey system) and are able to duplicate it, you can answer any question like this.

44. **(D)** Chapter 9

Benchmarks and monuments are markers used by surveyors for location and distance measurement, but a datum is specific to measuring elevation. A meridian is a feature of the government survey system and has nothing to do with elevations.

45. **(A)** Chapter 10

Dedication it is! The government gives land to people with grants. Avulsion is the sudden loss of land by natural forces. A sale is, well, selling property to someone else.

46. **(C)** Chapter 10

The government voluntarily gives land to people with grants. The other choices are involuntary ways of losing property.

47. **(C)** Chapter 10

Partition is a legal proceeding that divides property when the owners can't agree on how to do it themselves.

48. **(D)** Chapter 10

Probate is the way that a will is legally processed. It's done in surrogate's court, so surrogacy may have confused you.

49. (B) Chapter 10

The key word in this question is "give." The government gives property to a person in a public grant, but a sale involves the exchange of money or something of value for a piece of property.

50. (C) Chapter 10

A suit to quiet title is what you sue for when you claim ownership through adverse possession. A suit for partition involves co-owners who can't agree on how to divide the property they own. The other two answers sound good but are made up.

51. (D) Chapter 11

The statute of frauds governs certain kinds of contracts, including real estate contracts, and says that contracts must be in writing to be enforceable. Contract law itself has no such requirement; other kinds of contracts can be oral. RESPA deals with closing title, and as far as I know, no statute of contracts exists.

52. (B) Chapter 11

STATE SPECIFIC

An implied contract occurs because of the parties' actions. An express contract clearly states what the parties agree to do or not to do, and in a unilateral contract, one party has to act only if the other party acts. An executed contract has all of its terms fulfilled. In some states the absence of a written contract may affect your ability to collect a commission.

53. (B) Chapter 11

The contract is voidable, because Joey wasn't of legal age when he signed the contract, but he can go ahead with it if he wants to, and it is enforceable on the other person. A void contract never actually existed because it didn't meet some requirement to be valid. An implied contract exists because of the actions of the parties rather than any express agreement. An unenforceable contract is one that may appear valid but cannot be legally enforced by either party.

54. (B) Chapter 11

Remember that a contract in general requires consideration. It logically requires legally competent parties and mutual agreement about what is being promised. A real estate sales contract has all this and more. Because each piece of property is unique, a real estate sales contract would have to have the description of the property being sold to be valid.

55. (A) Chapter 11

As long as neither person accepts the other's offer, no valid deal exists. A person absolutely can raise his offer as long as no other offer has been accepted.

56. (B) Chapter 11

An option will enable Jim to get his approvals while the property cannot be sold. With an option, in the event that Jim can't get the approvals, he would not have to buy the land, whereas with a standard sales contract he would.

57. (C) Chapter 11

A novation is a new lease agreement to replace the old one. The other answers, which don't involve completely new leases, are explained in Chapter 12.

58. (A) Chapter 12

The key in this question is that the tenants want to move out rather than get the items repaired, so lease violation — on the part of the landlord, in this case — is not a good answer. In actual eviction, the landlord seeks to evict the tenant for some reason and goes to court to do it. I made up invalid possession.

59. (C) Chapter 12

The best answer is percentage lease because it involves some payment based on a percentage of something, usually sales in a store. This lease may be a net lease, but you would need to know if the tenant is paying building expenses as well as rent.

60. (D) Chapter 12

The proprietary lease entitles the cooperative owner to use the apartment for which he has purchased shares in the corporation that owns the building. A gross lease is a typical apartment lease. A net lease is often used in commercial buildings. A ground lease is one where only vacant land is leased.

61. (B) Chapter 12

In an estate at sufferance, the tenant remains in possession of the apartment after the lease expires without the landlord's permission. An estate at will is when the tenant can stay in the apartment with the landlord's permission for an indefinite period of time. An estate for years is one that has a definite period of time associated with it. A periodic estate keeps automatically renewing itself from period to period.

62. (A) Chapter 12

TIP

I use the word "tenancy" here. Remember that when talking about leases, it means the same as "estate." In a tenancy for years, the lease is for a definite period of time, providing a beginning and ending date for the commercial tenant.

63. (D) Chapter 13

EPA is the Environmental Protection Agency. HUD is the Department of Housing and Urban Development. The other two are environmental laws, not enforcement agencies.

64. (D) Chapter 13

Joint and several liability means that if there is more than one owner of a contaminated property, each one is personally liable, and if only one is able to pay, he must bear the total cost and attempt to collect from the other owners. Strict liability means that the contaminated property's owner has no excuse for any injury done by the contamination.

65. (A) Chapter 13

The Superfund Amendments and Reauthorization Act increased funding of the Superfund, which was created by CERCLA. It also created innocent landowner status for current owners not responsible for contaminating property.

66. (B) Chapter 13

The phases of environmental assessment are 1) a review of records and a physical inspection of the property; 2) testing; 3) cleaning up the contamination; and 4) managing the contamination.

67. (B) Chapter 13

The main difference between the first two answers is that with sick building syndrome, the symptoms disappear on the way home, and with building-related illness, they remain even after you leave the building. Asbestosis is a disease specifically caused by exposure to asbestos. And there is no such thing as building radon illness.

68. (A) Chapter 13

The goal of the Leaking Underground Storage Tanks program is to identify and prevent the failure of underground storage tanks. The main provision is tank registration.

69. (A) Chapter 14

Analysis of value may sound right, but the market gets analyzed to estimate the value. A calculation of value is wrong because while calculations may be used, the result is still an estimate of value. A guess, educated or not, is still a guess. An estimate of value is the definition as used in the appraisal industry. Sometimes the word *opinion* is also used to mean the same thing.

70. (D) Chapter 14

The first three answers are some of the things that real estate agents use to measure a location's value. However, it is the fact that property cannot be moved that makes location so important as a determining factor in the property's value.

71. (C) Chapter 14

If the comparable is better than the subject, what must you do to make it like the subject? You take something away. So, it is a negative adjustment to the comparable. You never adjust the subject.

WARNING

72. (C) Chapter 14

There's no such thing as straight-line deterioration. However, there is a straight-line method of estimating depreciation. Beware answers that have one or two words that sound right (like straight-line).

73. (B) Chapter 14

Progression is the positive effect on value that larger houses have on a smaller house. Regression is the opposite or negative effect on value that smaller houses have on a larger house.

TIP

74. (C) Chapter 14

Don't get put off in a question like this because it doesn't have the exact wording like "gross rent." Rent to value is the best answer because the gross rent multiplier technique uses rents and converts them to value using the GRM. Net income to value may look right, but that's the technique used with the income capitalization approach to value. As for the other two answers: You never convert expenses to value.

75. (C) Chapter 14

Gross income minus vacancy and collection loss plus other income is effective gross income. When you subtract operating expenses from the effective gross income you get net operating income, so the other three answers don't give you any meaningful numbers.

76. **(A)** Chapter 15

With mortgage loans, the borrower gives the mortgage to the bank. The borrower is the mortgagor; the bank is the mortgagee. The bank is the lien holder and the note holder. The mortgage lien entitles the bank to foreclosure for nonpayment, and the note signifies that the borrower owes money to the bank.

77. **(C)** Chapter 15

The discount rate has to do with loan rates established by the federal government (and has nothing to do with the APR). The other three answers are all related to the APR. Take special care not to confuse discount points and the discount rate.

78. **(C)** Chapter 15

The difference between the value and the debt attributable to the property and the amount of cash taken out after the house is sold are pretty close. The difference is that you don't have to actually sell the house to calculate equity. Note the use of the phrase "best defined" in the question; the difference between the value and the debt attributable to the property is the best answer.

79. **(B)** Chapter 15

The Certificate of Reasonable Value is required for a Veterans Administration guarantee.

80. **(C)** Chapter 15

Freddie Mac (not Freddie Mae) is part of the secondary market for mortgages. Always read the questions carefully.

81. **(D)** Chapter 15

A variable loan refers to how the interest rates are set. A term loan and a balloon loan require a payment at the end of the term.

82. **(C)** Chapter 15

A shared-equity mortgage allows for a share of the profit on the property to be given to someone else in return for help purchasing the property. You must be able to distinguish among types of mortgages by a few of their principal characteristics.

83. **(A)** Chapter 16

Remember the term "equalization rate" simply with the word "equalize," which is what it does. The capitalization rate is used to estimate value in the income capitalization approach. The mill rate is an actual tax rate in any community. The assessment ratio is the percent of market value used to calculate the assessed value.

84. **(B)** Chapter 16

Divide the town budget by the total assessed value of the town, which is also called the tax base, and you get your answer.

85. **(B)** Chapter 16

TIP

Here's a trick to remember: *E*, for equitable right of redemption, comes early in the alphabet, so it's what you can do before the tax sale. The statutory right of redemption (*S* for statutory) comes late in the alphabet; it's what you can do after the tax sale. In rem right of redemption and post foreclosure right of redemption are made up, but the phrase "in rem" relates to taxes and means "against the thing," meaning the property.

86. (D) Chapter 17

A combination Real Estate Investment Trust (REIT) invests in equities, which are real estate investments, and mortgages. The others are partially correct, but REITs don't invest in stocks and bonds. An equity REIT invests only in properties; a mortgage REIT invests only in mortgages.

87. (B) Chapter 17

A real estate exchange is designed to defer payment of taxes on capital gains. The exchange takes the place of a regular sale.

88. (D) Chapter 17

Remember that depreciation is the government's way of helping you recover the cost of the building, which is wearing out, so to speak.

89. (B) Chapter 17

A credit comes off taxes owed, whereas a deduction is subtracted from income. The other two answers don't really apply here.

90. (B) Chapter 17

Negative cash flow is when you have to put money into a building every month because its income cannot cover its expenses. Positive cash flow is the opposite: You have money left over each month after expenses are paid out of the building's income.

91. (A) Chapter 17

WARNING

The answer that the harder the property is to manage may be true, but don't overthink the question. The expected answer is "the higher the expected return."

92. (D) Chapter 18

What you know here is that after you deduct your commission, the owner is getting 94 percent of some dollar amount (the sales price). Just divide the dollar amount to the owner by the percentage to the owner, and presto! You have the selling price.

100 percent − 6 percent = 94 percent

$200,000 ÷ 0.94 = $212,765

93. (C) Chapter 18

Multiply the length times width, and you get the area in square units (in this case, feet). To find the area in acres, you divide the number of square feet by 43,560 square feet, which is how many square feet are in an acre.

264 feet × 264 feet = 69,696 square feet

69,696 square feet ÷ 43,560 square feet (one acre) = 1.6 acres

94. (C) Chapter 18

You're looking for the volume of the peaked roof part of the barn. For you city folks, that's like the attic. The formula for the volume of a triangular-shaped structure is

½ Base × Height × Length

0.5 × 40 feet × 15 feet × 60 feet = 18,000 cubic feet

95. (C) Chapter 18

First you find the difference between the number of houses sold this year and the number sold last year. Because you want to find the percentage of more houses sold this year than last year, you need to divide by last year's amount.

500 − 400 = 100

100 ÷ 400 = 0.25 = 25 percent

96. (D) Chapter 18

Calculate any cost recovery problem like this by dividing the number of years of cost recovery into the number 1.

1 ÷ 25 = 0.04 or 4 percent or directly by dividing the number of years into 100.

100 ÷ 25 = 4 percent

97. (A) Chapter 18

Multiply the rent by the gross rent multiplier to find the value. Easy!

$20,000 × 16 = $320,000

98. (D) Chapter 18

You always pay interest on the unpaid balance of the mortgage, which is the whole thing in the first year.

Mortgage amount × interest rate = total first year's interest

$250,000 × 0.07 (7 percent) = $17,500

99. (B) Chapter 18

Always divide the mill rate by 1,000 to get the number you have to multiply by. Then multiply that number by the assessed value.

22 ÷ 1,000 = 0.022

$42,000 × 0.022 = $924

100. (C) Chapter 18

If you have a dollar figure and the portion of 100 percent that the figure represents, you can get the total number (100 percent) by dividing the dollar figure you have by the percent it represents. In this problem, $200,000 is 80 percent of some number.

$200,000 ÷ 0.80 (80 percent) = $250,000

Chapter **21**

Practice Exam Two

A re you ready for another round of test-taking fun? Like the first practice exam in Chapter 19, this practice exam has 100 questions and is laid out with similar subjects grouped together, even though on the actual exam, subjects will be distributed randomly. I've grouped the questions so you can have an easy time determining what your strong and weak areas are. Also remember that a number of state-specific questions on the actual exam will deal with particular laws and practices unique to your state. Review the items marked with the State-Specific icon throughout this book, and study both the materials that you get in your prelicensing course (such as a textbook) and your state's license law.

Download a fill-in-the-bubble answer sheet from www.dummies.com/go/relebubblesheets and use it as you take the practice exam. Try to complete the entire test in less than two hours. Chapter 22 contains the correct answers to this exam, plus explanations and cross-references to chapters for review. (Be strong: Don't check out the answers until you finish the exam.)

You should take this exam only after you've completed the first practice exam in Chapter 19 and reviewed the chapters featuring your weaker areas. You also may want to take this exam a second time right before you take your state exam as a refresher. Good luck!

1. A rental building has several different types of insurance. A property manager may want to have which of the following?

   (A) Fire and hazard insurance

   (B) Errors and omissions insurance

   (C) Casualty insurance

   (D) Rent loss insurance

2. Rents are typically set

   (A) after an analysis of the building by a certified appraiser.

   (B) somewhat arbitrarily.

   (C) based on the expenses of the building.

   (D) based on market rents and vacancy rates.

3. Salesperson Sally works for Broker Bob. Unknown to Bob, Sally has been particularly rude to Vietnamese customers. If she is charged with a fair housing violation, will Broker Bob also be held responsible?

   (A) Yes

   (B) No

   (C) Only if she is an employee

   (D) Only if Bob had known

4. A property manager analyzing a building's risk may recommend all except which of the following?

   (A) Retain risk

   (B) Transfer risk

   (C) Avoid risk

   (D) Contain risk

5. Broker A and Broker B meet to discuss a listing that both of them are working on. They discuss the commission they will share. Which of the following is true?

   (A) They have violated antitrust laws on price fixing.

   (B) They have violated local real estate board practice if the fee they are discussing is beyond the standard fee schedule.

   (C) They really can't discuss anything because the state real estate commission sets fees.

   (D) No violation of the law has occurred.

6. Broker A and Broker B, who have real estate agencies on opposite sides of town, meet at the beginning of the year and agree that each one will handle sales only in his part of town and not interfere with sales in the other broker's area.

   (A) They have violated the antitrust law prohibiting price fixing.

   (B) They have violated the antitrust law prohibiting market allocation.

   (C) They have violated the antitrust law on group boycotting.

   (D) They have violated no antitrust law.

7. Seller Sam hires Broker Bob to sell his house. Bob brings Buyer Betty to see the house. Assuming there is no dual agency, which of the following is correct?

   (A) Sam is the customer; Bob is the agent.

   (B) Sam is the customer; Betty is the client.

   (C) Sam is the client; Betty is the customer.

   (D) Betty is the client; Bob is the agent.

8. An agency established with a written document is always

   (A) an express agency.

   (B) an implied agency.

   (C) an agency by estoppel.

   (D) an agency by ratification.

9. Fran notifies all the brokers in her area that her house is for sale and says she will work with any broker who brings a buyer. She is creating

   (A) a seller's listing.

   (B) a free-for-all listing.

   (C) an open listing.

   (D) an exclusive right to sell listing.

10. Seller Sara agrees to let Broker Ben keep any amount over the $200,000 that she needs if he sells her house. This is called

    (A) an open listing.

    (B) a gross listing.

    (C) a net listing.

    (D) a buyer's listing.

11. You are representing Seller Sharon and bring Buyer Barbara, your customer, to see the house. Barbara makes an offer. Barbara has confidentially told you about the bankruptcy she went through two years ago, but she thinks she will be financially approved to buy the house. What, if anything, should you do with the information about the bankruptcy?

    (A) Tell Sharon.

    (B) Keep the information confidential as Barbara asked you to.

    (C) Keep the information confidential unless the deal doesn't go through.

    (D) Contact the bank to verify Barbara's financial status.

12. Several people are involved in most real estate transactions. The duty of loyalty requires you to put their interest in what order of priority?

    (A) Yourself, customer, client

    (B) Yourself, client, customer

    (C) Customer, client, yourself

    (D) Client, yourself, customer

13. A homeowner refuses to rent an apartment in his two-family house to an African American family. Which of the following is true regarding this action with respect to fair housing laws?

    (A) This is legal because there is an exception to the law for one- to four-family houses.

    (B) This is legal only if the owner lives in the house himself.

    (C) This is legal as long as the homeowner does not use discriminatory advertising.

    (D) This is illegal.

14. "Christians only" is the advertisement for a house that's for sale. This is

    (A) legal if the house is owner-occupied.

    (B) illegal unless a real estate agent is used.

    (C) legal because it's a one-family house.

    (D) illegal.

15. A young married woman's income is discounted by 50 percent by a bank when she applies for a mortgage loan because she is of childbearing age. This is

    (A) illegal discrimination.

    (B) legal discrimination because of the business aspects of banking.

    (C) called redlining.

    (D) legal because protection of a depositor's money supersedes other laws.

16. A Portuguese couple looking for a house asks a real estate agent to show them houses in Portuguese neighborhoods. Which of the following is correct?

    (A) The agent can accommodate this request because the buyers are asking for it.

    (B) The agent should tell the buyers that she will show them houses in a number of different neighborhoods that meet their needs.

    (C) The agent should refuse to work with the buyers.

    (D) The agent should agree, then show the buyers houses in other neighborhoods.

17. Advising people on which neighborhoods they would be happy in may be construed as

    (A) redlining.

    (B) blockbusting.

    (C) steering.

    (D) canvassing.

18. The *Jones versus Mayer* decision basically confirmed

    (A) the constitutionality of fair housing laws.

    (B) the legality of the various exceptions to fair housing laws.

    (C) no exception for race in fair housing laws.

    (D) the owner-occupied exemption for fair housing laws.

GO ON TO NEXT PAGE

19. A young woman is refused the right to buy a condominium in a complex that restricts purchases to people 50 years of age or older. This is

(A) illegal.

(B) legal.

(C) legal if there is a restrictive covenant in the condominium deed.

(D) legal if the complex is specifically designated as senior citizen housing for people over the age of 50.

20. The lumber for a deck that has not yet been built is

(A) personal property.

(B) a fixture.

(C) a trade fixture.

(D) real estate.

21. The interest of a tenant in a rented building is most properly known as

(A) leasehold.

(B) leased fee.

(C) tenant's rights.

(D) tenancy in fee.

22. Reversion of title is a feature of what type of interest?

(A) Fee simple

(B) Fee simple condition precedent

(C) Fee simple condition subsequent

(D) Fee simple determinable

23. I give my sister permission to live in a house I own until the death of her son. I have created

(A) an ordinary life estate.

(B) a life estate pur autre vie.

(C) a leased hold interest.

(D) a tenancy for life.

24. Littoral rights for properties abutting the ocean give ownership

(A) to the mean high water mark.

(B) to a point 200 feet out from the shore.

(C) to the state ownership line.

(D) to nothing because littoral rights have to do with non-navigable rivers.

25. Jewelry cases in a jewelry store are an example of

(A) fixtures.

(B) personal property.

(C) trade fixtures.

(D) real estate.

26. A fixture

(A) is always assumed to accompany a property that is sold.

(B) is always assumed to belong to the seller and may be removed.

(C) is usually sold separately with a bill of sale.

(D) is not considered real estate.

27. In what way does a PUD generally differ from a condominium?

(A) Condominiums have homeowners associations; PUDs do not.

(B) Condominiums have monthly common charges; PUDs do not.

(C) Condominium owners own the air-space occupied by their unit and the land under and around their units as tenants in common; PUD owners own the land under and around their units individually.

(D) Condominium owners own shares in a corporation; PUD owners own the real estate individually.

28. Three people each buy pieces of property next to each other for farm use. As a matter of efficiency, they hire one person to manage the farm as a single unit even though the properties are owned separately. How is the property owned?

(A) Joint tenancy

(B) Tenancy in common

(C) Tenancy by the entirety

(D) Tenancy in severalty

29. A proprietary lease is a unique characteristic of what form of ownership?

(A) Condominium

(B) Cooperative

(C) Time share

(D) PUD

30. A corporation usually owns property in

(A) joint tenancy.

(B) tenancy in common.

(C) tenancy by the entirety.

(D) tenancy in severalty.

31. Liability that is limited to the investment does not apply to

(A) partners in a general partnership.

(B) a corporation's shareholders.

(C) limited partners in a limited partnership.

(D) limited liability corporations.

32. The type of co-ownership that allows an owner's property to be left to her heirs is

(A) tenancy by the entirety.

(B) tenancy in severalty.

(C) tenancy in common.

(D) joint tenancy.

33. You want to build your house ten feet closer to the road than the zoning ordinance permits. You will likely try to get

(A) a zoning ordinance change.

(B) a variance.

(C) a deed restriction amendment.

(D) an infrastructure change.

34. You own a factory that has been in your family for 100 years. Houses have sprung up all around it, and the zoning is now residential. How would your factory most likely be classified?

(A) Temporary use

(B) Transitional use

(C) Interim use

(D) Nonconforming use

35. The drawing showing an entire subdivision and the lots it is being divided into is most properly called

(A) a survey map.

(B) a plat map.

(C) a filed map.

(D) a metes and bounds map.

36. A mortgage is most accurately described as what type of lien?

(A) Involuntary and general

(B) Voluntary and general

(C) Voluntary and specific

(D) Involuntary and specific

37. A restriction in the deed says you cannot run a business out of your home. The zoning ordinance says you can. Which of the following is true?

(A) You cannot run a business out of your home.

(B) You can run a business out of your home.

(C) You can run a business out of your home if you get the town to give you a special permit.

(D) The deed restriction is invalid because it is against the public interest.

38. The loss of a right to enforce a deed restriction is called

(A) prescriptive rights.

(B) adverse possession.

(C) escheat.

(D) laches.

39. The assignment of costs between the buyer and the seller at the closing is called

(A) finishing fees.

(B) proration.

(C) closing accounting.

(D) real estate settlement and procedures.

40. How many acres does a section contain?

(A) 640

(B) 320

(C) 160

(D) 40

GO ON TO NEXT PAGE ➤

41. The deed that provides warranties only for the duration of the grantor's ownership is called a

    (A) general warranty deed.

    (B) special warranty deed.

    (C) quitclaim deed.

    (D) grantor's deed.

42. If the seller paid taxes in advance for the whole year on January 1 and he sells the house on July 1, which of the following is true?

    (A) The grantor gets a credit, and the grantee gets a debit.

    (B) The grantor gets a debit, and the grantee gets a credit.

    (C) The grantor and grantee both get credits.

    (D) The grantor and grantee both get debits.

43. A deed often used to clear up a cloud on a title is

    (A) a trust deed.

    (B) a referee's deed.

    (C) a special warranty deed.

    (D) a quitclaim deed.

44. The act of recording a deed provides or accomplishes

    (A) actual notice of ownership.

    (B) constructive notice of ownership.

    (C) proof of ownership.

    (D) transfer of ownership.

45. Which of the following is not a form of voluntary alienation?

    (A) Gift

    (B) Sale

    (C) Dedication

    (D) Forfeiture

46. You have just lost a large portion of the hill you live on due to a sudden mudslide. You are the victim of

    (A) erosion.

    (B) avulsion.

    (C) escheat.

    (D) forfeiture.

47. A religious group was given property for use in building a church. Instead, they lease the property out to raise money for their missionary work. The group loses the property for violation of the deed condition through a process called

    (A) avulsion.

    (B) escheat.

    (C) foreclosure.

    (D) forfeiture.

48. The process by which multiple owners can accumulate the statutory time necessary to claim adverse possession or a prescriptive easement is called

    (A) accumulation.

    (B) accretion.

    (C) tacking.

    (D) notorious possession.

49. If you die intestate, the law distributes your assets according to the laws of

    (A) descent.

    (B) inheritance.

    (C) probate.

    (D) surrogacy.

50. The court that handles wills is called

    (A) inheritance court.

    (B) civil court.

    (C) surrogate's court.

    (D) devisee's court.

51. You sign an option agreement to purchase some land while a zoning change is being sought. Which of the following is true?

    (A) You must purchase the land.

    (B) You must purchase the land if the zoning change is granted.

    (C) The seller must sell you the land.

    (D) The seller must renegotiate with you if you want.

52. A buyer wants to make sure everything is okay with the house he's buying. He most likely would

- **(A)** have every house he looks at inspected by a qualified home inspector.
- **(B)** sign an option on a house he likes so that he doesn't lose it while it is inspected.
- **(C)** put an inspection contingency clause in the sales contract.
- **(D)** not sign the contract until the house is inspected.

53. The parol evidence rule generally says that

- **(A)** written contracts take precedence over oral contracts.
- **(B)** oral contracts take precedence over written contracts.
- **(C)** written contracts can be modified by oral contracts.
- **(D)** real estate sales contracts may be oral or in writing.

54. Forcing a buyer to go through with a property purchase that he does not want to do is

- **(A)** a novation.
- **(B)** an assignment.
- **(C)** a suit for compensatory damages.
- **(D)** a suit for specific performance.

55. A contract for the sale of property is said to be

- **(A)** executed.
- **(B)** executory until the closing.
- **(C)** executory until the closing whereupon it is executed.
- **(D)** executed until closing whereupon it is executory.

56. Joe agrees to buy Sally's house. When Joe can't come up with the money, Tim agrees to take over the contract and buy Sally's house under the same terms. This is called

- **(A)** a mutual agreement.
- **(B)** a novation.
- **(C)** an assignment.
- **(D)** a delegation.

57. A landlord who is selling a building allows a tenant to stay until the building is sold. This is

- **(A)** an estate at sufferance.
- **(B)** an estate at will.
- **(C)** an estate for years.
- **(D)** a periodic estate.

58. A tenant's lease expires, and the landlord does not give the tenant a new lease but instead allows her to stay and collects rent from her every month. Which of the following is true?

- **(A)** An estate for years has become a periodic estate.
- **(B)** A periodic estate has become an estate for years.
- **(C)** A periodic estate has become an estate at will.
- **(D)** An estate for years has become an estate at sufferance.

59. The fact that a lease of longer than a year must be in writing is a typical provision of

- **(A)** RESPA.
- **(B)** UCC.
- **(C)** the statute of frauds.
- **(D)** the parol evidence rule.

60. Landlord *A* rents space to Tenant *B*. Tenant *B* agrees to rent the same space to Tenant *C*. This is most likely

- **(A)** an assignment.
- **(B)** a novation.
- **(C)** a sublease.
- **(D)** a net lease.

61. A tenant rents an apartment from a landlord. The tenant pays rent and the landlord pays all the building expenses. This is

- **(A)** a net lease.
- **(B)** a proprietary lease.
- **(C)** a triple net lease.
- **(D)** a gross lease.

GO ON TO NEXT PAGE

62. A feature unique to a ground lease is that

(A) the tenant pays all expenses.

(B) the tenant pays no expenses.

(C) the term may be unusually long.

(D) the tenant pays rent based on the revenues the property generates.

63. What phase of environmental assessment creates a management plan for the hazardous waste area?

(A) 1

(B) 2

(C) 3

(D) 4

64. Various allergic and respiratory symptoms that develop in an office building and then persist even after leaving the building may be

(A) BRI.

(B) SBS.

(C) OSHA.

(D) CERCLA.

65. Homes built before what year require lead paint disclosures?

(A) 1978

(B) 1979

(C) 1980

(D) 1981

66. A colorless, odorless gas that may cause cancer is

(A) asbestos.

(B) electromagnetic fields.

(C) radon.

(D) BRI.

67. Typically, individual on-site sanitary waste disposal systems are sized by the number of

(A) square feet.

(B) bedrooms.

(C) bathrooms.

(D) people.

68. The test done to determine the soil's capability to absorb leachate from a septic system is called

(A) a site test.

(B) an absorption analysis.

(C) a percolation test.

(D) a leach field analysis.

69. Investment value is

(A) the same as market value.

(B) the same as value in use.

(C) the value to a typical investor.

(D) the value to an individual investor.

70. The value usually associated with real estate taxes is

(A) market value.

(B) appraised value.

(C) assessed value.

(D) tax value.

71. A transaction in which a father sells property to his son would not be used in an appraisal because

(A) it is not an arm's length transaction.

(B) it is an invalid transaction.

(C) it is a value in use transaction.

(D) such a sale can use only the cost approach.

72. A comparable sale has four bedrooms compared to the subject's three bedrooms. The fourth bedroom is worth $30,000. What do you do with that number?

(A) Add it to the subject's value.

(B) Subtract it from the subject's value.

(C) Add it to the comparable's sale price.

(D) Subtract it from the comparable's sale price.

73. The method of estimating replacement or reproduction cost that requires you to know the original cost of construction of the building is

(A) the square foot method.

(B) the quantity survey method.

(C) the unit in place method.

(D) the index method.

74. The total number of years a building is considered to contribute to the value of the property is a good definition of

(A) chronological age.

(B) effective age.

(C) economic life.

(D) remaining economic life.

75. A number that relates net operating income to value is

(A) the gross rent multiplier.

(B) the capitalization rate.

(C) the depreciated cost factor.

(D) the effective gross income factor.

76. Which of the following does not fit in a group?

(A) Consumer Credit Protection Act

(B) Truth in Lending Act

(C) Regulation Z

(D) Equal Credit Opportunity Act

77. A person buys a furnished house and wants to finance the purchase of both the house and the furniture through a mortgage loan. She tries to get

(A) a blanket mortgage.

(B) a purchase money mortgage.

(C) a temporary loan.

(D) a package mortgage.

78. Which of the following is not a typical obligation of the mortgagor?

(A) Maintain the property.

(B) Keep a hazard insurance policy in force.

(C) Get permission for alterations.

(D) Advise the mortgagee of a change in the escrow account balance.

79. Which one of the following does not affect the interest rate adjustment in an adjustable-rate mortgage loan?

(A) Index

(B) Equity

(C) Margin

(D) Cap

80. In a fixed-rate amortized loan, which one of the following does not vary from month to month?

(A) Monthly payment

(B) Interest paid

(C) Principal paid

(D) Remaining principal owed

81. The discount rate is

(A) the amount of points you pay to reduce your interest rate.

(B) the amount of interest federal reserve banks charge each other for loans.

(C) the amount of interest paid on treasury bonds.

(D) the amount of money as a percent of total deposits that banks must keep in cash.

82. A property is foreclosed and sold for nonpayment of the mortgage loan. The sale does not cover the remaining balance of the mortgage loan. The bank goes to court to seek

(A) judicial foreclosure.

(B) statutory redemption.

(C) equitable redemption.

(D) deficiency judgment.

83. The term most closely associated with real estate taxes is

(A) ad valorem.

(B) appraised value.

(C) market value.

(D) cost approach.

GO ON TO NEXT PAGE ➡

84. The assessment ratio is used to
    (A) determine the tax rate.
    (B) convert market value to value in use.
    (C) convert market value to assessed value.
    (D) determine property tax exemptions.

85. Someone protesting his assessment has to prove that
    (A) his taxes are too high.
    (B) his taxes are higher than those of similar properties.
    (C) his assessment is too high.
    (D) his assessment is unequal to those of similar properties.

86. Capital gains is calculated using
    (A) the depreciated basis.
    (B) the original price of the property.
    (C) the adjusted basis.
    (D) the capital gains basis.

87. A reason people invest in real estate is because real estate is
    (A) low risk.
    (B) highly liquid.
    (C) easy to manage.
    (D) highly leveraged.

88. Real estate investors expect to make money all the following ways except through
    (A) tax benefits.
    (B) staying liquid.
    (C) capital appreciation.
    (D) positive cash flow.

89. When calculating the adjusted basis for capital gains purposes, depreciation is
    (A) subtracted from the total cost of the property.
    (B) subtracted from the value of the building only.
    (C) added to the adjusted basis.
    (D) subtracted from taxes due.

90. In analyzing a possible real estate investment, potential gross income minus vacancy and collection loss plus other income minus operating expenses equals
    (A) effective gross income.
    (B) net operating income.
    (C) debt service.
    (D) cash flow.

91. If properties are not equal in value in an exchange, one person will have to pay the other
    (A) capital gains.
    (B) loot.
    (C) boot.
    (D) adjusted basis value.

92. A property was sold for $260,000, which was 130 percent of what the owner paid for it. What had the owner paid for the property?
    (A) $100,000
    (B) $160,000
    (C) $200,000
    (D) $230,000

93. A building generates gross rent of $30,000 and just sold for $360,000. What is the gross rent multiplier?
    (A) 12 percent
    (B) 8 percent
    (C) 10
    (D) 12

94. A building has a net operating income of $45,000. Buildings like this are appraised using a capitalization rate of 11 percent. What is the estimated value of the building?
    (A) $409,000
    (B) $450,000
    (C) $495,000
    (D) $540,000

95. How many cubic feet are in a warehouse that measures 80 feet by 50 feet by 18 feet high?

    (A) 72,000

    (B) 4,000

    (C) 2,340

    (D) 145

96. Seller Sally pays $1,200 in taxes in advance for the year on January 1. She sells her house to Buyer Brian and closes on June 1. Who owes what to whom?

    (A) Seller owes the buyer $700.

    (B) Buyer owes the seller $700.

    (C) Seller owes the buyer $500.

    (D) Buyer owes the seller $500.

97. If the tax rate is $30 per $1,000, what are the taxes on property assessed at $80,000?

    (A) $240

    (B) $2,400

    (C) $800

    (D) $300

98. The payment factor for a 25-year loan at 6 percent interest is $6.85. What is the monthly payment on a mortgage loan of $175,000?

    (A) $1,199

    (B) $875

    (C) $583

    (D) $618

99. What is the commission if a property sold for $250,000 and the commission rate is 5 percent?

    (A) $15,500

    (B) $12,500

    (C) $10,500

    (D) $7,500

100. What is the total interest you will pay on an 8 percent amortized 25-year mortgage loan of $200,000 if the monthly payments are $1,400?

    (A) $420,000

    (B) $300,000

    (C) $220,000

    (D) $200,000

Chapter 22

Answers and Explanations to Practice Exam Two

Your performance on the second exam in Chapter 21 should tell the story of how well you've mastered the material and how ready you are for the state exam. Give yourself one point for each correct answer and note the blocks of questions by subject. You'll have two scores: an overall exam score and a score for each of the sections by subject. At this point, I'm assuming you took the practice exam in Chapter 19, reviewed the answers in Chapter 20, and studied your weakest areas. If you've done that and your score for this exam is below 80, take a close look at your weakest areas on this exam. If you got more than two or three questions wrong in any subject, go back and review the corresponding chapter. Spend some time reviewing the material in your weakest areas, but unless you got everything right in a particular subject, don't neglect the areas that you did well in. Remember: Every point counts. After you've finished reviewing all the material, you need to continue on to the next two exams in Chapters 23 and 25. Take all the practice exams more than once. I bet you'll be amazed at how much your score improves.

STATE SPECIFIC

Don't forget that no matter how well you did on this exam, the information here is general to most states. You still need to study the information specific to your state. Review the material marked with the State-Specific icon throughout this book as well as the list of state-specific subjects in Chapter 27. You also can get state-specific information from your prelicensing course materials, textbook, and instructor.

1. **(B)** Chapter 3

   A property manager gets errors and omissions insurance for his own protection and the other three for a building. Reread the question in light of this explanation, and you'll see how the correct answer makes sense.

2. **(D)** Chapter 3

   The word "typically" is important. An owner usually looks at market rents of similar buildings and the vacancy rate of other buildings and his own to determine a proper rental rate.

3. **(A)** Chapter 3

Broker Bob is responsible for everything that Salesperson Sally does. Her status as an employee or an independent contractor doesn't matter. And if Answer (D) confused you, the point is that Bob should have known.

4. **(D)** Chapter 3

Retaining, transferring, and avoiding risk are three ways to deal with risk. The fourth way to deal with risk (which isn't listed) is to control it.

5. **(D)** Chapter 3

The antitrust law doesn't apply to cooperating brokers for a particular transaction. All real estate commissions are individually negotiated, so Answers (B) and (C) don't exist.

6. **(B)** Chapter 3

The question describes market allocation, or dividing up the market, and it's illegal.

7. **(C)** Chapter 4

The agent represents the client, who may be a buyer or a seller. The person not represented by the agent is the customer.

8. **(A)** Chapter 4

If the agreement is in writing, it's expressed. All of the other choices are agencies established by the actions of the parties rather than any specific agreement.

9. **(C)** Chapter 4

An open listing gives several brokers a chance to sell the property. Seller's and free-for-all listings are not types of listings. An exclusive right to sell a listing is an agreement with one broker who is paid whether the broker or the owner sells the property.

STATE SPECIFIC

10. **(C)** Chapter 4

Be sure to check out whether net listings are illegal in your state. An open listing gives several brokers a chance to sell a property. Gross and buyer's listings are made up.

11. **(A)** Chapter 4

Your fiduciary duties include disclosure to your client of all important information, even if it's personal to the customer and you've been asked to keep it confidential. You don't owe your customer the duty of confidentiality.

12. **(D)** Chapter 4

The fiduciary principal of loyalty requires you to put the client's interest above all others, even your own. You don't owe loyalty to the customer; you owe only honest and fair dealing, reasonable care, and disclosure of material facts and latent defects.

13. **(D)** Chapter 5

There's no exception for race as per the Civil Rights Act of 1866.

14. **(D)** Chapter 5

Even if there's an exception to one of the antidiscrimination acts, discriminatory advertising, which includes any mention of religion, isn't permitted.

15. (A) Chapter 5

Gender is a protected class in housing discrimination including lending practices.

16. (B) Chapter 5

Real estate agents may not participate in steering, even if the customer directs it. Steering is directing people to various neighborhoods on the basis of any protected class. Keep in mind that you can accommodate someone's request to see properties in a particular neighborhood or subdivision if he specifies it by geographic location.

17. (C) Chapter 5

Advising people on where they would be happy may not appear to be steering because you may not be doing it to discriminate, but the word "construed" indicates that it can appear to be steering.

18. (C) Chapter 5

The 1866 Civil Rights Act, which prohibited discrimination on the basis of race, allowed no exceptions. It was largely forgotten. The 1968 Federal Fair Housing Act, which also prohibited discrimination on the basis of race, among other things, permitted some exceptions. The *Jones vs. Mayer* decision confirmed that the 1866 law was still in effect and superseded the 1968 law, permitting NO exceptions for race.

19. (A) Chapter 5

Housing may be restricted to people 62 years of age and older or 55 years of age or older in cases where at least one occupant per unit is 55 and at least 80 percent of the units are occupied by people 55 or older.

20. (A) Chapter 6

Personal property is tangible, moveable, and not permanently attached to real estate. The lumber can become a fixture (and therefore, real estate) if the deck is built. A trade fixture is something used in conjunction with a business.

21. (A) Chapter 6

The words "most properly" signal that the exam writers are looking for a precise legal answer (if possible), so the best answer is leasehold.

22. (D) Chapter 6

You may have been tempted to answer fee simple condition subsequent, which allows the right of reentry (the grantor's right to go to court to reclaim the property). In fee simple determinable, the title reverts back to the grantor if a certain condition isn't met.

23. (B) Chapter 6

In an ordinary life estate, the length of time of the estate interest is the lifetime of the person receiving the life estate. The length of a life estate pur autre vie is for the lifetime of a third party rather than the person actually receiving the life estate.

24. (A) Chapter 6

Littoral rights give owners of property next to large bodies of water ownership of land up to the average or mean high water mark. Riparian rights involve rivers and streams.

25. (C) Chapter 6

Jewelry cases may be considered personal property because they're usually removable by the owner, but the best answer is trade fixtures, which are used in association with a business use of property.

26. (A) Chapter 6

A fixture becomes real estate when it is attached and is always assumed to go with the property when sold. Personal property is normally sold with a bill of sale.

27. (C) Chapter 7

Both PUDs and condominiums generally have homeowners associations and monthly common charges. Cooperative owners own shares in a corporation.

28. (D) Chapter 7

TIP

Look for key words in a question, and above all, read the question carefully and completely. Don't confuse how a property is owned with how it is managed. The key words are "each buy pieces of property" and "owned separately." This is a case of three individual owners. Sole ownership is tenancy in severalty. Joint tenancy, tenancy in common, and tenancy by the entirety all apply to ownership of one property by more than one person.

29. (B) Chapter 7

Cooperative ownership provides for ownership of shares in a corporation that owns the building. The proprietary lease allows occupancy of the unit.

30. (D) Chapter 7

Corporations are considered a single person, and ownership by a single person is tenancy in severalty. The other choices are all forms of ownership with other people.

31. (A) Chapter 7

WARNING

TIP

Watch the negative in this question; three of the choices feature limited liability, and only one (a general partnership) doesn't.

This question is a good example of what to do if you have no clue. Two answers have the word "limited" in them, as does the question. I know you think the exam writers want to trick you, but your best bet is to eliminate those two answers. If you think about how most corporations work (many stockholders and a few people running the company), it may seem logical that liability would also be limited in that case as well. That leaves you with the correct answer of general partnership.

32. (C) Chapter 7

WARNING

Tenancy in common has no right of survivorship, which means that a person's shares of property go to heirs upon the person's death, not to the other owners of the property. And watch out for especially tricky wrong answers. In this case, tenancy in severalty is not a form of co-ownership; it's ownership by one person.

33. (B) Chapter 8

You can try to get a change in the actual zoning ordinance itself, which you're unlikely to get because it involves only one property. You'll apply for a variance, which is a change in the zoning ordinance for one lot.

34. (D) Chapter 8

A nonconforming use is one that existed before the current zoning and isn't in accordance with current zoning.

35. (B) Chapter 8

A plat map is the technical term for a map of lands that have been approved for subdivision. A discussion of a survey map, the filed map system (another name for the lot and block system), and the metes and bounds system can be found in Chapter 9.

36. (C) Chapter 8

No one can force you into a mortgage agreement, so it's voluntary. And a mortgage applies to only one property, so it's specific.

37. (A) Chapter 8

If a conflict arises between a deed restriction and public law, the stricter rule applies.

38. (D) Chapter 8

Laches is correct. Two wrong answers may have thrown you off. Someone may gain prescriptive rights over the property of another by continuous use. Adverse possession is similar to prescriptive rights, only it may involve actually obtaining ownership.

39. (B) Chapter 9

In the proration process, costs and payments are debited and credited between the buyer and the seller. If "real estate settlement and procedures" looks familiar, that's because the Real Estate Settlement and Procedures Act governs most closings.

TIP

40. (A) Chapter 9

Remember that a section is one mile long (5,280 feet) on each side. If you do the area math (5,280 feet × 5,280 feet), and then convert square feet into acres (by dividing by 43,560), you'll come out with 640 acres.

41. (B) Chapter 9

The general warranty deed provides warranties back to the beginning of time (basically). "general" is broader than "special," so you may remember that a special warranty deed provides warranties only for the ownership period of the grantor.

42. (A) Chapter 9

The grantor is the seller, and the grantee is the buyer. A credit means an amount is owed to you. A debit means that you owe an amount. The grantor paid for the whole year, and the grantee will live in the house for part of the year. Therefore, the grantee owes the grantor money for that part of the year.

43. (D) Chapter 9

A quitclaim deed provides no warranties and often is used to clear up title problems. Make sure you have a basic knowledge of the different types of deeds.

44. (B) Chapter 9

Constructive notice is essentially setting up a situation in which someone who's interested can get information. Recording the deed in the public records does that.

45. (D) Chapter 10

Voluntary alienation is giving up title to property of your own free will. Gifts, sales, and dedication are voluntary. Forfeiture is an involuntary loss of the title to a property because of a violation of a condition in the deed.

46. (B) Chapter 10

Avulsion is the sudden loss of land through natural processes such as earthquakes. It's often grouped with erosion, which is the loss of land through a gradual natural process, so you may have answered (A).

47. (D) Chapter 10

The two you may confuse are forfeiture and foreclosure. Forfeiture is the loss of ownership of a property because of a violation of a deed condition. Foreclosure is the seizing of your property for nonpayment of a debt such as taxes or the mortgage loan.

TIP

48. (C) Chapter 10

"Tacking equals time" may be a good way to remember this answer. And time is what you're accumulating.

49. (A) Chapter 10

Exam writers expect you to know that "intestate" means without a will. The laws of descent govern the distribution of your assets after death. Some of the other answers may ring true; probate, which is the processing of a will, occurs in surrogate's court.

50. (C) Chapter 10

TIP

Surrogate's court handles an estate on behalf of someone else, namely the deceased. (Think of surrogate mothers to help you remember this.)

51. (C) Chapter 11

A simple option agreement is a unilateral agreement, in which only one person is obligated to do what is promised. In this case, the seller has to sell the land to the buyer (option holder) if the buyer wants to purchase the land. The simple option agreement doesn't require the buyer to act. If the buyer refuses to buy at the terms originally stated in the option agreement, the seller is under no obligation to renegotiate the deal. Answer B would apply if this were a conditional contract instead of an option.

52. (C) Chapter 11

The buyer can choose to do any of the options listed, but he probably will add an inspection contingency clause to the sales contract. A contingency clause in a contract requires that something be completed before the closing can take place.

53. (A) Chapter 11

The parol evidence rule says that written contracts take precedence over oral contracts and that oral modification of written contracts may not be enforceable. All real estate sales contracts must be in writing.

54. (D) Chapter 11

You want the buyer to perform, that is, to do or act in the manner he agreed to and buy your house. Novation involves a whole new contract, assignment is the same contract with a different buyer, and a suit for compensatory damages is a suit for money.

55. (C) Chapter 11

WARNING

I wanted to give you a taste of a bad question. Executory until the closing is technically correct, but executory until the closing whereupon it is executed is the better, more complete answer. A real estate sales contract is said to be executory until closing because all the terms have not yet been fulfilled. It is executed at closing because at that point, all the terms have been fulfilled. Look out for answers that are partially correct; the test writers want you to give the best, most complete answer possible.

56. (C) Chapter 11

There is mutual agreement for Tim to take over the contract, but it's an assignment of the existing contract. The tricky part is telling the difference between assignment and delegation. Assignment is when Party B takes over the obligations of Party A and Party A no longer has any liability. Delegation is when Party A asks Party B to fulfill the terms of Party A's contract. Party A is still responsible.

57. (B) Chapter 12

In an estate at will, the tenant will stay as long as the landlord lets him. In an estate at sufferance, the landlord "suffers" when the tenant stays, because the landlord wants him to leave. A year is a period of time, and an estate for years lasts for some definite period. And a periodic estate renews itself as each period expires.

58. (A) Chapter 12

An estate for years is the regular lease tenancy with a beginning and ending date. A periodic estate is (in this case) a month-to-month lease that automatically renews itself from period to period and in which the landlord accepts the rent.

59. (C) Chapter 12

The statute of frauds (adopted in some form in every state) usually requires that all real estate contracts, including leases of more than a year, be in writing.

60. (C) Chapter 12

In a sublease, the original tenant remains responsible for the lease provisions but executes a lease between herself and the new tenant. An assignment is similar, but it's in fact taking over the original tenant's lease as is, with the new tenant liable.

61. (D) Chapter 12

A gross lease is the one described in the question. In a net lease, the tenant pays some part of the building's expenses. In a triple net lease, the tenant pays all of the building's expenses. A cooperative apartment owner has a proprietary lease.

62. (C) Chapter 12

Because ground leases often involve someone leasing vacant land to build a building, they tend to be for unusually long terms, 50 to 100 years not being unusual.

63. (D) Chapter 13

The phases of environmental assessment are 1) a review of records and a physical inspection of the property; 2) testing; 3) cleaning up the contamination; and 4) managing the contamination.

64. (A) Chapter 13

The symptoms of building-related illness persist even after you leave a building, and the symptoms of sick building syndrome are present only when you're in a building. The Occupational Safety and Health Administration can make employers sick when it finds safety violations in the workplace, and the Comprehensive Environmental Response, Compensation, and Liability Act is designed to prevent everyone from getting sick by cleaning up contaminated sites.

65. (A) Chapter 13

Sorry, gang; this is something you're just going to have to memorize. The federal government requires lead paint disclosure for houses built before 1978.

66. (C) Chapter 13

Radon is gas formed from radioactive rocks usually beneath a house. It comes up through basements and can be alleviated by ventilation.

67. (B) Chapter 13

The problem with this question is that answers like bathrooms and square footage make sense. Just remember that you can have many bathrooms in a very large house and still have only a few people. The number of bedrooms, however, often determines a choice in buying a house for a family. By the way, the specific onsite sanitary waste disposal system in the question is usually called a septic system.

68. (C) Chapter 13

An absorption analysis may sound right, but an absorption analysis actually looks at how fast space, houses, or apartments will be absorbed by the market. "Site test" is too vague. A leach field analysis may look right, but remember that you're testing the soil. The leach field, which is part of the septic system, isn't there yet.

69. (D) Chapter 14

Investment value can be the same as market value by coincidence. A typical investor will pay market value for a building. A specific investor will look at investment value for a particular use.

70. (C) Chapter 14

There's technically no such thing as tax value. Market value may be used in tax work, but real estate taxes are based on assessed value; it's the best answer. Appraised value is an estimate of value and is usually but not exclusively associated with market value.

71. (A) Chapter 14

If this question was tricky for you, remember that all appraisals depend on the use of market value transactions, which presume an arm's length transaction. An arm's length transaction technically is one in which no relationship exists between the parties. (The transaction is valid because no law forbids a father from selling his property to his son, or anyone else for that matter; the transfer of ownership took place.)

72. (D) Chapter 14

Remember, you never touch the subject in the sales comparison approach. Instead you make adjustments to the comparable. If the comparable is better than the subject, you subtract; if it's worse than the subject, you add.

73. (D) Chapter 14

The three incorrect answers all are methods for estimating reproduction cost or replacement cost that involve either calculating building costs per square foot or pricing out the various construction components.

74. (C) Chapter 14

The economic life of a building reflects the number of years it contributes to the value of the land. Chronological age is the actual age of the building. The effective age is the current apparent age of the building taking into account the level of maintenance and upgrades the building has had. Remaining economic life is the number of years left in which the building will contribute to the value of the land.

75. (B) Chapter 14

You divide the net operating income by the capitalization rate to get value.

76. (D) Chapter 15

The first three answers are essentially interchangeable names for the same act, which controls advertising and the provision of information with respect to loans. The Equal Credit Opportunity Act prohibits discrimination in granting credit.

77. (D) Chapter 15

A package mortgage loan covers real and personal property. You need to be able to identify all the types of mortgage loans covered in Chapter 15.

78. (D) Chapter 15

This question requires you to know who the mortgagor (borrower) and mortgagee (lender) are. The first three answers relate to the borrower's duties. The mortgagee does the advising about the escrow account balance; the borrower contributes money to the escrow account only according to the lender's accounting of what it needs.

79. (B) Chapter 15

Equity is the difference between the value of the property and all the debts owed on the property. It bears no relationship to adjustable-rate mortgages.

80. (A) Chapter 15

In an amortized loan, the monthly payment remains the same while the portion of the principal you pay goes up, the amount of interest goes down, and you pay off more and more of the overall principal.

81. (B) Chapter 15

The two answers to watch out for are discount points (A) and the discount rate (B). Discount points are prepaid interest that you pay at the beginning of a loan to reduce the interest rate that you pay.

82. (D) Chapter 15

A deficiency judgment makes a borrower personally obligated to pay the balance of a debt. Judicial foreclosure is wrong here because foreclosure has already happened. Statutory and equitable redemption are rights of the person whose property was foreclosed to pay off the debt and get the property back.

83. (A) Chapter 16

Appraised value and market value can be used to figure out assessed value for tax purposes. However, the term "ad valorem," which means "based on the value," relates directly to real estate taxes because taxes are based on the value of the property. The cost approach is an appraisal technique for estimating value.

84. (C) Chapter 16

Multiply a property's market value by the assessment ratio to get the assessed value.

85. (D) Chapter 16

Note the word "assessment" in the question. This should help you eliminate Answers (A) and (B), which are about taxes, not assessments. Although you may think your assessment is too high, remember that assessments are about being equal among similar properties.

86. (C) Chapter 17

WARNING

Some of these answers *almost* make sense. For example, the adjusted basis is calculated using depreciation and the original value of the property, so you may have thought Answers (A) or (B) was correct. But the adjusted basis is the best answer because it's the last number you use in figuring capital gains. (I can't stress it enough — watch out for wrong answers that may be partially correct.) I made up the capital gains basis.

87. (D) Chapter 17

Believe it or not, real estate isn't considered a low-risk investment unless it can be held for an unknown length of time. It also isn't considered liquid, which means you can't get your money out of it quickly. Those midnight phone calls about the broken furnace don't make real estate easy to manage. Generally you can borrow money easily to buy property. And that's what leverage is.

88. (B) Chapter 17

Real estate isn't considered a liquid investment; you can't get your money out of it quickly.

89. (A) Chapter 17

Depreciation is subtracted from the total cost of the property (for instance, the purchase price plus capital improvements) to get the adjusted basis. Remember that depreciation is calculated only against the value of the building; buildings depreciate, but land doesn't.

90. (B) Chapter 17

Here's the whole breakdown of the pro forma (analysis of an investment):

Potential gross income – vacancy and collection loss + other income = effective gross income

Effective gross income – operating expenses = net operating income

Net operating income – debt service = before-tax cash flow

91. (C) Chapter 17

I know, it may be loot, but that's still not the right answer — boot is. And watch out: Don't be thrown off by capital gains. A capital gains tax is deferred in a real estate exchange, but one person doesn't pay that tax to the other.

92. (C) Chapter 18

The question says 130 percent of what he paid for the property, not 130 percent *more than* what he paid for it. State the problem this way: $260,000 is 130 percent of some number. When you can state a problem like that, you can divide the number you have by the percentage you're given and get the number you're looking for. And don't forget: You can convert any percentage into a decimal number you can work with by dividing the percentage by 100 or moving the decimal point two places to the left.

130 percent ÷ 100 = 1.30

$260,000 ÷ 1.30 = $200,000

93. (D) Chapter 18

A multiplier always is just a number. A rate is a percentage, so you know 12 percent and 8 percent are wrong. The formula for finding the gross rent multiplier follows:

Price ÷ gross rent = gross rent multiplier

$360,000 ÷ $30,000 = 12

94. (A) Chapter 18

Net operating income ÷ capitalization rate = value

$45,000 ÷ 0.11 = $409,090 (Answers like this are usually rounded, hence the given answer of $409,000.)

95. (A) Chapter 18

Length × width × height = volume

80 feet × 50 feet × 18 feet = 72,000 cubic feet

96. (B) Chapter 18

A credit is an amount owed to you, and a debit is an amount you owe. Seller Sally paid taxes for the whole year, but she lives in the house for only five months. Buyer Brian lives in the house seven months and paid nothing. Brian owes something to Sally.

$1,200 of taxes ÷ 12 months = $100 per month

The seller is in the house 5 months, and the buyer is in the house for 7 months. So, 7 × $100 = $700.

97. (B) Chapter 18

Assessed value × tax rate = taxes owed

$80,000 × ($30 ÷ $1,000) = taxes owed

$30 ÷ $1,000 = 0.03 tax rate

$80,000 (assessed value) × 0.03 (tax rate) = $2,400 taxes owed

You also can do the following:

$80,000 ÷ $1,000 = $80

$80 × $30 = $2,400

98. (A) Chapter 18

Amount of mortgage ÷ $1,000 = units of $1,000

Units of $1,000 × payment factor = monthly payment

$175,000 ÷ 1,000 = 175

175 × $6.85 = $1,198.75 (rounded off to $1,199)

The payment factor includes the interest rate (6 percent) and the loan term (25 years), so this information actually isn't needed for your calculation. And no, the exam writers don't expect you to be able to calculate the factor.

99. (B) Chapter 18

The formula for calculating a commission, which I'm sure you'll grow to love, follows:

Sales price × commission rate = commission earned

$250,000 × 0.05 (5 percent) = $12,500

100. (C) Chapter 18

Each payment in an amortized mortgage loan contains principal and interest, and at the end of the loan, you've paid a lot of interest and the original amount of the mortgage loan (principal). The following formula will handle a typical problem like this.

Monthly payment (principal and interest) × 12 months × term of loan in years = total payments of principal and interest

Total payments of principal and interest – original loan amount (principal) = interest

$1,400 × 12 months × 25 years = $420,000 in total payments

$420,000 – $200,000 (original loan amount) = $220,000 interest

Chapter 23

Practice Exam Three

You've completed two exams, but you can't get too much practice. So here is another exam with the answers in the following chapter. This exam offers you some new questions as well as some old questions asked in a different way. Download a fill-in-the-bubble answer sheet from www.dummies.com/go/relebubblesheets and use it as you take the practice exam. I group the questions by chapter so you can easily analyze your weak areas.

Don't get over confident. Read the questions and answers carefully. By the time you're done with all four practice exams, know you are ready for the state test.

1. Maximizing income and maintaining property value are the general goals of what aspect of the real estate business?

   (A) Appraising

   (B) Brokerage and sales

   (C) Property management

   (D) Property inspection

2. When managing risk, transferring it usually means

   (A) making the property manager responsible.

   (B) making the owner responsible.

   (C) complying with all local laws so that the municipality is responsible.

   (D) purchasing insurance.

3. What type of insurance would usually pay a financial claim for injury by a person who falls on the icy sidewalk in front of a building?

   (A) Liability

   (B) Errors and omissions

   (C) Casualty

   (D) Fire and hazard

4. Although a property management agreement can be for any length of time, the generally recommended minimum is

   (A) six months.

   (B) one year.

   (C) two years.

   (D) no minimum.

5. An agent who represents someone in a group of activities such as a property manager is considered what type of agent?

   (A) Special

   (B) General

   (C) Universal

   (D) Individual

6. In general, which of the following is not an agent's duty to a customer?

   (A) Confidentiality

   (B) Honest and fair dealing

   (C) Disclosure of material facts

   (D) Reasonable care

7. Which of the following is true?

   (A) A latent defect is always a material defect.

   (B) A latent defect is never a material defect.

   (C) A latent defect always affects a buyer's decision.

   (D) A material defect may affect the buyer's decision.

8. Seller Sam agrees to allow Broker Betty to keep anything she makes above the $250,000 Sam wants for his house. This is an example of

   (A) an open price listing.

   (B) a violation of accounting.

   (C) a net listing.

   (D) an auction listing.

9. A seller can be

   (A) a principal only.

   (B) a principal but not a client.

   (C) a principal, a client, but not a customer.

   (D) a principal, a client, and a customer.

10. A buyer wants to be represented by only one broker and understands that the broker will spend time and money working for him. He agrees that it is only fair that the broker be compensated even if he, the buyer, finds a house on his own. The buyer signs

    (A) an open buyer agency agreement.

    (B) a buyer agent guaranteed compensation agreement.

    (C) exclusive agency buyer agency agreement.

    (D) exclusive buyer agency agreement.

11. Disclosure as part of an agent's fiduciary duties mean

    (A) full disclosure of all facts to buyer and seller equally.

    (B) disclosure of latent defects to the seller only.

    (C) disclosure of all material facts to the client.

    (D) disclosure of all pertinent information to the client.

12. A seller's agent earns her commission when

(A) she is the procuring cause of the transaction.

(B) produces a ready, willing, and able buyer.

(C) there is a meeting of the minds.

(D) all of the above.

13. There are no exceptions to the

(A) 1866 Civil Rights Act.

(B) 1968 Fair Housing Act.

(C) Community Development Act of 1974.

(D) Fair Housing Amendments Act of 1988.

14. A landlord requires a higher security deposit from families with children than those without children. According to Federal Law this is

(A) not discriminatory.

(B) not discriminatory if there are more than two children.

(C) discriminatory in all cases.

(D) not discriminatory if the owner only rents one single-family house.

15. "There are a lot of children in this neighborhood" said by a real estate agent to a buyer

(A) is acceptable if there are a lot of children in the neighborhood.

(B) is acceptable steering since people want to know about the demographics in a neighborhood.

(C) is considered steering and is therefore illegal.

(D) is not steering because it's stating a fact.

16. A real estate agent

(A) is subject to all fair housing laws with no exceptions.

(B) can assist clients with legal exceptions to fair housing laws.

(C) cannot use federal exceptions but can use local state exceptions.

(D) can only use the exception to the 1866 Civil Rights Act.

17. "This apartment/house is not available"

(A) is permitted as a polite way to avoid renting to an African American couple.

(B) is a good way to avoid discriminatory advertising as an exception to fair housing law to the owner of four or more single-family houses.

(C) is permitted if the apartment has already been rented.

(D) is never permitted because a reason for not renting always has to be provided.

18. The fact that you could own an office building but rent it to someone else is explained

(A) by the theory of prior possession.

(B) by the bundle of rights theory.

(C) by the theory of eminent domain.

(D) by the unlimited estates theory.

19. When using the term *estate* with respect to property rights, it

(A) refers only to ownership of a large piece of property.

(B) refers only to ownership through inheritance.

(C) refers only to purchased property.

(D) does not necessarily refer to ownership.

20. Which of the following is not considered an estate with limitations?

(A) Fee simple absolute

(B) Fee simple defeasible

(C) Fee simple qualified

(D) Fee simple determinable

21. The right of a husband to a portion of his wife's property is called

(A) community property or curtesy.

(B) community property or dower.

(C) dower or curtesy.

(D) community property and homestead.

GO ON TO NEXT PAGE ➡

22. The best definition of tenancy is

    (A) being a residential apartment renter.

    (B) being a property owner.

    (C) being a commercial property renter.

    (D) having an interest in real estate.

23. Property inherited by one spouse under community property law

    (A) is considered community property.

    (B) is considered separate property.

    (C) may only be sold by joint action of both spouses.

    (D) becomes community property after five years.

24. Which of the following is not a unity required in joint tenancy?

    (A) Unity of trust

    (B) Unity of time

    (C) Unity of title

    (D) Unity of possession

25. In a condominium you generally own your unit

    (A) as a tenant in common.

    (B) as a tenant in severalty.

    (C) as a joint tenant.

    (D) under a proprietary lease.

26. A subdivision is zoned for one acre lots. The town agrees to allow the developer to build all the houses on quarter-acre lots and leave the remaining land in open space. The developer is likely being subject to

    (A) density zoning.

    (B) limited zoning.

    (C) a special permit.

    (D) cluster zoning.

27. When a property owner sues the government because an action it has taken reduced the owner's property value, she will claim what as a basis for her lawsuit?

    (A) Escheat

    (B) Eminent domain

    (C) Due process

    (D) Inverse condemnation

28. An owner who fails to exercise his right of legal actions against his neighbor for violating a deed restriction, and then loses that right because he failed to exercise it in a timely fashion, has fallen victim to the doctrine of

    (A) prior authority.

    (B) laches.

    (C) escheat.

    (D) adverse possession.

29. Property owner A has a driveway easement across property owner B's property. Property owner A eventually buys property owner B's property. The easement

    (A) continues despite the joining of the two properties.

    (B) is considered abandoned.

    (C) continues by prescription.

    (D) disappears by merger.

30. A shared driveway is usually a case of

    (A) easement in gross.

    (B) easement appurtenant.

    (C) easement by prescription.

    (D) easement by necessity.

31. A judgment lien is

    (A) specific and voluntary.

    (B) specific and involuntary.

    (C) general and voluntary.

    (D) general and involuntary.

32. The dominant tenement in an easement situation

    (A) is the one who benefits from the easement.

    (B) is the one who gives the easement.

    (C) can be either party.

    (D) does not exist in an easement in gross.

33. Demographics is the study of

    (A) job growth.

    (B) topography.

    (C) earthquake activity.

    (D) population characteristics.

34. Title to property is actually conveyed by

    (A) deed.

    (B) contract.

    (C) title insurance.

    (D) acknowledgement.

35. The words "to have and to hold" are typical of

    (A) the words in the sales contract.

    (B) the words in the habendum clause of the deed.

    (C) the words in the acknowledgement.

    (D) the consideration clause.

36. The words "for love and affection" in the deed usually mean

    (A) the property is part of an estate.

    (B) the property is jointly owned by a husband and wife.

    (C) the property is a gift.

    (D) the property is to be retained in a life estate.

37. What kind of deed has most likely been executed when Person A conveys his property to Person B to hold as security for a loan made by Person C to Person A?

    (A) Quitclaim

    (B) Bargain and sale with no covenants

    (C) General warranty

    (D) Deed in trust

38. A legal description of property is any description

    (A) that can locate the property for the U.S. postal service.

    (B) that can locate the property for tax purposes.

    (C) that can be used in a deed.

    (D) that can clearly identify the location of property in the community.

39. In the government survey system

    (A) a township has 36 sections.

    (B) a section has 36 townships.

    (C) a quadrangle has 36 sections.

    (D) a township has 36 quadrangles.

40. What do surveyors use to measure elevations?

    (A) Datums

    (B) Benchmarks

    (C) A and B

    (D) Neither A nor B

41. In the proration process a credit for an item can be owed

    (A) to the buyer only.

    (B) to the seller only.

    (C) to the buyer and seller.

    (D) to the buyer or seller.

42. RESPA is monitored by

    (A) the Department of Commerce.

    (B) the Department of Justice.

    (C) the local Department of State.

    (D) the Department of Housing and Urban Development.

43. The estate of a person who dies without a will is usually divided according to state laws of

    (A) infestation.

    (B) testation.

    (C) probate.

    (D) descent.

44. An owner of property in common with others who wants to divide the property against the will of the other owners would file a suit to

    (A) divide the property.

    (B) partition the property.

    (C) dissolve the tenancy in common.

    (D) create a joint tenancy.

45. The sudden loss of land through natural forces is called

    (A) erosion.

    (B) declination.

    (C) accretion.

    (D) avulsion.

GO ON TO NEXT PAGE

46. A contract formed by the actions of two parties is

 (A) express unilateral.

 (B) express bilateral.

 (C) implied unilateral.

 (D) implied bilateral.

47. An unenforceable contract where the parties choose to honor the agreement is said to be

 (A) valid in law.

 (B) unvoided.

 (C) enduring between the parties.

 (D) valid as between the parties.

48. A person two weeks under the legal age of consent signing a contract is likely to create a situation known as a

 (A) void contract.

 (B) unenforceable contract.

 (C) fraudulent contract.

 (D) voidable contract.

49. A real estate sales contract is usually

 (A) an express bilateral contract.

 (B) an express unilateral contract.

 (C) an implied bilateral contract.

 (D) an implied unilateral contract.

50. Person A makes an agreement to let his neighbor (Person B) buy Person A's house at a certain price within the next six months if Person B wants to. What kind of agreement have they reached?

 (A) Express bilateral

 (B) Express unilateral

 (C) Implied bilateral

 (D) Implied unilateral

51. What does the landlord own in a lease situation?

 (A) A leasehold interest

 (B) A leased fee interest

 (C) A reversionary interest

 (D) B and C

52. A month to month tenancy is an example of

 (A) a tenancy at will.

 (B) a periodic tenancy.

 (C) a tenancy at sufferance.

 (D) an estate for years.

53. Generally a lease longer than a year has to be in writing according to

 (A) the Statute of Frauds.

 (B) the Uniform Residential Landlord and Tenant Act.

 (C) the Uniform Commercial Code.

 (D) the State Real Estate Commission.

54. In which of the following might it be said that no actual tenancy exists?

 (A) Tenancy at will

 (B) Periodic estate

 (C) Estate for years

 (D) Tenancy at sufferance

55. The federal agency responsible for most environment rules and regulations is

 (A) HUD.

 (B) CERCLA.

 (C) HTMA.

 (D) EPA.

56. Innocent land owner status was established by

 (A) the Comprehensive Environmental Response, Compensation, and Liability Act.

 (B) the Superfund Amendment and Reauthorization Act.

 (C) the Environmental Assessment Act.

 (D) the Landowner Liability Release Act.

57. Development of a management plan for a contaminated site too large to remove would fall under which phase of environmental assessment?

 (A) 1

 (B) 2

 (C) 3

 (D) 4

58. A colorless, odorless, hazardous gas originating from rocks under the earth would most likely describe

(A) carbon monoxide.

(B) radon.

(C) chlorofluorocarbons.

(D) electromagnetic fields.

59. The number of bedrooms most likely determines

(A) whether or not you can connect to the public sewer system.

(B) whether or not you can use well water.

(C) the size of your septic system.

(D) the amount of sanitary waste the house produces.

60. In an estate appraisal for tax purposes, what date is used as the appraisal or valuation date?

(A) Date the appraisal is ordered

(B) Date the person died

(C) Date set by probate court

(D) Any time within the calendar year of the death

61. All other things being equal, what characteristic of real estate makes location the most important value factor?

(A) The federal government's policy of encouraging home ownership

(B) Ready access to mortgage money in certain communities

(C) The dependence on the automobile

(D) The immobility of real estate

62. A real estate broker who obtains special permission from the town to use part of his house as a real estate office may have his house appraised for

(A) value in use.

(B) market value.

(C) assessed value.

(D) all of the above.

63. A surplus of condominiums in a town may be the result of the principle of

(A) balance.

(B) conformity.

(C) competition.

(D) substitution.

64. A man wants to buy a warehouse and convert it into a movie theater. What types of value will he most likely want to know?

(A) Assessed and market

(B) Investment and assessed

(C) Market and value in use

(D) Investment and market

65. House A is worth $300,000 and is surrounded by $500,000 homes. In a neighborhood of homes similar to House A, it would be worth $250,000. This is an example of

(A) conformity.

(B) competition.

(C) progression.

(D) regression.

66. Curable deterioration

(A) can be fixed.

(B) is just a paper loss.

(C) costs more to fix than it's worth.

(D) costs less to fix than the value it adds to the property.

67. Which one of the following is not a method by which to estimate a property's value?

(A) Capitalize the net income

(B) Multiply the gross rent by a multiplier

(C) Compare the values of several similar properties

(D) Estimate the cost to replace the building

GO ON TO NEXT PAGE

68. The formula for estimating a property's value by comparing similar properties and making adjustments is

(A) comparable better, add the adjustment to the comparable.

(B) comparable worse, subtract the adjustment from the comparable.

(C) comparable better, subtract the adjustment from the comparable.

(D) comparable worse, add the adjustment to the subject.

69. Who does what with respect to mortgages?

(A) Mortgage broker lends money.

(B) Mortgage banker arranges loans.

(C) Real estate broker and mortgage broker arrange loans.

(D) Mortgage banker lends money, mortgage broker arranges loans.

70. Why is the person lending the money called the mortgagee and not the mortgagor?

(A) Because they receive the mortgage payments.

(B) Because the mortgage industry language evolved that way.

(C) Because the borrower gives the mortgage to the lender.

(D) Not correct. The lender is called the mortgagor because he gives the mortgage to the borrower.

71. The clause that enables the lender to declare that the entire balance of the loan is due is called the

(A) acceleration clause.

(B) due on sale clause.

(C) forfeiture clause.

(D) lien clause.

72. Which of these does not insure mortgage loans?

(A) The Veterans Administration

(B) The Federal Housing Administration

(C) Private insurers

(D) The Government National Mortgage Association

73. The Certificate of Reasonable Value is a requirement of what type of loan?

(A) VA

(B) FHA

(C) Credit union

(D) Jumbo

74. The difference between a property's value and the debt on the property is a good definition of

(A) the loan to value ratio.

(B) equity.

(C) investment value.

(D) A and B, but not C.

75. What type of loan is expected to convert to a conventional mortgage in a relatively short time?

(A) Construction loan

(B) Home equity loan

(C) Package loan

(D) Reverse mortgage

76. An index is a feature of what type of mortgage loan?

(A) Adjustable rate mortgage loan

(B) Reverse mortgage loan

(C) Package loan

(D) Jumbo loan

77. In a 30-year amortized mortgage loan, the interest for the third year is calculated by multiplying the interest rate by

(A) the original amount of the loan.

(B) the original amount of the loan and dividing by 30.

(C) the original amount of the loan and dividing by 27.

(D) the unpaid balance of the loan.

78. A feature of the growing equity mortgage is

(A) that the interest rate starts low and steadily increases.

(B) that the principal payments increase over time.

(C) that the principal payments decrease over time.

(D) that the interest rate decreases over time allowing more rapid payoff.

79. An interest-only loan is called

    (A) an adjustable rate loan.

    (B) a blanket loan.

    (C) a straight loan.

    (D) a reverse loan.

80. The formula for calculating a tax rate is

    (A) municipality budget / (divided by) total assessed valuation.

    (B) total assessed valuation / (divided by) municipality budget.

    (C) total assessed valuation × assessment ratio.

    (D) total assessed valuation × equalization rate x municipality budget.

81. If there are three towns in a county, each using different assessment ratios, what does the county need to do to make the assessments and the taxes fair to each taxpayer?

    (A) Reassess all the properties in the county.

    (B) Make the towns reassess all the properties in each town.

    (C) Equalize the assessed values using an equalization rate.

    (D) Nothing because assessments are up to each town.

82. If you multiply the market value by the assessment ratio, you get

    (A) the tax rate.

    (B) the assessed value.

    (C) the equalization rate.

    (D) the total municipal budget.

83. Market value × tax rate = taxes due under what circumstances?

    (A) Always

    (B) Never

    (C) When the assessment ratio is 50 percent

    (D) When the assessment ratio is 100 percent

84. The assessment ratio can be calculated by

    (A) dividing the assessed value by the market value.

    (B) dividing the market value by the assessed value.

    (C) multiplying the equalization rate by the market value.

    (D) dividing the assessed value by the equalization rate.

85. Which of the following would not be considered a liquid investment?

    (A) Bank certificate of deposit

    (B) Stocks

    (C) Real estate

    (D) Savings accounts

86. A group of investors wanting to invest in real estate could legally form

    (A) a syndicate and a corporation.

    (B) a partnership and a corporation.

    (C) a syndicate but not a corporation.

    (D) a corporation but not a syndicate.

87. The use of borrowed money to invest in real estate is called

    (A) leverage.

    (B) syndication.

    (C) selling shares.

    (D) investment trust.

88. Joe buys an investment property and three years later sells it for enough profit to buy two buildings. Five years later he refinances one building and buys two more. His actions may be described as

    (A) leveraging.

    (B) pyramiding.

    (C) capitalizing.

    (D) depreciating.

GO ON TO NEXT PAGE

89. A real estate investment that works like a stock market investment is probably

(A) an equity trust.

(B) a mortgage trust.

(C) a combination trust.

(D) any of the above.

90. Which is not one of the benefits of investing in real estate?

(A) Tends to keep pace with inflation

(B) Favorable tax treatment

(C) Non-liquid, making it a stable investment

(D) Annual returns on one's investment

91. A property is assessed at $225,000. What is the equalized value if the equalization rate is 2.35?

(A) $528,750

(B) $95,745

(C) $957,447

(D) $52,875

92. What is the principal balance of a $100,000, 30-year amortized mortgage loan at 6 percent interest after the first monthly payment of $600?

(A) $99,400

(B) $99,500

(C) $99,700

(D) $99,900

93. The taxes on a property are $3,575. The tax rate is $30 per $1,000. The assessment ratio is 70 percent. What is the market value of the property?

(A) $107,250

(B) $153,214

(C) $162,765

(D) $170, 238

94. If the net operating income of a commercial building is $156,000, and the capitalization rate is 12 percent, what is the value of the building?

(A) $1,872,000

(B) $1,300,000

(C) $1,560,000

(D) $15,600,000

95. A building has a potential gross income of $350,000, a vacancy and collection loss of 5 percent, and total expenses of $140,000. What is the effective gross income?

(A) $192,500

(B) $210,000

(C) $217,000

(D) $332,500

96. A comparable that sold for $280,000 has a fourth bedroom valued at $20,000 that is not present in the subject. You think the subject might be worth about $290,000. What is the indicated value of the subject?

(A) $260,000

(B) $270,000

(C) $290,000

(D) $300,000

97. A house sells for $480,000 with a commission rate of 4 percent. The listing salesperson receives 40 percent of the listing side commission, which is 50 percent of the total commission. How much does the listing broker receive after paying the salesperson?

(A) $3,840

(B) $4,800

(C) $5,760

(D) $9,600

98. Taxes for the year of $3,600 are paid in arrears on January 1 for the previous year. The sale of the property closed on September 23. Use 12 months, 30 days per month, and the buyer owns the property on the day of closing — now prorate the taxes.

(A) $2,620 debit to buyer and $2,620 credit to seller

(B) $2,620 debit to seller and $2,620 credit to buyer

(C) $3,600 credit to buyer and $3,600 debit to seller

(D) $3,600 credit to buyer and $2,620 debit to seller

99. If effective gross income is $180,000, the vacancy and collection loss is 7 percent, and expenses are $73,000, what is the net operating income?

(A) $167,400

(B) $107,000

(C) $99,510

(D) $94,400

100. If a building sells for $1,200,000 and has a net operating income of $130,000, what is the capitalization rate?

(A) 9.23 percent

(B) 11 percent

(C) 12 percent

(D) 12.34 percent

DO NOT TURN THE PAGE UNTIL TOLD TO DO SO **STOP** DO NOT RETURN TO A PREVIOUS TEST

Chapter 24

Answers and Explanations to Practice Exam Three

I assume you've already taken the first two practice exams, so by the time you're done review-ing your answers for this exam there should be a big smile on your face. Once again, review the answers carefully. I wrote the explanations of the correct answers in such a way as to give you a little more than the basic information, so study these answers as another way to learn and remember the material.

As you did with the last two exams, go through all the answers and give yourself one point for each one correct. After you've noted all your correct and incorrect answers go through the exam answers one more time and note how many wrong answers you got by chapter. Both your overall score and your chapter-by-chapter score should be getting higher at this point. But keep study-ing. You've put a lot of effort in so far, and the finish line is almost in sight.

1. **(C)** Chapter 3

   The key to this answer is that only the correct answer has any actual control over what hap-pens to a piece of real estate. The three incorrect answers are all specific functions that an agent or other real estate professional may perform to provide a limited service that would have no ongoing impact to the property.

2. **(D)** Chapter 3

   There's a tendency when answering questions to look for the most complicated answer as the correct one. This question is an example of the simplest answer being correct. The idea of dealing with risk by transferring it is that no individual involved in the property has to assume the risk. One must always comply with municipal laws.

3. **(A)** Chapter 3

   This can be a tricky question because of the titles of some of the other insurances. You might think that words like *hazard* or *errors* would relate to the fact that you didn't clean the side-walk, and that casualty might be correct because the person who fell was a casualty of your negligence. Just remember that liability insurance covers the owner for injury that someone sustains due to negligence.

4. (B) Chapter 3

The generally recommended minimum is one year. This gives the manager time to recoup his initial investment in setting up systems to manage the building and provides sufficient time for the owner to adequately judge the performance of the manager.

5. (B) Chapter 4

Review the other types of agents. There is no such thing as an individual agent unless you consider the fact that every agent is an individual.

6. (A) Chapter 4

Not only do you not owe confidentiality to the customer, but your duty to your client requires that you reveal all information to your client that you may learn from your customer.

7. (D) Chapter 4

A latent defect is something not readily visible and may or may not affect a buyer's decision. A material defect is one that may affect a buyer's decision and, therefore, a reasonable buyer would want to know about and will most likely affect a buyer's decision. Latent defects may be material or not.

8. (C) Chapter 4

Answers (A) and (D) are made up. Answer (B) doesn't apply as long as the client is kept fully informed of all financial dealing. Remember net listings may or may not be illegal in your state or if legal may be subject to specific requirements which you should learn about for the exam.

9. (D) Chapter 4

The terms *principal* and *client* mean the same thing. A seller can be the client of the broker he hires to represent him and the customer of the buyer's broker.

10. (D) Chapter 4

Answer (B) is made up, though descriptive of what happens in the case described. The open buyer agency agreement allows the buyer to work with multiple brokers and pay only the one, if any, who finds him a house. The exclusive agency buyer agency agreement, Answer (C), is with one broker, but compensation is earned only if the broker finds the buyer a house.

11. (D) Chapter 4

An admittedly tricky question that should be read through carefully and all answers considered. When you see *client* instead of *buyer* or *seller* in this kind of question, it's a good bet that *client* is the answer. Remember you owe fiduciary duty to the client and this question did not provide enough information to determine if the buyer or seller was the client. Answers (C) and (D) are both correct, but (D) is more correct because you should disclose any and all information to your client that might affect the transaction and allow the client to decide what is material or not.

12. (D) Chapter 4

Procuring cause and producing the buyer (Answers [B] and [C]) describe the agent's role. The meeting of the minds describes the point at which all the sale conditions are agreed to and met.

13. (A) Chapter 5

The 1974 and 1988 Acts in effect amended the 1968 Act by expanding the protected classes but the 1968 exceptions remained in place. The 1866 Act is the only one with no exceptions.

14. (D) Chapter 5

This is generally always discriminatory. The exception is when an owner of three or fewer single-family houses offers them for rent.

15. (C) Chapter 5

Any language directing people to or from a neighborhood based on a protected class is steering, and it is illegal whether based on facts or not.

16. (A) Chapter 5

A real estate agent may not participate in any exceptions even if they are legal to an individual. There are no exceptions to the 1866 Act.

17. (C) Chapter 5

Answer (A) is incorrect in that there are never any exceptions with respect to race. For rentals, the exception in Answer (B) applies to owner-occupied, two- to four-unit houses. Answer (D) is incorrect. Provided one is not discriminating or is partaking of an acceptable exception to the law, one need not provide a reason for not renting to someone.

18. (B) Chapter 6

Answer (A) is made up but I made it sound like the prior appropriations theory related to water rights. Eminent domain has to do with government rights of taking. Answer (D) is also made up. Remember that the bundle of rights theory explains the ability of someone to separate rights like ownership and occupancy or possession.

19. (D) Chapter 6

The term *estate* refers to the extent or type of interest someone has in a piece of land. It includes any interest including non-ownership interests like a lease or an easement.

20. (A) Chapter 6

Answers (B) and (C) are almost the same thing. Answer (D) is a form of conditional estate.

21. (A) Chapter 6

This is a tricky question because at least two of the answers — (C) and (D) — are partially correct. Community property deals with the rights of either spouse. Curtesy deals with the husband's rights specifically, so Answer (A) is the most correct answer.

22. (D) Chapter 7

Technically all of the answers are correct but the first three answers are limited because they each deal with only one aspect of tenancy. The most inclusive and therefore best answer is (D).

23. (B) Chapter 7

Only property purchased during the marriage is considered community property and would require joint action to sell it.

24. (A) Chapter 7

The missing one is unity of interest. I have no idea what unity of trust is but it sounded like a good false answer.

25. (B) Chapter 7

Don't get confused here by Answer (A). Condo owners usually own the common areas as tenants in common but they own their individual units — or more accurately the air space their unit occupies — as sole tenants or tenants in severalty. The proprietary lease is associated with cooperative ownership.

26. (D) Chapter 8

This is a classic description of the cluster zoning subdivision. The density zoning subdivision would have lots of varying sizes. Some town may have something called *limited zoning*, but it's generally not a common term associated with zoning.

27. (D) Chapter 8

Inverse condemnation is essentially the owner claiming that the government has taken away her land value without due process or proper use of eminent domain.

28. (B) Chapter 8

There is no such thing as prior authority. Escheat has to do with the government claim of ownership. Adverse possession actually conveys ownership of property that has been used against the owner's will.

29. (D) Chapter 8

Answers (A) and (C) are incorrect; the easement disappears because it's no longer needed. It could be considered abandoned, though that's not precisely what's happened because an easement could be abandoned if the properties were not joined.

30. (B) Chapter 8

A shared driveway could be created in a number of ways, but generally speaking (and the best answer because you don't have any other facts) the answer is (B). Remember an easement appurtenant or appurtenant easement is one where the adjacent property benefits from the easement. In this case the property on the right half side of the property has an easement for use of the left side. The left side owner has an easement for the right side.

31. (D) Chapter 8

Keep in mind what a judgment lien is. A judgment lien is usually the result of a lawsuit someone has filed (and won) against you for money. This is certainly involuntary. And because it's about money, it's not about a specific piece of property like a mortgage.

32. (A) Chapter 8

There is always a dominant and servient party in any easement. The servient tenement (remember to serve) is the one giving the easement even if it was not given voluntarily.

33. (D) Chapter 8

Demographic studies are associated with creating master plans for the community. Things like age, salary, gender, and marital status are typically studied.

34. (A) Chapter 9

A contract is an agreement to transfer title to the property at some future date. Title insurance insures against any problems with the title after it's conveyed. The acknowledgement is witnessing the grantor's signature for filing purposes.

35. (B) Chapter 9

The sales contract would not contain these words. The consideration deals with what things of value are being exchanged for the property. The acknowledgment is a witnessing of the signature of the grantor.

36. (C) Chapter 9

These words are peculiar to the consideration clause in the deed when a property is a gift since there has to be something of value mentioned even if it's not monetary. The words would not normally be found in property conveyed in an estate or owned by a married couple. It's possible that the property could be conveyed as a gift AND be required to be held in a life estate, but (C) is the best answer with the information given.

37. (D) Chapter 9

All of the incorrect answers are types of deeds, which are distinguished by the warrantees they provide. The situation described would have the grantor use a deed in trust to accomplish creating security for the loan.

38. (C) Chapter 9

The term legal description has a specific meaning, which none of the other answers fit.

39. (A) Chapter 9

The correct order of division is quadrangle to townships to sections. A quadrangle has 16 townships; a township has 36 sections.

40. (C) Chapter 9

Datums are the primary points used for measuring elevations, but benchmarks — which are used primarily for ground surveys — are also used to help surveyors measure elevations.

41. (D) Chapter 9

This is a tricky question, mostly because of the last two choices. You need to read this question and the answer choices carefully. It would be impossible for the buyer and the seller to receive credit for the same item, though a buyer and seller could receive a credit for different items for the same property.

42. (D) Chapter 10

Just remember that RESPA — the Real Estate Settlement and Procedures Act — has to do with closing for homebuyers as in housing.

43. (D) Chapter 10

The first two answers are made up and are derived from the words *testate* (with a will) and *intestate* (without a will). Probate occurs when there is a will. Your state may call these statutes of descent and distribution.

44. (B) Chapter 10

This is a tough question unless you memorize the answer because all the answers seem logical except Answer (D), which wouldn't solve the problem. But you are going to be real estate agents and need to know proper terminology, which is a suit to partition the property.

45. (D) Chapter 10

Erosion is gradual loss of land. I made up declination. Accretion is actually adding land through natural processes.

46. (D) Chapter 11

A contract formed by the actions of the parties instead of a written or oral agreement (express) is considered implied. A contract formed by two parties implying promises made to each other is bilateral. Unilateral would be if only one party promised anything.

47. (D) Chapter 11

I got very creative here with three answers that sound good but are made up.

48. (D) Chapter 11

The most correct answer is "voidable" because in a very short time the person could choose to void the contract or go ahead with it. You could argue that the contract is void, but because it can be validated in a few weeks, (D) is the better answer. The contract itself isn't fraudulent because there's nothing in the question that implies that the underage party was agreeing to something they had no intention of doing.

49. (A) Chapter 11

Two parties agreeing in writing to do something is the definition of an express bilateral contact. Remember unilateral means only one party promises, and implied usually means that no agreement has ever been discussed or signed.

50. (B) Chapter 11

The contract is express because they have both reached the agreement. The contract is unilateral because A must act if B wants the house, but Answer (B) has the choice not to act. This kind of agreement would go by the more common name — option.

51. (D) Chapter 12

The leasehold is the interest the tenant has. Note that in the questions on leases I use both the terms tenancy and estate because I don't know which terms your particular exam will use. As noted in Chapter 12, the terms are interchangeable. When the lease expires the lease interest in the property reverts (goes back) to the landlord. So answers B and C are both correct.

52. (B) Chapter 12

A tenancy or estate at will is where the landlord allows the tenancy to occupy the premises but there is no definite point at which the arrangement will expire. A tenancy or estate at sufferance is where a tenant remains in the premises after the lease has expired against the landlord's will. An estate for years has a definite beginning and ending date.

53. (A) Chapter 12

All states have adopted some form of the statute of frauds. The Uniform Residential Landlord and Tenant Act has other provisions that should be addressed in the lease. The Uniform Commercial Code, which all states have in some form, governs personal property transactions.

The real estate commission — your state may have a different name for it — generally handles license law issues rather than real estate transactions themselves.

54. **(D)** Chapter 12

In the case of tenancy at sufferance, in which the tenant remains against the landlord's will, the landlord doesn't collect the rent. In effect no tenancy, therefore, exists.

55. **(D)** Chapter 13

This is an easy question if you remember the meaning of all the acronyms, which you should. The Department of Housing and Urban Development; The Comprehensive Environmental Response, Compensation, and Liability Act; and the Hazardous Material Transportation Act are all important but not the correct answer.

56. **(B)** Chapter 13

Answers (C) and (D) are made up, but they sound good, don't they. Answer (A) was the original Superfund funding act, but innocent landowner immunity was not conveyed until SARA.

57. **(D)** Chapter 13

Phase 1 is examination of the site records; phase 2 is testing; phase 3 is remediation.

58. **(B)** Chapter 13

Carbon monoxide and chlorofluorocarbons don't come from rocks, and are byproducts of other materials or processes. Electromagnetic fields are just that, not gasses.

59. **(C)** Chapter 13

REMEMBER

Connecting to a sewer system is usually a matter of location. The use of well water is governed by quality and quantity of water available through a well. The amount of sanitary waste produced is generally a function of the number of people in the house.

60. **(B)** Chapter 14

None of the other answers have any bearing. For tax purposes the value of the estate on the date of death must be established.

61. **(D)** Chapter 14

If Answer (A) were correct, it would affect all locations. Mortgage money is now available from regional banks that may not even be in the same community as the property. Dependence on the automobile is certainly one factor that contributes to the idea that location is very important, but it's not the only factor. Remember exam writers expect you to know the meaning of words like *immobility* as they apply to real estate.

62. **(D)** Chapter 14

You probably were tempted to go for Answer (A) because this is a case where value in use would apply. But there may be an occasion to want market value to see how it compares to value in use or assessed value to fight a high assessment.

63. **(C)** Chapter 14

These questions about the economic factors at work in real estate value can be tough because the various factors can be hard to distinguish. In all cases, try to go for the best answer that most closely fits the definition and examples given in the book. In this case, builders, the supply side, usually go in when they see a demand until that demand is satisfied. The building cycle is slow, however, so by the time the last project is built there is often a surplus.

64. (D) Chapter 14

The investor may eventually want assessed value, and it is unlikely that he would want a value in use appraisal. He wants to know what the property should cost him in order to make his project successful — investment value. He also should want to find out whether the market value is higher or lower than the investment value because he might be getting a bargain if it's lower, or the property may not be a good investment if the market value is higher than the investment value.

65. (C) Chapter 14

Conformity creates value by houses being similar. Competition often results in a surplus, driving values down. Regression is the opposite of progression. Remember, in progression a smaller house benefits from being near larger, more expensive homes.

66. (D) Chapter 14

Curability when speaking of deterioration is an economic concept not necessarily a physical one. Answer (C) could be applied to incurable deterioration; it can be fixed but costs more than the value it would add to the property.

67. (D) Chapter 14

Okay. Stop yelling. If you answered this question correctly, I won't worry about you passing the state exam. This is probably not the normal way a question like this would be asked, but just in case some state examiners decide to get cute you're ready. You may wonder why Answer (D) wasn't correct because the cost approach calls for determining the replacement or reproduction cost of the building. You're half right, and that's why this answer is wrong. Without subtracting depreciation and adding land value, you won't even come close to the appraised value of the property.

68. (C) Chapter 14

Answer (D) is wrong because you never add or subtract the adjustment to or from the subject. In Answer (A) the market has already increased the value of the comparable (added) due to its superior features. The same is true in reverse for Answer (B). The adjustment process is designed to compensate for what the market has already done.

69. (D) Chapter 15

This is a basic question of definitions. Real estate brokers may recommend sources for mortgage loans but generally don't actually arrange loans unless they are also certified in some way by their state to be mortgage brokers.

70. (C) Chapter 15

The lender gives the money to the borrower, but the borrower gives the mortgage to the lender. Remember — the mortgage is the document that the borrower signs to allow the lender to take the property in the event of a foreclosure.

71. (A) Chapter 15

Answers (C) and (D) are made up. The due on sale clause which is typical in most mortgages is that the loan must be paid off if the property is sold.

72. (D) Chapter 15

The Government National Mortgage Association (Ginnie Mae) is a secondary market organization that buys mortgage loans.

73. **(A)** Chapter 15

All lenders require an appraisal to determine the value of the property. The CRV, which is based on an appraisal, is unique to the VA.

74. **(B)** Chapter 15

This is a tricky question because Answer (A) could be correct at the time at which the property is purchased. A good way to understand this is to think of the amount of money one might get out of a sale or refinance even though it's not necessary to sell or refinance to calculate equity. As the mortgage is paid off and the property's value changes (hopefully upward), the equity changes. Investment value is an appraisal concept.

75. **(A)** Chapter 15

REMEMBER

A construction loan is used to build a house and is expected to convert to a conventional mortgage at the end of construction. A home equity loan can be refinanced into a new mortgage, but that's not the general expectation. A package loan covers the real estate and personal property and continues without the necessity of conversion to anything else. The expectation with a reverse mortgage is that it will be paid off (not converted) upon the death of the property owner.

76. **(A)** Chapter 15

Given the information in the question, Answer (A) is the best answer because it's always a feature of these loans and is part of the way the interest rate is calculated. Any of the other types of loans could have adjustable rates, but an index would not be considered a standard feature of these loans because they could just as well be fixed interest rate loans.

77. **(D)** Chapter 15

First of all, I'm finding more of these no-number math questions in exams. So you need to know how the math works without having to actually do any calculations. Don't worry — I've got plenty of math questions with numbers coming in a little while. Meanwhile, the amount of interest due on this type of mortgage is always calculated on the unpaid balance of the principal at any point in time. No need to divide by the number of years because the mortgage rate is an annual rate.

78. **(B)** Chapter 15

I tried to make all the wrong answers seem plausible, especially Answer (D). The fact of the matter is that the interest payments (not the interest rate) would likely decrease over time because you pay off a reducing balance. See the answer to Question 77.

79. **(C)** Chapter 15

An adjustable rate loan deals with how the interest rate is calculated. The other two incorrect answers are types of loans for special purposes. The straight loan, also called a term loan, calls for payment of interest only until the end of the loan when the whole principal is due.

80. **(A)** Chapter 16

I'm afraid you're going to have to remember this. One hint might be that taxes are expressed as dollars of taxes per thousand (or hundred) of assessed value, which means that assessed value is always the bottom number in a fraction, or the number you're dividing by.

81. (C) Chapter 16

Answers (A) and (B) could be possibilities under certain circumstances, none of which are mentioned in this question. So the best answer given the information is (C). In fact, this is the purpose of the equalization rate.

82. (B) Chapter 16

Market value × assessment ratio = assessed value

83. (D) Chapter 16

There are so few circumstances in which something is always or never, it's a good bet these answers are incorrect. You need to think through this question, or just remember it. When municipalities assess properties at full market value, they're essentially using a 100 percent assessment ratio. In that case, the assessed value used to calculate taxes is the same as the market value, making (D) the answer.

84. (A) Chapter 16

Assessed value ÷ market value = the assessment ratio. This is a reverse of the formula to find assessed value: market value × assessment ratio = assessed value. Answers (C) and (D) must be incorrect because the answers to these equations are in dollars. Remember a number representing a rate or ratio is always a percentage.

85. (C) Chapter 17

Liquid means that you can get your cash relatively quickly. If you're wondering about certificates of deposit, you can usually cash them in any time; you most likely have to pay a penalty to access it, but the money is readily available.

86. (A) Chapter 17

A syndicate is a descriptive term rather than a legal entity. Corporations and partnerships are two forms a syndicate may take but not at the same time.

87. (A) Chapter 17

You may have been fooled by some of the other answers that implied use of other people's money like selling shares. The difference is shares are not borrowed money. Investors in syndicates and corporations expect a direct return on their money. In a sense they are actual owners of the real estate investment.

88. (B) Chapter 17

You might argue that leveraging applies because he's using refinanced (borrowed) money to build his empire. But of the four choices Answer (B) is the most correct.

89. (D) Chapter 17

You might have gotten fooled into thinking that (A) was the answer because equities are the properties themselves, but all of these are ways to invest in the real estate market.

90. (C) Chapter 17

Real estate isn't liquid, but that doesn't make it stable or unstable; that's the work of the economy having nothing to do with liquidity.

91. **(A)** Chapter 18

Assessed value × equalization factor (rate) = equalized value

$225,000 × 2.35 = $528,750

92. **(D)** Chapter 18

Remember that the monthly payment in an amortized mortgage consists of principal and interest, so each month a portion of the payment goes to reducing the principal balance.

Mortgage amount × Interest rate = Annual interest owed

$100,000 × .06 (6 percent) = $6,000

Annual interest ÷ 12 months = first month's interest because the whole balance is due at this point

$6,000 ÷ 12 = $500

Monthly payment − monthly interest = principal portion of the payment

$600 − $500 = $100

Total principal due − monthly principal payment = balance due

$100,000 − $100 = $99,900

The fact that the loan is for 30 years is irrelevant.

93. **(D)** Chapter 18

You're being asked to work backwards to arrive at the market value of the property. Generally these kinds of problems involve division rather than multiplication.

Taxes ÷ the tax rate = assessed value

$3,575 ÷ $30/$1,000 ($30 of taxes per $1000 of assessed value) = 119,166.67

The logic of this equation is that each $30 in taxes represents $1,000 in assessed value. So divide by $30 and multiply by $1,000.

Assessed value ÷ assessment ratio = market value

$119,166.67 ÷ .70 (70 percent) = $170, 238.10

If you know the number and the percentage it represents, divide to find the whole.

94. **(B)** Chapter 18

Net operating income ÷ capitalization rate = value

$156,000 ÷ .12 (12 percent) = $1,300,000

95. **(D)** Chapter 18

WARNING

This is a trick question. I know how much you love them. You don't need to know the expenses to calculate effective gross income.

Potential gross income − vacancy and collection loss = effective gross income

$350,000 − 5 percent = $332,500

Note that I also didn't include any "other income" in this question. Some buildings may not have any.

96. (A) Chapter 18

The rule for this is comparable better, subtract. And you never, ever touch the subject regardless of what you think it's worth.

Sales price of comparable − adjustment amount = indicated value of subject

$280,000 − $20,000 = $260,000

97. (C) Chapter 18

After you've calculated the commission, the easiest way to do this unless you're very comfortable with math is to break down the entire commission into everyone's shares. Also you need to read this question carefully because the information leads you to believe that they want to know the listing salesperson's share when in fact they want to know the listing broker's share.

Sale price × commission rate = commission

$480,000 × .04 (4 percent) = $19,200

The first split is between the buyer's broker and the seller's broker. Because they each get 50 percent you can just divide by 2.

$19,200 ÷ 2 = $9,600

Commission × percentage shares = dollar amounts

$9,600 × .40 (40 percent salesperson's share) = $3,840

Total listing side commission − salesperson's share = broker's share

$9,600 − $3,840 = $5,760

Saving one step, you could also conclude that if the salesperson gets 40 percent, the broker gets 60 percent, and multiply the $9,600 by that.

98. (B) Chapter 18

Proration questions always seem more complicated than they really are. It comes down to finding out the monthly and daily amounts of money involved and apportioning it out taking into account whether the buyer or the seller has paid. I kept the numbers themselves easy because I want you to see the methodology clearly. Expect more difficult numbers on the exam.

Because taxes are paid in arrears and the house has closed prior to the tax due date, you know that the buyer (the new owner) has to pay the entire year's taxes a few months after he's moved in even though he's only lived in the house for less than the full year. So the seller is going to owe the buyer money at closing — a debit to the seller and a credit to the buyer.

Annual taxes ÷ 12 months = monthly taxes

$3,600 ÷ 12 = $300

Monthly taxes ÷ 30 = Daily taxes

$300 ÷ 30 = $10

The buyer owns the property on the day of closing so the seller owns the property for 8 months (January through August) and 22 days of September.

8 months × $300 (monthly taxes) = $2,400

22 days × $10 (daily taxes) = $220

$2,400 + $220 = $2,620 that the seller owes the buyer for the time he owned the house without paying the taxes which the buyer had to pay later.

99. (B) Chapter 18

This question requires you to remember the format for arriving at the net operating income.

Potential gross income − vacancy and collection loss + other income = effective gross income

Effective gross income − expenses = net operating income

Note that the question already provides the effective gross income. The vacancy and collection rate is an unnecessary number to solve the problem.

$180,000 − $73,000 = $107,000

100. (B) Chapter 18

Income ÷ value = rate

This formula assumes the value and sales price are the same. In questions like this, you can assume that value and sales price are the same.

$130,000 ÷ $1,200,000 = .11 or 11 percent

Chapter 25

Practice Exam Four

Okay. This is it, your fourth practice exam. If you've completed the first three practice exams, regardless of how well you did, you should be very comfortable answering the type of questions you'll see on the state exam. You've gotten comfortable with the material and the vocabulary. You've reviewed your strong areas and studied your weak ones. In short, you are ready!

You're familiar with the routine by now. Download a fill-in-the-bubble answer sheet from www. dummies.com/go/relebubblesheets and use it as you take the practice exam. Check the clock to time yourself, and get to it. Go through the exam as quickly as you can, answering the questions to which you immediately know the answers. There are a lot of them. Then go back through to take your time with the others. Make sure you do each math question twice. Not that I think you will, but don't start to slow down your studying as you get close to the finish line. You may have done well on the first three practice exams. In fact, I'm sure your scores are improving. I try to ask different questions and tackle the same subject matter in different ways in these exams, so use this exam as one more opportunity to be as absolutely prepared as you can be for the state exam. I'd wish you good luck, but you won't need it. So I say congratulations in advance of you passing your state exam and becoming a licensed real estate agent.

1. A property management fee should not be based on

   (A) a fixed fee.

   (B) a percentage of gross income.

   (C) a lease fee.

   (D) amount of remuneration from contractors.

2. One of the primary differences between independent contractors and employees is that independent contractors

   (A) pay their own social security.

   (B) don't have to obey office policy.

   (C) can't deduct work-related expenses.

   (D) work a different set of standard hours than an employee.

3. Broker A and Broker B met on January first and agreed that during the year A will service only sellers on the north side of town and B will service only sellers on the south side of town.

   (A) This is legal market division because everyone is guaranteed to get service

   (B) This is illegal price fixing.

   (C) This is boycotting because they left Broker C out of the arrangement.

   (D) This is illegal market allocation.

4. The case that dealt with real estate broker price fixing was

   (A) Brown vs. the Board of Education.

   (B) United States vs. Foley.

   (C) Dred Scott.

   (D) Jones vs. Mayer.

5. A special agent is one who

   (A) handles a single transaction.

   (B) is appointed by the broker only in dual agency situations.

   (C) is the typical agency for a property manager.

   (D) always represents the seller.

6. "The landscaping on this house is beautiful," which in reality consists of two scraggly bushes in the yard, is an example of

   (A) puffing.

   (B) fraud.

   (C) negligent misrepresentation.

   (D) intentional misrepresentation.

7. Which of the following need not be disclosed to a seller client?

   (A) Recent customer bankruptcy

   (B) Self-dealing

   (C) Current customer divorce

   (D) All of the above must be disclosed

8. Joe is Mary's seller client. Fred is Sally's buyer client who is interested in Joe's house. Based on this information, which of the following relationships is accurate?

   (A) Mary and Sally are each other's sub agents.

   (B) Mary and Sally are dual agents.

   (C) Joe is Sally's sub agent whereas Fred is Mary's sub agent.

   (D) Fred is Mary's customer and Joe is Sally's customer.

9. Using your best efforts on behalf of your client even if they conflict with your own self-interest is

   (A) loyalty.

   (B) care.

   (C) obedience.

   (D) accountability.

10. Broker Allen has a listing and is the agent for the seller Sam. Buyer Ben hires Broker Allen as his buyer's agent and wants to see Sam's house. Broker Allen

    (A) must refuse to work with Buyer Ben as his agent.

    (B) must disclose his relationship to Sam and Ben.

    (C) must engage another broker to represent Ben.

    (D) must obtain informed consent to continue with this arrangement.

11. Seller Cindy asks Broker Bob to help her sell her house. Broker Bob agrees, and they settle on a fee but nothing is put in writing. This appears to be

    (A) an express agency.

    (B) an implied agency.

    (C) a designated agency.

    (D) an agency by ratification.

12. Seller Slim agrees to let Broker Barbara list his house for sale and agrees to pay her a 4 percent commission if the sale goes through. But Slim continues to advertise the house himself, and Barbara agrees that there will be no commission owed if he sells his own house. What type of listing agreement did Slim sign?

    (A) Open listing

    (B) Owner acting as seller listing

    (C) Exclusive right to sell

    (D) Exclusive agency

13. A buyer asks you to show them homes in a Christian neighborhood.

    (A) You can comply with their request because they initiated the request.

    (B) You must immediately stop working with the buyer.

    (C) You can tell them where the Christian neighborhoods are, but you can't show them houses there because real estate agents are held to a higher standard.

    (D) You may show them houses in a variety of neighborhoods that meet their financial and other housing needs.

14. Which of the following is not a protected class under federal fair housing law?

    (A) Gender

    (B) Race

    (C) Marital status

    (D) National origin

15. The unique enforcement provision of the 1866 Civil Rights Act is that

    (A) all complaints are brought to the department of Housing and Urban Development.

    (B) suits are always brought in state court.

    (C) suits are brought directly in federal court.

    (D) the FBI is charged with investigating the complaint.

16. What is the rule regarding a housing exemption for religious organizations?

    (A) No limits on the exception due to freedom of religion

    (B) Limited to three or fewer units

    (C) No limits as long as no real estate agent is used

    (D) The religion itself must not discriminate in its membership rules

17. Because there's a significant Jewish population in a particular community, two multiple listing organizations have been established — one Jewish and one non-Jewish. Real estate agents may belong to one but not both.

    (A) This is legal market allocation.

    (B) This is no problem.

    (C) This is discriminatory but not a fair housing violation.

    (D) This is a fair housing violation.

18. The rights of an owner to the waters of an abutting river or stream are called

    (A) littoral rights.

    (B) riparian rights.

    (C) prior appropriation rights.

    (D) homestead rights.

GO ON TO NEXT PAGE

19. Title to property donated to the county park system has automatically reverted back to the original owner because the parks department is no longer using it for the purpose for which it was donated. The donation was probably made as

(A) fee simple absolute.

(B) fee simple condition precedent.

(C) fee simple condition subsequent.

(D) fee simple determinable.

20. You give your aunt the right to live in your second home until your cousin dies. You've likely given her

(A) curtesy rights.

(B) homestead rights.

(C) a life estate pur autre vie.

(D) an ordinary life estate.

21. Personal property attached to a building

(A) remains personal property.

(B) becomes a fixture.

(C) becomes personalty.

(D) is assumed to not remain with the property upon sale.

22. Another term for tenancy in severalty is

(A) sole ownership.

(B) common ownership.

(C) joint ownership.

(D) community property.

23. Tenancy by the entirety

(A) means one owns the entire property rather than shares.

(B) is the way several people can own equal shares of the property.

(C) is characterized by the four unities.

(D) is specific to property ownership by a married couple.

24. A person who buys the interest of someone who owns property in joint tenancy becomes

(A) a new joint property owner.

(B) a tenant in common.

(C) a tenant by the entirety.

(D) a tenant in trust.

25. Tenancy in common owners always have

(A) equal shares.

(B) the right of survivorship.

(C) divided ownership.

(D) the ability to sell without permission of the other owners.

26. Which of the following statements is correct?

(A) All encumbrances are financial limitations on property ownership.

(B) Encumbrances are only physical limitations on properties.

(C) Easements are not considered encumbrances.

(D) Encumbrances may be physical or financial.

27. A mortgage lien is

(A) voluntary and specific.

(B) involuntary and specific.

(C) voluntary and general.

(D) involuntary and specific.

28. An easement by prescription is created by

(A) the actions of a person.

(B) utility companies only.

(C) agreement.

(D) eminent domain.

29. An easement that benefits a person rather than a property is called an easement

(A) by necessity.

(B) by prescription.

(C) in gross.

(D) appurtenant.

30. The fact that I must paint my house white is probably because of

(A) an easement.

(B) a deed restriction.

(C) a lien.

(D) an infrastructure clause.

31. Which of the following is not considered a public land use restriction?

(A) Deed restriction

(B) Zoning

(C) Building code

(D) Special permit use

32. If a density zoning ordinance is applied to a subdivision all the lots must

(A) be grouped in a small area.

(B) allow for at least 30 percent of the land to be left open.

(C) total the lot count in a normal subdivision.

(D) be below the normal size called for by the zoning.

33. If a person dies without a will and without heirs, the state government obtains the property by

(A) eminent domain.

(B) claim of prior appropriation.

(C) escheat.

(D) lien rights.

34. Title to property is actually conveyed

(A) when the contract is signed.

(B) when all the conditions in the contract are met.

(C) when title insurance is issued.

(D) when the deed is delivered to the buyer and accepted by him.

35. The allocation of certain expenses between a buyer and a seller is called

(A) proration.

(B) settlement and procedures.

(C) kickbacks.

(D) payoffs.

36. The section due east of section 36 in the rectangular (government) survey system is section

(A) 36.

(B) 31.

(C) 25.

(D) 1.

37. In the rectangular (government) survey system a principal meridian and a baseline cross to form a

(A) township.

(B) section.

(C) quadrangle.

(D) nothing; they never cross because they are parallel.

38. A deed commonly used in family property transfers that gives no warrantees is a

(A) bargain and sale deed.

(B) deed in trust.

(C) grant deed.

(D) quitclaim deed.

39. Whose signature is required to make a deed valid?

(A) Grantor only

(B) Grantee only

(C) Grantor and grantee

(D) Grantor, grantee, and the title company representative

40. In a warranty deed the covenant of quiet enjoyment means

(A) that no one will come along to claim ownership of the property.

(B) that the grantor must compensate the grantee if any later claims of ownership turn out to be valid.

(C) both A and B

(D) neither A nor B

41. In the proration, an accrued item

(A) is paid by the seller.

(B) is paid by the buyer.

(C) could be paid by either.

(D) has been paid by the mortgage lender.

GO ON TO NEXT PAGE

42. Constructive notice of a real estate transaction is generally provided by

(A) registered mail.

(B) the title company notifying the town tax assessor.

(C) the buyer to the seller.

(D) registering the deed in the public records.

43. The continuous use of property by someone other than the owner could result in a claim of

(A) eminent domain.

(B) avulsion of title.

(C) adverse possession.

(D) grant of title.

44. Title to a park created as part of a new development might be given to the local town by

(A) grant.

(B) dedication.

(C) possessory interest.

(D) partition.

45. When the town takes property for unpaid taxes the process is called

(A) foreclosure.

(B) eminent domain.

(C) public grant.

(D) forfeiture.

46. Person B wants $300,000 for her house. Person A offers $250,000. Person B counteroffers $280,000. Person A counteroffers $252,000. Person B gets disgusted and counteroffers $310,000 back to Person (A) Can Person B do this?

(A) Yes

(B) No

(C) Only if the negotiations are conducted verbally

(D) Only as long as both real estate brokers agree

47. A contingency in a real estate sales contract

(A) must be satisfied for the contract to be enforceable.

(B) can be dropped from the contract by mutual agreement.

(C) can be dropped by the party who placed the contingency in the contract.

(D) All of the above

48. The words vendor and vendee are often associated with what type of contract?

(A) Lease

(B) Real estate sales contract

(C) Option agreement

(D) Installment or conditional sales contract

49. Forcing someone to sell you their house in accordance with the contract you both signed is called

(A) specific performance.

(B) forfeiture.

(C) compensatory damages.

(D) rescission.

50. A building contractor taking over the contract of another builder is called

(A) the assignee.

(B) the vendor.

(C) the subcontractor.

(D) the contractor of record.

51. The owner of a two-family (duplex) house with two tenants might want to put what clause in the lease that would allow the new owner to evict either or both of the tenants.

(A) Sale clause

(B) Use clause

(C) Occupancy clause

(D) Subleasing clause

52. What kind of lease is typically used in an office building?

(A) Gross lease

(B) Percentage lease

(C) Proprietary lease

(D) Net lease

53. If the date/day is not stated in the lease, legally when is the rent due on a rental apartment?

   (A) The monthly anniversary of when the lease was signed

   (B) The last day of the month

   (C) The first of the month

   (D) Whenever the state stipulates as the default payment date

54. The principle difference between a net lease and a triple net lease is

   (A) There is no difference other than terminology.

   (B) the type of building.

   (C) the number of different expenses paid by the tenant.

   (D) the term of the lease.

55. Friable is a term generally associated with

   (A) lead paint.

   (B) asbestos.

   (C) sewage disposal.

   (D) brownfields.

56. Which phase of environmental assessment deals with remediation of the polluted area?

   (A) Phase 1

   (B) Phase 2

   (C) Phase 3

   (D) Phase 4

57. The cutoff below which tanks are generally exempted by the LUST program is

   (A) 2,600 gallons.

   (B) 2,100 gallons.

   (C) 1,600 gallons.

   (D) 1,100 gallons.

58. Brownfields refer to

   (A) former military bases.

   (B) former industrial sites.

   (C) farms where the soils are depleted.

   (D) sanitary landfills.

59. Chlorofluorocarbons are associated with

   (A) lead in water.

   (B) mold.

   (C) sewer gases.

   (D) air-conditioning equipment.

60. At what vacancy rate is potential gross income calculated?

   (A) 100 percent

   (B) The actual rate

   (C) 0 percent

   (D) 80 percent

61. Reconciliation in appraising involves

   (A) averaging the value estimates from each approach.

   (B) weighing the value estimates from each approach and relying on the most appropriate approach for that type of property.

   (C) adjusting the three values so they're no more than five percent apart.

   (D) eliminating any value that doesn't meet the expectation of the client.

62. Which of the following is not a formula in the income capitalization approach?

   (A) Value ÷ income = rate

   (B) Value × rate = income

   (C) Income ÷ rate = value

   (D) Income ÷ value = rate

63. Vacancy and collection loss is subtracted from

   (A) potential gross income.

   (B) net operating income.

   (C) effective gross income.

   (D) gross rental income.

64. The formula for determining the gross rent multiplier is

   (A) gross rent × gross rent multiplier.

   (B) potential gross income ÷ capitalization rate.

   (C) sales price ÷ gross rent.

   (D) value × rate.

GO ON TO NEXT PAGE

65. Of the various approaches to apprising property, what approach would be most suitable to
appraising a unique nonresidential property
with few comparables?

    (A) Sales comparison approach

    (B) Gross rent multiplier approach

    (C) Income capitalization approach

    (D) Cost approach

66. In the cost approach, a severely broken foundation that could be repaired would be classified as what kind of depreciation?

    (A) Functional obsolescence curable

    (B) Functional obsolescence incurable

    (C) Physical deterioration curable

    (D) Physical deterioration incurable

67. A gas station near a house is a form of

    (A) functional obsolescence.

    (B) external obsolescence.

    (C) physical deterioration.

    (D) straight-line depreciation.

68. If the subject has a newly remodeled kitchen
and the comparable does not, you

    (A) add the adjustment value to the
comparable.

    (B) add the adjustment value to the subject.

    (C) subtract the adjustment value from the
comparable.

    (D) subtract the adjustment value from the
subject.

69. Other than the borrower's ability to repay the
loan what is the most important thing in consideration of how much the lender will lend?

    (A) LTV

    (B) NOI

    (C) Property value

    (D) Property cost

70. Which piece of federal legislation dealt with
banks making loans within their communities?

    (A) The Community Reinvestment Act

    (B) The Equal Credit Opportunity Act

    (C) The Truth in Lending Act

    (D) The Neighborhood Affordable Housing
Act

71. In which case does the buyer become
personally liable for the balance of the
mortgage loan?

    (A) Estoppel

    (B) Presumption

    (C) Subject to

    (D) Assumption

72. You can calculate the first month's interest on
an amortized 30-year mortgage by multiplying

    (A) the loan amount by the interest rate and
dividing by 30.

    (B) the loan amount by the interest rate and
dividing by 12.

    (C) the loan amount by the interest rate and
dividing by 30 then dividing by 12.

    (D) the monthly loan payment by the
interest rate.

73. The interest rate on an adjustable rate
mortgage is calculated as follows:

    (A) Index plus margin

    (B) Annual cap plus margin

    (C) Lifetime cap minus margin

    (D) Index minus margin

74. What is negative amortization?

    (A) Additional money borrowed on a home
equity loan

    (B) An increase in the principal balance of a
loan due to money owed but not paid

    (C) The total payment due at the end of a
term loan

    (D) The result of a drop in the index from
one year to the next in an adjustable rate
loan

75. The total monthly payment on an amortized
loan is composed of

    (A) principal and interest.

    (B) principal only.

    (C) interest only.

    (D) principal, interest, taxes, and insurance.

76. I'm in contract to sell my house. I've bought another house and the seller wants to close before I can close on my own house. What kind of financing might help me?

    (A) Temporary loan

    (B) Swing loan

    (C) Bridge loan

    (D) All of the above

77. Mom and Dad lent you money to buy a house with the stipulation that you not only pay them back what you borrowed but also a portion of the profit you make on the house when you sell it. This is probably a

    (A) blanket mortgage.

    (B) package mortgage.

    (C) purchase money mortgage.

    (D) shared equity mortgage.

78. A partial release provision is characteristic of what kind of mortgage?

    (A) Blanket mortgage

    (B) Construction loan

    (C) Package mortgage

    (D) Open end mortgage

79. Another name for the estoppel certificate is

    (A) reduction certificate.

    (B) certificate of reasonable value.

    (C) assumption certificate.

    (D) payoff certificate.

80. Which of the following is not the same tax rate as the others?

    (A) $8 per $100

    (B) $80/$1,000

    (C) 8 mills

    (D) 80 mills

81. Assuming no special exemptions, properties with the same market value should

    (A) pay the same taxes but not necessarily have the same assessments.

    (B) pay the same taxes and have the same assessments.

    (C) have the same assessments but may pay different taxes.

    (D) not be concerned if their taxes differ periodically.

82. An equitable right of redemption with respect to a tax sale comes

    (A) after the tax sale.

    (B) before the tax sale.

    (C) either before or after the tax sale.

    (D) after the in rem proceeding.

83. What priority does a tax lien have over other liens?

    (A) All liens are prioritized by date.

    (B) Tax liens come last.

    (C) Tax liens take priority over all other liens.

    (D) Tax liens take the second position right after the mortgage regardless of when other liens were filed.

84. A protest against high taxes should be brought to

    (A) the tax grievance board.

    (B) the tax assessor.

    (C) small claims court.

    (D) elected officials.

85. When rent from an investment is used to pay off an amortized mortgage it's called

    (A) capital appreciation.

    (B) cash flow.

    (C) depreciation.

    (D) equity buildup.

GO ON TO NEXT PAGE

86. An owner of an investment building gets to deduct from the taxes he owes a certain amount of money he spent making his building environmentally more efficient. Most likely the government has given him

   (A) a grant.

   (B) a tax credit.

   (C) an exemption.

   (D) a tax deduction.

87. The cash owed to someone in an uneven property exchange is called

   (A) boot.

   (B) like kind.

   (C) capital gains.

   (D) deferred depreciation.

88. In a real estate investment, which of the following is correct with respect to risk and expected return?

   (A) Risk up, return up

   (B) Risk up, return down

   (C) Risk down, return the same

   (D) Risk up, return the same

89. Another term for cost recovery is

   (A) capital gains.

   (B) profit.

   (C) return on investment.

   (D) depreciation.

90. The fact that equal amounts of deprecation are taken every year is referred to as

   (A) accelerated.

   (B) cost recovery.

   (C) straight line.

   (D) limited.

91. You're selling the NW1/4 of the SW1/4 of the S1/2 of the W1/2 of Section 31. How many square feet of land are you selling?

   (A) 435,600

   (B) 43,560

   (C) 21,780

   (D) 4,356

92. An owner wants to net $300,000 from selling his house after she pays you a 5 percent commission. What price must she sell her house for?

   (A) $315,000

   (B) $315,789

   (C) $300,000

   (D) 320,000

93. You sold 20 houses last year and 25 houses this year. What percent fewer houses did you sell last year than this year?

   (A) 25 percent

   (B) 20 percent

   (C) 10 percent

   (D) 5 percent

94. A couple gets a 30-year amortized mortgage loan for $200,000 at 5 percent interest. The monthly payment for principal and interest is $1,074. They make 15 years of payments when they come into some money and are able to pay off the remaining $120,000 balance of the loan. Approximately how much total interest did they pay on the mortgage loan?

   (A) $113,000

   (B) $105,000

   (C) $93,000

   (D) $78,000

95. What is the first month's interest on a 20-year mortgage loan for $90,000 at 4 percent interest?

   (A) $3,600

   (B) $300

   (C) $200

   (D) $180

96. A couple has $24,000 a year available to buy a house. Annual taxes are $4,000; one year's insurance is $1,000. The mortgage rate they've secured calls for a payment of $4.50 per month per $1,000 of mortgage. The couple has $30,000 to put down on the house. What is the highest price house they can afford?

   (A) $474,444

   (B) $444,444

   (C) $381,851

   (D) $138,000

97. The market value of a property is $400,000. The town's assessment ratio is 80 percent. The tax rate is 15 mills. What are the annual taxes for this property?

(A) $480

(B) $600

(C) $4,800

(D) $6,000

98. Six months taxes of $3,600 are paid in advance on February 1. Sale of the house closes on August 1. Who owes how much to whom?

(A) Buyer owes the seller $3,600

(B) Seller owes the buyer $3,600

(C) Seller and buyer owe each other $1,800

(D) Buyer owes seller nothing

99. The subject property has a third bathroom that is not present in the comparable; however, the comparable has a renovated kitchen that the subject property does not have. If the bathroom is valued at $5,000, the renovated kitchen has a value of $10,000, and the comparable recently sold for $330,000, what is the indicated value of the subject?

(A) $315,000

(B) $325,000

(C) $335,000

(D) $345,000

100. Three multifamily properties sold as follows:

Sales Price	Gross Annual Rent
$700,000	70,000
$650,000	$65,000
$720,000	$72,000

The property you are interested in purchasing has a gross annual rent of $68,000. Using the gross rent multiplier method, what's the value of the property you want to buy?

(A) $680,000

(B) $710,000

(C) $780,000

(D) $6,800,000

Chapter 26

Answers and Explanations to Practice Exam Four

I assume that you took these practice exams in order, at least the first time through. If so, your score on this should be great. If not, don't worry. After you've checked through all your answers, go back as you did in the earlier exams and see in which areas you need more study. You'll see that once again I've grouped the questions by chapter to make it easier for you to identify the subjects that you may need to go over.

Your goal on all of these exams is to get at least 85 correct answers out of a 100. This should give you a safe margin for the actual state exam. If you've used a separate piece of paper for your answers, re-do any and all of these exams until you get an 85 or better. And you'll soon be on your way to your first million dollars in real estate.

1. **(D)** Chapter 3

    Remuneration is one of those four-dollar words exam writers occasionally like to use. It simply means *pay* and in this case means kickback, which is a payment the owner doesn't know about from a contractor hired by the property manager. It's illegal.

2. **(A)** Chapter 3

    Everyone must obey office policy. In fact it's the independent contractor rather than the employee who usually can deduct work expenses. The word standard in Answer (D) should tip you off that this is wrong because independent contractors can't be made to work certain hours.

3. **(D)** Chapter 3

    There is no such thing as market division though I imagine some who engage in market allocation might call it that. No matter what you call it though, it's illegal. Although leaving Broker C out of it could be considered a boycott, leaving someone out of an illegal scheme is not what boycotting refers to. Price fixing has to do with illegally setting commission rates.

4. (B) Chapter 3

The three wrong answers may look familiar because they're all cases that dealt with fair housing or other discrimination issues.

5. (A) Chapter 4

A special agent is typically the type of agency created for a single real estate transaction. Property managers are usually general agents. As you already know, agents can represent either the seller or buyer. An agent might be appointed in a dual agency situation but it's not the "only" case in which this might happen.

6. (A) Chapter 5

You might argue that the statement intentionally misrepresents the quality of the landscaping but the term is generally used for cases of misrepresenting items that can't be readily checked and is usually another term for fraud. Negligent misrepresentation is not revealing something you should have known but didn't.

7. (D) Chapter 4

Both Answers (A) and (C) are situations that could affect the buyer's ability to buy the property. Self-dealing is where an agent wants to buy his own listing.

8. (D) Chapter 4

This is an easy question to get lost in because of the poor wording. Yes, I did this on purpose. First thing to do is to organize the players on scrap paper if you can.

Mary = Agent representing

Joe = Client/seller

Sally = Agent representing

Fred = Client/buyer

The third party in a transaction is the customer. So in this case from Mary's perspective Fred is the customer. From Sally's perspective Joe is the customer. Give yourself a pat on the back if you got this one right.

9. (A) Chapter 4

No fair, you say! Using your best efforts is care, but putting your client's interests above your own is loyalty. Don't be too literal here. Loyalty is the best answer because care doesn't address the self-interest issue.

10. (D) Chapter 4

This is often the way dual agency occurs. Informed consent means giving full disclosure to both parties and obtaining both their consents to represent both of them.

11. (A) Chapter 4

A designated agency occurs when there is a possibility of a dual agency. Agency by ratification occurs after the fact when an implied agency is accepted. The tough choices here are Answers (A) and (B) because nothing in writing would imply an implied agency. (Sorry I couldn't resist.) But the fact that an agreement was made orally makes this an express agency, though in some states the agent would have a hard time collecting her commission.

12. (D) Chapter 4

I made up Answer (B). Exclusive right to sell guarantees Barbara a commission regardless of who sells the property. Open listing allows multiple brokers to sell the property.

13. (D) Chapter 5

As a real estate agent you may never initiate or participate in steering, which this is.

14. (C) Chapter 5

Marital status may be a protected class in some states, but it's not one of the protected classes under federal law.

15. (C) Chapter 5

All civil rights complaints are brought to HUD for enforcement except the 1866 Civil Rights Act.

16. (D) Chapter 5

The limitation is that the religion may not discriminate as to who may become a member. Even though a real estate agent and no advertising should be used the limits still exist so Answer (C) is wrong.

17. (D) Chapter 5

WARNING

This question can be tricky since it included a reference to an antitrust issue: market allocation, which is never legal. If you're wondering how something can be discriminatory but not illegal, think about some of the exceptions to the fair housing law that in effect permit legal discrimination.

18. (B) Chapter 6

Littoral rights involve large bodies of water like lakes. Prior appropriation rights are the state's rights to water in certain states. Homestead rights have nothing to do with water rights.

19. (D) Chapter 6

You're really going to have to memorize the fine points of these definitions, especially Answer (C) and (D). The big difference is that (C) requires action on the part of the owner. Answer (D) is an automatic reversion of the title.

20. (C) Chapter 6

Answers (A) and (B) have nothing to do with the question. An ordinary life estate gives the right for the life of the person receiving the life estate. *Pur autre vie* means for the life of another person, in this case your cousin.

21. (B) Chapter 6

Answers (A) and (C) are both incorrect. Personalty is another word for personal property. A fixture is assumed to remain with the property upon sale.

22. (A) Chapter 7

The three wrong answers describe some form of ownership by more than one person. You have to memorize this one.

23. **(D)** Chapter 7

This is another one of those definitional questions. Tenancy by the entirety is only for use by married couples. Answer (A) most likely is tenancy in severalty. Answers (B) and (C) refer to joint tenancy.

24. **(B)** Chapter 7

Answer (A) seems to be the logical answer, but in fact because of the unity of time a new owner buying into an existing joint tenancy becomes a tenant in common.

25. **(D)** Chapter 7

Tenants in common can have equal or unequal shares. The right of survivorship is a feature of joint tenancy. Both tenancy in common and joint tenancy have undivided ownership.

26. **(D)** Chapter 8

An encumbrance is a limitation on property ownership. As such it can be either physical like an easement or financial like a lien.

27. **(A)** Chapter 8

Answer (A) is a voluntary action for one piece of property.

28. **(A)** Chapter 8

An easement by prescription may result when an individual continually uses the property of another person without an agreement. Such a situation may arise with a utility company, but it's also possible for this to occur by the actions of a private individual.

29. **(C)** Chapter 8

WARNING

This is a tricky question because Answers (A) and (B) Answers, are strictly speaking not types of easement but rather two ways an easement can be created. An easement appurtenant benefits an adjacent property.

30. **(B)** Chapter 8

An *easement* allows someone else to use a portion of your property. A lien is a financial encumbrance on the property. Infrastructure clause sounds like it should mean something, but I made it up.

31. **(A)** Chapter 8

These negative questions — pick the wrong answer (really it's the answer that doesn't fit the group) — are not the easiest because you'll be generally doing most questions looking for the right answer. It's a good reminder to always read the question carefully. The three incorrect answers are all types of public land use controls.

32. **(C)** Chapter 8

You're going to have to re-read this section to fully understand the concept. Density zoning allows lots to be various sizes, bigger or smaller than what zoning requires, but the total lot count must be the same as if it were a regular subdivision. Grouping the lots close to each other is a characteristic of cluster zoning.

33. **(C)** Chapter 8

Eminent domain is the government's right to take one's property against the owner's will. The claim of prior appropriation has to do with water rights. A lien usually means that property taxes haven't been paid and the town or city, not the state, seized the property.

34. **(D)** Chapter 9

Delivery and acceptance of the deed, usually at closing (which is why I didn't include that as a choice) is when title to a property transfers. The other three conditions are typical as preliminaries leading up to the transfer of title.

35. **(A)** Chapter 9

Settlement and procedures might remind you of the RESPA act that applies to closings. Kickbacks are illegal payments. If you've watched too many gangster movies you know what a payoff could be, but remember one of your goals as a homebuyer is to pay off your mortgage loan.

36. **(B)** Chapter 9

Check out Figure 9-1 and remember that every township is divided into 36 sections in the same manner. So if you lay one township grid next to the other, you'll always know what sections are next to each other.

37. **(C)** Chapter 9

Quadrangles are the principal divisions in this system and are further divided into townships and sections. Principal meridians run north and south whereas baselines run east and west, so they aren't parallel.

38. **(D)** Chapter 9

Bargain and sale deeds are used in many typical real estate transactions and may or may not have certain warrantees. Deeds in trust are used for loan guarantee purposes. Grant deeds have limited warrantees.

39. **(A)** Chapter 9

You have to remember this because it is a little tricky. Most people think that the buyer (grantee) should have to sign the deed to accept the property but the only required signature is the grantor. The title company representative is not involved in signing the deed because he or she has no ownership interest in the property.

40. **(C)** Chapter 9

You might want to remember the differences of each of the warrantees in the general warrantee deed. Because these are generally legal terms there is no easy way to remember them other than to memorize them.

41. **(B)** Chapter 9

I suggest you read through this section and the math examples carefully since this can be complicated. An accrued item is one that's owed by the seller and paid by the buyer, usually at a later date. A seller who lives in a house for the first six months of the year then sells it where the taxes for the year are paid on December 31 for the previous year owes the buyer the six months taxes that he used for the first half of the year. So the seller owes the taxes to the buyer for those six months, because the buyer will pay an entire year's taxes in December.

42. (D) Chapter 9

Constructive notice is accomplished by making the transaction records available to the public. This is done by recordation. The other activities may occur incidentally but have nothing to do with constructive notice.

43. (C) Chapter 10

Eminent domain is taking property by the government. There is no such thing as avulsion of title. A land grant is usually given to someone by the government.

44. (B) Chapter 10

Grant is the government giving you land. Possessory interest may be an interest in property but it's not a way to transfer title. Partition involves a lawsuit to divide property between owners.

45. (A) Chapter 10

Eminent domain is used by the government to take property against the owner's will and has nothing to do with unpaid taxes. A public grant is where the government gives property to private individuals. Forfeiture is where property may be lost due to the owner disobeying some condition in the deed.

46. (A) Chapter 11

You'll most likely have to think through this question as you read the offer and acceptance, or in this case counteroffer pattern. Because real estate contracts including offers and acceptances have to be in writing to be valid, if negotiations are conducted verbally anything goes until a contract is signed. Agents work for clients, not the other way around. An agent must obey all lawful orders of a client. In these circumstances, every time a counteroffer was made, it negated the previous offer so Person B is free to raise the price as she did.

47. (D) Chapter 11

Many exams are dropping questions that have "all of the above" as Answer (D), so I wanted to include one, and I thought this would be a good place to give you all the information about contingencies that you need to know after you read the section in the chapter. The contingency is usually placed by one party and agreed to by the other, so if both agree to drop the contingency or the party that the contingency protects wants to drop it, the contract can proceed. If neither of those things happens, the contingency must be satisfied. You sharp readers may also note that if Answer (A) is correct, because I use the word *must*, Answers (B) and (C) can't be correct.

48. (D) Chapter 11

The installment contract that usually conveys title after a number of payments have been made often uses the terms in the question. A typical real estate sales contract uses the words *grantor* and *grantee*. A lease uses the words *lessor* and *lessee*. An option agreement may use the words *optionor* and *optionee* but can also use the terms *grantor* and *grantee*.

49. (A) Chapter 11

Compensatory damages might be storage costs for the buyer's furniture. Forfeiture might be when the buyer refuses to buy and forfeits his deposit. Rescission is when both parties agree to rescind, that is dissolve the contract.

50. (A) Chapter 11

This could be a little tricky because in fact the new contractor might now be considered the contractor of record by the town. Also in some cases anyone selling a service or product could be called the vendor. So I admit this is probably not a great question, but you may get some not so great questions, which is why I include one or two. The best answer is assignee because it appears from the information in the question that the existing contract was assigned to the new contractor.

51. (A) Chapter 12

The sale clause (sometimes called the *termination on sale clause*) allows the new owner after proper notice to evict the tenant. In case you're wondering, the reason that this may be a good idea is that many two-family houses are sold to buyers who want to live in one of the apartments. The use clause controls the uses to which the rental unit can be put. The occupancy clause limits the number of people who can live in the unit. The subleasing clause governs subleasing activity.

52. (D) Chapter 12

Net lease is the best answer of these choices but see Question 54. Meanwhile the gross lease is usually used in residential rental situations. A percentage lease is generally used with retail stores. The proprietary lease is given to cooperative owners.

53. (D) Chapter 12

This is a state-specific question but I wanted to use it to remind you to check what your state's default date is. In some places the usual practice of payment on the first of the month is nothing more than the standard language in a lease, without which the rent would be due on the last day of the month.

54. (C) Chapter 12

All the wrong answers essentially have no bearing on anything to do with this question. In a net lease the tenant will pay some of the expenses like taxes or insurance of the building. In a triple net lease the tenant will pay all of the expenses. Note that even in a triple net lease the tenant never pays the mortgage.

55. (B) Chapter 13

Friable refers to how easily asbestos can crumble or give off particles and dust.

56. (C) Chapter 13

Memorize the various phases.

57. (D) Chapter 13

All the other answers don't relate to anything in particular. Another one you have to memorize.

58. (B) Chapter 13

Brownfields are former industrial sites that may have pollution issues. Although the other answers may or may not have environmental issues, brownfields generally focus on industrial, manufacturing, and storage facilities that may have hazardous waste from a previous use. This could be a tricky question, but the best answer is (B).

59. **(D)** Chapter 13

Chlorofluorocarbons (CFCs) are elements in the gases in older air-conditioning equipment and aerosol cans.

60. **(C)** Chapter 14

Okay. Read this question carefully. Potential gross income in the income capitalization approach to value is calculated at 100 percent occupancy, which is zero percent vacancy.

61. **(B)** Chapter 14

I thought I'd go easy on you and give you one obviously false answer, (D). An appraiser never averages the values nor does he manipulate the values in any way.

62. **(A)** Chapter 14

Value is generally larger than income. If you divided value by income you'd come up with a multiplier (whole number) not a rate (percentage).

63. **(A)** Chapter 14

You have to memorize the sequence to arrive at net operating income, and it starts with vacancy and collection loss being subtracted from potential gross income.

64. **(C)** Chapter 14

The other three answers were a variety of terms thrown together none of which result in anything useful. There are several formulas in this chapter that should be memorized. Make every effort not to mix up terms from one appraisal approach to another, as I did in this question.

65. **(D)** Chapter 14

Technically you could use the cost approach on residential property also but I didn't want you to get confused and pick (A) as the answer because you know that's the approach most suitable to appraising homes. Answers (B) and (C) are both ways to appraise income producing properties that are usually bought for investments.

66. **(D)** Chapter 14

Functional obsolescence usually includes design flaws in the building not deteriorating physical condition. Curable and incurable are economic not construction concepts. Curability means that the cost to fix the item will add at least the same or more value to the property. Incurability means that the cost to fix the item will not result in a commensurate increase in value even though the item is fixable.

67. **(B)** Chapter 14

Physical deterioration is wear and tear on the building itself. Functional obsolescence is design flaws in the building. Straight-line depreciation is a method for estimating depreciation. External obsolescence are things negative to value that occur off the property. It's always incurable, by the way.

68. **(A)** Chapter 14

You never touch the subject in the sales comparison approach, so Answers (B) and (D) are incorrect. If the subject has something that the comparable does not have it, makes the comparable inferior to the subject. If the comparable is inferior you have to compensate for that lack by adding the adjustment. Remember, what do you have to do to the comparable to make it like the subject?

69. (C) Chapter 15

This is a pretty sophisticated question that I think at this point you're ready for. The loan to value ratio is important, but the ultimate amount of the loan is based on the value. The lender considers the cost in determining the loan amount, but only if it's lower than the value. The net operating income contributes to the determination of the value of a commercial property, but it isn't the basis for the loan.

70. (A) Chapter 15

Answers (B) and (C) do provide for nondiscrimination and greater information respectively in the mortgage lending process. I made up Answer (D) by changing one word National to Neighborhood in the title of the actual act. I didn't want to make the question too easy.

71. (D) Chapter 15

Estoppel is the certificate signed to verify the loan balance. Presumption is made up. In a subject to the mortgage purchase the new buyer is not personally responsible for the balance, though he would make the payments on the loan.

72. (B) Chapter 15

In an *amortized loan*, the interest rate is stated as an annual rate so multiplying the total amount of the loan — because that's the unpaid balance in the first year — by the rate gives you that year's total interest. Divide by 12 months and you have the first month's interest.

73. (A) Chapter 15

The three wrong answers are completely made up.

74. (B) Chapter 15

In an *adjustable rate* loan, if the annual interest rate exceeds the annual or lifetime cap there is money owed to the lender but not paid. It is sometimes added to the outstanding loan balance creating negative amortization.

75. (A) Chapter 15

You already know that an amortized loan is paid off over time rather than in a lump sum at the end, so each payment has a portion of the principal as well as the interest. The confusing answer might be Answer (D) because many of us pay our property taxes and insurance through an escrow account with the bank. The fact is, however, that the total we may send to the bank each month is not the mortgage payment but is the payment plus these other items.

76. (D) Chapter 15

This is a pretty simple question if you did your reading (which, of course, you did). This should give you a chance to review all the names that this type of gap or interim (two more names) financing goes by.

77. (D) Chapter 15

WARNING

This is a difficult question because Answer (C) may technically be correct also because the mortgage loan is used to purchase the property. But the better and more correct answer is D. You will probably get some questions on your exam that require you to pick the best answer out of two or more that are very close.

78. (A) Chapter 15

A blanket mortgage covers more than one piece of property. The partial release provision is used to release the lien on each individual piece of property as it's sold.

79. (A) Chapter 15

The Certificate of Reasonable Value (CRV) is part of the VA loan process. There is no such thing as an assumption certificate. Although payoff certificate sounds right, it too is made up though you may get something like that when you pay off your mortgage loan, but it's more properly called a *mortgage satisfaction*.

80. (C) Chapter 16

Answers (A) and (B) are pretty obviously the same; (B) being (A) with both numbers multiplied by 10. Remember when using a mill rate you move the decimal, which is at the end of the number, three paces to the left. 8 mills is 8 dollars per thousand of value so it's the one unlike the other three.

81. (B) Chapter 16

People should always be concerned about paying unequal taxes for the same market value property. If market value is the same, a consistent application of the assessment ratio will result in the same assessed value and the same taxes due, which is the desired result.

82. (B) Chapter 16

Remember E comes before S as in statutory right of redemption, which comes after the tax sale. In rem refers to foreclosure, which is a different procedure.

83. (C) Chapter 16

Memorize this and remember that this is why banks want escrow accounts for taxes so mortgages won't go into second place behind an unpaid tax lien.

84. (D) Chapter 16

Read this question carefully and remember what my tax assessor friend said. Complaints or grievances about unfair tax *assessments* can be brought to any of the agencies named in the first three answers depending on your state. But if taxes are too high, that's the responsibility of the elected officials no matter where you live.

85. (D) Chapter 17

Remember equity is the difference between what the property is worth and the debts attributed to the property. If the mortgage is getting paid off there is less of a balance to pay at the end; therefore, equity has been — you guessed it — building up.

86. (B) Chapter 17

A *tax deduction* is deducted from income before taxes are calculated. A *grant* is actual money given. An exemption is usually something we don't have to pay taxes on that we own or certain types of income that might not be subject to taxes.

87. (A) Chapter 17

Tax on the boot is payable by the person receiving it. The boot can be due to capital gains but not necessarily.

88. (A) Chapter 17

Yes, there are questions this easy on the exam, though not many. As the risk goes up, so does the expectation of a higher return.

89. (D) Chapter 17

Profit can be anything you make beyond your investment. Return on investment is much the same as profit. Capital gains is the positive difference (if there is one) between what you paid and what you sold a property for.

90. (C) Chapter 17

Accelerated depreciation allows more depreciation to be taken in the early years of an investment.

91. (A) Chapter 18

Remember to drop the directions and replace them with multiplication signs. Also remember two important facts needed to answer this question: A section is always 640 acres and an acre is 43,560 square feet.

$1/4 \times 1/4 \times 1/2 \times 1/2 \times 640 = 10$ acres

10 acres $\times$ 43,560 sq. feet = 435,600 sq. ft.

92. (B) Chapter 18

You and the owner are partners in this deal whether the owner knows it or not. Because the commission comes off the sale price, she gets what's left after you get your 5 percent commission, which means she gets 95 percent of the sale price. If you know the dollar amount and the percent of the whole it represents, you can calculate the whole by dividing the percent into the dollar amount.

$300,000 ÷ .95 (95 percent) = $315,789

93. (B) Chapter 18

You know the numerical difference is five houses. The trick is knowing which number to divide by. Because you're "going backward," you use this year's number.

$5 ÷ 25 = 20$ percent

94. (A) Chapter 18

This question looks far more complicated than it is. The total loan was for $200,000 and the couple paid off in a lump sum $120,000 right after the 15th year, so in the first 15 years of the loan they must have paid off $80,000 in principal.

$200,000 – $120,000 = $80,000

But they made 180 monthly payments of $1,074, which included principal and interest.

15 years $\times$ 12 months = 180 months

180 $\times$ $1,074 = $193,320 in total payments

If they paid $80,000 in principal during this time the rest must be interest.

$193,320 – $80,000 = $113,320 interest

95. (B) Chapter 18

Interest is always calculated for the year on the unpaid balance.

$90,000 × .04 (4 percent) = $3,600 interest

$3,600 ÷ 12 months = $300 for the first month

96. (C) Chapter 18

This is a typical problem in real world real estate as you help someone determine the most he or she can afford to pay for a house. The idea is to work backward from their income.

Note, the couple doesn't have $24,000 available to pay the mortgage. They actually have:

$24,000 − $4,000 − $1,000 = $19,000 because the lender includes taxes and insurance in their affordability calculation.

If every $4.50 buys $1,000 worth of mortgage on a monthly basis, then

$19,000 ÷ 12 months = $1,583.33 per month available

$1,583.33 ÷ $4.50 = $351.85 units of $1,000 worth of mortgage

$351.85 × $1,000 = $351,851.85 mortgage amount

$30,000 down payment + $351,851.85 mortgage amount = $381,851 rounded total maximum house price

97. (C) Chapter 18

You may be doing this calculation a lot and not just on the exam.

Market value × assessment ratio = assessed value

$400,000 × .80 (80 percent) = $320,000

Assessed value × tax rate = taxes due

$320,000 × .015 = $4,800

Don't forget when dealing with mills to move the decimal point three places to the left before multiplying.

98. (D) Chapter 18

The taxes are paid in advance to cover the period February 1 to July 31. The new owner takes title the day the new tax period begins.

99. (B) Chapter 18

Don't get overwhelmed by the fact that this question has two adjustments. Just take one at a time.

Remember, if the comparable is better than the subject, subtract the adjustment from the comparable. If the comparable is inferior to the subject, you add the adjustment amount to the comparable.

Subject has a third bathroom. The comparable does not have a third bathroom, which makes it inferior to the subject, so you add the adjustment value of $5,000 to the comparable's selling price of $330,000.

The comparable has a renovated kitchen that the subject does not have, which makes the comparable superior to the subject so you subtract the $10,000 kitchen value.

$330,000 − $10,000 + $5,000 = $325,000

100. **(A)** Chapter 18

Two formulas to memorize for this problem:

Sales price ÷ gross annual rent = gross rent multiplier

Gross annual rent × gross rent multiplier = value

$700,000 ÷ $70,000 = 10

$650,000 ÷ $65,000 = 10

$720,000 ÷ $72,000 = 10

The gross rent multiplier derived from comparable properties – 10

$68,000 × 10 = $680,000 value of subject property

7

The Part of Tens

Get a look at a list of important state-specific subjects that you need to research. Real estate laws can be extremely specific from one state to another and are ever-changing either by legislative action or court decree.

Enhance your test-taking skills with more test-prep techniques to help you sail through the exam with less stress and worry.

Discover how to get unstuck on a question and understand about going with your first instinct and not overthinking the answers.

Chapter 27

Ten Things to Find Out from Your State's Real Estate Law

icenses for real estate brokers and salespersons are granted by each state. The problem that creates in writing a book about taking the real estate license exam is that every state has its own laws governing real estate procedures, practices, and license law. Enough factors don't vary from state to state to fill an exam review book, which, of course, is what you're reading right now. On the other hand, some space inevitably must be devoted to information that may be specific to each state.

This chapter gives you a list of issues (in alphabetical order) that you need to find out about in your own state before you take the real estate exam. I touch on ten categories of subjects that you need to research. For more information on the general subject matter, you can consult the chapter on that particular issue. (Fear not — I provide handy cross-references for you. Now that's service!)

The two things I need to warn you about are the following:

» This is my list of the most important state-specific items. Some instructors and exam writers may disagree with what's on the list. The research I did in writing this book led me to create this list, and I constantly was on the lookout for topics that may have state specific items within the general topic.

» Real estate laws can be extremely specific from one state to another and are ever-changing either by legislative action or court decree, even as you're reading this book. So as you're researching these topics in your home state, try to get the most current and complete information you can find. Often you can go online to get your state's latest version of its real estate license law. You can be assured that there will be questions on the exam based on what's in that law. You also need to consult your prelicensing course textbook, handouts, and the instructor.

Agency Law

Agency law, simply stated, is the law that governs the relationship between a client and an agent, in this case a buyer or seller and you their real estate agent. Every state has its own version of how it defines the relationship between a broker/salesperson and a client (the person represented by a broker/salesperson). Of all the state-specific exam information, agency law is perhaps the most complicated and the most important. See Chapter 4 for more info. Look for what your state has to say about the following topics:

>> Agency disclosure

>> Buyer agency

>> Buyer agency agreements

>> Dual agency

>> Listing agreements (including net listings)

>> Transactional or facilitating brokerage

>> Any other types of permitted or prohibited agencies in your state

Fair Housing

In essence, the goal of fair housing laws is to prevent discrimination in housing sales and rentals. Most fair housing laws come from the federal government. Many states, however, and some municipalities, have supplemented the federal regulations with their own. The local rules and regulations usually are stricter than the federal rules. In the case of two different laws covering the same thing, the stricter law applies. (See Chapter 5 for more.) Check out

>> **Protected classes:** Federal fair housing laws cover a number of groups. You need to check out additional groups that are protected by fair housing standards in your state, for example, sexual orientation may be a protected class in your state even though it's not a protected class in the federal law.

>> **Exceptions to the exceptions:** Some municipalities may not permit the same exceptions to the rules that the federal government does.

>> **Additional prohibited activities:** Federal law is pretty complete in addressing prohibited activities, but check out any supplemental state or local laws.

License Law

Every state has its own procedures for obtaining and maintaining a real estate license. Find out everything you can about your state's licensing law. Something as minute (and silly, in my opinion) as knowing the fee for filing a change of address has been asked on exams. So study your state's law carefully. You probably can check out your state license law online, and you may get a copy of it when you take your prelicensing course. For more, flip to Chapter 3.

Limitations on Land Use

A variety of local governmental controls govern how you use your property; see Chapter 8 for the scoop. Questions you may want to ask about local regulations include the following:

» What board or agency adopts and amends the zoning ordinance?

» What board or agency grants variations (variances, special permits) from the zoning ordinance?

» What local procedures are required for approval of a subdivision and who or what board or agency gives the approval?

» What are the statutory time limits for protesting deed restriction violations?

» Are any statewide historic preservation programs or environmental review laws in effect?

» Does your state require you to know something about construction?

Money Stuff

Money makes the world go round, including the world of real estate. A few things that you may want to check out in your state with respect to money issues include:

» State-sponsored mortgage loan or guarantee programs that may make money available to homebuyers under favorable conditions like lower-than-normal interest rates.

» Special incentive, rebate, or exemption programs for property taxes, such as a senior citizen tax exemption.

» How you protest your property tax assessment.

For the scoop on mortgages, see Chapter 15. I cover taxes (including property tax assessments) in Chapter 16.

Ownership Rights, Forms, and Theories

You may want to check out the following ownership issues in your home state:

» The applicability of the following terms in your state: community property, curtesy, dower, and homestead.

» Whether your state recognizes the right of survivorship in joint tenancy.

» Whether the terms town house and condominium mean the same thing.

» If your state is a title theory, lien theory, or intermediate theory state.

» Whether your state uses tenancy by the entirety or some other form of ownership specific to married couples.

Chapter 6 provides details about the rights involved with owning real estate; Chapter 7 covers the different forms of real estate ownership. For specifics on title theories, see Chapter 15. And check out the two sections about transferring ownership later in this chapter.

Property Disclosure

The general fiduciary duties (the overall responsibilities of an agent to a client) regarding disclosure of information to your principal or client (the person an agent represents) are pretty standard from state to state. The issue of what must be disclosed to the customer, which in most cases is the buyer, can vary. As an agent, you may want to check out the following responsibilities of an agent as well as an owner with respect to disclosure:

- Latent defects
- Material defects
- Stigmatized property
- Megan's Law
- Disclosure procedures
- Penalties
- Special environmental hazards such as earthquake prone areas

See Chapter 4 for more, and check out your state licensing law for fraud and negligent misrepresentation penalties.

Tenants' Rights and Rent Control

Check out any laws in your state that specifically guarantee certain protections to tenants in rental buildings. If any are in effect, they may be on a state level or an individual municipal level. These types of laws can cover anything from placement of window guards and other security features to notification about rent increases. Pay particular attention to the number of units a building must have for the laws to apply.

The other thing to check out is whether your state or any municipalities in your state have laws that control rental rates and rent increases. I'm not talking about public housing here but rather control over rents in privately owned rental buildings. Check out what the rules are and to what buildings or tenants they may apply. And be aware that even within the same state, two ways for controlling rents may be in effect — one in the cities and one in the suburbs. Head over to Chapter 12 for more about renting and leases in general.

Transferring Ownership Involuntarily

To find out more about involuntarily giving up property, check out Chapter 10. Two state-specific factors to check out regarding the loss of property against your will are

- The statutory time period needed to claim adverse possession or prescriptive rights against someone else's property.
- The laws of descent, which govern the distribution of your estate if you die intestate (without a will). Because as an agent you may help heirs dispose of real estate that they've inherited, many states want you to know something about these laws.

Transferring Ownership Voluntarily

Voluntary transfer of property ownership is the area where you'll be spending most of your time after you get your real estate license. Perhaps the most important item you need to check out for exam and for practical purposes is to what extent you'll be involved in the legal side of things. In some places, real estate agents handle most, if not all, of the work in actually transferring ownership of the property from one person to another. In other parts of the country, attorneys pick up the ball right after an offer is accepted on a piece of property.

Regardless of your role in the actual ownership transfer process, some of the specific things that you need to check out for your state's exam include:

>> The type of deed most commonly used.

>> Requirements for a valid deed. These can vary a little from one state to another.

>> The type of property description most commonly used in a deed.

>> The use of title insurance, abstract of title, or other systems for certifying marketable title to the property.

>> Who pays what closing costs.

>> Who owns the property on the day of closing.

>> Who's responsible if the property is destroyed while under contract for sale.

>> Whether property transfers commonly close in escrow.

With respect to property descriptions, you folks who live in states that came along after the original 13 colonies should know something about how to calculate area and locate property in the rectangular survey system as well as the other property description systems.

Chapter **28**

Ten Tips to Help You Succeed on the Exam

I once had to go to the doctor, and I knew he would test my blood pressure. I stayed up all night studying so I could pass the test. (Groan!) But seriously, everyone's taken tests, and yes, even the calmest, most well prepared of all of us get nervous about being tested. As you know, there are tests and then there are tests. You probably don't want to fail your blood pressure test. And you sure didn't want to fail your driving test back when you first took it. That, after all, is serious stuff. So I won't minimize the anxiety you're probably already feeling about taking the state real estate exam. Yet I do want to put this into perspective for you. The worst that can happen is that you have to take the exam again. And, of course, the best thing that can and will happen to you is you'll pass the first time around. I had a student take the test twice in the same day, figuring that would double her chances of passing at least one of them. Yes, she did pass both. So don't let exam anxiety get in your way. If you've done your homework in your prelicense class and used this book to help you prepare, you're there. Trust me. You'll be selling real estate before you know it.

But just to give you one last bit of help, I wrote this chapter to provide you with a few more strategies to use while you're taking the exam and a few ideas for preparing for the exam. Don't think of these ten topics as guarantees for success; just know that if you follow the advice in this chapter, you can maximize your chances of passing the state license exam the first time you take it. For more exam preparation tips, check out Chapter 2.

Taking the Exam as Soon as You Can

Given the fact that the vast majority of states require some kind of coursework before you can get your real estate license, most of you probably will have completed a number of hours of real estate classes before taking the exam. You never will know the material better than you do right when you finish the course. And you're likely to forget the specifics that you need from the material soon after your coursework is completed, especially if you must take an exam to complete the course. Your mind will actually think it's done with all of this, even though you're not and you'll start forgetting important information. One of the most creative exercises you'll ever do in your life is to come up with a laundry list of excuses for putting off taking the state exam. Don't! A few of my students have actually taken the state exam near the end of their course but before the course exam. Some states may allow you to do that.

I hope you use this book along with the course material as you complete the prelicensing course. If you haven't taken the practice exams in Chapters 19, 21, 23, and 25, do so. Take a quick review of your weakest points, and then go take the state exam. If you need to make an appointment to take the exam, make the appointment before you finish your course so there is little delay after you finish real estate school.

Knowing the Rules (and Following Them)

STATE
SPECIFIC

You must adhere to a number of rules for any state exam. Find out what they are and obey them. Although you may encounter others, here are a few rules that you may want to check out. (For more on figuring out the rules of your state's exam, see Chapter 1.)

>> **Calculators:** What kind can you bring and what kind are forbidden? Some states forbid any calculator (or electronic device with a calculator) that can store text, so no cellphones.

>> **Entry permit:** If your state requires an entry permit, don't forget to bring it. States that require them typically have some sort of application procedure for you to go through just to take the exam. Follow all the instructions to apply for your entry permit, put it in a safe place when it comes in the mail, and then (did I say this already?) don't forget it when you go to take the exam.

>> **Exam fee:** If you must pay the fee at the time you take the exam, make sure you have it and can pay it the way the test makers want it, by check, credit card, in cash, or with a money order; but you need to know which so you are prepared. Most of the time, though, you pay the exam fee when you apply to take the test.

>> **Food:** You may be prohibited from bringing food to the test. If you have a medical condition that requires you to eat at certain times, get permission ahead of time by contacting the state licensing agency or the people administering the test since some states use contracted services.

>> **Handicapped accessibility:** If this is an issue for you — say, for example, you use a wheelchair — find out ahead of time how your state licensing agency is making accommodations.

>> **Identification:** Find out the specific types of identification you need and whether more than one is necessary. Photo IDs are common requirements, but check it out first and make sure you bring what you need.

>> **Location:** Some states have more than one exam location. Pick the one most convenient and least stressful to you. Note, I didn't say the one closest. You may be more relaxed driving a longer distance to a suburban location, knowing that you won't have to struggle for parking downtown.

>> **Time:** Find out what time you need to arrive at the exam and be there at least 30 minutes early. At the very least, doing so can help relax you by avoiding the last-minute rush and possibly being late.

>> **Writing implements:** If the test materials say to bring two No. 2 pencils, then bring at least two or more. And you may want to bring a pen with you, just in case you have to sign something.

Studying Your State License Law

STATE SPECIFIC

Make sure that you read your state's real estate license laws (see Chapter 3) before you take your state exam. These laws can cover everything from agency relationships, which you can read about in Chapter 4, to how much continuing education you have to have to keep your license. Even if you've covered some of the material in your real estate course, you're expected to be familiar with the law itself. You may be given a copy of the law when you take a prelicensing course. If not, you usually can obtain a copy directly from your state licensing agency, and often can do so online with your computer. Try using a search engine like Google and type in your state's name followed by the words real estate license law. Because states vary in who issues real estate licenses, you can also type in your state's name followed by the words real estate license commission or real estate license board.

WARNING

Don't neglect knowing about the silly little stuff like license fees. Every real estate exam I've ever taken asked some question or another about how much it costs to get a license or change an address or something like that.

Remembering Important Vocabulary

Not having taken the real estate exams in all 50 states, I can't say the following with absolute certainty, but I believe you can pass most state license exams for real estate salesperson by simply mastering the vocabulary (no small task). At the initial stage of licensing, state officials want to make sure that you at least understand the basics. If you can master all the terms that are in italics in this book, the glossary terms, the terms on flashcards, and any other words that are new to you, I think you'll pass the state exam. By master them, however, I mean committing to memory a one- or two-sentence definition for each term. As for the more complicated concepts, memorizing the major differences between two similar terms probably will get you through. The online flashcards should be especially helpful because they contain most of the important terms in this book.

WARNING

Exams beyond the salesperson exam, such as the broker's exam, require you to memorize more terminology and be able to apply it in various situational questions, almost like mini-case studies. A mastery of the vocabulary, however, shouldn't be overlooked, even for the broker's exam. That mastery can help you answer case studies and other questions on the broker's exam.

Focusing on Key Concepts

Real estate studies include many key concepts that go beyond simple vocabulary (see the previous section). For example, the fact that a salesperson must work under a broker is a key concept (see Chapter 3). The idea of fiduciary responsibility is a key concept (see Chapter 4). Math formulas are key concepts (see Chapter 18). Most key concepts can be reduced to a few sentences. The way this book is organized, every key concept has its own heading. Look for the words in italics and a few key sentences that describe what I'm talking about. If it helps, reduce it all to a sentence or two or a list of important characteristics. In addition, when a key concept doesn't warrant its own section, I highlight it with the (you guessed it) Remember icon. Make sure that you learn, understand, and remember them for the exam.

Eating Something

I'm a big believer in the food, energy, blood sugar, and alertness relationship. Eat your normal meals for the day. If eating and the exam schedule are a problem, make other arrangements. For example, if you're traveling to an exam site or actually taking the exam when you normally would be eating, get some energy or meal replacement bars or some other healthy snacks and eat them as close to your regular meal time as possible. If you're allowed to bring food into the exam, by all means, bring something if you want — just don't go overboard.

Staying Cool, Calm, and Collected

Okay! I grant you staying calm before a test always is easier said than done. But let your nerves work for you rather than against you. Get just anxious enough to motivate you to study, do the practice exams in this book, and review the material you didn't do well on in class and practice questions. At some point, you'll begin to feel comfortable enough with the information that you'll begin to relax. Keep in mind that you probably have accomplished much harder things in your life, that you're being tested on real estate issues and not rocket science, and that you can always take the test over if you don't pass.

I think activities like relaxation exercises, meditation, and deep breathing all can help. Before any exam that I take, I close my eyes for just a few seconds and take a couple of deep breaths. If you're so inclined, say a short prayer. What you're looking for is to become calm and focused.

Paying Attention (without Overthinking)

Take what is presented in each question at face value. Avoid "what-iffing" as you read the question. Don't be afraid to select the obviously correct answer. Examiners don't write questions that are intentionally designed to trick you. They do write questions that sometimes require knowledge of the fine differences between two points. Pay attention to unnecessary material that is designed to give the question a sense of reality or throw you off. Here's an example with a topic from Chapter 7.

Question: Tenancy in common is a common form of ownership for

Answers: married couples, cooperative apartment owners, time share owners, condominium owners.

The answer is condominium owners, and you can read why in Chapter 7. If you started to overthink this question, you may want to pick cooperative apartments, because that's a form of group ownership, and married couples can own property as tenants in common, but it isn't typical.

Time share ownership generally is individual ownership. So if you overthink this question, you may find justification for at least one if not two of the incorrect answers. This question, again, points out the benefits of mastering terms and key concepts that I discuss in "Focusing on Key Concepts" earlier in this chapter. I've tried to give you examples of various types of test questions in the four practice exams in this book.

Going with Your Initial Instinct

The advice you've been given since the time you started taking multiple-choice tests needs to be engraved on Mount Rushmore: Go with your first answer on a multiple-choice question. I have corrected enough of these types of exams and have seen enough right answers changed to wrong answers to tell you that for the most part, it's true. I don't know enough about how the brain works to explain it, but on recognition-type exams, or exams where the answers are right in front of you if you have prepared well, the first answer that comes to mind usually is the best one.

The two exceptions to this rule are:

>> If a later question gives you information that makes a better choice likely in an earlier question.

>> When checking your answers to the math questions. Do the math questions at least twice or until you get the same answer twice. Once upon a time, I decided that 100 minus 4 equaled 94. That cost me a perfect score on a math test in seventh grade. Although not that important in the grander scheme of things, I never forgot after that to do math questions twice over just in case.

Finishing the Job

Above all, don't leave any answers blank. Go through the test quickly the first time to answer as many of the easy questions that you know the answers to right away. Then go back and take your time with the harder ones. Guess if you have to. There will inevitably be a few answers you know right off the bat in the last 10 or 15 questions. It would be a shame to miss those answers because you spent too much time on a few questions earlier in the exam. If you're a little mathphobic, don't get stuck wrestling with the math questions. Skip them, if you have to, and come back to them after you've gone through the entire exam.

The last thing you need to do is actually count the number of marks on the answer sheet to make sure that the number corresponds with the number of questions on the exam. While you're at it, make sure you didn't fill in two answers for the same question. Many states are using computerized testing. Make sure you understand how the system works, how to finalize your answers or leave them open to change, and to make sure you've answered all the questions. And if you're not sure, ask the exam proctor, and don't be embarrassed to ask in front of the kids in the room who probably grew up with computers in their cribs.

Appendix A

Glossary

abstract of title: A report based on what was found in a title search, which is an investigation of the legal records concerning the title to a property.

acceleration clause: A clause in a mortgage loan that allows the lender to declare the entire balance of the loan due immediately once the loan is declared in default after the borrower misses a certain number of payments.

accessory building: A separate building on a property that supports or is related to the main use of the property, such as a free standing garage on a residential property.

accretion: The gaining of land due to natural forces.

accrued depreciation: The total loss in value of a building from all causes; part of the cost approach to value.

accrued item: In terms of proration at a real estate closing, an item that is owed by the seller but paid by the buyer.

acknowledgement: In a deed, shows proof of witnessing the signature of the grantor.

actual eviction: Occurs when the landlord takes legal action, generally through a lawsuit, to re-possess the premises.

ad valorum: Used in connection with real estate taxes that are based on the value of the property.

add on factor: The percentage that is added to the useable space to arrive at the rentable space in a commercial building.

adjustable rate mortgage: A mortgage loan in which the interest rate can change throughout the life of the loan.

adverse possession: The claim of ownership of one person's property by another based on how the encroaching person is using it and the length of time involved.

agency by estoppel: An agency created when the principal doesn't stop the agent from going beyond his normal duties thereby giving the impression that an agency relationship has been created.

agency by ratification: An agency created by accepting the circumstances after the fact.

agency coupled with an interest: An agency relationship where the agent has some kind of interest in the property being sold.

agency relationship: The relationship between the agent and the client — in real estate, the broker and the buyer client or seller client. The salesperson is the subagent of the buyer client or seller client.

air rights: Rights of a property owner to the infinite air space above her land that may be limited by government regulations regarding aircraft traffic.

alienation clause: A clause in the mortgage loan that requires the loan to be paid off upon sale of the property. Also known as a *due on sale clause, call clause,* or *resale clause.*

amortized loan: A type of mortgage loan in which the entire balance of the loan is paid off by the end of the term (period) of the loan. Also known as a *direct reduction loan.*

annual cap: In an adjustable rate loan, the maximum amount the interest rate can be adjusted upward in any given year.

annual percentage rate (APR): The real interest rate one is paying on a loan taking into account the interest rate charged for periodic payments as well as prepaid interest (points).

anti-trust laws: Federal laws designed to protect the public from various unfair business practices.

anticipation: The economic influence on value that indicates that present value is created by the valuation of future benefits.

appraisal: An estimate or opinion of value or as being completed by an expert for a particular purpose. The term refers to both the activity and the report.

appreciation: A rise in the value of a piece of property. Also called *capital appreciation.*

appurtenant easement: An easement that benefits a neighboring property. Also called an *easement appurtenant.*

aquifer: The location of an underground water supply.

area variance: A one property exception from the zoning regulations due to a physical hardship on the property that allows for an exception to rules such as the location of the placement of the building on the property.

arm's length: A reference to a type of transaction where there is no relationship between the two parties, such as being members of the same family.

assemblage: The act of putting together several properties into one larger property generally to create addition value (plottage).

assessed value: The value of a property that is used to calculate real estate taxes. It may or may not be equal to the market value but is based on the market value.

assessment ratio: The percentage by which the market value is multiplied to arrive at the assessed value for properly tax purposes.

assignment: In contract terms someone else takes over (the assignee) the obligations and responsibilities of one of the parties to the contract.

associate broker: A person, although holding a broker's license, who has a status similar to that of a salesperson, in that the associate broker is allowed to perform certain real estate activities but only under the supervision of a real estate broker.

avulsion: The sudden loss of land due to natural forces.

balance: The economic influence on value that states that a relationship exists between the value of the land and the value of the buildings on the land.

balloon payment: The amount remaining to be paid in a single payment at the end of a partially amortized loan.

bargain and sale deed: Provides no warranties unless specifically inserted in which case it is referred to as a bargain and sale deed with covenant against grantor's acts. Title by the grantor is implied.

basis: The initial price paid for a property. Once capital improvements are added and depreciation (cost recovery) is subtracted, it becomes the adjusted basis.

beneficiary: In a trust arrangement, the person on behalf of whom a property is administered by a trustee. In a mortgage loan situation, the lender who will receive the deed from the trustee in the event of a default.

bilateral contract: An agreement that is created in which two parties each agree to do something, in effect exchanging promises.

binder: An agreement in writing signifying the intention of the parties to move forward with the sale and containing the basic terms of the agreement. Also called an *offer to purchase.* The binder may be accompanied by a deposit or earnest money.

blanket mortgage: A mortgage loan used to cover more than one piece of property. Sometimes used to buy multiple lots in a subdivision.

boot: The additional cash or a thing of value other than real property paid to either party in a tax deferred exchange that will be taxed at the time of the exchange. Taxable to the person receiving it.

broker: A person, licensed by the state, who is permitted to perform certain listed activities related to real estate transactions. A broker's license is required in order to perform these activities for another person for a fee. An individual may always perform these same activities on his own behalf without a license.

brownfield: A former industrial, factory, manufacturing, or storage site that may have environmentally hazardous waste on or under it from previous use.

building code: A regulation that establishes minimum standards for construction, electrical, and plumbing work.

building permit: Usually issued by the local government in accordance with the building code allowing construction of a project to proceed.

bundle of rights: The theory of ownership of land that incorporates the idea that various rights in the land can be separated, such as separating ownership and possession, by leasing the property.

buydown: These points are pre-paid interest that are paid at the beginning of a mortgage loan in order to lower the interest rate on the periodic payments.

buyer agency: The establishment of an agency relationship that allows the buyer to be represented by his own broker.

buyer default: When the buyer in a real estate contract refuses to proceed with the purchase of a property.

capital gain: The profit realized from the sale of a property for more than one paid for it.

capital improvement: A permanent improvement that usually adds value to the property, such as a new roof.

capitalization rate: Similar to a rate of return, that is, the amount of income an investor hopes to receive from an investment as a percentage of the value of the investment. In the income capitalization approach to value it's used to convert a stated amount of income into the value of the investment.

cash flow after taxes: The amount of money left for the year from a property investment after all expenses including the mortgage and income taxes are paid. The same as *after tax cash flow*.

cash flow before taxes: The amount of money left for the year from a property investment after all expenses including the mortgage are paid but before income taxes are paid. The same as *before tax cash flow*.

casualty insurance: Covers losses caused by theft, vandalism, and burglary.

certificate of occupancy: A document issued by the local government at the end of a project certifying that the building has been completed according to approved plans (building permit) and is ready for occupancy.

certificate of title: An opinion about the validity of the title without a guarantee of title.

Civil Rights Act of 1866: A federal law that prohibits discrimination in the purchase, sale, leasing, or conveyance of real and personal property on the basis of race or color. This law is important because unlike future laws there are no exceptions.

client: The person you represent as an agent. Another term for *principal*.

closing in escrow: The process of closing a real estate transaction that takes place through a third party who gathers all the paperwork and funds and distributes them to the proper parties.

cluster zoning: A regulation that permits the same number of lots in a subdivision as regular zoning would allow but permits them to be grouped together on smaller lots.

co-ownership: When more than one person owns the same piece of real estate. Also called *concurrent ownership.*

codicil: An addition or change to an existing will made by the person for whom the will is written.

collateral: Something of value that is used as security for a loan.

combination trust: A real estate investment trust (REIT) that invests shareholders money in property equities and mortgage loans.

commingling: Combining a client's funds with your own business funds. Usually considered to be some type of violation even if the money is accounted for.

community property: A legal life estate in which the spouse is entitled to a one-half interest in real property acquired during the marriage.

Community Reinvestment Act: A federal law requiring banks to reinvest in their service area by making mortgage and other type of loans available.

comparable: A property that has recently been sold that is very similar to the property being appraised (subject property). Based on the principle of substitution the comparable is a good indicator of the value of the subject property.

compensatory damages: Moneys that may be paid in a default situation where one party (may be the buyer or seller) sues the other party for money they believe they have lost as a result of the default by the other party.

Comprehensive Environmental Response, Compensation, and Liability Act (CERCLA) of 1980: Federal legislation designed to identify sites of environmental pollution and provide funds, called the Superfund, for cleanup.

condominium ownership: A form of group ownership where the owner receives a deed for the individual ownership of her unit as well as an ownership interest as a tenant in common for all common spaces.

conforming loans: A type of mortgage loan that meets the requirements necessary for the loan to be sold on the secondary mortgage market.

consideration clause: The mandatory words in a deed that indicate that something of value is being received in exchange for the title to the property.

construction loan: A loan made to a builder to finance a construction project whereby the funds are released periodically during the life of the project.

constructive eviction: When the landlord takes illegal actions that make the premises uninhabitable.

contract: A voluntary agreement to do or not to do something.

contribution: The economic influence on value that states that an improvement to a property is worth what the real estate market will pay, not what it cost.

conventional loans: Mortgage loans that meet criteria set by the lender but which also often meet the criteria set by Fannie Mae in the secondary mortgage market.

corporation: A legal entity that for property ownership purposes is treated as a single person that will own property in severalty.

cost approach: One of the three approaches to value used to appraise properties, based on the cost of the various components of the building and property. Especially used for unique properties for which there aren't many comparable sales.

cost recovery period: The period of time, set by the government, over which an asset may be depreciated.

credit: In terms of proration at a real estate closing, the amount that is owed to the buyer or seller or something for which they have already paid.

curable deterioration: Damage or wear and tear to the property that is economically feasible to repair, that is, the increase in value of the property as a result of the repair exceeds the cost of the repair.

customer: The third party to a transaction in which an agent is used. Example: If the agent represents the seller/client, the buyer is the third party/customer.

debit: In terms of proration at a real estate closing, an amount that the buyer or seller owes.

debt service: The mortgage payment.

dedication: The voluntary transfer of ownership of property from an individual to the government without payment.

Deed: The document that transfers title (ownership) to property from one person to another.

deed in lieu of foreclosure: A deed signed by the owner giving the property to the lender to avoid foreclosure. Also called a *friendly foreclosure.*

deed restriction: A limitation on the use of property that appears in the deed, put there by one owner and will affect all future owners unless there is an expiration time limit. May also be referred to as *covenants, conditions, and restrictions (CCRs)* or *restrictive covenants.*

default: When a borrower doesn't pay off the debt.

deficiency judgment: A judgment rendered against a property owner after a successful lawsuit on the part of the lender requiring payment of the difference between the mortgage loan amount and the proceeds of a foreclosure sale.

density zoning ordinance: A regulation that permits the same number of lots as the normal zoning would but allows for varying lot sizes.

depreciation: In the cost approach to value, the loss in value to any structure due to various factors such as wear and tear.

depreciation (cost recovery): The recovery of the cost of an asset that wears out; used for tax purposes.

devisee: The person named in a will who will receive the title to the real property.

direct costs: Those expenses directly associated with the actual construction of a building, such as labor and materials. Also called *hard costs.*

discharging a contract: A term that describes the end of the contract in one of several ways.

discount rate: The interest rate set by the Federal Reserve that member banks charge each other for loans.

doctrine of prior appropriation: A state-specific right regarding use of water, especially where water is scarce.

dominant tenement: As it applies to an easement, the person or property that receives the benefit of the easement. Also called the *dominant estate.*

dual agency: A situation where both the buyer and seller are represented by the same agent. Sometimes called *limited agency.* May be illegal in some states.

duties of a property manager: They are to maximize the income and maintain or increase the overall value of the property.

earnest money: A relatively small amount of money given at the time the binder is signed to indicate good faith on the part of the purchaser to move ahead with the purchase.

easement: The right of a person or entity to use someone else's property for his own benefit.

easement by necessity: A court-ordered easement usually associated with gaining access to a property.

easement by prescription: An easement that is created by the actions of one person against the interests of another person. Also called a *prescriptive easement.*

easement in gross: A type of easement that benefits another person rather than a property; for example a utility company easement.

economic life: When speaking of a building, the length of time the structure contributes value to the land.

effective age: When speaking of a building, an estimate of the age the structure appears to be, given wear and tear, maintenance, and upgrades.

effective gross income: The income available for property expenses after deducting a vacancy and collection loss from potential gross income and adding in other income.

eminent domain: The right of the government to take property against the owner's will for a public purpose.

encroachment: The unauthorized or illegal use of someone's property by another person.

encumbrance: A right or interest in a piece of real estate that belongs to someone other than the property owner. May be either a financial claim or a limitation on use.

environmental assessments: The examination of a property for the presence of environmentally hazardous material. The four phases include document review, testing to determine the extent of hazardous materials, remediation recommendations, and management recommendations.

environmental impact statement: A study of the potential environmental impacts of a project; often required as part of the approval process by the local government.

Equal Credit Opportunity Act: A federal act prohibiting discrimination in the granting or arranging of credit.

equalization rate: The rate used to equalize the differences between taxing units when calculating taxes to be paid to a higher authority.

equitable right of redemption: As it relates to a tax sale for nonpayment of taxes or a foreclosure sale for nonpayment of a mortgage loan debt, the right to redeem a property by paying the taxes and penalties or the loan debt before the sale of the property.

equitable title: Gives the holder of the equitable title the right to the transfer of title when all the conditions of a contract are met.

equity buildup: The reduction of the mortgage loan debt by paying off the loan through the income of the property investment.

equity trust: A real estate investment trust (REIT) that invests in a number of different types of real estate and sells shares to investors.

erosion: The gradual loss of land due to natural processes.

escheat: The process by which the government obtains property from those who die intestate (without a will) and without heirs.

escrow account: An account maintained by the lender into which the borrower deposits money from which the lender pays the property taxes and insurance. These funds may also be called *reserves, impounds,* and *trust account.*

estate: The extent and type of interest or rights that someone has in a piece of land. Also called *estate in land.*

estate at sufferance: A situation where a tenant who had a legal right to occupy the premises continues to occupy the space after the right of occupancy has expired against the landlord's will.

estate at will: A situation where the landlord allows the tenant to occupy the premises, but there is no definite period of time when the arrangement will expire.

estate for years: A lease agreement with a definite starting and ending date. Also called a *tenancy for years.*

estoppel certificate: A statement of the amount of debt owed by one party to another. In the case of a mortgage loan, executed by the mortgagee (the lender). In the case of a lease, executed by the lessee tenant. Also called a *reduction certificate.*

exclusive agency buyer agency agreement: Where the broker is the exclusive agent to the buyer and gets paid only if the broker finds the property the buyer ultimately purchases.

exclusive agency listing agreement: Where a broker is given an exclusive right to market the property but is only paid if the broker sells the property. If the owner sells the property, no fee is paid to the broker.

exclusive buyer agency agreement: Where the broker is the exclusive agent to the buyer and gets paid no matter who finds the property the buyer ultimately purchases.

executed contract: A contract in which all the terms of the contract have been completed.

executor: The person named to carry out the instructions in a will.

express agency: An agency relationship established through an agreement.

express contract: An agreement where the parties to the contract (the participants) clearly state in words what they agree to do or not to do.

external obsolescence: A form of depreciation (loss in value) caused by factors external to the land itself.

Fair Housing Act of 1968: Part of the 1968 Civil Rights Act, it prohibited certain discriminatory acts related to property transactions, identified protected classes, and defined exceptions.

Fair Housing Amendments Act of 1988: This act added handicapped and familial status (presence of children) to the list of protected classes.

Fannie Mae: The Federal National Mortgage Association, part of the secondary mortgage market that buys and sells mortgage loans.

Federal Housing Administration: A federal agency under the Department of Housing and Urban Development that provides loan guarantees for mortgage loans.

fee simple condition precedent: Ownership of the real estate that doesn't pass until a certain condition is met.

fee simple condition subsequent: Ownership that can be reclaimed by the grantor if a certain condition isn't met by the new owner.

fee simple determinable: Ownership of the property that remains with the new owner as long as the conditions of ownership are being met. Violation of the conditions results in automatic reversion of the ownership to the previous owner.

fee simple qualified estate: A fee simple estate with some limitations. Also called *fee simple defeasible estate.*

fiduciary: Describes the relationship between the broker and the client; meaning faithful service.

fixed expenses: Expenses that aren't dependent on building occupancy, when calculating net operating income. Fixed expenses are real estate taxes, property insurance, special assessments, and license fees.

fixed rate mortgage: A mortgage loan where throughout the life of the loan the interest rate doesn't change and the monthly mortgage payments remain the same.

fixture: Personal property that becomes real estate usually by physical attachment.

foreclosure: The involuntary loss of property due to nonpayment of a debt related to the property such as a mortgage loan or property taxes.

forfeiture: The loss of property by disobeying some condition in the deed or not using the property for the purpose required in the deed.

forfeiture of the contract: A buyer default, when the buyer formally declares the contract forfeited (ended).

fraud: The intentional misrepresentation or lying about the property or important issues related to the transaction.

freehold estate: Ownership in real estate that lasts for an indefinite or indeterminate period of time.

friability: The tendency of asbestos to break down and give off dust and fibers that can be dangerous if inhaled.

functional obsolescence: Outmoded design in older structures or unacceptable design (by modern standards) in newer structures.

general agent: Someone hired to represent a person in a range or group of transactions. In real estate, the usual agency relationship of a property manager.

general lien: A lien attached to a number of properties.

general partnership: A form of ownership by two or more people (partners) coming together for business purposes who share management responsibility, profits and losses, and liability.

general warranty deed: Provides the greatest protection and warrantees for the grantee. Also called the *full covenant* and *warranty deed.*

grant deed: A deed used in some states to provide limited warranties.

grantee: The person receiving title (ownership) of a piece of property.

granting clause: The words in a deed indicating that the grantor is conveying title (ownership) to the grantee.

grantor: The person who is the current owner of the property who is conveying title (ownership) to someone else.

gross income multiplier: A method for calculating the value of a property based on a multiple of the annual gross income.

gross lease: A lease where the tenant pays the same rent each month and the landlord pays all the building's expenses. This is the lease used in a typical residential lease arrangement.

ground lease: A lease where a tenant rents a vacant piece of property specifically to build a building on the land. This is usually a long-term lease. Also called a *land lease.*

group boycotts: In the case of real estate brokerages, when two or more brokerages agree not to work with another broker.

growing equity mortgage: A fixed rate mortgage loan where the principal payment increases periodically to allow the loan to be paid off faster.

habendum clause: A statement in the deed further defining the rights being granted to the grantee and characterized by the phrase "to have and to hold."

highest and best use: The economic influence on value that states that every property has a single use that results in the highest value for that property.

home equity: The difference between the value of the property and the debt attributed to the property.

home equity loan: A loan made against the equity in a property which allows withdrawal of all or part of the equity in the property.

homestead: A legal life estate that grants the family home a certain level of protection from creditors during the owner's lifetime.

honest and fair dealing: One of the obligations that the broker has to the customer (third party).

Housing and Community Development Act of 1974: Federal law that protects against gender (sex) discrimination in housing; added to the protected classes in the 1968 Fair Housing Act.

hypothecation: The process of using property as security for a loan.

implied agency: An agency relationship established by the actions of the parties rather than an expressed agreement.

implied contract: A contract that is created by the actions of the parties rather than a formal agreement.

impossibility of performance: In contract terms where the activity for which the contract was entered into can't legally be performed.

in rem: Results in the debt being tied to the property and obligating a future owner if it's not paid before transfer of ownership. A term usually associated with real estate taxes.

income capitalization approach: An appraisal method used for commercial properties that converts the net operating income into value using a capitalization rate.

incurable deterioration: An economic term meaning that even if an item can be fixed, the cost of the repair exceeds the value it adds to the property.

independent contractor: An independent contractor is self-employed and is the way most real estate agents work even though salespeople must work under the supervision of a broker.

index: A rate, not under the control of either the lender or the borrower, used in calculating the interest rate for an adjustable rate mortgage loan.

indirect costs: Those expenses not directly related to the physical construction process, such as permit fees and architectural costs. Also called *soft costs.*

infrastructure: The physical facilities of a community that are important to the maintenance and growth of the community such as water lines, sewers, and roads.

interest rate lock: A fee paid to the lender to maintain the interest rate of a mortgage loan in situations where there may be a significant period of time between loan approval and closing.

intermediate theory mortgage: Where the borrower retains title to the property and the mortgage is a lien. Title is conveyed to the lender in the case of a default but the mortgagee (lender) must go through the foreclosure process before the property can be sold.

Interstate Land Sales Act: A federal law governing the practice of offering land in one state for sale to buyers in another state, usually sight unseen.

intestate: A situation where a person dies without a will.

involuntary alienation: The loss of property against one's will.

involuntary lien: A lien placed on the property against the owner's wishes.

joint and several liability: A legal concept that in the case of environmental pollution says that if more than one person is responsible for the hazardous waste site, the law is enforceable on the group as well as each individual involved.

joint tenancy: A form of co-ownership created by four unities: interest, possession, time, and title.

judgment lien: A lien placed on property as a result of a court judgment. Also called *judgments* or *money judgments.*

judicial foreclosure: The most common type of foreclosure where the court orders the property to be sold as a result of a foreclosure action brought by the lender.

kickback: An undisclosed fee, usually paid for referring business to someone.

laches: The loss of a right by not using it; connected to not enforcing deed restrictions.

land: The unimproved surface of the earth.

land contract: An agreement made to purchase property without immediately paying the full price, eliminating the need for a mortgage loan. The agreement generally requires a down payment and periodic installment payments thereafter. Also called an *installment contract, conditional sales contract, contract for deed,* and *land sales contract.*

landfill: An area that is excavated, filled with solid waste, and then covered.

latent defects: Problems with the property that may not be visible in a normal inspection.

laws of descent: State laws governing the distribution of assets when one dies without a will. Also called *statute of descent* or *law of descent and distribution.*

leachate: The liquid that comes out of the septic tank after the solids have settled.

lead: A mineral widely used in various forms in residential and commercial construction. Under various conditions it's considered a health hazard.

Lead Based Paint Hazard Reduction Act: A 1992 federal law requiring homeowners of homes built before 1978 to fill out a lead paint disclosure form that is then provided to the buyer.

lease: An agreement between two parties for possession and use of a particular space, usually for a certain length of time.

lease rent: The rent that is being paid in accordance with a lease agreement; also referred to *scheduled rent* or *contract rent.*

leased fee estate: The owner's (lessor's or landlord's) interest in a property in a lease situation. Also referred to *leased fee interest.*

leasehold estate: The tenant's interest in the property in a lease situation. Also called *leasehold interest.*

leasehold interest: See *leasehold estate.*

legal description: The type of description of property boundaries and location that is acceptable for deed purposes to transfer ownership.

legal life estate: A life estate created by state law.

legal title: The title or ownership that normally transfers in a property sale.

leverage: The use of borrowed money to increase the return on your investment by using less of your own funds.

liability insurance: Insurance that covers losses due to negligence on the part of the building owner or property manager.

license: The temporary right of one person to do something on another person's property.

lien: A financial claim against someone's property.

lien theory mortgage: Where the borrower retains legal title as well as equitable title to the property. The lender is granted a lien against the property.

life estate: It grants possession and limited ownership of a property to a person for the duration of the recipient's life or the life of another person.

life estate pur autre vie: Life estate that lasts for the lifetime of a third party rather than the person actually receiving the life estate.

lifetime cap: In an adjustable rate mortgage loan, it limits the upward adjustment of the interest rate over the life of the loan. Also called the *ceiling*.

Limited Liability Corporation (LLC): A hybrid organizational structure that has elements of a partnership and a corporation.

limited partnership: A form of ownership by two or more people where there is a general partner that manages the investment and limited partners who have no management responsibilities. The limited partners' liability is limited to their financial contribution.

liquidated damages: A clause that deals with how much money the seller is entitled to in the event of buyer default.

liquidity: The speed with which an investment may be turned into cash. Real estate isn't considered a liquid investment.

listing agreement: The agreement that establishes an agency relationship between an agent and a property seller.

littoral rights: The rights commonly granted to owners of property that borders a bay, a large lake, the ocean, or sea.

loan to value ratio: Known as the LTV, the percent of the property's value that may be borrowed.

loss factor: The percentage that is subtracted from the rentable space to arrive at the useable space.

lot and block system: A system used for legally describing the boundaries of a property using a map showing individual lot lines often used in conjunction with a new subdivision. May also be called the *recorded plat system,* the *recorded map system,* the *lot block tract system,* the *recorded survey system,* and the *filed map system.*

margin: In an adjustable rate mortgage loan, a set amount added to the index to arrive at the interest rate for the loan.

market allocation: When different brokerages agree to not compete with one another by dividing up an area along geographic lines or according to some other division, for example price.

market rent: The normal rent that is charged for a particular type of space in the market place.

market value: The price a property will bring in a typical real estate transaction, subject to certain conditions such as the buyer or seller being free of undue influence. Appraisers are most often interested in this type of value.

marketable title: A description of a title to the property where the title is free of any reasonable doubts as to who the owner is and is free from any defects.

master plan: A plan for the future development of a municipality based on current conditions and future projections. Sometimes called a *comprehensive plan.*

material defects: Important defects in the property that the average person would want to know about and usually must be disclosed.

mechanic's lien: A lien placed on the property for nonpayment of work done the on the property.

meeting of the minds: The point at which a commission on the sale of a property is earned. The buyer and seller are in agreement on all terms and are prepared to complete the transaction. Also called *mutual assent.*

Megan's Law: The law regarding the registration of sex offenders.

metes and bounds: The system for legally describing the boundaries of a piece of property using specific locations, distances, and compass directions.

mill rate: The method of calculating taxes due based on a rate of one mill equals one-tenth of a penny. Also called *millage*.

mineral rights: The right to extract minerals from the property. This right is often associated with subsurface rights.

mitigation measures: The actions that may be taken to minimize the environmental impact of a project.

mortgage: The document that the borrower (mortgagor) gives to the lender (mortgagee) creating a voluntary lien on a property that is being used as security for a loan.

mortgage assignment: The transfer of the person or institution to whom the mortgage debt is owed from the current person or institution to a new one.

mortgage assumption: The process of taking over of the obligations of a mortgage debt of one person by another person.

mortgage contingency: A clause in the sales contract that allows time for the buyer to secure a mortgage loan to purchase the property and allows for the possibility of cancelling the contract if the loan isn't approved.

mortgage lien: A voluntary lien placed on the property as security for a mortgage loan.

mortgage trust: A real estate investment trust (REIT) that uses shareholder's money to buy and sell mortgage loans rather than properties.

mortgagee: The lender, that is the one who receives the mortgage from the borrower.

mortgagor: The borrower who gives the mortgage to the lender.

Multiple Listing System (MLS): A marketing tool to allow brokers to share listings by acting as buyer's agents or cooperating brokers.

negative amortization: Additional moneys due at the end of an adjustable rate mortgage loan due to the effect of a payment cap.

negative cash flow: A property investment situation in which the property's expenses are greater than the property's income.

negligent misrepresentation: An agent's failure to disclose information important to a buyer's decision due to the agent not being aware of the information. In this case the information was either common knowledge or was something the agent, as an agent, should have known, such as the location of a new highway adjacent to the property.

net lease: A lease where the tenant pays part of the building's expenses in addition to the rent. This is a typical lease in commercial property rentals.

net listing: A way to calculate the broker's fee as well as establish a listing agreement where the broker is hired to sell the property at a certain price and is permitted to keep anything above that as the fee. Illegal in some states and discouraged in others.

net operating income: The amount of annual income remaining after all building expenses except debt service (the mortgage payment) are deducted from potential gross income.

nonconforming use: A structure or use of property that was once permitted but due to a change in the regulations wouldn't now be permitted. Sometimes referred to as a *grandfathered use* or *building*.

nonconforming loan: A mortgage loans that doesn't meet the criteria of the secondary mortgage market.

nonjudicial foreclosure: A procedure permitted in only some states that allows sale of property in the case of a default without going through a court proceeding.

novation: In contract terms, where a new contract with different terms replaces the old one.

oil/gas rights: Rights conveyed by a lease giving the leaseholder the right to extract oil or gas from the property.

open buyer agency agreement: Where the buyer is able to enter into agreements with any number of brokers and only pays the one who finds them the property they ultimately purchase.

open end mortgage: A mortgage loan that can be reopened and borrowed against after some of it has been paid down.

operating statement: A statement that tracks the actual income and expenses of an investment property for one year. Also called an *income and expense statement.*

option: A unilateral agreement in which a seller agrees to sell property to a buyer at an agreed to price within a certain time frame if the buyer wants to purchase the property. In an option agreement the buyer can choose not to purchase the property.

option listing: A clause in a listing agreement that permits the broker to purchase the property. May be illegal or highly regulated in some states.

ordinary life estate: A life estate in which the length of time of the estate interest is the lifetime of the person receiving the life estate.

origination fee: An administrative charge paid by the buyer related to processing the mortgage loan.

ownership in trust: A type of ownership where a third party holds title for the benefit of another person, the beneficiary.

package mortgage: A loan that covers both the real estate and the personal property being sold with the real estate.

partial performance: In contract terms, when one party agrees to accept partial completion of the contracted obligations as fulfilling the contract.

partially amortized loan: A combination of an amortized loan and a straight loan where part of the principal is paid during the term of the loan.

partitioning: A legal proceeding that is undertaken to divide a single piece of property that is owned in shares (undivided ownership) by two or more people.

party wall: The outside wall between two buildings that is shared by both buildings.

payment cap: A limit on the amount the monthly payment may be raised in an adjustable rate mortgage regardless of the change in the interest rate. It may result in negative amortization.

percentage lease: A lease sometimes used in retail commercial rentals where the tenant pays the same base rent each month plus a portion of their sales volume that may vary each month.

percolation test: The test done to determine the capacity of the soil to absorb leachate and therefore to determine where a septic field can be located. Also known as a *perc test.*

periodic estate: In a tenancy situation created when the original agreement doesn't contain any definite period of time. Also called an *estate from period to period* or *periodic tenancy.*

personal property: Anything that is portable, moveable, and not permanently attached to the real estate. Also called *personalty.*

physical deterioration: The normal wear and tear that a building experiences as it ages; dependent on the quality of the original construction and the level of ongoing maintenance.

planned unit development: A single development having mixed uses that may include different types of residential uses as well as nonresidential uses.

plottage: The influence on value that states that the whole may be greater than the sum of its parts. Also refers to the additional value created by assembling various properties into one larger property (assemblage).

points: Each *point* is one percent of the mortgage loan amount and is paid at the beginning of the loan to lower the interest rate that will apply to payments going forward. In this case they're called *discount points.* Points may also be used to calculate such things as origination fees and interest rate locks.

police power: The right of the state to pass laws for the protection of the public. The state's right to limit the use of privately owned property.

positive cash flow: A property investment situation in which the property's expenses are less than the property's income.

potential gross income: The total annual income a building will generate at 100 percent occupancy, based on market rent, lease rent, or a combination of the two.

pre-payment penalty: A fee charged by a lender when a mortgage loan is paid off earlier than the normal schedule.

prepaid item: In terms of proration at a real estate closing, an item the seller has paid but from which the buyer benefits.

prescriptive easement: See *easement by prescription.*

price fixing: When business competitors meet to decide on common prices for their services.

primary mortgage market: The place where a person will go to borrow money to buy a piece of property. Also called *primary lenders.*

principal: The person you represent as an agent. Also called the *client.*

priority of liens: Applies in the case of multiple liens and determines the order in which lien holders get paid in the event of a court ordered sale of the property. The government is usually the first in priority to be paid.

private mortgage insurance: Commonly referred to as PMI, this insurance coverage, purchased by the borrower, protects the lender in case the borrower defaults on the mortgage loan.

pro forma: A one-year potential income and expense projection for a property investment. Also called a *reconstructed operating statement.*

probate: The process for making sure that a will is legal and valid, the deceased's wishes are carried out, and the assets are actually in the estate.

promissory note: An agreement to repay a loan according to certain terms and conditions.

proprietary lease: The type of lease given to an owner in a cooperative building since the owner owns shares in the corporation owning the building rather than owning real estate.

proration: The allocation or dividing of certain money items at the closing.

protected classes: Those groups, defined by characteristic, such as race or religion, that are protected by the Federal Fair Housing Act and various state and local laws, from discrimination.

public grants: The conveyance of property from the government to an individual.

puffing: Exaggerating the virtues of a property. It isn't illegal because the exaggeration is usually fairly simple to verify.

purchase money mortgage: The mortgage that is used to purchase real estate. Sometimes specifically refers to a mortgage loan made by the seller directly to the buyer.

quitclaim deed: Provides no warrantees to the grantee and gives no implication of how much or how good the grantor's title to the property is.

radon: An odorless, colorless, tasteless, radioactive gas produced by the decay of natural materials such as rocks that are radioactive. At certain levels considered hazardous.

real estate: The land and all natural and artificial improvements permanently attached to it.

real estate exchange: A process for exchanging one property for another that allows for taxes on capital gains to be postponed. Also called a *1031 exchange* or a *tax-deferred exchange.*

real estate investment syndicate: An ownership structure (rather than a legal form of ownership) in which a number of people join together to invest in a single project or property.

real estate investment trust (REIT): A form of investment similar to stocks that pools the money of multiple investors to invest in real estate.

The Real Estate Settlement and Procedures Act (RESPA): The federal act taken together with the Truth in Lending Act (TILA) that governs various paperwork and procedures to be followed before and at the closing where a mortgage loan is involved.

real property: The land, natural and artificial improvements, and all the rights, benefits, and interests that go with owning a piece of land and the improvements.

reconveyance deed: Used in a trust arrangement to convey title back to the trustor by the trustee when the debt is paid off.

rectangular survey system: A system for legally describing the boundaries of a piece of property based on a system of lines throughout the United States forming squares and rectangles. Also called the *U.S. Governmnet Survey System.*

redlining: A prohibited action whereby lenders deny mortgage loans based on location rather than an individual's eligibility for the loan.

rent loss insurance: Insurance that covers losses to the owner due to the building not being available to be leased due to damage such as from fire. Doesn't covers rent losses due to normal vacancies. Also called *business interruption insurance* or *consequential loss insurance.*

rentable space: The space the tenant pays for when renting nonresidential space, such as in an office building or shopping mall.

renunciation by the agent: Where the agent in a real estate listing agreement dissolves the contract against the wishes of the seller or buyer.

replacement cost: Used in the cost approach, the cost to construct a building with the same utility (usefulness) as a comparable structure using today's materials and standards.

reproduction cost: Used in the cost approach, the cost to construct an exact duplicate of the subject structure at today's costs.

rescission: In contract terms, when one party decides not to fulfill its obligations under the contract and considers the situation as if the contract never existed.

reserves: Funds that are put aside by the owner of the building to pay for periodic expenses that don't occur annually, such as replacing a stove in an apartment. Sometimes called *reserves for replacement.*

reverse mortgage: A loan that allows the property owner to use the equity in his home without selling the home. The primary feature that differs from a regular home equity loan is the ability to delay repayment until the property owner leaves the home.

reversionary right: The right of someone to get back her property automatically. In a lease situation the owner has a reversionary right to possess her property at the end of the lease term. Sometimes called *leased fee estate with reversionary rights.*

revocation by the principal: Where the principal (client) in a real estate listing agreement dissolves the contract against the wishes of the agent.

right of quiet enjoyment: The tenant to exclusive use of the premises for the term of the lease, without the landlord's interference.

right of survivorship: A characteristic of joint tenancy but not tenancy in common whereby the interest of a deceased member of the joint tenancy automatically goes to the remaining co-owners.

sale leaseback: A situation where the owner of a property sells the property in order to obtain cash while remaining in the property as a tenant.

sales comparison approach: The method most often used to appraise residential properties. Also called the *market analysis approach* and the *market comparison approach.*

salesperson: A licensed person who is allowed to perform certain real estate activities but only under the supervision of a real estate broker.

sanitary waste: The water that drains from such things as showers, toilets, sinks, and washing machines. Wastewater is often treated at sewage treatment plants.

secondary mortgage market: A series of institutions that purchase mortgages from banks and other primary lenders in order to allow the primary lenders to replenish their funds to permit further loans.

section: In the rectangular survey system, a subdivision of a township. There are 36 sections of one square mile each (640 acres) in a township.

seller default: When the seller in a real estate contract refuses to proceed with the sale of a property.

seller incentive: A situation where a seller will pay points (pre-paid interest) to lower the interest rate for the buyer. The cost of the points is usually added to the price of the property.

septic fields: A part of an onsite septic system that absorbs the sewage into the ground. Also called *leach fields* or *absorption fields.*

septic system: An on-site sewage disposal system usually for one house.

servient tenement: As it applies to an easement, the property that is burdened by the easement.

shared equity mortgage: Allows a portion of the profit made when selling a property to be shared with another party in return for that party's financial help in purchasing the property.

sheriff's deed: A court-ordered deed used in the case of a foreclosure by a local government or bank. Individual states govern its use and form.

single agency: When the agent represents only one party, the buyer or the seller.

special agent: An agent hired to represent a client in a single transaction. The arrangement most common to a real estate sale/purchase.

special assessment: Taxes that are levied against a specific group of properties rather than all of the properties in a municipality; usually to finance a local improvement such as sidewalks.

special assessment district: An area designated in which the properties are subject to a special tax levy usually used to finance a local improvement such as sidewalks.

special permit use: A type of variation from the zoning regulations that allows for a series of listed uses that may require extra control by the local government granting agency. Also called a *special exception use permit, a conditional use permit,* and a *special use variance.*

specific lien: A lien attached to only one piece of property.

specific performance: Occurs in a default situation when a lawsuit that is brought by a seller or buyer requires the other parry to go ahead with the sale.

statute of frauds: A state law, found in all states, that governs various transactions. The law generally requires most real estate contracts to be in writing.

statutory right of redemption: The right of the original owner to redeem a property that has been sold for back taxes after the sale has occurred.

steering: Encouraging or discouraging people from buying or leasing property in a certain area as means of discrimination.

stigmatized property: A property where something occurred that makes the property less desirable to some people.

straight line depreciation: The cost recovery process used for tax purposes based on the concept that a building loses an equal amount of value each year over the cost recovery period.

straight line method: In the cost approach to appraising property, a method of calculating depreciation that presumes that the structure deteriorates at the same rate each year. Also called the *economic age life method.*

straight loan: Loan's primary feature is that during the term of the loan, only interest must be paid. Also called a *term loan.*

strict foreclosure: A process permitted in some states where the borrower must be given proper notice and a time frame established by the courts during which the borrower may pay off the debt.

strict liability: In terms of environmental pollution, the owner of the property has no excuse with respect to his liability.

subdivision: A single property divided into smaller pieces (lots, parcels) usually for sale or development.

sublease: A situation where a tenant leases the space to another tenant (the subtenant). Provisions to allow or not allow subleasing are usually contained in the original lease.

subordinate lien: Any lien that is in the line of payment after the lien in first position. Also called a *junior lien.*

subordination agreement: An agreement that allows a new mortgage loan to be placed in first position ahead of previous loans, for repayment if a foreclosure become necessary.

substantial performance: In contract terms, when the work under a contract is nearly completed and for one reason or another the determination is made to discharge (end) the contract. Monetary damages may be due to the injured party from the party who didn't complete the work.

substitution: The economic influence on value that states that a buyer will pay the least he can for a property that satisfies their needs.

Superfund Amendments and Reauthorization Act (SARA): Passed in 1986, authorized more funding for the Superfund program, created stronger hazardous waste cleanup standards, and created innocent landowner immunity.

surety bond: Insurance that pays for losses due to dishonest acts by employees such as the owner's rent collector stealing the rents.

surface rights: The rights of the owner to do whatever is legally permitted on the surface of the land.

surrogate's court: The court that handles the process of validating a will and distributing the assets. Also called *probate court.*

tacking: As applied in the case of adverse possession, the ability to add periods of continuous use by different owners to achieve the required total period of continuous use.

tax base: The total assessed valuation of taxable property within the community.

tax credit: Subtracted from the taxes you owe.

tax deduction: Subtracted from income to reduce your taxable income.

tax lien: A financial obligation attached to a property based on taxes due.

temporary loan: A type of loan used when funds are needed for a short period of time between real estate transactions. Also called *interim financing, bridge loan, swing loan,* and *gap loan.*

tenancy: Having an interest in a piece of real estate. May refer to ownership as well as a leasehold interest.

tenancy by the entirety: A form of ownership only available to married couples geared to protecting the interest of each of the partners.

tenancy in common: A form of co-ownership with several distinct features one of which is the ability to leave the interest to heirs.

tenancy in severalty: A form of ownership of real estate by one person. Also called *sole tenancy*.

tenant: Someone seeking to rent space from the owner (landlord) of a property.

termination on sale clause: A clause in a lease that, in the event the property is sold, allows the new owner to terminate the tenant's lease otherwise the lease would remain valid.

tie-in arrangement: When a customer who wishes to purchase one service or product is required to purchase another product or service as a condition of the sale. Also called *tying agreement*.

time share: An arrangement where a person has either a fractional interest in a property or the right to use a property for a limited period of time each year or both.

title closing: The point in time when a real estate transaction is finished and title (ownership) of a property is transferred from the grantor to the grantee.

title insurance: An insurance policy that covers various defects in the title that may be discovered after closing.

title theory mortgage: A mortgage lien theory that gives title of the property to the lender while the borrower retains equitable title. This theory makes it easier for the lender to claim the property in the event the borrower defaults.

townships: In the rectangular survey system a division of a quadrangle and measuring six miles on each side.

transactional brokerage: When the agent represents neither buyer nor seller but handles the transaction for both. Not available in all states.

triple net lease: A lease where the tenant pays all of the buildings expenses. A typical lease in commercial property rentals.

trust deed: Used to convey title by a trustor to a trustee for the benefit of a beneficiary as security for debt. Also called a *deed of trust* or a *deed in trust*.

trustee: The person who holds the deed during the life of the loan in a trust deed situation.

trustee's deed: Used to convey (ownership) title of a property held in trust to someone else.

trustor: The borrower who gives a deed for the property to the trustee as security for the loan in a trust deed situation.

The Truth in Lending Act (TILA): The federal act taken together with the Real Estate Settlement and Procedures Act (RESPA) that governs various paperwork and procedures to be followed before and at the closing where a mortgage loan is involved.

unenforceable contract: A contract that seems valid and may, in fact, have all the elements of a valid contract, but for one reason or another can't be enforced by one party on another.

uniform commercial code (UCC): A state law governing sales and contracts involving personal property.

unilateral contract: A one-sided agreement in which only one party is obligated to do what is promised.

unity of interests: A requirement for joint tenancy whereby each owner must have the same interest in the property.

unity of possession: A requirement of joint tenancy whereby each owner has an undivided interest in the property.

unity of time: A requirement of joint tenancy whereby all the owners must take ownership of the property at the same time.

unity of title: A requirement of joint tenancy whereby the names of all owners must be on the same deed together.

universal agent: Someone who acts on a client's behalf in all transactions.

use variance: A one property exception to the regulations of the zoning ordinance regarding use of the property.

useable space: The space in a nonresidential property in which the tenant has exclusive use.

vacancy and collection loss: A percentage number derived from the market place that reflects a loss of rent due to short-term periodic vacancies and nonpayment of rents.

vacancy rate: The amount of a particular type of space that is vacant as a percentage of the total amount of that type of space in a given area.

valid contract: A contract in which all the required elements are present.

value: What something is worth usually in exchange for something else. Sometimes referred to as *value in exchange.*

value in use: The value a property has to a specific person who may use it for a specific purpose that's generally unavailable to the typical buyer.

variable expenses: Property expenses that may vary with the occupancy of the building. All annual expenses that don't fall into the fixed expense category or the reserves category. Sometimes called *operating expenses.*

variance: A one property exception from the regulations of the zoning ordinance.

void contract: A contract in which one or more of the required elements is missing.

voidable contract: A contract that usually involves a situation in which one of the parties may not have the legal ability to enter into the contract but may confirm the contract at a later date.

voluntary alienation: The voluntary transfer of ownership of a property from one person to another.

voluntary lien: A lien in which the property owner willingly takes some action which allows a lien to be placed on the property, such as a mortgage loan.

wetland: Land where the soil type and location allows for the extra absorption of water from natural sources such as rain. These areas act as sponges to help prevent flooding of other areas.

wraparound mortgage: A mortgage loan where the seller retains the original mortgage loan, and the new mortgage loan includes payment of the new debt as well as payments on the original mortgage.

zoning district: An area designated for a certain type of use by the zoning ordinance.

zoning ordinance: A law, adopted by the municipality, that controls what property can be used for and the size and placement of structures on a property. Sometimes called a *zoning code.*

Index

About the Author

On the first night of class, **John Yoegel** always quotes one of his former real estate teachers to his students: "Most of us don't start out in real estate, but an awful lot of us end up there."

After serving in the United States Air Force and with a master's degree from New York University in hand, John pursued a career in his chosen field — urban planning. Working in local government, specifically Westchester County, New York, he earned a PhD in public administration and urban planning, also from New York University. During this time, John found himself getting more involved in county real estate matters, first as property supervisor for the county parks department and eventually as director of real estate for Westchester County. Along the way, John picked up his New York State broker's license and studied appraising with the Appraisal Institute.

After teaching courses in urban planning and public administration at the college and graduate-school levels, John began teaching real estate courses in 1987. He currently teaches prelicensing and continuing education courses for salespeople, brokers, and appraisers. John has served on a number of professional committees, including test-preparation review committees for the New York State Department of State and an ad hoc curriculum study committee of real estate educators. The recommendations of this committee resulted in a complete overhaul of real estate licensing requirements in New York State.

John is a member of the Real Estate Educators Association (REEA) and was awarded the DREI (Distinguished Real Estate Instructor) designation. He also holds the C-CREC (Consumer-Certified Real Estate Consultant) designation from the International Association of Real Estate Consultants and completed real estate instructor training with the Instructor Training Institute. In addition to this book, John also has written four other real estate books as well as articles that were published in the *REEA Journal* and *The Real Estate Professional* magazine.

When John isn't teaching or writing about real estate matters, he serves as a priest with the Orthodox Catholic Church of America. He is also an ordained interfaith minister and has taught at The New Seminary for Interfaith Studies from which he graduated. And when time permits, he's an avid amateur home winemaker.

He lives with his wife, the lovely Marina, in Connecticut.

Dedication

This book is dedicated to my beautiful and loving wife, Marina. Throughout this book she was there every day, scheduling things around my writing schedule and taking care of what needed to be taken care of as I wrote. I owe her at least one vacation that she canceled and much more. Thanks, honey, for being my biggest fan. I love you.

Author's Acknowledgments

No book ever is written alone. Even if it's a work of pure fiction that comes straight from an author's imagination, other people still must inspire that imagination, teach the author the discipline to write it all down, support and encourage the author's writing, and generally take care of business while the author writes. It's those people, past and present, whom I want to acknowledge.

For this revised edition I'd like to thank Lindsay Lefevere for initiating the project and Chad Sievers, the editor. I'd also like to thank my technical editor, Becky Rogers, real estate professional.

Many people are connected to the chain between the idea for a book and its production. Without my agent, Grace Freedson, this project never would've happened for me. Thanks, Grace, for that first phone call 16 years ago, for keeping me in your address book, for getting me this project, and representing my interests through this and other books.

Who I am today is in no small measure the result of the influence of a few very important people in my life. First of all I want to thank my parents, John and Angela, for giving me the education to get where I've gotten. I regret that my father, for whom education was an unfulfilled dream during his lifetime, is not here to see his son's name on the cover of a book. As an educator, I value the role teachers play in their students' lives, so it's with great humility that I attest to the inspirations that Remo Ianucci and Perry Norton were in my life.

On the professional side, I want to thank my fellow members of the Real Estate Educators Association for all their knowledge and willingness to share it. In particular, I want to express my appreciation to Eileen Taus, director of education with the Hudson Gateway Association of Realtors. She gave a fledgling instructor his first real estate teaching job and since then has served as mentor and cheerleader. I also want to thank my friend Richard O'Donnell for being there (as always) with his expertise when I needed answers to questions for the chapter about taxes. I also want to thank all the students I've taught over the years. It was a rare class that I did not learn something from them.

While writing the different editions of this book, my friends and extended family were supportive, encouraging, and wonderfully patient I want to thank them all: Dr. John Paulmann, Victor and Gloria Consiglio, Greg and Janice Arcaro, They never failed to ask how the book was going and were enthusiastic in the most supportive of ways — as if the project were their own, listening patiently as I ruminated about the joys and pressures of writing a book. Thanks, pals. You're the best.

The most important thanks go to my family: my children Alex and his wife Porscha, my daughter Angelique and her husband Joseph Capozzi, both talented writers in their own right, for their enthusiasm and love; Christine, who someday may read this and know that her father is thinking about her; and Jennifer, who is always with me. I also want to acknowledge my grandsons Alexander, Aydin, Anthony, and Gavin. Someday they will be old enough to know that they were never far from their grandfather's thoughts while he worked on this book.

Finally, I want to thank my wife, Marina. Her support and enthusiasm for this project never wavered, even as she was rearranging our lives around my writing. You wouldn't be reading this book if it weren't for her.

Publisher's Acknowledgments

Executive Editor: Lindsay Lefevere

Project Editor and Copy Editor: Chad R. Sievers

Technical Editor: Becky Rogers

Production Editor: Mohammed Zafar Ali

Cover Photos: © Kenishirotie/Shutterstock

DISCARD

Mac® OS X
Version 10.1
Little Black Book

Gene Steinberg

CORIOLIS™

President and CEO
Roland Elgey

Publisher
Al Valvano

Associate Publisher
Katherine Hartlove

Acquisitions Editor
Charlotte Carpentier

Product Marketing Manager
Jeff Johnson

Project Editor
Karen Swartz

Technical Reviewer
Pieter Paulson

Production Coordinator
Wendy Littley

Cover Designer
Laura Wellander

The Coriolis Group, LLC
14455 North Hayden Road
Suite 220
Scottsdale, Arizona 85260

(480) 483-0192
FAX (480) 483-0193
www.coriolis.com

Library of Congress Cataloging-in-Publication Data

Steinberg, Gene
    Mac OS X Version 10.1 little black book / by Gene Steinberg.
       p. cm.
    Includes index.
    ISBN 1-58880-294-9
    1. MacOS. 2. Operating Systems (Computers). 3. Macintosh (Computer)--Programming I. Title.
QA76.76.O63 S736785 2002
005.4'469--dc21
                                            2001052950
                                          CIP

Printed in the United States of America
10 9 8 7 6 5 4 3 2 1

 CORIOLIS

The Coriolis Group, LLC • 14455 North Hayden Road, Suite 220 • Scottsdale, Arizona 85260

A Note from Coriolis

Coriolis Technology Press was founded to create a very elite group of books: the ones you keep closest to your machine. In the real world, you have to choose the books you rely on every day *very* carefully, and we understand that.

To win a place for our books on that coveted shelf beside your PC, we guarantee several important qualities in every book we publish. These qualities are:

- *Technical accuracy*—It's no good if it doesn't work. Every Coriolis Technology Press book is reviewed by technical experts in the topic field, and is sent through several editing and proofreading passes in order to create the piece of work you now hold in your hands.

- *Innovative editorial design*—We've put years of research and refinement into the ways we present information in our books. Our books' editorial approach is uniquely designed to reflect the way people learn new technologies and search for solutions to technology problems.

- *Practical focus*—We put only pertinent information into our books and avoid any fluff. Every fact included between these two covers must serve the mission of the book as a whole.

- *Accessibility*—The information in a book is worthless unless you can find it quickly when you need it. We put a lot of effort into our indexes, and heavily cross-reference our chapters, to make it easy for you to move right to the information you need.

Here at The Coriolis Group we have been publishing and packaging books, technical journals, and training materials since 1989. We have put a lot of thought into our books; please write to us at **ctp@coriolis.com** and let us know what you think. We hope that you're happy with the book in your hands, and that in the future, when you reach for software development and networking information, you'll turn to one of our books first.

Coriolis Technology Press
The Coriolis Group
14455 N. Hayden Road, Suite 220
Scottsdale, Arizona
85260

Email: ctp@coriolis.com
Phone: (480) 483-0192
Toll free: (800) 410-0192

Look for these related books from The Coriolis Group:

Mac OS X Administration Basics Exam Cram
By Samuel A. Litt

Mac OS X Version 10.1 Black Book
By Mark R. Bell and Debrah D. Suggs

Dr. Mac: The OS X Files
By Bob LeVitus

Also Recently Published by Coriolis Technology Press:

Visual Basic .NET Programming with Peter Aitken
By Peter Aitken

Visual Basic .NET Black Book
By Steven Holzner

Windows 2000 System Administrator's Black Book, Second Edition
By Deborah Haralson, Stu Sjouwerman, Barry Shilmover, and J. Michael Stewart

C++ Black Book
By Steven Holzner

C# Core Language Little Black Book
By Bill Wagner

I wish to pay special thanks to my "muse" (she knows who she is) for always helping me to find the right things to say and the means to say it.

≥∢

About the Author

Gene Steinberg is a full-time writer and computer software and systems consultant. He is the author of more than two dozen books on computing, the Internet, and telecommunications, and he has written articles for such diverse sources as CNET, ZDNet, *MacAddict*, *MacHome*, and *Macworld*. His weekly column, "Mac Reality Check," is carried by *The Arizona Republic*/azcentral.com and his Mac support site, The Mac Night Owl (**www.macnightowl.com**) is regularly visited by thousands of Mac users each day. In his spare time, Gene and his teenaged son, Grayson, are developing a science fiction adventure series, *Attack of the Rockoids*.

Acknowledgments

Mac OS X is a simple yet an extraordinarily complex operating system, and there is no way to complete a project of this scope without outside assistance. During the course of researching and writing this book, I've been pleased to receive the help of a number of folks who have made this daunting task far more pleasant.

First and foremost, I want to thank the folks at Apple's corporate communications department for letting me see the future of the Mac OS and answering all my questions, whether simple, complex, or just downright silly. I'm particularly grateful to Natalie Sequeira and Bill Evans for their able assistance. Apple's Director of OS Technologies, Worldwide Product Marketing, Ken Bereskin, was especially helpful in delineating the key aspects of Mac OS X for both this book and my ongoing online articles on the subject.

This book would not have been possible were it not for my friend Pieter Paulson, who took on the task as technical editor to make sure every single fact in this book was as accurate as possible. In addition, an author cannot work without a publisher and editors, and the terrific folks at The Coriolis Group were especially helpful in putting up with my quirks and demands without protest. I'm particularly thankful to Charlotte Carpentier, acquisitions editor; Karen Swartz, project editor; Tiffany Taylor, copyeditor; Wendy Littley, production coordinator; Laura Wellander, cover designer; and Jeff Johnson, product marketing manager for ensuring that the words I wrote were understandable to all of our readers, and for making this book look good.

Finally, I am especially thankful for the help and support from my little family—my beautiful wife, Barbara, and my brilliant son, Grayson—for putting up with the long hours I spent at the keyboard in order to deliver the manuscript for this book on schedule.
—*Gene Steinberg*

Contents at a Glance

Table of Contents

Introduction

Ever hear of the boy who cried wolf? Sure enough, if you were told for nearly a decade that a company was going to bring a product to market in the near future, you'd probably chuckle sadly and then get on with your business, or just ignore it altogether.

This is, no doubt, the dilemma Apple faced when they first announced plans for Mac OS X. Apple's road for producing a modern operating system to replace the Mac OS was, for years, littered with failed projects, wrong turns, and missed deadlines. So it almost came as a relief when I attended a press briefing on Mac OS X Public Beta at the San Francisco headquarters of CNET, the online and broadcast technology news service, in September of 2000.

Within a few hours I was back at my home office, installing the future of the Mac OS on my computer. I examined the documentation and checked my notes as the installation proceeded. Within less than fifteen minutes, my Mac restarted. A short trip to the Setup Assistant and a second restart, and I was a believer! Mac OS X was at last a reality, not vaporware to be touted strictly for public demonstrations.

However, that was only the beginning. By January 2001, Apple had poured through tens of thousands of feedback messages from devoted Mac users. In the Macworld Expo keynote, CEO Steve Jobs announced some important changes to the user interface to satisfy the clamoring of thousands to restore the Apple menu, restore disk icons to the desktop, bring back the menu bar clock and, if need be, allow the Finder to work just as the old "Classic" version did.

By March, the first official release of Mac OS X hit the streets, but it still wasn't quite a finished product. During Apple's rollout of what was dubbed "the world's greatest operating system," it had to admit that it was strictly a version for early adopters and systems administrators who wanted to test the new system for eventual widespread deployment.

After several bug-fix updates, Apple finally rolled out the "mainstream" version, Mac OS X 10.1, in September 2001. The hallmark of the new release was a huge performance improvement, plus the addition of features missing from the original release, such as the ability to burn a CD or DVD from the Finder and DVD playback.

The Mac OS X Version 10.1 Little Black Book is designed to be your companion as you migrate to Apple's Unix-based operating system. From installation to setup to troubleshooting, you'll find the information you need is readily available, all tested with the release version of the software for maximum accuracy.

The Bill of Fare

Because this book is part of The Coriolis Group's Little Black Book series, it covers the essential information you need to install, configure, and use Mac OS X. There are no frills and no fluff. Useless tips and tricks that will satisfy one's intellectual curiosity or perhaps trigger a chuckle but not enhance your productivity, aren't included.

The 23 chapters here are divided into four parts, each covering a particular area of your Mac user experience.

In "Part I: Mac OS X Arrives," I run through the important new features, and then help you plot installation strategies. You are then taken step-by-step through the actual installation and configuration. From here you'll be introduced to the new Mac OS X Finder, the Dock, multiple user features, search features, as well as the big changes in the networking architecture. This part closes with information about AppleScript and how to install and use your programs. There's even a section covering the new Open and Save dialog boxes, which are sure to simplify file management.

Next, there's "Part II: Mac OS X and Hardware." Are you planning to install Mac OS X on a new Mac, or just one you've upgraded with extra memory, drive space, and other additions? These critical subjects are dealt with here. You'll also learn how to add peripherals, such as printers, scanners, and removable drives, on your Mac. Finally, there's a section on using Mac OS X with one of Apple's iBooks or PowerBooks.

Moving on to "Part III: The Software Review," you'll discover some of the new Mac OS X applications, how to run older "Classic" software on your Mac, and how to handle fonts, perform backups, and check for computer viruses. Finally, there's a comprehensive section on troubleshooting, plus a visit to the Unix command line of the new operating system to perform hard drive diagnostics and to navigate the underbelly of the new operating system.

The last part of this book, "Part IV: Taking Mac OS X Online," covers Internet access from stem to stern. You'll have a birds-eye view of the newest Web browsers, Apple's Mail application, and the iTools feature.

How to Use This Book

The *Mac OS X Version 10.1 Little Black Book* isn't designed to be read from cover to cover as you might read a novel, though I don't particularly mind it if you do it all in a single sitting. You'll probably just want to read the chapters that answer your questions about the new Mac OS.

As part of the Little Black Book series, each chapter is divided into two sections. The first, *In Brief*, gives you the basics and theories about the subject. The second, *Immediate Solutions*, offers step-by-step instructions on how to accomplish tasks, along with guides on what to do if something goes wrong.

Although the Mac OS X user interface is ultra simple and smooth, it's a highly complex operating system, one that will be updated regularly as time goes by. If you were one of the early adopters to the new operating system, you can see the vast number of changes between the original release and the 10.1 version (the first "major" upgrade). As a result, a book of this sort is also a developing process, and future updates for this book will reflect those changes, plus what I've learned as I continue to use Mac OS X.

I also welcome your comments, questions, and suggestions for future editions. If you have a problem with the new operating system or discover something totally unique and utterly cool, let me know. You can either email The Coriolis Group directly at **ctp@coriolis.com** or email me directly at the address below. Erratas, updates, and more information about *The Mac OS X Version 10.1 Little Black Book* can be found at **www.coriolis.com**.

Gene Steinberg
Scottsdale, AZ
Email: **gene@macnightowl.com**
www.macnightowl.com

Part I

Mac OS X Arrives

Mac OS X:
New Features from A to Z

One of the most important developments in the PC industry in recent years was the arrival of Mac OS X, a major upgrade to the aging Mac operating system. For years, Apple had tried and failed to provide a completely stable, robust operating system of a sort that would appeal to both newcomers and power users alike.

Apple's previous efforts to deliver a modern operating system were doomed to failure. In the most notable (and perhaps notorious) example, Apple spent tens of millions of dollars, thousands and thousands of man (and woman) hours, and several frustrating years developing an operating system (code-named Copland) that was designed to offer all the industrial-strength features needed to bring the Macintosh user experience into the twenty-first century. The project, though laudable in its intentions, fell apart when serious problems were encountered in such areas as offering back-ward-compatibility with older Mac software.

Eventually, the original expected shipping name for Copland, Mac OS 8, was used for a modest system upgrade that offered interface improvements but none of the under-the-hood features expected of a modern operating system. The upgrade and subsequent system versions used some of the appearance features left over from Copland, but with only minor improvements in overall system reliability.

Apple Goes Operating System Shopping

When its own in-house talent was unable to finish the job, Apple went operating system shopping in 1996. According to published reports at the time, Apple flirted with acquiring a fledgling operating system called BeOS from a company run by a former Apple executive, Jean-Louis Gassée. The BeOS was briefly offered in a series of twin-processor computers, but the company soon abandoned the hardware and concentrated on the software.

Although the BeOS still works on the older PowerPC Macs, Apple would not deliver support for the G3 or G4 CPUs, and thus the company went to the Intel world in search of more enthusiastic support. However, the operating system never quite caught on as its developers hoped, and the BeOS was finally acquired by Palm; it may find its way into future iterations of Palm OS software for handheld devices.

Apple finally took what has become the action that saved its neck. It agreed to spend some $400 million to acquire NeXT Inc., which had been established by Apple cofounder Steve Jobs after he was ousted from the company he helped create back in 1985, nine years after he and Steve Wozniak founded the company. The company's product, NeXTSTEP, was a Unix-based operating system that provided the basic underpinnings and technology Apple needed to develop its next-generation Mac OS. As soon as the former NeXT folks were on board, Apple began developing a new operating system bearing the code name Rhapsody, which would, in effect, merge NeXTSTEP with the Mac OS. In short order, Steve Jobs was back at the helm of Apple, where he diced and sliced and brought the company into sharp focus with a new line of striking consumer-oriented products.

Although Rhapsody's focus, direction, and release dates changed, the first realization of the technology was delivered with the arrival of Mac OS X Server in 1999. It was a mixture of the old and the new, combining a large portion of NeXT Inc. core technology with elements of the traditional Mac user interface.

Once the server version was released, it was time to focus on a consumer version. The end result, the subject of this book, is Mac OS X.

A Brief Look at the New Features

The striking new look of the Mac OS X interface, called Aqua, is just a small part of the changes wrought by the new Mac operating system. Under the surface are a tremendous number of changes designed to provide improved support and make the Mac run more reliably than ever. Before we look at the new, however, it is fitting to examine where we've come from. For example, when the Macintosh first shipped in 1984, its graphical interface was unique for an affordable personal computer (see Figure 1.1). Instead of typing commands to make your computer perform a given function, you used a pointing device—a mouse—and you clicked on icons and command menus representing common functions, such as files, folders, and disks.

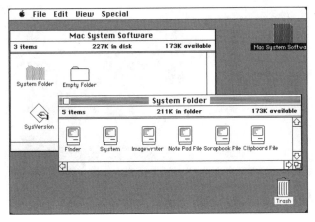

Figure 1.1   This is the Macintosh desktop that was introduced with the very
first models.

NOTE: *It's fair to mention that the Mac wasn't the first Apple PC with a graphical interface. Prior to the Mac, Apple introduced a high-priced desktop computer, called Lisa, which never quite caught on. In those days, some firms who provided typesetting computers, such as Agfa CompuGraphic (now Agfa), were offering the Lisa as a simple-to-use front end for some of those systems.*

Over the years, a number of changes have been made to the Mac. However, even the user interface of Mac OS 9, the last "Classic" or traditional Mac operating system version, bears a striking resemblance to the original, despite its more colorful, more delicately constructed desktop and icons (see Figure 1.2).

Now that you've taken a before and after look at the evolution of the Mac OS, the following sections detail what Mac OS X brings to the table.

Darwin

The open source core of Mac OS X, Darwin, is based on a Unix microkernel, consisting of the Mach 3 microkernel and FreeBSD. The Apache Web server, which powers a majority of Web sites, has been tamed and forms the basis of the new operating system's Web-sharing capabilities.

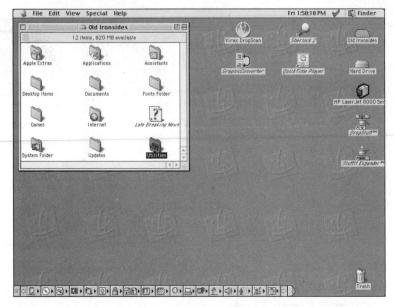

Figure 1.2   The traditional Mac OS has grown in complexity and size by
quantum leaps, yet retains many of the core visual elements of
previous versions.

NOTE: *Apple's Darwin is also an open-source project, where the core components of the
operating system are to be made available free of charge to software developers, with Apple
retaining full rights to the code. These developers can test and debug the software, and then
make available bug fixes and enhancements to the entire developer community. For more
information about this feature, feel free to visit Apple's Darwin Web site, **www.apple.com/
darwin**.*

Although its Unix underpinnings are well hidden beneath Aqua's striking user interface, they are not invisible. Power users can easily pour
beneath the surface, bypassing the graphical user interface, and run
regular Unix-based applications under Mac OS X via a command-line
interface. Apple has even provided a Terminal application in the Utilities folder (see Figure 1.3), so power users can visit the command
line and access the core Unix functions.

In addition, the new Mac operating system offers the same industrial-
strength features that are the hallmark of Unix. These include the
following:

- *Protected memory*—Each Mac OS X native program you run
  resides in its own address space, walled off from other programs.

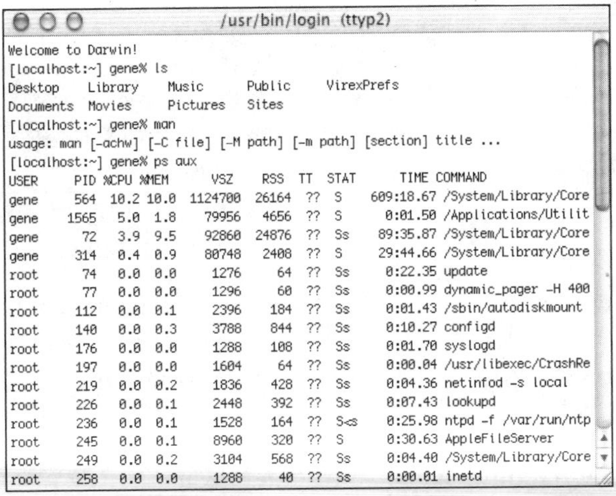

```
  ⊖ ⊖ ⊖              /usr/bin/login  (ttyp2)
Welcome to Darwin!
[localhost:~] gene% ls
Desktop    Library    Music     Public     VirexPrefs
Documents  Movies     Pictures  Sites
[localhost:~] gene% man
usage: man [-achw] [-C file] [-M path] [-m path] [section] title ...
[localhost:~] gene% ps aux
USER     PID %CPU %MEM    VSZ    RSS  TT STAT    TIME COMMAND
gene     564 10.2 10.0 1124700 26164 ??  S    609:18.67 /System/Library/Core
gene    1565  5.0  1.8   79956  4656 ??  S      0:01.58 /Applications/Utilit
gene      72  3.9  9.5   92860 24876 ??  Ss    89:35.87 /System/Library/Core
gene     314  0.4  0.9   80748  2408 ??  S     29:44.66 /System/Library/Core
root      74  0.0  0.0    1276    64 ??  Ss     0:22.35 update
root      77  0.0  0.0    1296    60 ??  Ss     0:00.99 dynamic_pager -H 400
root     112  0.0  0.1    2396   184 ??  Ss     0:01.43 /sbin/autodiskmount
root     140  0.0  0.3    3788   844 ??  Ss     0:10.27 configd
root     176  0.0  0.0    1288   108 ??  Ss     0:01.70 syslogd
root     197  0.0  0.0    1604    64 ??  Ss     0:00.04 /usr/libexec/CrashRe
root     219  0.0  0.2    1836   428 ??  Ss     0:04.36 netinfod -s local
root     226  0.0  0.1    2448   392 ??  Ss     0:07.43 lookupd
root     236  0.0  0.1    1528   164 ??  S-s    0:25.98 ntpd -f /var/run/ntp
root     245  0.0  0.1    8960   320 ??  S      0:30.63 AppleFileServer
root     249  0.0  0.2    3104   568 ??  Ss     0:04.40 /System/Library/Core
root     258  0.0  0.0    1288    40 ??  Ss     0:00.01 inetd
```

Figure 1.3   Mac OS X brings something totally new to the platform: a
command-line interface that allows you to make changes right
in the underbelly of the system.

If a single program crashes, that application is shut down, along
with the memory address space it occupies. You can continue to
run your Mac without the need to restart. This feature will help to
sharply reduce the Mac OS's tendency to crash at the least sign of
a software conflict.

- *Preemptive multitasking*—Apple's previous multitasking
  method was cooperative, meaning that each application would,
  in effect, have to share CPU time with other programs. This
  meant that if you were working in a program, such as typing in a
  word-processing document, background tasks, such as printing
  or downloading a file, could come almost to a screeching halt,
  particularly if a program hogged processor time unnecessarily.
  With Mac OS X, the operating system serves as the traffic cop,
  performing the task management and allowing programs to run
  more efficiently and with fewer slowdowns when multiple
  processes are running.

- *Advanced virtual memory*—With previous versions of the Mac
  operating system, virtual memory meant slower performance,
  poor performance with multimedia programs, stuttering sounds,
  and other shortcomings. Under Mac OS X, virtual memory
  management is dynamic. Programs are automatically given the
  amount of memory they require, via either RAM or virtual
  memory disk swapping. Performance is optimized, so you get the
  maximum-possible performance from your programs.

NOTE: Virtual memory in Mac OS X is super-efficient, but it can't do miracles. To get the best possible performance, there is no substitute for having sufficient RAM to run your high-energy programs (such as Adobe Photoshop or Apple's Final Cut Pro). But you will no longer have to visit the Mac OS X equivalent of the Get Info window (Show Info) to keep changing a program's memory allocation to meet your needs (except, of course, for Classic applications).

Quartz

In previous versions of the Mac OS, Apple used an imaging model called QuickDraw to generate pixels on your display. For Mac OS X, Apple has given up this technology, moving instead to Adobe's Portable Document Format (PDF). As you probably know, most electronic documents are available in PDF trim, which retains the exact formatting, fonts, pictures, and colors of the original.

Full system-wide support is provided for the major font formats—bitmap, PostScript, TrueType, and the new OpenType format. As a result, Adobe Type Manager (ATM) is no longer needed to render fonts crisply on the screen, although font management is not quite as extensive as the Deluxe version of ATM.

NOTE: ATM will still work normally from Mac OS X's Classic environment, including the font-management features for the Deluxe version, but it will not be upgraded to Mac OS X. Chapter 16 covers the subject of font handling and includes information on the available options for font management.

The Quartz 2D graphics system is extremely powerful, with speedy rendering of images and anti-aliasing, providing sharp screen display. You'll see some of this elegance in the illustrations provided in this book, but you have to see the real thing to get the flavor of the effects of this unique technology.

There's also system-level support for PDF, which makes it easy for Mac software developers to provide built-in support to save documents in this format. In addition to PDF, Apple includes support for ColorSync to ease color management from input to display to output; the industry-standard OpenGL, which provides superlative performance for many 3D games and graphic applications; and Apple's famous QuickTime, used worldwide for generating multimedia content.

Cocoa

One of the technologies inherited from NeXTSTEP, which forms the basis for a large part of Mac OS X's capabilities, is Cocoa. This is the new name for an advanced object-oriented programming environment that's supposed to allow programmers to develop new applications much more quickly than with other programming tools. In one spectacular example, Stone Software's integrated illustration program, Create, which features drawing, HTML, and page layout capabilities, is largely the work of one programmer. With traditional programming tools, a large, highly skilled team would be required to perform the same work.

NOTE: *If there's a downside to all this flexibility, it's that programs created in this fashion cannot run on older Macs. However, that situation may be of less significance as more Macs are shipped or upgraded to Mac OS X in the years ahead.*

Carbon

Once referred to by Apple CEO Steve Jobs as the "basis for all life forms," Carbon is, in fact, a new set of application programming interfaces. These interfaces are designed to offer software publishers a relatively easy upgrade path to deliver Mac OS X–savvy applications. Most major Mac developers, including such heavyweights as Adobe, Macromedia, Microsoft, and Quark, have been hard at work porting their products to Mac OS X; many of these applications will be available when you read this book, including Office v. X for Mac. (I used Word X, in fact, to write this book.)

NOTE: *Even though Carbon greatly simplifies conversion of software to Mac OS X, it's not a cakewalk. Microsoft Office 2001, for example, consists of millions of lines of computer code. Microsoft has the largest Mac programming team outside of Apple Computer, and yet it didn't complete work on the Mac OS X version of the application suite until late fall 2001.*

The main advantage of an application that is "Carbonized" is that it supports the major features of Mac OS X, such as preemptive multitasking, protected memory, and advanced virtual memory, plus the eye-catching Aqua interface. In addition, when Apple's CarbonLib extension (which first appeared as part of Mac OS 9) is installed, many of these programs can run on older Mac operating system versions— though, of course, without the advanced features of Mac OS X.

NOTE: *Not all Carbon applications have backward-compatibility. The Mac OS X versions of both Internet Explorer and Office run only under Mac OS X, but Adobe's and Macromedia's Mac OS X applications run fine with the older Mac OS. As with any development effort, there are trade-offs, and it's up to each company to decide how to address these issues.*

Classic

Although a reasonably useful number of Mac OS X–savvy programs have shipped since the release of the new operating system, you will want to use some of the thousands of older programs. Fortunately, you can do so by virtue of the Classic feature.

Classic is, in effect, Mac OS 9.1 and later (9.2.1 came with Mac OS X 10.1) running as a separate application under Mac OS X. You can think of it as being somewhat similar to running Connectix Virtual PC to emulate the Windows environment on a Mac. But it goes further than that. Apple's Classic feature runs transparently under Mac OS X. The feature lets you run most of your older applications with good performance and a high level of compatibility, but without taking advantage of the Aqua user interface or the robust underpinnings of the new operating system. It is designed to ease the transition to the new Mac computing paradigm.

NOTE: *The Classic environment is not a panacea. Some cherished system extensions, particularly those that modify Finder functions and hardware drivers for such peripherals as scanners and CD writers won't run. You'll need to get Mac OS X–compatible drivers for all these products.*

Aqua

The Macintosh user interface is reborn with Aqua (see Figure 1.4). Although at first glance Aqua clearly comes across as eye candy—a software interface that is consistent with the striking industrial designs for Apple's latest computers—much more is involved here.

Aqua's translucent, shimmering, ocean-blue look is designed to address many of the usability problems with older graphical user interfaces (both Mac- and Windows-based). It is designed to be relatively easy for novice computer users to master; such users form a large percentage of purchasers of Apple's consumer-level products (the iBook and the iMac). But it's also intended to provide the power that will appeal to the sophisticated computer professional.

NOTE: *Apple is also offering a slightly more subdued graphite version of its user interface as an appearance option, paying attention to professional users who might consider Aqua just a bit too imposing for an office environment. You'll learn more about setting this option in Chapter 3.*

From large, photo-quality icons to translucent menus, drop shadows, and real-time object dragging (without a performance penalty), Aqua is designed to provide Mac users new and old with a convenient,

Figure 1.4. After you boot a Mac with OS X installed, you will witness a bold,
new, eye-catching user interface.

easy-to-manage user experience. The standard single-window mode,
for example, which keeps Finder displays to one window, helps reduce the clutter and confusion of previous operating system versions.
However, the new Mac OS X Finder has many options for adjustment, so you can easily configure it to spawn additional Finder windows when you open a folder, just like the Classic Mac OS.

NOTE: *In prior versions of the Mac operating system, when you moved an object about the
screen, you'd see its outline or bounding box rather than the object's contents. With Mac OS X,
the power of the Quartz graphic layer allows you to see the actual object while it's moving
(except for a few applications that do not support this feature). Although some third-party
programs, such as Power Windows (a shareware utility), allow you to do this under prior Mac
operating system versions, it requires a powerful Mac to avoid a serious performance penalty.*

One common interface problem addressed with the new operating
system is the Save dialog box. Even experienced Mac users have sometimes had trouble navigating through complex folder hierarchies.
Under Mac OS X, however, when you're ready to save an open document for the first time, the Save As dialog box opens as a sheet of
paper right below the title bar of the document in question (see
Figure 1.5). Unlike the present Mac operating system, you aren't
prevented from doing something else while the dialog box is open.

11

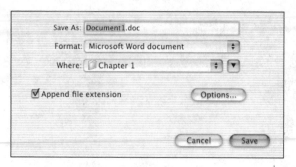

Figure 1.5   The new translucent Save As dialog box stays hooked to the document window you're going to save.

You can simply switch to another document window, and the Save As dialog box remains anchored to the document you want to save. Then, you just return to it when you're ready to save the document. In addition, the expanded column view arrangement provides Finder-like navigation of folder hierarchies.

The Mac OS X Finder

The core of the Mac user experience is the Finder, an application that runs full-time on a Mac, providing the desktop appearance as well as performing file- and disk-management chores. For Mac OS X, the venerable Finder has undergone a complete redesign (see Figure 1.6), ending up as a composite of technologies from the original Finder

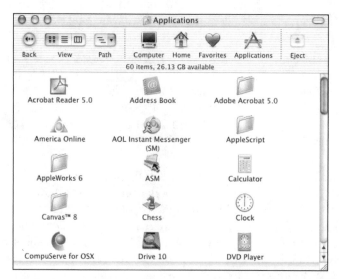

Figure 1.6   The new face of the famous Mac Finder has striking differences, yet retains some familiar elements.

and from the NeXTSTEP file viewer. The combination is designed to make it possible to access your applications, files, and disks easily, without having to dig deep into numerous nested folders, scattered icons, and directory windows.

At the top of the Mac OS X Finder are large, clearly labeled toolbar buttons that take you directly to the most frequently accessed areas on your Mac. The Computer button, for example, displays your mounted disks, those available for file access, and network connections. The Home button takes you to your main or personal Users directory or folder, regardless of whether it's on your Mac's hard drive or on a local or Internet-based network. There are also standard buttons for your favorites (files, folders, disks, and sites) and documents. However, that is just the beginning. The toolbar can be customized with a variety of icons (see Figure 1.7) that can also be sized to your taste. You can even hide the toolbar altogether and have the Finder behave very much like the old Mac OS, despite the daringly different look.

TIP: *Combining local, network, and Internet access in a single interface is part of Apple's Internet integration efforts. These also include the iTools feature at Apple's Web site, which provides a set of Web-based enhancements that work only with Macs fitted with Mac OS 9 and Mac OS X. I cover the subject in more detail in Chapter 23.*

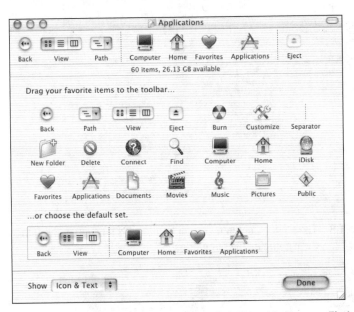

Figure 1.7   A wide range of possibilities is inherent in the new Finder toolbar setup window.

The Finder offers not only new, more colorful variations of the list and icon views that exist on the original Finder, it also offers a new column view that makes locating deeply nested items easier (see Figure 1.8). You single-click on a folder or disk, and the contents quickly display in the window at the right. Reminiscent of Greg's Browser, a popular Mac shareware program, this file-viewing feature allows you to more easily locate anything from a file to a networked drive.

The Dock

The Apple menu was once the principal repository on the Mac for your frequently accessed files, folders, and disks. Apple's Control Strip was a floating palette of control panels and other programs, offering one-click access. The latter is history, replaced (at least in part) by the Dock (see Figure 1.9). This picturesque taskbar puts a set of colorful, almost cartoonish icons at the bottom of your Mac's display (or at the side, if you prefer). It contains files, folders, disks, programs—whatever you choose to store there. The icons are designed to easily reflect their contents. For example, a picture file contains a preview of the image, so you can recognize it immediately. If you prefer to

Figure 1.8   The Finder's column view option speeds navigation through even complex file directories.

Figure 1.9   The Dock automatically resizes to accommodate additional items.

view titles, you'll be pleased to see the title of an item displayed as soon as the mouse passes over it.

To access an item on the Dock, just click once on it, and it will open in a new window. When you minimize a window, it transfers to the Dock in a flashy motion that looks like a sheet of paper being folded (in a sense, the end result is similar to the way a minimized window is moved to the Microsoft Windows taskbar). The motion is sometimes known as the *Genie Effect*. With the standard single-window mode, you'll find that your previous open window is closed and moved to the Dock. You can also use the Mac's drag-and-drop feature to add items to the Dock.

TIP: *If the Genie Effect is too distracting, Mac OS X 10.1 includes a scaling option that drops a minimized window to the Dock or returns it to full size with much less flourish.*

Even the venerable Mac trashcan is now part of the Dock, although it performs precisely the same functions as in previous Mac operating system versions.

Desktop

The famous Apple desktop isn't left untouched by Mac OS X. Although on the surface it looks very different (again, see Figure 1.3), looks can be deceiving. The versions of Aqua that were first displayed showed a clear desktop, without even a disk icon to clutter the landscape. Apple answered the call of devoted Mac users and has restored much of the desktop behavior of previous versions of the Mac OS.

Mac OS X 10.1 vs. Mac OS X 10.0

Are you one of the early adopters? When Apple first released Mac OS X, it conceded the software wasn't quite finished, and promised a steady stream of updates. With 10.1, which was released in September 2001, Mac OS X finally came into its own. Apple made the upgrade available for a limited time free from Apple dealers, and also offered an almost free upgrade that Mac users could order ("almost free" meaning there was a $19.95 shipping charge) to get up to date as painlessly as possible.

The 10.1 upgrade delivers a tremendous number of system enhancements; virtually every function, from booting to application launching, is noticeably faster. I'll cover both fresh installations and upgrading in the next chapter.

If you gave up on Mac OS X with the initial release, the 10.1 upgrade may make you reconsider the new operating system. If you are already a user of the original version of Mac OS X, here are some of the most significant changes:

- *Speedier performance*—Apple boasts that menus are up to five times faster and applications launch two to three times faster. File copying has also been speeded up, as have startup, login, and real-time resizing of Finder and application windows.

NOTE: *This isn't just a claim. I have personally verified the tremendous speed boost on a number of Macs, with both G3 and G4 processors. In many cases, performance should pretty much equal that of Mac OS 9, with some functions (such as basic file copying chores) running even faster.*

- *Interface improvements*—The Dock is not frozen at the bottom of the screen but can be moved to hang vertically at the left or right end of your display (a feature third-party utilities also offer). Common system-related functions, such as volume level, display resolution, modem connection status, and AirPort and battery indicators, can be put on the menu bar for single-click access. You can resize Finder columns in column view.

- *New system preferences*—The System Preferences application, used to adjust all sorts of settings for your Mac, has been redesigned. The settings panels are divided into four convenient categories for fast access. Some system settings have been redesigned and new features have been added, such as a Full Keyboard Access feature that lets you navigate menus and the Dock via the keyboard, and a Universal Access option for disabled users. In addition, the interface has been opened up to third parties, so you can expect to see a growing number of Mac OS X utilities that are controlled via System Preferences.

- *Enhanced networking*—The original release of Mac OS X couldn't network via AppleShare with older Macs. That feature has been added, along with the ability to network with Windows and Unix servers courtesy of a built-in SMB/CIFS (SAMBA) client.

- *Missing features added*—The ability to burn a CD or DVD from the Finder has been added; you can also view DVDs on any Mac or Apple laptop that has Accelerated Graphics Port (AGP) capability. Additional printing support has been included for both ink jet and network laser printers. There is also improved AppleScript support, including the ability to run scripts direct from a Finder menu or Finder toolbar icon. Musicians will appreciate built-in support for 32-bit/96kHz audio, multichannel sound, built-in MIDI, and more.

Before Installing Mac OS X

If you're ready to take the plunge into a whole new world of ultra-reliable, speedy Macintosh computing, you should make sure that your Mac is ready for the upgrade.

Here are some points to consider when moving to Mac OS X:

- *System requirements*—Mac OS X will work on almost any Apple Macintosh computer that shipped with a PowerPC G3 or G4 CPU. This includes even the original Bondi Blue iMac. There is, however, one important exception—the first generation PowerBook G3, which was built on the original PowerBook 3400 chassis. In addition, Apple specifies a minimum of 128MB of RAM. If you don't plan to use Classic programs, you'll probably get away with 64MB of RAM; but it's highly unlikely you'll be able to avoid using such software, because it will take a while for most of the major programs to show up in Mac OS X trim. What's more, Mac OS X really does work better if you have 256MB of RAM or greater. You'll also want to allow 1.5GB of disk storage space for the installation. Apple includes Mac OS 9.2.1 or later in the package, so you won't have to buy a separate copy to use Classic.

TIP: *If you have a very large hard drive, you might want to consider making a separate partition for Mac OS X. Check the Mac OS X ReadMe that comes with the version you have, to find out about any partition limits, such as putting it on the first 8GB of a drive on Rev. A through Rev. D iMacs.*

- *Peripheral compatibility*—If your Mac has a non-Apple expansion card of any sort, such as a graphic card, SCSI accelerator card, or video capture card, contact the manufacturer about driver software that might be required for full compatibility with Mac OS X. Although the Classic feature lets you run older Mac software, it doesn't provide the hardware-level support you need for unsupported hardware.

- *Software compatibility*—Most older programs ought to run fine in the Classic mode under Mac OS X. You should contact the publishers directly, however, to be sure that the programs will run without a hitch. System extensions, for example, are not part of the Mac OS X architecture but might, within limits, work under Classic. However, programs that directly access the hardware, such as a CD writing program or hard disk formatter, will need an update to work properly—more than likely a Carbon version that's tuned to recognize Apple's updated hardware driver model.

- *Printer and serial devices*—Regular PostScript laser printers should work reasonably well under Mac OS X. Other printers, especially ink jets, will need driver updates to function with the new OS. Mac OS X printer drivers from such major companies as Canon, Epson, HP, and Lexmark are included with Mac OS X, but not all product lines are included. As far as other peripherals are concerned, in each case, you'll need to check with the manufacturer about compatibility. Apple Computer has provided tools to help developers make its products Mac OS X–aware, but how quickly this is done depends on each particular company, its priorities, and the amount of work required.

WARNING!   *Apple Computer doesn't officially support Macs or Mac OS clones upgraded from older PowerPC CPUs to G3s or G4s. If you decide to take the risk anyway and attempt to install Mac OS X on one of these unsupported models, you cannot depend on Apple for support. Be prepared to make a full backup of your data, in case you run into a disk-related problem or want to return to your previous Mac OS version. Some of the companies that make G3 and G4 upgrades promise to deliver Mac OS X support, but it won't come with Apple's blessings; you will have to depend on those companies to provide help if something goes wrong when you use the products.*

Chapter 2

Upgrading to Mac OS X

In Brief

All right, the time has come. Are you ready to install your new operating system? Mac OS X is a huge leap over previous versions of the Mac OS. As explained in Chapter 1, there is really no comparison under the hood. Many of the familiar elements are no longer present. If anything, the new operating system, because it is Unix-based, has more in common with high-end workstations that are used to power Web and network servers around the world.

Don't be put off by all this sophistication. Despite the complexity of the underlying software, Apple has gone the extra mile to simplify installation. However, don't be lulled into a sense of complacency by the ease of the process. A lot of complicated things are happening very, very fast to install the new operating system as quickly as possible without undue delay. During that time, the Mac OS X installer is copying literally thousands of new files to your Macintosh. It's not something to take lightly, and you should take a few precautions to make the process as seamless as possible.

Preparing for Mac OS X

Before you attempt to install Mac OS X, you should make sure that your Mac has been prepared for the installation. First, you should review Chapter 1 to see if your Mac can run the new operating system. Take the warnings about attempting an installation on unsupported hardware very seriously. Although it's possible to perform unsupported installations with the help of a shareware utility, such as Ryan Rempel's Unsupported UtilityX (see **http://eshop.macsales.com/OSXCenter/ framework.cfm?page=UnsupportedUtilityX.html** for more information), or a utility provided by a processor upgrade manufacturer, you should be guided by their recommendations and cautions.

Don't say I didn't warn you.

NOTE: *If you decide to take the chance and install Mac OS X on a Mac not supported for the installation, be guided by the instructions provided with the software you use, which are apt to change as Mac OS X itself is updated. The information provided in this book assumes you will be doing your installation on a Mac officially supported by Apple for Mac OS X.*

In the following pages, I cover the basics of getting ready for the installation. Once you're prepared, proceed to the "Immediate Solutions" section for step-by-step instructions that walk you through the entire installation process and let you know what to expect along the way.

Make Sure You Have Mac OS 9.1 or Later for Classic Applications

Despite the arrival of more Mac OS X software, many of the Mac OS programs you'll be running probably are of the older Classic variety; so, you'll need an installed copy of Mac OS 9 on your Mac. Fortunately, Apple included the Mac OS 9.2.1 CD as part of the Mac OS X 10.1 package. Feel confident that you can install it if necessary to use your older applications. You can place Mac OS 9.2.1 on the same disk volume as Mac OS X. If you choose to install it on a separate partition, be guided by the instructions later in this chapter in the section "Mac OS X: Hardware-Related Issues."

NOTE: *If you have Mac OS 9.1 installed, you aren't forced to upgrade to a later version for Classic to function. But the later versions of Mac OS 9 are more stable and offer better performance in the Classic environment, so you'll want to consider the upgrade seriously. In addition, Mac OS X will "suggest" you upgrade to a later version of Mac OS 9 the first time Classic runs.*

Check Your Hard Drive

During the installation process, the Mac OS X Installer has a lot of work to do. Whereas older versions of the Mac operating system generally consisted of hundreds of files, this time literally thousands of files (taking up nearly one gigabyte of storage space) are part of the agenda. All that work is done behind the scenes in minutes, which means your Mac and its disk storage system will be taxed to the limit to keep up.

As a result, you should make sure that the target drive for Mac OS X is working properly. Fortunately, this isn't hard to accomplish. Apple provides a free hard drive diagnostic and repair utility—Disk First Aid (see Figure 2.1)—in the Utilities folder of every Mac. This program, although not as full-featured as the commercial alternatives, should be able to do the job. Although it is true the Mac OS X Installer will also check the drive during the setup process, it doesn't hurt to run an extra verification.

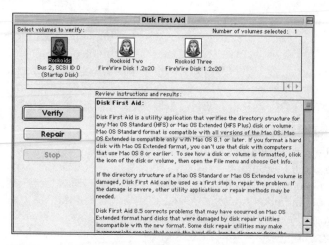

Figure 2.1   The best part of Disk First Aid is that it's free with every new Mac and included with every Mac OS installation.

NOTE: *One of the great features of Disk First Aid is its ability to repair directory damage to a startup drive without having to boot from a separate volume or system CD. Only Symantec's Norton Utilities (see below) can boast a similar capability.*

If you want to make doubly sure that your drive is in tip-top shape, however, you may want to look at one of these three commercial alternatives:

- *Norton Utilities*—This is the oldest existing hard drive utility package. The latest versions of the Disk Doctor application (see Figure 2.2) are, like Disk First Aid, capable of repairing drive directory problems on a startup disk. This ability saves trips to the program CD except when the startup drive won't boot or when you wish to optimize it. Norton Utilities, by the way, is also included as part of Norton SystemWorks.

NOTE: *At the time this book went to press, Symantec was in the process of developing a version of Norton Utilities that would run from the Mac OS X environment, so check the company's Web site for updates. However, Norton Utilities 6 was designed to examine problems with a drive running Mac OS X as long as you boot from the Norton Utilities CD or a drive running Mac OS 9.x.*

- *TechTool Pro*—MicroMat's upstart utility application (see Figure 2.3) performs many of the same tasks as Norton Utilities, plus the application can run an extensive set of hardware checks on your Macintosh, including several levels of RAM tests. In

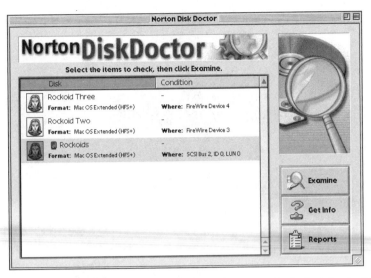

Figure 2.2   Norton Disk Doctor provides a far more comprehensive level of disk repairs than Disk First Aid.

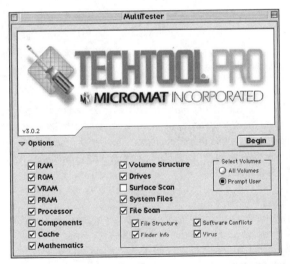

Figure 2.3   You can use TechTool Pro 3 to check a hard drive for directory damage prior to the Mac OS X installation.

addition, beginning with version 3, virus protection capability is part of the package. A Mac OS X derivative of TechTool Pro called Drive 10 (see Figure 2.4) is fully compatible with the new operating system, but must be run after booting from another drive or the application's CD to fix problems.

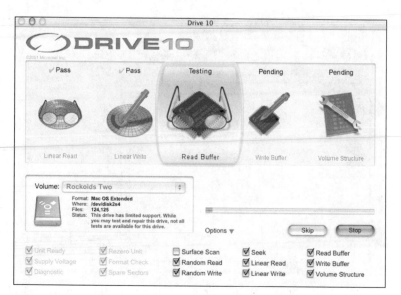

Figure 2.4   MicroMat's Drive 10 is a single-purpose utility designed to check
and fix directory problems on your Mac's hard drive.

NOTE: *A limited-feature version of TechTool Pro—TechTool Deluxe—is provided under Apple's
AppleCare extended service policy. However, that particular version of the program doesn't offer
disk drive maintenance, nor does it offer virus protection.*

**WARNING!   TechTool Pro is supported only under Classic Mac OS versions; it cannot
repair directory problems on the startup drive, so you have to boot from the program's
CD or another startup volume to handle those problems. However, the publisher
assures me that current versions of TechTool Pro 3 can fix directory problems on a
drive on which Mac OS X is installed.**

TIP: *Both Norton Utilities and Drive 10 are capable of doing surface scans of your hard drive
(the option is to check for defective media in Norton Utilities). Whereas the scanning process
takes longer, it will identify media-related problems that might present problems in copying
data to the drive. If you do see a media-related error (bad blocks, for example), you will want
to back up and reformat the drive before proceeding.*

- *DiskWarrior*—Reviewers call Alsoft's DiskWarrior (see Figure
  2.5) a "one-trick pony" because it's limited to checking and
  replacing hard drive directories. However, it does that task
  extraordinarily well. Rather than just fixing damage found in a
  hard drive's directory, it prepares a new, optimized directory,

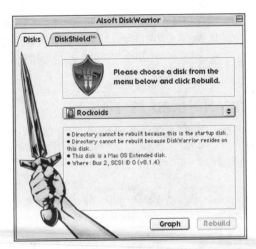

Figure 2.5   DiskWarrior performs its lone function so well that it merits a
place in any Mac user's software library.

delivering the promise of speedier performance. You need to boot
from the CD or another volume to rebuild a drive's directory.

NOTE: *A Mac OS X version of DiskWarrior was under development when this book was written.*

**WARNING!   You should try to restrict installation of Mac OS X to a hard drive
formatted with Apple's Drive Setup. The installation makes major changes to the file
structure, and although third-party disk formatting tools might be just fine, the safest
course is to stick with the tried-and-true. If Apple's disk formatter won't work with
your drive (and it doesn't support many third-party SCSI devices), you should check
with the manufacturer of the formatting utility you're using for compatibility information. At the time this book was written, the folks at FWB, publishers of Hard Disk
ToolKit, had not yet delivered a compatible version of their hard drive formatting
application.**

Back Up Your Data

Backup chores tend to be put off until the next day, but it is super-
critical for any operating system installation. The most effective
backup is complete, covering all your data. If you have backups of
all your applications (such as the original CDs) and your original
System Install or System Restore disks for your Mac, you can, as a
time-saver, restrict the backup to the documents you've created with
your software, along with critical program settings, such as your
Internet preferences.

However, having your entire drive backed up on a single set of disks is far more convenient, and it makes the process of restoring your files much easier. I cover the subject of backups in more detail in Chapter 17.

Mac OS X: Hardware-Related Issues

You should consider some hardware issues and strategy suggestions before proceeding with the installation. Doing so will avoid problems and confusing performance later on.

NOTE: *This information is based on the release notes for Mac OS X 10.1. As Apple updates its operating system, some of the limitations are apt to be addressed, and perhaps new ones will appear.*

Here's a list of primary concerns:

- *Firmware*—You should make sure firmware is current. Many Macs produced since the summer of 1998 have firmware (a boot ROM) that can be upgraded by software. Because the updates enhance the boot process and stability of your Mac, you'll want to stay current for the best experience with your new operating system. The Mac OS X installer disk includes a selection of firmware updates for various Macs, but you'll also want to check Apple's support Web site (**www.info.apple.com/support/ downloads.html**) to be sure that the firmware on your computer is up to date.

NOTE: *Recent Apple firmware updates have also been known to prevent use of some third-party RAM in your Mac. Apple's reasoning is that the memory is out of spec and may cause performance problems or frequent system crashes. If you run a firmware update, and some of your memory isn't recognized, you'll want to contact the vendor about a replacement (most will replace memory disabled as a result of this update).*

- *Beige PowerMac G3, PowerBook G3 (non-USB versions), and Rev A through D iMac (those with pop-up CD trays)*—For these models, if you choose to divide your hard drive into multiple partitions or volumes, make sure that the Mac OS X installation is performed on the first 8GB of the drive (it will appear first in your list of available volumes in the Mac OS X installer).

NOTE: *It is perfectly possible to install Mac OS X on a drive with a single partition and have it coexist with Mac OS 9.2.1. In fact, Apple ships all its new Macs this way. Partitioning a drive can be done for protection, as a way to start your Mac if the other partition goes down, or just to more easily organize the contents of your drive. However, it's not required.*

- *FireWire and USB drives*—Sorry, such an installation isn't supported. Although most FireWire drives—from such companies as Evergreen Technologies, LaCie, Maxtor, SmartDisk, and others—will work just fine under Mac OS X; don't think of attempting to use them for the new operating system. Apple says it won't support such an installation, which means if something goes wrong, you'll have to sort it out. At worst, your Mac will simply not boot from any of these drives.

- *Third-party SCSI cards*—If you can't boot your Mac after Mac OS X is installed, place a drive or terminator on one of the ports of your third-party SCSI card.

WARNING! Check your card maker's support Web site for information about compatibility between your SCSI card and Mac OS X. You may need to upgrade software, flash ROM, or a ROM chip, or perhaps even replace the card to avoid trouble with your new operating system. For example, Adaptec is not supporting many of its older cards with Mac OS X, and as this book was written, Orange Micro's SCSI cards weren't compatible, although an update was under development.

- *AirPort*—Apple's fancy wireless networking hardware works fine under Mac OS X, and the Mac OS 10.1 update added network and base station administration tools. But you can only set up a direct computer-to-computer AirPort network by upgrading to AirPort 2.0 or later. If you're using a third-party 802.11b wireless networking card, such as the Asante AeroLAN or the Farallon (now Proxim) SkyLINE, check with the manufacturer about updated drivers for Mac OS X.

- *Third-party graphics cards*—Some third-party graphics cards aren't supported. Mac OS X only works with graphics chips and cards from ATI, IX Micro, and NVIDIA, all of which have supplied products for a number of Macs over the years. It's up to manufacturers of graphics cards such as Formac and any other entrants into this arena to supply Mac OS X–compatible drivers for their own products. With the departure of 3dfx Interactive from the scene in late 2000, it's not at all certain when, if ever, its products will become compatible, although a small number of third-party developers were trying to deliver updated drivers.

- *Processor upgrade cards*—Again, it's the responsibility of the manufacturers of these products to make a processor card function. Some of these products use special software to activate a G3's or G4's backside cache. Even if they worked otherwise, there might be a severe performance penalty. However, most existing products from such makers as PowerLogix, Sonnet Technology, and XLR8 do work fine under Mac OS X, although software updates may be necessary. In addition, the Sonnet processor cards designed for the Blue & White Power Mac G3 line do not require software.

NOTE: *Sonnet has included support for Newer Technology MAXpowr products in its Mac OS X–compatible software updates. Also bear in mind that if you plan to boot your Mac under Mac OS 9.2.1, you should install the traditional Mac OS version of such software so your processor card runs at full efficiency in both environments.*

Immediate Solutions

Preparing for Mac OS X

Before you install Mac OS X, you'll need to make a few decisions about how to proceed:

- *Determine where to install*—You can install Mac OS X on the same drive partition as Mac OS 9 or on a separate partition. Be guided by the instructions in the previous section about partitioning and hard drive support on certain Macs. If you plan to install on a separate partition, the Mac OS X installer can handle the job of erasing the partition for you.

- *Install Mac OS 9.2 or later*—If you need to run Classic applications, you should install the Classic system first before proceeding with Mac OS X. That way, if something goes wrong with the Mac OS X installation, you can still return to the older operating system to remove Mac OS X files or just to use your Mac until you decide to reinstall the new system. A copy of the installation CD comes with Mac OS X at no charge with the shipping package.

- *Copy Internet and networking setups*—During the installation of the Mac OS X, you'll need to enter information manually to get access to a local network or the Internet. This information is not cataloged during the Mac OS X installation process. You'll then need to copy all these settings from the Modem, Internet (see Figure 2.6), Remote Access, and TCP/IP control panels.

NOTE: *If you are an EarthLink member, you can use the Mac OS X Setup Assistant to pick up your account settings.*

TIP: *You can quickly capture these settings with a screenshot. To take a picture of just the Control Panel window (rather than the entire screen), press Command+Shift+4+Caps Lock. Then, click on the window that you want to capture to complete the action. You'll hear the sound of a shutter clicking in confirmation. Each file will be identified by the name Picture plus the number (1, 2, and so on). You can then open these files in SimpleText and print them, so you'll have a copy to refer to when needed for Mac OS X's Setup Assistant.*

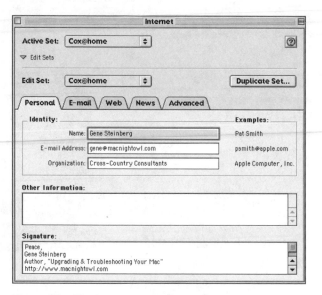

Figure 2.6   The Internet control panel has several tabs you need to check to pick up all your configuration information.

Installing Mac OS X

Now that you're ready to proceed, these instructions will take you through the entire installation process, including the actual restart:

NOTE: *These instructions are based on the installer screens used for Mac OS X 10.1. As the operating system is updated, the setup dialog boxes may change, but your basic choices will be essentially the same as described here.*

---

1. Insert the Mac OS X CD into your Mac's drive.

2. Restart your Mac, holding down the C key, so that it boots from the CD. After you restart, the Installer will take several minutes to begin, so be patient. During each step of the process, you'll have to click a button or click a checkbox or pop-up menu to make a choice before proceeding. Therefore, read the onscreen instructions carefully, in case they've changed from those present when this book was written.

NOTE: *If you just double-click the Installer from Mac OS 9.2.1 or an earlier version of Mac OS X, it will put up a prompt that lets you click the Restart button to automatically restart from the installer CD. There's no other way to do the installation.*

---

3. The first screen that appears allows you to select the default language kit used for the installation. You're not restricted to English. After you've made your selection, click Continue to proceed.

NOTE: *Because the Mac OS X Installer takes over a Mac during the setup process, I could not capture illustrations of the process in the usual way. If you follow the steps precisely as described, however, you'll get through the process like a champ.*

---

4. The Welcome screen appears. This is just a message telling you to get ready for the main event. Click Continue to move on to the next step in the process.

5. The Important Information screen appears. You should consult this ReadMe file to see if you must consider any factors before proceeding with the installation. Spend a few moments reading this document. You'll see for the first time the ultra-clear text display afforded by Mac OS X. After you're finished reading the document, click Continue to proceed, or click Go Back to review the previous screen.

6. The next screen shows the Software License Agreement. This is a fairly standard license agreement covering Mac OS X. Click Continue after reviewing the information. You'll see a dialog box in which you must click the Agree button and accept the agreement to continue with the installation; if you click Disagree, you'll end the process then and there. You have only two alternatives. Click Agree to continue.

7. The Select A Destination screen appears, showing the available drive volumes. Click the icon representing the drive on which you want to place Mac OS X. Even FireWire drives will be shown, but you cannot, of course, install Mac OS X on those (they'll be grayed out if you select one of them). You also have another option: If the volume has no other data on it, or has only data you no longer need, you can click the Erase Destination And Format As checkbox to format the drive and then select the file format from the pop-up window. Should you take this route, keep the default file system—Mac OS Extended (also known as HFS+)—because it will provide maximum compatibility with Mac OS 9.2.1. Click Continue after your destination and disk-formatting options are selected.

NOTE: *The second option, Unix File System (UFS), is useful only if you plan to work primarily in the Mac OS X environment or plan to do application development. You cannot run Mac OS 9.2.1 from a UFS partition, nor will the older Mac OS recognize such a partition.*

WARNING!   Formatting a hard drive can be a destructive process. If you select that option, all the data on the selected volume will be wiped out with little or no chance of recovery. Be certain that's the decision you want to make—there's no going back.

TIP: *If you cannot locate the right startup volume on the Select A Destination screen, go to the Installer application window and quit the Installer so you can cancel the process and reboot your Mac. You should then verify that the drive on which you want to install Mac OS X is indeed available. After everything has been rechecked, you can attempt installation again by restarting from the CD.*

---

8. The Easy Install screen appears. If you click Customize, you'll see a dialog box where only two packages cannot be un-checked: Base System and Essential System Software. For maximum networking compatibility, and for running Unix applications with the terminal application, you'll also want to select BSD Subsystem. The Additional Printer Drivers option is useful to provide support for a variety of ink jet and laser printers. You can, however, save storage space on your hard drive if you uncheck the extra language options, if you do not intend to use those language systems on your Mac.

NOTE: *If you add up the space required by the four components of Mac OS X's installation, you'll find the total isn't quite 1.5GB. Where does Apple get the 1.5GB figure? Simple. Mac OS X needs elbow room for movement, copying files, and virtual memory storage space. It uses a large virtual memory file to provide its extraordinary memory management.*

After the installation process begins, the hard drive on which Mac OS X is to be installed is examined for drive directory issues, and minor problems are repaired. If everything is all right, the installation proceeds with several status messages and a progress bar estimating the amount of time left. You should expect installation to take anywhere from 15 minutes to half an hour, depending on the speed of your Mac's processor, the speed of your CD (or DVD) drive, and the speed of your hard drive. When the installation is complete, your Mac will restart automatically under its new operating system version. Then, you'll experience a brief multimedia presentation, and you'll be guided through the Setup Assistant, where you'll be asked to make some very basic system settings to get Mac OS X up and running to your satisfaction. These steps include registering your copy of Mac OS X, optionally registering Apple's iTools feature, plus setting up your Mac for Internet access. I cover these and other settings in Chapter 3.

Related solutions:	Found on page:
Configuring the Setup Assistant	40
Configuring System Preferences Under Mac OS X	44

Chapter 3

Mac OS X User Preferences

In Brief

Once your Mac OS X installation hits the finish line, your Mac will restart. As soon as the new Mac desktop appears, you'll be introduced to a pleasant multimedia presentation, providing a musical introduction to the new operating system, followed by the appearance of Apple's Setup Assistant. You use the Setup Assistant to register Mac OS X with Apple, and then configure a basic set of user and networking settings for Mac OS X. Typical of a Unix-based operating system, Mac OS X is designed for multiple users, allowing each person who works on the Mac to have a different level of access. If you're upgrading from Mac OS 9 or later, you'll find that this concept is nothing new. In almost every installation, more than one person is using a Mac. Even in a home setup, the family computer may be used by parents and children, each of whom may have a different set of requirements—and an equally diverse need to restrict certain elements of user access. (I cover the subject of configuring your Mac to work in such an environment in much more detail in Chapter 6.)

This chapter first discusses the various preference settings you'll make right after installing Mac OS X using the Setup Assistant. In large part, these settings cover access to your Mac by you as administrator of the system and by other users to whom you will grant access. You'll also make basic network setups, including your Mac's network name and various types of Internet access. In addition, time zone adjustments are necessary so that your Mac will put the correct time on your documents and email messages.

Control Panel Settings: A Mixture of the Old and New

After you've completed the basic setups, you can use your Mac and your favorite programs without altering anything further. However, to get the optimum performance from your computer, you'll also want to tackle the preference panels. Rather than offer each item as a separate control panel, Mac OS X merges them all into a single System Preferences application. This arrangement greatly simplifies the setup process, because you don't have to hunt down multiple applications from the Control Panel's submenu in the Apple menu or directly from that folder to enter the settings you want. For convenience, the preference panels are divided into four distinct categories: Personal, Hardware, Internet & Network, and System.

NOTE: *Although the Apple menu is still present, it is a rather different breed from the one with which you're familiar from the Classic Mac OS. For one thing, it replaces the functions of the Finder's Special menu, and it adds a few elements from the original version. I cover that subject in more detail in Chapter 4.*

In some ways, the new design is a throwback to the way system setups existed under older versions of the Mac operating system prior to System 7. Even though control panels were separate items then, they all displayed in a single window. Apple has apparently taken the simplicity of this design to heart, except for making the icons a horizontal Finder-like display rather than the vertical array of icons you clicked to get to a particular setting.

Click an icon to bring up the labeled function, which will launch essentially as a separate application within the Preferences window. You'll see how the System Preferences application is set up in the "Immediate Solutions" section of this chapter.

NOTE: *Like the Classic Mac OS's Control Panels, the System Preferences application is open to third parties to configure their software. If you install a program that uses System Preferences, such as ASM or TinkerTool (two shareware utilities that enhance system setups), they will appear in a new System Preferences category called Other.*

Before I discuss the various preference settings, let's look at some new Finder-level features of Mac OS X. The rest are explained in Chapter 4. Unlike previous Mac OS versions, you don't click a square box to close, minimize, or maximize Finder windows. Instead, three separate traffic-light-colored buttons mounted at the left provide these functions:

- *Red ("X" symbol)*—Close the window. Clicking this button may or may not quit the application (in most cases, it won't).

- *Yellow ("–" symbol)*—Minimize the window. When you click this button, the window is collapsed and appears as an icon on the Dock.

- *Green ("+" symbol)*—Maximize the window. This command expands the window to the largest size necessary to encompass its contents, limited only by the size of your Mac's display.

NOTE: *When you pass your mouse over any of these buttons, you'll see a symbol inside representing its function. If you choose the Graphite interface as a General preference, as described in the "Setting General Preferences" section later in this chapter, the button colors will all switch to the same color (graphite), but the symbols will still appear whenever the mouse is brought to the vicinity of these buttons.*

Additionally, you no longer quit a Mac OS X application from the File menu. Apple Computer decided to move that function to the Application menu (the one in bold at the left end of the menu bar, next to the Apple menu).

Selecting Printers Without a Chooser

In every version of the Mac operating system prior to Mac OS X, you used a somewhat clumsy little application—the Chooser (see Figure 3.1)—to both select a printer and connect to a Mac or PC with the proper networking software installed across a network.

TIP: *To learn more about networking Macs and Windows-based PCs, check out a book that I wrote with networking guru Pieter Paulson,* The Windows 2000 Mac Support Little Black Book. *This fairly technical instruction book covers networking Macs with Windows NT servers and Windows 2000 servers.*

For Mac OS X, Apple has moved to a more conventional solution called Print Center. As you will learn later in this chapter, this application can ferret out the printers on your network or directly connected to your Mac. You can then select the ones you want to use,

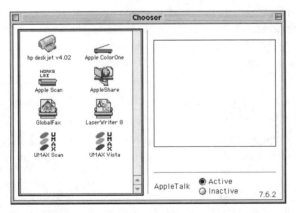

Figure 3.1   The venerable (and clunky) Apple Chooser is now history.

configure custom features, and monitor and adjust your print queue while printing is in progress (in a fashion similar to the Desktop printer or regular PrintMonitor applications).

One big advantage over the older Chooser is that Print Center can search for any available printer, even if it's on a USB port or accessible via TCP/IP across the Internet, without having to fiddle with multiple network adjustments other than turning to AppleTalk (for a network printer). What's more, if you have a USB printer connected to your Mac and the correct drivers installed, Print Center automatically recognizes the device—no extra setup is needed. Once all your printers are configured, you can use the regular Page Setup and Print dialog boxes to switch among the available printers.

No more awkward visits to the Chooser, at least for Mac OS X applications. If you're using a Classic application, however, you'll still have to select your printer the old-fashioned way, in the Chooser. When a document is being printed, PrintMonitor (or the print driver's custom print window) will appear to show its progress.

NOTE: *You will also have to install the Classic version of the driver software for your printer if you intend to use a Classic application. The Mac OS X printer drivers don't function in the Classic user environment.*

**3. Mac OS X
User Preferences**

Immediate Solutions

Configuring the Setup Assistant

As you go through the setup screens in the Setup Assistant, check the instructions carefully. They will change from time to time as Apple updates Mac OS X. As you progress through the setup process, click the right arrow at lower right to move to the next setup screen, and click the back or left arrow to review or change a previous setting. At the top left of the screen, you'll see the title of the setup category you've entered.

WARNING!   After the Setup Assistant runs during the initial Mac OS X configuration process, it is no longer functional. From here on, you need to run System Preferences to configure your Mac; except for the initial registration process, you can do all the same settings, and much more, as you'll see later in this chapter.

The introduction will consist of a short multimedia presentation, punctuated by music with a nice beat (as the music reviewers are apt to say), but you don't need to dismiss it. Soon, you'll see the message, "We'll have you up and running in no time." Follow these steps:

NOTE: Aside from the initial registration of Mac OS X, all user settings you make now can be changed in the System Preferences application as needed. Nothing is set in stone.

1. *Welcome*—When you see the Welcome screen, select the country in which you're located from the list. Click Show All to see more options. After you've checked the appropriate country, click Continue.

2. *Registration Information*—There are several screens where you will enter the information needed to register your product with Apple Computer. The first screen asks for your name, address, phone number, email address, and so forth. The next screen inquires about some simple marketing information (you don't have to answer). Then, click Continue to receive an acknowledgement that your registration information has been recorded and will be sent to Apple when you have connected to the Internet.

NOTE: *You won't have to toil through the registration process again if you reinstall Mac OS X, unless you've removed the original installed files (in other words, only if you're doing a clean installation).*

3. *Create Your Account*—Enter your username as owner or administrator of the Mac. For convenience, press the Tab key to move to the next text field; press Shift+Tab to return to the previous field. You also need to enter a short name or nickname for yourself containing eight lowercase characters; when you enter that text field, Mac OS X's Setup Assistant will create a shortened version of your name by default, but feel free to change it. In the next three text fields, enter a password, reconfirm your password, and enter a password hint—a word or phrase that will remind you of the password in case you forget it.

NOTE: *If you are using your Mac in a home or small office, a secure password probably doesn't matter. However, if you want the utmost in security, try to use what is considered a strong password: a password that consists of random numbers and mixed upper- and lowercase letters so that it cannot easily be guessed by anyone who might try to break into your computer. An example is 0Bfusc8. However, you should pick a password that is easy for you to remember (or at least write it down and put it in a safe place).*

4. *Get Internet Ready*—After you've created a username and password, you'll move on to a setup screen where you can configure your Mac for Internet access. Click the button to indicate whether you already have an ISP or want Apple to set you up with an EarthLink account or retrieve your EarthLink settings from its servers. Assuming you are already connected and select the option to add your existing settings, you'll have the following options:

NOTE: *This particular range of settings can be separately duplicated in the Network preference panel later on, but doing so now is simpler, because you get the proper range of dialog boxes you need depending on the type of connection you specify. On new Macs with Mac OS X installed, you will usually find EarthLink sign-up software in the Utilities folder; otherwise you would need to install a copy from EarthLink's Web site or from an installation CD.*

- *Telephone Modem*—This option is for a standard, garden-variety, dial-up connection to an ISP. When you check this option and click Continue, you'll be greeted with a Your Internet Connection screen where you enter the basic login information required to connect to your ISP.

3. Mac OS X User Preferences

NOTE: *The Setup Assistant will not work with AOL or CompuServe 2000 because their client software must be separately configured to access these services. To use their software for direct dial-up connections, you'll have to get the Mac OS X–savvy versions or run the Classic software atop another ISP hookup.*

- *Local Area Network*—If you log on to the Internet via your local area network (perhaps using a server for the connection), choose this option. In the next screen you see, enter your network setup information.

- *Cable Modem*—This setting is used for high-speed Internet provided by a cable service. Click Continue to see a setup screen where you enter your setup information. You might have to put in a DHCP client ID number to allow your cable modem to connect, or PPP over Ethernet (PPPoE) settings, as required.

- *DSL Modem*—Another connection option for high-speed Internet service is accessing the Digital Subscriber Line broadband option. Again, if you click Continue after selecting this option, a setup screen will appear for you to enter the required information.

NOTE: *You'll need to check with your ISP for the specific settings you need, if you haven't recorded them from a setup book or your Mac OS 9.x installation.*

- *AirPort*—When you use Apple's AirPort wireless networking system, click this option to access the wireless network.

NOTE: *Because AirPort is based on an international standard known as 801.11b, or Wi-Fi for short, you can use your Mac's AirPort system to connect to a number of third-party wireless devices, which greatly increases your flexibility when it comes to connecting to a Mac or cross-platform network.*

5. *Get iTools*—One of Apple's better ideas to move the platform beyond the box is iTools, a set of special features at the Apple Web site that enhances the user experience. In this settings screen, choose whether you want to create an iTools account or use the one you already have, by entering the appropriate information.

NOTE: *If you need to set up a new iTools account, be sure your Mac has been set up to connect to your ISP so that Apple's Web site can be checked to establish your account and make sure your username hasn't already been taken (in which case you'll be given a chance to try a different one).*

6. *Now You're Ready To Connect*—Click Continue to send your registration to Apple via your ISP and do the next stage of setups for your Mac. A progress screen indicates that you're connecting to Apple. Once you're done, continue to the next screen to perform the last setups.

7. *Set Up Mail*—Mac OS X includes a brand new email application called Mail that provides speed and reasonably powerful mail-handling features. Indicate whether you want to use your iTools account or choose the option Add My Existing E-mail Account. The setup screen will ask for your email address, incoming mail server, account type (POP or IMAP), user account ID, password, and outgoing mail server. These settings are the same ones you've always used for your email.

NOTE: *Don't have the settings? If you didn't follow my suggestions in Chapter 2 to copy your ISP settings from your Classic Mac OS, you'll need to refer to the documentation provided by your ISP or just ignore this setting right now. You can return to it later under the System Preferences application.*

8. *Select Time Zone*—In order for such things as your email and documents to display the proper time, you first need to click and move the slider in the map until it points to the correct time zone. Then, choose the time zone or city nearest you from the pop-up menu if a special time setting is required (such as in Arizona, which doesn't observe daylight savings time).

9. *Thank You*—This final setup screen gives you one last chance to recheck all the entries you've made before they are stored in Mac OS X. You can use the back arrow to return to any setting and change it now. If you accept the setup, click the Go button to move on.

NOTE: *Once again, your setups aren't set in stone. Feel free at any time to change everything from networking to passwords in the System Preferences application. I explain how later in this chapter.*

10. *Logging In*—Once you're done, your Mac will proceed through the login process and finish the startup process. When you first see the Mac OS X desktop (see Figure 3.2), you'll feel for a moment as if you've visited an alien environment. The new Aqua interface has familiar elements, but there are unfamiliar elements as well. In the next few chapters, I cover every aspect of the revised look of the Mac OS. For now, get comfortable, and get ready to explore the system setup and printer setup options.

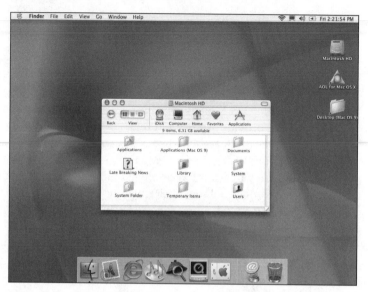

Figure 3.2   Your first exposure to Mac OS X, with your computer already given a name, based on your user name.

NOTE: *This is the last time you'll see the Setup Assistant under Mac OS X, unless you want to reinstall the operating system on a different volume. If you launch the application again (it's located in a folder called Core Services, within the folder path System>Library), you'll be reminded that settings are made in the System Preferences application (unless your registration information hasn't been sent to Apple, in which case it will give you a chance to review the information).*

Related solutions:	*Found on page:*
Preparing for Mac OS X	29
Setting Up Multiple-User Access	133

Setting System Preferences Under Mac OS X

Once you've configured your basic Mac settings with the Setup Assistant, you can compute without having to change any other settings. However, if you want to make adjustments to the look and feel of your Mac, use the System Preferences application (see Figure 3.3).

You'll find the System Preferences application on the Dock when you've done a normal installation of Mac OS X. If for some reason the

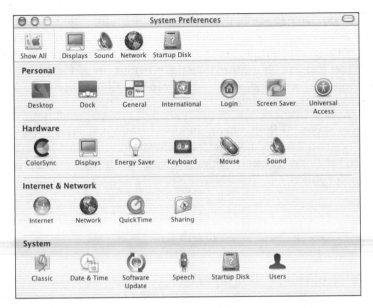

Figure 3.3   Click an icon to access a specific system setting.

program isn't where you expect it to be, click the Applications button on the Finder's Toolbar (or use the same command in the Apple menu) to locate and launch the application.

TIP: *If a program isn't already on the Dock, drag its icon to the left side, and the Dock will expand to accommodate it; icon sizes will be reduced as needed, should the Dock expand to the ends of your screen. Applications go on the left, and documents appear at the right, separated by a white vertical line. Don't worry if you miss the separator line—sometimes you have to glance twice to notice it.*

To switch from one program setting pane to the next, click the icon you want. If the icon isn't shown in the application's toolbar, click Show All to see the entire lineup. After making your settings, press Command+Q to quit the program. Depending on the settings you make, such as ones involving your network or ISP connection, you may see an additional confirmation dialog box with a Save button you have to click to store your settings. Some system-critical functions can be secured by clicking the padlock, in which case only users granted "administrator" status will be able to change those settings after entering the correct username and password.

NOTE: *If you've used previous versions of the Mac operating system, you'll find some of these preferences are quite familiar. Aside from the distinctive Aqua interface, they work pretty much the same as in the previous versions.*

You do not have to set all the settings in the Preferences application right now. You can try each one for size, or experiment with one setting without changing any of the others. If the setting isn't what you like, you can quickly restore it to the previous one. In addition, depending on your specific Mac setup, you may find additional preference components to adjust.

Although System Preferences components are divided into categories, I've opted to put them in alphabetical order so that you can easily find the one you want without having to concern yourself over what category it's in.

3. Mac OS X
User Preferences

TIP: To quickly bring up the settings pane you want, click the application's View menu and choose from the pop-up menu. That's the way I do it.

Setting Classic Preferences

The Classic mode lets you use traditional Mac OS applications by opening the older version of the operating system within Mac OS X. In a sense, it's similar to running Windows applications on a Mac using Connectix Virtual PC. The major difference is that the Classic mode runs applications transparently, without inheriting the Aqua interface, using the Mac OS X Finder. What's more, performance is better than any of the emulation programs, because you're not emulating a foreign processor.

NOTE: A Mac OS 9.2.1 or later CD-ROM comes with your Mac OS X 10.1 package. In order for you to use the Classic environment, you need to install the older system if you're not already using it. The earliest Classic OS you can install is 9.1, but later versions offer better compatibility and performance.

The Classic preferences panel (see Figure 3.4) lets you specify the startup volume for the Classic operating system, which is especially important if you have more that one volume with a System Folder installed. If your Mac has Mac OS 9.1 or later on another hard disk (or partition), you'll see the drive's name displayed in the list (drives without a 9.1 or later partition will be grayed out). You can click the disk from which you want to run the Mac in Classic mode, and then specify whether you want to have the Classic environment automatically start when you boot (log into) your Mac. This is not an essential selection unless you want to begin using Classic applications without having to wait for Classic to boot. You can also choose Restart or Force Quit

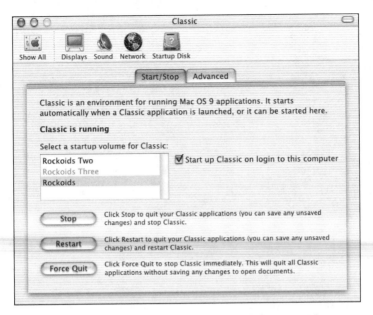

Figure 3.4   Choose your startup disk for Classic mode on this screen.

Classic. The Advanced preference panel is used to configure additional options, such as whether to rebuild the Classic Mac OS system's desktop, restart with extensions off, or bring up Extensions Manager when Classic opens. (I cover this subject in more detail in Chapter 15.)

TIP: *If a preference panel is already open, you can access another panel by its icon on the top of the screen; if that icon isn't there, click the Show All button to see the rest of the list.*

Setting ColorSync Preferences

Apple's ColorSync technology is tightly integrated into Mac OS X. You can use this settings pane (see Figure 3.5) to choose a ColorSync profile for input devices (such as a scanner), your Mac's display, output devices (a printer), or a proofing device. Click the pop-up menu to select the profile you want. To choose the color management method (CMM), click that tab in the ColorSync pane. The final tab is designed strictly for custom color workflow settings that may be required when you are working in an art department or prepress establishment.

NOTE: *Many manufacturers of input and output peripherals provide their own ColorSync profiles. If one didn't come with a particular device, ask the manufacturer how one might be obtained or whether an existing ColorSync profile will do.*

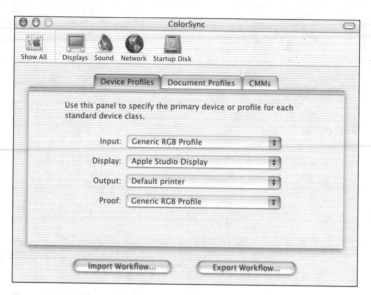

Figure 3.5   Select a ColorSync profile in this pane.

Setting Date & Time Preferences

In effect, the settings you create here (see Figure 3.6) mirror the ones you've already configured in the Setup Assistant. However, these settings have a new wrinkle. At the bottom left of the settings screen, you'll notice a button labeled Click The Lock To Prevent Further Changes. You can protect this panel and any other panel with a padlock icon so that only users with administrator's permissions can access them.

TIP: If you plan to access a particular preference panel often, drag its icon to the top of the System Preferences window.

You can access any of the four settings categories by clicking on the appropriate tab:

- The first tab (Date & Time) and the second (Time Zone) offer the same settings you already performed in the Setup Assistant. You can leave them alone or make further adjustments now.

- The third tab—Network Time (see Figure 3.7)—allows you to have your Mac's clock synchronized to another computer on your network or to an Internet-based NTP time server (such as Apple's, which is offered by default). The latter setting requires that you connect to the Internet to adjust the time, but when it's done, both the date and time will be configured automatically as needed.

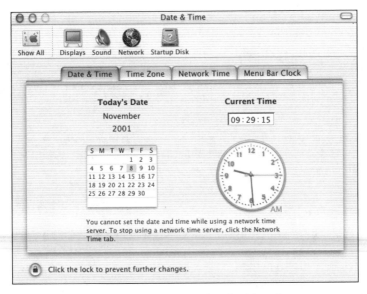

Figure 3.6   Make your various time-related settings here.

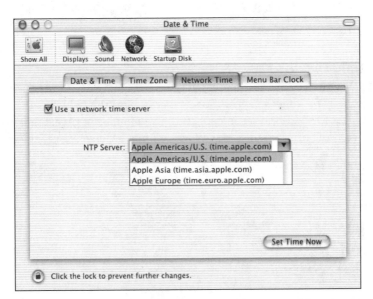

Figure 3.7   You can synchronize your Mac's clock via a network server.

NOTE: *If you check Use A Network Time Server, Mac OS X will attempt to contact the server during the boot process to synchronize the clock. The only downside is that the boot process will be slower if you don't have a full-time ISP hookup or access to a time server on your own network. In addition, some network firewalls may prevent access to an Internet-based time server unless specially configured.*

• The final tab—Menu Bar Clock—allows you to specify whether you want to show the clock in the menu bar (it's on by default) and whether you want it to display seconds, AM/PM, the date of the week, or flashing time separators. The settings are identical to those available under the Classic Mac OS, except for the inability to change the font and size of the menu bar clock's display.

TIP: *If you're not happy with the limitations of Apple's menu bar clock, check for a shareware alternative. One resource is **VersionTracker.com**, a popular Web site that includes information about software plus links to download sites.*

Setting Desktop Preferences

Don't like the default Aqua or ocean-blue background for Mac OS X? The Desktop preferences panel (shown in Figure 3.8) can be used to change it to your liking. I'll cover this subject in more detail in Chapter 5.

Related solution:	*Found on page:*
Setting Desktop Preferences	118

Setting Display Preferences

The Display screen (see Figure 3.9) is used to configure the size (resolution) of the images on your Mac's display and the color depth setting. The Resolutions setting specifies the number of pixels that are shown on your Mac's display. When you make this adjustment, you

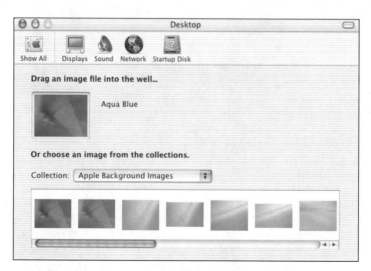

Figure 3.8   Pick another desktop backdrop from Apple's collection or yours.

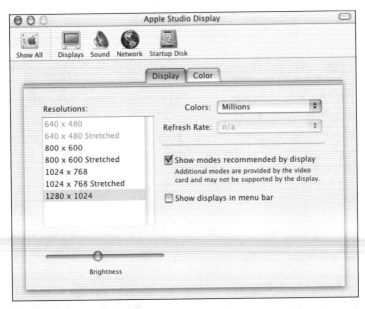

Figure 3.9   Choose your Mac's display preferences on this setup screen.

should weigh the range of your Mac's desktop against the clarity of the items on it. To change resolution, click the setting you want.

NOTE: *On some Macs, you can configure contrast and brightness settings from the Display pane; on others, the settings will be grayed out. iMacs and some models equipped with an Apple display also have a tab labeled Geometry, where you can make sure your display's image is as wide as possible and that the shapes are straight and true.*

To change color depth, click the Colors pop-up menu. For most purposes, the difference between thousands and millions is slight. But if you do graphics work, configure your Mac for the latter (unless you have a Mac with a slower graphics processor, such as a first-generation iMac, where the thousands setting will deliver noticeably better graphics performance).

NOTE: *Click the checkbox to put a display system menu in your Mac's menu bar.*

The Show Modes Recommended By Display checkbox restricts settings to those that the operating system expects your monitor to support. But if you uncheck it, you might gain additional choices, with which you can experiment (don't be concerned—if you pick one that can't be used, your Mac will revert within a few seconds to the previous setting).

Click the Color tab (see Figure 3.10) to adjust the color balance or calibration of your display. These settings take advantage of Apple's ColorSync technology so that your display more nearly matches the color balance of your printer or other output device.

The settings on the Color tab are pretty much identical to those present in Mac OS 9.1 or later:

1. To establish a color profile for your Mac's monitor, select the model display you have or choose a generic profile from the Display Profile scrolling list. Then, click the Calibrate button. Apple's Display Calibrator Assistant (see Figure 3.11) will be launched.

NOTE: You can also find the Display Calibrator Assistant application in the Utilities folder, inside the Applications folder, if you want to access it directly and bypass System Preferences.

---

2. Before proceeding, take a quick look at the introductory text in the Assistant's dialog box. For the most accurate color calibration, click the Expert Mode checkbox, if it's not already selected. Click the right (forward) arrow to proceed, and the left (back) arrow to review a setting. When you click the right arrow, you'll move to the Set Up screen (see Figure 3.12).

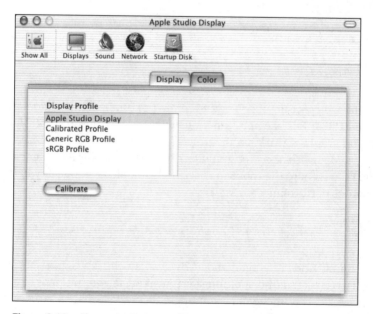

Figure 3.10   You can create a calibrated color profile to give your Mac a more accurate color balance.

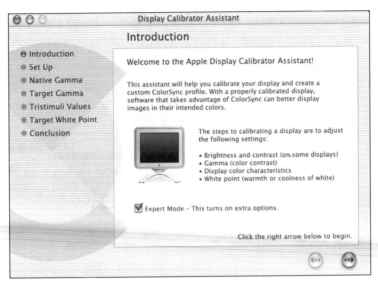

Figure 3.11   Apple's Display Calibrator Assistant helps you create a
ColorSync profile for your monitor.

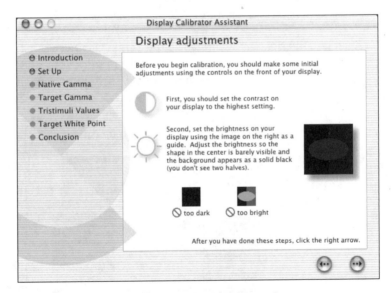

Figure 3.12   Adjust your Mac's optimal brightness here.

3. Use your display's brightness control to increase the brightness
   so that the center shape is visible but the two halves of the
   background square appear as one.

NOTE: *If you have a regular CRT display, you'll need to redo brightness as the unit ages. Users of LCD displays shouldn't have to revisit these settings unless lighting conditions change substantially or you move the unit to a different working environment.*

4. When you click the right arrow, you'll see the Native Gamma screen (see Figure 3.13). This setting lets you calibrate the gamma (center point) for the three RGB (red, green, blue) colors of your display by moving the slider back and forth. At the proper setting, the color of the Apple picture within the squares will seem to almost disappear into the background.

TIP: *It's a good idea not to sit too close to your display when making these adjustments. You get the most accurate view of gamma settings if you sit back from the display as far as possible. Otherwise, you might find that the inner and outer portions of the square never seem to come together.*

NOTE: *A number of Apple's own displays have an automatic ColorSync capability built in, where settings are adjusted as the display ages. Thus the gamma settings windows will not appear. No, there's nothing wrong with your setup; this is the way it's supposed to work.*

5. A click of the right arrow brings up the Target Gamma setting (see Figure 3.14). Move the slider to configure the setting and observe the picture in the preview screen to see the end result.

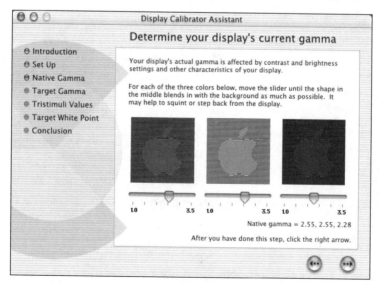

Figure 3.13   The gamma settings for each color are made here.

If you work in a mixed-platform environment, you might want to choose the PC Standard setting. Otherwise, use Mac Standard.

6. You are near the finish line. Click the right arrow to see the Target White Point screen (see Figure 3.15). The slider will set white point (or color temperature) for your display. D65, or 6500 degrees Kelvin, is normal. A setting of 9300 will brighten the display somewhat.

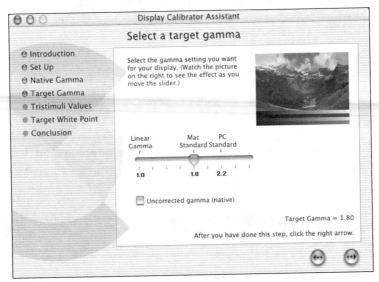

Figure 3.14   When Native Gamma is done, Target Gamma is next.

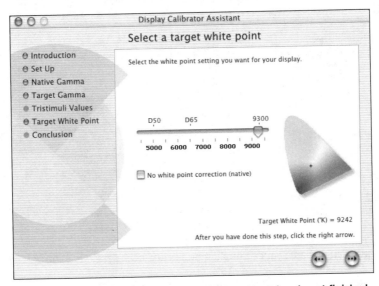

Figure 3.15   Choose the white point setting and you're almost finished.

55

> **NOTE:** You may find that some displays benefit from one setting as opposed to another, depending on their design characteristics. Apple's LCD monitors, for example (such as the 17" and 22" models), seem to provide a brighter, more brilliant picture at the 6500 settings; other LCD displays I've used, such as the ViewSonic ViewPanel VP181 (18.1-inch) and the Sony SDM MD-81 (also 18.1") work best at 9300. Feel free to experiment.

7. Click the right arrow to reach the final stage of the process (see Figure 3.16). Name your profile (Calibrated Profile is the default). Then, click Create to finish and close the Display Calibrator Assistant.

> **NOTE:** By default, the Display Calibrator Assistant will simply overwrite a previous setting with the same name without warning. So, be careful about naming your profile.

Setting Dock Preferences

Apple's Mac OS X taskbar (see Figure 3.17) can be configured in several ways to adjust the display. I'll cover these settings in more detail in Chapter 5.

Related solution:	Found on page:
Using the Dock	121

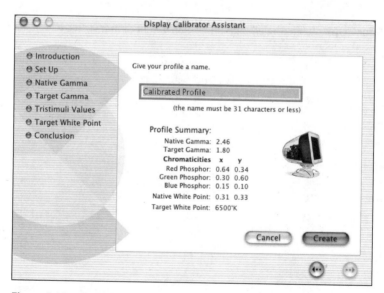

Figure 3.16   Name your calibration profile and click Create to wrap up.

3. Mac OS X User Preferences

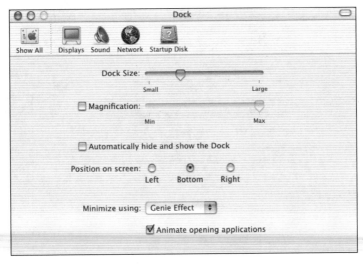

Figure 3.17   Adjust how you interact with the Dock here.

3. Mac OS X
User Preferences

Setting Energy Saver Preferences

The Sleep settings screen (shown in Figure 3.18) will be the same regardless of which Mac you're using. The following adjustments are offered:

- The first setting puts the system into sleep mode after it's been idle for the preset period of time. The most recent desktop Mac models, beginning with the Power Mac G4, are designed to operate most efficiently by leaving the unit in sleep mode rather than shutting it down (in fact, they use hardly more current than a small light bulb). Move the slider to change the idle time from the minimum of 30 minutes to Never (which deactivates the function).

- The second setting lets you establish separate adjustments for your display, to preserve screen life and put it into sleep mode when not in use for a specific interval.

- The final setting puts the hard drive to sleep. To activate this or the previous option, select the checkbox, and then drag the slider to the interval you prefer. If you have an iBook or a PowerBook, you'll have separate Energy Saver settings for AC Power and Battery; the latter settings can be used to maximize battery life.

WARNING!   Some older displays are not Energy Star–compliant and will not go into sleep mode, even though you've activated that setting. If you're not certain whether your display supports the feature, check the manufacturer's documentation, the

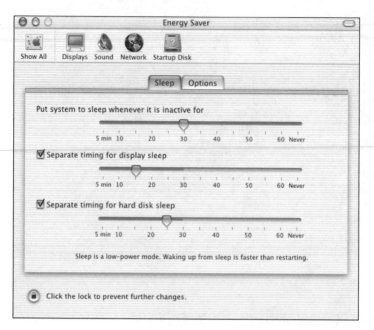

Figure 3.18   Use the slider to adjust your Energy Saver options here.

shipping box, or the manufacturer's technical support division. Some displays ship with front panels peppered with all sorts of compliance information, but most users rip off these decals before putting the products into use.

NOTE: *Some programs make continuous demands on the hard drive, and thus putting the drive into sleep mode won't work efficiently. The best time to use this feature is when you do not intend to work on your Mac.*

The second set of preferences appear when you click the Options tab. The first choices, Wake Options, will awaken your Mac when the modem detects a ring (useful if you use your Mac for faxing) or when a network administrator needs to access it.

The Other Options choices depend on the kind of Mac you have. The first, Restart Automatically After A Power Failure, is useful if you need your Mac on all the time (otherwise you can uncheck it and not worry over it). If you have an iBook or PowerBook, there will also be an option labeled Show Battery Status In Menu Bar, which is enabled by default if you install on an Apple laptop.

NOTE: *Whenever you see a lock icon at the bottom of a preference panel, as you do with the Energy Saver preferences, it requires administrator access to change.*

Setting General Preferences

If you thought you'd see the Mac OS X equivalent of the General control panel from previous versions of the Mac OS, think again. What you see is the Aqua equivalent of the Appearance control panel, at least part of it, along with a pair of settings for the Apple menu. So much for consistency.

You have six sets of appearance-related settings in the General pane (see Figure 3.19) from which to choose:

- *Appearance*—If the default Blue (or Aqua) color isn't to your liking, click the pop-up menu to choose the Graphite setting to adjust the look of buttons, menus, and windows.

WARNING! *When you switch the appearance to Graphite, the colorful buttons at the left of a Finder or document window become gray when they can be used. The only visual indication of what they do is a symbol within each clear button when the mouse is brought near it.*

- *Highlight Color*—This option sets the color you see when you select text. Feel free to experiment with different settings to see which colors set off highlighted text to your liking.

- *Place Scroll Arrows*—How would you like it? At the top and bottom, or all together at the bottom (this option may be easier on the mouse)? Take your pick.

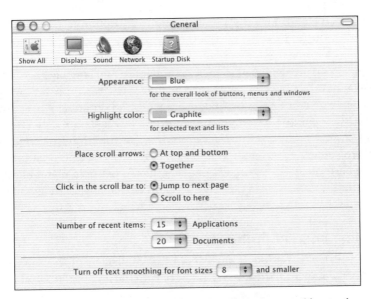

Figure 3.19   Choose your Mac's appearance settings on this panel.

- *Click In The Scroll Bar To*—This setting is supposed to direct how far a screen jumps when you click in the scrollbar (to the next page or to the point at which you click). For most programs, however, there will be no difference, so the setting is best left at its default.

- *Number Of Recent Items*—This is, in a small part, the Mac OS X equivalent of the Apple Menu Items Control Panel under the Classic OS. Click a pop-up menu to pick the number of applications and documents displayed in the Apple menu's Recent Items list.

- *Turn Off Text Smoothing For Font Sizes*—Choose the threshold at which smoothing is activated, in one-point jumps from 8 point to 12 point. If you find that smaller type is hard to read with smoothing on, you may want to choose 9 point or larger.

WARNING! *It's a good idea to check a few programs when you switch the text smoothing starting point. You may find, for example, that the text with smoothing disabled may be poorly spaced and look worse than with smoothing on. This is particularly true of Carbon-based rather than Cocoa-based applications, such as Microsoft Internet Explorer.*

Setting International Preferences

Mac OS X is designed to be a worldwide operating system, with built-in support for some of the major languages. Under older system versions, you had to install separate modules for different parts of the world or buy a different product. But Apple has moved to selling a single operating system version, and the preferences available (see Figure 3.20) are designed to localize keyboard and language settings as needed. You have settings for Language, where you can move a language to a different position by dragging and dropping it to set its priority. Separate tabs let you adjust display formats for Date, Time, and Numbers. These options combine the functions of several control panels from older versions of the Mac OS. The final tab—Keyboard Menu—lets you choose whether to put up a menu bar label from which you can quickly switch from one keyboard layout to another.

Setting Internet Preferences

This settings pane (see Figure 3.21) is reminiscent of the Internet Control Panel from the Classic Mac OS, with the notable addition of a

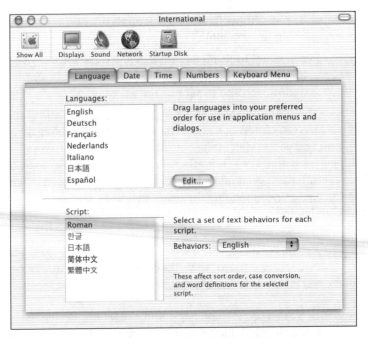

Figure 3.20   Choose your language settings on this screen.

Figure 3.21   Configure your Internet application settings here.

category for Apple's iTools feature. Click a tab to enter a particular setup screen. Four are available:

- *iTools*—Put in your iTools member name and password. If you don't have an account, click the Sign Up button; you'll be connected to Apple's Web site to set up your account.

- *Email*—These are settings you would have retrieved from your Classic Mac OS's Internet Control Panel. Specify which email program you want (Mail is the only Mac OS X–savvy program shipping with Mac OS X, but others are available, as you'll see in Chapter 22), the incoming and outgoing mail servers used by your ISP, the type of account, and the username and password required to log in.

TIP: *If you failed to write down this information from your Classic Mac OS installation, you can launch any Classic application to bring up the Classic environment. After you switch to that application, use the Apple menu to get the settings from the Internet Control Panel.*

- *Web*—Pick a browser, a home page, and a default search page. You can also select a default location on your Mac's drive where downloaded files are placed; the default, and probably the best locale, is your Mac's desktop.

- *News*—To access Internet newsgroups, click this tab, choose a news-reading application, and then enter your ISP's news server information.

NOTE: *For some ISPs, you'll have to enter your username and password as a registered user to access newsgroups. This is done to protect against relaying messages from one news server to another as a means to post junk messages. EarthLink is one of the services to require authentication.*

In case you're wondering, no there is no Advanced setting panel, as you'd find under the Classic Mac OS version of the Internet Control Panel. Mac OS X sets most settings behind the scenes, though individual applications may overwrite them. In addition, Internet Explorer and other programs do let you control some of these settings, such as helper applications. Settings for proxies, required by some ISPs and network administrators, are moved to the Network preference panel.

Related solution:	Found on page:
Setting Up Your User Account	450

Setting Keyboard Preferences

You can configure two types of settings here. The first, under the Repeat Rate tab, affects your Mac keyboard's Automatic Repeat modes. Here's the list of the available choices:

- *Key Repeat Rate*—Specifies the time you hold down a key before it repeats.

- *Delay Until Repeat*—Specifies the speed at which a key repeats.

Move the sliders to make the needed changes. You can also enter text in the text box to get a feel for the changes you'll be making.

The second set of preferences is accessed by clicking on the Full Keyboard Access tab (shown in Figure 3.22) and is used to give you more control of Finder functions via the keyboard. When you click the Turn On Full Keyboard Access checkbox, you'll harness the power of the seldom-used function keys.

3. Mac OS X User Preferences

TIP: *Full Keyboard Access can also be activated (or deactivated, if it's already on) by pressing Control+F1.*

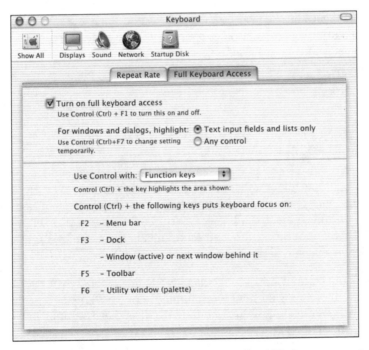

Figure 3.22   Full Keyboard Access gives you the ability to access certain functions via the keyboard.

The end result? When you activate these functions, you'll switch the focus to a specific area of your Mac's desktop. With the menu bar selected, for example, the Apple menu will drop down, and the left and right arrow keys can be used to move through the menus. Up and down arrows will travel up and down the commands, and the Return or Enter key will activate the functions.

Once Full Keyboard Access is working, you can do the following:

- *Highlighting in windows and dialogs*—By default, the emphasis is on text input fields and lists, but the Any Control option switches the emphasis. Pressing Control+F7 switches the setting from what you've checked.

WARNING!   *Individual programs have keyboard shortcuts that might work in place of the various Full Keyboard Access shortcuts. This is especially true if the program has its own brand of function key support, such as the various applications in Microsoft Office.*

- *Use Control With*—This option lets you choose whether the function keys or other keys activate the various features.

- *Keyboard focus*—When you press F2, it points to the menu bar. F3 focuses on the Dock, F5 focuses on a toolbar, and F6 focuses on a utility window or palette. Try it; you might find that changing focus via keyboard is a faster way to go.

NOTE: *If you've used Windows, you might find that Full Keyboard Access has some familiar elements.*

Setting Login Preferences

You use these settings (see Figure 3.23) in a fashion similar to the Startup Items folder under previous versions of the Mac OS. The programs that appear in this window launch when you log in. Click the Add button to locate and select startup applications that will open when you boot or log into your Mac, and click the Remove button to delete a selected item.

Click the Login Window tab to display a login prompt when your Mac boots. To set up your Mac for multiple users, you'll need to uncheck the Automatically Log In checkbox. I cover these settings in more detail in Chapter 6.

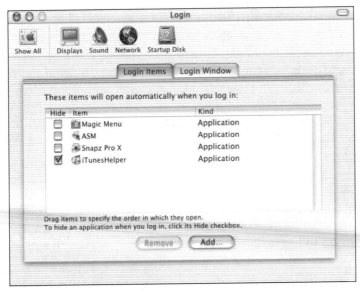

Figure 3.23   Add the programs that will launch when you boot your Mac.

Setting Mouse Preferences

Most Macs ship with the Mouse speed in the middle setting, and that can be somewhat slow. However, the middle setting can be helpful for those new to personal computing and pointing devices and who need to get accustomed to a mouse's feel and movement. Generally, though, you will find that the standard speed setting is just too slow, especially if your Mac has a large screen display. The Mouse Speed slider adjusts the tracking speed; the Double-Click Speed setting is used to configure the ideal interval for a double-click to activate a Mac OS function. There is no correct setting. It's entirely up to your taste, and you can experiment with different adjustments to see which are most comfortable. You'll also find that the ideal settings change as you move from one Mac to another, or to a different brand of pointing device. If you have an iBook or PowerBook G4, the Mouse panel window provides direct support for your trackpad rather than the mouse. On some older Apple laptops, however, a separate Trackpad tab controls these settings.

NOTE: *Some non-Apple input devices, such as those from Kensington and Microsoft, come with special software to allow you to access extra button features plus custom tracking routines. For such products, the Mouse panel probably will not work.*

Setting Network Preferences

This configuration screen has four tabs (see Figure 3.24) that control various aspects of your network settings. You can make two types of settings. One is for your internal modem, used for connecting to your ISP. (I cover those in more detail in Chapter 8.) The other, under the Built-in Ethernet category, includes four tabs to configure different settings (these are mirrored in the settings panels for an AirPort card, if one is installed):

- *TCP/IP*—The settings you make here, labeled Manually using DHCP Router, BOOTP or DHCP, are for TCP/IP-based connections, if you have one. They activate these services for a local network, cable modem, or DSL. They're very similar to those used in the TCP/IP control panel of older Macs. The required settings will come from either an ISP or network administrator.

NOTE: *To access a dial-up connection to the Internet, you'll make your settings in the Internal Modem category, available from the Show pop-up menu. AirPort users will find a category devoted to that product (with settings pretty much the same as the Built-in Ethernet category) if an AirPort card is installed on your Mac.*

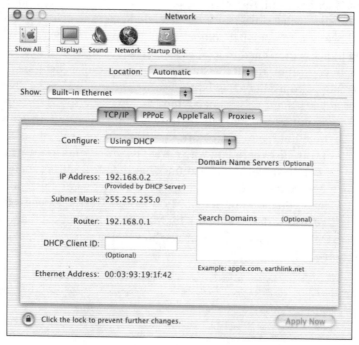

Figure 3.24 Select a tab to make a network-related adjustment on your Mac.

- *PPPoE*—Some broadband ISPs, such as those using cable modems or DSL, use PPP over Ethernet (PPPoE) software or settings. When you click this tab, you'll be able to enter information for Service Provider, PPPoE Service Name, Account Name, and Password. You can also save your password and click the PPPoE Options button to make settings that might be required by your ISP.

NOTE: *Your ISP is the source for updated information about the settings required for the PPPoE panel. The settings will vary from service to service.*

- *AppleTalk*—To access Macs and network printers on a standard AppleTalk network, select the checkbox to activate AppleTalk.

- *Proxies*—Depending on the requirements in your network or for your ISP, you might have to enter proxy settings to access the Internet. Contact your network administrator or ISP for the appropriate settings information.

After you've made your changes to your network services, click Apply Now to store your settings. If you quit System Preferences without saving your settings, you'll see a prompt asking if you want to save your settings before you move on. If you don't click Save, the network changes will be discarded.

Related solution:	Found on page:
Using Internet Connect for Dial-Up Networking	182

Setting QuickTime Preferences

Apple's QuickTime is a multimedia standard around the world. Use this settings pane (shown in Figure 3.25) to establish five sets of user preferences:

- *Plug-In*—These settings determine how your Web browser works with the QuickTime plug-in. The Play Movies Automatically checkbox turns on a QuickTime movie as soon as it's downloaded. Save Movies In Disk Cache stores a movie in the browser's Web cache (not a good idea if it's a big file). Enable Kiosk Mode turns on Kiosk mode, which allows you to save movies and adjust your QuickTime settings from within the browser.

- *Connection*—Click this tab to optimize QuickTime to work best with your specific ISP connection. Choose the speed at which you access your ISP and whether to allow multiple streams of net traffic

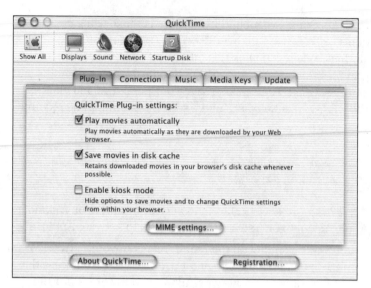

Figure 3.25   Choose your QuickTime user preferences on this pane.

(this option is best only with broadband Internet access). The Transport Setup button should be left to network administrators.

NOTE: *By default, the Connection settings are configured for a 56K modem. Although QuickTime Player will remind you to change the settings if you activate that program with a faster network hookup, it's better to save a little time and do it now.*

- *Music*—Use this setting to choose a music synthesizer package. You don't need to use it unless you've added such a package from a music program.

- *Media Keys*—Use this setting to store passwords to access secured multimedia files. Specify the fashion in which Mac OS X's built-in QuickTime features are used.

- *Update*—The final tab lets you check for updates to QuickTime from Apple's Web site. You can also enter your registration information, in the event you've opted to purchase QuickTime Pro (and get rid of those annoying messages about doing so when you try to view multimedia content on the Internet).

NOTE: *The upgrade to QuickTime Pro gives you more options with which to edit and export movies in the QuickTime Player application. It also allows you to save at least some of the movie trailers that you download from the Internet. In some cases, you may not be able to access a larger movie trailer without buying the Pro license. This was true, for example, with* Star Wars: Episode Two.

Setting Screen Saver Preferences

If you've used Microsoft Windows, no doubt you've discovered that it has a built-in screen saver. Apple has finally delivered one of its own. The setup screen is ultra-simple. Pick a module, and then click the Activation tab to set the idle time before the screen saver activates. The intervals are in 5-minute jumps up to 60 minutes. The Hot Corners option lets you automatically activate a screen saver when moving the mouse to the selected corner.

NOTE: *By default, the screen saver interval is activated when you install Mac OS X 10.1, but you can change the interval or switch it to Never if you're not a fan of screen savers. On the other hand, you can also opt to password-protect your screen saver in the Activation pane, using your regular username and password to unlock it and dismiss the display.*

Setting Sharing Preferences

Peer-to-peer file sharing is one of the delights of the Mac OS. You don't need a network administrator to set up a network over which you can share files with other users. You just have to open this pane (see Figure 3.26) and click the Start button for file sharing and the

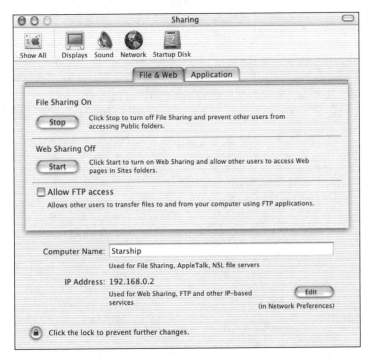

Figure 3.26   Choose whether file sharing and some sharing services will be available on your Mac.

Start button for Web sharing (which uses the Apache Web Server soft-ware to let you host a site), plus a checkbox for FTP sharing. The final display shows your Network Identity (the name you gave your Mac) and its IP address for TCP/IP connections. I'll cover this subject in more detail in Chapter 8.

NOTE: *If you want to network with an older Mac that cannot share files via TCP/IP, you'll need to turn on AppleTalk in the Network preference panel before activating file sharing here.*

WARNING!   *The FTP sharing feature is, like Web sharing, a potential security hole, so use this feature with caution. If you must share files in this fashion, consider setting up a firewall to control access.*

Related solution:	Found on page:
Setting Up a Web or FTP Server on Your Mac	Chapter 8

Setting Software Update Preferences

Starting with Mac OS 9, Apple offered a Software Update option. It's intended to provide an effective way to check Apple's Web site for the latest Mac OS X software updates (see Figure 3.27 for Mac OS X's version).

You can opt to update your software manually whenever you want, or select the Automatically option to have Apple's Web site checked on a daily, weekly, or monthly basis for needed updates. The status dis-play will show the last time you attempted the update. Click Update

Figure 3.27   Update your OS using this panel.

Now whenever you want to recheck for updates. When an update is available, a separate Software Update application will launch, and that's where you can select the updates you want to install from the list (yes, sometimes there's more than one).

NOTE: *The Software Update feature is not always as effective as it should be. However, Apple assures us that the version used for Mac OS X will deliver the goods. Regardless, you may want to check the* **VersionTracker.com** *Web site periodically to see if you missed a needed update for your Apple system software.*

TIP: *When you access the Software Update application, choose Save As from the Update menu to store a copy of the update on your drive right after it's installed. This is a great way to ensure that the update is available should you need to reinstall it later (perhaps after reinstalling Mac OS X), without having to access the Internet to retrieve it again.*

Setting Sound Preferences

Your Mac is, at heart, a multimedia computer with the ability to create and play audio and video productions (with the right additional software for making such productions, of course). There are two categories of settings. Alerts (see Figure 3.28) perform the following:

- *Choose An Alert Sound*—Select the audible warning you get when an alert is displayed. When you pick a sound from the scrolling list, you'll hear it played in your Mac's speaker.

- *Alert Volume*—Choose the level at which the Mac plays alert sounds, such as those warning you of a problem with your Mac. If the little beeps and blurbs irritate you, you can make them lower than the overall volume.

- *Play Alerts Through*—Do you have an extra set of speakers on your Mac? In the example shown in Figure 3.28, I had a set of Harman Kardon SoundSticks attached to my Power Mac G4, which is why SoundSticks is shown. Otherwise, the choice would be confined to Built-in Audio Controller.

- *Main Volume*—This setting controls the system volume. The checkbox puts a system menu volume control on your Mac's menu bar.

When you click the Output tab, you'll be able to pick a device for audio (assuming you have a second choice) and also choose Balance, moving the slider to match up the levels between your left and right speakers.

Figure 3.28   Set your volume and choose alert sounds in this pane.

NOTE: *The Sound preferences you see also depend on the kind of Mac you have. For example, if you have a slot-loading iMac, you may see additional adjustments for use if you're using Harman Kardon's iSub, a woofer module that enhances the sound reproduction on these models.*

Setting Speech Preferences

Some Mac programs support Mac OS X's Speech Manager, which allows you to activate Mac functions via spoken commands and have text read back to you. In the first Speech settings pane, Speech Recognition (see Figure 3.29), you can decide whether to activate the speech recognition feature. Click On and then click Listening to specify whether you can speak a command with or without a listening key (a keyboard shortcut that precedes the speech command). The standard setup calls for saying "computer" prior to a command. With recognition turned on, you'll be able to access the Speakable Items folder to see the available commands.

The Text-to-Speech tab brings up a screen where you can choose a voice from a list, and then specify the rate at which the voice is played back. As the rate increases, the pitch of the voice is raised, and the speed at which it reads to you is also increased proportionately. Moving the slider to a slower rate has the reverse effect.

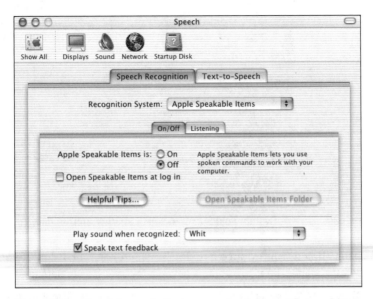

Figure 3.29   Speak to me. Activate your speech recognition preferences here.

NOTE: *It's not a good idea to be overly dependant on Apple's speech features. The "recognition" feature is limited to some simple commands and doesn't work terribly well in a crowded room. The Text-to-Speech feature works after a fashion, but many words simply are not pronounced correctly. To use speech recognition for dictation, you may want to look for a separate program, such as the Mac OS X version of IBM's ViaVoice, which also allows you to verbally access some of your Mac's commands—but it's still a far cry from the way it is done on* Star Trek.

Setting Startup Disk Preferences

This setting lets you switch startup disks, if you have additional volumes with system software on them on your Mac. In Figure 3.30, you can see selections representing the names of the volumes connected to my Mac when I wrote this book and the system versions they contained. For most of you, the option will be to switch from Mac OS X back to Mac OS 9.2.1 or 9.2.2. To change the startup disk, follow these steps:

1. Click the icon representing the name of the volume from which you want to boot your Mac.

2. Click the Restart button.

3. You'll see an acknowledgement prompt; click Save and Restart to boot from a different startup volume. Click Cancel to simply save your settings, in case you want to restart at a later time.

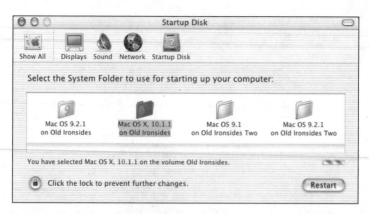

Figure 3.30   Click a System Folder icon to select another startup disk.

This choice will produce a dialog in which you'll be asked if you want to save the new settings (even they are the old settings).

4. If you opt to restart later, choose Restart from the Apple menu to boot your Mac from the previously selected startup volume.

WARNING! For your Mac to boot properly from another startup volume, it must contain system software that's compatible with your computer. The Startup Disk preferences screen only displays the disks on which a Mac OS System Folder is present; it won't always know whether your Mac can run from it. Should your Mac not be able to boot from the specified volume, it will, instead, boot from another volume with a compatible version of the Mac OS (perhaps the one from which you just switched).

5. When you're finished setting your Mac's preferences, choose Quit from the application menu. The changes you make go into effect as soon as you apply them.

Setting Universal Access Preferences

This settings panel (see Figure 3.31) is a direct descendant of the EasyAccess feature of the Classic Mac OS. It's designed for those who are physically disabled, or anyone for whom the keyboard and mouse are difficult to use. The Keyboard panel, shown in the figure, has a Sticky Keys option that lets you enter a keyboard shortcut as a separate sequence, rather than all at once. There are two checkboxes: one to beep when you've used your modify key, and the other to show the keys on your Mac's display.

3. Mac OS X
User Preferences

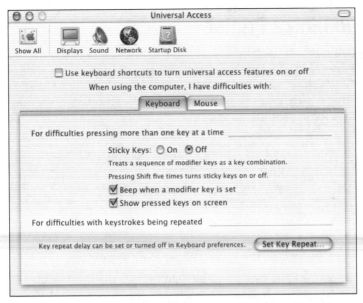

Figure 3.31   For those with disabilities, or for whom mouse and keyboard movement is painful, Mac OS X has a possible solution.

The Mouse tab allows you to use the numeric keypad on your keyboard to emulate the functions of the mouse, using just the number keys to control mouse action.

TIP: To quickly access the Sticky Keys function, press the Shift key five times in a row (repeating the action turns the function off). The Mouse Keys function is activated by pressing the Option key five times in a row (repeat the action to turn the feature off).

Setting User Preferences

Bring up this screen to change your login password or add additional users to your Mac, to take advantage of its multiple-users features. To make the change, click your username, click the Edit User button, enter the new password twice in the appropriate text fields, and then enter the appropriate hint, if you want a reminder. Once you click the OK button, your new password goes into effect. The Cancel button undoes the changes you've made. Chapter 6 covers this subject in more detail.

Related solution:	*Found on page:*
Setting Up Multiple-User Access	133

Configuring a Printer

As mentioned at the start of this chapter, under all previous versions of the Mac OS, you would use the Chooser to select and configure a printer. With the departure of the Chooser, your printer choices are now made with an application called Print Center. You'll find it in the Utilities folder, within the Applications folder.

NOTE: If you're using a printer hooked up to your Mac's USB port, you don't need to use Print Center except to set a default printer (the one listed first in your Page Setup and Print dialog boxes). Once the drivers are installed, the printer is automatically recognized as soon as it's connected and turned on. The following steps, however, are needed if you want to connect a network printer.

After you've located the application, follow these steps:

1. Go to the Utilities folder and double-click the Print Center application icon to launch it.

2. If you have no printers selected, you'll see a dialog box (see Figure 3.32) asking if you want to add a printer. Click the Add button.

WARNING!   What happened to your networked printers? Before you can check an AppleTalk network, you need to make sure AppleTalk is turned on. It's a setting in the Network pane of the System Preferences application.

3. On the next screen, click the Connection pop-up menu and select the network or peripheral connection on which you want to check for printers. Depending on the kind of Mac you have, you can choose from AppleTalk, LPR Printers Using IP, or USB. The Directory Services option can locate an enterprise printer located on your network. In the example shown in Figure 3.33, I chose AppleTalk to locate a printer on my Ethernet network.

4. If your printer is located in another AppleTalk zone, click the second pop-up menu to pick that zone.

You have no printers available.
Would you like to add to your list of printers now?

Cancel   Add...

Figure 3.32   This dialog box comes up if no printer has been configured.

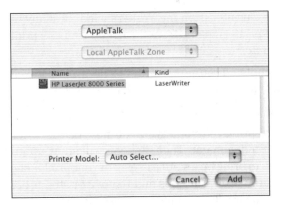

Figure 3.33   The author's laser printer as it appears in the Local
              AppleTalk Zone.

5. Continue browsing for printers until they are all displayed.

6. Under Printer Model, leave the Auto Select option selected, or
    pick a printer from the list of PostScript Printer Description
    (PPD) files to provide maximum support for your output
    device. A PPD file will recognize the custom features of your
    network printer, such as extra paper sizes, extra trays, custom
    resolutions, and, if available, the ability to duplex or print on
    both sides of the paper. If you don't have the right PPD file
    available, your selections will be limited to the standard paper
    tray and a limited range of paper sizes.

NOTE: *Mac OS X 10.1 shipped with files for a number of printers, including those from Apple,
Hewlett-Packard, Lexmark, Tektronix, and Xerox. To install a PPD file, just drag it to the proper
folder. You'll find it via the following hierarchy: Library>Printers>PPDs>Contents>Resources>
en.lproj (for the English language version). You can obtain PPD files from the manufacturer,
using a special installer provided by the manufacturer, or from Adobe's Web site at:*
www.adobe.com/products/printerdrivers/macppd.html*.*

7. Click the red button to close the window. At this point, all your
    available printers should appear in the main Printers window.

8. To select a default printer (the one normally selected when you
    want to print a document), click the name of the printer to
    select it, and then choose Make Default from the Printers menu
    (or press Command+D). The name and icon of the printer will
    appear at the top of the Print Center window. However, you'll
    still be able to pick other printers connected to your Mac or
    your network directly from the Page Setup and Print dialog
    boxes.

9. You can remove a printer from the Printers window at any time by selecting the printer's name from the list of available printers and clicking Delete.

10. After you've completed setting your preferences, click the close box or choose Quit from the application menu to close the program.

If you have no more printers to add, you will not see Print Center again until you print a document. Then, its icon will show up in the Dock. Click the Dock to bring up a status display of your printer queue, where you can monitor your print jobs and remove or stop processing of specific documents. This window is very similar to the one shown in Apple's desktop printer window from earlier versions of the Mac OS.

NOTE: *When a job is being printed from a Mac OS X application, Print Center's Dock icon will display the number of pages remaining to be processed in the current document. If there's a problem with a job, you'll see an onscreen prompt and an exclamation point within the Printer Center icon.*

Chapter 4

Introducing the Mac OS X Finder

In Brief

The more things change, the more they remain the same. Although the Mac OS has been upgraded time and time again since it debuted in 1984, there has been one constant—the Finder, Apple's famous file-access and management software. Although it has been enhanced and refined over the years, its basic look and goals have persisted substantially unchanged.

Not so with Mac OS X. The Finder (shown in Figure 4.1) has metamorphosed into a totally new application, bearing more than a passing resemblance to the file viewer for the NeXT operating system and even some of the Mac shareware programs that have been introduced over the years. At the same time, however, it retains characteristics of the Finder you know and love, although some contents appear in a very different form.

NOTE: Greg's Browser is another application that offers a similar look in some respects. This file-viewing or browsing program is produced by the folks responsible for Kaleidoscope, a popular shareware program that alters the entire appearance of the Mac with various themes. However, neither Greg's Browser nor Kaleidoscope appear to be Mac OS-bound.

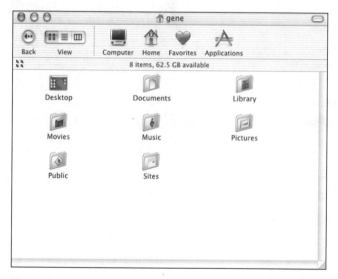

Figure 4.1   The Mac OS X Finder, the 10.1 edition, retains basic elements from the original Mac Finder, but in an entirely new uniform.

Aside from the function of the new Finder, there's plenty to be said about its form. Using Apple's Quartz imaging technology, the new Finder is carefully crafted from an artistic standpoint. You can drag it across the screen in realtime; the image is anti-aliased, with clearly defined corners that cast a shadow behind them as the Finder is dragged across the desktop.

Despite the surprisingly new look and feel, however, you'll see more than a passing resemblance to the traditional or Classic Mac OS Finder. The basic functions—viewing the contents of a hard drive, as well as opening, copying, and moving files—are, of course, little different despite the highly changed Aqua interface. But in some respects, the way you look for files may be substantially changed; and, as you'll see later on in this chapter, you have more options with which to customize the Finder's look and feel. To start with, look at the ways in which you can now view your files with Mac OS X's Finder. To change the display motif, simply click one of the three small View buttons at the left end of the Finder window. Here's what they do, from left to right:

- *Icon View*—This is familiar territory (see Figure 4.1); it's quite similar to the way you examine files with the original Mac Finder. Each Finder item is identified by a unique icon, ranging from the simple folder picture to a far more complicated rendering for some applications. You just double-click any item to open it.

- *List View*—The icons in List View (see Figure 4.2) are small (unless you change the Finder option to make a larger icon, as

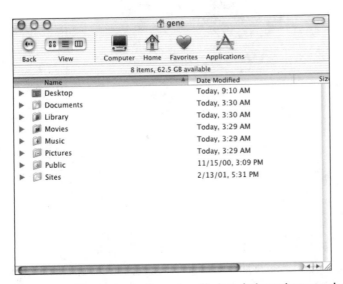

Figure 4.2   You see more items in a Finder window when you choose the List View option.

explained in the "Immediate Solutions" section titled "Setting Viewing Preferences," later in this chapter). As with previous versions of the Mac OS, the contents of a disk or folder are displayed as a list, in four distinct categories: Name, Date Modified, Size, and Kind. You can use the Finder List View preferences to add or remove categories. To open an item, just double-click it.

TIP: *It's easy to change the sorting order in List View. Just click the title of the category under which you want the listings sorted. Normally, items are sorted by name; but if you click Date Modified or another category, the list will be organized in that fashion. Click the arrow at the right of the Name or Date Modified category to reverse the sorting order.*

- *Column View*—This choice is new for Mac OS X, although as mentioned, it is not unfamiliar to users of the NeXTSTEP operating system or some shareware file-browsing programs (such as Greg's Browser, mentioned earlier). It gives you a full hierarchical view of the contents of a folder, from left to right (see Figure 4.3). Just click an item to see its contents, which are displayed at the right. If you click a file or application icon, a graphic preview describing the item you selected is displayed. This viewing method is ideal for navigating deeply into nested folders without having to produce endless numbers of open folders on your Mac. In addition, if you click a folder in one of the two rightmost columns, the view shifts to the left.

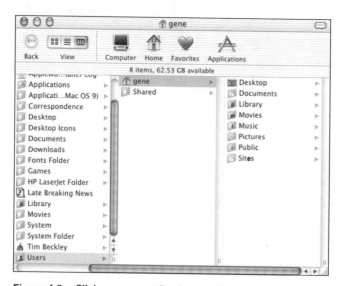

Figure 4.3   Click once on an item at the left to see the contents at the right.

Additional Finder Navigation Features

After you've opened a folder, you can Command+click the title bar to produce a pop-up menu to see the direction (path) of your folder navigation and access the higher-level folders through which you've traveled. This feature is a carryover from earlier Mac OS versions. You can also move back through previous folders one at a time (regardless of path) if you click the back arrow. In that sense, it works similarly to the back arrow of a Web browser.

NOTE: *The back arrow functions in the Finder's single window mode. If you change the setting, under Finder Preferences, to open folders in a new window, the back arrow no longer functions.*

Visiting the Finder's Toolbar

Another highly useful feature of the Mac OS X Finder is a colorful customizable toolbar, which gives you one-click buttons (or icons) to provide fast access to specific folders, files, or other features (depending on what choices you make). Let's start with the four icons at the right of the separator bar, because the other two were explained earlier:

- *Computer*—This is the Mac OS X Finder's display for the disk icons that also inhabit the desktop (see Figure 4.4). When you click this button, you'll see icons for available drives and a Network icon, to access network or Internet-based services. Disk icons will differ, depending on the type of drive, such as a fixed drive, FireWire drive, or CD. The iPod, for example, when the cute little jukebox player is put in FireWire disk mode, has a typically unique icon that's instantly recognizable. The name on the title bar will reflect the name you've given your Mac (a name that can be changed in the Sharing preference panel).

- *Home*—The Home folder is part of the multiple-user feature of Apple's operating system. When you click this button, you'll see the directory that contains your personal file folders in your User's folder. Figure 4.5 shows the standard layout, neatly categorized for convenient organization of your stuff. In the Public folder, you place files that you want to share across a network when file sharing is activated.

NOTE: *Each person who uses your Mac can get his own Home folder, as I explain further in Chapter 6.*

Figure 4.4   The Computer toolbar button takes you directly to your disks and servers.

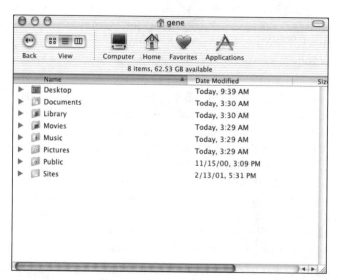

Figure 4.5   Several folders make up a user's personal Home directory under Mac OS X.

- *Favorites*—Probably the closest equivalent of what you could do with the Classic Apple menu, this locale can be used as a repository for items you want to access again and again. By default, it has aliases to your Home and Documents folders, but you can easily add more. I cover this topic in more detail in the "Immediate Solutions" section of this chapter.

Figure 4.6   This Applications folder shows some of the standard applications that are distributed with Mac OS X, plus a few I've added.

- *Applications*—This folder, shown in Figure 4.6, is meant to be the repository for all your installed Mac OS X programs (although they can run if put elsewhere). This rigidity is useful from an organizational standpoint, because you don't have to hunt all over your Mac's drive for a specific program.

TIP: Don't want the Finder's toolbar to intrude on your Mac's desktop? No problem. Just choose Hide Toolbar from the View menu, press Command+B, or click the little oval icon in the upper-right corner of the Finder window. If the toolbar has already been hidden, the View menu displays Show Toolbar instead; the keyboard combination stays the same. When you hide the toolbar, the Finder acts like a Classic Mac OS Finder, and double-clicking on an item spawns a new Finder window rather than showing everything in one window. Double-clicking with the Command key pressed produces the same result.

The New Finder Menus

The Mac OS Finder has had essentially the same display options from day one. But certain elements have changed with Mac OS X, and in some respects, the changes are drastic. In this section, I cover the new menu bar commands and how they differ from the previous versions of the Mac OS.

If you used the Mac OS X Public Beta or watched all those cool demos of early versions of the Aqua interface at Macworld Expo keynotes, the first thing you'll notice when you look at the menu bar is that the

Apple menu has been restored (shown in Figure 4.7). In addition, the application menu is now situated at the left side of the menu bar rather than the right.

Although the Apple menu looks the same, you'll notice some big changes in the contents. Part of this is the result of the elimination of the Finder's Special menu. All those commands, and some extras, are now available system-wide in the Apple menu. So, you don't have to return to the Finder to activate these functions.

NOTE: *In the initial releases of Mac OS X, it was not possible to customize the Apple menu in any way, as you could with previous Mac OS versions, aside from the number of recent items displayed, which was added in version 10.1. This limitation could be changed for future versions. In addition, the new Apple menu only shows itself in the Finder or with Mac OS X native applications. If you use a Classic application, the Apple menu you see is the old one, from your Classic Mac OS.*

Here's the list of the Apple menu features:

- *About This Mac*—Very little is different here. Choose this command to see a window displaying the Mac OS X version you are using, the amount of memory installed, and the kind of processor your Mac has. The big change is that the amount of virtual memory is no longer listed, because virtual memory is a full-time function and is never turned off.

TIP: *Mac OS X version numbers are also classified by build numbers, which are used by Apple's Mac OS X development team to catalog the process. Just click the version number in the About This Mac window to see the actual build number. On some Macs, a third click will produce your computer's serial number. Either way, once you've gone through the options, the next click takes you back to where you started.*

Figure 4.7   A familiar menu, but in a new guise.

- *Get Mac OS X Software*—Select this command to be taken to a page on Apple's Web site where you can order new programs for your Mac. This is one of the few concessions to commercialization in Mac OS X (as distinct from Microsoft Windows XP, which includes a number of links to sites where you can take advantage of commercial offerings for specific features, such as working with digital photos).

- *System Preferences*—Access the System Preferences application from here.

- *Dock*—Configure the settings for the famous Dock, such as whether you'd like to hide it, magnify the icons when you pass the mouse over them, anchor the Dock in a different position, and so on. Chapter 5 covers this subject in more detail.

- *Location*—Location may be the watchword for realtors, but it's also a feature of Mac OS X that lets you customize network and Internet setups for different locales. It is especially helpful if you move your Mac from place to place (invaluable with an iBook or PowerBook). Chapter 8 covers this feature in more detail.

NOTE: By default, Mac OS X is multihoming, which means it can automatically switch between a single set of network and ISP hookups, including an AirPort network, Ethernet network, and dial-up connection.

- *Recent Items*—A carryover from the Apple Menu Options software of previous Mac OS versions, this feature displays up to 5 recent applications and documents in the submenu by default, or up to 50, each, courtesy of the General preference panel in the System Preferences application.

- *Special menu items*—The remaining five items—Force Quit, Sleep, Restart, Shut Down, and Log Out—are Special menu–type commands moved to the Apple menu for convenient access without returning to the Finder. You can also access the Force Quit dialog box via the Command+Option+Esc keystroke.

TIP: Commands with one or more letters beginning with the Command (or Apple) key are keyboard shortcuts you can use to access a feature without using the mouse.

Following is a list of how the remaining menus have changed:

- *Application menu*—As mentioned, the application menu has been moved. In addition, the name of an application is now in bold (see Figure 4.8) for clear identification. When you click the

4. Introducing the Mac OS X Finder

Figure 4.8   The Finder's application menu has new features for Mac OS X.

application menu, you'll see commands that apply to that program. Another new feature of Mac OS X is the Services submenu, which gives direct links to programs that extend the features of the one you're using; you can, for example, take a selected text passage that's actually a URL and open the site in a Web browser window. You can use the various hide options to hide the program in which you're working or to hide other programs for a cleaner desktop. The biggest change is the Quit command; it has now moved from the File menu to what Apple feels is a more logical location—the application menu. Empty Trash is also found under the Finder's application menu.

NOTE: *Older, Classic Mac applications will still have their Quit commands in the File menu, and their application menus will still appear in the accustomed spot at the right side of the menu bar.*

TIP: *If you hold down the Option key while selecting another application's window, all windows for other programs are hidden from view; the exceptions are applications that run in the Mac OS 9 or Classic environment. The Show All feature in the application menu reverses the effect. This feature works the same as in earlier versions of the Mac OS.*

- *File menu*—The Finder's File menu (see Figure 4.9) isn't much different from the one in Mac OS 9. The big change is the replacement of the Get Info window with the Show Info window. It has some of the same functions, plus some new ones I'll get to shortly. The other notable changes include: Command+N now produces a new Finder window, and the keyboard command for a new folder is Command+Shift+N. To make an alias, you press Command+L (Command+M previously). You now use Command+M to minimize a window and consign it to the Dock. (Don't ask me to explain the wisdom of changing things in this fashion; I just work here.)

Figure 4.9   New keyboard commands and a new Show Info window
highlight major changes to the Finder's File menu.

NOTE: *Our fearless technical editor, Pieter Paulson, suggests that the use of the Command+L combination also signifies the fact that, under Unix, what we call an alias is referred to as a link. Makes sense.*

- *Edit menu*—Some things have remained nearly the same. The Edit menu, shown in Figure 4.10, is functionally identical to the Edit menu of older versions of the Mac OS, except for one big addition: You can actually copy a file or folder in addition to text or a picture object. You do so in the same way you would in Windows. This technique lets you copy these items without having to navigate or manipulate Finder windows to allow for a normal drag-and-drop operation. What's more, the Undo command also affects the last copy or move operation.

- *View menu*—The first three options (see Figure 4.11) simply mirror those available in the Finder itself. You can select to view items as icons, as a list, or as columns. The other choices let you hide a Finder window's toolbar, customize the toolbar, or set view options. I explain the latter in detail later in this chapter.

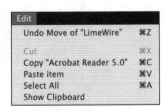

Figure 4.10   The contents of Mac OS X's Edit menu have not changed from
the menu in Mac OS 9.

Figure 4.11   Choose the manner in which Finder contents are displayed
from this menu.

- *Go menu*—This menu inherits at least some elements of the
  original Apple menu in Mac OS X (see Figure 4.12). Four of the
  first five choices mirror the standard toolbar options in the
  Finder, plus add the ability to bring up your iDisk, part of Apple's
  iTools feature. The Recent Folders option provides a submenu of
  recent Finder folders you've accessed. Another new command to
  the mix—Go To Folder—lets you type the actual path of a folder
  in order to bring it up. An example would be "/users/<*your
  username*>", which would immediately transport you to your
  Home directory. The Connect To Server option accesses a shared
  volume (Mac OS, Windows, and Unix, courtesy of built-in SAMBA
  and NFS support), whether it's on a local network or on the
  Internet.

- *Window menu*—This menu is found in many applications. It first
  appeared in Mac OS 9.1 and has been carried over to X's Finder
  (see Figure 4.13). The second option—Minimize Window—
  shrinks an application or Finder window to the Dock. Bring All
  To Front makes all open Finder windows accessible (you'll use
  this option if the windows were previously hidden from view).

Figure 4.12   The Back feature shown in the Go menu works in the Finder's
Column View mode.

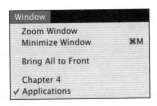

Figure 4.13   Adjust the display of Finder windows from this menu.

The items at the bottom of the display are the names of the Finder windows presently open. Select the one you want to bring to the front.

NOTE: *If you click Mac's desktop, the Zoom Window and Minimize commands are grayed out.*

- *Help menu*—This menu is just what the name implies. Most of the information that Apple provides about Mac OS X is situated here, rather than in a printed document and a lot of it requires knowing the right material to search. (But at least you have this book to learn the rest.) In addition, just about every Mac application has some sort of Help support.

4. Introducing the Mac OS X Finder

Immediate Solutions

Setting Finder Preferences

As with any feature of Mac OS X, there's no need to customize or alter the new Finder. You can continue to use it in its pristine form if you prefer, running applications on your Mac, surfing the Net, and so on, without needing to alter its appearance. But there are many ways to customize its look and feel.

By default, the Mac OS X Finder displays its contents in single-window mode. You open the contents of a folder in the Finder, and the Finder replaces the contents in the window with the contents of the opened folder. If you want to change this functionality to the way it worked with the previous Mac OS, where opening a folder opened a new Finder window, you can take any of the actions described in the following sections.

Keeping Folder Views Consistent

This preference setting establishes the default behavior when you double-click a folder icon to open it. Just follow these instructions:

1. Choose Preferences from the Finder's application menu to bring up the Finder Preferences window shown in Figure 4.14.

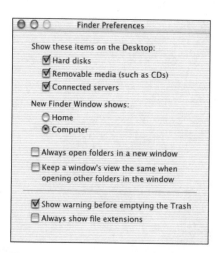

Figure 4.14   Select the way the Finder displays the contents of an opened folder.

NOTE: *I cover the desktop-related preferences in Chapter 5.*

2. Click the Keep A Window's View The Same When Opening Other Folders In The Window checkbox in the Preferences window. The following Finder preferences are also available:

   • *New Finder Window Shows*—Choose Home directory or Computer (which displays available drives and network shares).

   • *Always Open Folders In A New Window*—This option makes Finder behavior similar to what you had in the Classic Mac OS. Opening a new folder will spawn a new Finder window. Although you will probably prefer the Mac OS X way of doing things when you get used to it, you aren't forced to stay with single-window behavior.

   • *Show Warning Before Emptying The Trash*—This setting mirrors what you could do with the Classic Mac OS. When you uncheck this box, there will be no warning when you attempt to empty the trash from the Finder's application menu. If you want a second chance before deleting, you may want to leave this option checked.

4. Introducing the Mac OS X Finder

TIP: *Another way to avoid the Finder's warning about emptying the Trash is simply to click the Trash icon in the Dock and, while it's held down, choose Empty Trash from the pop-up menu. There will be no backing out.*

   • *Always Show File Extensions*—By default, Mac OS X will hide file extensions unless you specifically add them to a file name (except for some applications that do it anyway). However, the file extensions will always be present for cross-platform compatibility, except for older Classic applications that do not offer the option to put a file extension at the end of a file name. For a simpler Finder and desktop, you may want to leave this option unchecked.

3. When you're finished configuring the Finder, click the red light button to close the window and save your preferences. From here on, all folder windows opened within a Finder window will inherit the same view setting, whether Icon, List, or Column View.

NOTE: *No, I didn't skip the other preference settings. I discuss the rest of the Finder Preferences options in Chapter 5, because they relate to how the desktop is displayed.*

If you don't want to make a permanent change in the way an opened folder displays, just hold down the Option key to reverse the behavior when you double-click a folder icon. That way, you can decide on the fly whether a new Finder window is opened.

Related solution:	Found on page:
Setting Finder Preferences	119

Setting Viewing Preferences

As with the previous Mac OS Finder, you can set the way items appear in the Finder, but your options are far more extensive under Mac OS X. Settings can be made on a global basis, so they apply to all open Finder windows and all display categories, or to a specific Finder window. The options you have depend on the view setting, so they'll be explained separately:

1. With a Finder window with Icon View selected open, go to the View menu and choose Show View Options, or press Command+J. The window shown in Figure 4.15 appears.

2. Click the Global button if you want all Finder windows to inherit your changes, or This Window Only to affect just the selected Finder window. You can choose from the following changes:

   - *Icon Size*—By default, icons are fairly large—at least compared to older versions of the Mac OS. You can move the slider to change their size as you look.

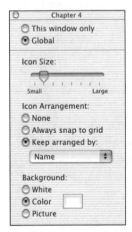

Figure 4.15   Choose a global or individual preference here.

- *Icon Arrangement*—Whether you like your desktop automatically arranged or not, the choice is yours. Just click the appropriate radio button. The default—None—means you can place your disk, file, and folder icons as you wish, anywhere in a Finder window. The Always Snap To Grid option is similar to what you find in some drawing programs. The icons are spaced by an invisible grid, at fixed distances apart. The final option—Keep Arranged By—gives you a pop-up menu of sort sequences: Choose from Name, Date Modified, Date Created, Size, and Kind.

NOTE: *Is something missing? Well, in the Classic Mac OS, you could also view by Label and apply a specific color to an item for convenience or appearance. At least through Mac OS X 10.1, labels are no longer available.*

- *Background*—This Finder feature is new for Mac OS X. You can leave it set at White if you prefer the default background. Otherwise, you can give your Finder background a unique color by clicking the Color radio box, then on the box at the right to bring up an Apple Color Picker (see Figure 4.16). After you click the kind of color adjustments you want, moving the sliders with the mouse changes the selected colors. When you click the final Background option—Picture—you'll see a Select button that you click to bring up the Open dialog box. There, you can choose a picture.

After you've made your settings, you can click the close button to activate the changes. Or, go to the next section if you want to make further Finder changes.

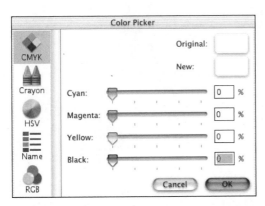

Figure 4.16   Drag sliders to produce a color scheme that suits your taste.

NOTE: *Remember that a background color or picture you select will apply only to the selected Finder window unless you click Global.*

---

3. If you prefer the Finder's List View, the selections change. With List View selected, the View Options window is different (see Figure 4.17). Under Show Columns, choose which categories you want displayed. The Use Relative Dates option gives you such selections as Yesterday and Today (but never Tomorrow—that was a bad joke!). As with the Classic Mac OS, Calculate All Sizes will give you the size of items in a folder, but at the expense of slowing down performance. The final option is Icon Size. Make it small or make it large—those are all the choices you have.

TIP: *You can still view the size of an item without checking it in the View Options window. Instead, select a folder and choose Show Info from the Finder's File menu, and you'll see a visual display of the size in the first or General Information window.*

---

4. When you're finished setting Finder preferences, click the close button.

Changing Finder List View Columns

The new Mac OS Finder can be customized extensively in List View. In addition to adjusting preferences as to which categories are displayed, you can further modify it in two ways:

* *Resize Category Lists*—Move the mouse between the columns, and you'll see the cursor change to reflect two opposite pointed

Figure 4.17   A new variation of View Options shows up in List View.

arrows. Then, simply click and drag the column to resize it. The change you make is reflected in all new Finder windows.

- *Change Order Of Categories*—You can also move an entire category into a new position in the Finder window. Just click and drag the Finder category to its new location, and let go of the mouse button. This change can be made in all categories except Name. After a category is in a new position, the change is reflected in all new Finder windows.

Resizing Columns in Column View

If you opt for the Finder's Column View, you aren't locked into the default size either. Just click the two vertical lines at the bottom in the space between columns and drag back and forth to resize the columns. If you hold down the Option key, the change is confined to the column at the left.

The changes you make in this fashion will affect all the new Finder windows you open in Column View.

TIP: *Want to see how much disk space is left on a drive or removable disk? Choose Show Status Bar from the View menu. From here on (until you select the option again—it's now labeled Hide Status Bar), you'll see a display showing both the number of items in a Finder window and the amount of available disk storage space.*

Customizing the Finder's Toolbar

You can simply hide the Finder's toolbar, if you prefer the old ways of the Mac OS—the ability to open a folder and spawn a new Finder window. If you decide to keep the toolbar open, you can customize it in a variety of ways. Here's how it's done:

1. Choose Customize Toolbar from the Finder's View menu to bring up a convenient window displaying lots of cool icons (see Figure 4.18).

2. To add an icon, drag it to the toolbar. You can use the Separator icon to categorize your selections.

NOTE: *If you add too many icons, you can drag the resize bar to the right to make the Finder window wider; otherwise, you can click the arrow at the end of the toolbar to access the remaining icons.*

---

3. To limit the toolbar icon to either the icon or the text, make your choices from the Show pop-up menu at the bottom of the screen.

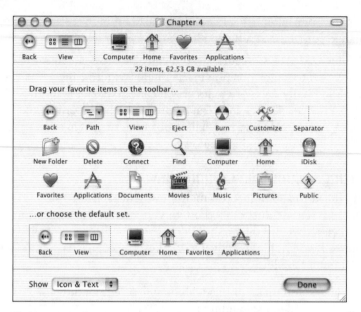

Figure 4.18   Go ahead and drag icons to the toolbar.

TIP: If you make a mistake and put the wrong icon in the toolbar, you can click and drag it to a new position.

4. Click the Done button to complete the process.

TIP: To restore the toolbar to factory issue, click the default set on the Customize Toolbar screen and drag it to the toolbar. It will replace the contents.

NOTE: Don't fret if the icon you want to add isn't shown. You can drag and drop any application, file, or folder icon onto the Finder's toolbar, and it will be added immediately.

After you've changed the toolbar, you can remove an icon by holding down the Command key and dragging the icon off the toolbar. The default toolbar icons, however, cannot be removed this way. They can be removed only when you bring up the Customize Toolbar screen.

TIP: The Path icon in the Customize Toolbar screen is useful. When you add it to the toolbar, clicking it will show the folder path of the item you've selected, which lets you quickly move to higher folder levels. Of course, holding down the Command key and clicking the title of a Finder window gets the same result.

Using the New Finder on a Day-to-Day Basis

After you have configured the Finder the way you want, you'll find that it's easy to get accustomed to the new way of handling your Mac's files and even the somewhat restricted organizational requirements. In the next few pages of this chapter, I discuss basic file management techniques. For the most part, you'll see they aren't terribly different from earlier versions of the Mac OS.

Moving a File

To move a file from one folder to another, simply click to select the file, and then drag it to the new folder. You might need to open another Finder window to move between widely disparate folders.

Copying a File

To copy a file from one folder to another, hold down the Option key as the file is being dragged to its new location. This copying function is automatic if you are moving an icon from one drive's folder to a folder on another drive.

TIP: *If the folder to which you want to copy a file is buried deep and not easily accessed, just use the Copy command in the Finder's Edit menu to copy the entire file or folder. Now open the folder into which you want to copy the item, and then choose Paste from the Edit menu to put a copy there. This is, of course, similar to the way it happens in the Windows platform.*

Making an Alias

An *alias* is a pointer to the original file that aids in file navigation (it's similar to a shortcut in Windows or a symbolic link under other Unix-based operating systems). You can put the alias where you want without having to depend on Mac OS X's organizational structure for applications and other files. Many Mac users place aliases for files on the desktop, putting them a double-click away from launching without having to burrow deep through nested folders.

To make an alias, simply select the item, and then choose Make Alias from the Finder's File menu or press Command+L. The alias can then be moved or copied to your preferred location.

TIP: *To make an alias of an item and move it at the same time, simply drag it to its new location while holding down the Command and Option keys.*

Creating Favorites

The Favorites folder is a great place to keep the documents you use over and over again. To make an item appear in that folder, select it and then choose Add To Favorites from the Finder's File menu or press Command+T. Favorites are available as a default Finder toolbar item, or via the Go menu.

Accessing Contextual Menus

This feature, which debuted with Mac OS 8, produces a pop-up menu related to the item selected. It's quite similar to the right-click feature of Windows. To access the contextual menu, select an item and hold down the Control key.

NOTE: *Some third-party input devices, from such companies as Kensington, MacAlley, and Microsoft, have extra buttons that you can program to access the contextual menus. This will be familiar territory for Windows users.*

Ejecting a Disk

This function works the same as in previous versions of the Mac OS, with a small exception. The normal behavior is to drag the disk icon to the Trash. You can also press Command+E after the drive has been selected. The Put Away command (Command+Y) has been removed. When you drag a disk icon to the Trash, the icon for the Trash changes to an eject symbol, no doubt a response to complaints from user interface experts that you aren't trashing a disk when you eject it.

TIP: *If you have an Apple Pro keyboard, you can also use the Eject key or F12 to remove a CD or DVD from the desktop and eject it in a single operation. Having a drive access key on the keyboard is especially useful for many Apple computers that do not have CD eject buttons on the drives themselves.*

Using the Show Info Window

In older versions of the Mac OS, you'd use the Finder's Get Info window to adjust a program's memory allotment and get information about a program's version. Mac OS X has a Show Info window (see Figure 4.19) with one key feature no longer present: the ability to change the memory given to a program. You no longer need to do so under Mac OS X, because the operating system dynamically allocates the memory a program requires. What you see depends on the kind of

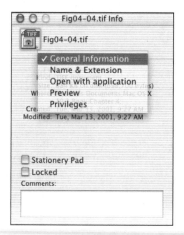

Figure 4.19   The Show Info window lets you access information about a file
or change the application that will automatically open a
document.

item selected. A document will provide one set of options, an application another. Here are the basic features:

NOTE: *When you use the Show Info command with a Classic application, you will still see a
Memory option, which you can use to control allocation of memory for that application. Mac OS X's
superior memory management doesn't help your older Mac applications.*

- *General Information*—This screen presents general information
  about a selected item, including its location and size. If you've
  selected an application, it shows the version information.

- *Name & Extension*—For documents, this option lets you change
  the file's name and specify whether the file extension that applies
  to that document will appear.

- *Open With Application*—If you've selected a document, this
  option lets you change the application that launches that document, or all documents of the same type.

- *Languages*—This window (available for Mac OS X applications
  only) shows the languages supported by an application. You can
  uncheck some of them, if you wish; doing so might improve
  performance at the expense of limiting the application's ability to
  handle multilingual material.

- *Preview*—This feature appears only when you select a document
  icon. You can use it to view a preview image of the document.

NOTE: *If the icon you've selected belongs to a Classic application, all you'll see is an enlarged picture of its icon.*

- *Privileges*—Use this window to set access privileges to the selected item. That way, you can extend the range of users who can view that item via file sharing.

TIP: *You can easily change the icon for an item. Just select the item, bring up the Show Info window, and paste the new icon atop the previous icon in the General Information window. This is best done for drives and folders. Changing a file icon may make it difficult to visually identify which application opens the file.*

---

4. Introducing the Mac OS X Finder

Taking Screenshots

In previous versions of the Mac OS, you could take a screenshot of the contents of your desktop or a selected item via simple keyboard shortcuts. Although this feature was missing from the initial release of Mac OS X, parts of it are restored in Mac OS X 10.1. Here's a brief run-through of the built-in screen capture capabilities:

- *Command+Shift+3*—This is the original shortcut. When you press this combo, a picture of your entire screen is captured and saved as a TIFF file. The file itself will be named Picture 1, Picture 2, and so on, and placed on your desktop.

- *Command+Control+Shift+3*—This awkward combination also captures the entire screen, but puts the data in the clipboard, so you can paste it within an open document window via the Paste command.

- *Command+Shift+4*—This combination changes the cursor to a crosshair. Just drag the cursor across the area you want to capture. When you release the mouse, the area is captured as a screenshot and also saved as a TIFF file on your desktop, named Picture 1, and so on.

- *Command+Control+Shift+4*—This combination also lets you select an area for capturing. The saved area is stored in the clipboard for pasting into another application.

TIP: *Mac OS X includes Grab, in the Utilities folder, which can also do timed screen grabs and save the results with the file name you choose. However, if you do lots of screen captures, my personal recommendation is Snapz Pro X, a shareware application available from Ambrosia Software (**www.ambrosiasw.com**). I used this program to capture all the illustrations in this book.*

Finder Keyboard Shortcuts

You don't have to mouse around in Mac OS X. A liberal number of keyboard shortcuts can help you navigate without a mouse click. Some of these, in fact, will work in many of your Mac programs. The shortcuts listed in Table 4.1 will work in the Finder as listed.

Table 4.1   Finder keyboard shortcuts.

Shortcut	Result
Command+N	Opens a new Finder window
Command+Shift+N	Creates a new folder
Command+M	Minimizes the window and shrinks it to the Dock
Command+L	Makes an alias
Command+A	Select All
Command+C	Copies items (including files and folders)
Command+V	Pastes items (including files and folders)
Command+X	Cut (does not work on files and folders)
Command+Z	Undo (including file/folder copy or move operations)
Command+I	Opens the Show Info window
Command+T	Adds the selected item to Favorites
Command+H	Hides an application
Command+J	Displays the View Options window
Command+F	Launches Sherlock
Command+D	Duplicates the selected item
Command+O	Opens a file or folder
Command+K	Brings up the Connect To Server window
Option+drag	Copies an item
Command+drag	Lines up icons
Command+Option+drag	Makes an alias of the selected item
Command+double-click	Opens the folder in a new Finder window
Option+Right Arrow	Opens a folder and all its subfolders in List View
Option+Left Arrow	Closes a folder in List View
Command+Option+Right Arrow	Opens all the folders of the selected folder in List View
Command+Option+Left Arrow	Closes all the folders in the selected folder
Option+click close button	Closes all open windows
Option+click minimize button	Minimizes all open windows and shrinks them to the Dock

(continued)

4. Introducing the Mac OS X Finder

Table 4.1 Finder keyboard shortcuts *(continued).*

Shortcut	Result
Option+click zoom button	Enlarges the window to fill the entire screen
Option+click window	Hides the previous program
Option+click Dock icon	Hides the previous program
Command+drag window	Moves a window without making it active
Command+click window title	Chooses the folder containing the current folder
Command+Tab	Moves the focus to the Dock and displays the next active application.

Using the Finder to Burn CDs and DVDs

When Apple got the message and added built-in CD burners, it also added a feature that lets you burn your CDs from the Finder. Under Mac OS X, it works essentially the same as in your Classic Mac OS:

1. Insert a blank CD, CD/RW, or DVD-R disc into the drive. After a short time in which the optical media is analyzed, you'll see a screen prompt where you can prepare the media (see Figure 4.20).

NOTE: If you need to format the CD/RW, Disk Utility will open to the proper screen where you can erase it.

WARNING! *The Finder's CD burning feature works only with Apple's built-in CD and DVD burners (DVD-R support requires the SuperDrive), and a small selection of supported third-party devices. If you want to see the current supported list, check with Apple's iTunes site at www.apple.com/itunes. Whatever drives are supported by iTunes will, in large part, work with Finder-level disk burning as well.*

2. Name your CD or DVD and then choose the type of data you want to copy (data or music files) from the pop-up menu.

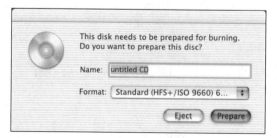

Figure 4.20   Prepare your optical media from this dialog box.

3. With your selections made, click Prepare to complete the initial setup process. In a few seconds, you'll see an icon on your Mac's desktop identified by the type of media you prepared.

4. Drag the files you want to copy to the optical disc's icon.

WARNING!   Depending on the kind of media you use, you'll be limited to 700MB for an 80-minute CD, 650MB for a 74-minute CD, and 4.7MB for a DVD-R. You will receive a Finder warning if you attempt to copy over too many files.

5. If you want to organize the layout of the optical media before it's burned, open its window and reorder the icons as you like and the position of the window. This will simplify locating the material on the disc later.

6. After the layout is set up, choose Burn Disc from the Finder's File menu to begin the process. You'll get a final warning from the Finder to confirm that you really want to burn a disc.

7. After you OK the prompt, the disk burning process will begin, followed by a verification procedure in which the data will be read back to make sure that the data is good.

8. When the disc burning process is complete, you can insert more media and continue to create CDs or DVDs.

WARNING!   Not all optical media work with all drives, even if the labels say they're compatible. If you run into consistent problems with a specific brand, where burning is halted or the media isn't successfully verified, try another brand. If you're using a third-party CD or DVD burner, contact the drive manufacturer for additional help, because Apple won't provide direct support for its disc burning feature except with an Apple computer that shipped with a factory CD or DVD burner.

Restoring Classic Mac OS Application Switching

When Mac OS X was first unveiled, sharp criticisms were leveled at the disappearance of the oh-so-useful application-switching menu, which was located at the right end of the menu bar. Although the Dock (see Chapter 5) is meant as a substitute, there is another alternative, in the form of a donationware (meaning you send a voluntary donation) utility. ASM (see Figure 4.21) is installed as a System Preference component. Once installed, it can be configured to restore an application-switching menu in its accustomed spot.

Two of the most interesting features of ASM are the ability to hide other applications automatically courtesy of its Single Application Mode, so you see only the active application. This is a sure way to

4. Introducing the Mac OS X Finder

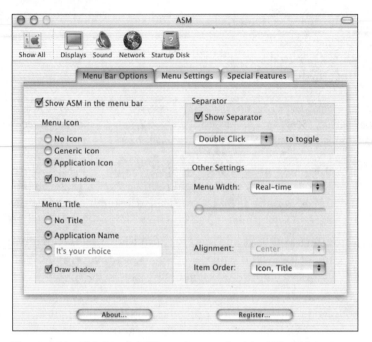

Figure 4.21   This handy utility restores a cherished Mac OS feature.

reduce screen clutter and confusion, especially if you have a smaller display on your Mac. The other key feature is Classic Window Mode, in which all windows in an open application come forward, rather than just the one you select (the Mac OS X way).

ASM also sports an extensive array of adjustments to the way the application menu looks, from icon size to whether labels and icons appear, or just one or the other. You can also suppress application hiding for individual programs, in case you need to see both applications at the same time (or even use a modifier key such as Shift to suppress the feature altogether).

Related solution:	Found on page:
Using the Dock	121

Chapter 5

Mac OS X Desktop Management

In Brief

Mac OS X is a clever mixture of the old and the new. For example, the Mac OS X desktop looks very similar to the one from previous Mac OS versions. It has a decorative background pattern and, unlike the versions of the new operating system that were shown during the initial development process, the familiar icons for your hard drive are present and accounted for. But something appears to be missing. Where's the trash? As you've probably noticed, it's migrated to the Dock, which, in part, forms the main subject to be dealt with in this chapter.

The pristine desktop is part of the normal behavior of Mac OS X, but as you'll see in this chapter, it's not necessary to keep things neat and clean. One of the rights of the Mac user is to arrange, even clutter, a desktop to suit your taste, and the new Mac operating system, as with the Classic Mac OS, gives you lots of freedom to change background images and clutter it with icons to a fare-thee-well.

The Dock Dissected

Previous versions of the Mac OS gave you several ways to access a file quickly, whether a document, a folder, or a program. Apple has merged a number of these functions into a single taskbar—a colorful, almost cartoonish, and almost infinitely resizable palette of icons that resides at the bottom of your Mac's display (or elsewhere if you prefer, as you'll see shortly). It's called the Dock (see Figure 5.1).

NOTE: Although it's easy to find the Dock's roots in Windows, actually the Dock is more closely aligned to the original application-launching palette used for the NeXT operating system, on which Mac OS X is based.

Here's what the Dock replaces:

- *Apple menu*—The original Apple menu (see Figure 5.2) was the former repository of frequently used items and Control Panel

Figure 5.1   The Dock is a single location where you check and open applications, documents, and folders. Note the white separation line (barely visible) to divide the Dock into two usually unequal parts.

Figure 5.2   The original Apple menu was infinitely customizable and was easily set to reflect the tastes of its user.

access. It was immensely customizable, but doing so required a trip to the System Folder and then to another folder called Apple Menu Items. For Mac OS X, the Apple menu has gotten an overhaul, after disappearing entirely in prerelease versions (see Figure 5.3). It now incorporates the functions of the Finder's

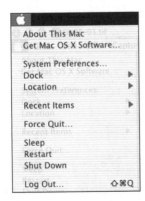

Figure 5.3   The new Apple menu is designed in a more rigid fashion, merging the old and the new and replacing the functions of the Finder's Special menu.

Special menu, system-wide customization, and just the core of the recent items features of the previous version. The list of recent folders has been moved to the Go menu, as explained in Chapter 4. Control Panels have been replaced by the System Preferences application, which consolidates the various system settings into one program; it gets a featured spot in the Dock. I discussed setting your Mac OS preferences in detail in Chapter 3.

- *Control Strip*—Some Control Panel functions and settings for a number of applications were put in the Control Strip (see Figure 5.4), a floating palette that first debuted as a feature on the Apple PowerBook. It later spread to all Macs. Some of the functionality has been rolled into the System Preferences application, and other functions for a handful of preference panels, such as Airport, Display, Internet Connect, and Sound, can be placed as system menu items on the menu bar.

- *Application menu*—Part of the function of working with open applications stays in the menu bar, with the bold application menu now at the left of the screen. The ability to switch between open applications is now a function of the Dock.

NOTE: *If you prefer something more akin to the Control Strip of old, don't despair. Independent programmers have plenty of opportunities to get in the game. The OpenStrip shareware program is meant to replace some of the functions of the original Mac OS Control Strip. One popular application menu replacement is ASM, which deposits the same sort of application menu on the right side of the menu bar that you'd see in the Classic Mac OS. As with all such useful Mac OS X enhancements, you can find a good collection at the **VersionTracker.com** Web site (**www.versiontracker.com/macosx**).*

The Dock is divided into two parts, and some of the icons have clearly identifiable functions. Here's a description of how they work:

- *Left side*—Application icons, including those representing open programs, stay here (see Figure 5.5).

- *Right side*—Icons representing documents, folders, servers, Web sites, QuickTime TV channels, and the Mac OS Trash exist on the right end of the Dock (see Figure 5.6).

- *Finder*—Click this icon to open a Finder window (see Figure 5.7).

Figure 5.4   Depending on the programs you have installed on your Mac, the contents of the Control Strip will change; this version has lots of extras.

Figure 5.5   The items at this end of the Dock consist strictly of applications. Icons with the triangles beneath are open.

Figure 5.6   The rest of the icons you put in the Dock reside at the right, regardless of political content.

Figure 5.7   This icon represents the Finder.

- *System Preferences*—As part of the Dock when you install Mac OS X, this icon allows you to set your Mac's preferences (see Figure 5.8). It replaces the Control Panels, at least in part.

TIP: *Missing an icon? Although several application and document icons are part of the standard installation of Mac OS X, it's easy to drag them off the Dock. If you want an icon back, just locate the original icon for that item, which will usually be in the Applications or Documents folder, and drag it back to the Dock.*

- *Mail*—This icon represents Apple's powerful new email software (see Figure 5.9). When you receive email, you'll see a display on the Mail icon indicating the number of unread messages waiting for you. I'll cover this program in detail in Chapter 22.
- *Document*—This icon represents a document that's been placed in the Dock (see Figure 5.10).

Figure 5.8   Click this icon to launch the System Preferences application.

Figure 5.9   This icon represents Apple's Mac OS X exclusive email software.

Figure 5.10   When you add documents to the Dock, they'll look something like this.

- *Web Sites And Servers*—Another great feature of the Dock is the ability to store icons that link you to your favorite Web sites or provide direct access to a networked server (see Figure 5.11).

- *Minimized window*—When you click the minimize icon in an open document window, the document shrinks to the Dock (see Figure 5.12). It remains there until you click it to restore or maximize the document window. This is a difficult effect to capture, and it took a clever little application, Andrew Welch's

Figure 5.11   Whether a networked server or a favorite Web site, it's just a click away in the Dock.

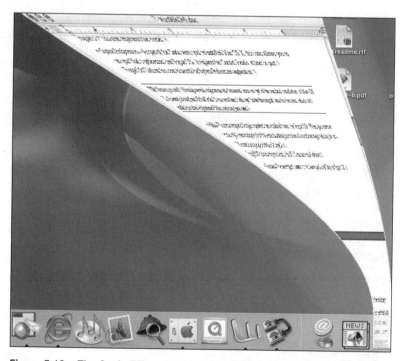

Figure 5.12   The Genie Effect ends with the icon lodging itself in the Dock.

Snapz Pro X (shareware from **www.ambrosiasw.com**) to capture it for posterity. Pressing Command+M, by the way, will also minimize a window.

TIP: *If you want to see the ultraslow Genie Effect demonstrated at Macworld Expos by Apple CEO Steve Jobs, hold down the Shift key when minimizing a document. You'll see the reverse effect with the same keyboard shortcut when you click an icon representing a minimized document in the Dock.*

- *Trash*—The Mac OS Trash is no longer a resident of the desktop (see Figure 5.13). It now always sits at the right end of the Dock.

- *Pop-up menus*—Click any item in the Dock and hold down the mouse button to see a pop-up menu related to that item. With a word-processing program, such as Microsoft Word, for example, you'll be able to directly access an open application window. The best effect occurs when you click a disk or folder icon (see Figure 5.14). The end result is a menu with lots of submenus, similar in scope to what you used to see in the Apple menu. The display for a regular application is more pedestrian. Click the icon to access a Show In Finder command. If the application is open, you'll be able to quit it from the pop-up menu.

TIP: *Some applications, such as Apple's iTunes, display application controls in the Dock-based pop-up menus. That way, you can access functions without going to the program itself. Apple has opened the programming interface for this feature, so you can expect to see a number of programs supporting it over time.*

NOTE: *The pop-up menu you see when you click a Dock item is similar to what you get when you command-click an item to see its contextual menu, but it doesn't require a modifier key, and it's strictly limited to items placed in the Dock.*

The Mac OS X desktop is ripe for changing, and you'll be pleased to know it's quite possible to organize it in many ways depending on your particular needs. In the following pages, I'll describe the various desktop preferences and then cover how you can tailor your Mac's desktop to resemble the one used in prior versions of the Mac OS, or

Figure 5.13　The Trash gets a new home for Mac OS X.

5. Mac OS X Desktop Management

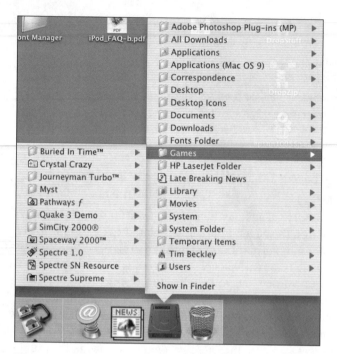

Figure 5.14   Up to five levels of pop-up menus can be displayed when you click and hold a folder or disk icon in the Dock.

in ways you might not have imagined before. You'll also get a gander at a third-party utility that will take the desktop farther than you might have expected.

Immediate Solutions

Setting Dock Preferences

In Chapter 4, I discussed the Finder preferences, one type of preference you can establish under Mac OS X that may impact your desktop. Now I'll give you, as long-time radio broadcaster Paul Harvey says, the rest of the story. You can follow these steps to change the way your Mac's desktop and the Dock function:

1. To change Dock settings, choose Dock from the Apple menu and select Dock Preferences from the submenu. Doing so brings up the Dock settings pane from the System Preferences application (see Figure 5.15).

2. Set all or some of the following six Dock preferences:

   • *Dock Size*—This setting lets you configure the size of the icons by moving the slider. You're apt to find that the Dock is just too imposing on your Mac's screen except for a very large display, so you'll probably want to make it smaller.

TIP: *You can also resize the Dock by clicking the bar on the Dock that separates applications from documents and dragging it up or down. If you hold down the Option key while resizing the Dock, the Dock will default to fixed-sized icons, such as 32 pixels, 64 pixels, and 128 pixels. Otherwise, the adjustments are infinitely variable. When you Control-click the Dock, you'll have immediate access to its preferences.*

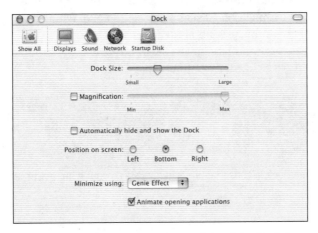

Figure 5.15   Change the look and actions of the Dock here.

5. Mac OS X Desktop Management

- *Magnification*—Select this checkbox to make the Dock magnify the icons as you drag the mouse over them (see Figure 5.16). It looks flashy, but it may be a little bit much after you use it for a while. The slider bar lets you decide how much the icons will expand.

- *Automatically Hide And Show The Dock*—The Dock sits above your open application windows, and you cannot grab anything beneath it, so this adjustment may be a great convenience. It's also a good way to save screen real estate. The Dock stays hidden unless you drag the mouse to the bottom of the screen to make it visible. You'll find this adjustment particularly useful for a smaller Mac's display.

TIP: *You can also make the Dock hide itself when the mouse isn't near by pressing Command+Option+D. Repeating the command will undo the change. This shortcut won't work if you're in a Classic application or in a program that has a keystroke that duplicates this one.*

- *Position On Screen*—This is the answer to many requests to move the Dock from its bottom position. You can center it at the left or right end of your screen, if you prefer (see Figure 5.17).

NOTE: *As you'll see later in this chapter, you can pin the Dock at the end of the screen or even at the top, courtesy of a third-party utility such as TinkerTool. This handy System Preferences add-on also can change other Dock settings, such as the one that follows.*

- *Minimize Using*—The Genie Effect is regarded by some as totally cool, but others regard it as totally annoying. This setting lets you choose a scaling effect instead, which rapidly reduces an item in size and puts in on the Dock. You may prefer this option if you have a slower Mac and the Genie Effect slows things down too much.

Figure 5.16   The Dock's icons magnify when you drag your mouse over them.

Figure 5.17   Right or left—make the Dock go where you want.

- *Animate Opening Applications*—When this feature is shown at a presentation, it looks cool; but the idea of having an application's icon bounce up and down in the Dock may grow tiresome. You can switch off the option here and wait for programs to open for you without warning.

NOTE: *The Dock provides another level of animation, where an icon bounces up and down to alert you that another application is calling for your attention. It may mean there's a problem with the application or, for example, that a Web site opened in Internet Explorer cannot be retrieved. This option can't be switched off (although some programs, such as Print Center, manage to limit alerts to an icon that doesn't bounce).*

3. After you've set your Dock preferences, you can quit the System Preferences application or make further settings, such as the one that comes next.

Setting Desktop Preferences

In addition to modifying the Dock in various ways, you can change your Mac's desktop backdrop or control a handful of Finder preferences to make your desktop take on more of the look and feel you like. To begin with, let's change the desktop pattern:

1. To change your Mac's desktop settings, launch System Preferences and click the Desktop preference panel. The dialog box shown in Figure 5.18 appears.

2. Select a picture from those displayed in thumbnail form at the bottom of the dialog box (use the horizontal scrollbar to see more).

3. Drag the image into the well or double-click it and, within seconds, your background image will change to the one selected.

TIP: *If your new background doesn't appear right away, log out and log in again. This time, the changeover should work as you expect.*

---

4. If you don't see a background image that suits your taste, or if you want to use one of your own photos, click the Collection pop-up menu (see Figure 5.19) to see additional choices. The pictures in the folder you choose will appear in the Desktop preference dialog box in thumbnail form.

5. When you've made your selection, you can quit System Preferences or choose another preference icon for further changes.

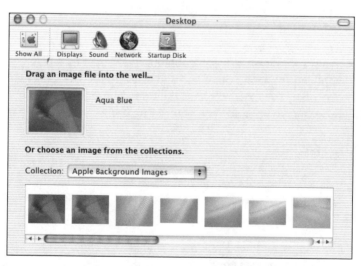

Figure 5.18   Alter the Mac's desktop backdrop here.

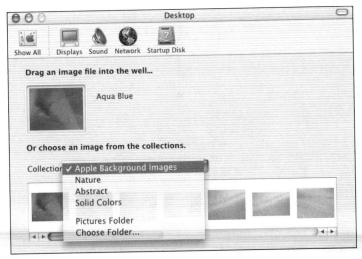

Figure 5.19   Pick a suitable source for desktop patterns from the ones on display.

NOTE: *You should be able to use just about any JPEG or TIFF image file as a background, but remember that a large or complicated image may take longer to display on your screen, particularly if you don't have the latest and greatest Mac with the fastest graphics accelerator. Should screen refresh slow down, pick a simpler image (or just try a few and see which work best).*

Setting Finder Preferences

After you've established the way you want the Dock to look and the desktop background that meets your needs, setting Finder preferences is the final step of the equation. Here's how it's done:

1. Click the Finder.

2. Choose Preferences from the Finder's application menu to bring up the dialog box shown in Figure 5.20.

3. Click a checkbox or button to establish your personal settings. Here are the changes you can make:

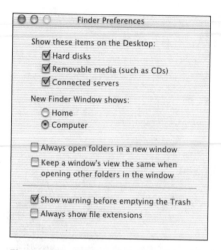

Figure 5.20   Click a checkbox to establish your preference.

- *Show These Items On The Desktop*—One of the controversial features of prerelease versions of Mac OS X was the fact that drive icons didn't show up on the desktop automatically. Now a clean desktop is an option. If you don't want certain items to appear automatically on the desktop, just uncheck the options for hard disks, removable media, or connected servers. Even if you turn them all off, you can click the Computer icon in the Finder to show a display of available disks and servers.

- *New Finder Window Shows*—Choose whether a new window will go to your Home or Computer directory (Computer is the default).

- *Always Open Folders In A New Window*—When you check this option, Finder behavior is changed to that of the Classic Mac OS, in which opening a folder spawns a new Finder window, rather than display the contents in the existing Finder window. Checking this option is a sure way to increase desktop clutter, if that's what you want.

These options control how your Mac's desktop is populated under Mac OS X. If you want to go further and set the entire range of Finder preferences, refer to Chapter 4 for more information. When you're done, click the Close button to dismiss the Finder Preferences screen.

Related solution:	Found on page:
Setting Finder Preferences	92

Using the Dock

In day-to-day use, the Dock is highly intuitive. It provides clear status messages about your open applications and documents, and it can be, as explained previously, customized in many ways for your convenience. Here are some basic hints and tips for getting the maximum value out of the Dock:

- *Adding icons*—Because the Dock expands dynamically to accommodate the number of icons you've added, all you need to do is drag an icon to the Dock to have it display (the actual file, of course, remains where it was). The left side of the Dock carries your application icons. The right side handles the rest, such as documents, folders, links to servers and Web sites, and Quick-Time channels. You can't put the wrong icon in the wrong side; the icon will only be accepted in the proper side of the Dock.

NOTE: *Icons in the Dock are not automatically sorted for you. You can click and drag them to new positions, depending on whether you prefer alphabetical order or some random sequence.*

- *Application switching*—As explained earlier, open applications are indicated by a black triangle below the application's icon in the Dock. Click the icon of any opened application in the Dock to move directly to that program.

TIP: *To hide all other open application windows when opening a new one from the Dock, hold down the Command+Option keys while clicking any application icon. Hold down the Option key to hide just the application window from which you're switching (but not all windows opened with that application). The Show All command in the application menu brings back the windows.*

- *Single-click access*—Just like the Launcher in older versions of the Mac OS, you can access any item in the Dock with a single click.

TIP: *You can use the keyboard to switch between open applications. Press Command+Tab to open the next application icon, as shown from left to right. Repeat the action to select other applications. To reverse the process, press Command+Shift+Tab.*

- *Reordering icons*—To change the order of an icon in the Dock, click and drag it to its new position. You cannot, of course, put application icons on the right end of the Dock; but otherwise, feel free to reorder items as you prefer.

5. Mac OS X Desktop Management

NOTE: *Did the application icon disappear? Some applications, such as Mac OS X's Print Center, stay open only as long as the print queue has a job being processed. After the processing is finished, the application automatically quits (except, however, if you double-click the print queue, in which case it stays open until you quit Print Center). It may take a few moments, however, for the actual document to finish, depending on the speed and the need for extra processing by the output device itself. The same vanishing effect holds true for the Classic environment; the Mac OS 9 icon vanishes when Classic has loaded (even though it remains active).*

- *Removing icons*—Did you change your mind? You can discard a Dock icon you no longer need. Just click and drag it away from the Dock. In just a second, it will disappear in a puff of smoke, like magic.

NOTE: *You cannot remove the icon for an open application.*

- *Pop-up menus*—When you click and hold a Dock icon, you'll see a menu related to the contents of that icon. For Mac OS X applications, you have the option to jump to an open document window, to display the folder in which the item is located in the Finder, or to quit the application. In addition, some applications, such as Apple's iTunes, let you access additional control functions courtesy of the Dock, such as playing a song from your playlist or moving to other tracks on the list. This feature is optionally available to program developers, and you may see it in a specific application from time to time.

- *Dock notifications*—Are you trying to access a Web site while working in another program, and the browser needs to tell you the site can't be found or you have to OK a security window? Or, is there a problem with an application you need to know about? If you see a bouncing icon from an open application, click the icon to see what's up. Some applications, such as Mail and Print Center, will simply alter the Dock icon to present a notice, such as the number of messages waiting to be read in your mailbox or how many pages are still to be processed in a job queue.

NOTE: *Sorry, you cannot turn off the bouncing icon feature, even if you switch off the Dock preference to animate the process of opening applications.*

- *Dock icon shortcuts*—The Dock gives you a fast way to gain access to your hard drive. Drag a drive icon to the Dock and then click the Dock to see a hierarchical menu of the drive's contents. If that seems to be overkill, just drag a folder's icon to the Dock (such as your Favorites folder in your personal Users directory).

The contents of that folder, up to five levels deep, are now just a click away from fast access.

TIP: *Another way to speed access to the Dock is to use the Full Keyboard Access feature, which is an option in the Keyboard panel of the System Preferences application. With this feature enabled (see Chapter 3 for details), the Control+F3 command will highlight the Dock for instant access to any Dock icon.*

Related solution:	Found on page:
Setting Keyboard Preferences	63

The TinkerTool Alternative

If Apple hasn't implemented a feature, you can bet a third party will find a way. TinkerTool is a useful alternative (see Figure 5.21); it's a shareware utility that can configure a whole range of default preferences for Mac OS X. When installed, TinkerTool occupies the Others category in the System Preferences application.

The Desktop settings in TinkerTool include the following features that will enhance your desktop control far beyond the standard range of Mac OS X settings:

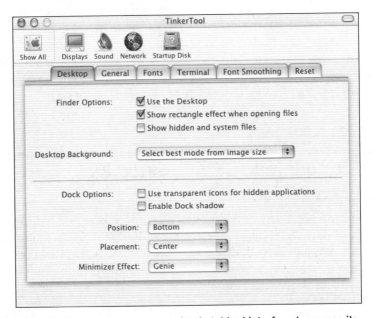

Figure 5.21   TinkerTool uses a simple tabbed interface to access its powerful features.

NOTE: As with most System Preferences settings, TinkerTool can be configured to offer a separate set of options for each person who has a user account on your Mac.

- *Finder Options*—Uncheck Use The Desktop and, next time you log in or restart, your Mac's background will revert to a plain, ocean blue regardless of the background image you selected. In addition, all icons will be gone. This is the ultimate desktop cleanup. The option to Show Rectangle Effect When Opening Files may make things slower on an older Mac, so you may want to turn it off.

- *Dock Options*—Even though Apple allows you to place the Dock at the left or right sides of your screen, TinkerTool adds the ability to place the Dock at the top or at any corner of the screen. In addition, a new Minimizer Effect called Suck-In displays a rapid shrinking motion when an open window is minimized. The Use Transparent Icons For Hidden Applications option will make it easier to see background applications that may be open on your Mac.

NOTE: Many TinkerTool settings require a logout and a login (or a regular restart) to take effect. You'll see a message at the bottom of a TinkerTool settings window if this is required.

- *Other TinkerTool options*—Click a tab to see additional settings for TinkerTool. Other available options let you put twin scrollbars at each end of a document window, determine whether multimedia CDs or DVDs will play automatically when inserted, switch font smoothing off and on (it doesn't work in all cases), adjust the terminal interface, and choose different default system fonts and sizes (another feature that not all applications support).

Making Your Mac OS X Desktop as Cluttered as Ever

One of the good or bad features of Mac OS X, depending on your point of view, is the new desktop. It can be clean and uncluttered when you remove the disk and network volume icons. However, if you leave them intact, you are well on your way toward producing the requisite degree of disorder.

Under Mac OS 9.2.1, my Mac's desktop traditionally has about 100 items on it, ranging from mounted drives and available desktop printers, to files I need to send to my son's computer for our joint writing projects, to folders containing recent downloads, to files I need to access . . . well, one of these days. Every so often, I put most of these files in another folder called, with no attempt at originality, Desktop Icons. The desktop is clear, at least for a few days, after which it becomes just as cluttered as before.

Apple has made a concerted effort to organize your desktop and file organization patterns under Mac OS X. The desktop is clear as water, unless you decide to pollute it with some icons. Here's how to return your Mac's desktop to its former glory:

1. In Mac OS X's rigid organizational system, applications are meant for the Applications folder and documents for the Documents folder. Mac OS X–savvy applications are meant to stay put, but if you hold down the Command+Option keys and drag the icon to the desktop, an alias is placed there.

NOTE: *The Command+Option shortcut also works with all files and Classic applications.*

2. After your application icons are on the desktop, go ahead and locate your favorite document files and place them there as well. A few minutes of clicking and dragging and, presto (see Figure 5.22), your Mac OS X desktop can be as cluttered as you wish, precisely as it was in previous versions of the Mac OS.

Figure 5.22   If your taste is for a busy Mac desktop, don't worry. Mac OS X will not prevent you from organizing it the way you want.

5. Mac OS X Desktop Management

Chapter 6

Setting Up Mac OS X for Multiple Users

In Brief

Although most Mac users are individuals, it has long been recognized that more than one person might use a single computer. Thus, beginning with Mac OS 9, Apple introduced a Multiple Users feature. It was an outgrowth of AtEase, a no-frills security program that allowed the owners of Macs to create a simplified user environment for children and inexperienced users. The program was popular in the educational environment because it gave teachers and system administrators the ability to restrict student access to certain files and disks on the Macs in their classrooms and computer labs.

NOTE: *In addition to being offered in workgroup form for network use, AtEase was bundled as standard equipment on many of Apple's mid-1990s consumer computers in the Performa series.*

Mac OS X extends the Multiple Users feature on a more professional level, allowing any Mac user with appropriate access privileges to easily configure his or her computer to offer a customized user experience. The great value of this feature is to give each user a personal workspace. As a result, those who work on your Mac can customize their Mac's desktop and Finder appearance to their needs without impacting the settings made by other users. They can also have a separate set of applications, documents, fonts, and other items, plus their own user settings, from mouse tracking speed to Dock location and keyboard options.

Mac OS X Multiple Users Features

Because it is based on Unix, Mac OS X is, at heart, a multiple-user system in its own right. Although it inherits some of the features that were first introduced in Mac OS 9, Mac OS X has its own unique variation. However, once you get used to its simplified user interface, you'll find that Mac OS X provides a fairly secure working environment with lots of options to help you set it up for all the people who will use your Mac.

NOTE: *Not all multiple-user features available in Mac OS 9 have been carried over to the new operating system. For example, the ability to create limited-function interfaces isn't present. Customization and access settings are limited to the standard Aqua user interface.*

---

6. Setting Up Mac OS X for Multiple Users

Here are some of the basic features of Mac OS X that provide customized user environments and security:

- *Owner as administrator*—When you first install Mac OS X, you'll establish your user account as the administrator of the computer. After you've set up your username and password, you can add users to and remove users from your system, and you can unlock and use certain system preferences that are available only to the administrators (see Figure 6.1). These preferences include Date & Time, Energy Saver, Login Window, Network, Sharing, Startup Disk, and Users. Chapter 3 talks more about using these preference settings.

NOTE: *Items in the System Preferences application that can be accessed only by the administrator are always identified by a padlock icon. In large installations, it is usually recommended that a dummy account, separate from the administrator's real user account, be created for systems administration. Doing so provides even greater security.*

- *Keychains*—If you use a number of different passwords to access your Internet accounts, online ordering and banking services, and various applications and server connections, no doubt you have to keep a record or memorize many passwords. It's easy to forget those passwords and thus lose your access to programs and services. With Apple's Keychain Access application (see Figure 6.2), located in the Utilities folder, you can store all those disparate passwords in a single location—called a *keychain*—and enter a single password to access all of them. Only you or someone with your password can unlock those passwords. When the passwords are unlocked, applications and services that need them can get them, but casual users cannot see them. When you finish using them, you just lock your keychain.

You need an administrator password to make changes using Users.

Name: Gene Steinberg

Password: ••••••••••••••••••••••••

Cancel   OK

Figure 6.1   When you click the padlock icon, you must enter your administrator's username and password to gain access to certain Mac OS X features and System Preferences settings.

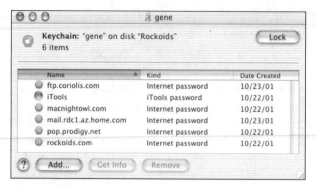

Figure 6.2   You can use the Keychain Access application to set up your personal account and store all your user passwords.

NOTE: In order for a keychain to work, the application for which you want to store a keychain must support that feature. Not all do, so you'll want to check the appropriate documentation to see which Mac OS X features are supported before you attempt to use passwords stored in a keychain.

- *Shared folders*—All users who have accounts on your Mac have their own personal user or Home folder for their own sets of applications, documents, system-related preferences, fonts, Internet accounts, and so on. These files are available only to the administrator or the individual user who logs in to that user account, unless additional sharing privileges are granted. The Public folder, however, serves as a place where you can put files and make them available to anyone who accesses your Mac. That way, those users do not need special access privileges. You can also create a Drop Box folder, where other users can place files, but only the individual user (who created the Drop Box) or the administrator can access the files inside.

NOTE: The Public folder is also used as a reasonably safe location where users who access your Mac from across a network can send and receive files. You'll want to read Chapter 8 for information on how to configure network file-sharing privileges so that access to your Mac is restricted.

- *System logins*—When you log out, only a user with a valid username and password can use your Mac. That rule provides the maximum possible degree of security for system-related access. However, if you are usually the sole user of the Mac and you have no qualms about letting others—perhaps family members or coworkers—work on your Mac, you can continue to bypass the Login prompt at startup. This is the default setting, so nothing need be changed.

WARNING!   *Although you need the proper password to access a Mac under Mac OS X, nothing prevents you from restarting your computer under Mac OS 9, or with a Mac OS 9 or Mac OS X startup disk, and then gaining access to files in that environment. If maximum security is important to you, you'll want to set up the Multiple Users feature of Mac OS 9 as well so that users cannot casually access your Mac. It would also be a good idea to hide system startup CDs (and third-party utilities, such as Norton Utilities, that come with bootable CDs) so that access cannot be gained in that fashion.*

*   *Dedicated security software*—Under previous versions of the Mac OS, a number of dedicated security programs were available from such publishers as Intego and Power On Software. Although these programs have not yet been updated for Mac OS X, Intego, which took over the products from ASD Software, was working on Mac OS X upgrades for DiskGuard and FileGuard when this book was written. In addition, Power On Software was still considering whether to upgrade DiskLock and On Guard to the new operating system. Regardless of which program you choose, however, you'll find that it can totally lock out your Mac from access from different operating systems or from external or CD-based startup disks. For the highest level of security in a workplace, you might want to seek further information about the availability of Mac OS X versions of such programs.

WARNING!   *Because of changes in the file structures of Mac OS X, do not even consider using a Classic security program with the new operating system. If you must secure your Mac to a level beyond what is available via the combination of Mac OS 9 and Mac OS X Multiple Users settings, you may want to delay deploying Mac OS X until dedicated security software is available for the new environment.*

Using Strong Passwords

If you are running your Mac in a family environment or in a small office, you might not have to be overly concerned about your choice of passwords, because it might not be a critical issue if another user in your environment works on your Mac. But if you need the maximum amount of security, you'll want to use a password that is difficult for others to guess. The best password is a random combination of upper- and lowercase letters intermixed with numbers. Such a password is extremely difficult for anyone to guess, and thus you have the maximum level of security. An optimal password should contain at least eight characters to provide a good level of security.

WARNING!   *Once you set up your Mac with Mac OS X, there is no way to gain user access without the proper password. Even if you use the Login preference panel to bypass a password request at startup, many features will not be available to you until you can manually enter that password. Should you forget it, you will have to reset your password using the Password Reset utility available in the Mac OS X Installer application. Chapter 19 explains how, and this is why you should also keep your Mac OS X installer CD in a safe place.*

6. Setting Up Mac OS X
for Multiple Users

Immediate Solutions

Setting Up Multiple-User Access

Each user of your Mac can be given his or her own personal password and user environment, which allows each user to set, within the guidelines you establish, a custom font collection, user preferences, desktop layout, applications, and documents.

Follow these steps to create a new user account:

1. Launch the System Preferences application. You'll find it on the Dock or in the Applications folder.

2. Click the Users icon to bring up the Users settings panel (see Figure 6.3).

3. If the padlock is closed, click the padlock to open it, and enter the username and password for your administrator account.

NOTE: *If you are logged in under your administrator account, the padlock is normally open. You might want to consider closing it in various system settings until you can establish separate user accounts for others who are going to use your Mac.*

---

4. With the padlock open, click the New User button to open the New User dialog box shown in Figure 6.4.

5. Click the Identity tab and, in the Name field, type the actual name of the new user.

6. Setting Up Mac OS X for Multiple Users

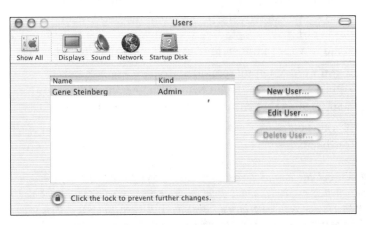

Figure 6.3   You can establish a new user account from this dialog box.

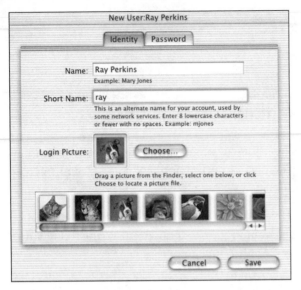

New User:Ray Perkins

Identity   Password

Name: Ray Perkins

Example: Mary Jones

Short Name: ray

This is an alternate name for your account, used by
some network services. Enter 8 lowercase characters
or fewer with no spaces. Example: mjones

Login Picture: Choose...

Drag a picture from the Finder, select one below, or click
Choose to locate a picture file.

Cancel   Save

Figure 6.4   Create a new user account on your Mac here.

6. In the Short Name field, type a username (nickname). By
   default, Mac OS X will suggest a possible username based on a
   shortened version of the real name, containing up to eight
   lowercase characters (spaces aren't allowed).

7. Choose a Login Picture from those provided and drag it into the
   picture well. You can also click Choose and select a JPEG or
   TIFF picture in an Open dialog box from among the ones you
   might have on your Mac.

8. Click the Password tab to continue (see Figure 6.5).

9. In the Password field, type a password containing at least four
   letters. Then, retype the password in the Verify field. If the
   password isn't accepted, retype it again. It must be entered the
   same way (both upper- and lowercase letters) in both places.

10. If you want a helpful reminder about a forgotten password,
    enter a question in the Password Hint text field (but don't make
    it so obvious that a third party can guess the answer).

11. If you want to give the user the authority to act as administrator
    for the Mac, select the checkbox at the bottom of the dialog box.

WARNING!   *Before allowing another user to act as administrator for your Mac, consider*
carefully whether you really want to grant those access privileges to someone else
(other than a family member, of course). Remember that any user who can log in as
administrator will have the same authority that you do as owner of the Mac.

6. Setting Up Mac OS X
for Multiple Users

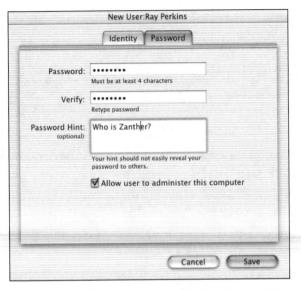

Figure 6.5   Choose your password on the Password tab.

12. Click Save to store the new user account. If you opted to use the auto-login feature to avoid manually entering the username and password each time you boot your Mac, you'll see the dialog box shown in Figure 6.6. Click Turn Off Automatic Login to turn off the feature, or click Keep Automatic Login to let the new user log in at the next restart.

NOTE: *If you turn off auto-login, you'll see a prompt whenever you boot your Mac. If one person uses the Mac most of the time, this may be an impediment rather than a convenience. You may want to leave auto-login on, as long as you have no qualms about security in your particular setting.*

13. Repeat Steps 4 through 12 to add more user accounts.

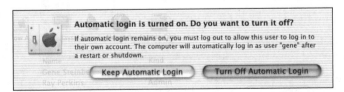

Figure 6.6   Do you want to turn off the auto-login feature? Decide here.

6. Setting Up Mac OS X for Multiple Users

14. Quit the System Preferences application by choosing Quit from the application menu or by pressing Command+Q.

Related solution:	Found on page:
Setting System Preferences Under Mac OS X	44

Editing a User Account

A user account can be changed easily at any time. If you need to reset a password or change other user information, follow these steps:

1. Launch the System Preferences application from either the Dock or inside the Applications folder.

2. Click the Users icon to launch the settings panel.

3. Click the padlock (if it's not already open) and enter the username and password for your administrator account.

4. With the padlock open, click a user's name. Then, click the Open User button or press Command+O to access the user account information.

5. Make the appropriate changes to the user's name and password information and enter a password reminder question if you wish.

6. If you intend to grant this user the authority to act as administrator for the Mac, select the checkbox at the bottom of the dialog box.

7. Click Save to save the edited user account.

8. Exit System Preferences by choosing Quit from the application menu or pressing Command+Q.

If you need to remove a user account, follow these steps:

1. Launch the System Preferences application.

2. Click the padlock if it's closed and enter the username and password for your administrator account.

3. With the padlock open, click the name of the user account you want to delete.

4. Click the Delete User button, and then click Delete to respond to the acknowledgment prompt (see Figure 6.7). (Or, if you change your mind, click Cancel instead to leave the user account.)

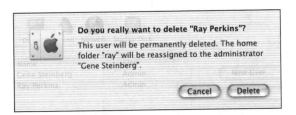

Figure 6.7   Are you sure you want to remove that user account?

NOTE: *When you delete a user, the Home folder for that user will still be present and will inherit the label Deleted. The administrator(s) of your Mac will have control over the material inside that folder.*

5. Quit the System Preferences application by choosing Quit from the application menu or by pressing Command+Q.

Setting Up Keychain Access

The keychain, first introduced in Mac OS 9, is a valuable feature that helps simplify management of all your passwords by storing them in a single place.

NOTE: *To be precise, the keychain feature appeared previously in System 7.1.1, commonly called System 7 Pro, but that system version didn't quite catch on (it was a failure in the marketplace). It was several years before the feature returned.*

Here's how to use the feature:

1. You need to create a keychain so you have a place to store all those passwords. To do so, locate the Keychain Access application, which is located in the Utilities folder inside your Applications folder.

2. Double-click the Keychain Access application to launch it and display the screen shown in Figure 6.8.

NOTE: *When you set up a username, a Keychain under that name is already made for you.*

3. Choose New Keychain from the File menu to name your new keychain (see Figure 6.9).

4. Type a name for your keychain, and then click the Save button.

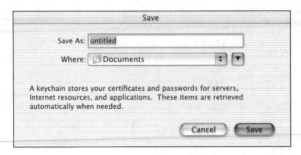

Figure 6.8   This message appears only if there is no existing keychain.

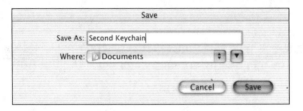

Figure 6.9   Give your keychain a name.

5. On the next screen, type a user password, and then retype the password to confirm it. Use a strong password, as explained earlier in this chapter.

6. Once you've created a keychain, it's time to populate it. If you have several keychains, there will be a Keychains menu; otherwise, your new keychain will be displayed. Click Add and type a name for the item you want to add. (Use a name that identifies the item's contents.)

NOTE: *If you are entering a Web site, be sure you include the exact access URL in the Name field. Otherwise, you won't be able to use that password to access the site.*

TIP: *A quick way to enter a complicated password is simply to access it via your Web browser and then copy the address in the URL field. You can then paste it into the Keychain Access application.*

---

7. Type the user password you need for that particular program or service.

8. Repeat Steps 6 and 7 for each password you want to enter.

9. When you're finished using Keychain Access, quit the application by choosing Quit from the application menu, pressing Command+Q, or clicking the Close button.

NOTE: *You can easily create multiple keychains, each of which stores a different set of user passwords. This method may help you from an organizational standpoint.*

With your keychains active, the first time you use a keychain, you'll see a prompt asking whether using the keychain should be allowed for this one time only or in all situations (Always Allow). If others are using your Mac under your account, you may prefer not to use that option.

Checking and Using Your Keychain

Once you've configured Keychain Access to store your user passwords, it's very simple to launch the program and check or use your passwords. Just follow these steps:

1. Locate Keychain Access in the Utilities folder, inside the Applications folder, and double-click the program to launch it.

2. If you have more than one keychain, select the Keychain Access menu and choose the keychain you want to open. If you have only one keychain stored, there will not be such a menu.

3. To unlock a keychain, click the Unlock button, and then enter your keychain password.

4. To learn about a specific password, click Get Info and then click View Password.

5. Click Allow Once to see the password.

6. Keep your keychain unlocked if you want to use it with your applications or services.

7. When you're finished working with your keychains, choose Quit from the application menu, press Command+Q, or click the Close button to close the program.

Changing Keychain Settings

The Keychain Access application has just a few settings, but you'll want to consider all the options to see what fits your work environment. Here's how to change the settings:

1. Launch the Keychain Access application.

2. Choose My Keychain Settings from the Edit menu (the words *My Keychain* will reflect the actual name of the keychain you want to configure). Doing so opens the dialog box shown in Figure 6.10.

3. If you want to change your password, you can do so now, by clicking the Change Passphrase button (see Figure 6.11). You'll have to confirm your password to make it active.

NOTE: *If you use a password that the software thinks isn't secure, such as a simple word or recognizable name, you'll get a warning prompt. If you need a strong password, I suggest you heed the warning and create a new password, preferably one with mixed upper- and lowercase letters and numbers to make it more secure.*

---

4. Once your password is changed (assuming you want it altered), you can also have your keychain lock automatically after a specified period of inactivity (you set the number of minutes) or when your Mac slips into sleep mode. Go ahead and check the settings you want.

5. To change the name of a keychain, choose Keychain List from the Edit menu, and then select the name of the keychain.

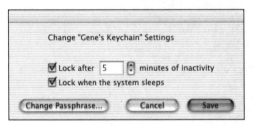

Figure 6.10   Choose your keychain settings here.

Figure 6.11   You can alter your password from this dialog box.

6. Type a new name for the keychain.

7. When you're finished making your changes, quit Keychain Access by choosing Quit from the application menu or pressing Command+Q.

Running a Keychain on Another Mac

When you create a keychain on your Mac, the keychain is not limited to that one computer. You can easily access the very same keychain on another Mac, which is quite convenient if you need to run the same applications and services on home and office computers or on an Apple laptop. Here's how to work with a mobile keychain:

1. Locate your personal keychain file. You'll find it in the Your Keychains folder, inside the Library folder, within your Users folder. Your keychain file will be stored using the name you specified when you set it up.

2. Drag the file to a mounted disk to make a copy, or make a copy in your Public folder by holding down the Option key when you drag the file to that folder.

3. On the other Mac, you can access the keychain file from across the network or from another drive simply by locating the file and double-clicking it.

4. If you want the keychain to appear in another Mac's Keychain List, drag the other keychain file into the Keychain List you have open to place the file on the other Mac as well.

5. Once the keychain is available, you can open it by entering the proper username and password.

6. When you're finished using the keychain, close the application by choosing Quit from the application menu, pressing Command+Q, or clicking on the Close button.

Coping with Problems Involving Keychains and Multiple Users

The Users features of Mac OS X are quite straightforward and usually work without a hitch. They just require a little attention to detail. But if you run into trouble, here are some likely problems and solutions:

- *Password isn't recognized*—Are you sure you entered the password correctly? Did you leave the Caps Lock key engaged by mistake? If you followed my suggestions about using a strong password, the keyboard combination might not be something you readily remember. It would be a good idea to write it down somewhere and put it in a safe place. Type the password again, just in case you made a mistake the first time (which you wouldn't see because the only feedback on your screen are the bullets in place of the characters you type). If you cannot get your keychain or multiple-users password to work, you'll have to consider reinstalling Mac OS X and starting again, unless you can delete the individual keychain file or user account via your administrator's access using the Reset Password feature of the Mac OS X Installer (it's in the Installer's application menu when you restart from the installer CD).

WARNING!   Being able to reset a password via the Mac OS X installer CD represents a potential security issue. If you are in an office environment, you may want to keep this CD under lock and key and accessible only if you need to reinstall Mac OS X or reset a password. The other issue, of course, is that individual users can bring in their own CD and do the deed, but this is an issue between you and your employees and beyond the scope of this book.

- *Keychain doesn't work with a program*—Not all applications support keychains or other multiple-user features. Check with the software publishers about their plans to support these features.

- *User forgets password*—Log in as administrator and recheck the user's account. You should keep a written record of all user accounts in a safe place, so you can access the users' computers whenever necessary or simply give them a lost password. As administrator, you can easily log in via the Multiple Users feature, open the user's account, and reset the password with a new one, if necessary.

NOTE: You cannot readily reset a password for your keychain. The best solution is just to trash it and start again if you forget the password.

- *User doesn't have permission*—If you used the original release of Mac OS X (10.0 through 10.0.4), perhaps you ran into a problem with not having permission to access, copy, or move a file. One sure way to fix this problem is to modify the permissions via the Terminal, after logging in with your administrator's account. Launch Terminal from the Utilities folder. With Terminal open, type "sudo chmod –R u+rw nameoffile". Press Return, and then enter your password at the password prompt, followed by another press of the Return key. In this command, **sudo** calls up your super user access. The **chmod** command and the subsequent instructions tell Mac OS X to give you both read and write access to the named file.

---

*TIP: Another way to deal with permissions settings is courtesy of the GetInfo shareware application, which allows you to change both groups and usernames for files, folders, and disks from a single handy graphical interface. You'll find this program and other handy Mac OS X utilities at the VersionTracker.com Web site (**www.versiontracker.com**).*

WARNING! From a security standpoint, when you set up an administrator's account, it's never a good idea to leave a password setting blank. If nobody else will access your Mac, or only friends and family, you can just as easily create a password identical to your username.

Related solution:	Found on page:
Solving Mac OS X Installation Problems	382

Suggestions for Setting Up Multiple Users for Use with Children

Many new Macs are purchased for home or small business use, where they'll be used frequently by children, ranging from those barely out of the toddler stage to those in the teen years. Parents are often surprised that young people take to personal computers far more easily than they did. My son, for example, was actively trying to trash all my files from my Mac's desktop when he was three or four years old. But more seriously, they learn mouse skills and develop good typing skills (with a little parental or school-based direction) far more speedily than the older generation. As a result, they can get on the Internet more easily and perhaps get into trouble more easily, as well.

Here are some considerations for setting up Mac OS X for use with children:

- *Keep passwords hidden and hard to guess.* Just as you would hide your password from outsiders, consider making your user password difficult for children to detect. Today's kids have a remarkable ability to figure out such things, if you make your password too easy to guess. Make sure they cannot log on to your

administrator's account and do mischief (even if unintended).
That way, they will be limited to system preferences that are
padlocked or secured.

- *Consider AOL or CompuServe 2000 for a kid's Net access.* Both
  AOL and CompuServe have Mac OS X–savvy software available
  (see Figure 6.12). AOL, for example, has a powerful set of Parental Controls that allow you to restrict your child's access to
  various features of the service, such as instant messages, email
  from strangers, and various Web sites. This family-friendly
  approach is one reason AOL has risen to the top of the heap in
  terms of online services (not to mention its hugely successful
  promotional campaigns).

- *Use email filtering.* Apple's Mail application and the other
  alternatives have filtering options that let you prevent email from
  specific locations from arriving. By extending these tools, you
  can restrict a user to receiving email only from approved locations, such as family members or friends. That way, unacceptable
  material doesn't arrive. Another ISP that will help you in this
  regard is EarthLink, Apple's default ISP partner. It inherited a
  feature called Spaminator when it merged with MindSpring. This
  feature automatically blocks email from known purveyors of junk
  mail. That, plus careful filtering, will go a long way toward
  protecting children from unacceptable email solicitations.

6. Setting Up Mac OS X for Multiple Users

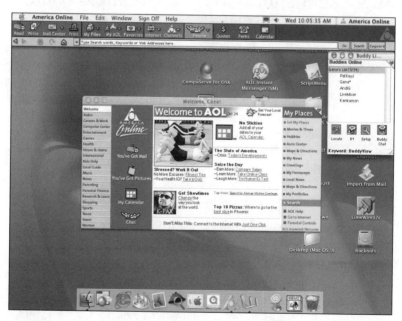

Figure 6.12   Here is AOL for Mac OS X.

Chapter 7

Mac OS X's Search Feature

In Brief

"Where is it?" is a common refrain when you're trying to locate a missing file. Hard drives are constantly getting cheaper and bigger, which means you can store more of your stuff on them. However, with so much data (and some new drives with capacities greater than 100GB), it gets increasingly difficult to find the files you want. In addition, the World Wide Web contains literally millions of sites, with content that dwarfs the largest libraries in the world. With so much material out there, what can you do to find the information you want without spending endless amounts of time in the process?

For Mac OS X, Apple has enhanced its Sherlock search utility (see Figure 7.1) to run faster and more efficiently, using its plain-English language technique for making requests. This approach makes it much easier to find the information you want without having to know special search techniques or arcane instructions.

Figure 7.1   Apple's fancy search utility handles local, network, and Internet searching with aplomb.

Sherlock Searches Locally and Internationally

Where did you put that document containing information about a great new stock opportunity? Can you find the right news story about your favorite movie star? Are there online resources where you can search for new homes in that city to which you've been transferred?

Before Apple created its highly flexible searching tool, no central resource existed to access these kinds of information. On your computer, you had to use the built-in search mechanism, and you had to get a third-party program to check the content of a file. The Internet has a number of popular search engines, but knowing which one will work for your specific range of requests is a matter of trial and error. In addition, you have to learn the right search syntax for any but the most simple information requests.

Beginning with Mac OS 8.5, Apple introduced Sherlock, an all-purpose search utility that grew out of the original Find File application. Searches were once limited to drives connected to your Mac or from a network, but Sherlock brought the Internet into the picture by allowing you to extend your search capabilities across the world. In addition, it added the ability to search the content of files, a capability previously available only in third-party software, such as Now SuperBoomerang, an Open and Save dialog box enhancer that's no longer being developed.

For Mac OS X, Apple has made Sherlock faster and more efficient. The basic user interface from the Mac OS 9 version—Sherlock 2—is essentially the same, other than inheriting the Aqua look. Why mess with a good thing?

Sherlock divides its search feature into nine buttons, or *channels*, each of which accesses a different type of search routine. Here's a brief description of what they do; I'll cover all these features in detail later in this chapter:

- *Files*—This channel confines the search to files on a drive available to your Mac, whether attached to your computer or accessible by a local or Internet-based network. As you'll learn later in this chapter, you can also use this feature to customize the search extensively and even to search for the contents (text) in a file.

- *Internet*—Select from one or more popular Web-based search sites (see Figure 7.2) to search for almost any accessible Internet-based location.

- *People*—Let your Mac replace your phone directory. This feature lets you look up people around the world by name or by email address.

- *Shopping*—This channel is a very useful feature of Sherlock, although only a small number of online merchants are supported. Just enter a word or phrase that describes the item that you seek, and Sherlock will not only search for it but also display a list of current prices so you can do instant comparisons.

- *News*—Before information reaches your daily paper, you can search several popular news-oriented sites for stories on the events of the day, business, technology, personal finance, lifestyle information, and more.

- *Apple*—Need more help with your Mac? Or, do you just want to check out the latest models? This channel has direct links to several of Apple Computer's Web sites.

Figure 7.2   Click the checkbox to include or not include a site in your search request.

- *Reference*—Take advantage of online encyclopedias for general information, help with homework, or perhaps just the definition of a troublesome word. Do your online research courtesy of Sherlock.

- *Entertainment*—Consult such Web-based entertainment resources as *E! Online*, the Internet Movie Database, and *Rolling Stone* magazine for the latest news and views from the world of show business.

- *My Channel*—This channel isn't populated yet. It's there for you to enter your own custom-selected search sites.

You can launch the Sherlock application, choose a category or channel, and then enter your search request in plain English. Sherlock will go to work finding the information you want. Whether you're searching your Mac's drive, an attached drive, a network, or the Internet, you'll be taking advantage of one of the fastest search tools available on a personal computer. You can also easily customize both requests and features of Sherlock. You'll learn how in the following section.

7. Mac OS X's Search Feature

Immediate Solutions

Searching for Files

In seconds, you can easily locate a file on any drive connected to your Mac or accessed across a network. Whether you're looking for a document, application, or folder, Sherlock can handle the job for you. Here are the simple steps to follow:

1. Launch Sherlock by clicking its icon in the Dock or double-clicking the Sherlock icon in your Applications folder. If you prefer keyboard shortcuts, it's the same as in the Classic Mac OS, Command+F.

2. If it's not already selected, click the Files button (or channel).

3. Click the File Names radio button.

4. Enter your search request in the text field.

5. Click the magnifying glass. In seconds, Sherlock produces results that match your request (see Figure 7.3).

Figure 7.3   Sherlock has located files on my Mac's hard drive with names that match the request.

6. To see the location of an item found by Sherlock, click its name to select it. The information is displayed in the results pane at the bottom of the window.

7. To open the item, double-click its name. If it's an application or document file, the application will be launched, followed (if necessary) by the document. The process is the same as if you double-clicked on the original item.

8. To move the selected item, drag it to an open Finder window or to the desktop. Remember that some Mac OS X files cannot be moved, only copied.

9. To make a copy of the item, hold down the Option key as it's being dragged.

10. Should you want just an alias of the file, hold down the Command+Option keys as the item is being dragged to its new location.

TIP: To delete selected items from the Sherlock window, press Command+Del. This action moves the selected item to the Trash, but the Trash won't be emptied until you either perform that action in the Finder's application menu or click and hold the Trash icon in the Dock and select Empty Trash from the menu.

Searching Files for Content

It's not enough to simply find a file by its name. Sometimes, you need to find files that contain a specific word or phrase. Fortunately, Sherlock can handle that chore as easily as any other search routine.

NOTE: Your personal Users folder is indexed automatically by Sherlock. Your startup drive cannot be indexed, because it may hold information that's exclusive to other users on your Macs. Other drives and folders must be indexed separately. If you haven't indexed a drive, check the next section for information on how to perform this procedure.

To search the text inside a file, follow these steps:

1. Launch Sherlock.

2. Click the Files button.

3. Click the Contents radio button to confine your search to the text inside a document.

7. Mac OS X's Search Feature

4. If you do not find the information you want, refine your search by trying a different combination of words or phrases contained in the file for which you're searching.

NOTE: *The text-parsing process isn't perfect. Sherlock should be able to search for the text in most documents from word processor, page layout, graphic, and Internet applications, but the possibility always exists that a program will encode text in a manner that Sherlock can't read.*

---

5. After you've found the item you want, click once on the listing. Information on the contents appears in the results pane at the bottom of the Sherlock window.

6. When your search is done, quit Sherlock.

NOTE: *If your file and text search doesn't yield results, you might want to refine your request still further. Read the section "Customizing Your Information Request," later in this chapter.*

Indexing a Drive

To use Sherlock to examine the contents of a drive, you must first index the drive; the process is automatic only for the contents of your personal Home or Users directory. When a drive is indexed, keywords to locate the text strings are all placed in a special file so Sherlock can access the information quickly. Here's how to perform the indexing process:

1. Launch Sherlock.

2. Select the drive you want to index from those listed in the Sherlock window.

3. Go to the Find menu and choose Index Now (see Figure 7.4). The process begins. If the drive contains a lot of data, the process can take a considerable amount of time.

4. Repeat the process for each drive you want to index, or just select them all and they will progress in sequence, usually two at a time (see Figure 7.5).

Figure 7.4   Choose Index Now to update Sherlock's database.

Figure 7.5   These drives are being indexed as we watch.

NOTE: *You can add individual folders for indexing, which gets around the limitation on your startup drive. You'll learn more about this handy feature later in this chapter.*

WARNING!   Because a new index procedure can take a long time, as will an index of a drive on which lots of changes have been made, you might want to schedule the process for times when you're not using your Mac. Even though Mac OS X's preemptive multitasking feature can handle multiple tasks at the same time (more so if you have a dual-processor Power Mac), you should do the indexing when you're not apt to be changing the files that are being indexed.

Setting Sherlock Preferences

You can configure Sherlock's indexing settings in the Preferences screen (see Figure 7.6). As with most Mac OS X applications, the preferences are located in the Application menu. Here are the settings you can change:

- *Automatically Index Items When Sherlock Opens*—Speeds up the index process of your Home directory. Unless the process seems to slow down your Mac, you should keep this option checked.

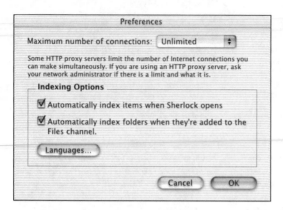

Figure 7.6   Click the checkbox to change a setting.

- *Automatically Index Folders When They're Added To The Files Channel*—Speeds things up, particularly if you're adding extra folders for custom searches. I'll explain how to add folders later in this chapter.

Searching the Internet

As mentioned, Sherlock doesn't distinguish between local, network, and Internet-based searching. It can handle all with equal flexibility. Here's how to search for information on the Internet:

1. Log on to your ISP. (See Chapter 8 for information on how to configure Mac OS X to make your Internet connection.)

2. Launch Sherlock, and then click the Internet channel button or any other channel button that reflects the information you want to search online. A screen listing the search options available in that channel appears (see Figure 7.7).

NOTE: *By default, some of the search sites are checked and some aren't. Feel free to check and uncheck items as desired to refine the search to the sites that interest you.*

3. Make your search request. Enter the word or phrase that best describes what you're searching for in the text field. For example, if you are interested in buying a new Ford, enter "Ford" or, more specifically, the model, such as "Ford Taurus".

4. Click the magnifying glass to start the process.

5. Sherlock produces a list of items that match your search request. Depending on the number of sites you've activated and

Figure 7.7   Click the checkboxes to add or remove search sites.

the speed of the connection to your ISP, this process may take anywhere from a few seconds to several minutes. A progress bar indicates the status of your search. By default, items are listed in order of relevance (how closely they match your search query). When Sherlock is done, click any item in the search list to see more information in the results pane at the bottom of the Sherlock application window (see Figure 7.8).

NOTE: *Not all search requests will yield a response. If you don't receive any matches to your request, try refining the request a bit, perhaps by using a more descriptive phrase. I'll get to the process of customizing your search requests later in this chapter.*

6. If you've found an item you want to know more about, click the link in the results list to open your Web browser. This takes you right to the page you've selected (see Figure 7.9).

7. Repeat the process to search for additional information.

8. Quit Sherlock when you're done using it.

Related solution:	*Found on page:*
Using Internet Connect for Dial-Up Networking	182

Figure 7.8   The bottom pane provides a summary or further description of the selected search result.

Figure 7.9   Success! Sherlock has found a site that has information that matches your needs.

Finding People on the Internet

In the old days, if you wanted to find out someone's physical address, you had to check a phone directory or call the telephone company for the information. Now, there's a new way to let your fingers do the walking, with the help of Sherlock—and you can find email addresses as well. To find someone on the Internet, just follow these steps:

1. Log on to your ISP in the usual fashion.

2. Launch Sherlock, and then click the People channel button.

3. Enter the name of the person you want to find in the text field. You can enter the real name or the email address, if you know it.

4. Click the magnifying glass. Sherlock goes to work searching the Internet for the person you want to contact. A progress bar indicates the status of the search.

5. After you see a list of likely candidates, if any, click the item to bring up a summary in the results pane of the Sherlock application window (see Figure 7.10).

6. If you don't find the right person the first time, continue to check likely candidates from the list.

Figure 7.10   Here are possible matches when I search for myself with Sherlock.

7. Should your initial request not be successful, ask the question differently. Instead of the real name, try an email address or vice versa. If the person is listed on the Internet in some fashion, one technique or the other may produce a successful match.

NOTE: *I don't want to overstate the accuracy of "people" searches on the Internet. There are gaps in the databases, and sometimes information will be highly out of date or simply unavailable. I still find listings showing email accounts and ISP affiliations that I abandoned long ago; the items in Figure 7.10 are a prime example.*

---

8. When you're finished with the search request, make another or quit Sherlock.

Customizing Your Information Request

Not every request will be successful, and it's not always because you've done something wrong. There is so much information on the Internet that sometimes you must fine-tune your request or try a few different ways of asking.

As mentioned, Sherlock works with plain English to send your requests, whether they're made locally, on a network, or on the Internet. However, you can narrow the information so you get what you need. Here are some suggestions:

- If you want your search request to include all the words of a phrase, type a plus (+) character between each word. So, if you're looking for a Ford Taurus, try "Ford+Taurus" if the original request isn't specific enough.

- To exclude a word, you'd think you'd type a minus sign, right? Well, no; you need to use an exclamation point (!). To refine that request on Ford products to exclude the Taurus from the search, use "Ford!Taurus".

- Now we get a bit more complicated. If you'd like to search for a group of items, use parentheses. You can even group items, yet exclude specific categories in this fashion: "(cars|Ford)! Taurus". Again, this request excludes the Taurus.

NOTE: *That vertical bar character, described above as a means to group items (which looks like a slash in some typefaces), is accessed by pressing Option+Shift+1.*

- If the simple additions to your search request don't deliver what you want, you can customize your request still further, although the options I'll discuss now are strictly confined to file-based searches, not Internet site searches. With the Files button selected, click Sherlock's Find menu and choose More Options (see Figure 7.11). In the example shown, I've clicked on the Advanced Options arrow to bring up still more possibilities. From the More Search Options window, select the checkboxes that cover your search category and enter the appropriate information, or click the pop-up menu and make your selection. Here are the categories available:

NOTE: *The search criteria described next can be refined only when you first select the checkbox that describes that category. Otherwise, text entry fields and pop-up menus remain unavailable.*

- *File Name*—Click the pop-up menu to decide whether the file name is included or excluded from the search request in several ways.

TIP: *Is the Find menu grayed out? Make sure you've clicked the Files button in Sherlock's window first.*

- *Content Includes*—Refine your file search by making sure that a certain bit of text (a word or phrase) is included.
- *Date Created*—Decide how closely the search will look at file creation dates in making your request. You can click a date and use the up and down arrows to change it. Then, you can click the pop-up menu and choose from the selected day, the

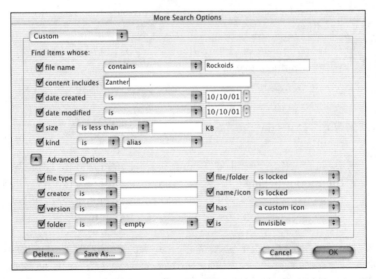

Figure 7.11   You can customize search criteria in a number of ways. I've checked all the categories in this screen for clarity.

previous day, or from a range of criteria that includes a fixed period from that day.

- *Date Modified*—The settings are the same as in the preceding item, except the search covers the modification date of the file.

- *Size*—This option limits or includes files of a particular size. It's especially helpful for content searches—particularly if you want to look at text in a small document but don't want to wait until large documents are also searched.

- *Kind*—Is the file an alias, a document, or a font, or does it fit into a wide range of categories? Choose the one you want from the pop-up menu.

- *File Type*—Under Advanced Options, this category lets you enter whether a file is a document created in a specific program. You can find out this information by selecting a file's icon, choosing Show Inspector from the Finder's File menu, and then selecting Application from the Show pop-up menu.

- *Creator*—This is a more complicated category. The creator identifies the name of the application that made the file. Normally, you won't know this code unless you have a file viewer that can read such attributes.

- *Version*—Here, you specify the version of a program or the program that made the file.

- *Folder*—In this category, you indicate whether the folder has files.

- *File/Folder*—Is the file/folder locked or not? You decide which applies here.

- *Name/Icon*—Is the name/icon locked or unlocked? Here's where you make your choice.

- *Has*—Does the file have a custom icon? Here's where you decide.

- *Is*—Is the file invisible? Some files are declared invisible by the Finder because they are system-related and not intended for general access. Sherlock lets you search for them anyway, although you won't use this option often, if at all.

WARNING!   *A number of system-related files under Mac OS X are set in a specific way or located in a specific place because they are required for your Mac to run properly. Don't attempt to seek them out and manipulate them with Sherlock, or you might find that your Mac fails to run properly or will not even boot when you try to restart.*

After you've fine-tuned your information request, click OK to return to the main Sherlock window. Now Click the magnifying-glass button. Sherlock comes up with a list of results that match your request. If you find that it's not successful in getting you what you want, you can refine the searches still further. When you're finished using Sherlock, quit the application.

TIP: *You can deselect all the checkboxes quickly in the More Search Options window by going to the Edit menu and choosing Turn Off All. Or, press Command+T. The Edit menu is grayed out if no checkboxes have been selected.*

Saving Your Custom Searches

With all those choices available to you to customize your file search, no doubt you'll want to use a complex search pattern more than once. If that's the case, you'll be pleased to know that it's possible to save a search routine for regular retrieval. Here's how:

1. With the More Search Options window opened, click the Save As button. Then, give your search routine a name.

2. When a new search routine has been saved, it will show up as a selection in the Custom pop-up menu on the opening Sherlock window.

TIP: *You can also save a set of search preferences as a separate file. To do so, choose Save Search Criteria from Sherlock's File menu, and then give your search routine a name. Once you've saved it, you can double-click that file to activate Sherlock and your custom search setup.*

Searching for Files in a Single Folder

As you saw in the preceding section, Sherlock can be customized in an almost infinite number of ways to search for precisely what you want. If you want to keep it simple, however, and look for files in a specific folder, here's a quick way to do it:

1. Launch Sherlock.

2. Click the Files button.

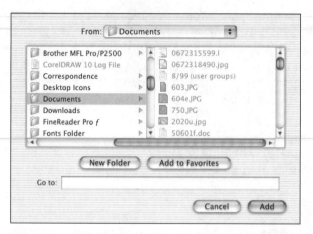

Figure 7.12   Drag a folder icon to this screen to search it via Sherlock.

3. Go to the Find menu, and select Add Folder (see Figure 7.12).

4. Drag a folder from a Finder window into this dialog box so that it's included in your Sherlock request. Repeat this action for each folder you want to add before clicking Choose to close the dialog box.

5. Enter your search request, and then click the magnifying-glass button to perform your search.

6. If you don't intend to search a folder again, go to the Files menu and return to Add Folders.

7. Select the folder you no longer need to search and drag it to the Trash. Don't fret; this action won't delete the folder, it will just remove the folder from Sherlock's list.

8. When you're done, quit Sherlock.

Making Your Own Sherlock Channel

As explained at the beginning of this chapter, Sherlock's application window has nine buttons that access the various channels. The last, labeled My Channel, is one you can customize to your taste. You can even add more channels, but you'll want to widen Sherlock's window to accommodate the extra entries. Here's how to create or customize a channel:

1. Launch Sherlock.

2. Go to the Channels menu and select New Channel to bring up the dialog box shown in Figure 7.13.

3. Give your channel a name, or just rename the one that's opened.

4. Choose an icon from the list. You can move the arrows up and down until you see the icon you want.

5. Select the type of channel you want from the Channel Type pop-up menu. You can choose from Searching, People, Shopping, and News, depending on what you want to do. Be certain of what you want, because you can't mix and match and you can't change the category without deleting the channel. If necessary, make an extra new channel.

6. Adding a search site is simple. Just open another channel that has the search site you want, select the folder and click Add. Once again, only the items in the category you've created can be added.

WARNING! *If you fail to hold down the Option key when transferring a search site, it will be removed from the source channel (not just copied).*

7. To rename a channel, click the Channel button.

8. Go to the Channels menu and pick Edit Channel.

9. If you want, enter a description to explain the purpose of your channel, and then click the OK button to save your changes. From here on, the new or modified channel appears in the Channels window (see Figure 7.14) and as a button in the Channels menu.

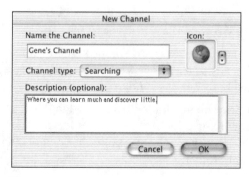

Figure 7.13   Name your channel, and you're ready to begin.

Figure 7.14   The author's custom channel now gets its own spot in the Sherlock search window.

Installing Additional Search Modules

Mac OS X comes with a small selection of search sites, but you're not limited to these offerings. You can add search areas to further extend the reach of Sherlock. You'll find additional plug-in modules for Sherlock at Apple's Web site, **www.apple.com/sherlock/ plugins.html**. Here's how to install a new module for Mac OS X:

1. Download the module to your Mac's drive.

2. Make sure the file is not compressed. It will be named with an .src extension if it's ready to use. Go to your Home directory by clicking on the Home button in the Finder.

3. Locate the Internet Search Sites folder. It's located in the Library folder in your Home directory. The folder has additional folders, each identified by channel. Drag your Sherlock plug-in to the correct channel's folder.

TIP: *To install a Sherlock plug-in in more than a single folder, select the plug-in's name, hold down the Option key, and drag it to another folder so that it's duplicated, not moved.*

Once installed, the search site appears in the appropriate channel when you launch Sherlock again.

NOTE: *Modules can be removed simply by taking them out of the folder in which they were installed, but you'll want to do it after you quit the Sherlock application. The changes will appear the next time you launch the program.*

7. Mac OS X's Search Feature

Chapter 8

Networking Overview

In Brief

When you use a Mac, you don't have to contend with setup wizards or complex configuration to join a network. Although the Macintosh was originally designed as a computer that empowered the individual, easy networking was always a part of the picture. The first example of simple networking was the ability to set up a network-capable laser printer in just a minute or so simply by plugging it in, turning it on, and selecting the driver that worked with the output device in the Chooser. The same easy networking extended to more powerful printers. Even an imagesetter, used in the printing industry for high-quality output, could be hooked up to a Mac just as easily as the cheapest laser printer. If you wanted to network Macs with each other, however, you needed special software.

NOTE: *There was one no-cost exception to the rule of having to buy commercial sharing software, such as Apple's own AppleShare or Mac OS X Server, both of which are used for larger networks. A free program, produced but unsupported by the former Claris division of Apple, allowed for limited file sharing. It was called Public Folder, but its value ended when Mac users moved past System 6.*

When Mac OS 7 came around in 1991, Apple made a logical extension of networking by offering built-in support for personal file sharing. This support allowed Mac users on a small network to activate peer-to-peer file transfers without special software by attaching cables among the computers and turning on file sharing. In minutes, the shared Mac's drive was visible in the Chooser as an AppleShare volume available on your network (see Figure 8.1).

For larger setups, it was easy to use the Get Info window to set user access privileges for file sharing. Using this limited set of user controls, you could restrict the ability of those connected to a Mac to see or modify files. As file sharing evolved, Apple also added the capability of sharing a Mac across the Internet with almost the same ease as connecting to a Mac on a local network.

For Mac OS X, Apple has advanced its networking architecture, using industry-standard technologies to provide faster performance, greater reliability, and better cross-platform compatibility. The Darwin core of the new operating system includes the BSD networking stack, which includes TCP/IP, the protocol used to power the Internet. You don't have to abandon your existing techniques for getting

8. Networking Overview

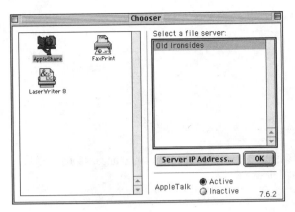

Figure 8.1   The late and definitely not lamented Mac Chooser was used to access printers and networked Macs.

connected, either; there's native support for Point-to-Point Protocol (PPP) connections, so you can access your ISP as easily as before—perhaps more easily. (I'll cover the subject of Mac OS X's Internet features in Chapter 21.) AppleTalk is also supported, so you don't have to do anything extra to access your existing Macs and printers. In all, Mac OS X, beginning with version 10.1, includes built-in network support for such file services as AFP (AppleShare), Server Message Block / Common Internet File System (SMB/CIFS), WebDAV, and Network File System (NFS), which means you can mate not only with a Mac, but also with computers running Linux and other Unix operating systems, Novel NetWare, Windows 3.1, Windows 95, Windows 98, Windows Me, Windows NT, Windows 2000, and Windows XP. All of this is accomplished under Mac OS X without your having to learn special skills or trip through a complicated series of dialog boxes and interpret arcane commands.

Accessing Networked Macs from Mac OS X

When you look over your new operating system, you'll see that something's missing. Where's an application for accessing networked computers?

The method for accessing shared volumes is closer in concept to the Network Browser application that first appeared under Mac OS 8.5 (see Figure 8.2). Networked Macs appear in the Connect To Server dialog (see Figure 8.3), available from the Mac OS X Finder's Go menu. Your network installation, whether local or Internet-based, is divided into *neighborhoods*, each of which consists of a set of networked Macs.

Figure 8.2   The Network Browser application could access local and
Internet networks.

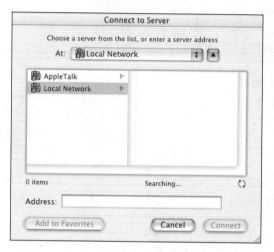

Figure 8.3   The Connect To Server feature in Mac OS X's Go menu is the
new method of taking advantage of file-sharing features.

A Different Way to Share Files

With older versions of the Mac OS, the normal situation was to share
an entire disk or folder. For Mac OS X, the safest routine is to place
items you want to make available to others on your network in your
Public folder. That way, everyone who uses your computer can have
access to the files without having to log in via any of your user accounts. That folder can also be used as a repository for the files you
want to share or to receive across your network. In the "Immediate
Solutions" section of this chapter, I'll explain how to establish access
privileges so that only the users you specify can connect to your Mac
without going through a login process.

TIP: *To share a large number of files in other parts of your Mac's drive and see other files on your Mac's drive, without having to provide access to the rest of the volume, create an alias for each of those items and place them in your Public folder. Doing so will provide easy access to these items for users who connect to your Mac directly or across a network.*

You can limit file access even further by using the Drop Box folder, which is located within your Public folder. The Drop Box folder can be used to receive files, but those who network with your Mac will not be able to see any files in that folder or anywhere else on your Mac other than in the Shared folder.

A Look at Mac OS X's Networking Components

The tools to network your Mac require settings in two System Preferences panels and a dialog box. I'll describe them here, and then, in the "Immediate Solutions" section, I'll discuss how they're used:

- *Network*—This settings pane (see Figure 8.4) is used to configure your AirPort, Ethernet, and modem connections, all from a single set of screens. This tool helps ease the setup process. Moreover,

Figure 8.4   The Network settings pane is used to configure all your modem and network hookups.

most of the setups are essentially the same as the ones you used in the Classic Mac OS. There's even a Location Manager feature, which can automatically switch network settings when you move your Mac to different locales.

NOTE: *If you are working in an organization where a systems administrator handles network-related issues, you should consult with that person before you attempt to change any of the existing network settings on your Mac.*

- *Sharing*—You'll use this settings pane (see Figure 8.5) to switch file and Web sharing on and off. Web sharing uses the features of the Apache Web server software to let you run an Internet site from your Mac. You can also allow others to access your Mac via FTP or Telnet (remote login)—an option that adds to the flexibility of the new networking features.

- *Connect To Server*—This dialog box, available from the Go menu, is used to access all shared volumes (again, see Figure 8.3). You'll notice that aside from the Aqua user interface and a few additions, it bears a striking resemblance to the Network Browser application from the Classic Mac OS.

Figure 8.5   The Sharing settings pane is used to switch sharing services on and off.

Immediate Solutions

Sharing Files with Mac OS X

If you want to share files with a Mac running Mac OS X, you'll find the process familiar, even though you have to use a different set of dialog boxes to set things up and access your shares. The really sophisticated stuff happens behind the scenes, as Mac OS X's highly flexible network services are activated to do your bidding.

Here are the basic steps to follow to activate file exchanges with Mac OS X:

1. On the OS X Mac, open the System Preferences application, click the Network pane, and choose Built-In Ethernet from the Configure pop-up menu (see Figure 8.6). I'll discuss the modem option in the section entitled "Using Internet Connect for Dial-Up," later in this chapter.

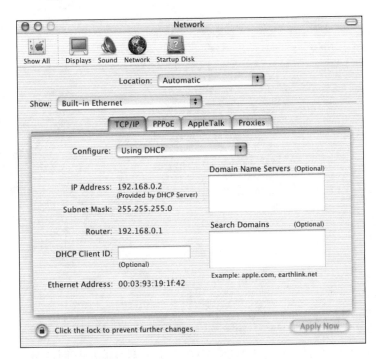

Figure 8.6   Change your network setups here.

2. If the padlock is locked, click its icon, and then enter your administrator's username and password. If the login window shakes, it just means that you entered the wrong username and/or password—try again.

NOTE: *If you do not have the username and password handy, please consult with your network administrator, if applicable. There's no way to access the protected features of Mac OS X without entering this information. The padlock remains open whenever you log in with an account that has administrator access.*

---

3. If you're going to share files with an older Mac running a Mac OS version prior to 8.5, you'll need to network via AppleTalk (it's also required for many network printers). In this case, click the AppleTalk tab and click the Make AppleTalk Active checkbox (see Figure 8.7). To change the name of your Mac for network access, move on to the Sharing pane.

4. Click the Apply Now button to store your settings. If you forget, you'll see a reminder prompt in which you can click the Save button.

Figure 8.7   AppleTalk is activated when you select the checkbox.

5. Click Show All at the top left of the System Preferences application window to display the other settings panes in System Preferences.

6. Go to the Sharing pane and click the Start button to activate file sharing. Note the Network Identity of your Mac, because either the Computer Name or IP Address is needed to access your computer from elsewhere on the network. You can change the name of your Mac before sharing is activated, by the way. Once sharing is activated, it may take a few minutes to start up.

NOTE: I'll discuss Web, FTP, and Telnet access later in this chapter.

7. Access privileges can be changed only for the contents of an active user's folder, not for your entire drive (unless you have administrator's access, of course). To set custom access privileges for that folder or another disk volume on your Mac, return to the Finder or desktop, click on the icon, and then click on the name of the item you want to share.

8. Choose Show Info from the Finder's File menu (the Mac OS X equivalent of Get Info), and then choose Privileges from the pop-up menu (see Figure 8.8).

9. The Privileges window offers three sets of access privileges, in a fashion very much like previous versions of the Mac OS. These are:

    • *Owner*—This is the name of the owner or administrator of the files on this Mac. The normal access setting is Read &

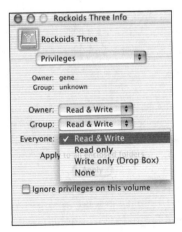

Figure 8.8 Set file access and sharing privileges in this window.

Write, which gives the owner the ability to access and modify files. By design, you can restrict your own access to files, but I'm not sure why you'd want to do that.

- *Group*—Each selected user of your Mac can be given a specific set of access instructions. Click the pop-up menu to change privileges, choosing Read & Write, Read Only, or Write Only. The Write Only setting lets the user place files in a Drop Box folder within the Public folder but not see any other files.

- *Everyone*—These settings are identical to those for a group, except that when you set them here, anyone who connects to your Mac as a guest can have that level of access—even if they haven't been given specific user privileges.

Set your access privilege settings. They are activated as soon as they are changed. To keep the same settings for all the files and folders within a folder, click Apply to incorporate the settings.

NOTE: *Depending on your needs, you may prefer to establish separate settings for individual files and folders. So, use the Apply function with caution, because it will only duplicate the permissions you've established for the main folder or file. In addition, copying privileges to a folder with lots of files (or en entire drive) can take several minutes.*

---

10. The next step requires setups on the other Macs on your network. If you want those Macs to be available in your list of shared volumes, the users of those Macs need to launch the File Sharing Control Panel (see Figure 8.9) or, as it's known on older Macs, Sharing Setup.

11. With File Sharing open, make sure the Network Identity fields are filled in with Owner Name, Owner Password, and Computer Name.

12. Click Start to activate file sharing.

NOTE: *The Network Identity is automatically configured when you use the Mac OS Setup Assistant to configure your Classic operating system. However, it's not uncommon for folks to change the settings; if your new Mac was pretested before delivery (perhaps to install a RAM upgrade due to those prevalent free RAM offers), you may find that the Assistant doesn't launch when you boot your Mac.*

---

13. Once sharing has been activated (it can take a few minutes, particularly on a Mac with several large drives attached to it), click the Close box to dismiss the File Sharing Control Panel.

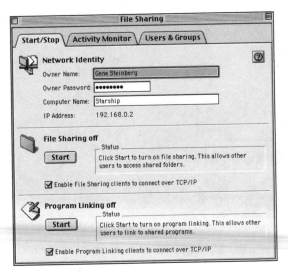

Figure 8.9   Make sure File Sharing is set up for your Classic Mac OS
computers.

NOTE: If your Mac supports TCP/IP-based file sharing and you have an always-on Internet connection, you'll see the IP address of your computer displayed. If you are using an AirPort or compatible 802.11b wireless network, you should use TCP/IP file sharing, where possible, for maximum performance in file transfers. AppleTalk file sharing with a wireless network can be mighty slow. In addition, for security reasons, you'll want to enable the maximum level of encryption supported by your wireless network. Otherwise even folks driving past your home or office will be able to access your computer network.

Accessing Shared Volumes with Network Browser

Depending on the Classic Mac OS version you're using, you can access shared volumes two ways: with Network Browser or the Chooser. These techniques are described in this section and the next.

Follow these steps to use Network Browser to access a shared volume:

NOTE: These file-sharing tools work only when you boot under a Classic Mac OS. If you are accessing shares under Mac OS X, you'll need to use the Connect To Server feature from the Finder's Go menu, described in the next section.

1. To access the Mac OS X computer from the other Mac (if it's running Mac OS 8.5 or later), launch the Network Browser application (it should be in the Apple menu), as shown in Figure 8.10. For earlier Mac OS versions (or as an alternative), you can also use the Chooser to access shares (see the next section).

Figure 8.10   You'll see your shared Mac listed here.

NOTE: *Be patient here. Each step might take up to a minute to complete, because the Mac takes a while to find that other computer with Network Browser.*

---

2. Click the right arrow next to Network to display the name of your Mac OS X computer.

3. Double-click the other Mac's name in the list to display the standard file-sharing login dialog. After you enter the proper user name and password and click Connect, you'll see a list of shared volumes that are just a double-click away from access.

4. When you've mounted the share volumes, you can quit Network Browser.

Accessing Shared Volumes with the Chooser

The other way to access a shared volume with the Classic Mac OS is with the famous (or infamous) Chooser. Follow these steps to use that feature:

1. Launch the Chooser from the Apple menu.

2. Click AppleShare to bring up the list of available file shares (see Figure 8.11).

3. Click the name of the share, and click OK.

NOTE: *To access the shared volume via TCP/IP (which is available only for Macs running Mac OS X or Mac OS 8.5 through Mac OS 9.x on which the option to enable file sharing via TCP/IP is checked), click the Server IP Address button and enter the IP address of the computer you want to access in the text field.*

---

4. Enter the user name and password in the login dialog box, and click Connect. You'll see a list of available shared volumes. Choose one or more to mount on your Mac's desktop.

5. Click the close box on the Chooser when you've finished mounting file shares.

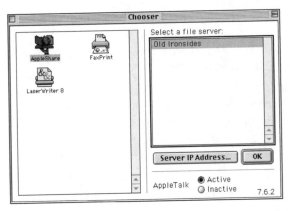

Figure 8.11 Select a networked computer from the list.

Connecting to Shared Macs Under Mac OS X

For Mac OS X, the Go menu becomes a neat substitute for the Chooser and the Network Browser application. To access other shared computers, follow these steps:

1. Click on the Mac's desktop or the Finder icon in the Dock.

2. Choose Connect To Server from the Go menu to open the dialog box shown in Figure 8.12. Or just press Command+K.

3. From the pop-up menu at the top of the screen, choose the type of server you need to access. The normal options shown are

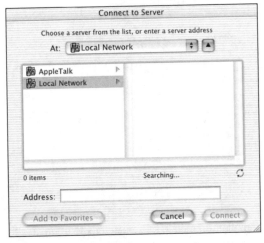

Figure 8.12 Your available network shared volumes are shown here.

AppleTalk (if AppleTalk is switched on) and Local Network, but this may change depending on the number of network zones available to your Mac and whether the item you want to share is available via the Internet.

4. You see a list of available network neighborhoods in the Connect To Server dialog box. Unless you have a network with several zones, however, there will be just one listing for Local Network, as in the example shown in this book, and, if AppleTalk is enabled, an AppleTalk option.

5. Click a network connection, and the network will be provided for available shared computers.

NOTE: *If the computer you want to connect to isn't displayed, enter its IP address in the Address field and click Connect. If the computer is on your network or accessible via the Internet, the login window should appear in a few seconds. See the next section for information on accessing Windows or Unix file shares.*

---

6. Double-click the name of the networked computer you want to access.

7. In the login window (see Figure 8.13), enter the username and password needed to access the Mac's shared volumes. When you choose guest access, your choices are usually limited to the Public folder.

NOTE: *You may need to check with your systems administrator to get the login information for the other computers on the network. The Options button also lets you attach a password to your Mac's keychain. Chapter 6 covers this subject in more detail.*

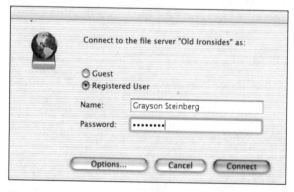

Figure 8.13   Enter the login information in this dialog box to bring up a list of available shares.

8. In the next dialog box, double-click the name of the volume you want to access or just select it and click the OK button. You'll see it mounted on your Mac's desktop momentarily. It's also added to the Finder's display when you click the Computer icon in the Finder's toolbar (see Figure 8.14).

The shared volumes can be handled just like local volumes on your Mac's desktop, and can be accessed by the Mac OS X Finder in the same fashion. The only significant difference is when you trash a file from the shared volume. If you drag the item to the trash, you'll see a prompt notifying you that the file must be deleted immediately (you can't leave it in the trash and decide later whether to zap it from your computer).

NOTE: *If the shared volume is no longer accessible because either sharing has been turned off on the other Mac or there has been a system crash or restart, you'll see a prompt saying the file server has closed and when it happened.*

Related solution:	*Found on page:*
Setting Up Keychain Access	137

Figure 8.14   When a volume is shared, its icon appears on your Mac's desktop and the Finder (note the special globe icon).

Connecting to Shared Windows and Unix Servers

In addition to providing easy access to Macs on your network, Mac OS X (beginning with the version 10.1 update) also makes it possible to access Windows and SAMBA Unix file shares, via the Connect To Server feature. The main difference, at least through the Mac OS X 10.1.2 update, is that you cannot just browse for an available computer: You have to enter the actual name or IP address to connect.

Here's how it works:

1. Click on the desktop or click the Finder icon in the Dock.

2. Choose Connect To Server from the Go menu.

3. In the Connect To Server dialog box, enter the name or IP address in the Address field, using the following naming format: "smb://[*nameofserver*]/[*directoryname*]". A typical example might be "smb://workgroup;server/share".

4. Click Connect to access the login prompt.

5. In the login prompt, enter the Workgroup/Domain name, your username, and your password.

6. Click the OK button to bring up the shared volume. As with Mac volumes, the ones you access from a Windows or Unix network will appear just like any drive on your Mac's desktop.

Using Internet Connect for Dial-Up Networking

In the days of Apple Remote Access, you could call up your Mac from a remote location in order to access or send files. Your modem was used to hook up to the other computer's modem, and then—within the limits of dial-up file transfers, of course—your remote Mac was as easy to access as one connected to your local network. Mac OS X has no Remote Access Control Panel. Instead, you make your connection with the Internet Connect application, with more than a little help with the settings you make in the Network pane of the System Preferences application.

NOTE: *Depending on your ISP, these settings might be made courtesy of an installer. You had the chance to install them when you ran the Setup Assistant right after you installed Mac OS X. I'm covering the process here in case you didn't enter the settings then or you want to change them now.*

Here's how it's done:

1. Launch System Preferences from the Dock or from the Applications folder.

2. Click the Network pane and make sure the Internal Modem (or Modem) option is chosen from the Configure pop-up menu (as shown in Figure 8.15).

NOTE: *One of the reasons for being able to enter separate settings for your AirPort, Ethernet, and dial-up TCP/IP access is to allow you to access any available network via Mac OS X's multihoming feature. Working with the built-in Location Manager software, you can automatically switch from AirPort to Ethernet to dial-up, depending on which port is available and which provides the speediest access.*

---

3. If it's not already selected, click the TCP/IP tab.

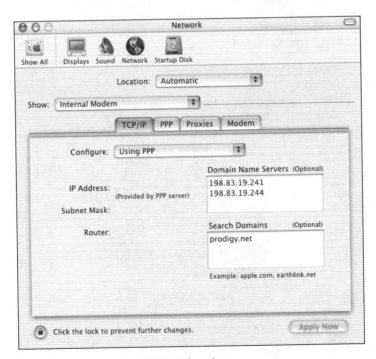

Figure 8.15   Enter your ISP's settings here.

4. Make sure the Using PPP option is shown in the pane's Configure menu. The second setting, Manually, is used only for specialized situations that may be required by your network setup.

5. If required by your ISP, enter the correct numbers in the Domain Name Servers field.

6. Under Search Domains, input the proper information. Again, your ISP may not need this setting. The example shown in Figure 8.15 has the regular settings for making a dial-up connection to Prodigy Internet.

NOTE: *Where did these settings come from? In Chapter 2, I suggested that you obtain your setup from the Remote Access and TCP/IP Control Panels. Here's where they go. If you don't have the information, contact your ISP directly.*

---

7. Click the PPP tab to enter your dial-up information (see Figure 8.16).

8. Enter the telephone number, account name, and password for your account. When you click the Save Password checkbox, the

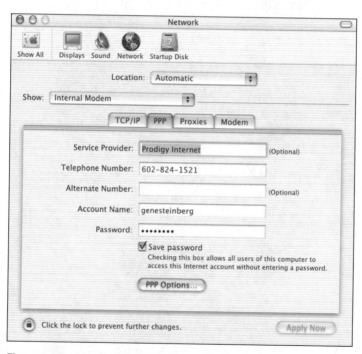

Figure 8.16   This is a standard set of dial-up entries for a Prodigy Internet access number in Phoenix.

password will be stored, but you can skip this process and enter it manually if others may have access to your Mac.

NOTE: *You don't have to enter an alternate number, but it's a good idea, because then you have a choice if the first number is busy. You should put the name in the Service Provider field for identification, or to help you choose the proper option if you've created multiple Location setups (that's coming in the next section).*

---

9. To fine-tune your session, click the PPP Options button and enter the appropriate information in the dialog box (see Figure 8.17). All the items shown are defaults, except Connect Automatically When Starting TCP/IP Applications, which you may want to activate. This option will log you in to your ISP whenever you launch applications such as your browser or email client. Here are the options from which to select:

NOTE: *If you have both cable modem and dial-up access to an ISP at your location, it's a good idea not to enter the option to connect automatically, because it will result in an attempt to dial up your ISP, rather than use your network-based Internet access.*

- *Session Options*—In addition to making your connection when you launch your Internet application, you can also get a warning prompt if you've been idle for a while, or automatically disconnect after a selected interval. Another option, which is checked by default, redials your ISP in the event of a busy signal.

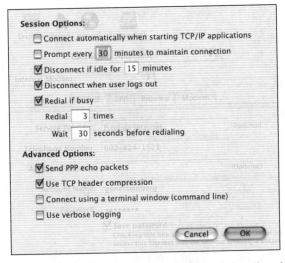

Figure 8.17 Choose your special connection options here.

- *Advanced Options*—Depending on the needs of your ISP, you may have to select one or more of the options beyond those already checked. Your ISP or network administrator can give you this information.

10. When your settings are made, click the OK button.

11. To double-check your modem setup, or if you're not using a standard Apple Internal Modem, click the Modem tab (see Figure 8.18). You can select from a wide variety of modem scripts by clicking the Modem pop-up menu.

TIP: *Although Mac OS X has built-in support for most popular modems, if you don't find any from the manufacturer of the one you own, try a Hayes or Apple model and see which provides the best connection. You can ask the company that makes your modem for a modem script, which would be installed under Mac OS X via the following folder path: Library>Modem Scripts.*

---

12. When you're done, click Apply Now to store your setup. Now you're ready to get connected.

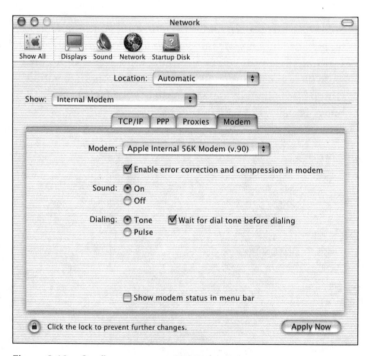

Figure 8.18   Configure your modem here.

Related solution:	Found on page:
Preparing for Mac OS X	29

Verifying Connectivity

Once you've established your dial-up settings, you should try logging on to your ISP and making sure everything works properly. Here's where you'll see Apple's replacement for the Remote Access Control Panel. To get connected, follow these steps:

1. Locate the Internet Connect application, which you'll find in your Applications folder.

TIP: If you intend to use Internet Connect frequently, check the option labeled Show Modem Status In Menu Bar, available in the Network preference panel, at the bottom of the Modem tab. To access your ISP, click on the modem icon in the menu bar and choose Connect (it becomes Disconnect when you're logged in). The status of your connection will be displayed graphically. In this sense, the function is essentially the same as the Remote Access Control Strip under the Classic Mac OS.

2. Launch Internet Connect (see Figure 8.19). It will display the name of your modem, along with the settings you made for your ISP. If you didn't enter a password, the Password field will be blank for you to type that information.

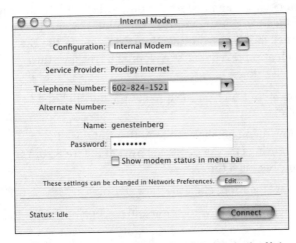

Figure 8.19   The settings previously made in the Network pane are duplicated here.

NOTE: You can redo the settings from the Internet Connect application simply by clicking the Edit button, which launches the Network pane in the System Preferences application for you to reconfigure your setup.

3. Click the Connect button to establish your connection. A status window will appear, indicating when your connection is established.

4. When your online session is done, click the Disconnect button (which toggles to Connect). The process is no different from the way it was done under the Classic Mac OS.

NOTE: Internet Connect will work even if your Internet application runs from the Classic environment, but it doesn't support the ability to connect with an application that uses its own dialing method, such as AOL or CompuServe.

Using Apple's Location Manager to Create Custom Setups

As with the Classic Mac OS, sometimes you want to move your Mac to different places, particularly if it's an iBook or a PowerBook. Apple's location feature lets you create custom AirPort, modem, and network setups for each particular location. That way, you can easily connect to the right local network and access the proper ISP without having to redo the settings. As you move from one place to another, just choose the correct location from the Network pane in the System Preferences application. Frequent travelers will treasure these features. Here's how it's done:

1. Launch the System Preferences application and click the Network pane.

2. Click the Show menu and select the Active Network Ports option, which brings up the display shown in Figure 8.20. You will see your present setup.

3. To create a new location, click the New button.

4. Type the name for your new location and select a port from the pop-up menu.

5. Click the OK button.

6. Make the Ethernet, modem, and connection settings for that location, and click the Apply Now button to store them.

Figure 8.20   This is your standard setup for a typical Mac.

7. Repeat this process for each location you want to create.

8. To switch locations, choose Location from the Apple menu and select the name of the location you want to use from the submenu. The default is Automatic, which simply accesses whatever available network service is required for a particular purpose.

NOTE: *The default setting is smart enough to sort out most routine differences in network setups as you move from location to location.*

Setting Up a Web or FTP Server on Your Mac

One of the extra networking features afforded by Mac OS X is the ability to run your Mac as a Web server or to allow others to access files via FTP, which greatly expands your ability to make files available to others—with proper security precautions, of course (such as having a strong password).

Here's how to turn on Web sharing:

1. Launch System Preferences from the Apple menu, Dock, or Applications folder.

2. Click the Sharing panel.

3. With the File & Web tab displayed, click the Start button under Web Sharing.

NOTE: *To allow FTP access to your Mac, click the Allow FTP Access button located just below the Web Sharing access control.*

---

4. Check the bottom of the Sharing panel to see your Mac's IP number. Once activated, other users can connect to your Mac via this URL: **http://[computerIPaddress]/~[shortusername]/**. An example, to use a typical IP number, might be **http:/ 192.168.123.254/~gene/** to access a site I might make available under Web sharing (the IP number is actually the default number of an Asante cable/DSL sharing router).

NOTE: *When you turn on Web sharing, the files placed in the Sites folder in your Home or Users folder will be available for Web access. The default index.html file that's already present in that folder includes more information about using the Web Sharing feature; you might want to print this file or save under a different name if you want to refer to it later on.*

WARNING!   Some ISPs prohibit Web sharing as part of the end-user agreement, and they will cancel your account if you violate their terms. Before setting up your Mac for full-time duty as a Web server, you may want to contact the ISP first. Just making your Mac available for a short time to share files or information with another user probably will be all right. If you want full-time access, consider one of the free Web spaces provided by your ISP or Apple's iTools feature. For business use, you may want to contact your ISP or a third-party hosting service to set up a Web server.

5. If you want to allow other users to access your Mac and transfer files via an FTP client, such as Fetch or Interarchy, click Allow FTP Access. This setting is helpful if those with non-Apple operating systems are going to be connecting to your Mac.

6. To allow remote login to your Mac via a terminal application, click the Application tab in the Sharing panel (see Figure 8.21) and check the option labeled Allow Remote Login. To send Apple events to your Mac (required for using AppleScript across the network), click the checkbox labeled Allow Remote Apple Events.

8. Networking Overview

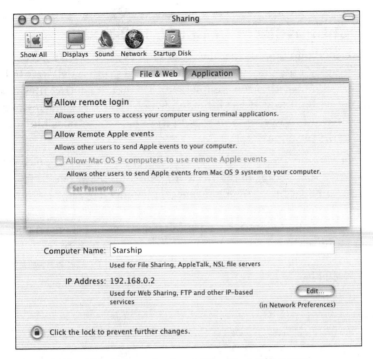

Figure 8.21   Choose your sharing options from this screen.

*WARNING!   I mention this feature for your information only. You should use this feature with extreme caution, as it allows your user name and password to be clearly transmitted over the Internet, and thus make your Mac vulnerable to access by hackers. If you want to set up this sort of tool, you might consider downloading an SSH program instead. Check **versiontracker.com** for some choices for Mac OS X users.*

7. Quit the System Preferences application after you've set your Web and FTP sharing options.

Can't Access a Drop Box?

Here's the problem. You attempt to copy or write files to the Drop Box folder on an AppleShare IP Server. But instead of seeing a progress bar to indicate that the files are being copied, you see a warning: "The operation cannot be completed because you do not have sufficient write privileges." The solution is to make sure that you attempt to send files only to a shared volume that has read/write privileges established. If you cannot change access privileges, contact your network administrator.

Correcting Network Access Problems

One of the hallmarks of the Mac operating system is easy networking. You plug one Mac into another, or into a printer, network hub, and so on, and with a few simple setups, you are sharing files and printing without any great difficulty. Should your network installation not work, however, you should look into these possible solutions to the problem:

- *Recheck your settings.* Your first troubleshooting step should be to verify your setups in the Network pane of the System Preferences application. Remember that you will need to click the Apply Now button for changes to become effective (fortunately you'll be reminded by a Save prompt if settings are changed and not stored). One common problem is the failure to turn on AppleTalk, which means that standard network printers may not be available.

NOTE: *Don't assume Mac OS X is at fault. You should also recheck the settings on the other computers involved in the network connection. If the setup is good, see if your Mac OS X computer can work with a different computer or printer. By checking this, you will be able to isolate a probable source for your problem.*

- *Examine your networking hardware.* Consider rechecking the networked cables and your hubs. Whenever there's a complete connection to the network hub or switch, one or two green lights will appear on that jack on a hub to indicate a proper connection is being made. If there's no activity or connection light, consider swapping cables to see if the problem transfers itself to the other computer or printer to which the cable was connected. If the problem travels, replace the cable. If networking still doesn't work, consider whether your hub itself might be defective.

- *Use the Network Utility application.* Mac OS X supplies a handy tool that can help you examine the condition of your network in a more sophisticated fashion. You'll find the application in the Utilities folder, inside Mac OS X's Applications folder. After you launch the application, click a tab to access your network scouring features. Ping is the most common utility to check whether a network connection is being made; it sends a signal to the target Mac and then records whether the signal has been returned to you. Just enter the IP number of the Mac, click Ping, and see if you get a result on repeated probes. Click the Stop button when you're finished. Another useful feature is Traceroute, which displays the path packets take during their travels. It's useful in locating the source of a possible network problem. If these probes don't yield successful results, you should return to your network hardware and configuration to be sure you didn't miss anything.

Protecting Your Network from the Internet

More and more folks these days have high-speed Internet connections. From cable to DSL, homes and businesses are joining the fast lane. (I discuss these and other fast access options in Chapter 21.) However, an always-on connection doesn't just deliver convenience; it also means your Macs are vulnerable to attack from Internet vandals who might want to play pranks with your computers, or attempt to retrieve passwords and other personal information. Nobody is immune from such intruders. Even Microsoft was the victim of highly publicized network attacks on the secured servers that contain the source code for some of the company's software. Here are some ways to protect your network:

- *Use a hardware router to share connections.* Several companies manufacture Internet router products that will feed your Net connection across an Ethernet network to other computers (Macs and PCs). They include Apple's AirPort Base Station, plus products from Asante, Proxim (formerly Farallon), LinkSys, and MacSense, to name just a few. These products are all designed to distribute the connection, and some include a hub or network switch. Most of these products also offer a built-in firewall, which sets up a secured barrier to prevent outsiders from entering your network. The common form of security employs a network address translation (NAT) feature that, in effect, manages requests to and from the network and hides the true IP numbers of your workstations. As a result, network intruders will find it far more difficult to invade your systems.

- *Set up software firewalls.* If you use a software router to share your connection, such as Sustainable SoftWorks IPNetRouter, or your Internet connection has no other means of protection, you should buy a program that sets up a firewall. Current entrants in the Mac marketplace include Symantec's Norton Personal Firewall (based on another program called DoorStop from Open Door Networks) and Intego's NetBarrier. Both programs will help to block unauthorized traffic from reaching your Macs and can be adjusted to selectively allow certain traffic, as needed.

NOTE: *Symantec has also bundled Norton Personal Firewall with Norton AntiVirus and Aladdin's iClean (which deletes old cache files and other items) to form an integrated package called Norton Integrated Security. A shareware alternative, FireWalk X, harnesses the power of the firewall built into Mac OS X (but not available from Apple's graphical tools)*

- *Restrict distribution of administrator passwords.* Many of you have heard horror stories about vengeful former employees of a company stealing confidential files and other proprietary information. Although you may have legal remedies to get this material back, the cost in manpower and legal action can be tremendous, with no guarantee of success. The best approach is to be careful who gets access to passwords in your company, and perhaps to consider a non-disclosure agreement if employees have access to company secrets that could give a competing company an advantage. You should also follow through with my suggestion to use strong passwords when setting user accounts to further protect your network.

Related solution:	*Found on page:*
Choosing Personal Firewall Software	373

Chapter 9

The New AppleScript

In Brief

Yes it's true. Despite a powerful operating system and incredible processing power courtesy of the Mac's G3 and G4 processors (and whatever is to come in the future), a lot of the work you do on your Mac is manual. Every step requires an operation of keyboard and mouse. You locate a document in a specific folder with the Finder, and then double-click on the document to open it in the appropriate application. You then examine or edit the document. As necessary, you save it, print it, and proceed to the next document.

When you navigate the World Wide Web, you might enter a site's address or select one from your list of Favorites. During the course of a day, you carry out a number of repetitive steps.

What if you could make your Mac perform a complex set of repetitive steps just by running a single application or by accessing a simple command within a program? What if the tools to provide all that complex functionality didn't cost an extra cent and didn't require installing additional software? A dream? Something only a skilled computer programmer can do? Read on.

For years, the Macintosh operating system has had a built-in feature that lets you automate complex tasks. This capability is not reserved for computer programmers and highly technical power users. It's in use today in the graphic design departments of major companies around the world. This feature is used for creating print publications, editing videos, producing Web content, and automating everyday tasks, such as copying and printing files.

Did I say it was free? In fact, its origins can be traced way back to Mac System 7 in 1991. It's called AppleScript, and this powerful feature is already on your Mac and has no exact equal in the Windows world.

NOTE: *To be perfectly technical, you can use Visual Basic for automating tasks in a number of applications from Microsoft and other companies. But AppleScript is far more user-friendly, and it's a standard part of the Mac OS.*

What AppleScript Can Do

The word *script* connotes an arcane language that is apt to confound and befuddle all but the most experienced Mac users. Yet AppleScript, although not quite plain English, is close enough to make it possible for folks like you and me to create scripts. What's more, using the scripts already available, you might be able to get all or most of the desktop automation you want without having to make anything at all.

In effect, AppleScript lets Mac programs communicate with one another and with the operating system. The scripts you make tell these programs what to do. For example, you might want scripts to automatically copy a file from one disk to another, to batch-process a series of images and apply certain Photoshop filters to them, and to save and print documents. And that's just the beginning. Many popular Macintosh productivity programs depend on AppleScript to exploit some of their most useful features.

NOTE: *To learn what sort of support an application has for AppleScript, check the application's documentation. AppleScript's uses range from the simple to the complex, and all variations in between.*

In the "Immediate Solutions" section of this chapter, you'll discover some of the tools Apple has already provided to let you exercise AppleScript. For now, here's a brief idea of what you can do with AppleScript:

- *Automate use of the Mac OS X Finder*—Many common Finder functions can be scripted. That means you can harness complex file-management features by launching a single script.

- *Automate Mac OS system functions*—From searching the Internet, to querying and directing XML-aware applications, to automatically adjusting a specific set of settings, AppleScript can handle operations that require repeating steps.

- *Automate workflow*—This is where AppleScript comes into its own in a working environment. Users of the popular desktop publishing application QuarkXPress, for example, can create scripts that access specific templates for pages, flow in text, import images, and scale and crop the images. In Adobe Photoshop, a script can be used to open all the images placed in a single folder, apply a specific set of program filters to them, and then save the images in a specific file format. Canvas 8 for Mac OS X can perform such functions as activating any of its extraordinary range of tools and functions, or preparing Web graphics without direct user intervention. Imagine if you had to do all this work manually, one step at a time, every time you needed to handle these chores.

- *Record your actions*—You don't have to write all your scripts from scratch. Many programs let you record a series of actions, using Apple's Script Editor application. After the steps have been recorded, you can save them as a script, and then have them run the same as any other AppleScript.

NOTE: *Which programs support the record function? Check the program's documentation. None of the shipping programs that come with Mac OS X 10.1 include the record feature, although many are scriptable.*

AppleScript, however, is not the only desktop automation feature. Some commercial programs, such as CE Software's QuicKeys, perform similar functions, but have the added advantage of working with all Mac software, not just programs that can be specifically scripted. QuicKeys for Mac OS X (see Figure 9.1) includes the ability to record mouse actions and multistep actions (formerly called sequences), so that you can script complicated procedures.

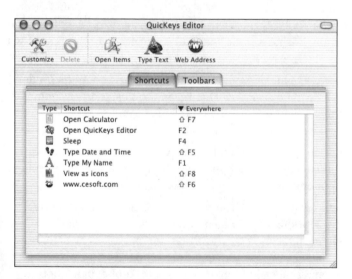

Figure 9.1   A long-time favorite of many Mac users, QuicKeys has made the migration to Mac OS X.

What Doesn't Work in Mac OS X

Some features of the Mac OS X version of AppleScript might not be completely functional, at least as of version 10.1. For example, the Folder Actions feature doesn't work; it allowed you to attach specific functions to a folder when it's opened and was a convenient way to automate such actions as moving files to another volume for backup. However, AppleScript features are works in progress, and more features will be added over time.

Fortunately, your existing scripts should work pretty much the same under Mac OS X as they did under the Classic Mac OS. Apple suggests that when you create scripts, you identify the operating system version, in case problems arise when switching from one to the other. Doing so will simplify the process of testing and removing bugs from the script.

Mac OS X Script Features

When you get started with AppleScript, you'll find that a number of Mac applications support this feature and thus will provide quite a bit of exposure to what this valuable tool can do. These include such standard applications as the Finder, Image Capture, Internet Connect, Mail, Print Center, QuickTime Player, Sherlock, Terminal, and TextEdit. In addition, AppleWorks 6.2x, which has been rewritten to support Mac OS X, can be scripted, as can Microsoft Entourage X, Stone Studio (a set of graphic applications and tools), and lots more.

The Tools for Using Scripts in Mac OS X

Aside from the built-in functions of some programs that use AppleScript behind the scenes, an AppleScript can come in several forms—as an applet, as a fully compiled script, or as a text file containing the script commands. Which form to use depends on the program you're running, but the most common form of script is the applet. An *applet* is a small application; you can double-click it to start it, or you can drag and drop onto it an item that is subjected to the scripting action.

NOTE: *In addition to double-clicking and dragging and dropping, you can place an AppleScript applet in the Dock so that it can be activated with a single click, use a toolbar script that is identified by a Finder icon, or use a handy utility Apple has placed at its Web site, ScriptMenu, which puts up a menu bar icon to access your scripts. Once you've downloaded ScriptMenu, just drag the little application to the menu bar and it will show up automatically.*

For Mac OS X, Apple has included a convenient way to run your scripts. It's an application called *Script Runner,* which allows you to execute any number of scripts from a single floating palette (see Figure 9.2). I tell you how to set it up in the "Immediate Solutions" section of this chapter.

AppleScript: The Future

The future of AppleScript is vast. Apple has made no bones about the fact that the present iteration of its system-wide scripting language works fine with both the Carbon and Cocoa environments, so it doesn't matter whether software developers use either. In addition, AppleScript continues to function with Classic applications, so there's no fear of losing the functionality of scripts made with such programs as Adobe Photoshop and QuarkXPress.

NOTE: *Both Adobe and Quark have committed to bringing their applications into the Mac OS X environment. You'll want to check with these publishers for estimated timetables. At the time this book was written, Adobe Illustrator 10 had shipped, and the company promised that all its major applications would make the migration to the new operating systems by the spring of 2002. QuarkXPress for Mac OS X was also expected to appear in early 2002.*

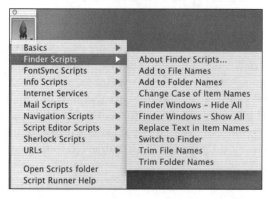

Figure 9.2   This Script Runner has been loaded with a number of useful scripts for Mac OS X.

Apple plans to extend AppleScript support for the Unix environment as well. You'll get an indication of how AppleScript works in the "Immediate Solutions" section of this chapter, where I show you how to run a script from the command line.

Immediate Solutions

Locating Mac OS X's AppleScript Collection

Before you get started making a script of your own, you might want to try using the ones Apple has provided. You'll get a good idea of what an AppleScript can do, and by examining the script in the Script Editor application, you'll learn the scripting language; this will go a long way toward helping you develop your scripting skills. To locate the scripts, follow these steps:

1. Open the Applications folder.

2. Double-click on the AppleScript folder.

3. Open the Example Scripts folder, and then open the folder that contains scripts in the category you want to try.

After you've located the scripts you want, you can open them and see how they do their stuff. You'll find, by and large, that the lingo is clear enough that you can see how they accomplish the various actions.

Choosing Mac OS X's Sample Scripts

As explained in the previous section, Apple has assembled a small collection of useful scripts that you can use to learn how AppleScript works. Here's a list of the script folders and some of the scripts provided:

- *Basics*—These scripts are designed to help you discover the fundamentals of preparing your own AppleScripts. The scripts provided will transport you to the AppleScript pages at Apple's Web site, launch the Script Editor application, and give you a tour through the handy Help menus on the subject.

- *Finder Scripts*—These scripts are designed to direct the Finder to perform various functions. They can alter file and folder names in various ways, from changing case to searching and replacing the names of files in a folder. In addition, file and folder names can be trimmed to look more readable in a Finder window.

- *FontSync Scripts*—A boon for those with huge font libraries. The two scripts available with Mac OS X 10.1 let you create and match up your FontSync profiles.

- *Info Scripts*—One lets you change your Date & Time setting, and another produces a font sample sheet in TextEdit with all your installed fonts.

- *Internet Services*—These scripts exploit AppleScript's XML capability to query Web sites. They provide the current temperature in any USA location and retrieve stock quotes (assuming you want to know whether your favorite stock has gone up or down).

- *Mail Scripts*—One entrant in this folder can be used to set an address and a subject line for an email message. Once you enter these values (you have to set a default address first), the script will automatically open the Mail application and then populate a new message window with the information.

- *Navigation Scripts*—These scripts are designed strictly to work with the Finder. They will activate a new Finder window pointing directly to a specific folder. There are scripts for the Applications, Documents, Favorites, and Home folders.

- *Script Editor Scripts*—These all have a single purpose—to help you write a script that runs properly. Each is designed to test a particular script function, such as checking for syntax errors. They are all useful if you want to hone your AppleScript skills.

- *Sherlock Scripts*—The sole entrant when this book was being written allowed you to use Sherlock's handy Internet searching features. You'll learn more about Apple's search application in Chapter 7.

- *URLs*—The scripts in this folder are designed to access specific Web sites. These scripts contain the examples I use when I show you how to modify or create your own scripts.

Related solution:	Found on page:
Searching the Internet	154

9. The New AppleScript

Using Script Runner

To get started with AppleScript in Mac OS X, you'll want to set up Apple's Script Runner application. You can use this program to both organize and run your scripts (see Figure 9.3). Here's how to work and add scripts with Script Runner:

NOTE: By default, Apple installs its sample collection of scripts for you. So, when you launch Script Runner, it's ready to roll.

1. Locate your copy. Script Runner is in the Applications folder.

2. Double-click Script Runner to launch it.

3. Click the button on the little Script Runner floating icon, and select Open Scripts Folder from the pop-up menu. The Scripts folder will be displayed in a Finder window (see Figure 9.4).

4. Put the scripts you want to access (or the folder in which they're contained, if you want Script Runner to display a submenu of its contents) in the Scripts folder.

5. Click Script Runner's close button. Now, launch Script Runner again. Your newly added scripts are available.

6. Removing a script is a simple matter of dragging it from the Scripts folder. The next time you launch Script Runner, the script will no longer be available.

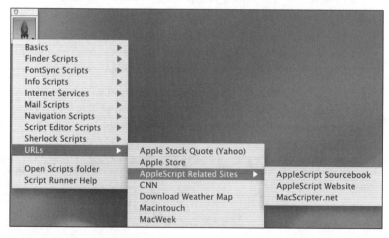

Figure 9.3   Script Runner is a convenient way to access all your scripts from a single interface.

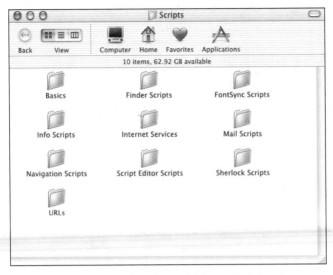

Figure 9.4   Put your scripts in this folder so that Script Runner can find them.

Making or Editing Your First AppleScript

Although AppleScript is a plain-English language, you need to use some basic commands to make your scripts work. In this section, I'll show you how to create your first script, just to give you an idea of how it's done. Using these techniques, after you learn the syntax, you'll be able to make scripts as easy or complex as you want.

NOTE: *I am not trying to minimize the learning curve for AppleScript. It takes time, study, and some practice to become flexible in writing reliable scripts. To learn more about the subject, visit the AppleScript Web site at **www.apple.com/applescript**. There, you'll discover sample scripts and online tutorials that will help you learn both simple and complex scripting skills.*

In this script, you will tell Microsoft's Internet Explorer to access a Web site—in this case, mine. Here's how to make your first script:

1. Locate the Script Editor application, which is in the Utilities folder inside the Applications folder.

2. Double-click the program to launch it (see Figure 9.5).

3. When the program is running, a blank script window should be on your screen. If it's not, choose New Script from the program's File menu.

Figure 9.5   Creating an AppleScript starts here.

4. In the Description field, enter a sentence or two that describes the purpose and function of your script.

5. The first element in your script is a property. The property defines the item you will be acting on in the script. In this case, the URL **www.macnightowl.com** will be accessed. So, type the following text and then press the Return key (don't worry about writing commands in bold as you see them in a completed script; it's not necessary):

```
property target_URL: "http://www.macnightowl.com/"
```

6. Type the following command, which tells the script to ignore how an application responds to the command:

```
ignoring application responses
```

7. In the next set of commands, specify the application that you want to script, tell it what action to perform, and then close this set of commands:

```
tell application "Internet Explorer"
Activate
GetURL target_URL
end tell
end ignoring
```

NOTE: *You don't use Internet Explorer? No problem. You can put the name of the browser you prefer, such as OmniWeb, in its place.*

---

8. You are almost at the finish line, and your Script Editor window should look much like the one in Figure 9.6. The next step is to make sure the script was written properly. Click the Check Syntax button. The script you just wrote will be checked for errors. AppleScript is very literal-minded, so if a single letter in a command is wrong, you'll see what it is and what you need to do to fix it.

NOTE: *When a script is examined for syntax, it will take on the text formatting shown in Figure 9.6, with bold commands. Before you check the syntax, the script is all straight text; you don't have to format any of it manually.*

---

9. If the script has an error, now's the time to recheck the script and fix the problem. If the script checks out, choose Save As from the File menu.

10. Type a name for your new script that corresponds to its purpose, choose Compiled Script as the format, and specify the location where the script will be saved. (The best place to save the script is in the Scripts folder so that it will be recognized by Script Runner.)

11. Click the Save button.

12. To make sure your script truly does what you want, go ahead and run it via Script Runner. Launch Internet Explorer. If the script to access a specific URL was compiled correctly, it will access the Web site you specified (see Figure 9.7).

Figure 9.6 Here's the completed script, already formatted.

Figure 9.7   Success! The author's Web site was opened, courtesy of the
script you created.

Running a Script from the Unix Command Line

To try running an AppleScript from Mac OS X's Unix command line,
here's what to do:

1. Locate the Terminal application in the Utilities folder, within
   the Applications folder.

2. Double-click the Terminal application to launch it.

3. In the command line, type "osascript" and then type the name
   of the script.

4. Press Return to activate the script. If you enter the correct file name, the script should run precisely the same as if it were accessed via Script Runner.

Using Toolbar Scripts

Another way to access a script is via the Finder's toolbar. Apple has provided a set of scripts that perform a variety of Finder-related functions, such as opening and closing folders and hiding open applications. You can find these and more at the AppleScript Web site, at **www.apple.com/applescript/macosx/toolbar_scripts/**.

To use one of these scripts, just follow these steps:

1. Open any Finder window.

2. Drag the script you want to the Finder's toolbar.

3. To use the script, just click its icon.

TIP: *If you would also like to use these scripts via the ScriptMenu application, place them in the Scripts folder, within the Library folder. The advantage of the ScriptMenu is that it's available from all Mac OS X applications (no, you won't see it when you run a Classic application).*

Chapter 10

Installing Programs Under Mac OS X

In Brief

What goes around, comes around. Way back when, you could install an application on your Macintosh simply by dragging the application's icon from a floppy disk to your hard-drive icon. In a few moments, the program would be on your Mac, a double-click away from running.

Over time, however, things became a lot more complicated for the Classic Mac OS. A single application might consist of hundreds of files, and not all those files are placed in the same folder. Some go into disparate locations inside the System Folder. More often than not, it isn't even readily apparent which file belongs to what program. So, the installation is handled by an installer that is designed to sort out all these files for you and, if necessary, to restart your Mac.

Removing an application can be totally frustrating unless the installer has an Uninstall option. There's even a third-party program—Spring Cleaning, from Aladdin Systems—that is designed to remove all vestiges of a program. I'm reminded of the Add/Remove feature of Windows (which persists even in Windows XP) as an example of how complicated a program installation can get; some Windows software installations require multiple restarts.

NOTE: *Yes, there is indeed a Mac OS X version of Spring Cleaning, but as you'll see shortly, the need for uninstalling an application is sharply reduced.*

Introducing the Package

Beginning with Mac OS 9, Apple came up with a better idea for Mac users (although it's not unique to the Mac)—the *Package*. A Package is simply a folder that contains an application and all its support files, whether 1 or 1,000. But all these elements are hidden from the end-user. The Package appears on your Mac as a single icon that you can double-click to launch the application located within the Package folder.

Installing is a dream—a throwback to the earliest days of the Macintosh. Just drag the application's package icon to the appropriate folder (usually the Applications folder) and launch it.

Removing an application involves the same process. You drag it to the trash and empty the trash, and all elements of that program (except for preferences files) are removed. It's remarkable that the best way to install and remove a program was the way it was done originally, back in 1984 when the first Mac appeared on the scene.

The Microsoft Way

Microsoft, which has paid more attention to the Mac platform in recent years, has been featuring drag-and-drop installation of its software since Office 98 came out in 1998. The process involves dragging a folder to your Mac's hard drive. However, you still have a visible folder containing a lot of separate files, and you still must open that folder to run any of the applications you've installed.

Also, when you first launch any recent Microsoft application, it will populate the older Mac OS Extensions folder with a bunch of files, and these must be manually removed if you decide to uninstall the software. So, Microsoft's drag-and-drop installation is only part of a solution—but it's a step in the right direction.

NOTE: *To be perfectly fair, there is an installer on the Office v. X CD. But it's designed for optional installs of fewer or extra components, and isn't needed just to install the software in its standard form.*

Exploring New Application Features

As I explain throughout this book, any application written to support Mac OS X inherits a bevy of beautiful interface features and Unix-based reliability. In addition to preemptive multitasking and protected memory, you'll see visible differences to enhance your computing experience. These differences include:

NOTE: *Although older, Classic Mac applications can run under Mac OS X, they do not inherit any of the features about to be discussed. These are all the province of programs developed for the Carbon or Cocoa programming environments.*

- *Services*—Available in the Applications menu of many applications, the Services command produces a submenu that makes it possible for you to access the features of another application. This feature allows you to select text or a picture in your document and then go to the Services menu, choose a command from another application, and have that command executed in that program. In effect, you can send the text from one program to another without having to launch the second application, drag text between them, or use Export and Import features.

NOTE: *Although Services is available for both Carbon and Cocoa applications under Mac OS X 10.1 and later, it's up to Carbon application developers to add specific support for its powerful features.*

- *Open dialog box*—The venerable Mac Open dialog box has been one of the most confusing features of the operating system. It can be difficult for folks to navigate through large collections of nested folders and various disks to find a file. Although the Open dialog box was updated in Mac OS 8.5 with a new scheme, called *navigation services*, this was only part of what needed to be done. For Mac OS X, Apple has redesigned this dialog box yet again, and the new version, affectionately called *sheets* (see Figure 10.1), simplifies navigation tremendously. In addition, it's non-modal, which means that it doesn't prevent you from doing something else on your Mac until it's dismissed. You can bring up the Open dialog box and then switch to another application, and the Open dialog box will still be there when you return; the operation of your Mac is not affected.

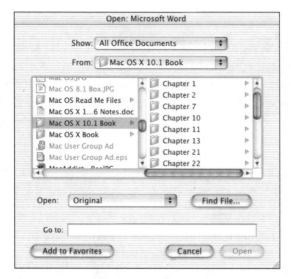

Figure 10.1   The new Open dialog box makes it easier for you to locate the file you want to use.

TIP: *Users often overlook the Open dialog box. A prime example is the common practice of many Mac users to double-click a file's icon to open it, even if the application used to make the file is already open. Apple has had to do its homework here, and it has made things much better for Mac OS X.*

- *Save As dialog box*—Another bugaboo of the older versions of the Mac OS was the Save As dialog box. When you wanted to save your document, where were you putting it? How often did you waste time figuring out the correct place (if there was one) to put a file? The Mac OS X version of the Save As dialog box opens as a sheet in the document window in which you're working (see Figure 10.2). There's no question about what you're saving, and the simple elegance of its interface makes it easy for you to specify precisely where your document is going so you can easily locate it later—without a headache or constant use of the Sherlock file-search utility.

- *New location for the Quit command*—This is a logical issue rather than a critical one. Instead of putting the Quit command in the customary place in the File menu, Apple put it in the application menu. The logic is that the command affects the application, not the file (except indirectly, because files are closed before an application is closed). If nothing else, logic wins here.

TIP: *Regardless of the location of the Quit command, pressing Command+Q still activates this feature. Some things never change, thank heaven.*

- *Font panel*—Not all applications designed for Mac OS X will inherit this feature (just those programmed in the Cocoa environment, unless Apple changes it), but those that do use the Font

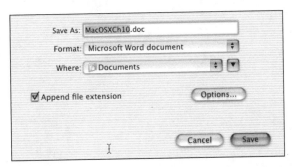

Figure 10.2 A new way to simplify the process of saving your document; this is the version you see in Word for Mac OS X.

panel will enjoy enhanced abilities to access fonts and manage a font library. As described in Chapter 16, Mac OS X has native support for PostScript, TrueType, and OpenType fonts, plus the original bitmap fonts that date back to the original versions of the Mac OS. With the Font panel (see Figure 10.3), not only can you select your fonts, but you can preview them in the sizes you want and create special collections to ease font management.

Figure 10.3   The Mac OS X Font panel, when available in your application (at least the ones developed via Apple's Cocoa API), eases font handling.

Immediate Solutions

Handling Complex Application Installations

Mac OS X's Package feature greatly simplifies the installation and removal of applications, but some programs have, for one reason or another, more complex installation processes. This can happen when you're trying to install a Classic application. The following sections describe some of the installation options.

Using an Installer

The normal way to install an application—when you're not using Mac OS X's new techniques—is to load a CD and double-click an installer application. After an installer is launched, read the prompts and other on-screen instructions. Should the installer application ask for a location for the application, specify the Applications folder for ease of organization.

At the end of the installation, you might see a Restart prompt. Click it to restart your Mac. After the restart, you'll be able to use the application normally.

NOTE: *In my experience, Restart prompts are quite rare in Mac OS X installations. You usually see them only if the installer needs to install certain system-related software (or one of Apple's own Mac OS X updates). An example is MouseWorks, which is used to provide custom scrolling, mouse movement, and direct access features for Kensington's line of input devices.*

Using a Disk Image

Another way to distribute software is to use the disk image. The disk image has the virtue of being a copy of the original distribution disk for the software, so you can use it without needing to have the disk media present. A disk image can consist of just the installation files or the full installation CD.

NOTE: *Just about all of Apple's software files are distributed in disk image form for convenience. Many other publishers (and even shareware developers) are using a similar technique for efficient transfer of their products.*

To use a disk image, follow these steps:

1. Locate the disk image file. It will usually be identified by a file name with the extension .img or .smi and an icon that looks like a small hard drive embedded into a document. Double-click the file's name. Over the next few seconds, the file will be checked to make sure it isn't damaged. If it turns out to be damaged, you will have to get another copy (download it again, for example).

> **TIP:** *If the file was compressed for distribution to save download time from the Internet, the file may come as a compressed archive, which sports a .sit or .hqx extension. If you have a file of this sort, double-clicking it ought to be sufficient to activate the decompression software (StuffIt Expander, which comes with Mac OS X). StuffIt Deluxe 6.5 and StuffIt Expander 6.5, available from Aladdin Systems, include full support for Mac OS X. The latter is free, so you should consider downloading it from the publisher's Web site at* **www.aladdinsys.com**. *The installation process fully supports Mac OS X.*

2. When the file opens, it will put a disk image icon on your Mac's desktop. Double-click the icon to reveal its contents (see Figure 10.4).

3. If the file contains an installer, double-click the installer to proceed.

Figure 10.4   A disk image's contents appear in the Finder window.

NOTE: *When you open the contents of a disk image file, you'll want to see if they include any ReadMe files. If there are ReadMe files, open them to see if you need to follow any special instructions to install the application or prepare for the installation.*

4. Should the disk image contain the actual file or files to be installed, look for instructions on how to proceed. Microsoft's Office v. X (see Figure 10.5) and Internet software might even include a text description on the disk image or on the CD itself explaining what to do (usually just drag the installation folder to your Mac's hard drive).

5. When the installation is done, you can proceed with using the new software.

Making a Startup (Login) Application

To have your application launch as soon as you boot your Mac, follow these steps:

NOTE: *Mac OS X uses no system extensions in the traditional sense (although there are kernel extensions that run at the core of the operating system). The alternative is to run your program as an application that starts up with your Mac. Some installers might set this up for you behind the scenes. These instructions tell you how to do it yourself.*

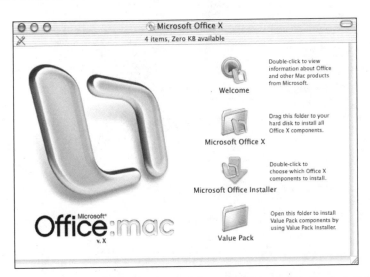

Figure 10.5   As you see from this Microsoft software disk, the installation file consists of a single installation folder, a Welcome message, a custom installer, and a folder of extras.

1. Locate the System Preferences application icon in the Dock and click it, or double-click its icon in the Applications folder.

2. Click once on the Login pane to open the Login Items window, shown in Figure 10.6.

3. Click the Add button.

4. In the Open dialog box that appears next, select the application or file that you want to open when you log in as a user on your Mac (see Figure 10.7).

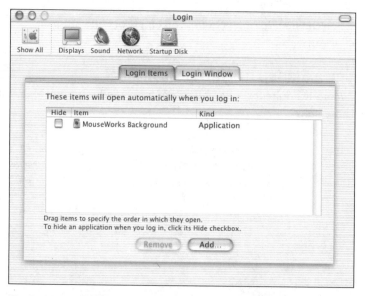

Figure 10.6   Add startup applications in this window.

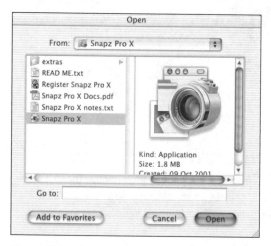

Figure 10.7   Select your startup application in this dialog box.

5. Click the Open button to store the file in your Login Items window.

6. To hide the application (so its window is available only from the Dock), click the Hide checkbox.

TIP: *Some applications, particularly those providing system-wide enhancements, may include a preference to make the program a login application. That can be a time-saver.*

---

7. Choose Quit from the application menu or press Command+Q to quit System Preferences (or click the close button). The next time you boot your Mac and log in under that username, the selected application will launch.

NOTE: *Startup applications apply strictly to a single user's account. Each user of your Mac can select from a different range of startup applications. If you want to make a system-wide startup application, place an alias to it in the StartupItems folder inside the Library folder at the root level of your hard drive. If such a folder isn't there, just create one.*

Using the New Open Dialog Box

If you're used to double-clicking a document to open it, rather than going through the Open dialog box, here's Mac OS X's better way:

1. Launch the application in which you want to open the document.

2. Choose Open from the File menu or press Command+O, which produces a dialog box much like the one shown in Figure 10.8, featuring a Finder-type column display. The pop-up menu lists the folder hierarchy from bottom to top, also easing navigation.

NOTE: *Open dialog boxes include options that apply to a specific application. I used Microsoft Word X for this illustration. You will find that some choices are different for other Mac OS X applications.*

---

3. Click a folder's name to reveal its contents.

4. Should you want a folder or document added to your Favorites, select its icon and click the Add To Favorites button before opening the document.

5. If the document you want doesn't appear, see if your application's Open dialog box has a pop-up menu listing

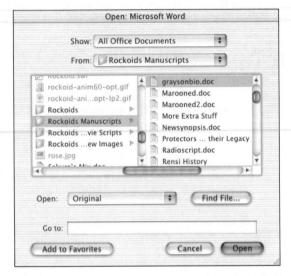

Figure 10.8   Easily locate the document you want to open.

alternate file formats supported. Use them to see if the document appears.

TIP: *If a document's name is grayed out, the program you're using cannot open it.*

---

6. When you locate the document you want to open, either select it and click the Open button, or double-click the document's name.

TIP: *If a document you open is a template or was created in an older version of a program, you might see a new, untitled document on your screen, rather than the name of the document you selected. If this is the case, you can simply save the document with the original name to replace it, or give it a new name and store it in a new location, if necessary.*

---

7. If the document you wanted to locate isn't shown, click the Cancel button or press Command+. (period) or the Esc key to dismiss the Open dialog box. Then, use Apple's Sherlock search application to find the document. You'll find more information about Sherlock in Chapter 7.

Related solution:	*Found on page:*
Searching Files for Content	151

Using the New Save As Dialog Box

On the surface, saving a new document ought to be an especially easy process, but it hasn't always been thus in the Mac OS. The new Save As dialog box for Mac OS X offers both basic and advanced options to help you quickly find a place to put your document, so you can easily locate it later. Here is how to use this feature to its best advantage:

1. When you're ready to save your new document for the first time, choose Save As from the File menu. A virtual sheet will drop down from the document's title bar (see Figure 10.9).

NOTE: *When the Save As dialog box is displayed, you can move on to another document in the active application or to another application on your Mac. The dialog box will stay put, anchored to the original document's title bar, so you can return to it later without storing the wrong document by mistake.*

2. Type a name for your document in the Save As text field. It's always a good idea to be as clear as possible when creating a name, so you can easily recognize the document when you need to open it again.

NOTE: *Although, in theory, Mac OS X supports file names with a total of 256 characters, you should keep a file name to a reasonable length.*

3. To select a location for your document, click the pop-up menu to the right of the Where field. The default location is your Documents folder, inside your personal user's folder, but you can click the menu and specify another location.

TIP: *The most logical place to put your file is in the Documents folder, which is where the Save As dialog box will usually point by default. But if you plan to generate lots of documents for a single category or a single business contact or friend, you should consider making a separate folder within the Documents folder, to avoid having to comb through long lists of files to find the ones that apply.*

4. To see more locations and additional choices, click the down arrow at the right of the Where pop-up menu. You'll see the expanded view reminiscent of the Finder's column view (see Figure 10.10).

NOTE: *When you choose an expanded Save As dialog view, the selection will usually stick for that particular application until you switch to the standard, simplified display by clicking on the up arrow to the right of the Where field.*

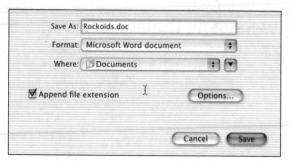

Figure 10.9   Where do you want to put your document?

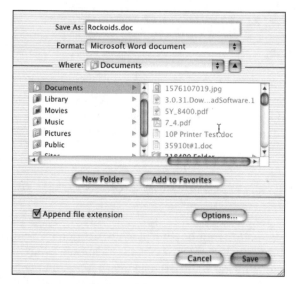

Figure 10.10   You have additional choices as to how to handle your new document.

5. Click a folder in the left column to see the contents in the right column.

6. To put your file in a new folder, choose the location for the folder from the column display, and then click the New Folder button to open the New Folder dialog box (see Figure 10.11).

7. Type a name for the new folder.

8. Click the Create button. The new folder will be placed in the location selected in the Save As dialog box.

9. You can also make the document a favorite so that it will appear in your Favorites folder for fast access. To do this, click the Add To Favorites button.

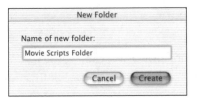

Figure 10.11   Name your new folder.

10. When your save options are selected, click the Save button to store the file. If the document name you selected is already in use, you can either replace the document with the duplicate name or give your new document a different name; the document you are replacing must be closed for this to work.

NOTE: *Depending on the application you're using, there may also be an Options button, which gives you access to program-specific features related to the Save As function.*

WARNING!   Once you replace a document with the duplicate name, the replaced document is history. Consider carefully which choice to make if you run into this situation.

TIP: *If the column display isn't big enough to show a thorough view of the contents of your Mac's drive, click the resize bar at the bottom-right corner and drag to expand the Save As window.*

Using the Services Menu

Wouldn't it be nice if applications could communicate with one another easily without your having to go through the confusing processes of cutting and pasting and dragging and dropping? The Services menu for Mac OS X helps to minimize this problem. Here's an example of how it can be used to make two programs work together:

NOTE: *This example is for demonstration purposes only. I used TextEdit and OmniWeb, a Web browser described in Chapter 21, but any Web browser that accesses the Services feature can accomplish the same task. You can download a copy of the latest version of OmniWeb from* **www.omnigroup.com**.

---

1. Open a word-processing or text-editing program. For the sake of this exercise, I'm using TextEdit, the replacement for Apple's SimpleText.

2. Type the URL for your favorite Web site.

3. Select the URL.

4. Go to the application menu, choose Services, and scroll to Omni-Web, where the submenu will read Open URL (see Figure 10.12).

When you select this option, the selected URL will open in OmniWeb (see Figure 10.13). Depending on the program you're using and the

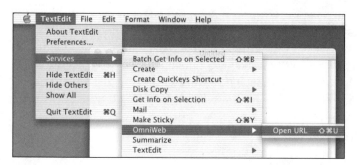

Figure 10.12   This feature takes longer to describe than to show.

Figure 10.13   OmniWeb displays a Web site whose URL was selected in TextEdit.

kind of text or picture objects you've selected, the Services menu will display different choices, and different commands will be available to apply to the selected material.

Troubleshooting Software Installation Problems

Mac OS X makes software installation easy, but sometimes things simply won't work. Here are some common problems and solutions:

- *The application won't launch.* Is it a Mac OS X application? If the program is Mac OS X–savvy, consider restarting your Mac to see if doing so makes a difference. If it doesn't, reinstall the application. If this doesn't work, contact the publisher about possible compatibility problems.

NOTE: *Most applications designed to work with specific hardware, such as scanning software, may have a problem working in the Classic environment of Mac OS X. You may need to wait for a genuine Mac OS X version.*

- *The application keeps quitting.* Usually, this is an installation or compatibility problem. Your first line of attack is to try launching the application again. Mac OS X's protected memory will close down the memory space with the application (unless it runs in the Classic environment). If that doesn't work, restart your Mac. You might also want to consider reinstalling the program. Otherwise, consult the documentation or the publisher's support department or Web site for information about possible bugs.

NOTE: *In the scheme of things, Mac OS X is quite new. So, don't be surprised to find applications failing from time to time. You should check with the publishers about possible updates. In particular, you'll find that the Classic environment sometimes won't quit or will quit very slowly.*

- *The application is installed in the wrong place.* Drag the application icon or folder to the Applications folder. Although this shouldn't make a difference, there may be other support files in a separate folder in the Applications folder that the program needs to run. It never hurts to try.

If you continue to run into problems with an application, whether newly installed or not, check Chapter 19 for more information about troubleshooting Mac OS X.

Related solution:	Found on page:
Solving System Crashes and Freezes	384

Part II

Mac OS X and Hardware

Chapter 11

Hardware Management

In Brief

Whether you have a brand-new Mac or an older model, the arrival of Mac OS X greatly simplifies the process of handling your system and application software. Ease of installation, simplified file management, and improved performance and reliability are hallmarks of the new operating system and the programs that come with it.

Most of the other chapters in this book deal primarily with the software, except for those devoted to adding new hardware accessories and using a Mac on the road. But another factor is important on the road to setting up and maintaining a Mac system: the Mac itself. In this chapter, I cover the basics of surviving a new Mac hardware installation, some of the special features Mac OS X provides to support that hardware, and some of the problems you may encounter and their solutions.

Mac OS X's Special Hardware Features

It's not just the system software that provides the performance advantages and reliability for Mac OS X. The new operating system includes special support to harness powerful features you might already have on your Mac.

Here are some of the main capabilities that can make your Mac more powerful and productive:

NOTE: To fully exploit these powerful technologies, you need to run Mac OS X–savvy applications. Your older programs will run with good performance in the Classic compatibility environment, but no faster (except in a few rare circumstances) and no more reliably than they did before. If any of these applications crashes, it will bring down the entire Classic environment, although the crash won't affect the rest of the system. In some cases, you could experience a performance hit, particularly if you're using programs heavily dependent on 3D graphics.

- *Advanced graphics management*—The Quartz imaging layer has built-in support for technologies such as PDF, OpenGL, and QuickTime. The superlative visual display of the Aqua interface, with shadings, shadows, transparency, and real-time object dragging, is one of the features that maximizes the potential of the graphics chips in your Mac. Even the first-generation iMac with a 233Mhz processor (the original Rev. A model) and the entry-level graphics chip from ATI Technologies can provide decent performance, but these work best in the thousands-of-colors mode. Of course, if you have a top-of-the-line Power Macintosh computer with an NVIDIA GeForce 3 graphics chip, you will realize the maximum possible benefit from the new features, regardless of resolution settings.

WARNING! **If you do not have a Mac with a graphics chip from ATI, IX Micro, or NVIDIA, you will have to contact the manufacturer about driver updates to address Mac OS X compatibility. This problem could be difficult if you have a graphics card from a defunct maker, such as 3dfx Interactive (although a third party has been trying to build Mac OS X–compatible drivers for these cards). Check such software information sites as VersionTracker.com to see if any outside parties will provide updates.**

- *Symmetric multiprocessing*—Some Macs come with more than a single processor chip. Although previous versions of the Mac OS and a very few applications (such as Adobe Photoshop) offer limited support for multiprocessing, as a practical matter, the extra brainpower doesn't do much good, except to help Apple's marketing department push new Macs. This situation changes, however, with Mac OS X, which has built-in support for multiprocessing and can efficiently parcel out tasks between processors to speed up performance. Any multi-threading application can also take advantage of multiprocessing, so that you get the maximum level of performance from the extra processors.

NOTE: Multiple threading *means simply that a program can handle more than a single chore at the same time.*

- *Preemptive multitasking*—The original Mac version of multitasking was cooperative, which meant that the programs themselves were designed to play nicely with one another. Under Mac OS X, the operating system is the traffic cop, parceling out tasks at a system level, providing better management of multiple applications.

Together, these features can make the same Mac that served you well under previous versions of the Mac OS behave almost as if you bought a new computer. Your Mac will start faster, will launch applications more quickly, and won't bog down at inopportune times when you're trying to make it do two things at once.

11. Hardware Management

NOTE: *Multiprocessing isn't a panacea. Other systems on your Mac, such as your graphics card and hard drive, can conspire to put limits on overall performance.*

With preemptive multitasking, the operating system parcels out the tasks among programs (rather than the programs themselves divvying things up), so your Mac will be able to play a QuickTime movie, download software from the Internet, and print documents without slowing down or coming to a screeching halt.

TIP: *One way to test the effect of Mac OS X on your Mac is to pull down a menu while performing all the functions I just listed and see if performance changes. Then, try doing the same thing under Mac OS 9, one of the more reliable Mac operating system versions, and see how long it takes for the multiple processes to stop.*

---

11. Hardware
Management

Immediate Solutions

Installing New Hardware

The arrival of a new Mac in your home or office can be a special event. It may be your first Mac or your tenth, but you'll want to get it up and running right away. The promise of getting on the Internet in 10 or 15 minutes flat is tempting. But here are some things to consider before you deploy that new computer in a production setup:

1. Check the Mac for obvious damage. Macs are packed pretty carefully by Apple and its dealers, but sometimes they don't survive the trip to your home or office. If the box has severe visible signs of damage, let the shipper or dealer know right away. Then, open the box carefully and see if the computer also seems damaged. If so, don't use it. Wait for a thorough diagnosis or replacement.

NOTE: In early 2000, I was assigned to review a snow-white iMac DV SE for CNET, a large online tech news resource. When the computer arrived at my home office via overnight carrier, the box was a mess. I opened it, and the top of the case was cracked. Such a thing has happened to me only once, but it was a jarring experience.

2. Assuming your computer looks fine, carefully follow the instructions to hook it up. If you intend to connect it to a network and/or hook up a bunch of peripherals, it's a good idea to first run the new Mac system all by itself, with just mouse, display, keyboard, and a modem or other Net connection to handle registration.

NOTE: On a rare occasion, a Mac with no visible damage will be dead on arrival. If the Mac refuses to boot properly or crashes constantly even before you can perform simple functions, you should stop using it and contact your Apple dealer or Apple Computer about repair or replacement. Although Mac dealers usually will not exchange a Mac for another unit or give you a refund, most (even The Apple Store) will replace a DOA unit.

3. Turn on the Mac and follow the setup prompts to store your user settings and register the product. Registering from the Mac requires that you connect to Apple's Web site to send the information.

11. Hardware Management

NOTE: *If you don't have ready Net access, check the documentation with the new Mac for a registration card that can accomplish the same task via the post office.*

---

4. Once the Mac is registered, try running a few programs and see if everything works.

5. If the Mac is running all right, connect your peripherals and/or network connections and see if everything functions normally.

6. If the computer seems to work, but you run into problems with one accessory or another, be sure you have installed the latest drivers for those products. I cover the subject of adding extras to your Mac in Chapter 12.

If your Mac comes through like a champ, you're ready to deploy it for production purposes.

Related solution:	Found on page:
Determining What to Do If It Doesn't Work	258

Maintaining Your Mac on a Daily Basis

If your Mac runs fine, you may be tempted to use it day in and day out and never concern yourself about proper hardware maintenance. Although a personal computer is nowhere near as sensitive to lack of proper care as the family car (where a missed oil change or two, or the failure to change worn brakes or tires, can be catastrophic), you should periodically give your Mac a once-over (or two or three) to keep it purring. Here's a simplified maintenance schedule:

- *Check the hard drive regularly.* Every week or so, use the First Aid component of Apple's Disk Utility or your favorite hard-drive diagnostic program to check all the drives connected to your Mac. Directory damage has a habit of creeping up on you: You'll receive reports of simple problems, and then they'll grow worse, until finally you lose files or the drive can't mount. But if you perform regular diagnostics, you'll be able to fix problems before they become too serious.

NOTE: *You cannot use Disk Utility to check your startup drive, but you can run Disk Utility after booting from another drive, or you can access it from the Mac OS X Installer CD, in the Installer application menu, once you boot from that CD.*

TIP: You can't use Disk Utility to check your Mac OS X startup drive. Drives are scanned at each startup; so, even if your Mac has been running fine for days or weeks without a restart, it wouldn't hurt to restart occasionally to allow the disk scans to run.

WARNING! **Many older hard-drive diagnostic programs are not designed to work with Mac OS X, even if you restart your Mac from the Mac OS 9 environment. You should check with the publisher directly about compatibility issues. The file structure under Mac OS X is different enough to cause bogus reports of disk problems, and attempts to fix those problems could create real ones.**

11. Hardware Management

- *Keep it clean.* I live in a Southwest desert state, so I have a chronic problem with dust buildup. In just a few weeks, the surface of the Macs in my home office can become dusty, and don't ask about the interior of the computers. On a regular basis, it's a good idea to dust the case with a soft cloth (not abrasive). Stay away from caustic cleaning solutions, but sometimes a light dose of a window-cleaning solution on a soft cloth is useful. If your display has become dusty, check the manufacturer's instructions about cleaning. Be especially careful with the soft surface of an LCD display—damage can be mighty expensive. Every few months, you might want to open your Mac (powered off, of course) and blow out the dust. Excessive dust buildup could affect the integrity of the items, such as RAM, connected to the logic board or the expansion bus (PCI or AGP). It can also hurt the performance of a cooling fan, or block the convection cooling vents on the iMac and PowerMac G4 Cube.

NOTE: Excessive dust inside your Mac can cause performance anomalies. I once visited a client who had chronic crash problems. His software seemed up-to-date, and he had recently reformatted the drive, yet the problems persisted. Before sending him to the repair shop, I opened the Mac. A cloud of dust filled the room (and I suppressed a cough). A dose from a compressed air canister, placed just close enough to do some good, cleared out the Mac in short order. After removing and reseating the RAM and expansion cards, I closed the Mac. It ran perfectly; no more chronic crashes.

- *Optimize sparingly.* The process of optimizing (or *defragging*) a hard drive rewrites all the files and puts them adjacent to each other, rather than spread across the drive as they are normally (although Mac OS X's advanced file system handles the process of writing files more efficiently). In theory, sufficient fragmentation might cause performance to suffer. In practice, it takes a lot to make a difference. Besides, Mac OS X's improved file handling can reduce the problem. However, if you remove and reinstall huge numbers of files, which is common in the graphic arts industry, you might experience a slight speed boost if you optimize. Video capture performance can be especially affected by such problems.

NOTE: *The ultra-efficient nature of the Unix File System (UFS) option means you shouldn't have to optimize your drive if it's formatted that way. The downside is that you can't run Classic from a UFS volume, nor can the UFS volume be seen if you restart from your Classic Mac OS.*

- *Check for driver/software updates.* Software and device drivers are all in a constant process of evolution and change. You should stay in contact with the manufacturers about needed updates for better support of Mac OS X. A good resource for such information is the **VersionTracker.com** Web site (see **www.versiontracker.com**).

- *Check your Mac after a power failure.* If a weather or power company problem has resulted in loss of power at your home or office, you should check your computers carefully when power is restored. Normally, when you restart or shut down your Mac, a "housecleaning" process writes cached files to the drive and updates the drive's directory. If the process is interrupted, files could be damaged, and drive directory problems might occur. Your hard drives will be scanned when you restart your Mac, but you may also want to use your favorite commercial hard-drive program (such as DiskWarrior, Drive 10, Norton Utilities, or TechTool Pro) to make sure everything is all right before you get back to work.

- *Shut down everything before you install something inside your Mac.* The delicate electronic components in your Mac, from the logic board to the processor, can easily be damaged by static electricity or a short circuit. If you need to add or remove a peripheral card or RAM, touch the power supply (with the plug in) to get rid of any static charge you might have and then pull the plug. Some of the better memory and peripheral card dealers will supply a wrist strap to help with the process. You may feel like a surgeon beginning an operation while thus equipped, but the benefit is that your installation can be done with the maximum degree of safety and the maximum protection to the delicate internal workings of your computer.

NOTE: *If you remove RAM or a peripheral card from your Mac, try to store it in a static-resistant bag. You may want to keep them around for warranty service or for storing old hardware.*

Should You Buy a New Mac?

You've probably been to someone's home or office and seen an original compact Mac still purring away in the corner, working almost as reliably as the day it was purchased. Although it's possible to keep a Mac for many years without encountering more than the customary range of system crashes and reinstallations, sometimes you might just want to give the old computer to the kids, or donate it to your favorite charitable institution.

Here's what to consider when you're deciding if your Mac should be retired:

- *It's too expensive to fix.* You've encountered problems that appear to be hardware related. Although there are dealers who can supply used or reconditioned logic boards, RAM, graphics cards, and hard drives, do the addition before you take this route. It could be time to give your Mac a well-deserved permanent vacation.

NOTE: *One of my clients has an older Mac (a Mac OS clone computer from Motorola) upon which he has lavished attention and considerable expense. Between paying my fees for troubleshooting and installation, and buying parts, he has long since exceeded the cost of a new computer. He still persists; however, the arrival of Mac OS X, with its great user interface and promise of greater performance and reliability, is tempting him to upgrade so that he can run the new operating system. That is, unless he attempts to do an unsolicited installation of Mac OS X on his older Mac (I don't recommend it).*

- *It won't run Mac OS X.* This is a judgment call. Just because you can't run the latest and greatest doesn't mean your Mac will stop working and play dead. It could take years before most major applications are updated for Mac OS X. Even the initial updates will probably be Carbonized, which means the application may (but not always) work under both Mac OS X and the Classic Mac operating systems from 8.6 or 9.0 and on. That means you can use the updated program now on the older Mac, and it will also work great with Mac OS X when you buy a new computer. You can compare this situation to the so-called "fat" applications of the early PowerPC Mac era. Such programs contained both the older 680x0 Mac code and PowerPC code, and thus could be transported easily from a computer with one processor to the other and work fine. That's why software publishers are taking Carbon so seriously.

- *It's slow and won't run the latest software.* Do you really need to use AppleWorks 6 if ClarisWorks 3 works all right? That's just one example, and it's significant. You may find that you're perfectly happy with the older version of a program and you don't want to learn new tricks. Although older software will work on a newer Mac, if you're happy with your old computer and applications, don't let this book or the flashy "Think Different" ads you see from Apple deter you.

- *You just have to have Mac OS X.* All right, that's a good reason to upgrade; but before you do, consider whether you'll also have to update your favorite programs before you make the jump and how much those upgrades will cost. If the applications you want are not yet Mac OS X–savvy, you won't get much advantage from the new operating system, because you'll still see the old interface much of the time in the Classic environment and not experience the joys of Aqua. On the other hand, Mac OS X includes programs you can use to surf the Internet, so that may be partial compensation. In addition, although new Macs or recently discontinued models are much cheaper than the older models, you should consider what you'll do with the computer to see if the upgrade is justified.

NOTE: *One of my clients, a semiretired hairdresser, restricts his first-generation Power Mac to sending and receiving email and occasionally surfing the Net. However, he finally decided to buy a new Power Mac G4, and when I set it up for him, I took him on a tour of Mac OS X. Because all the software he needed was native, he happily switched to the new operating system without any regrets.*

Looking at Extended Warranties

Whether you buy a new Mac from a local store or a mail-order house, before you finish your order, the salesperson probably will ask you to consider just one more purchase—an extended warranty. Apple's computers, as of the time this book was written, had a one-year limited warranty on parts and labor, with just 90 days of free telephone support. If you plan to keep your new Mac for a while, the prospect of extended support might be tempting.

Consider this, though: Dealers often rely on the sale of extended warranties to shore up their profit margins, particularly in these troubled times when sales of new computers have stalled. More often than not, a hardware failure will occur early in an electronic component's life, during the warranty period. As with any insurance policy, you need to weigh the possible expense of an out-of-warranty repair against the certain expense of the extended warranty.

If you are using an Apple iBook or PowerBook, however, such a warranty might be a good idea. Laptop computers are potentially subject to far greater abuse than desktop computers, because they are dragged around so frequently. Having that extra protection might be worth the expense.

WARNING! *If you opt to buy an extended warranty, double-check with the dealer to find out whether the warranty is Apple's (known as AppleCare) or comes from another company. I have seen instances where customers ordered AppleCare and got something else. When checking into such a program, compare the cost and benefits before signing on the dotted line—and look at the actual policy information (don't just depend on what the salesperson tells you).*

Solving Hardware and Software Problems

This is an eternal difficulty. Your Mac crashes constantly, and you've gone through all the possible software troubleshooting you can, following the steps outlined in Chapter 19. But still your Mac misbehaves. Here are some additional choices to consider, along with cases when you might want to have the Mac's hardware serviced:

- *Chronic hard-drive errors*—Every time you check your hard drive with the First Aid component of Disk Utility or one of the commercial hard-drive programs, it comes back with reports of directory damage that needs to be fixed. Sometimes, you'll even see a message that the repairs can't be performed. Should this happen, first try restarting your Mac with a System CD or one of the CDs provided with the commercial drive utility. If you continue to run into problems that recur or can't be fixed, back up your data and reformat the drive. Leaving directory damage unfixed can eventually result in a loss of files or the inability of your Mac to recognize your drive.

TIP: *It's a good idea to back up your important data regularly, not just in response to a report of a drive directory problem. Not all drive problems announce themselves in advance; sometimes the drive just fails.*

WARNING!   If you see a prompt on your Mac's display offering to initialize your hard drive, don't do it! This destructive act will erase the data. Although it sometimes may be possible to restore a drive with a program such as Norton Utilities or with an expensive trip to a drive recovery service, you should try other diagnostic methods before going this route.

11. Hardware Management

- *Hard drive doesn't work properly after it's reformatted*—You bit the bullet and reformatted your hard drive, but problems still occur. You continue to get reports of hard-drive directory errors, or the worst happens and the drive doesn't appear on your Computer directory in the Finder or the desktop. You should have both the drive and your Mac checked by a technician. It's possible one or the other has failed.

- *Mac makes a startup sound, but the screen is dark*—If you just installed Mac OS X and you're using a graphics card that isn't from ATI, IX Micro, or NVIDIA, you should consult the manufacturer about Mac OS X support. You may need to restart with an Apple-approved graphics card to install updated software.

NOTE: *At press time, one or more independent programmers were at work trying to develop Mac OS X drivers for the Voodoo graphic cards produced by the now-defunct 3dfx Interactive. If you still have a Voodoo card, there may be hope; otherwise, you should seriously consider retiring it to an old Mac that will not be upgraded to Mac OS X.*

- *Mac with an upgrade card fails to boot*—Mac OS X requires a Mac that shipped with either a G3 or G4 processor. If you have an older Mac and upgraded the processor, don't expect it to work or to receive support from Apple. However, you may want to check with the manufacturer of the upgrade card to see if it has a way to make it run. Such companies as PowerLogix and Sonnet Technology have special software that will allow some of their cards to run under Mac OS X (some of Sonnet's upgrade cards don't need software), but you must depend on these companies for support for installations not supported by Apple Computer.

- *Mac fails to boot and doesn't make a startup sound*—Recheck the power cord, the power strip, and the devices attached to your Mac. If you recently installed a new peripheral card or RAM upgrade, remove each item in turn (closing the Mac each time) and see if you can get the Mac to run. If removing one fixes the problem, reinstall the item and try again. Should the problem return, contact the manufacturer for repair or replacement. If you cannot get the Mac to run, it's time for a trip to the dealer's service department.

NOTE: *Another potential cause of a Mac's failing to boot is a defective peripheral card, particularly the graphics card. Shut down, and then remove and reseat the video card, and see if doing so brings your Mac back to life.*

- *Mac fails to boot with peripheral device attached*—The blame should be placed on the device. If it's a SCSI device, make sure it's powered on before you boot your Mac. One key test is to remove the device (after powering down); if your Mac then works all right, you have a good idea as to the culprit.

NOTE: *If your Mac has a SCSI adapter card, you should check with the manufacturer about Mac OS X support for its products. As this book was written, Adaptec had released drivers for some of its newer cards, while retiring some older models. Orange Micro was still at work developing Mac OS X–savvy firmware for its SCSI cards.*

- *Mac crashes constantly early in the startup process or right after restart*—Follow the software diagnostics covered in Chapter 19. If a reinstallation of Mac OS X fails to fix the problem, consider backing up and reformatting your hard drive. From here, continued problems could be traced to bad RAM, a faulty hard drive, or your Mac's logic board. Take it to your dealer for diagnosis.

NOTE: *Can you do your own hardware diagnostics? Possibly. MicroMat's TechTool Pro (and the TechTool Deluxe application that comes with Apple's AppleCare service warranty) can test the various systems on your Mac. A number of new Macs also include an Apple Hardware Test CD that can be used to perform a basic set of hardware tests. However, if you see a report of a potential problem, let a technician make the final call. In general, some motherboard and RAM defects would result in a Sad Mac, but sometimes they'll just result in more system crashes or the failure to complete a startup process.*

- *You smell smoke or see a spark from your Mac*—What can I tell you? Although laser printer toner can sometimes smell a little smoky, if you see symptoms of this sort, don't try to use your Mac. Unplug it immediately and move away from any flammable material. Let a dealer's service representative do a diagnostic first.

NOTE: *A slight spark could just be static electricity. If you have thick carpeting or you're in a particularly dry climate, walking around may build up static electricity. If you touch a metal object, you may see a slight spark.*

Related solution:	Found on page:
Solving Other Common Mac OS X Problems	393

11. Hardware Management

Chapter 12

Hooking Up Accessories

In Brief

Although the original compact Macintosh may have started out as a device with just an internal floppy drive, a keyboard, and a mouse, your Mac isn't an island. Even if you have an iBook or PowerBook (especially the flashy Titanium G4 version), sometimes you'll want to add extra devices to enhance its capabilities. Fortunately, the promise of the Macintosh operating system that has endeared it to millions upon millions of customers is easy (well, fairly easy) plug-and-play ability. That means you can attach a peripheral device and have it function with the absolute minimum of fuss.

Mac OS X expands on this promise. When you install the new operating system, you'll find built-in support for a huge number of devices, including ink jet printers from Canon, Epson, HP, and Lexmark; laser printers from a number of major companies; third-party CD burners and input devices; and most digital cameras. If you install any of these devices, you'll find that they work without your having to do a special software installation (beyond a visit to the Print Center application for networked laser printers).

Support isn't 100 percent. If drivers aren't included with Mac OS X, you will have to look to the manufacturer of the product for the drivers you need (this is especially true for scanners, which have no built-in support under Mac OS X). However, when the drivers are all in place, the combination of easy installation and the powerful system management of Mac OS X makes it possible to get the maximum value from any peripheral you want to buy.

In this chapter, I cover many of the types of devices you can buy and how to install and use them as speedily and efficiently as possible.

A Review of Mac Peripheral Ports

In the old days of the Macintosh, you attached your input devices to an ADB port, a printer to the printer port, a modem to the modem port, and an external storage device to the SCSI port. All that changed, however, with the 1998 arrival of the computer credited with Apple's resurgence—the iMac.

The iMac begat a new peripheral standard on the Mac (although it wasn't new in the personal computing world) and eliminated some of the ports that were considered standard issue. Here's a brief rundown of the various peripheral standards present on Macs that can run Mac OS X and where they fit in the overall picture:

- *Apple Desktop Bus (ADB)*—This was an early standard input port for input devices, such as the keyboard and mouse you use on your Mac, a trackball, and joystick, and such extras as digital cameras. Even some modems use this port. However, it can only support a very few devices, performance tends to be slow for demanding accessories, and the plug-and-play aspect is a little murky. You have to shut down your Mac to remove and add devices, or you risk damage to the computer's logic board. The ADB port vanished with the arrival of the iMac and later new models, both desktop and laptop; it was replaced with Universal Serial Bus (USB), a much more flexible standard.

- *Serial port*—Some Macs had two serial ports, and some PowerBooks had just one. A regular desktop Mac had one port for printers (it doubled as a LocalTalk port) and another for modems. PowerBooks combined the two and added built-in modems so that there was no conflict or need for a switch to allow you to use an extra device. These ports are, in theory, plug and play. You can usually switch devices without a restart, although it's recommended you restart when you can. As far as performance is concerned, a serial port is more than adequate for printing and for modems. But networking speed is a fraction of that available for Ethernet, and thus the process of transferring files can be cumbersome if the files are too large.

NOTE: *The original Mac serial ports simply are not supported for Mac OS X. If you have a LocalTalk printer, then the iPrint from Proxim (formerly Farallon) or the AsanteTalk will convert to Ethernet. But serial printers, such as the Apple StyleWriter, should be replaced with USB versions even if you must use a USB adapter on your Mac, because driver support won't be offered; a simple serial-to-USB converter isn't enough.*

- *SCSI port*—Except for the very first Mac (which used the floppy drive port to add a hard drive), the SCSI port was the original standard for adding storage devices, scanners, and some specialty printers to your Mac. This is the closest thing to plug and *pray* on your Mac, because SCSI can be problematic, especially when the SCSI chain is large. For regular SCSI, you can connect up to seven daisy-chained devices. Each device has a unique ID number, from 0 through 6 (up to 15 for some high-speed SCSI cards), and the last physical device on the chain (regardless of ID number) must be terminated. With large SCSI chains, sometimes devices won't work properly or your Mac will crash frequently. The diagnostics include reordering devices (observing proper ID numbering and termination), swapping cables, taking two aspirins, and trying again. With millions of SCSI devices out there, Mac users still need to employ this peripheral standard, although better ones are available.

- *Ethernet*—This high-speed networking standard is in use in homes and both large and small offices. The standard Ethernet protocols in use on Macs are 10Base-T and 100Base-T, and recent generations of desktop Power Mac G4s and the fall 2001 version of the PowerBook G4 include Gigabit Ethernet. At its maximum speed, Ethernet can deliver networking throughput nearly as fast as a big hard drive. This is a true plug-and-play standard. You can connect multiple devices to a central connecting point, such as a hub or switch, and remove and reconnect as needed. Ethernet devices aren't limited to computers and printers. You can also add network routers and special modems for broadband Internet, such as cable and DSL.

- *Universal Serial Bus (USB)*—This low- to medium-speed serial port is standard issue on all shipping Apple computers. Most Macs, except the iBook, have two USB ports (the iBook has just one). To add more devices, you need hubs. In theory, you can connect up to 127 devices with full plug and play, but to do so you must install driver software for many products and unmount a storage device first before removal. Up to 12 megabits per second speed is shared on a single USB bus, which is enough for input devices, low-cost scanners, digital cameras, and storage devices where speed is not a concern.

NOTE: *An updated USB standard, version 2.0, promises to offer speeds that exceed those of FireWire. However, as of the time this book was written, support on the Mac platform was reserved to third-party adapters and peripherals.*

- *FireWire*—This is an Apple invention, a high-speed peripheral port that puts the kibosh on SCSI for all practical purposes. It delivers up to 400 megabits in performance, coming closest to all but the fastest SCSI standards. Devices can be daisy chained, and there's a high level of plug-and-play compatibility, including hotplugging. Drivers are needed on some devices, and storage devices must be dismounted from the desktop, but that covers most exceptions. FireWire devices include digital camcorders, which makes all recent Macs ideal desktop video-editing computers. FireWire storage devices and scanners are available, and

Apple's stylish music player, the iPod, uses the FireWire port to update the music on its internal drive or to serve duty as a regular storage device.

NOTE: *This is not to say that FireWire is free of conflicts. I once installed a FireWire scanner, and it had to be the last item on the peripheral chain. Otherwise, weird startup problems, problems copying large files to FireWire storage devices, and occasional system crashes resulted. The file-copying problems persisted after I installed Mac OS X, so it wasn't a driver issue (no drivers were available at the time). So, I never say never.*

Adding a Missing Port

What do you do if you want a peripheral, but your Mac doesn't have the correct port? For desktop Macs with expansion slots, you can get relief in the form of PCI-based peripheral adapter cards. They come in many shapes and sizes, offering the following:

- *FireWire*—Two or more FireWire ports can be found on a single expansion card. Best of all, such cards usually don't need any special software (aside from Apple's FireWire extensions for Mac OS 9) and can cost less than $50.

- *USB*—With so many USB products available, it would be nice if older Macs could use them. All it takes is a peripheral card that costs less than $20. Make sure Apple's USB extensions are installed if you're using Mac OS 9.x (USB support is standard issue with Mac OS X).

NOTE: *When you're buying a FireWire or USB adapter, check the documentation that comes with the product closely. Some companies bury the Mac OS compatibility information on the back of the box. I ran across a $20 Belkin USB adapter at Wal-Mart that was labeled in this rather confusing fashion.*

- *High-speed Ethernet*—Although the newest Mac desktops offer Gigabit Ethernet, you don't have to feel abandoned with an older Mac. Expansion cards fill this gap as well, but they're costly.

- *Combo cards*—If you don't have enough slots, take heart. Combination cards offer both FireWire and USB. Now, you don't have to choose just one.

- *SCSI cards*—If you need to find a home for your existing SCSI devices, a ready collection of SCSI cards are available with various price points and speeds. The cheapest cards, at roughly $50, are up to twice as fast as the built-in SCSI on most Macs, and they get much faster as the price increases.

NOTE: *Before buying a SCSI card, make sure it supports the devices you already have. For a scanner, removable drive, and a regular SCSI hard drive, the cheaper cards are fine. But some external drives and even backup drives require cards with "wide" SCSI ports.*

- *SCSI-to-FireWire converter*—This is another way to have the best of both worlds. Several brands of such converters are available that allow a single SCSI device to connect to the FireWire ports on your Mac. Because they're single devices, you don't have to consider issues of termination and ID.

- *Serial-to-USB converters*—These modules let you attach products that work on regular Mac serial ports, such as older ink jet printers and modems, to a newer Mac's USB port. The major limitation is the occasional software conflict and the inability to work with LocalTalk devices, such as AppleTalk printers that attach to a standard Mac printer port.

- *SCSI-to-USB converters*—This type of product would appear to be a blessing, because it lets you continue to use those old SCSI products on a Mac that has only USB, such as the iMac. However, because USB is slower than SCSI, the conversion works best for a scanner or low-speed storage device (such as a Zip drive or tape drive).

- *LocalTalk-to-Ethernet bridge*—If you have an older Mac where Ethernet is an option or a network printer that only has a LocalTalk port, this device allows you to continue to use these products on your Ethernet network. You won't get any faster speed, but you won't have to buy a new printer or spend extra money on a peripheral card for an old Mac that is near the end of its useful life.

- *ADB-to-USB adapter*—If you still cherish that old keyboard, mouse, trackball, or similar input device, fear not. You can still use it on your new Mac with this type of adapter. On the other hand, many terrific input devices are available for Macs these days— particularly Apple's new Pro Keyboard and Pro Mouse (I love these and use them all the time), which ship standard on new Macs and are available from the Apple Store for older models. You may find the money better spent acquiring something new.

WARNING! Not all peripheral cards work seamlessly with Mac OS X. Before you purchase one of these products, contact the manufacturer or check its Web site directly to see its plans. For example, older Adaptec SCSI cards are not guaranteed to run with Mac OS X (which does not, of course, mean they won't). If you have an older product, you can try it at your risk, and keep your fingers crossed.

- *Expansion cards for PowerBooks*—PowerBook users shouldn't feel abandoned by the new peripheral buses. Both USB and FireWire PC cards are available that will add this capability to just about any PowerBook that can run Mac OS X.

NOTE: *Unfortunately, the iBook and the iMac were conceived as inexpensive consumer computers and thus lack extra expansion ports and the ability to add them (except for FireWire on later models of both). So, you must live with the ports you have, should you be using one of these models.*

Peripherals Available for Macs

What do you need? Although some folks decry the limited availability of products for Macs, they aren't really paying attention to the lists in today's Mac mail-order catalogs or the shelves in stores that specialize in the platform.

Literally thousands of Mac products are available. Many, in fact, are cross-platform—the same product is available for both Mac and Windows users, with the sole difference being the driver software or the label on the box.

NOTE: *Some companies with cross-platform products will, for some unaccountable reason, put their software drivers only on their Web sites, rather than on the CD that comes with the product. If a product seems to work only under Windows, check the box and the manufacturer's Web site, in case you get lucky.*

Here's a short list of the kinds of products you can add to your Mac to help harness the power of Mac OS X:

NOTE: *This list is meant for information only, to give a sampling of the sort of products you can connect to your Mac. Check with a particular manufacturer to find out whether a special upgrade is needed for Mac OS X. Some of these products will plug in and run, regardless of whether you have Mac OS X or Mac OS 9.x.*

- *Scanners*—Once, desktop scanners were the province of professional graphic artists. They were expensive, with color models of reasonable quality running from one to two grand. Although there are still products in that price range, literally dozens of models are available from less than $100 to around $200. A scanner allows you to capture and digitize artwork and photos and even convert printed material to text that you can edit in your favorite word-processing program (with special optical character-recognition software). Once the artwork is scanned, you can convert it into a format that you can use on your Mac for word processing or desktop publishing, or send to your friends and business associates. Scanners are available in FireWire, SCSI, and USB form; some models support more than one peripheral standard.

TIP: *Is the manufacturer of your scanner a little late in developing Mac OS X drivers? Try VueScan, a clever third-party solution. I used this demoware scanning application (you need to buy a user license to get it to scan without a watermark on your image) until Microtek was able to deliver drivers for my scanner. Available as a download from the publisher's Web site at **www.hamrick.com**, VueScan supports a huge number of flatbed and slide scanners. It's also updated almost weekly, so if your scanner isn't working with it, just be patient or write to the publisher and see if support is coming.*

- *Digital cameras*—Is film obsolete? Perhaps not, but digital cameras offer a convenient way to take a picture and not have to wait for it to be developed by a processor lab. Although the cheapest models provide pictures that hardly rate in comparison with those offered by even a low-cost film camera, a few hundred dollars can now get you a digital camera that compares favorably to traditional models. Some of the more expensive models match film cameras with special features, such as single-lens reflex viewfinders (where you see the same image picked up by the camera's lens), and even the ability to do limited motion videos. Most of these products store data on small memory cards. Best of all, beginning with Mac OS X 10.1, the Image Capture application provides built-in support for most available digital cameras. Just plug the camera into your Mac, and Image Capture launches to download your pictures.

- *Hard drives*—This type of device can be essentially the same as the one in your Mac now, except that it's in an external case. Hard drives come in FireWire, SCSI, and USB formats; the first two provide the highest degree of performance. In terms of speed, there should be no difference between external and internal drives. The Power Macs, except for the Cube, sport extra drive bays for additional internal storage devices, in case you want to put everything on one case.

- *Removable drives*—As I explain in Chapter 17, backing up your data is critically important. Even though Mac OS X is a superbly stable, industrial-strength operating system, problems can happen to a drive's directory, and individual applications can still fail.

That, plus the possibility of external dangers, such as a burglary, natural disaster, or weather-related problems, makes it imperative that you keep regular backups of your most valuable material. A removable drive is a convenient backup tool and just as handy for moving files to another location—particularly files that are too large to send online. Two removable formats are the venerable Zip drive, which has found its way into millions of computers, and the Imation SuperDisk, which also reads older-style floppy disks.

NOTE: *Although the SuperDisk drive is quite handy and the technology seems robust enough, such drives are usually found in the closeout bins these days. The primary manufacturer, Imation, has apparently given up competing with the Zip drive, but still makes regular floppy drives. QPS Inc. also makes a SuperDisk drive, as well as a big line of CD burners and FireWire hard drives.*

- *CD writer (or burner)*—This type of product became standard equipment on a Mac only in early 2001. The closest equivalent is the DVD-RAM drive on some older Power Macintosh G4 models, which records on a special DVD-based medium with a capacity of up to 5.2GB. A CD writer, or *burner*, lets you make a CD of data or music. Such devices are ubiquitous and available in FireWire, SCSI, and USB trim (also ATA for use in a present-day desktop Mac's internal drive bay). There are two basic types of CD formats for writing data: CD-R, which can be recorded only once, and CD-RW, which can be rewritten up to 1,000 times (but the disk can't be read on all drives). Although a CD drive is slower than a regular removable hard drive, a CD has the added benefit of permanence. A CD can last for many years without suffering damage or possible loss of data, unless given ultra-severe abuse. In addition, you can buy a DVD-R burner, similar to the one used for the SuperDrive on G4 desktop computers, from such companies as LaCie and Que. These drives not only make DVD movies, but they can also be used for data storage via the Finder's Burn feature (check with the manufacturer about support for Mac OS X).

NOTE: *There are two basic types of CD-R media. The data type is designed to record any kind of data from a computer. The music CD consists of the same media, but higher priced, to cover the royalty paid to artists whose material you are copying.*

- *Wireless networking*—Apple's AirPort wireless networking modules are available for all new Macs. They allow Macs to network with each other at near standard Ethernet speeds at distances of up to 150 feet. The AirPort Base Station lets you share an Internet connection.

NOTE: *If you have an older Mac without AirPort capability, other choices are available for wireless networking. Among these choices are the SkyLINE from Proxim (formerly Farallon) and Asante's AeroLAN, both of which use the same industry standard protocols as AirPort (802.11b or Wi-Fi) and can function as part of the same network. Both firms also offer Wi-Fi base stations that work on both Macs and Windows-based PCs.*

- *Loudspeakers*—Yes, most loudspeaker systems you add to a computer plug in to your audio output or earphone jack, but some speakers connect directly to your USB port. These include the Harman Kardon iSub and SoundSticks. They take advantage of the Mac OS's own sound control features to adjust volume, balance, and tone.

- *Handheld computers*—These devices include the popular Palm OS products from Handspring and Palm, as well as dedicated electronic book readers, such as the Rocket eBook. They aren't designed to be attached to your Mac all the time, but they need to interface with your computer for installing and removing software, or for just synchronizing information. You'll need special software to allow this connection to work.

- *Digital music players*—MP3 has taken the music world by storm. Millions of PC users have assembled music libraries, and these little devices allow you to collect your tracks on a memory card or storage device. They work in the fashion of the famous Sony Walkman, letting you take music with you. Apple's iPod, a tiny, steel-clad player the size of a deck or cards, mates seamlessly with Apple's iTunes 2 software to sync the music library on your Mac with the one on the player.

NOTE: *I'll avoid the issues of the copyright disputes involving the recording industry and certain MP3-related Web sites. But I will mention in passing that Apple's iPod lets you share music only with a single Mac when run in its standard, or automatic mode, so you can't copy music from the player onto other computers.*

Although installing an accessory on your Mac is fairly easy, you should always take a few extra precautions to make sure everything is set up properly. This is particularly important if you are setting up a complicated peripheral device, such as a scanner, and some extra steps might be necessary. In addition, because many products come with very sparse documentation, these steps will help you get things working without extra fuss or confusion.

In the next section, I cover some basic recommendations for installing a peripheral device on your Mac and how to cope with problems, should they arise.

Immediate Solutions

Installing a New Scanner

After unpacking the device, check the manual or installer card for basic setups and follow these basic guidelines:

1. Locate the lock on the scanner. It might be identified by a padlock icon, and unlocking can be done with a screwdriver or just by turning a latch. This is critical, because you risk damaging a scanner if you attempt to run it while the optical mechanism is locked.

NOTE: *If you plan to move your scanner to a new location outside your workplace, remember to lock the optical mechanism first to protect the unit. Also, not all scanners have locks. If there's no indication of one on the unit, check the setup documentation. If it's not there, you may be lucky (although only really cheap scanners seem to lack those locks).*

2. If another user has logged in to your Mac, you'll need to use your administrator's account. Installing anything that requires system-wide access can be done only in this fashion. If the installer requires a login, you'll see a prompt at the beginning of the installation process.

WARNING! *Before you install any software for new hardware, be sure to consult the documentation or contact the publisher about Mac OS X compatibility. Even if you bought the product long after the new operating system was released, don't assume the unit is compatible unless the package or the product's label provides specific information about the subject such as a "Built for Mac OS X" label. If you can't find this information, check with the publisher.*

3. Install the software. It should be on a CD that shipped with the scanner. Some scanners include an integrated installation process, which handles the scanner drivers, image-editing software, and other extras. Others offer each element as a separate, clickable install. Follow the prompts about selecting installation options. Depending on the installer, you may have to restart your Mac (usually you don't).

WARNING! *If, for some reason, the scanner uses an old-fashioned floppy disk installer, you can be assured the scanner drivers aren't compatible with Mac OS X. Contact the manufacturer about this problem, or use it under the Mac OS X Classic environment until a new version of the software is available.*

12. Hooking Up Accessories

4. Connect the scanner to your Mac. If it's a SCSI product, shut down your Mac and attach SCSI devices first, then restart after the hookup. For FireWire and USB, shutting down isn't necessary, because of the plug-and-play nature of these two peripheral standards.

NOTE: *If you are installing a SCSI device, make sure there are no duplicate ID numbers and that termination switches on the product are turned on or off as needed for your installation. If you're using a third-party SCSI card, verify its compatibility with Mac OS X before attempting to install devices on it.*

---

5. Launch your scanning software and run the scanner through its paces for scanning and processing images. If you have problems, consult the documentation (it might be on the CD) for further assistance.

NOTE: *Some scanner drivers don't work separately from a photo-editing program. So, you'll need to see if a copy of Adobe Photoshop or a similar program is on your Mac and use that program's Acquire feature to activate the scanning driver.*

Installing New Storage Devices

Depending on the sort of storage device you have, you may not need to add any extra software. Here are the basic steps to follow:

1. Consult the documentation or look for a CD to see if special software needs to be installed.

NOTE: *Mac OS X has built-in support for a number of popular removable devices, such as Imation SuperDisk drives, Iomega Zip and Jaz drives, and a number of FireWire storage devices. You can run them without adding any extra software, and they will function normally. If you are installing a device in the same category, you may, as an experiment, want to hook it up and try to make it run before you attempt to use the software, because it's possible the drivers aren't updated for Mac OS X.*

---

2. If software is required, make sure it's Mac OS X compatible. You will see a login prompt for your administrator's password if required for the installation.

3. Launch the installer application and follow the prompts.

4. If necessary, restart your Mac (this step is necessary only for devices that load as part of the Mac's startup process).

12. Hooking Up Accessories

5. Connect the drive to your Mac. If you're hooking up a SCSI device, make sure that your Mac and attached SCSI devices are turned off first; you can safely restart after hookup.

NOTE: *Don't forget to check for SCSI ID and termination settings before powering up.*

6. Verify that the drive works properly. If it's a hard drive, copy files to and from it. For a removable device, insert the removable media and run it through its paces.

WARNING! *On a CD burner, it's worth trying one CD-RW disk just to be sure that you can copy data satisfactorily; the benefit of using a CD-RW disk is that you can reuse it after determining the drive is all right. You do not want to back up critical data and then find out, too late, that there was a problem reading the CD.*

Installing Digital Cameras, eBook Readers, Palm OS Handhelds, and Other Products

The process of setting up a device that's not connected full time to your Mac is essentially the same as connecting a device that's always hooked up. Here are the steps to follow:

1. Unpack the device and check for interface plugs. If there's no USB or FireWire cable, check to see if a serial cable is available. Depending on the kind of Mac you have, you might need an interface adapter, such as a serial-to-USB converter, to make it run.

2. After verifying Mac OS X compatibility, locate the installer CD and install the software. In many cases, you'll have to enter your administrator's password in the login prompt.

3. Check the device for proper operation, and then attach the unit to your Mac as instructed.

4. Consult the instructions about synching or interfacing with your Mac.

5. If the product doesn't run as expected, check manuals or the manufacturer's support Web site or telephone support line for further advice.

NOTE: *Most digital cameras mate perfectly with Apple's Image Capture software out of the box. So before you install anything, just take a few shots, attach the camera to your Mac, and see if Image Capture loads. This application will appear only if the camera is supported.*

12. Hooking Up Accessories

Determining What to Do If It Doesn't Work

Despite some of the concessions to mass production and competition to keep prices low, it's a rare product that will fail out of the box. Usually, when something doesn't work, you can take steps to address the problem.

Here are some items to check in case the accessory you've bought for your Mac isn't working as you expected:

- *Is the device compatible with Mac OS X?* Even if the box or documentation says it is, don't expect seamless compatibility in every case. You may need to double-check with the manufacturer to see if additional updates are required. If the box or documentation doesn't specifically address the issue, assume the product won't run unless there's built-in support under Mac OS X. Except for a limited number of products, the answer is probably no.

NOTE: *The promise and non-delivery of Mac OS X–compatibility information was brought home to me shortly after I first installed the new operating system. I bought a new software product whose box had a sticker promising details about a Mac OS X upgrade inside. I checked thoroughly, and no information whatsoever was provided. A call to the manufacturer yielded the worst news of all—the label was a mistake. The company hadn't made any decisions about when such an upgrade would be available and in what form.*

- *Have you installed the wrong software?* New products are apt to have different installers for Mac OS X and for the Classic Mac OS. Double-check to make sure that you ran the correct installation. You might want to do it again and see.

- *Did you forget to restart?* It may or may not be necessary, but if a product won't work, this step is worth taking just to make sure the proper drivers load.

- *Are you experiencing peripheral application crashes?* Even though the Darwin core of Mac OS X is highly robust and crash resistant, individual programs still may crash from time to time. Fortunately, protected memory means that even if an application quits, you can continue to use your Mac. Should the program continue to quit or freeze, contact the manufacturer about needed updates.

- *Is the device plugged in?* Even if the AC adapter is connected to the wall socket or a power strip, you may have to tear through a spaghetti-like maze of cables to see if everything is hooked up properly. Cables sometimes separate during spring cleaning.

NOTE: *This issue isn't as obvious as it seems. I once got a frantic call from a client who wondered why her printer had stopped working. I asked her to double-check her cables, and she assured me everything was plugged in. But when I visited her office to check, I discovered the loose printer cable lost behind a mass of similar-colored wiring that was extremely difficult to sort out. Apparently, a cleaning person had mistakenly pulled the cable from a USB hub in a futile attempt to make the wiring mess look neat.*

- *Is a cable bad or broken?* It's not always easy to see such a problem, because of the sometimes thick shielding on a cable. Try another cable, if you have one, as a test. Frayed or otherwise damaged cables should be replaced right away. Naked wires could cause a short circuit, which would fry the delicate electronic circuitry in the component.

- *Is the device faulty?* Perhaps the problem isn't your Mac or something you did. Sometimes, new products just fail out of the box or shortly after they're placed in service. That's the purpose of the new product warranty, and don't hesitate to read the fine print and find out what you need to do to get the unit repaired or replaced. Some companies will replace a product that's dead on arrival, by the way.

You may hope that you can continue to work full time in Mac OS X, although doing so is apt to be difficult in the early days of Mac OS X (at least until all your software has made the transition). Situations will do doubt arise where a product just won't run under Mac OS X, even if the manufacturer claims compatibility. If this is the case, bite the bullet and return to your old operating system.

12. Hooking Up Accessories

Taking Mac OS X on the Road

In Brief

Are you a road warrior? The rise of mobile computing means that you can truly take it with you—your laptop, that is. That way, you can sit on the beach and finish that business proposal, or write your great American novel while on a Caribbean cruise. Apple Computer even ships some iBooks and PowerBooks with DVD drives, so you can catch your favorite flick on that cross-country or cross-continent flight and not have to depend on the often-mediocre fare the airline selects for you.

With Mac OS X, Apple Computer has made your portable computing experience even more pleasant, with clever touches that will make your iBook or PowerBook run faster and more efficiently.

Exploring Mac OS X Tools for Laptops

Laptop computers nowadays are extremely powerful, in many respects on a par with desktop computers. A notable example is the striking Titanium PowerBook G4, which offers a brilliant 15.2-inch LCD display and great processor performance. In addition, using the built-in peripheral ports, you can easily attach a regular keyboard and mouse and, on PowerBooks, an external display, and use the laptop for double duty as a stationary desktop computer. If you need to take your work on the road, disconnect the laptop, pack it in a case, and you're ready to roll.

Superior Power Management

Year after year, as computer processors get more powerful, they also require less power. Today's iBook and PowerBook can crunch numbers with the best of them, yet the low power requirements of their microprocessors and Mac OS X's power-management features allow you to maximize the amount of time your computer can run without requiring a battery recharge or a nearby AC outlet.

Integrated Mouse Preference Panel

Under Mac OS X, a separate system setting for trackpad speed is usually not present on newer Apple laptops (you'll still find it on older PowerBooks). When you launch the System Preferences application and click the Mouse settings pane (see Figure 13.1), you'll be able to

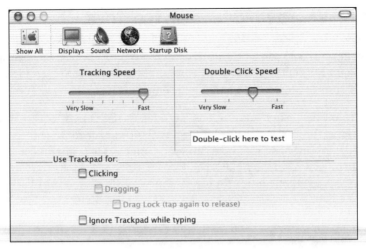

Figure 13.1   The Mouse settings pane handles trackpad settings for your Apple laptop.

adjust trackpad speed and double-click speed directly. With some models (such as various PowerBook G3s), you'll see a separate Trackpad tab, similar to the one in Mac OS 9.x.

Superfast Sleep and Awake Features

In the old days (before Mac OS X), when you put your PowerBook to sleep, your Mac would take a few seconds to do its disk drive and network housecleaning chores before going into idle mode. The reverse process could take even longer; it might take up to a minute for your Mac to return to normal operating mode after being brought back to life.

NOTE: *The process of awakening from sleep mode is quicker for Mac OS 9 and later, but it's still not as fast as in Mac OS X.*

For Mac OS X, Apple has made both processes ultra-efficient and super-quick. Just choose Sleep from the Apple menu, and your iBook or PowerBook will close almost immediately. Best of all, you can bring it back to life almost instantaneously by pressing any key on the keyboard or, with most models (check your documentation to be sure), opening the case. It almost seems as if it was never placed in sleep mode to begin with. This side effect can help speed your passage through airport security in case they want to see the computer's desktop to confirm it's really a laptop.

Editing Vacation Videos on the Road

If your iBook or PowerBook has FireWire capability (and all the recent models do), you'll be able to edit videos of the family vacation or presentation on the road, using Apple's iMovie software (see Figure 13.2) or any video-editing tool you prefer.

After you have shot your videos, you can easily copy them to your iBook's or PowerBook's hard drive and then edit the footage the way you like, adding special effects and sound effects. Then, after the movie has been prepared, you can save it in a variety of formats, including QuickTime, which allows for easy online distribution.

In addition to making and editing videos, you can also use programs such as AppleWorks 6 and Microsoft PowerPoint X for Mac to make slide shows. After you're finished, you can attach your Apple laptop to a TV or projector and use it for a portable presentation.

TIP: *Apple iBooks equipped with FireWire have an AV output port that you can use to attach these cute laptops to a regular TV with composite video or camcorder ports. The PowerBook's output capabilities include S-video.*

NOTE: *Because video fills a large amount of drive storage space, consider bringing an extra drive with you if you intend to capture a large video. Remember that USB-based drives are very slow and absolutely unsuitable except for lower-resolution video capture and playback. Expansion bay, FireWire, and SCSI-based devices can provide sufficient speed for good performance.*

Figure 13.2   iMovie is the flexible yet super-simple desktop video-editing software that's included with Mac OS X 10.1.

Immediate Solutions

Computing on the Road

Some day in the future, it's possible that most computers will be mobile devices, designed to work efficiently on the road, yet ready to plug into a desktop docking system at a moment's notice. Apple flirted with this sort of setup some years back with the Duo system, but the product never caught on as expected. In the meantime, you can enjoy a flexible Mac computing experience with the iBook, the PowerBook, and, of course, Mac OS X.

An Apple laptop comes complete with all the ingredients for performing the computing tasks you need when you're not at your home or office. The latest models include a built-in modem and Ethernet networking ports, and most models have a reasonable array of expansion ports so you can add extra devices to fill the gaps. Only the later models (the iBook and Titanium PowerBook G4) lack such niceties as a high-speed expansion bay for storage devices.

NOTE: *Why would newer Apple laptops make do with less expansion? In the drive to make them ultra thin, a few compromises were necessary, so you are left with an appendage if you want to connect an extra drive.*

Before you take your iBook or PowerBook on a trip, however, you'll want to be prepared for the worst and for the most effective computing experience, whether you're visiting someone's home, staying in a hotel, or camping out. With a little advance preparation, you can get the most value from your Mac computing experience regardless of your destination.

Checking Battery Life

With older versions of the Mac OS, you could check the state of your laptop's battery courtesy of a Control Strip module or an optional icon on the menu bar clock. For Mac OS X, Apple's new solution is a menu bar status display.

Where is it? You can enable this feature (if it doesn't already appear by default) in the Energy Saver preference panel (I'll get to this shortly) by clicking Options (see Figure 13.3).

Once you check the Show Battery Status In Menu Bar item, you'll see a graphical display of estimated battery life. You can use it to keep tabs on how much juice your battery has left.

NOTE: *By default, the battery status display is usually present on the menu bar when you set up a new iBook or PowerBook with Mac OS X or if you install the new operating system on an older model. But, if it's not there, it's easily activated.*

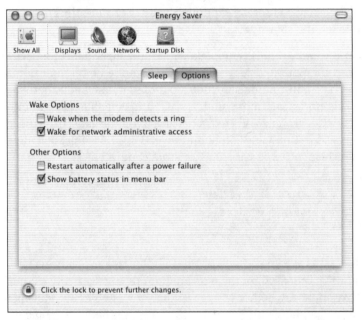

Figure 13.3   Activate the battery status display from this settings panel.

Getting the Maximum Amount of Battery Life

Whatever you do, your iBook or PowerBook won't run forever before the battery is spent. If you have an AC outlet and your power supply nearby, this may be a minor inconvenience at most. But if you're in a plane or power is otherwise unavailable, you'll want to stretch your battery as far as you can.

Here are some suggestions to get the most from your Apple laptop's battery power:

- *Let it sleep.* When you're not using your laptop, let it drift into sleep mode. Mac OS X will bring it to life in just a second when you're ready to use it again. While in sleep mode, all your applications remain open with your settings intact. Only your online or network connections will be deactivated.

WARNING! Sleep mode doesn't last forever if you're not near AC current. Over time, possibly a week or two, or maybe a bit more, battery power will be spent and when you fire up your Apple laptop, you'll have to recharge the battery. So it's worthwhile hooking up your baby to its power adapter from time to time during a long period of sleep, or just turn it off altogether if you're not going to use it for a while.

- *Use the Energy Saver preference panel.* Launch System Preferences and open Energy Saver (see Figure 13.4). You'll be able to adjust the intervals for system, display, and hard drive sleep. Because the hard drive can use a lot of extra juice, letting it go to sleep after a brief period of inactivity might conserve battery life far beyond the normal level.

NOTE: Some applications cause a lot of hard-drive activity when running, so a sleep setting won't save battery life. In addition, if your Apple laptop doesn't have a large amount of RAM, Mac OS X's advanced virtual memory feature will swap data to and from the hard drive frequently, again limiting the effectiveness of this setting.

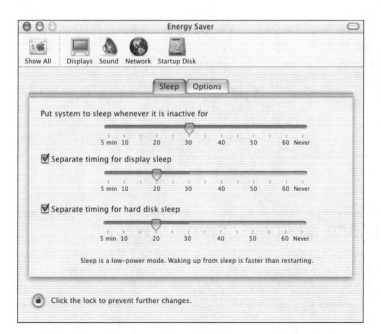

Figure 13.4   Use Energy Saver to give your battery greater longevity.

- *Turn down the brightness.* You probably like a brilliant picture, but the brighter the setting, the more power is required. If you can reduce brightness and not suffer too much from the dimmer screen, you might buy some extra time from your battery power.

- *Don't use the modem.* If you don't have to surf, your iBook or PowerBook won't need to draw as much current from the battery. Hence, you'll get longer life.

- *Remove expansion bay devices.* These devices are powered by your PowerBook's battery and thus will reduce battery life. Just remember, if it's a storage device, you need to eject the disk icon first by dragging it to the trash before you disconnect the device itself.

NOTE: *The Titanium PowerBook G4 and iBook lines do not have expansion bays.*

- *Remove FireWire and USB devices.* Some FireWire devices, including Apple's ultra-cool iPod jukebox player, draw current from your Apple laptop to run. Others, such as USB devices, just get trickle current. Regardless, unplug these devices if you don't need them and want to get maximum battery life.

- *Avoid PC Cards.* Don't use a PC Card expansion module if you can help it, because it will require additional juice.

- *Use headphones for audio.* Headphones draw less power, and you can turn the volume lower and save on precious battery life. The side benefit is that bystanders won't be annoyed if your sound, game, or musical preferences differ from theirs.

- *Forget the DVD.* If you have a model with a DVD player that's supported under Mac OS X, it's nice to be able to watch your favorite flick on the road, but doing so can sharply reduce battery life. It's a trade-off, but you might find the entertainment value to be worth the sacrifice.

Creating an Apple Laptop Travel Kit

When you take your iBook or PowerBook and Mac OS X on your next trip, you should consider adding a few items to your packing list so you can get the maximum level of convenience that portable computing has to offer. Here's a short list of items to take with you and the preparations to make:

- *Traveling bag*—You can pack your iBook or PowerBook into a suitcase, well cushioned with clothing, and it should survive the trip just fine. But you should consider buying a dedicated laptop travel bag. Such products usually have extra pouches and special storage compartments for removable media, extra drives, batteries, cables, software, and other items you might need for your work. There's also usually a shoulder strap in case the entire package gets a little heavy for you. When buying such a bag, consider a product that has a well-cushioned area to protect your laptop from the rigors of such things as airline turbulence and driving on rocky terrain in a sport utility vehicle.

WARNING! *Some older laptop cases aren't large enough to contain the first-generation iBooks or PowerBook G4s comfortably. Although the new Apple laptops tend to be lighter than many older models, they may be physically wider or deeper. I ran into this problem when trying to fit an original iBook into my favorite carrying case, although the ultra-wide Titanium PowerBook G4 fit perfectly.*

- *Protection from the elements*—As rugged as laptops are in normal use, if you're going to be outside in a damp environment or you're at sea, make sure your computer is well protected. Check with your dealer about getting a case that can protect your laptop, particularly in a damp environment.

NOTE: *This may seem at odds with a book about Mac OS X and Apple computers, but if you do travel to extreme environments, you may want to consider a notebook computer that's designed to withstand the elements. Called* ruggedized *notebooks, such products as the Itronix GoBook (a Windows-based notebook that can cost upward of five grand) and similar notebooks from such makers as Panasonic, are designed to withstand treatment that would cause any normal notebook computer to break or at least fail to run.*

WARNING! *Don't expect your iBook or PowerBook to run perfectly on your favorite ski slope or in the midst of a blizzard. According to Apple's spec sheets, the normal operating temperature is 50 to 95 degrees Fahrenheit. If you bring your laptop in from the cold, be sure to give it enough time to warm up before you use it.*

- *Backups for key files*—You plan to get some work done on the road, but your laptop's hard drive fails. Although these little computers are built to survive a reasonable amount of abuse, the fact is that storage devices fail at unexpected moments. It's easy for a repair shop to replace the drive, but recovering data from a defective drive can be costly, with no guarantee of total success. In addition to taking backup media for your most important files, you may want to include a copy of your laptop's system installer and restore disks in case you have to replace everything on a new hard drive.

TIP: *You might also want to take with you a backup for your home or office system. That way, should something happen at either location during your trip, you'll still be able to get up and running again upon your return.*

NOTE: *Having a hard drive fail on a notebook computer isn't as unusual as you might think. Just before I left to attend the Macworld Expo in San Francisco in January 2001, the drive on my nearly new iBook Special Edition began to make a frightening clicking sound and quickly failed. Fortunately, I made a CD of the files I needed to continue working, and I was able to borrow another laptop from a colleague and continue working with minimal delay.*

- *Extra storage devices*—Whether your Apple laptop has a built-in expansion bay port or not, plenty of convenient storage devices are small enough to pack in a PowerBook case. A number of external FireWire and USB storage devices, from such companies as Iomega, LaCie, and SmartDisk, are *bus powered* (meaning they are powered by your Mac's ports). As a result, you don't have to deal with power bricks and finding extra AC outlets in your hotel room. If you can put up with the little appendage, you can even use these devices during airline travel.

TIP: *If you have an iPod, you can also use its built-in FireWire drive for backups.*

- *Diagnostic or repair CDs*—In addition to a Mac OS system disk, you might want to bring along an emergency CD for such programs as Alsoft's DiskWarrior, Symantec's Norton Utilities, or MicroMat's TechTool Pro or Drive 10. These programs offer an extra measure of protection against drive directory problems and, in the case of TechTool Pro, potential hardware issues.

WARNING!   Some disk diagnostic programs won't work properly under Mac OS X, but they will function properly when you boot under Mac OS 9.1 or later. Before using any of these programs to diagnose a possible disk-related problem, check the compatibility information from the publisher.

- *Extra input devices*—Not everyone loves the feel of a laptop's keyboard; I have been hot and cold about the PowerBook G4 (the second generation model with gigabit Ethernet is a little better), although the iBook seems nice for my purposes. Such a keyboard might be fine for occasional use, but if you have to pound a keyboard or do lots of mousing around during your trip, you might want to pack a full-sized keyboard and mouse in your carrying bag. If you're into computer games, or the kids are part of the trip, consider buying a trackball or joystick, both of which are recommended for superior computer gaming.

- *Patch cables*—Need to hook up to a network, a phone jack, or an external drive or scanner? Don't forget to bring the proper cables, along with your laptop's AC power supply. Even if you're not 100-percent certain you'll need a specific cable setup for a specific purpose, having an extra cable isn't likely to weigh down your carrying bag much.

TIP: Don't assume that the phone in your hotel room is in a convenient location. It might be next to the bed, but you want to work on a table. It's a good idea to get a long telephone cable for just this purpose. Another good addition to your packing list is an Ethernet crossover cable, in case you need a direct connection (without a hub or switch present) to another Mac, network printer, or cable/DSL modem.

- *Consider a wireless connection*—Apple makes it possible to network or explore the Internet with the iBook and recent PowerBooks without a direct connection cable using its AirPort wireless networking system. You can install the AirPort module in your laptop and attach a base station to a phone. Then, you can stay connected for a distance of up to 150 feet (sometimes more). You can lounge on a patio or a beach, and surf the Net with your Apple laptop without having to run a long cable.

- *Special connection cables*—For trips overseas or when you are staying in a hotel or other locale where a convenient modem data port isn't available, you'll have to be creative to find a way to get connected. One useful resource is a company called TeleAdapt (**www.teleadapt.com**), which makes connection cables and power adapters for a variety of installations around the world. You'll be able to cope with foreign power connections, portable power supplies, and various forms of telephone hookups with the right connection kit. Although nothing is perfect, if you need to stay in touch, this is an option to consider.

- *Portable printer*—The major manufacturers of ink jet printers, such as Canon, Epson, and HP, all have smaller models that are designed for travel. What they lack in terms of print quality and speed is more than made up for in size and convenience.

- *Insurance*—Laptop computers are theft magnets. The convenient carrying handle of the first-generation "clamshell" iBook, for example, may tempt you to just carry it in your hand and leave the rest of the accessories in your suitcase or laptop accessory bag. But it can also attract thieves who'd love to separate you from your computer. Be wary of tight crowds at the airport and deliberate distractions—especially in light of the increased security since the September 11, 2001 terrorist attacks—and definitely don't put down your computer, even for a moment. Professional thieves know all the tricks. The best preparation you can consider, however, is simply to get a good insurance policy so you can replace the computer in case the worst happens. Some major insurance companies offer computer coverage, including units taken on the road, as part of homeowner's and small-business policies.

> **TIP:** If your insurance agent can't cover your computers, consider Safeware (see **www.safeware.com**). It has been in business for years, it's listed favorably with the Better Business Bureau, and many PC and Mac laptop owners swear by it. Remember, however, that insurance will cover only the cost of replacement hardware and software, but not your data. So have a backup ready in another location (at home or a bank vault, or both) if something goes wrong.

- *Airport X-rays*—Through the years, I've dutifully put my iBooks and PowerBooks under the airport security X-ray machines and haven't suffered any losses of data or computing power. Just let them do their job. If you are still concerned, however, you can ask for a personal inspection. Just remember to put your laptop in sleep mode rather than shut it down, to speed up the inspection process. The security personnel primarily want to see the computer's desktop display so they know it's really a computer. Imagine their surprise when they see how quickly Mac OS X starts up.

- *Games for the kids*—If you are taking your clan on a long trip, you may want to bring along some of their favorite computer games for relaxation. Games can keep them from getting into your hair, plus they can help you get the most value out of your iBook or PowerBook. The latest generations of both products are, in fact, decent game machines, with fairly good performance on high-action 3D games.

TIP: *If games are your "bag," or your children are picky, consider the PowerBook G4s released in the fall of 2001, which include an ATI Mobility Radeon graphics chip for superior 3D graphics and improved frame rates for more fluid gameplay.*

Related solution:	Found on page:
The No-Frills Daily Backup Plan	353
MicroMat's TechToolPro	366

Getting the Most Efficient Online Performance

Today, it's getting increasingly difficult to stay away from your email, unless you can afford to let the mail sit unopened until your return. Fortunately, if you must keep up with the messages, there are ways to stay in touch even if your ISP isn't available in the area you're visiting.

Here are some considerations to help you track your email in the event you need to surf the Net:

- *Check your ISP's access.* Such services as AOL, its sister service CompuServe, EarthLink (Apple's recommended ISP), Prodigy Internet, and other large services have access numbers in many major cities around the world. Before leaving, you should retrieve and print out a listing of the phone numbers in the cities you plan to visit. If your itinerary changes along the way, you can usually go online and look for additional numbers. If you're using a local service, however, you may have to consider other options. One possible solution is the EarthLink Mobile Broadband service, which uses a special high-performance wireless model to deliver speeds of up to 128KBps. Many services, such as AOL and EarthLink, also offer Web-based email options to retrieve your messages, or you can sign up for a free email account from such services as Microsoft's Hotmail or Yahoo. That way, if you can get online from, say, a public library, you can still retrieve your email. If you intend to travel to an out-of-the-way locale without convenient online access, check with the hotel or airline or travel agent for suggestions. On the other hand, it was once possible to survive on a trip without cellular telephones or email, so you may find that you can live without the luxury.

TIP: You may want to check whether your hotel offers high-speed Internet access. Some members of the Hilton chain, for example, offer DSL for a daily surcharge in some rooms, but you must make sure you reserve a room that's prewired for the Internet. Although you may have to redo your ISP settings (usually outgoing, rather than incoming mail), this is a way to speed up your on-the-road computing experience and have more time for rest and relaxation. The hotel should have an instruction booklet from the broadband ISP about how to access its services and your existing email.

- *Send messages to yourself for backup.* If you plan to get some work done on the road, consider sending copies of your documents via email so you can retrieve them at your home or office. That way, if something happens to your laptop during the trip, you'll still be able to get the files when you return.

NOTE: Some ISPs have strict limits on the size of file attachments you can send with your messages. For AOL, it's 2MB outside the service and 16MB within the service. Other online services limit the size to 5MB or 10MB. Apple's iDisk (part of the iTools service) affords you 20MB of storage for your personal stuff, and more if you are willing to pay a fee for the extra capacity. If you need to handle larger files, consider compressing them, or bring along extra disks and a removable device for storage.

- *Use a fax machine for a printer.* You can use your computer's fax modem to print a document by sending a fax to yourself. If you're using the hotel's fax machine, check the hotel's fees beforehand, because some charge several dollars per page. Or, perhaps you can find a local business or travel office that will lend a hand. Another way to get printed pages is to visit a print shop that can provide output for your files.

TIP: Some upscale business-oriented hotels even place fax machines in some rooms, but check the price list to see if there's a daily or per-page charge. You may also find a small business center at the hotel, where you can plug in your iBook or PowerBook to a networked printer. Again you'll want to know the costs of this service before outputting those pages.

Using FireWire Target Disk Mode

Once you return to your home or office, or you need to set up shop at another office, you'll be pleased to know that FireWire-equipped iBooks and PowerBooks offer a speedy way to retrieve files without having to concern yourself with a new network setting. The feature is called FireWire Target Disk Mode. Here's how to set it up:

TIP: Target Disk Mode isn't reserved for late-model Apple laptops. The feature is also available on any PowerMac G4 with AGP graphics, the PowerMac Cube, and slot-load iMacs with FireWire ports.

1. Shut down your Apple laptop.

WARNING!   Target Disk Mode is best used while your iBook or PowerBook is connected to AC current. Running out of juice during a copy operation may result in missing or damaged files.

2. Take a regular FireWire cable and attach your iBook or PowerBook to the host computer (which can be a desktop Mac or another Apple laptop).

NOTE: Because FireWire is a hot-pluggable technology, it's not necessary to turn off the other computer when you make the connection.

3. Boot your Apple laptop and hold down the T key. Keep pressing the key until you see a FireWire icon on the laptop's display. Wait a few seconds, and the laptop's drive icon should show up as another FireWire device on the host computer.

4. When you're finished transferring files, you can remove or dismount the drive icon from the desktop by selecting it and pressing Command+E or by choosing Eject from the Finder's File menu.

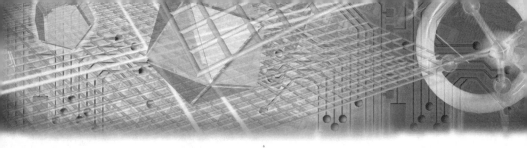

Part III

The Software Review

Chapter 14

Mac OS X-Savvy Applications

In Brief

No doubt about it: Mac OS X has a host of new interface elements and features that can provide a more productive, enjoyable, and reliable computing experience. But to be able to use those features, you have to run software that is specifically compiled to run under Mac OS X.

The situation is similar to what prevailed back in 1994 when Apple moved to PowerPC processors from the 680x0 processor family. An emulation mode let you run older software at reduced speed, but it took months and in some cases a few years for most Mac software companies to move their products over to the new architecture. Some applications never made the switch, but emulation was there to fill the gap.

The Two Forms of Mac OS X Applications

Back in the days when the first iteration of Mac OS X was announced (it was then known as *Rhapsody*), Apple announced that it expected software publishers to totally rewrite their products in a new programming language to be compatible. This requirement, of course, fell on deaf ears in the major companies, who didn't want to invest years and millions of dollars in the effort to rewrite millions of lines of computer code (over 30 million in Microsoft Office). So, Apple went back to the drawing board.

The company came up with two ways to provide programs that are compatible with Mac OS X:

- *Carbon*—This is Apple's trump card. Carbon is a special set of application programming interfaces (APIs) that can be used to modify an existing Mac program and make it support all or most of the features of Mac OS X. Rather than having to do all the work from scratch, only 10 to 20 percent (on average) of the program's code must be updated to support the new system architecture. Even better, most of these same applications can run normally on Macs equipped with Mac OS 8.6 through the various versions of Mac OS 9, by virtue of a system extension called *CarbonLib*. Depending on the program, the update could take days or months, so check with specific publishers about their plans.

NOTE: By "all or most of the features of Mac OS X," I mean that some capabilities, such as the Font Panel (described in Chapter 16) were still unavailable in the Carbon environment as of the time this book was published. Check with specific publishers about which features they choose to support and which they do not. Also, to be fair, not all Carbon applications are designed to also run in a Classic Mac OS. Microsoft Office v. X and AOL for Mac OS X are two examples.

- *Cocoa*—A native Mac OS X application can also be developed using either Sun Microsystems' Java programming language or one descended from the original NeXT-based Objective C. These programs will yield full support for all the core features of Mac OS X, but they won't run under the regular Mac OS. For new programs, it's a lot faster to build a program from scratch this way, but this isn't the best alternative for existing publishers that have to rewrite up to millions of lines of code.

The best thing about the way Mac OS X is set up is that you don't have to concern yourself with the choices publishers make to achieve product compatibility with Mac OS X. You can just install and use the program and take advantage of the features and improved performance and reliability.

Key Mac OS X Software Profiles and Previews

As of the time this book went to press, hundreds of new or updated applications had been announced for Mac OS X. Some were out, and others were promises of what was to come. The initial releases of Mac OS X included several offerings to sample the possibilities.

This section profiles some of the significant programs. In the "Immediate Solutions" section, I describe some useful features you'll want to try from three of the available Mac OS X-savvy programs—AppleWorks 6, Microsoft Office v. X, and Stone Design's Create suite.

Microsoft

One of the first publishers to declare support for Mac OS X was, believe it or not, Apple's former adversary, Microsoft. The original Public Beta of the new operating system included a Carbonized version of Microsoft's Internet Explorer browser (see Chapter 21), and the final version was bundled with Mac OS X 10.1. A Mac OS X version of Office 2001 for the Macintosh was announced in January 2001 and released in November of that year (see Figure 14.1).

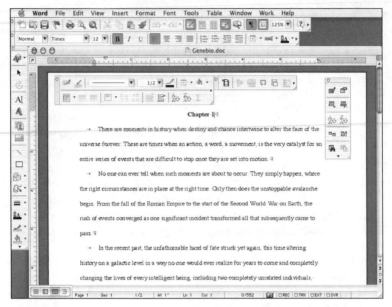

Figure 14.1   Dubbed Office v. X for Mac, the Carbon version of Microsoft Office takes special advantage of the Aqua interface.

The new version of Office includes extensive revisions for Entourage, Microsoft's new email client and personal information manager, in addition to support for Mac OS X's robust features. A handful of minor features are spread across the remainder of the suite (Excel, PowerPoint, and Word). Microsoft boasted in the product's rollout that over 700 icons and numerous dialog boxes were carefully redesigned to take best advantage of Aqua.

NOTE: *This book was written using Word X, courtesy of Microsoft, which gave the author prerelease versions to experiment with.*

Apple Computer

The standard installation of Mac OS X includes a number of utilities for you to try. These include the Mail application described in Chapter 22, plus old standbys such as the Calculator, Disk Utility (a combination of Disk First Aid and Drive Setup), Key Caps, QuickTime Player, Script Editor, Sherlock, and Stickies. In addition, Aladdin's StuffIt Expander is along for the ride, so you can open compressed files created in a variety of formats (even those from the Windows and Unix environments).

The installation includes quite a few new contenders, as well. Following is a brief description of a number of the most interesting programs included with Mac OS X, in the Applications and Utilities folders:

- *Acrobat Reader*—Adobe's popular application reads the many electronic documents that software publishers include in place of printed manuals these days.

- *Address Book*—This simple Rolodex application works with Apple's Mail application (described later in this list) to keep tabs on your personal and business address books.

- *Chess*—Pit yourself against your Mac's G3 or G4 processor and see how well you can do in an interactive Chess game (see Figure 14.2) designed to exploit the ultra-crisp graphics of Mac OS X.

- *Clock*—This program (see Figure 14.3) is intended as a replacement or supplement for the popular menu bar clock. It can also put a floating clock palette on your desktop. You have a choice of analog or digital clocks.

14. Mac OS X-Savvy Applications

Figure 14.2   A grayscale picture doesn't really do justice to Mac OS X's interactive chess game.

Figure 14.3   Clock is a different answer to putting a clock on your Mac's screen.

TIP: *If you prefer the menu bar clock, no problem. You can continue to use both. But if you prefer to eliminate the one on the menu bar, launch System Preferences, click the Date & Time pane, and click the Menu Bar Clock tab. Uncheck the option Show The Clock In The Menu Bar.*

- *ColorSync*—Mac OS X 10.1 comes with ColorSync 4.0 (in the Utilities folder), which provides automated support for color calibration between your Mac's display and an input or output device (such as a scanner or color printer). The ColorSync utility also includes a special First Aid feature that verifies a color profile against ICC specifications and repairs such problems, to ensure the best possible color matching.

- *Console*—As you use your Mac, you might, from time to time, see some strange error messages because of a printing problem or system-related issue. The Console application (see Figure 14.4) keeps a log of those messages. They may not be directly useful to the average Mac user, but you can use the information to help a software publisher figure out what went wrong with its product; you don't have to remember the arcane messages or prompts. This utility resides in the Mac OS X Utilities folder.

- *CPU Monitor*—Get a visual indication (see Figure 14.5) of how your Mac's processor is being accessed by Mac OS X. If you have a Mac with two processors, as I do, CPU Monitor (available in the Utilities

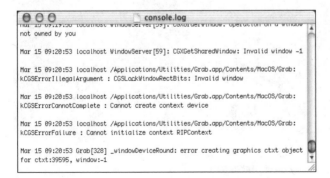

Figure 14.4   The log can display system-related error messages that might help you troubleshoot a problem on your Mac.

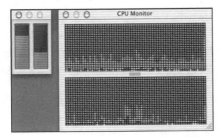

Figure 14.5   Two processors really share tasks under Mac OS X, and these little windows show what they're up to.

folder) provides a separate display for each, so you can see how both are handling the load. This utility is proof positive of the operating system's built-in support for symmetric multiprocessing.

- *Disk Utility*—Take one part Disk First Aid and one part Drive Setup, and the result (in the Utilities folder) is an application that will check and format a drive. The sole limitation of the First Aid component of Disk Utility is its inability to check a startup drive (but that's already done during the Mac OS X boot process).

NOTE: *Another useful feature of Disk Utility is its ability to format IDE and SCSI (FireWire isn't supported in the 10.1 release) drives in Redundant Array of Independent Disks (RAID) format, for the highest possible performance for content creators.*

- *DVD Player*—If you have a Mac with DVD drive (and it's supported by Mac OS X), you can watch your favorite flick at home or on the road. DVD Player's controls mimic what you find in a home DVD player.

NOTE: *By default, DVD Player is installed only on Macs with supported DVD drives. Version 3.0.1 supports Macs with AGP graphics and a handful of other models. Check your Mac's spec sheet to see what sort of graphics system it has, although the presence of the DVD Player is usually the best clue.*

- *Display Calibrator*—This application (in the Utilities folder) works directly with the Displays preference panel in the System Preferences application to calibrate your Mac's display.

NOTE: *When you calibrate your display, you give it the best possible color balance within its design limitations. A calibrated monitor along with color calibrated scanners or printers yields the best possible match between input and output. Although Apple's calibration process is not quite as perfect as a separate outboard calibration unit, it will suit for all but the most critical graphic artists and printers.*

14. Mac OS X-Savvy Applications

- *Grab*—So, what does this utility grab? A screenshot of your Mac, useful in providing illustrations for documentation. Although Command+Shift+3 (for a whole screen) and Command+Shift+4 (for a selected area) still work, Grab (in the Utilities folder) takes the concept a little further. Options let you capture the entire screen or a selected window. You can also perform a timed capture, which gives you 10 seconds to set things up before the shutter goes off.

TIP: *These aren't your only screen-capture options. I used a shareware utility, Snapz Pro X (from Ambrosia Software, **www.ambrosiasw.com**), to deliver all the illustrations in this book. This application can capture whole screens, selected areas, or objects (a single window, dialog box, or menu), and can save in a number of different formats. If you upgrade to the "Pro" version, you can even capture QuickTime movies.*

- *Image Capture*—Found in the Applications folder, this application launches automatically whenever you hook up a supported digital camera. It can then download files from the camera (see Figure 14.6); you don't need any extra software to get pictures.

- *iMovie*—Apple's great video-editing application is standard issue with Mac OS X. It will capture video from a DV or Digital8 camcorder via your Mac's FireWire port, or edit video files you already have on your Mac's hard drive.

- *Internet Connect*—This application (see Figure 14.7) incorporates some of the elements of Remote Access, with a direct link to the Network pane of the System Preferences application to help you set up your dial-up access. Chapter 8 discusses the subject in more detail.

14. Mac OS X-Savvy Applications

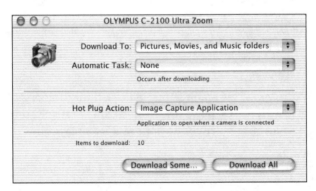

Figure 14.6   Dozens of digital cameras work with Image Capture to bring pictures over to your Mac.

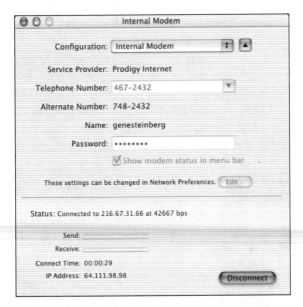

Figure 14.7 Use Internet Connect to dial up and log in to your ISP.

- *Internet Explorer*—For several years, Microsoft's browser has been included with new Macs. For Mac OS X, Microsoft has made it look good for the Aqua environment, but the features are the same as those in the Classic version. They include the Auction Manager, Scrapbook, and the ability to change the theme color to suit your taste.

- *iTunes*—Apple's popular jukebox program already sported an Aqua-inspired interface in its initial Classic Mac OS version. The version that comes with Mac OS X has hardly changed. It works with Apple's built-in CD drives and a host of third-party devices so you can burn music CDs containing your personal playlists.

NOTE: *iTunes 2, the version shipping when this book was written, also mates seamlessly with Apple's iPod, the ultra-slick jukebox player that keeps my son occupied when he's not doing his homework (or is that instead of doing his homework?).*

- *Key Caps*—This utility is an update of the Classic Mac program for checking obscure characters on your Mac's keyboard.

- *Keychain Access*—Beginning with Mac OS 9, Apple incorporated a keychain feature that lets you manage all your user passwords from a single application. This application, in the Utilities folder, is used to configure keychains. You can also do so automatically via such features as the Finder's Connect To Server function for accessing network shares.

- *Mail*—Email is often the most-used feature on the Internet, and Apple has delivered a brand-new application for the purpose (see Figure 14.8). Mail will handle most of your email accounts. It provides a bevy of features, including the ability to import your messages from several other email programs, multiple signatures, email rules, scheduled retrieval of messages, and a Finder-like interface where you can change the toolbar icons to meet your needs. Chapter 22 discusses the subject in more detail.

- *NetInfo Manager*—This application, in the Utilities folder, is a valuable tool for system administrators to manage Mac OS X users and directories. At the basic level, you can use it to create root access to your Mac (a kind of super-user). You can get a fairly extensive and technical explanation of how this powerful application is used from Apple's Web site at **www.apple.com/macosx/server/pdf/UnderstandingUsingNetInfo.pdf**.

- *Network Utility*—What's happening on your network? Are you encountering a problem connecting to a shared computer or printer, or is your Net access not functioning as you expect? This application (see Figure 14.9) can be used to perform such functions as **ping** (contact and return, like sonar) or **trace** to find the source.

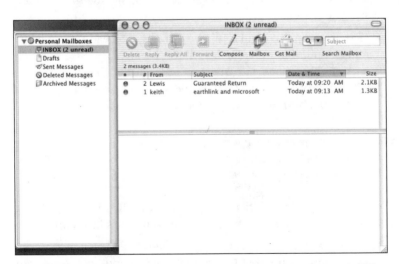

Figure 14.8   Manage a full range of email features with this speedy little application.

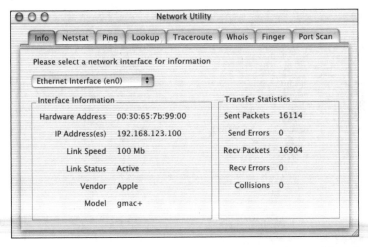

Figure 14.9   You can use this application to examine the condition of your
local network or Internet connection.

- *Preview*—This application can read both PDF files (and convert documents to that format as well) and pictures in such popular formats as GIF, JPET, PICT, and TIFF.

- *QuickTime Player*—This is yet another program that inherits nothing more than a new look for Mac OS X. It's used to play QuickTime movies from your Mac or from the Internet.

- *Stickies*—What's a Mac without Stickies, your personal post-it note system? For the Mac OS X version, Apple has taken the basic features of the Classic version, added some additional text formatting and import features, and put them into a familiar package. You can import all your Stickies from your Classic Mac System Folder, so you don't lose a thing in switching over.

NOTE: *Of course, nothing prevents you from running the Classic version of Stickies, but because the conversion is completely accurate, doing so shouldn't be necessary.*

- *System Preferences*—Apple's replacement for Control Panels, System Preferences is used to configure most of your system settings. In addition, beginning with Mac OS X 10.1, Apple has also made it extensible, so third-party software companies can put their own material in System Preferences (it will appear in a category labeled Other).

- *Terminal*—Apple has gone to great lengths to bury the native Unix command line for Mac OS X. As a result, Mac users can continue to use the new operating system without taking a

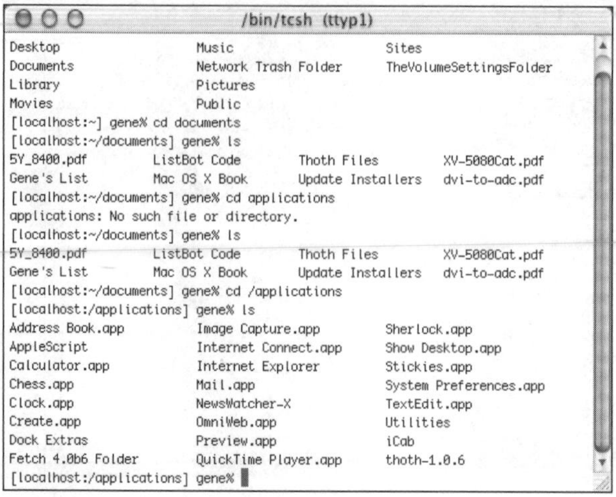

```
●  ○  ○                          /bin/tcsh  (ttyp1)
Desktop                Music                  Sites
Documents              Network Trash Folder   TheVolumeSettingsFolder
Library                Pictures
Movies                 Public
[localhost:~] gene% cd documents
[localhost:~/documents] gene% ls
5Y_8400.pdf            ListBot Code     Thoth Files        XV-5080Cat.pdf
Gene's List            Mac OS X Book    Update Installers  dvi-to-adc.pdf
[localhost:~/documents] gene% cd applications
applications: No such file or directory.
[localhost:~/documents] gene% ls
5Y_8400.pdf            ListBot Code     Thoth Files        XV-5080Cat.pdf
Gene's List            Mac OS X Book    Update Installers  dvi-to-adc.pdf
[localhost:~/documents] gene% cd /applications
[localhost:/applications] gene% ls
Address Book.app       Image Capture.app    Sherlock.app
AppleScript            Internet Connect.app Show Desktop.app
Calculator.app         Internet Explorer    Stickies.app
Chess.app              Mail.app             System Preferences.app
Clock.app              NewsWatcher-X        TextEdit.app
Create.app             OmniWeb.app          Utilities
Dock Extras            Preview.app          iCab
Fetch 4.0b6 Folder     QuickTime Player.app thoth-1.0.6
[localhost:/applications] gene% ▊
```

Figure 14.10   Experience the guts of Unix with this application.

gander at the core; but Terminal (see Figure 14.10) gives Unix mavens full access to the command line and a chance to explore the underpinnings.

WARNING!   *Unix is not a tool for the casual user. The wrong commands can get you in trouble and invoke the wrong functions or cause performance problems. Unlike most graphical software, there's no opt-out provision or Are You Sure message if you do something destructive, like trashing files by mistake or removing a directory the operating system needs in order to run. Before you explore the ins and outs of the command line, you should read Chapter 20, where I introduce you to this new element of the Mac OS. For additional information, visit the Web site http://public.sdsu.edu/ Docs/unixf/basic_unix_f/basic_unix.html.*

Just to give you a gander at what Terminal does, launch the application (it's in the Utilities folder) and then type the command **ls**. This command will list the contents of your Mac's drive. To move to an individual folder, type the command **cd <*name of folder*>**, which switches you to the specified folder. Now, an **ls** command will list the contents of the folder. All those text listings, even if they don't really change the way your Mac works, will look impressive to your friends.

• *TextEdit*—The Classic Mac OS had TeachText and later SimpleText, to open and view short text files, such as the ReadMe files that come with new computer products. TextEdit can view ReadMe files, but it's also a simple word processor complete with spell checking and a basic level of document formatting capabilities. It can create and open documents in Rich Text Format (RTF), so you can see files created in a wide variety of software.

By far the most interesting Mac OS X application, however, is not one of the handy utilities bundled with the new operating system, but an upfront and personal example of the potential of Carbon. This program was originally released for users of Mac OS 8.6 or later, but when the Public Beta came out, Mac users learned that the popular software suite had built-in support for Mac OS X. The program? AppleWorks 6 (see Figure 14.11), a major upgrade to the venerable program suite from Apple. I cover AppleWorks in more detail later in this chapter.

NOTE: *If you bought an iMac or iBook released since the Spring of 2000, a copy of AppleWorks 6 is already present in your Applications folder at no extra cost. A version that's more compatible with Mac OS X (the latest was 6.2.2 when this book was being written) is available in free update form from Apple's Web site.*

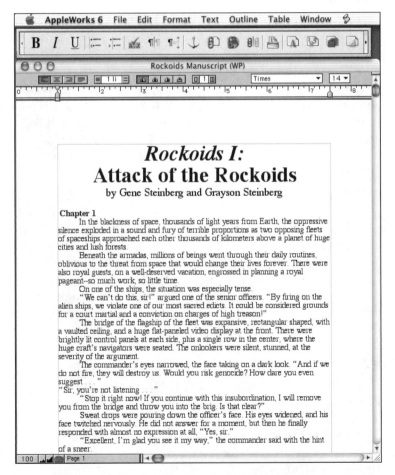

Figure 14.11   AppleWorks shows off the flexibility of a Carbon application.

Although its interface seems simple and uncluttered, a lot of power is packed into this program. I tell you more about it in the "Immediate Solutions" section.

FileMaker

Apple's spin-off, which handles development of FileMaker Pro, promises to produce a Mac OS X version. FileMaker Pro is a cross-platform database program (available in both Mac OS and Windows versions) that has existed since the early days of the Mac.

Adobe Systems

When Apple CEO Steve Jobs first demonstrated Mac OS X's Aqua interface in January 2000, he produced an early development version of Adobe Photoshop to show the potential of Carbon. The unique aspect of this application was the fact that it was all developed by a single Adobe programmer, working in his spare time, without actually seeing what Aqua looked like. The end result was rough, but functional. Adobe has committed to bringing all its current graphics programs to the new operating system. Shortly before this book was published, Illustrator 10, with Mac OS X native support, was released, with InDesign 2.0 close behind; the remainder of Adobe's flagship graphics applications were due in the first part of 2002.

Alias|Wavefront

One of the most significant developments for Mac OS X users is the arrival of new programs on the Mac platform. The $7,500 3D animation program Maya is one of the new entrants. Although the program isn't quite a household name, the work done with Maya has been prominent in a number of popular movies. Maya has been used to create spectacular effects for films such as *Star Wars Episode I: The Phantom Menace, Hollow Man,* and *The Perfect Storm.* A number of the major production houses have this application doing duty in their special effects labs.

Corel

This Canadian software publisher is best known for CorelDRAW, which has always been more popular on the Windows than Mac platforms. Corel Graphics Suite 10, released in September 2001, was designed to change that. In addition to CorelDRAW, a host of useful applications are provided for additional content creation capabilities, including Corel PHOTO-PAINT 10. The bundle also includes a Mac OS X version of DiamondSoft's Font Reserve for native font management, tons of clip art, and 2,000 PostScript and TrueType fonts.

Deneba

From sunny Florida comes Canvas 8, an application that combines superior graphics, page layout, and HTML tools in a single application. The feature-set is huge and not easily summarized. To make the package more compelling, Deneba bundles the collection with a healthy set of clip art and, like Corel, over 2,000 PostScript and TrueType fonts. Even if you buy it for the extras, you might find value in Canvas once you give it a workout.

Macromedia

Program for program, many of Macromedia's offerings are in direct competition with those from Adobe. It comes as no surprise, then, that Macromedia will also be in the forefront of Mac OS X development, promising to deliver new versions of its flagship products. FreeHand 10 was released for Mac OS X within weeks of the new operating system's initial release. The company was hard at work developing its Dreamweaver Web authoring application and other native software for Mac OS X when this book was written.

Quark, Inc.

The flagship program from this company, QuarkXPress, has already been demonstrated in Mac OS X form. This highly sophisticated page layout application is a standard for both advertising agencies and publishers. The built-in PDF feature of Mac OS X's Quartz imaging layer should be especially helpful in expanding the scope of Quark as it migrates to the new operating system. Release of the native version was promised after QuarkXPress 5 (with Web, layers, and table creation capability) came out.

Stone Design

This publisher has migrated from the NeXT world and has embraced Mac OS X. Among its most useful applications is Create (see Figure 14.12), an integrated illustration program that also incorporates elements of HTML authoring and page layout. Create treats every element, from text to pictures, as an object, which can then be dragged and dropped onto other objects to create sophisticated illustrations.

NOTE: *The various Stone Design applications stand as evidence of the power of Apple's Cocoa development environment. Considerable work on these programs was done by one person, Andrew Stone. Using traditional developer tools, it would have taken a programming team to create software of this level of sophistication in a reasonable amount of time.*

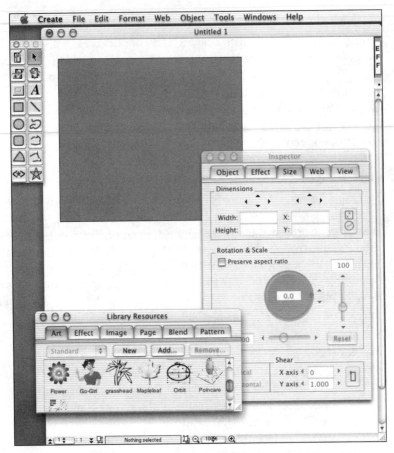

Figure 14.12   Create is the centerpiece of Stone Design's Mac OS X product line.

AOL

The world's largest online service is not ignoring Mac OS X. At press time, it had committed to developing a Mac OS X–savvy version of its software, so you'll be able to dial up your AOL account in the same fashion as before, under the Classic Mac OS. The initial native release is an update to version 5.0 of its Mac software, but AOL promises to deliver a 7.0 version (to bring parity with the Windows platform) at a later time.

NOTE: *As this book was written, however, AOL had abandoned development of the U.K. version of its Mac OS X client, although it's possible the USA version is being reskinned for the overseas market after release.*

Immediate Solutions

Introducing AppleWorks for Mac OS X

What's the good of having a modern operating system if no programs exploit its wide-ranging capabilities? Apple's integrated application suite, AppleWorks, underwent a huge change with version 6. But the biggest change of all was only hinted at if you checked a file placed in the System Folder after the installation—CarbonLib. This file allows Mac OS X applications that use the Carbon API to run on a Mac using Mac OS versions 8.6 through 9.1.

Here's a brief run-through of this cleverly designed program—the first Carbon application from a major publisher (which is fitting).

NOTE: *Starting Points has had some influence in big places. The Project Gallery featured in Microsoft Office 2001 is highly reminiscent of this feature.*

Using AppleWorks Starting Points

When you first launch AppleWorks, you'll be greeted by the program's Starting Points (see Figure 14.13), a floating tabbed palette. From here you can create new documents or open recent ones. Here is a brief description of what you get when you click each tab:

NOTE: *The following information applies strictly to version 6.2.2 of the program. If you're using an earlier revision, access the latest from Apple's Web site.*

- *Basic*—Access any of the six AppleWorks modules by clicking once on the kind of document you want to make. Depending on

Figure 14.13   Use Starting Points to originate or open documents in AppleWorks.

what you select, the user interface will vary in terms of menu bar commands, toolbars, and features.

TIP: *Where's Starting Points? If you don't see it, choose Show Starting Points from the File menu.*

- *Assistants*—AppleWorks is designed for users of all skill levels, from novices setting up their first Mac to power users. The Assistants palette provides step-by-step guidance in setting up a new document in several useful categories, from a business card to an envelope.

- *Templates*—To help get you started with a new document, you can choose from a collection of document templates. Click a preview icon to bring up a blank document with the template ready to roll.

- *Web*—Apple keeps an updated collection of clip art, templates, and tips about AppleWorks 6 at its Web site. When you click this tab, you can access a current list of what's available. If you're logged on to your ISP, a single click in the listing automatically downloads the templates to your Mac.

- *Recent Items*—This tab provides a fast way to open a document you've worked on previously. When you click here, you'll see a list of dozens of documents you've created in the program, sorted alphabetically.

- *+*—You can use this tab to make your own custom palette, and then drag and drop items to fill it in.

Using Tables in AppleWorks

One of the most important new features of AppleWorks 6, aside from the user interface and Mac OS X support, is the Table tool. You can easily add tables to any AppleWorks document and resize the tables to fit your needs. To use this handy feature, follow these steps:

1. Launch AppleWorks 6.

2. Start a new document.

3. Make sure the program's toolbar is open. If it's not visible, go to the program's Window menu and select Show Tools (see Figure 14.14).

4. Locate the Table Frame tool (see Figure 14.15) and select it.

Figure 14.14   The toolbar you see in AppleWorks changes depending on the kind of document you're creating.

Figure 14.15   Easy table creation in AppleWorks starts here.

14. Mac OS X-Savvy Applications

5. Place the cursor in the location in your document where you want to put a table, and then drag the mouse in a diagonal direction to set the approximate size of the table. The size can be changed easily.

6. In the Insert Table dialog box that appears (see Figure 14.16), type how many rows and columns you want to put in the table. These values can also be changed easily.

7. Click OK to finish the table setup process.

After you have set up the raw essentials of your table, you can easily adjust the table as you see fit. The entire table or rows and columns can be resized by clicking and dragging. When you're working in a table, a new Table menu appears on the menu bar; you can use it to add or delete rows and columns.

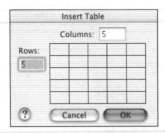

Figure 14.16   Choose how many rows and columns with which to populate your table.

Introducing Office v. X for Mac

When you first take a gander at any of the Office v. X applications, it's hard to get beyond the luscious Aqua interface; but some new features are particularly useful. I'll cover three of the highlights here, features new to the Mac OS X version. It would take a large book to even scratch the surface of what's offered in this sprawling business application suite.

NOTE: *Although Office v. X may seem an awkward name for this product, that's the way Microsoft refers to it, and that's the way I'll refer to it also.*

Profiling the Project Gallery

When Microsoft introduced the Project Gallery (see Figure 14.17), some people thought it was the company's answer to AppleWorks' Starting Points palette. But it does offer some neat features. One of them is the new Based On Recent feature, which is a super Save As capability that lets you automatically open a new document with all the formatting and content of the original.

Using Word X's Multiple Selection Feature

This isn't an original feature (such Mac word processors as Mariner Write and Nisus Writer already have it). But in practice, it's both simple and useful. When you want to select more than a single item in your Word document, hold down the Command key and click and select each item, in succession. Once you've done that, all you have to do is apply updated text formatting to these items. Or, just cut and paste or drag and drop into a new location.

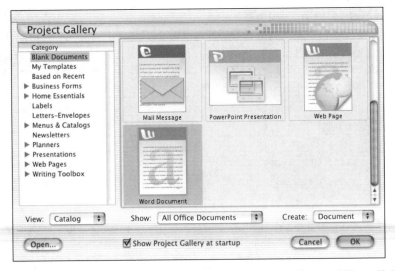

Figure 14.17   The Project Gallery is a flexible beginning for any Office v. X document.

Using Excel X's Auto Recover Feature

Suppose you are busy working on a long spreadsheet, and there's a power outage (I won't dwell on the possibility of a system crash, but it can happen, even in Mac OS X). You restart your Mac and find that your Excel spreadsheet is damaged beyond recovery or doesn't reflect all the changes you made since the last time you saved. Mimicking a feature already present in Word, you don't have to change anything to use AutoRecover. It's already in your Excel Preferences box under the Save category. The default setting is to save every 10 minutes, but you can change that. So, even if your original document is damaged or not up to date, when you launch Excel, you'll see the version automatically recovered; you can save and use that version without missing a beat.

Introducing Create for Mac OS X

Stone Design's clever illustration suite, Create, is an all-purpose illustration program that has elements of several applications rolled into one. In addition to being able to produce simple or highly complex drawings in its uncluttered interface, you can create special effects, manage complex text stylings, and build your own Web site.

Using the Inspector

A lot of the work you do in Create is directed by the Inspector window. It's a mélange of buttons, checkboxes, sliders, and text entry points where you can originate the look and feel of your document.

NOTE: The Inspector feature available with Create is not the same as the Finder's Inspector. It provides services strictly for the application, and not for the rest of the Mac OS.

To access the Inspector, follow these steps:

1. Launch Create.

2. Go to the Tools menu and choose Inspector (see Figure 14.18).

3. Click the tab that represents the type of project you are working on.

With the Inspector active, you'll find an easy way to manipulate your artwork, configure Web pages, and apply and change color selections.

TIP: You can use another terrific feature of Create—the Resources palette—for clip art and document templates. If the Resources palette isn't present, choose Library Resources from the Tools menu to bring it up.

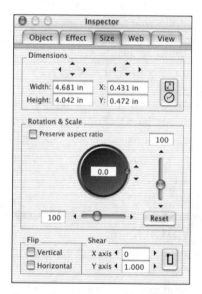

Figure 14.18   The Inspector has many faces, depending on the tab you select.

Starting a Web Page in Create

In addition to being a flexible object-oriented illustration environment, Create lets you generate a fully professional Web page. Here's how to get started setting up a Web page in this program:

1. Launch Create. A new Untitled document window appears, along with, by default, the Resources and Inspector windows.

2. Type your text and place your pictures in the document.

3. When you're ready to enter URL links to other pages or sites, click the area of your document where you want to place the link.

4. Click the Web tab of Inspector, as shown in Figure 14.19.

5. Enter the URL. To specify special options for this link, click the Use Custom HTML option.

6. When your Web page is finished, choose Create Web Pages from the Web menu and name your file. When you click Save, you'll see the page opened in the Web browser set as an Internet preference in the System Preferences panel, so you can check to see how it will look when it's published on the Web.

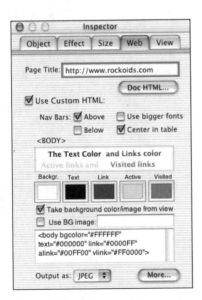

Figure 14.19   The multipurpose Inspector lets you configure your Web page. It is shown here with the Use Custom HTML option selected.

Chapter 15

Using Older Programs with Mac OS X

In Brief

It seems like only yesterday. When Apple Computer released the first Macintosh computer with a PowerPC processor in the early part of 1994, the landscape was quite lonely. Although these computers offered the promise of far greater levels of performance, it would only happen when programs were ported (or updated) to support the new chip architecture.

However, thousands of Mac applications were designed to run on the older 680x0 Motorola processors. With this in mind, Apple devised a plan to allow Mac users to continue to use the vast majority of these programs with decent performance, and then gradually migrate to the PowerPC versions as they were released. The ROMs for PowerPC Macs came with an emulator (extensively updated via patches to the system software). The emulator, shorn of the complex programming techniques involved, would, on the fly, emulate a 680x0 processor. It would thus allow those programs to run with good compatibility—except for software that required a Mac with an FPU chip for special math-related functions. At first, the speed of the emulator barely kept up with 68030 processors, let alone the fastest 68040 processors that were produced before the PowerPC took over. But as the emulator got better and the new chips got faster, performance of the older programs was so good, it was sometimes hard to see a significant difference.

Introducing the Classic Environment

For Mac OS X, the changes are far greater than the switch to the PowerPC's RISC code. The underlying structure of the operating system would seem, in comparison, to be from an alien world. It's Unix-based—the same operating system that powers some of the most powerful Internet servers—and thus the situation is rather more complex.

However, Apple has an inventive solution: the Classic Compatibility environment (see Figure 15.1). It's not an emulator, such as the one used for PowerPC Macs, nor is it in the tradition of software that emulates Windows on a Mac, such as Connectix Virtual PC.

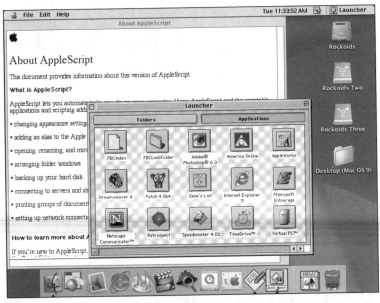

Figure 15.1   Yes, this is truly Mac OS 9.2.1, but it's running within Mac OS X.

The closest description would be that Classic runs as a sort of virtual machine in which Mac OS 9 runs as a separate process or application within Mac OS X, but without inheriting the Aqua user interface or the robust operating system features of the Darwin core. Basically, when you run a Mac OS 9 program, the old menu bar, Apple menu, Control Strip, Launcher, and most features of the older operating system take over your screen (see Figure 15.2). However, when you switch out of a Classic application, you're back in Aqua.

NOTE: *The real version of Office v. X came out in November 2001. But if you haven't upgraded to that version yet, you can continue to use the Classic version with good performance and compatibility (although the native version looks much better and offers some exclusive features).*

Classic Environment Limitations

As seamless as switching to a Classic application may seem (and I'll explain the best ways in the "Immediate Solutions" section of this chapter), there are limits to compatibility, more so than with the switch from 680x0 to PowerPC. Although you can run most of your applications with good performance, some programs just won't run until

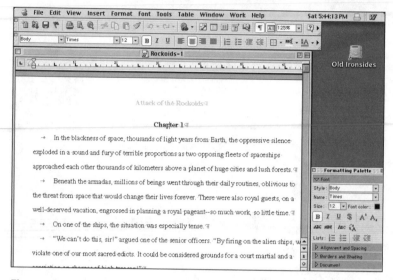

Figure 15.2   This is the Classic version of Microsoft Word 2001 running under Mac OS X, but with the Mac OS 9 look.

updated for the new operating system. Here's the short list of potential problems:

- *It still crashes a lot.* The Classic environment doesn't inherit the robust features of Mac OS X, such as preemptive multitasking and protected memory. It has the same limitations as the original Mac OS, which means that if a single application crashes, you will need to restart Classic. However, because it operates in its own protected memory space, that memory is walled off from the rest of the system, so you can continue to use your Mac OS X applications without a problem. If Classic crashes, just run it again.

- *Many system extensions don't run.* Mac OS system extensions that access hardware functions will probably fail, or will run only with limited compatibility. I'll explain ways to clean out your Mac OS 9 user environment for best performance in the "Immediate Solutions" section of this chapter.

- *CPU-intensive applications are slower.* Adobe Photoshop and other programs that tax the Mac's processor to the limit may run somewhat slower in the Classic environment. The amount that the performance suffers depends largely on the speed of your Mac's processor, hard drive, and graphics hardware. However, other functions, such as launching and screen refreshing, will seem not much different from a regular Mac OS 9 Mac.

NOTE: *Some Photoshop 6 filters, such as the processor-intensive Gaussian Blue, run slightly faster in the Classic mode on faster Macs with a G4. This isn't an across-the-board rule, just a tribute to great programming and compatibility that's better than you have a right to expect.*

- *Certain Mac peripherals fail.* Any product that requires special drivers to run will probably fail under Mac OS X, even if run from the Classic environment. Although it's possible that some of these devices will work after a fashion, don't expect consistent compatibility. Among the affected products are CD burners, DVD-RAM burners, removable storage devices (except for Imation and Iomega products), scanners, tape backup drives, and peripheral cards that provide such features as extended audio editing or video capture. Even graphics cards that were not provided by Apple's graphics chip partner, ATI Technologies, IX Micro (which is now defunct), or NVIDIA won't function unless the company that makes the product has produced drivers for Mac OS X. The best source of information about what works and what doesn't is the manufacturer of these products.

NOTE: *At press time, Formac, a German-based manufacturer of high-performance graphics cards for Macs, was working on Mac OS X drivers. 3dfx Interactive, which announced that the company was going out of business in late 2000, never updated drivers for its Voodoo cards for Mac OS X, though some third parties are looking for a solution. Fortunately, most digital cameras work fine under Mac OS X and the Image Capture application without the need for special drivers.*

- *Some printers won't work.* You can continue to use most laser printers by using the Print Center application of Mac OS X. But some special laser printers that do not have Adobe PostScript installed or that use the USB rather than Ethernet ports may not work without driver updates, except from the Classic environment. The same holds true for those ever-popular ink jet printers that have captured a large portion of the printer market. A core selection of printers from such companies as Canon, Epson, and HP work just fine. But you'll need to check with the manufacturer directly (probably at its Web site) for drivers that aren't supported by Mac OS X out of the box.

- *Third-party hard drive formatters won't work.* Any device that provides low-level support to storage devices probably won't work until a special Mac OS X version is delivered. Apple's own Disk Utility can handle most—probably all—ATA drives and many recent SCSI drives. Otherwise, you have to wait for the third-party manufacturer to come through for you.

NOTE: *FWB Software, publisher of Hard Disk ToolKit, informed me that its Mac OS X version of the popular drive utility application would be "late," meaning that you should consider trying Apple's disk formatter for the time being if you need to run a drive under Mac OS X.*

- *Some Windows emulators are not compatible.* Although Connectix released Virtual PC 5.0, which supports Mac OS X, there's no solace for users of the rival product, SoftWindows. FWB has made it clear that it won't update the product, and the chances of the Classic Mac OS version running under Mac OS X aren't terribly high. Ditto for PC processor cards from such companies as Orange Micro.

- *Internet software compatibility is a mixed bag.* If you have a high-speed (broadband) Internet connection, you may be all right, but dial-up connections have problems of one sort or another. Although a shareware program, PortReflector, may help resolve some dial-up problems, programs with their own dialers, such as AOL and CompuServe, must be updated to the Mac OS X.

- *Some classic games won't work.* Although Mac OS X is designed to be a gamer's paradise, the realization of that promise won't happen until games are truly ported to the new operating system. In the meantime, you can run many older games in the Classic environment, but do not expect stellar performance. Frame rates, for example, will not be quite as high as you experienced under Mac OS 9, because of less complete support for graphics acceleration.

Immediate Solutions

Launching Older Mac Programs

You don't have to do anything special to run your Classic Mac applications within Mac OS X. The operating system is clever enough to sort it all out for you and give you the proper environment for the program you run. To launch an older Mac program and have it work, just do the following:

1. Locate the document or program on your Mac's drive.

TIP: Have both a Classic and Mac OS X version of a program, such as Microsoft Word? In theory, the Mac OS X version should launch, but in practice, the Classic version may run instead. Should this happen, use the Finder's Show Info command on the document and use the Open with Application feature from the Show Info's pop-up menu to make the Mac OS X version the default (it won't affect how the document opens if you restart under Mac OS 9.x, when the available Classic application will launch).

2. Double-click the application icon or a document created with the application.

3. If the Classic environment isn't running, it will go through its regular boot process (see Figure 15.3).

4. The first time you launch Classic from Mac OS X, you'll see a dialog box notifying you that some resources (extensions) need to be added to the Classic System Folder to continue the startup process. You must click OK to accept the installation and continue running Classic. Otherwise, click Quit, and the process will stop.

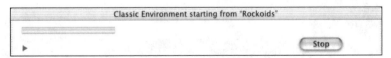

Classic Environment starting from "Rockoids"

Stop

Figure 15.3 This progress bar shows that the Classic environment is starting up.

NOTE: *Mac OS 9.2.1 included several Classic-related extensions to run under Mac OS X's Classic environment. However, the Mac OS X 10.1 upgrade uses later versions of these utilities, so don't be surprised if you see that message anyway and if it returns as more updates to Mac OS X arrive.*

---

5. If you click the disclosure triangle in the Classic window, you'll see a standard Mac startup screen (see Figure 15.4), but it happens within an application window within Mac OS X. Clever! Once the Classic environment is running, the application you launched will be opened as well. Then your document will appear on the screen, surrounded by a user interface that is essentially the same as what you experienced under Mac OS 9.x.

NOTE: *When Classic is launching, its icon will appear in the Dock and will (assuming you haven't changed the option) bounce up and down rhythmically as the environment is loading. You'll also see an icon representing the Mac OS 9.x application you opened. However, once Classic is open, its icon will no longer be present.*

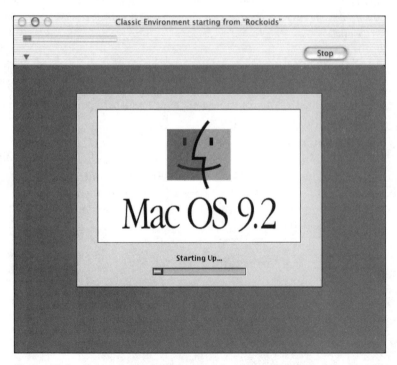

Figure 15.4   If you click the disclosure triangle, you'll see the standard Mac OS 9 startup screen.

Running Classic as a Startup Application

It's highly likely that, if you haven't yet upgraded your applications to Mac OS X native versions, you'll have to spend plenty of time in the Classic environment to run your older programs. Therefore, it may be a good idea to have Classic as a startup application so that you don't have to wait for it later when you're running those programs. Here's how to make it a startup program:

1. Launch the System Preferences application (it's normally in the Dock).

2. Click the Classic icon. The Classic preference pane, shown in Figure 15.5, appears.

3. Choose the startup volume that contains the Mac OS 9.x System Folder you want to use from the scrolling list.

NOTE: *Which to use if you have several? Well, you might want to have a backup System Folder on another partition or drive in case something happens to your Classic System Folder, or perhaps you have one with a lean set of system extensions for best Classic performance. So long as it's 9.1 or later (and the later the better), any of these will work.*

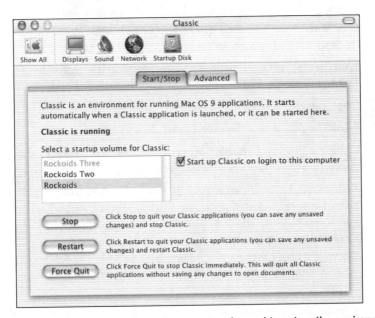

Figure 15.5   The Classic preference pane is used to set up the environment as a startup process.

4. Click the Start Up Classic On Login To This Computer check-box. Whenever you log in to your Mac OS X user account, Classic will be launched. You can still quit the environment in the normal fashion later, but you'll be all set when you're ready to run your older software.

5. If you want to begin Classic right away, click the Start button.

6. Choose Quit from the application menu or type Command+Q to leave the System Preferences application.

NOTE: *The next section discusses the settings found in the Advanced Classic settings pane, which will help you tailor performance and reduce potential hang-ups.*

Getting Reliable Performance from Classic Applications

Making it possible to run older Mac programs under Mac OS X is one of the main factors that will ease migration to the new operating system. Rather than fret over what works and what doesn't, the most efficient way to run Classic right now is bare bones. Here's the ideal way to set it up for maximum compatibility:

1. Launch the System Preferences application (it's probably in the Dock unless you removed it).

2. Click the Classic pane.

3. Click the Advanced tab (see Figure 15.6).

4. Click the Startup Options pop-up menu and select one of the configuration options you want. They are as follows:

- *Turn Off Extensions*—When you select this option and click the Restart Classic button, Mac OS 9.x will reboot with extensions off. This step offers maximum compatibility at the risk of losing access to system extensions needed to run specific programs (such as Microsoft's). Video acceleration in Classic mode is also turned off, so screen refresh will slow considerably.

- *Open Extensions Manager*—When you select this option and click the Restart Classic button, the Extensions Manager application will open as Mac OS 9.x boots, giving you a way

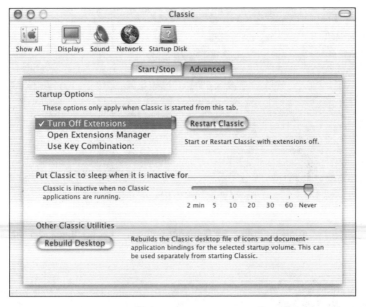

Figure 15.6   These Advanced settings help you tailor Classic performance and compatibility.

to fine-tune your extensions lineup to remove items that may cause performance hits or incompatibilities. I'll cover this in more detail shortly.

- *Use Key Combination*—When you select this option, you'll need to enter a keyboard combination in the data field that will appear below the pop-up menu to trigger Classic with System Preferences open.

5. The easiest management technique is to select the Open Extensions Manager option. When Classic starts, this option acts as the equivalent of holding down the spacebar at startup under Mac OS 9.x. The Extensions Manager window appears, as shown in Figure 15.7.

6. Choose the Mac OS 9.x Base set from the Selected Set pop-up menu.

7. Go to the File menu and select Duplicate Set. A window appears allowing you to name the set, as shown in Figure 15.8. This simply makes a copy of the Base set you've already selected.

8. Name the copy of the Base set something that will identify it for the purpose, such as "Mac OS X Classic Set."

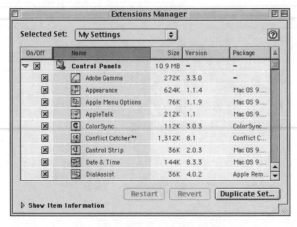

Figure 15.7   Apple's Extensions Manager helps you set up Classic for the best performance.

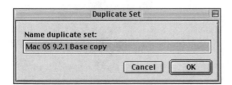

Figure 15.8   This is a copy of the extension set you selected.

NOTE: *If you run any recent Classic version of Microsoft's Internet programs or any Microsoft Office application while using this Mac OS X set, a number of system extensions required by these programs will be installed the first time any of those programs are launched. There's no reason to be concerned; the installation is normal.*

9. Close Extensions Manager to save your set. From here on, whenever you want to start your Mac under Mac OS X, make sure you activate this special "lean and mean" set for Mac OS X.

NOTE: *You can perform essentially the same operation if you use Casady & Greene's Conflict Catcher to manage your Mac OS 9.x System Folder. However, you should use version 8.0.9 or later. Earlier versions of Conflict Catcher had a peculiar bug when they interacted with the Classic environment, with recurring requests for the program's serial number. Free updates to any Conflict Catcher 8 version are available from the company's Web site, **www.casadyg.com**.*

After this special set has been created, you might want to consider adding a few of your cherished extensions and see if Classic continues to run efficiently. There's no reason to abandon your normal extensions set; just switch over before you install or run Mac OS X.

In my experience, a lean and mean Classic environment is a good way to get the most out of Mac OS X without a wasting a lot of time seeking out possible extension conflicts. If you need to return to Mac OS 9.x after restart (see "Returning to Mac OS 9.x" later in this chapter), hold down the spacebar until the Extensions Manager (or Conflict Catcher) window appears. Then switch back to your regular extension set (which will probably bring up a dialog from Conflict Catcher stating that it will restart your Mac yet again). That way, you can enjoy the best of both worlds.

NOTE: *If you switch extension sets with Conflict Catcher, on occasion you'll see a prompt indicating that you need to restart your Mac again. This happens if some of the extensions that were activated must boot before Conflict Catcher. It is normal behavior.*

Keeping Your Mac OS 9.x System Folder Safe and Sound

You can also protect your Mac OS 9.1 System Folder by using another startup drive for your regular setup when you're not using Mac OS 9.x. This way, you don't have to fret over special startup sets, extra extensions in the System Folder from Mac OS X, or other possible problems that might result from the switching process (although it should, in theory, work all right). Here's how to get the most value out of this multiple System Folder scheme:

1. Before you install Mac OS X, back up and reformat your Mac's hard drive into at least two partitions.

2. Install the version of Mac OS 9.x you want to use with Mac OS X on your first partition.

3. Install the System Folder you want to use for regular work on the second partition.

4. Proceed with your standard installation of Mac OS X, as described in Chapter 2.

5. When the installer proceeds to the dialog box where you select a disk for installation, choose the one on your first boot partition. Be sure not to check the box to erase the partition; otherwise, you'll wipe out the data on that drive.

6. Continue with the Mac OS X installation. For now, whenever you wish to use Classic, you'll choose the Mac OS 9.x System

Folder on the first partition. When you want to work full-time in the older operating system, you'll simply select the System Folder in the second partition.

TIP: If one or the other System Folder isn't recognized for startup or by the Startup Disk pane in the System Preferences application, open that folder and then close it again. This action has the effect of "blessing" the System Folder, making it possible to boot your Mac from it.

NOTE: Some folks feel that putting Mac OS X on a separate partition from the Classic Mac OS might improve performance and compatibility. Apple installs both operating systems on a single partition on all new Macs. My personal experience with a single partition and dual-partition setup yielded no significant differences. If you want to go through the trouble to back up your data and reformat your drives, it may be worth trying. Consider, however, that this might be best done on a new Mac, where you can partition the drive during the initial setup process and just restore all the standard files to one of the partitions.

Related solution:	Found on page:
Installing Mac OS X	30

Solving Classic Environment Problems

If you follow the steps in the previous sections, you should be able to continue to use your Classic Mac OS applications with decent performance and the maximum level of compatibility. However, if you choose to abandon the simple setup to add extra extensions, you may encounter some troubles along the way. Here are likely causes and solutions:

- *A slow startup of the Classic environment*—If it seems to take a long time to access a Classic application, consider this remedy: Pare down Mac OS 9.x system extensions to the Base set, and then create a new Mac OS X set from it. The startup process should be much faster, and your problems fewer.

- *Classic startup applications switch back and forth*—I have observed this phenomenon when the Launcher and Spell Catcher played a game of dueling launches (but it can happen whenever there are multiple Classic startup programs). The immediate solution is to click the menu bar and quit the Spell Catcher application, but the long-term remedy is to disable one or the other. Spell Catcher's compatibility under Mac OS X is questionable.

NOTE: *Spell Catcher is a terrific interactive spell-checking and thesaurus utility. It runs in virtually all programs and will flash warnings if you make an error. Its Ghostwriting feature stores keystrokes, in case you lose a file as a result of a system crash. It would be nice to see this program continued under Mac OS X, but author Evan Gross says it is doubtful he'll do it; it would have to be rewritten from scratch as a Cocoa-based application, because the tools he needs to make it work aren't supported in Apple's Carbon APIs.*

- *A nasty startup crash when returning to Mac OS 9*—More than likely, you will need to restart under Mac OS 9.x for one reason or another, unless the Mac on which Mac OS X is installed is de- voted to testing and nothing else. Shortly after the startup pro- cess begins, before extension icons appear, all or part of a blank bomb screen may bring the whole process to a halt. One of the causes could be a corrupted TCP/IP Preferences file. The solution is to restart with system extensions off (hold the Shift key down at startup), and then trash this file, which is located in the Prefer- ences Folder inside the System Folder. Then it will be safe to restart normally. You'll need to re-create the settings (or keep a backup around, just in case).

TIP: *One way to avoid this annoying file corruption is to remove your standard TCP/IP Preferences file and keep it for safekeeping. Upon restart, a new, empty file will be created. With no data entered, it is less apt to become corrupted when you try to run your old Mac Internet software from the Classic environment. Another way is to lock your settings, so that they cannot be modified. You do so by changing the user mode to Administration (via the File menu). Once you're in Administration mode, you can lock down any setting.*

- *Launching Internet programs doesn't get you connected*—If you have dial-up access to the Internet, you need to launch the Internet Connect application first and then connect. You can then use any Carbon or Cocoa Internet application. If you're trying to use a program that does its own dialing, such as AOL or CompuServe 2000, you'll need to check for Mac OS X updates to their client software.

15. Using Older Programs with Mac OS X

Returning to Mac OS 9.x

There is no reason not to switch back to Mac OS 9.x to run programs and hardware that aren't ready to work under Mac OS X (that's why it's part of the Mac OS X package). To return to your former environ- ment, do the following:

1. Launch the System Preferences application.

2. Double-click the Startup Disk pane (see Figure 15.9).

3. If you are not using an administrator's user account, click the padlock icon (if it's closed) and then type your username and password to get access to changing the startup disk.

4. Click your Mac OS 9.x startup disk.

5. Click the Restart button that appears at the bottom of the Startup pane in System Preferences and then in the confirming dialog box to save your settings and restart. In a few moments, your Mac will restart under Mac OS 9.x.

NOTE: *If you followed my recommendation to establish a special set in Extensions Manager or Conflict Catcher to use when running Mac OS 9.x in the Classic environment, be sure to hold down the spacebar when starting under Mac OS 9.x. Doing so will bring up your startup manager's screen, and you can then switch to your preferred Mac OS 9.x startup set for regular use and enjoy all your favorite system extensions. Apple calls your default extension setup My Settings unless you've renamed it.*

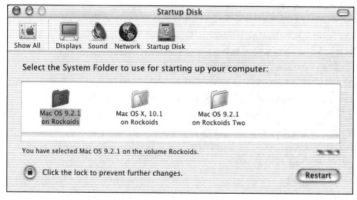

Figure 15.9   Choose your startup disk from this screen.

Chapter 16

Mac OS X Font Management

In Brief

You can't avoid fonts. The desktop publishing revolution is credited with giving the Macintosh platform credibility. Where you once had to use an artist's table, dedicated typesetting computers, and high-cost output devices to produce artwork for a brochure or publication, the Mac made it possible to do it all on your desktop at relatively low cost, even in your own home. Page layout applications, such as Adobe PageMaker and QuarkXPress, low-cost fonts, and relatively high-quality laser printers combined to bury much of the traditional typesetting industry, except for extremely specialized work.

However, the availability of thousands of fonts has proven to be the bane of the Mac user's experience, because it creates new concerns and sources of confusion.

There Are Fonts and There Are Fonts

It would be nice if fonts all came in just one format and were easy to install, but the situation has been otherwise. There are multiple font formats, and fonts of different types with the very same name. Where do you begin?

Font Formats Defined

Before you even select a font to use in your document, you are faced with choices of installation and organization. Here's a list of the types of fonts commonly used on Macs:

- *Bitmap fonts*—The original Mac font format, bitmap fonts are designed for printing and display in a single size. If they are scaled to one size or another, the quality of the image deteriorates in proportion to the size difference; the image can become an almost unreadable collection of pixel shapes when printed or viewed at a very large size.

- *PostScript fonts*—This scalable font format was developed by Adobe Systems in the 1980s and quickly came to dominate the printing and publishing industries. See the next item for a full description of what such fonts do.

- *Scalable fonts*—Whether PostScript or TrueType, these fonts can be printed in any available point size at the full resolution of the printer or other output device. However, the fonts come in a form that confuses many Mac users. The scalable fonts, called variously *outline fonts* or *printer fonts*, are separate from the fonts that generate images on your Mac's display, the *screen fonts*. This arrangement is a carryover from the way fonts were organized in the days of traditional typography, when font sets were divided into two parts for width or space values and for output. But it causes confusion because the lack of the screen font means your font won't show up in a Font menu, and the lack of a printer font means it won't print at full quality.

- *TrueType fonts*—In 1990, to avoid having to pay license fees for use of PostScript fonts, Apple (with a little help from Microsoft in its later stages) developed a new scalable font format. TrueType fonts include the screen font and outline font in a single file. For that reason alone, they are easier to handle. However, they have downsides. One is that you should not try to use a PostScript and TrueType font of the same typeface family. At worst, printing of the document will be inconsistent or output in the wrong font. Or, letterspacing may be distorted. The other problem with TrueType is that printers and service bureaus with high-resolution output devices may not fully support the format, particularly if they are using older hardware.

NOTE: *Although originally introduced on the Mac platform, TrueType fonts are the standard font format for Microsoft Windows. On the Mac platform, however, PostScript remains the font format of choice for the publishing industry, because the high-resolution output devices used may not always support TrueType (a situation that has been largely fixed with newer devices). New Macs and the Mac OS ship with TrueType fonts.*

- *OpenType fonts*—A recent entrant in the font arena, the OpenType font format can combine elements of PostScript and TrueType fonts in a single file, along with more extensive character sets. It hasn't quite caught on yet, although it's fully supported by Mac OS X.

Font Organization Under the Mac OS

Before Mac OS X arrived, Mac users had to rely on extra software for flexible font handling and, in fact, to use fonts with some printers. Here's a list of the options and what they did:

- *Adobe Type Manager (ATM)*—Originally introduced in 1989, this program is designed to provide clear screen display of PostScript fonts in all available sizes. It also has the side effect of allowing non-PostScript printers, such as ink jet printers, to use PostScript fonts and deliver the maximum quality they were capable of. An enhanced version of ATM, ATM Deluxe (shown in Figure 16.1), also allows you to activate and deactivate fonts that are not installed in the System Folder, check for duplicates and damaged fonts, and print font samples.

NOTE: *Although a Mac OS X version of ATM will never be produced, according to Adobe, you should still keep it at hand for clean display of PostScript fonts used in the Classic environment.*

- *Alsoft's MasterJuggler*—MasterJuggler is one of the early font management programs. As with ATM Deluxe, it's used to activate and organize a font library. It does not, however, do anything about font rendering, so you still need the basic version (now free) of ATM for that purpose.

- *DiamondSoft's Font Reserve*—This program provides a unique way to store and manage fonts. It places all fonts outside the System Folder in a database file, so you don't have to concern yourself with placing them in any particular location. It offers various sorting features, as well as the ability to print samples of your library. Again, ATM is needed for font rendering in the Classic environment. You'll learn how to set it up for best efficiency in the "Immediate Solutions" section of this chapter.

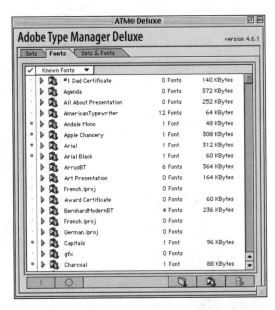

Figure 16.1   ATM Deluxe manages your font library and provides clear display of fonts, all in the same program.

- *Extensis Suitcase*—This is the original font manager, which has passed through several software publishers (such as the late Fifth Generation Systems and Symantec) before finding its current home with the popular publisher of add-on graphics utilities. It is somewhat similar to MasterJuggler in terms of its focus and features, but you still need ATM for clean display of PostScript fonts. A Mac OS X–native version of Suitcase was released in the fall of 2001.

Mac OS X's New Font-Handling Scheme

When developing Mac OS X, Apple Computer realized that font management was confusing for many Mac users and often the source of trouble in preparing and outputting documents. The response is the Apple Type Solution (ATS). This mechanism, which works with the Quartz 2D imaging layer of the new operating system, delivers system-wide handling of all the major font formats—PostScript, TrueType, OpenType, and even the original Mac bitmap fonts.

ATS handles font rendering of all the formats using Mac OS X's Portable Document Format (PDF) mechanism (which uses Adobe's popular open standard for creating electronic documents), so you don't need ATM for PostScript font display. In addition, built-in tools organize font collections and display samples, which may, to some extent, reduce or eliminate the need for a font management program.

Mac OS X applications can use fonts stored in all the Mac OS X Fonts folders, plus the Fonts folder in your Mac OS 9.x System Folder. Classic applications are restricted to the contents of the Classic Mac OS Fonts folder; that is, unless you install a font management program to manage your library (as described earlier).

NOTE: As you'll see in the pages that follow, the ATS font system isn't a panacea, and it doesn't work with all programs; nor will its font-handling features appeal to everyone. This is apt to leave plenty of room for third-party publishers to update existing font managers or develop new programs to provide needed features lacking in the core operating system.

Additionally, fonts are available in two ways to users of Mac OS X:

- *System-wide*—Fonts can still be placed in a Fonts folder, but several Fonts folders are in use under Mac OS X. The one you'll be using most often for system-wide fonts is in a new location, but it is used in a fashion similar to the Fonts folder under the Classic Mac OS. You'll find it in a folder labeled Library, where a number of folders related to system settings and preferences are

16. Mac OS X Font Management

located. Fonts in this folder are available to all users of that computer. Changing fonts or anything else on a system basis, of course, requires that you log in using an administrator's account name and password.

NOTE: *Is that all? Not quite. Within the Mac OS X System Folder, in a folder also labeled Library, is yet another Fonts folder. However, you cannot normally add or remove files to this folder, because it's protected. Another Fonts folder is located in another Library folder, located inside the Network folder (as accessible via the Computer directory). This font library is designed to be shared across a network and may be a useful alternative if you plan to use your Mac as a repository for fonts throughout your network (although a dedicated network server would be a more useful alternative if you want to divvy up files to lots of users from a single source).*

- *User-specific*—Each user can have a separate library, stored in the Fonts folder, in his or her personal Library folder. The Library folder is located within the Home or Users folder, which bears the user's name. Those fonts are available only to that user, but they behave transparently to Mac OS X otherwise and are indistinguishable in the Font menu.

NOTE: *Another advantage of Mac OS X is the number of fonts you can use. Under Mac OS versions prior to 9, the limit was 128 font resources, meaning bitmap and suitcase files. Some users would drag and drop font suitcases atop one another to combine them and get around this limitation. The limit went to 512 fonts under Mac OS 9, but Mac OS X has no limit to how many fonts you can install, other than the size of your Mac's drive and the agony you want to experience in looking at an endless font display.*

Introducing the Font Panel

Apple has made a significant stride toward more efficient font management with Mac OS X's Font panel (see Figure 16.2). This handy feature not only simplifies selection of fonts, but also allows you to organize your collection, regardless of size, according to your needs.

Figure 16.2   Choose, sample, and organize your fonts here.

The Font panel may even partially replace the need for a separate font management program—except that it has a serious limitation. When software publishers Carbonize their applications to work under Mac OS X, they must make a number of choices. One is to make the program run in the new environment and be compatible with the basic features, such as preemptive multitasking and protected memory. This option entails less work on the part of a publisher's programming team. Apple also provides tools to exploit the features of Carbon, should the publisher undertake the extra work. However, at least with the version of Mac OS X covered in this book (10.1.2), Font panel support wasn't available. As a result, an application that otherwise fully supports Mac OS X will have a plain-Jane Font menu (see Figure 16.3). Unfortunate, but true.

However, if the publisher has developed a Cocoa application, you'll find the Font Panel to be a flexible way in which to manage your font collection.

TIP: *One quick way to see whether a program was developed for the Carbon or Cocoa environment is to see whether it has a Font panel. However, regardless of which environment was used for developing the application, it should work fine under Mac OS X, with full support for its industrial-strength operating system features.*

16. Mac OS X Font Management

Figure 16.3   This particular application, although Carbonized for Mac OS X, yields only an old-fashioned Font menu.

Special Font Features of Mac OS X

If an application supports the Font panel, it also inherits some additional system-wide font features that used to be available only in separate programs. When you call up a Font menu in a Mac OS X program that offers the expanded font capability (see Figure 16.4), you'll see a number of those additional features (some will vary from program to program) in addition to the normal range of font formatting choices. They include the following:

- *Kern*—Used by graphic artists, *kerning* is the process of adjusting the spacing of letter combinations that would otherwise be wide apart visually. For example, in the word *To*, kerning tucks the lowercase *o* closer to the letter *T* for a more pleasing appearance and better readability. Mac OS X lets you use the kerning features of a font. You can also adjust the overall spacing between characters, which is sometimes called *tracking* or *range kerning*.

- *Ligature*—In high-quality books and ads, *ligatures* create single, integrated characters of such combinations as *fi* and *fl*, by joining the tops of the characters, such as fi and fl. The conversion is done automatically when you type a character.

NOTE: *Such programs as QuarkXPress and Adobe InDesign, two popular page-layout applications, can convert ligatures on the fly. Mac OS X lets you do it with all programs that support its font-handling features.*

With all the great font-handling features of Mac OS X, you may begin to cherish the ease with which you are able to manage your library, whether it includes a few dozen or a few thousand fonts. In the "Immediate Solutions" section, I'll cover the ways you can install or use fonts under the new operating system.

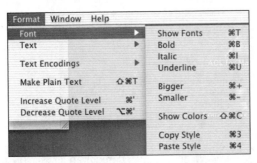

Figure 16.4   This submenu shows only some of the additional font management options for Mac OS X.

Immediate Solutions

Installing Fonts Under Mac OS X

As explained at the beginning of this chapter, fonts can be installed on a system for everyone who uses your Mac or on an individual-user basis (so only that user can access them). Here's how to install a font on a system-wide basis:

1. Log in as the administrator of that Mac or a user with administrator's rights. If another user has logged in, use the Log Out command in the Apple menu and then enter your username and password in the Login prompt.

2. Locate your Mac's Library folder, which is located on the startup drive and locate the Fonts folder within it.

3. Copy the fonts directly to the Fonts folder. The fonts will be recognized by your newly opened applications. If they don't appear right away, restart your Mac (this shouldn't be necessary, however).

The other way to install fonts is for the individual user only. Here's how it's done:

1. Log in under the individual user's or an administrator's account.

2. Locate the Home or Users folder, and then the folder with that user's name.

3. Locate the Library folder and copy the fonts directly to the Fonts folder located within it. Fonts installed in this fashion should show up immediately in your Font menu. If they don't, follow the steps in the preceding list and restart your Mac.

WARNING! *Fonts installed under a user's account are available only to an individual user. If you expect more than one user will work with a font, it's better to install the font on a system-wide basis.*

NOTE: *Am I missing something? I didn't mention the Mac OS X System folder and its Fonts folder, within the Library folder. You normally cannot copy or remove files from this folder without gaining root access, and you will gain no better level of font compatibility by doing so.*

16. Mac OS X Font Management

Using the Font Panel

Mac OS X's Font panel provides a feature-laden way to organize and access the fonts in your library, regardless of its size. Here's how to use the Font panel:

1. From within an application that supports the feature, go to the Format menu and choose Font. Select Font Panel from the submenu. The window in Figure 16.5 appears. To open it more quickly, press Command+T.

2. Under Family, select the font you want to use.

3. If the font has several styles, choose the one you want from the Typeface column.

4. Pick the size you want from the Sizes column (or type the size in the text field at the top of the column to get a size not listed in the display).

TIP: *If the Font panel is too large to fit comfortably on your Mac's screen in addition to your document window, resize it by moving the resize bar. Fonts are also organized into collections. If you expand the width of the Font panel, you'll see one more column, Collections, from which you can select a different group of fonts.*

---

5. Close the Font panel screen and continue to work in your document.

TIP: *If you plan to switch fonts back and forth from among your font collection, feel free to keep the Font panel window displayed so that you can return to it quickly from your document. Unfortunately, the Font panel doesn't have an active minimize function, so you can't leave it on the Dock for quick access.*

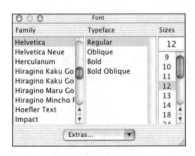

Figure 16.5   Many Mac OS X-savvy applications support the Font panel.

NOTE: *Commonly available weights of a font, such as bold or italic, can be selected directly from the Font menu without invoking the Font panel, although purists say you'll get better printing results if you choose the correct font weight from the panel itself.*

Adding Font Favorites

Another great feature of the Font panel is the ability to store fonts as favorites for fast retrieval. Here's how to set them up:

1. From within an application that supports the feature, activate the Font panel.

2. Select the font family, style, and size you want.

3. Click the Extras pop-up menu (see Figure 16.6) and select Add To Favorites.

4. Repeat the process for each font you want to use as a favorite. Favorites will list not just the typeface, but also the exact size you specified.

Using Favorites

To access a font from your Favorites list, follow these steps:

1. Activate the Font panel. Click the resize bar and extend it to the right, to expand the width of the Font panel.

2. From the Collections column, click Favorites to see the display in Figure 16.7. The Favorites list will show the selected fonts in their actual size and style.

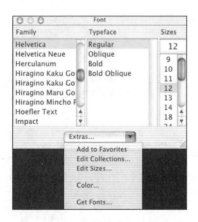

16. Mac OS X Font Management

Figure 16.6   Additional commands are available for you to organize your font collection.

329

Figure 16.7   Choose your favorites from this list.

NOTE: *If you used the Mac OS X Public Beta, you'll probably recall that the Font panel included a preview of all selected fonts. However, this feature wasn't carried over to the release version of Mac OS X, although we can always hope it will reappear in a future version.*

3. To remove a font from your Favorites list, select it and choose Remove From Favorites from the pop-up menu.

Creating a Font Collection

One of the more useful features of Mac OS X for managing a large font library is the ability to create a custom collection to match your specific needs. That way, you can have one font collection for personal use and another for business. If you're a business user, you can subdivide fonts by the name of your client, your document, or the type of fonts you're using, such as serif and sans serif, or title and text, to name a few.

The Collections feature of the Font panel makes easy work of this process. Just follow these steps:

1. Activate the Font panel.

2. Click the pop-up menu below the font sample area and choose Edit Collections to open the window shown in Figure 16.8.

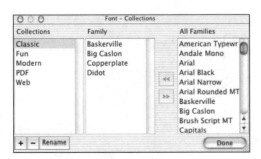

Figure 16.8   Manage and create new font collections from this window.

3. In the Collections column, click the plus (+) symbol to produce a brand-new collection with the name New-1, New-2, and so on, depending on how many you've made.

4. Click the Rename button to give the collection a more appropriate name, if you wish.

5. With the new collection selected, locate the font you want in the All Families column and click the left-pointing arrow to add it to your collection.

6. Repeat the process for each font you want to add to that collection.

7. To remove a font collection, select the item you want to delete and click the minus (–) button.

WARNING! *There is no warning prompt if you click the minus button when selecting a font collection. So, be certain you want to remove that collection before clicking the button. This feature may or may not be fixed in the final release of Mac OS X.*

8. Click Done when you're finished making your collections.

9. To add that particular font collection as a favorite, choose Add To Favorites from the Font panel's pop-up menu.

10. When you're finished creating font collections, close the Font panel.

11. When you need to use a specific collection, access the Font panel and click the collection's name in the Collections column.

12. Select your font in the same fashion described at the beginning of this section.

Choosing Custom Font Sizes

The Font panel includes a standard set of popular display sizes, but if your needs require more fine-tuning, follow this process:

1. Activate the Font panel from a program that supports the feature.

2. With the Font panel on display, choose Edit Sizes from the pop-up menu to bring up the screen shown in Figure 16.9.

3. In the New Size box, enter the size you want to include in the Sizes list, and click the plus (+) button. Alternatively, you can choose the Adjustable Slider button and move a slider to select the various font sizes.

16. Mac OS X Font Management

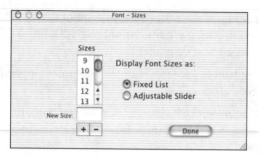

Figure 16.9   Add new font sizes here.

4. To remove a font size, select it and click the minus (–) button.

5. Click Done when you're finished. You'll be returned to the Font panel.

Checking the Characters in a Font

Some things never change, and the way you look for the extra characters in a font under Mac OS X is the same as in previous versions of the Mac OS: you use Key Caps (see Figure 16.10).

To use Key Caps, follow these steps:

1. Locate Key Caps in the Utilities folder, and double-click the program's icon.

2. Go to the Font menu and select the font you wish to use.

3. The keyboard layout displays the characters available. Press the appropriate modifier key, either Option or Option+Shift, to see the character you want.

Figure 16.10   Key Caps is still part of the Mac OS, and its functions remain essentially the same.

4. Type the character by clicking on the key with the mouse or pressing the appropriate key on the keyboard. That character shows up in the display window above the keyboard layout.

5. To use this special character, select it, and then copy it. You can then paste it into the text-entry point in your document.

Avoiding Too-Small Fonts in TextEdit

Apple's replacement for SimpleText, TextEdit (shown in Figure 16.11), can be used as a simple word processor, with full management of fonts with the Font panel. However, it can be quirky in an important respect, because you cannot specify an exact line width in the same fashion as a regular word-processing program. Instead, it uses the width of your document window to determine the size, and the line breaks made in the document on your Mac's display will match those in your printout.

However, if your printout uses a page width smaller than the screen, the font's size will be scaled down in proportion, and under some circumstances, it can get downright small. However, a simple solution to this dilemma exists:

1. Go to TextEdit's Format menu.

2. Select the Wrap To Page option. When this feature is active, lines will wrap on the basis of the page size selected in the Page Setup box. No more ultra-small (or ultra-large) letters, and the size that's printed will be the exact size you selected in the document itself.

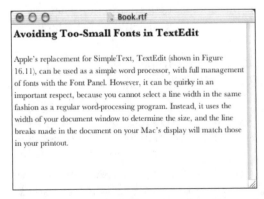

Figure 16.11   TextEdit is meant to be a less modestly featured replacement for the famous SimpleText application.

Using Font Reserve to Manage Your Mac OS X Font Library

Because most of the applications you are likely to use under Mac OS X that require extensive font handling are Carbon-based rather than Cocoa (such as the popular graphic applications from Adobe, Macromedia, and Quark), you'll appreciate the ability to use software that can manage a huge font library. The first available solution is DiamondSoft's Font Reserve; here's how to use it for maximum flexibility.

Begin by installing the software. The installer disk will usually include both the Mac OS 9.x and Mac OS X versions and runs the same as any other installation program.

TIP: You can get a free limited-edition version of Font Reserve for Mac OS X as part of the Corel Graphics Suite 10 package. The sole limitation is the number of fonts you can use: 2,000. But that isn't an issue unless you expect to use more than that many fonts.

WARNING!   The Mac OS X version of Font Reserve runs only with Mac OS X applications. If you plan to use Classic applications, you will need to install the Classic version of the software separately and set up two font databases. Sorry, but that's the way it is, at least until the publisher comes up with a better solution (or you switch to all-native Mac OS X software).

After performing the installion, here's how to set up the program to recognize your library. The first consideration, of course, is that for maximum efficiency, the program should manage all but your very basic operating system fonts:

1. Make sure none of your applications are running. Quit any that are still active (using the Dock as the guide to see which ones are open).

2. With all applications closed, go to your desktop and make a brand new folder. Call the folder, for lack of a better name, Temp Fonts.

3. Copy all the non—system-related fonts from your Mac OS 9.x and X Fonts folders and place them in the Temp Fonts folder.

NOTE: What's a system-related font? Keep such fonts as Charcoal, Chicago, Courier, Geneva, Lucinda Grande, Monaco, Times, and Symbol where they are. You can safely move the rest.

---

4. Locate the Font Reserve application in your Mac OS X Applications folder and launch the Font Reserve Settings application (see Figure 16.12).

5. Click the On button at the top of the application window to make Font Reserve active.

6. To avoid having to launch the application each time you log in or restart your Mac, click the Turn On When Mac Restarted checkbox, which will make the program a login or startup application.

7. Quit the Font Reserve Settings application and then launch the Font Reserve Browser application (see Figure 16.13), which you'll use on a regular basis to manage your fonts.

8. To add fonts to Font Reserve, they need to be placed in the Font Reserve Database, the program's font storage area, located in the Font Reserve Browser application window. Drag and drop the Temp Fonts folder you made into the lower pane of the Font Reserve Browser window.

NOTE: *The first time you add a fonts folder or set of files to Font Reserve, you'll see a Preferences dialog box in which you tell the program how to handle the fonts. The best option, Copy Into Font Reserve Database, will simply make a copy rather than put the original fonts in the database. This option leaves the fonts intact and will consume extra storage space, but it's useful if you need to install and use both the Classic and Mac OS X versions of Font Reserve and want to make duplicate Font Reserve Database files.*

16. Mac OS X Font Management

Figure 16.12   Activate Font Reserve from this application.

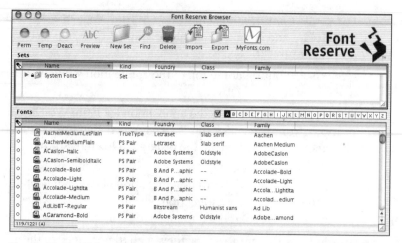

Figure 16.13   This application is used to locate, sample, and manage your Mac's font library.

After your font library has been compiled into Font Reserve, you can use the Font Reserve Browser application's toolbar to activate or deactivate fonts as needed. You must quit Mac OS X applications and relaunch them in order for newly activated fonts to be recognized (at least until DiamondSoft creates a method to allow for automatic activation). The Classic Mac OS version of Font Reserve includes special add-on modules (plug-ins or XTensions) that can be used with such programs as QuarkXPress to provide automatic activation of fonts stored in an opened document, or when fonts are activated with Font Reserve.

> **NOTE:** The biggest difference between Font Reserve and Suitcase 10 is that the latter can manage both Classic and Mac OS X fonts. However, both are limited in not being able to autoactivate fonts in documents opened under Mac OS X. Extensis told me it's not officially supported by Apple, but they are trying to do it anyway.

Handling Mac OS X Font Problems

The new, more robust font-handling features of Mac OS X usually make it far easier to handle a font library, whether small or large. But because of the interaction between Mac OS X and the Classic environment, for example, you may still run into problems.

Here are some common Mac OS X problems and the standard range of solutions:

- *Fonts not in the Font menu*—If a font was installed in a user's folder, it won't be available to any other user on your Mac. If you want more than a single user to access a font, install it under that user's account as well, or system-wide. If you did install the fonts in the proper fashion, try restarting your Mac just to make sure they are recognized by the operating system.

- *Fonts appear in some applications but not in others*—If you're using a Classic Mac application, only fonts installed in the Fonts folder within the Classic System Folder are recognized, unless you use a font-management program to handle additional fonts. Depending on whether you're using Font Reserve or Suitcase, you may have to have separate versions installed in both environments.

- *Garbled or bitmapped font output*—This is probably a font conflict, similar to those that afflicted earlier versions of the Mac OS. The best way to handle this problem is to make sure you have installed only one version of the font, and not both PostScript and TrueType versions. Another possible cause is installing two or more fonts of the same name from different sources. The operating system won't be able to sort them out.

- *Poor letterspacing*—Check the previous item to be sure you do not have fonts that are in conflict. Another possible problem is a damaged font suitcase or TrueType font, which may not provide the right letterspacing information.

- *Missing font collection*—Are you sure you didn't delete it by mistake? You get no acknowledgement if you click the minus button by accident. Otherwise, make sure the fonts added to a collection were not part of another user's account. That would explain why the collection isn't there when you try to access it.

16. Mac OS X Font Management

Chapter 17

Performing Backups

In Brief

Take a hint from that old TV commercial with the motto "nobody can eat just one." Although the comment applied to potato chips, the same theme can be carried over to the files you create on your Mac. Nobody should depend on just one.

There is no telling what might happen to your files during your day-to-day Mac computing experience. Although Mac OS X offers a robust computing environment, about as free of potential system crashes as the state of the art allows, both the operating system and application software can still fail under normal use. When the software fails, it could conceivably harm the document you're working on. In addition, hard drives, being mechanical devices, can fail unpredictably, even though they are supposed to have lengthy mean times between failures (sometimes 500,000 hours or more).

All sorts of potential issues beyond your Mac and computing environment could also conspire to cause data loss. They include weather-related problems such as hurricanes or tornadoes, natural disasters such as earthquakes and floods, and potential disasters like fire and theft. In addition, any factor that might cause a power outage or power spike, even if caused by a problem at the power company, can result in a damaged file or hard drive directory damage if it occurs at the wrong time.

Even if all your computing equipment is protected by insurance (and it should be, especially if used for business purposes), insurance cannot re-create the files you lose. However, if you have recent backups of all your critical data, you will be able to resume operation without having to re-create the material.

A Survey of Backup Software

Depending on your setup and requirements, different methods are appropriate to perform backups. The easiest is just to copy your critical files to another drive by dragging the files or folders to that drive's icon. If you don't have a lot of files to handle, this may be the perfect and highly practical solution, as long as you remember to do so on a regular basis.

NOTE: *All Macs of recent vintage have one or more Software Restore CDs that allow you to return the Mac to its shipping condition (minus the files you've added, of course). In addition, the vast majority of software shipped nowadays comes on a CD. So, even if you only back up the documents you create, you can restore your Mac's hard drive without a full backup, although at the expense of losing your user settings, such as those required for Internet access, and any applications you've added.*

The other method is probably more reliable, because you don't have to remember to make those backup copies. It's done for you on a more or less automatic basis, and it involves using dedicated backup software.

I'll list several of the popular backup applications here. No doubt, as Mac OS X continues to gain in popularity, additional backup options will be available to suit a variety of needs.

An Overview of Retrospect

Most people regard Retrospect from Dantz Development as the most popular backup program for the Mac (check **www.dantz.com** for more information). This program is bundled with a number of backup drives, which makes the choice automatic. It's also sold separately and is available at most Apple dealers. Besides its market share, the various forms of Retrospect routinely get top reviews from the Mac magazines.

Depending on your needs, there are three versions of Retrospect to consider:

- *Retrospect Express Backup*—Consider this the no-frills version of the program, although it doesn't scrimp on important features that you need for regular, robust backups. You can use its EasyScript feature to create a custom backup routine by simply answering a few basic questions about the sort of backups you plan to do and how often you want to do them. Based on this information, Retrospect Express will build an automated backup routine that suits your needs. Say, for example, you want to back up your Mac at 4:30 P.M. each afternoon, using your Jaz 2 drive. You just place your backup disk in the drive and leave the drive and your Mac on. At the appointed hour, Express will launch itself, and then run your scripted backup precisely as you specified. The program has its own compression feature to reduce the size of backup sets. Hundreds of fixed and removable storage devices are supported, including CD-R/RW and DVD-RAM.

Backups are stored in *sets*, which are special files containing all the data you've backed up. You can perform full backups and incremental backups (just the files that have changed). The Express version of the software only lacks support for networking backup and tape drives. It may be all the backup software you need, however, for a small home or business office setup.

TIP: *A particularly useful feature of Retrospect is multiple snapshots, which are, in effect, backups of your Mac taken at different points in time. Snapshots give you the power to restore your drive to the state it was in at a given point in time.*

- *Retrospect Desktop Backup*—This version of Retrospect (see Figure 17.1) has all the features of Express, including EasyScript. It adds support for a large variety of tape drives (including the hardware compression offered by these drives) and the ability to expand support to networked Macs and Windows-based PCs via Retrospect Client. These programs allow the files on each Mac on a network to be backed up to the same set of storage devices, in a single or separate backup session. Because Retrospect is also available for the Windows platform, cross-platform backups are possible. This version of Retrospect can also be configured to send backup status reports to you via email.

NOTE: *All versions of Retrospect include a robust security option. This allows the backup sets to be encrypted, so only those with the correct username and password can access and decrypt the backups or retrieve files from them. When I tested this feature with a security expert several years ago, efforts to crack the password encryption scheme proved unsuccessful. It doesn't mean it's perfect, but the results should deliver a greater feeling of confidence.*

- *Retrospect Workgroup Backup*—This is a fully packaged solution for automatic backups. The program comes with the standard Retrospect application and thus supports the entire set of features. You also get Client software (see Figure 17.2) for up to 20 networked computers.

An Overview of Intego Personal Backup

ASD Software (see **www.intego.com**), publisher of several popular Mac security products, targets Personal Backup for single users or small offices (see Figure 17.3). The program supports standard removable media, but it doesn't work with tape drives. In addition, it has no network client option.

NOTE: *At the time this book was written, the new publisher, Intego (also publisher of Internet, antivirus, and general security software), was promising to deliver a Mac OS X version of Personal Backup with a similar feature set.*

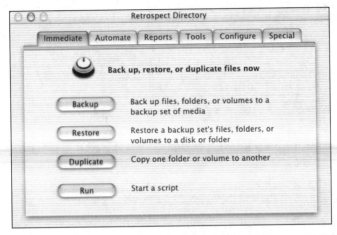

Figure 17.1   Retrospect Desktop Backup is bundled with a number of backup devices and is also sold separately.

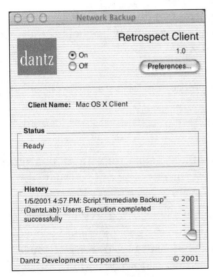

Figure 17.2   The Client version of Retrospect offers a simple interface that displays backup status.

17. Performing Backups

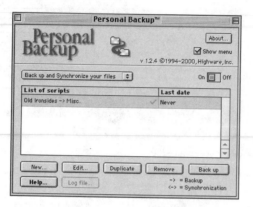

Figure 17.3   Easy configuration and keystroke backups are hallmarks of Personal Backup's feature set; the Mac OS 9 version is shown here.

The following are Personal Backup's features:

- *Single window interface*—The program's features can be accessed from a single, simple control-panel–like application. Only a small number of setup dialogs are needed to configure the program's various features.

- *Easy scripting*—You can schedule multiple sets of automatic backups without scripting knowledge simply by clicking the dates, times, and options you want.

- *File synchronization*—You can compare the files you create on your desktop Mac with the ones you make on your iBook or PowerBook (or any other Mac you use to work at a different location), so that you always have the latest versions on both systems.

- *Finder format backups*—The files you back up are simply copied in regular Finder format for easy access without your having to use a special restore feature.

- *Text backup*—Personal Backup can be set to record your keystrokes as you type. If you lose the original document because of file corruption or a system crash, you can easily retrieve the text (but not, of course, a program's special formatting).

Other Backup Programs

The choices listed in the preceding sections are not the only ones available. Here are some other backup programs:

- *Iomega's QuikSync 3*—This program is easy to set up for on-demand or scheduled backups. The new version overcomes the limitation of the previous edition, by supporting storage devices not manufactured by Iomega. Among the features of QuikSync 3 are:

  - *Easy setup*—A convenient setup wizard guides you through the process of setting up an unattended backup without your needing to understand scripting or complicated setups.

  - *Automatic copying*—You can specify certain folders on your Mac's hard drive for automatic backup. Files that are copied or moved to those folders will be duplicated automatically in the "sync" location, which is usually an external storage device.

  - *Multiple revisions*—By being able to save more than a single revision of an individual file, you can view documents in progress at different stages and restore the ones you need to use.

  - *Enterprise implementation*—As with Retrospect, QuikSync 3 can be administered from a central location, making it easy for IT managers to set up the program on a network system.

NOTE: *QuikSync 3.1 and later will run native under Mac OS X. Another program that was useful for backups, Connectix's CopyAgent, may not be developed for Mac OS X, according to the most recent information available from the company.*

- *FWB Backup ToolKit*—The publisher of Hard Disk ToolKit, a popular disk formatting utility, released a Mac OS X version of its Backup ToolKit software in the Fall of 2001. This application has three basic modes and does all its work via a simple application interface. The Automatic Backup feature performs your backups at regular intervals. An Incremental Backup feature, like the one in Retrospect, backs up only the files that have changed. For road warriors, a Synchronization feature eases the task of making sure both your Mac and your iBook or PowerBook have the same sets of files. Like Retrospect's EasyScript feature, a Configuration Wizard makes fast work of setting up your backup regimen. The notable missing feature is the ability to work with tape drives.

- *Power On Software's Rewind*—Suppose you install something new on your Mac, and suddenly the computer behaves like it's possessed. You can, of course, troubleshoot the problem and perhaps remove the application. But wouldn't it be easier just to turn back the hands of time? Rewind does that, by keeping a

17. Performing Backups

reference file of changes you've made to your Mac. Then, when called into action, it restores your Mac to the condition that existed before the event that triggered your problem. You can also use this clever application to recover a lost file, by going back in time to the point before you deleted the file. Although file recovery utilities are available, this may be a more robust way to regain lost ground.

NOTE: *At the time this book was being prepared, Power On Software was committed to updating several of its programs, which include security and personal information managers, to Mac OS X. An updated version of Rewind wasn't available for me to examine, however, so I'm summarizing the features of the Classic Mac OS version (based on the assurance from the publisher that features will be similar).*

In addition to the commercial programs, several freeware and shareware offerings promise many of the basic features of the commercial options. These include such entrants as FoldersSynchronizer, Gemini, Project Backer, Revival, SwitchBack, and Sync X. You'll want to check out the feature sets at VersionTracker.com (**www.versiontracker.com**) and see which ones might be worth a second look.

When you decide which program to deploy in your environment, consider the features offered and how they fit your situation. A simple file synchronization utility may be all you need if you just need to back up document files.

An Overview of Internet Backups

Beginning with Mac OS 9, Apple attempted to make Internet networking as transparent as connecting to a local area network (LAN). Mac OS X's user interface is designed to further blur the differences between the location of shared volumes, so it no longer makes a difference whether they're located at the other end of your room or at the other end of the world (except for file transfer speed, of course).

The ease of Internet networking and the lack of standard backup drives on some new Macs have resulted in a search for other backup methods. One of those methods harnesses the power of the Internet as a repository for your backed up files. Following are descriptions of two Internet-based backup resources. One is free, direct from Apple; the other comes at a modest monthly charge and requires special software:

- *iTools (www.apple.com/itools)*—Beginning with Mac OS 9, Apple introduced a new feature, iTools, which allowed for expanded access to the apple.com Web site. The initial features included a custom mac.com email address, the ability to create a personal home page, and iDisk (see Figure 17.4), which sets aside 20MB of storage space for your files. iDisk is easily accessed as a disk icon, which you can use in the same fashion as a volume connected directly to your Mac or your local network. iDisk is useful as a limited, fairly robust backup solution. It allows you to store your files in a private area, free from public access.

NOTE: *Apple Computer offers more storage space as an extra-cost option. Check the iTools Web site for current pricing and capacities.*

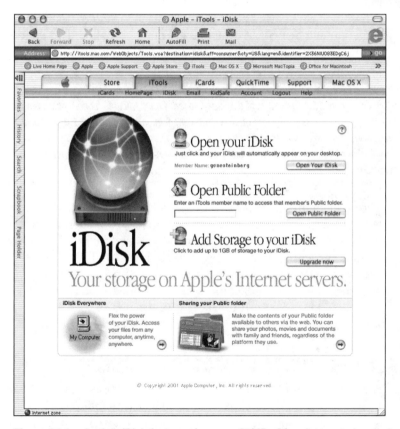

17. Performing Backups

Figure 17.4   Apple's iDisk feature gives you 20MB of free Internet storage to use for backups or to make files available to your Internet contacts.

- *BackJack (**www.backjack.com**)*—This Canadian-based company claims top ratings from Mac support Web sites. It offers a dedicated program that will provide automatic, unattended backups to its 128-bit secured Web servers. It also uses StuffIt compression technology to maximize the number of files you can send in a given amount of storage space. Pricing plans depend on the amount of storage space you need.

Although Internet backups are a reliable method of backing up critical files, and they offer the added benefit of being offsite, they have some decided disadvantages. Chief among them is throughput and capacity. Transferring even a few megabytes of files via a standard 56Kbps modem connection can be a tedious process. Worse, if you are disconnected during the transfer process (a fairly common occurrence), you must go through all or most of the process again to make sure all your files were sent. Consider broadband access, such as a cable modem or DSL (if available in your area), should you choose this backup solution.

> **TIP:** *Even if you have broadband Internet service, don't be surprised if your upload speed is throttled to a level far below that of download speed. Typically, cable modems limit uploads to 256Kbps (often less), even though they promise download speeds from 1 to 2Mbps or greater. The reason cited by some of these providers is to give maximum emphasis on downloads, and to limit use of their services by PC users who want to set up personal Web servers.*

The other shortcoming is capacity. iDisk limits you to 20MB total storage (unless you buy the extra storage space). Commercial Internet backup resources such as BackJack offer standard plans with fixed storage capacities (BackJack's are 40MB and 100MB) and additional per-megabyte charges for larger storage capacities. Even if you could send large amounts of data in a speedy fashion to such a service, the cost of backing up a fairly full hard drive in a new or recent Mac (with several gigabytes of files) on a regular basis can be considerable.

An Overview of Backup Media

A number of storage media are useful for backups—some more robust than others. When choosing a product, you should consider your specific needs, such as the amount of data you wish to back up and how robust the medium is for long-term storage, if that's one of your requirements. Here are your choices:

NOTE: *I have made no attempt to cover older, discontinued removable devices, such as SyQuest drives. Any of these products can be judged compared to the products mentioned here in terms of speed, capacity, and reliability. You should consider, however, whether it's a good idea to trust your backups to an obsolete product with little or no customer support.*

- *Floppy drive*—This was the original backup medium, not offered on Macs in several years. It isn't terribly robust; floppy disks are known to develop disk errors after being used just a few times. Worse, capacity is extremely limited. Even if you have an older Mac with a floppy drive, or you're using HD-style floppy disks on a SuperDisk drive or external floppy drive, you'll find this medium works best for small documents or pictures, when transferring them from one location to another.

- *SuperDisk drive*—This product was earmarked as a floppy drive replacement, but never managed to catch on (although some dealers still sell the product from such makers as QPS Inc.). It has the benefit of reading and writing to HD floppy disks at a speed greater than a standard floppy; it's most noticeable if you have the "2X" SuperDisk product. It allows support for legacy media (except for 800KB and 400KB floppies, of course). The SuperDisk medium is a 120MB disk that, at first glance, looks very much like a floppy (there's also a 250MB version). Although the product only became prominent in the last two or three years, it appears to be robust, and the medium is relatively inexpensive. Such drives are not particularly fast, however, which makes them less efficient for larger files, and the user base is still relatively small, despite the relative popularity of such devices as accessories for the iMac and other USB-based Apple computers.

NOTE: *Let me emphasize that the SuperDisk drive isn't the same as the SuperDrive, the Pioneer-built drive that is available in some Mac desktop computers and the flat-panel iMac. The SuperDrive can play and record to both CD and DVD media.*

- *Zip drive*—This is Iomega's most popular product; Zip drives are found in many business environments. The medium resembles a fat floppy disk, and it uses a mixture of floppy- and hard-drive technologies to provide storage capacities of 100MB and 250MB. Zip drives have been standard issue on many of Apple's desktop models, and millions of drives are out there, so it's easy to find compatible drives at other locations. The drives and media are considered quite robust, standing the test of time beyond some early reliability concerns about the mechanisms.

> **NOTE:** *One particularly vexing problem that still occurs sometimes is the so-called "click of death"—an annoying sound that emanates from the drive when you're using defective media or when the drive is poised for failure. Should you encounter this problem with a Zip drive, remove the disk and see if the sound persists when you insert another one. Should it still occur, have the drive serviced or replaced.*

- *Jaz drive*—The Iomega Jaz drive is, essentially, a portable drive using traditional hard drive technology. It comes in 1GB and 2GB formats (the latter product is called the Jaz 2), with media to match. It has the benefit of being relatively fast—about the equivalent of a slower hard drive. Long-term reliability of the media is something of a question, although the drive seems solid enough for part-time use and archiving.

- *Iomega Peerless drive*—This is an interesting variation of the removable drive scheme, brought up to date for the needs of twenty-first century PC users. A Peerless Storage System, to use the official term, consists of two parts. It starts with a Base Station, which works with a Mac's FireWire or USB port (the former is best to access this product's performance potential). Then there is the actual disk, which comes in 10GB or 20GB form. The product is sold as a bundle, with Base Station and disk, and separately (but why?), and is a clever way to handle the diverse needs of high capacity, good performance, and removable storage.

- *Castlewood ORB drive*—This product has superficial similarities to the now-departed SyQuest drives, perhaps because the founder of Castlewood was also the founder of SyQuest Technologies. The standard drive uses low-cost 2.2GB cartridges and employs a variation of standard hard drive technology called *magneto-resistive*, now standard on modern fixed drives. Its long-term robustness is not known, because the product has been on the market only a relatively short time at this writing. A review in *Macworld* magazine, however, suggested there might be some reliability concerns with the product. At the time this book was written, Castlewood had announced a 5.7GB version of the drive, using the same form factor (so older media can be read). But the initial release of the product didn't include a Mac OS version (although one might be available when you read this book).

- *Portable hard drive*—Because this standard hard drive is in a small case, it is suitable for easy transportation. Such drives are available in all the popular storage technologies, including FireWire, SCSI, and USB. Some notable examples include a

FireWire product line from SmartDisk (see **www.smartdisk.com**), which uses the FireWire bus for power. That and its Hot Plug feature make such drives easy to set up and move from workstation to workstation.

- *CD-R/CD-RW*—These products use special CD-based media, offering a high degree of longevity. The standard recordable CD technology is write-once, meaning that you cannot erase or replace the data already recorded. However, the medium is very cheap, so this isn't a serious problem. The more expensive CD-RW products let you rewrite data up to 1,000 times, but the discs themselves do not work on some regular CD drives, particularly older models. The shortcoming is speed, although newer 12x and 16x CD recorders promise to record a complete 650MB CD in just a few minutes. Optical media are great for archiving files for an extended period of time.

NOTE: *The figures 12x, 16x, and so on refer to multiples of the normal CD record speed, which takes approximately 74 minutes to write to a 650MB disc. In addition to the basic speed in recording data, you have to add the time it takes to read back the completed CD for verification (although that process is much faster, because standard CD readers on the Mac reach and exceed speeds of 32x, and third-party drives are even faster).*

- *DVD-RAM*—This product uses a variant of the newer high-density DVD form to reach a storage capacity of up to 5.2GB. Recording speed is equivalent to the fastest regular CD recording devices, and thus this is a useful method for backing up large amounts of data for long-term storage.

NOTE: *Apple no longer ships the high-end PowerMac G4 with a DVD-RAM drive, but it's available as a build-to-order option. In addition, a number of third-party peripheral companies, such as LaCie and QPS, offer drives using this format. However, the format is unfinished enough that the media recorded on one drive may not work on another brand.*

- *DVD-R/DVD-RW*—Still another variation of DVD technology is supported by the SuperDrive on Power Mac G4 and some flat-panel iMacs, and a number of third-party products incorporate the same Pioneer drive and similar products. Under Mac OS X, you can create movie DVDs using Apple's iDVD software, or store your data files via the Finder's disc-burning feature.

- *Tape drives*—Such drives come in several forms, using tapes that are roughly similar in setup to a cassette deck. Tape drives are not cheap, but the media are. You can buy DDS tapes for around

17. Performing Backups

$10 apiece or more, with storage capacities of up to 40GB (depending on the ability of the tape drive or software to compress data). Larger capacities are available for some tape drive formats, such as AIT. Tape drives tend to be slower than the other media, except for CDs, and the technology doesn't offer random access. Therefore, restoring files in different locations on a tape can take a while. In addition, although tapes are subject to wear and tear, the medium is easily and relatively cheaply replaced.

- *Network volume*—You can also back up your data to a drive on another computer (a Mac or a Unix- or Windows-based server), located on your local network. Such techniques are useful for each individual workstation, but the volume to which you are backing up should also receive a regular backup routine to ensure the highest amount of protection for the files. Consider the network backup, then, as just an intermediary to a full backup solution. At the other end of the equation, the system administrators should be using one of the previously described media for backup and archiving.

Immediate Solutions

The No-Frills Daily Backup Plan

This plan doesn't require special backup software. All it requires is a commitment to a regular program so you don't face the loss of crucial files in an emergency.

Before you begin your backup, you need the following elements:

- *Backup media*—Use a separate drive or networked volume (local or Internet-based). The "In Brief" section covers a number of backup products you might want to consider. You should also make sure you have backup media with sufficient capacity to store all the files.

- *A plan*—Create a small word-processing document listing the files and folders you want to back up on a regular basis.

TIP: *To keep track of your backups, you might want to include a list of dates and times on your backup list, along with an underscore or checkbox where you can easily mark your backups as you complete them.*

- *Logically named folders*—Create folders on the backup drive to easily identify the files you are backing up. If you plan to keep separate copies of each generation of your backup files, consider putting a date on each folder or other identification information that will help you quickly locate the files you need at a later time.

- *Reminder device*—It will help to have an alarm clock, clock radio, reminder program, or other means to notify you of the time of the scheduled backup.

- *Easy access to your original system or application CDs*—As mentioned earlier in the chapter, new Macs come with a Restore CD (or set of Restore CDs in the newest Macs), which can put the computer back in the form in which it shipped (at the expense of losing application and system updates and preferences).

17. Performing Backups

TIP: *The standard user license for most every program allows you to make a single backup copy. It is a good idea to make a backup of your software CDs and store them off site, in the event of theft or damage at your original location. Remember that if you are backing up a bootable CD, follow the instructions in the CD software to make your copy bootable as well.*

After you've got the raw materials set up, follow these steps:

1. Make sure you set your notification device to alert you of the appointed time for the backup.

2. Have your backup medium ready. If you're using a removable drive, such as a Zip drive, be sure that a disk is in the drive, ready to roll.

3. Refer to your backup list for the files and folders you need to copy.

4. Drag the files to the appropriate folders.

5. After the files are copied, put a note on your backup list confirming the day's backup is complete.

NOTE: *If your Mac is set up for multiple users, you may want to establish a single backup folder to which all users have access, such as a Shared folder. That way, each user does not have to run separate backup sessions (a potentially confusing, awkward process).*

These steps allow you to easily keep track of your daily backups, to make sure that you or one of your employees has performed the task as scheduled.

TIP: *If you are working on a mission-critical document that will take you a long time to re-create in the event of loss or damage, you may also want to perform frequent backups of the files throughout the workday. I do this regularly when I'm writing a book, because re-creating even a single chapter or portion can be an annoying, time-consuming process.*

The Special Software Backup Plan

The following steps are based on using one of the backup programs described in the earlier section, "A Survey of Backup Software." I'm assuming you will be installing the software according to the publisher's instructions and that you will be setting up your backup media as indicated.

First, take steps to prepare for your regular backup regimen:

- If you're using a removable device, be sure the disks or cartridges are inserted into the drive and ready to run at the appointed time.

17. Performing Backups

NOTE: *If you expect your backups to fill more than a single disk or tape, you should have spares available in case additional media are requested. You may, of course, recycle media if you want to discard older backups that are no longer useful. For tape-based media, however, you should replace the cartridges every year or two; they do wear out.*

- Make sure that the backup software is properly installed.

- Use the program's scheduling features to create a regular backup routine that meets your needs. You may schedule full backups once a week and incremental backups (which cover only the changed files) each day.

- If your backups are likely to consume more than a single disk or tape, be sure someone is available to insert extra media, if necessary.

- If your backup software includes automatic notification of problems via email, such as Retrospect offers, be sure the program is configured to contact you or your systems administrator at a location where they're likely to be at the time the backups occur. This may, for example, include the email address you use at home. If you have email service on your pager or mobile phone, that might be a convenient option to use for offsite notification.

WARNING! **If your Macs are located in an office, take the time to explain your backup schedule to your staff. Advise them to try not to use their Macs while files are being backed up, or to leave them on at the end of the day for after-hours backup duty. Files created or left open during the backup process may be copied in an incomplete form or not at all.**

After your backup program is in place, here are the steps you'll follow to make sure the process is done correctly:

1. Schedule your backups to occur at least once every workday, usually at a time when your Macs are not in use, so as not to interfere with your work schedule.

TIP: *Although some firms run backups at the end of the day or during the early morning hours, backups can also be conveniently done during lunchtime or any time when all or most employees aren't present, if the backups can be completed within that time frame.*

2. Before the scheduled backup is to begin, be sure the backup drive or drives and media are ready so that the process can occur (where possible) unattended.

17. Performing Backups

3. Make sure that the backup drive and all the computers from which files will be retrieved are left on and ready to run at the appointed time.

4. If the backups are unattended, check your software to see if it produces a log of the backup (Retrospect offers this feature). If a log is available, consult it regularly for information about possible problems with your scheduled backup.

Tips and Tricks for Robust Backups

Once you get accustomed to a regular backup routine, you'll appreciate the added security it offers. Consider the following additional procedures to customize your backups:

- *Store additional backup disks off-site.* Financial institutions, ISPs, and other companies store backups at other locations. That way, if something damages or destroys equipment and media at the original location, the valuable files are still available to be copied onto replacement equipment. A bank vault is one possible location. Although it may not be convenient to store all your files off-site, those most valuable to you should be considered as candidates for such storage.

NOTE: *Particularly tragic examples of lost data occurred during the bombing of the World Trade Center some years ago and the September 11, 2001 terrorist attack that destroyed the Twin Towers. Even if a firm managed to stay in business after this disaster, only an offsite backup would restore operations to a reasonable degree.*

- *Test your backups.* Don't assume you will be able to restore your files, even if the software reports the backups were successful. From time to time, do a test run to make sure you can easily retrieve files if necessary.

WARNING! *Tape drives need to be cleaned at regular intervals, because clogged read/write heads can result in premature wear of a drive or incomplete backups. Low-cost cleaning cartridges are available for such drives. The manufacturers of the mechanisms usually recommend cleaning them every 15 or 30 hours (check the documentation to determine the correct interval).*

- *Use the automatic backup or autosave features from your software.* A number of Mac programs include the ability to save documents at a regular interval or make extra copies. Check a program's preference dialogs or documentation for information about these features. Among the programs that offer one or both of these features are AppleWorks 6, Microsoft Word, and QuarkXPress. Financial programs, such as Intuit's Quicken 2002, also can create backup files of your financial records.

- *Perform extra backups of work-in-progress.* Whether you are compiling a financial profile, writing a novel, or creating an illustration for an important ad, it's a good idea to create extra copies from time to time. You can simply drag a copy of your document to a backup location, so there's always an extra one in case the original is damaged.

WARNING! *Although using the Save As feature is a possible method of making an extra copy, the end result is that you will end up working with the new document rather than the old, which means the original won't be updated.*

- *Save often.* The best protection against loss of a document in case of a crash or power outage is to have a copy on disk. Consider saving the document each time you make an important change and certainly after you create a new document.

- *Get file recovery software.* Even if you take extra steps to make sure you do regular backups, it's always possible you will trash a necessary file by mistake. Programs such as MicroMat's TechTool Pro, Power On Software's Rewind, and Symantec's Norton Utilities are able to restore files you delete by mistake. They work best when you install them first, because they are able to track files as you trash them.

TIP: *If you delete a file by mistake, try to recover it right away with one of the programs mentioned. When a file is trashed, it is not actually erased. The portion of the drive on which the file is located is simply marked as available, meaning new data can be written there. If you don't create new files, there is a greater possibility you'll be able to recover the file.*

- *Use a program's incremental backup feature.* Backup software will handle a backup in two ways: a full backup, in which all of your files are copied; and an incremental backup, in which only the files that have changed are added to your backup. The most effective, time-saving routine is to use a mixture of both. The initial backup should include all the files that need to be backed up, and the subsequent backups should be limited to changed files until the backup medium is filled. Then you should begin from scratch. In either case, you will probably want to do a complete backup once a week if you have a steady flow of files, or once every two weeks otherwise.

WARNING! *Backup programs that use tape-based media may restore files much more slowly if they have to check for a large number of new or changed versions of files when retrieving files. You should use this feature judiciously at best, particularly with tape media.*

- *Double-check your network setups.* In order for a networked backup to work, you need to make sure that your networked volumes are accessible when the backup is being performed. Pay particular attention to such issues as access privileges and whether your backup software is properly installed. Also make sure that your media are large enough to handle the available files. If not, an unattended backup won't be a good idea. If you run into problems in getting a useful network backup, examine your network configuration from stem to stern and also look at the backup logs made by your software to see what errors are being reported. Basically, if a shared volume is available for exchanging files, it should work fine for a networked backup.

WARNING! *If you want to back up an entire Mac OS X volume, including system files, you need software that's compatible with this operating system. Older backup software may work fine with application and document files, but it won't see the thousands of hidden or invisible files that are part of the Mac OS X installation, nor will such software work with volumes formatted in the Unix File System (UFS) format.*

Doing a Folder Backup via the Command Line

You can also copy your files courtesy of Mac OS X's Terminal application, which is located in the Utilities folder. If you're accustomed to dragging and dropping files in the Finder, you are used to some of its quirks and advantages. The Finder, for example, assumes that you want to move a file when you drag its icon from one location on the same disk to another and that you want to copy (not move) a file when you drag its icon to another disk.

17. Performing Backups

On the other hand, when you use a command-line interface, you have to tell the operating system specifically what you want to do, and not make assumptions.

WARNING! *Do not attempt to copy a Classic application via the command line. Unix doesn't understand the traditional Mac way of separating the elements of an application into data and resource forks; thus the file will be corrupted. But document files can be easily copied this way.*

To copy your Documents folder to a backup drive, follow these steps:

1. Launch Terminal if it's not already open.

2. In the Terminal screen, type "sudo cp –R Documents /Volumes/ Backup" and press the Return key. The first time you type a **sudo** command, you'll be asked for your administrator password, because the command grants you Super User access (a sort of temporary root access); it allows you to perform basically any system command via the terminal. Such access will remain in effect for five minutes, after which you'll have to authenticate again to perform more functions.

NOTE: *In the previous command line,* **cp** *is the copy command.* **-R** *is a flag that stands for recursive, which means that you are copying a folder, not a file, named Documents. The name* **Backup** *in this case represents the name of your backup medium; you can use any name you want. Also bear in mind this command requires the presence of a folder or file named Documents. Chapter 20 covers the Unix command line in more detail.*

---

3. To copy additional folders, use the same commands, substituting the name of the folder you want to copy.

NOTE: *When you want to copy a file rather than a folder, do not use the recursive command. Specify the path or location of the file, such as* **Documents/filename** *for a file in your Documents folder.*

Related solutions:	Found on page:
A Short List of Popular Command-Line Features	410
Using Mac OS X's Command-Line FTP Software	413

17. Performing Backups

Chapter 18

Security and Mac OS X

In Brief

Don't get complacent about computer viruses. Even if you use your Mac at home or in a small business, you are not immune from catching a computer virus. You've no doubt read the reports of email and macro viruses and felt that perhaps they were threatening only to users of other computing platforms and that folks who use Macs don't have to fret over such things. After all, the majority platform has been the victim of literally thousands of computer viruses, and programs are updated frequently to combat the latest strains. Therefore, it's often believed that the pranksters who create such viruses have no time to do their dirty work with Macs.

Of course, as those who have worked on Macs for many years may realize, this just isn't so. There have been several dozen Mac viruses over the years, some just annoying, others causing crashes and possible loss of data.

NOTE: *I have seen two serious instances of mass virus infections on Macs. In the early 1990s, a virus called WDEF infected the desktops of Macs running System 6. More recently, in 1998 and 1999, many Macs were infected by the AutoStart virus, which even managed to turn up on a few commercial CDs—ones quickly withdrawn, I might add.*

Worse, the proliferation of macro viruses that affect Microsoft's Office software haven't totally left alone our favorite Mac computing platform. Although these viruses won't cause some of the dire effects that may be prevalent in the Windows variations, such things as damaged documents and problems with document templates have been legion.

NOTE: *Folks tend to be overconfident about Word macro viruses. I have seen them in documents from software publishers that ought to know better (names omitted to protect the guilty).*

In addition, the growth of high-speed or broadband Internet connections, such as cable modems and DSL, and the recent support for Internet-based file sharing, have made Macs increasingly vulnerable to direct attacks from the Internet.

An Overview of Mac Viruses

It's common for movies to portray the use of computer viruses as something that's good—a clever scheme to beat the bad guys and win the day, or even save the world, depending on a particular situation. From *Independence Day* to *The Net*, the underdog who is smart enough to be able to write a virus manages to snatch victory from the jaws of defeat.

But in our real world, the author of a computer virus isn't the hero, and the victims of such viruses are not the villains. They are folks like you and me who just want to compute in comfort, without having to concern ourselves with invasions to our privacy and to the sanctity of our personal computing experience.

Types of Computer Viruses

There are three basic types of computer viruses, but extensive variations exist in each group:

- *Virus*—The standard form of computer virus is a piece of code that's attached to a program or other file. When the file is opened, the virus is activated. It can, in turn, be spread to other files as part of its function. Such a virus may be a simple joke, putting up a silly message on the screen. Others may cause system crashes or damage files and perhaps the hard drive directory.

- *Trojan horse*—This is the worst sort of virus-related affliction, because, on the surface, it appears to be a file or program that has a useful, productive function. However, like the Trojan horse of old, embedded within that file is a malicious application that's ready to wreak havoc on your Mac once it's unleashed. A recent example was the Graphics Accelerator or SevenDust virus. It was sent as a system extension called Graphics Accelerator, which supposedly was designed to enhance video performance. The virus would actually erase files on a Mac's drive. Complicating matters is that a Graphics Accelerator extension was indeed provided with older versions of the Mac OS to support models equipped with ATI graphics chips. Later, that extension and its associated files were renamed with ATI prefixes, so they are easy to identify and there's less confusion.

- *Email virus*—In a sense, you could call this a Trojan horse as well. You receive a message from someone you know, containing the file you were expecting—except you weren't expecting any file. But, because you know the sender, you launch it anyway, and it does its dirty work. Usually the net effect is to copy an email address list and send similar files to other users. Most such viruses do their thing under the Windows platform. However, the infamous Mac.Simpsons@mm virus, a macro virus that exploited AppleScript, was indeed a Mac-only variation that affected Microsoft's Entourage and Outlook Express users. The best approach to take is never to assume that it's all right to open a file you didn't expect to receive. Write to the sender and confirm what the file is and why it was sent to you. Get the OK before launching. Whenever you send a file to someone, it's a good idea to explain what kind of file is being sent and its purpose, so there is no room for error or suspicion.

NOTE: *The prevalence of email viruses has resulted in some companies setting up firewalls and mail servers to strip the .exe extension from an email attachment before delivery. Should you have a problem sending an executable file to a Windows user via email, send it as a Zip file instead.*

Viruses and Mac OS X

No doubt it will be a while before virus authors find ways to infect Macs running Mac OS X, because of its Unix underpinnings. The fact that computer viruses first started under Unix should be sufficient cause to be concerned and wary. In addition, because you may still spend a reasonable portion of your day running programs in the Classic environment, the potential exists for infection of your older applications and files too. So, you can't escape the need to use an antivirus program to ensure that you're protected. Fortunately, the available Mac OS X antivirus applications will scan all the files on your computer so that you can see if they're infected.

In the "Immediate Solutions" section, I'll describe the popular virus-detection programs available for Mac users. I've concentrated on the ones available in Mac OS X form, or those for which Mac OS X support was promised when this book was written. If you are cautious in your personal computing habits, you should be able to get the maximum amount of protection with the least amount of interference.

Broadband Internet and Invaders from the Outside

Another possible threat stems from the fact that more Mac users have upgraded to high-speed Internet services. Whether it comes by way of a cable modem, DSL, or a wireless connection (such as Sprint Broadband Direct or satellite), the primary difference between this sort of connection and regular dial-up is that you spend far more time online. It's rare for someone to be connected via a modem 24/7, but with a broadband connection, you're almost always connected to the Internet, in the same way that you may be connected to a printer or shared Macs or Windows-based computers on a local network.

In addition, Macs can share files via the Internet, a feature of Mac OS 9 and Mac OS X. Such networking, combined with a high-speed connection, can, in effect, minimize or eliminate the difference between a local and Internet-based network. As a result, your Mac may be more vulnerable to another form of attack, from outsiders who try to take control of your computer via your TCP/IP-based Internet connection.

To protect yourself from such invasions, consider getting a firewall program. Such programs monitor Internet traffic and warn you or even block attempts to access your Mac from outside.

NOTE: *In effect, a firewall program puts an armed guard on your Mac, monitoring traffic coming to and from your computer and preventing unauthorized access.*

Even before Mac OS X–savvy applications are available to seek out viruses, you can continue to use your existing software and have it function just fine in the Classic user environment. To learn more about how older programs interact with Apple's new operating system, please check Chapter 15.

The "Immediate Solutions" section profiles four programs designed to protect your Mac against computer viruses and four programs that are designed to act as software firewalls. You should contact the individual publishers of these programs to see whether you need a special version to support Mac OS X.

18. Security and Mac OS X

Immediate Solutions

Choosing a Mac Virus-Detection Program

In the early days of the Mac platform, a number of commercial and shareware virus-detection programs were available. Over time, many of these programs were acquired by other publishers or discontinued. Shareware antivirus offerings included VirusDetective, which was continued until the early 1990s, when its author decided that payments were too small to continue. Here are the currently available commercial Mac virus-protection applications.

NOTE: *One of the early Mac antivirus programs, Rival, went abroad and was developed strictly for the European market for several years. However, the publisher's Web site was down when I checked it for this book.*

MicroMat's TechTool Pro

This is an all-in-one application (see Figure 18.1) that not only checks for Mac computer viruses, but also handles hardware and hard drive diagnosis. Here's a quick look at the basic feature set of TechTool Pro 3:

WARNING!   *Some features of this program will not work under the Mac OS X environment until an upgrade comes from the publisher. You can check your hard drive with TechTool Pro when booting from a Classic Mac OS or from the supplied CD startup disk. Or, you can use MicroMat's Mac OS X disk diagnostic application, Drive 10, which works strictly under Mac OS X.*

- *Hardware diagnostics*—Does the problem lie in the RAM, the hard drive, or the logic board? TechTool Pro runs your Mac through a full diagnostic to determine whether all the systems on your computer and its attached peripherals are functioning properly.

- *Hard drive diagnostics and repairs*—You can check a hard drive from Mac OS 9.x or after restarting from the supplied CD. This program can also optimize a hard drive, which may, in theory at least, speed up performance somewhat.

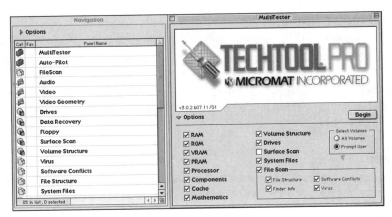

Figure 18.1   TechTool Pro performs a wide spectrum of analyses of your Mac.

NOTE: *MicroMat assured me that the latest updates to TechTool Pro 3 (3.0.5 as of this writing) would reliably analyze an HFS+ drive running Mac OS X when booted from a Classic OS or the CD. Volumes formatted in the UFS format aren't supported. If you have an older version of the program, contact the publisher about updates (any 3.x version can be updated free to a later 3.x version courtesy of a downloadable updater).*

- *Software conflicts*—Although this problem is less of an issue under Mac OS X, the consequences of application or system extension conflicts have been the bane of the Mac user's experiences for years. This program can check your installation for possible problems and report on the steps you should take to eliminate them.

- *Virus scans*—This powerful component of TechTool Pro scans your Mac for the presence of viruses. As with the competition, you can opt to perform scans in the background as you use your Mac, and at scheduled intervals for more comprehensive scans. TechTool Pro can repair or move an infected file or just leave it alone (your decision). To speed performance, you can configure the program to scan only files that have not been previously checked. You can also check for online updates to address program changes and newly discovered virus strains, but this process isn't done automatically.

NOTE: *The sole feature lacking in the virus-detection component of TechTool Pro that I examined for this book was the ability to check for the presence of Word or Excel macro viruses. If you work with a reasonable number of files created in those programs, you may want to look elsewhere for virus protection.*

18. Security and Mac OS X

Intego's VirusBarrier

The newest entrant to the antivirus application arena comes from the publishers of NetBarrier, a firewall program that will be discussed later in this chapter, and several security-based utilities. VirusBarrier has a particularly unique user interface that puts configuration panels in a drawer that can be opened and closed as needed, as shown in Figure 18.2.

NOTE: *Although I didn't have a chance to try a Mac OS X version of VirusBarrier in time to finish this book, the publisher assured me that the user interface and most or all of the features would run essentially the same in the Mac OS X native version.*

Here are the features of VirusBarrier that will help provide the maximum degree of virus protection:

- *Simple interface*—Unlike the other programs described in this chapter, the Classic Mac OS version of VirusBarrier consists of just one file—a control panel—where all features are activated. The other programs are an amalgam of applications, control panels, system extensions, and so on. This doesn't mean they are any less effective or more complex to use, but it's something you should consider when making your purchase decision.

- *Automatic repairs*—You can opt to have infected files repaired automatically by the program, a feature that matches the capabili-

Figure 18.2   Click a button to open a drawer that offers additional settings.

ties of the other contenders. A system log will report on such episodes, so you can see what was fixed and why and also if the file couldn't be fixed.

- *NetUpdate*—This feature allows the program to scan the Internet for program upgrades on a regular basis, or whenever you want to do a manual check. If an update is available, it'll be down-loaded automatically. Unlike other programs of this type, when new virus-detection capabilities are added, the control panel will sometimes (but not always) be updated, too.

- *Doesn't intrude on software installations*—Although it's best to disable an antivirus program before performing a software installation, VirusBarrier is designed to allow such processes to run without interfering.

- *Doesn't affect boot or system performance*—Because virus scans may slow your Mac's performance, VirusBarrier promises fully transparent operation, so you won't notice its presence unless a virus infection is found. My personal experience with the Classic version showed this claim to be largely realized on the G4 hardware on which I tried it.

Network Associates' Virex

One of the older Mac virus-detection programs, Virex (see Figure 18.3), has had a checkered history as far as having a steady manufacturer is concerned. It has gone through several software publishers, finally ending up in the hands of the McAfee division of Network Associates. This should not, of course, deter you from buying Virex; it continues to be developed and supported with regular program and detection string updaters. The version shipping at the time this book was printed was 7, fully native to Mac OS X.

Here are the basic features of Virex, based on the Classic version:

- *Drag-and-drop scanning and cleaning*—Just select a file, folder, or disk icon, and drag it to the Virex application icon, and the scanning process will commence in short order. Depending on the preferences you set in the application, you'll be able to see which files might be infected, or automatically repair them to the limits of the technology.

- *Advanced cleaning*—This feature essentially tries to remove the infection from a file and restore it to its normal condition. Once again, it's not a feature that differs materially from the competition.

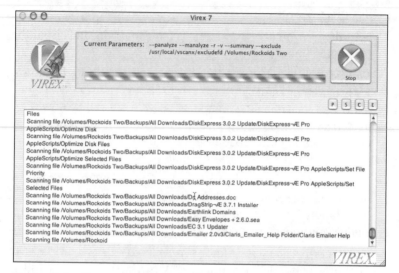

Figure 18.3   Virex continues to be updated to support newly discovered virus strains.

- *Checks for virus-like activities*—In addition to using detection strings to detect the presence of known virus strains, Virex can scan for what it considers to be virus-like activity. This way, Virex can help protect you against virus strains not already discovered.

NOTE: *Virex 7 was released without a big publicity flourish from its publisher and may be difficult to find at the company's Web site. The best site to check is the McAfee division, at* **www.mcafee.com**. *The home page should include links to available products and how to get a copy of the latest version.*

- *Automatic updates*—Virex has a NetUpdate feature that's supposed to check the publisher's Web site for the presence of program or detection-string updates. However, to be perfectly frank, I've not had great success in getting this feature to work with any consistency.

- *Command-line scanner*—If you want to get deeply involved with the Unix command line of Mac OS X, you can use the Terminal application to run on-demand scans or configure scheduled scanning runs.

- *Missing features*—Unfortunately, some of the features present in the Classic version of Virex are not part of the initial release of Virex 7. The most useful is background scanning, where the act of mounting a disk or launching a file causes Virex to check it for the presence of a virus. The scan-at-download feature, which checks files that you retrieve from the Internet or a network file share, also is not available, nor is a graphical interface for the scheduling operation. However, do not be surprised to see these features restored by the time you read this book.

Symantec's Norton AntiVirus

Once upon a time, the most popular Mac antivirus program was SAM, short for Symantec Anti-Virus Utilities for Macintosh. To keep the naming similar to the Windows version, the publisher reinvented the program as Norton AntiVirus. The version shipping when this book was printed, 7.0.2 (see Figure 18.4), runs fully native under Mac OS X.

The following is a brief list of the major features of Norton AntiVirus; you'll see that Symantec and Network Associates have added similar feature sets to their programs, leapfrogging one another as new versions appear. With the first release of a Mac OS X version, however, Symantec has not enabled certain features that are part of the Classic version:

- *Startup CD*—You can run Norton AntiVirus from its startup disk, which includes a bootable System Folder. This is the ultimate protection against a possible virus, because an infection can't contaminate a CD.

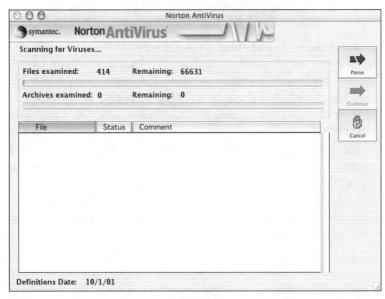

Figure 18.4   Norton AntiVirus in action, looking at my drive for potential virus infections.

18. Security and Mac OS X

NOTE: *As Apple releases new hardware, you'll need to order updated startup CDs for Symantec's utility products, so that they will start your Mac.*

- *Automatic repair of infected files*—This option is in the program's preferences dialog box and is on by default. The application will automatically attempt to repair any file that's infected. The downside to such a feature is that it's not always perfect, and the removal of the virus strain may also damage the file so that it's not usable. This is always a good argument for having recent backups of all your critical files.

- *Checks of suspicious files*—This feature appeared first in SAM, the predecessor to Norton AntiVirus. It lets the program check for system activities that may indicate the presence of a computer virus. Several levels of protection can be configured in the program's preferences. Keep in mind, however, that if made too robust, this feature can cause a number of annoying messages for tasks that really don't appear virus-like at all, such as expanding a compressed file that contains a system extension that is not infected.

- *Checks of compressed files*–Even though a virus in a compressed file cannot infect your Mac unless the file is opened, Norton AntiVirus gives you the added ounce of protection to scan the files anyway. The preferences dialog lists 10 common encoding or compression formats to scan, from BinHex to Unix GZip.

- *LiveUpdate*—This feature is shared with another Symantec program, Norton Utilities. As a result, it will seek out updates for both programs in a single operation. You can configure it to access the Internet regularly in search of the updates or only when you want. Unlike the Virex variation, this feature appears to work consistently.

- *Automatic warning of out-of-date preference files*—A common problem with virus-detection software is that many users do not upgrade their definitions. The result may make your computer vulnerable to virus infection by a strain that appeared after the last definitions update. Although LiveUpdate can help, it's nice to have a reminder that you should check for new definitions.

- *Missing in action*—As with Virex, certain features that were part and parcel of the Classic Mac OS version of Norton AntiVirus were not available in the first Mac OS X release. The most important of these features is background scanning: the ability to check files or disks when opened. The other key features that aren't available include scheduled scans, the ability to scan email for the presence of those pesky email viruses, plus a scan-at-download feature to check files retrieved from the Internet or a network. However, shortly before this book went to press, Symantec had announced a new version of Norton Anti-Virus that would include both background scanning and automatic email scans. This may be the version to which you'll want to upgrade.

Choosing Personal Firewall Software

With so many folks getting always-on Internet services, it stands to reason that there is a far greater vulnerability to potential invasions from the Internet. Although this would seem a fairly unlikely source of trouble, there have been some well-publicized instances of so-called *denial of service* attacks, where personal computers are commandeered by Internet vandals and used to flood popular Web sites with meaningless data, which prevents real access by visitors to those sites.

Until now, those problems haven't affected Macs, but that doesn't mean our preferred computing platform is immune. Although large companies often seek hardware solutions to such problems in the form of network routers or dedicated hardware-based firewalls, some relatively inexpensive Mac programs can offer good protection for homes and small-business users.

NOTE: *How bad is the risk? Well, many cable systems support equipment (including cable modems) that support the Data Over Cable Service Interface Specification (DOCSIS). Not only does it allow these services to use conventional cable modems you can buy at a computer or consumer electronics store, but also it encrypts the data flow from customers. This doesn't mean you are totally safe from Internet vandals, but it does reduce and usually eliminate the possibility that those who share your cable ISP's node can see your shared printers and disks. Vulnerability to denial of service attacks or similar invasions, however, still exists.*

Related solution:	*Found on page:*
Protecting Your Network from the Internet	193

Norton Personal Firewall

Open Door Networks, publisher of the Shareway IP software used by Apple Computer in Mac OS 9 to offer Internet-based file sharing, licensed its DoorStop software to Symantec. The result is Norton

Personal Firewall (see Figure 18.5), a Mac OS X–native firewall application that offers simple, solid protection against attacks from Internet vandals. You can configure several elements of protection, from Internet-based connections to your Mac, to FTP file transfers. The program displays a warning if an attempt is made to connect to your Mac via the Internet (I get several of these a day when I'm connected via cable modem), and it logs all access attempts.

NOTE: Norton Personal Firewall is also available in bundled form as Norton Internet Security. The package also includes Norton AntiVirus and Aladdin Systems's iClean; the latter is a program that can clear cache files, cookies, and other files you may want to discard from your Mac's hard drive.

Intego's NetBarrier

This program made Intego's reputation. NetBarrier (see Figure 18.6) shares a uniquely different interface with VirusBarrier. It lets you set several levels of protection, depending on the level to which you want to limit access to and from your Mac via the Internet.

Among the program's powerful features is the ability to protect against browser plug-ins and Java applets that may house hostile code. It also provides built-in protections against access of personal information on your Mac, such as passwords and credit card information.

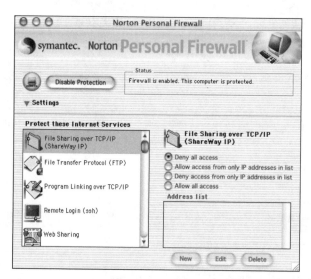

Figure 18.5   Norton Personal Firewall has flexible configuration options to ensure that you get the maximum level of protection against Net intruders.

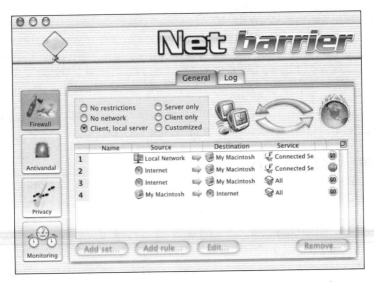

Figure 18.6   NetBarrier offers several levels of firewall protection.

Intego's ContentBarrier

The programs described so far will protect your Mac against outside Internet-based invasions or virus infections. Intego's ContentBarrier, on the other hand, is designed to monitor Internet access. It works for both home users and businesses, by allowing you to filter content that might be unacceptable to those using your Mac. Additionally, you can block Internet access at specific times of the day so that children don't waste time surfing rather than doing their homework assignments and household chores. It also helps increase employee productivity, because less time is wasted on unproductive pursuits.

ContentBarrier also logs Internet access, and settings can be password protected, so only those with access privileges can change program settings.

NOTE: *Another way to purchase these programs is in bundled form, courtesy of Internet Security Barrier, which includes all the features of ContentBarrier, NetBarrier, and VirusBarrier.*

Firewalk X

The final software option I'll mention, Firewalk X, doesn't have its own firewall capability. Instead, it harnesses the power of Mac OS X's built-in firewall capabilities, which are part of the Darwin core. Although it's possible for you to access these features via the command line, it's not necessary. This shareware application puts up a simple but sophisticated front-end to manage the firewall.

Like the commercial products, Firewalk X directs access to your Mac's ports and keep logs of attempts to penetrate your Mac's defenses. Setting up Firewalk X is quite easy, courtesy of its convenient setup assistant (see Figure 18.7), where you can select the level of protection you want.

As this book was written, Firewalk X cost just $12.00—well worth the huge degree of protection it provides.

Hardware Firewalls

Another route to firewall protection is hardware-based. Several Internet sharing hubs or switches work with your DSL or cable modem and distribute an ISP connection across your network. These products, from such companies as Asante, D-Link, MacSense, NetGear, and Proxim (formerly Farallon), and even the latest version of Apple's AirPort Base Station, include a feature called network address translation (NAT) firewall protection. With NAT activate, the IP numbers of the computers on your network are hidden, and thus outsiders cannot see them. This provides a high level of security.

Such routers offer other features, such as one or more ports for Ethernet hookups (Asante and Proxim have models with four ports, sufficient for most home office networks). Some even include a wireless capability, supporting the very same 802.11b protocol used by Apple's AirPort wireless networking system (which also includes NAT support in its latest software release).

TIP: *One way to test the resiliency of your firewall protection is to use a set of Web-based tools from Gibson Research called Shields Up. You can access the tools via **www.grc.com**. Although the company makes software primarily for the Windows platform, its Web-based firewall tests will function with the Classic Mac OS and Mac OS X.*

Figure 18.7   Firewalk X is a shareware firewall manager that lets you access hidden features of Mac OS X to protect your Mac from Internet vandals.

Chapter 19

Troubleshooting Mac OS X

In Brief

Personal computers are a far cry from appliances, despite what the manufactures may tell you. It's a normal part of the life of every personal computer owner to have a program suddenly quit or to find the entire computer frozen, totally unable to function. Such problems are not restricted to users of either Macs or Windows-based PCs. They are both quite capable of failing at unexpected moments, usually when you need to complete an important document and time is short. In fact, it has been said that if your everyday automobile had the same reliability as your computer, you could barely make it to the supermarket without brakes failing or the car stopping with neither rhyme nor reason.

Long-term experience on a personal computer is littered with system troubleshooting, reinstallations, and endless searches for program updates that address one problem or another. Beginning with Mac OS 9, Apple introduced a System Update control panel that was designed to periodically check the company's support Web site in search of necessary system updates. Even third-party publishers have gotten into the act. Programs from Intego, Network Associates, and Symantec have built-in features to seek out updates.

NOTE: Another solution to the software update dilemma is UpdateAgent X from Insider Software (**www.insidersoftware.com/**), which is designed to locate all the updates you need and make them available to you in a simple user interface.

Mac OS X promises to begin to liberate Mac users from regular diets of system-related troubles. Like Unix servers, which can run for days, weeks, or months (and sometimes years) without suffering breakdowns, the revolutionary new version of the Mac operating system is designed to be as resilient as possible to the trials and tribulations of daily computing.

Mac OS X's Crash-Resistant Features

Whether you surf the Internet, use heavy-duty graphics programs such as Adobe Photoshop or QuarkXPress, or use database software that must perform a lot of sorting and organizing, sometimes your Mac will be susceptible to problems. Here's a look at what Mac OS X has to offer to provide greater reliability:

- *Protected memory*—Every time you run a native application under Mac OS X, it gets its own memory partition, dynamically allocated by the operating system and walled off from other programs. Should that program quit or crash, the memory allocated to it is reallocated as part of the memory available to your Mac. You can continue to run your Mac safely without having to restart; try that under any previous version of the Mac OS without risking a serious crash. Although a Restart command is still available, now in the Apple menu, you will find yourself using Force Quit more often. Apple doesn't expect you to have to restart except when installing a new program or leaving Mac OS X to return to your Classic Mac OS.

NOTE: *As a matter of fact, shutdowns are no longer necessary with the newer Macs. You can use the Sleep command to have the Mac run in a super-low-power mode (using less power than a normal light bulb), ready to awaken in a second or two by a simple click of the mouse or by pressing any key on your keyboard.*

- *Advanced memory management*—Under previous versions of the Mac OS, an application received a specific portion of available memory. If this wasn't enough to run the program efficiently, you had to quit, open the Finder's Get Info window, and allocate more. In addition, if you didn't have enough free RAM to open a program, it would not run, or it would run so inefficiently that you risked poor performance, an out-of-memory error, or perhaps a system crash. Mac OS X dynamically allocates the memory a program needs and, if need be, provides virtual memory. Therefore, in theory, a program can never run out of memory.

NOTE: *Don't assume that a Unix-style virtual memory system is a panacea that has no downside. It's always better to have enough RAM to run a program—if the operating system has to use virtual memory instead, performance slows down and you'll see a spinning cursor when data has to be retrieved from your hard drive. Even though Apple recommends a minimum of 128MB of RAM for Mac OS X, having at least twice that amount delivers noticeably better performance. There's no free ride.*

- *Preemptive multitasking*—Can a superior way to manage multiple applications improve reliability? Very possibly. Some applications hog available processor time, making it difficult for other programs to run efficiently. Too many programs competing with one another can create the potential for a system crash. With Mac OS X, the operating system is the task or traffic manager, making performance better—sometimes much better—when multiple programs are performing complex tasks, such as downloading files, rendering a multimedia presentation, and printing at the same time.

NOTE: *One of the clever demonstrations Apple used to show how resilient Mac OS X is involves running a special application that repeatedly attempts to crash the operating system while a movie trailer continues to play flawlessly.*

Keep in mind, however, that although Mac OS X is resilient and reliable, this doesn't mean that your Mac will never crash, or that programs will never quit. As long as software is written by human beings, the potential for conflicts exists. In the Immediate Solutions section, I'll show you how to cope with common problems and how to get the most reliable performance from your Mac.

The Software Update Application

Beginning with Mac OS 9, Apple added a useful new feature, Software Update. Similar to some third-party applications that search for updates, such as the LiveUpdate utility that ships with Symantec's Mac utility programs, Norton AntiVirus, Norton Utilities, and Norton SystemWorks, Apple's utility checks the system-related files on your hard drive and seeks out updates at Apple's support sites on the Internet.

This utility continues in essentially the same form under Mac OS X (see Figure 19.1), but has migrated to the System Preferences application. When you activate this pane, just click the Update Now button to have Software Update check Apple's Web site for updates. If they're available, they'll be listed in a dialog box. Check the ones you want, click the Install button, and the program takes care of the rest, from downloading to installing. Depending on whether an update is system related or application related, you may have to restart your Mac for the changes to take effect.

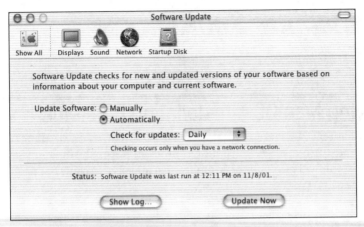

Figure 19.1   The Software Update pane from System Preferences will find
needed Mac OS X updates for you.

TIP: *It's a good idea to save a copy of the update installer. Right after an update has been downloaded and installed, while the System Update application is on your screen, click the Update menu, choose Save As, and select a location in the Save As dialog box for a copy of the update. That way you can easily access it in case of a system reinstallation and avoid a trip to the Internet to get it again.*

Immediate Solutions

Solving Mac OS X Installation Problems

In Chapter 2, I covered the simple installation process for Mac OS X. For most users, everything should proceed normally. In some situations, you will encounter problems, warnings, or errors that prevent the process from continuing.

The following is a list of potential problems and solutions:

- *The firmware isn't up-to-date.* Recent Macs have a small updatable boot ROM that's used to start your computer and perform small diagnostic checks (on older Macs, upgrading isn't possible). This firmware is updated from time to time to address hardware-related problems. If you receive a warning that the Mac OS X installation cannot proceed until you install the update, visit Apple's support Web site and see which updates apply to your model. The update site is located at **www.info.apple.com/support/downloads.html**.

- *The hard drive cannot be repaired.* At the very start of the installation process, the Installer examines the target volume (the one on which you're installing Mac OS X). Minor directory damage will be fixed before the installation starts. If the damage cannot be fixed, you'll see a prompt on your screen about the problem. If this happens, the installation will stop dead in its tracks. At this point, you can try other options to repair the drive. After you restart in your Classic Mac OS environment, you can try using the version of Disk First Aid that came with the Classic Mac OS or one of the hard-drive diagnostic programs described in Chapter 2. Should none of these remedies succeed, your remaining choice is to consider backing up your files and formatting the drive. Unless the drive has a hardware problem, that final drastic step ought to take care of the trouble and allow you to install Mac OS X.

- *The hard drive cannot be updated.* During the installation process, the Installer attempts to update the hard disk device driver. If the drive is already formatted with Apple's Drive Setup utility, this step should not present a problem. Drive Setup works with any ATA-based drive and many SCSI drives. But if you have a hard drive that didn't come from Apple, it's highly likely that the drive was formatted with a different program, such as FWB's Hard Disk ToolKit or LaCie's Silverlining. You only need to make sure that the program used is compatible with Mac OS X. Otherwise, you should update the drive with the right version of your disk-formatting program. In these two cases, the message can be ignored.

WARNING! *It's not a good idea to ignore messages about drive problems or to allow installation on a drive not formatted with a Mac OS X–compatible utility. The consequences can be serious—damage to your hard drive's directory and possible loss of data.*

- *Your Mac can't be restarted after installation fails.* When you run the Mac OS X Installer, it changes the Startup Disk selection so that it will boot from the new operating system. Should something happen to abort the installation, you need to change the setup manually. You can do so by starting your Mac with your Mac OS X CD. Just restart and hold down the C key to boot from the CD. Once you're running from the CD, the first installation screen will appear. Go to the Installer's application menu and choose Open Disk Utility. With Disk Utility launched, click the name of your target volume, and then click the Repair button. Let Disk Utility examine your Mac's hard drive for disk-related problems. If you get a clean bill of health or any drive problems are fixed, go ahead and reinstall Mac OS X. Should that installation fail, restart with your Mac OS 9.x CD, again holding down the C key. Locate the Startup Disk control panel (in the Utilities folder) and select your Classic Mac OS System Folder to restart your computer. At this point, you should consider backing up and reformatting your Mac's hard drive before attempting a new installation.

NOTE: *I am assuming that before you began the installation, you verified that your Mac is compatible with Mac OS X and that it has the right amount of memory and storage space. Although it is possible to install Mac OS X on a non-supported model, it's definitely not something I'd recommend doing unless the manufacturer of a third-party peripheral (such as a processor upgrade card) is willing to provide support in case of problems. Apple will not provide any help if you install Mac OS X on one of the unsupported models.*

- *You can't log in.* This is not as difficult as it may seem at first glance. Being a Unix-based operating system, Mac OS X expects you to enter the correct username and password unless the option to bypass the login panel is left selected in the Login pane of the System Preferences Application (this is the system default). If the problem affects an individual user of your Mac, you can log in as administrator, open the Users System Preferences panel, click the Password tab, and change the user's password. Should you be unable to access the administrator's account, restart with your Mac OS X CD by holding down the C key. When the Installer launches, go to the Installer's application menu and choose Reset Password. In the Password Reset application window, click the drive for which you want to reset the password, and then choose the name of the user whose password you want to reset from the pop-up menu. Type the new password in the first text field, and then verify it in the second. Click Save to store the new password and then quit the application. You'll be returned to the Installer application, where you can restart by quitting Installer and clicking the Restart button in the "Are you sure?" prompt. When you reboot your Mac, the new password should be in effect.

NOTE: *It's not uncommon for someone to activate the Caps Lock key by error, which means that the password would be typed in all caps. Look at the Caps Lock light on the keyboard to be sure when you're typing or creating a password.*

Related solution:	*Found on page:*
Installing Mac OS X	30

Solving System Crashes and Freezes

You may have hoped that Mac OS X would represent salvation from constant system crashes, but in the real world, it doesn't work that way. From time to time, you will encounter programs that behave as badly as they did under Classic system versions, but you'll be able to exit far more safely under Mac OS X.

The following sections address some common problems and solutions.

The Application Won't Quit

Whether the Quit command is in its accustomed place in the application menu or in the File menu, as in Mac OS versions of old, you've hit a blank wall. The application won't quit. It seems to be active, and you may even be able to open, edit, and save documents, but you cannot quit the program.

The solution is the Mac OS Force Quit feature, done as follows:

1. Choose Force Quit from the Apple menu or press Command+Option+Escape.

2. On the Force Quit Applications dialog box that appears (see Figure 19.2), scroll to the application you want to quit.

NOTE: *The new Force Quit feature, with its ability to selectively choose any open application, is not unique to Mac OS X. Even Windows works this way.*

---

3. Click Force Quit. The selected application will proceed to quit (well, usually).

After the application is forced to quit, you can continue to use your Mac in the normal fashion. Mac OS X's protected memory allows programs to crash or be forced to quit without affecting system stability. Now you can try running the application again and see if it works all right. If it still misbehaves, you should contact the publisher for technical assistance.

NOTE: *On some rare occasions, you may need to force quit an application twice before the action "takes." Such are the vagaries of software bugs even with an industrial-strength operating system.*

WARNING! *If a Classic application freezes, it's best to force quit the Classic environment instead, because it will be unstable otherwise. Classic applications do not take advantage of Mac OS X's robust system protection features. When you launch your next Classic application, Classic will come along for the ride. If you have open documents from a Classic application, however, you'll want to close those applications first before attempting to force quit Classic. Otherwise, you'll lose any unsaved changes to those documents.*

Figure 19.2   You can force quit one or more applications when this screen appears.

Applications Refuse to Launch

If the problem you encounter involves just a single application, try launching it again. If that doesn't work, you might need to reinstall the application.

If all your applications fail to run, however, restart your Mac and try again. Usually the restart will fix the problem. If the problems persist, contact the publisher of the software updates for Mac OS X.

NOTE: *If a number of applications that are supposed to be compatible with Mac OS X fail to launch, you should consider reinstalling Mac OS X. You can do this without losing your existing system settings or installed documents and software. However, you will have to reinstall updates as well (which is why I suggest you save all the updates you receive from Apple via the Software Update preference panel, as described earlier in this chapter).*

The Classic Environment Fails to Run

Do you have Mac OS 9.1 or later installed? The Classic feature simply doesn't support any earlier version of the Mac OS. In addition, many third-party system enhancements won't run in this setting. The best way to run a Classic System Folder is to configure it to be lean and mean. I cover the subject in more detail in Chapter 15.

NOTE: *The Classic environment works best with Mac OS 9.2.1 or later (9.2.2 was the version shipping at the time this book was written). The CDs that shipped with Apple's Mac OS X 10.1 update included the former. In addition to offering better performance, improved boot time, and improved stability, some of the Classic quirks (such as the missing-cursor symptom) are eliminated.*

If setting up an Apple-only System Folder fails to resolve the startup problem, consider reinstalling your Classic Mac OS using the original system CD that came with Mac OS X (the most recent full Installer) or your Mac. If you have applied a system update, you'll need to do a clean installation (click Option on the first Installer screen), and then apply any system updates you've received.

NOTE: *When you do a clean installation of your Classic Mac OS, you'll also have to transfer your system settings (for your ISP and Internet software) and third-party software from your older or previous System Folder to your newly installed System Folder.*

Related solution:	Found on page:
Getting Reliable Performance from Classic Applications	312

Solving Network Access Failure

Although Mac OS X has enhanced networking capability, that doesn't mean everything will work perfectly all the time. Here are some ways to handle common network problems:

- *Settings don't change.* You do not have to restart your Mac whenever you switch network configurations, but doing so doesn't hurt. In addition, you may want to redo the settings in the Network pane of the System Preferences application, just in case you missed something the first time out. Chapter 8 has more information on this subject.

- *Networked Macs and printers are not available.* Reopen your Network pane and make sure AppleTalk is turned on and you've given your Mac a name that's unique on your network. If everything is properly configured, check your network cables and hub configuration. Also make sure the other Macs on the network can recognize your Mac or other devices on the network. If other Macs encounter similar problems, complete network troubleshooting is in order. For a large system, you should contact your network administrator for further assistance.

- *Windows networking software doesn't run.* If you're using such programs as Thursby Systems' DAVE or MacSOHO, you should contact the publisher directly about support for Mac OS X.

Related solution:	Found on page:
Correcting Network Access Problems	192

Login Window Shakes

If you enter a username and password and the window shakes when you try to log in, it means the name or password you entered is not correct. The solution is to reenter the login information and make sure each keystroke is accurate. If the symptom happens with another user, you may need to reset his or her password.

Here's how to do it:

1. Login under your Administrator's account.
2. Launch System Preferences, and then open the Users pane.

19. Troubleshooting Mac OS X

3. If it's closed, click the padlock icon and enter your administrator username and password.

4. Click the name of the user whose password you want to change, click the Edit User button and, in the next screen, click the Password tab. The dialog shown in Figure 19.3 appears.

5. Enter the new password, and then close the window to store the settings.

6. Choose Quit from the System Preferences Application menu, or press Command+Q.

7. If necessary, log out again and log in under that user's new password.

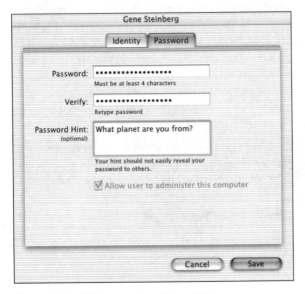

Figure 19.3   Edit a user's password here.

Desktop Folder Contents Aren't Visible Under Mac OS 9.x

You place a file or folder on Mac OS X's desktop, but when you reboot under Mac OS 9.x, the item is not there. What's wrong?

The answer is that the desktops for the two operating systems are totally separate. The contents of one are not mirrored on the other.

If you've installed Mac OS X on the same volume as Mac OS 9.1, you'll find a workable solution. There's an alias on your Mac's desktop labeled Desktop (Mac OS 9). When you open that folder, you'll see a folder that contains all of your Classic Mac OS desktop items. If the desktop is on another drive, just access that drive from a Finder window, and you'll see a folder labeled Desktop that contains the items you want.

Mac OS X Can't Boot after You Deleted a File by Mistake

When you run your Mac under Mac OS 9, by default you'll see the following files at the top or root level of the hard drive on which Mac OS X is installed (plus any additional files or folders you've placed on the top level of the drive):

- Applications
- Applications (Mac OS 9)
- Library
- mach
- mach.sym
- mach_kernel
- System
- System Folder
- Users

If you delete something from the Mac OS X Applications folder, that application is no longer available. In addition, deleting a user's folder removes that user from the system. Do not attempt to remove any of the files labeled *mach,* or the files in the folder labeled *Library* or *System,* because removal will probably keep Mac OS X from running. Should the worst happen, you will have to run your Mac OS X Installer CD to reinstall the system. The regular installation will preserve your system-related settings.

Performing a Clean Installation of Mac OS X Without Reformatting

The standard installation of Mac OS X is pretty much the equivalent of the Easy Install procedure under previous versions of the Mac OS. Your core system components and bundled programs will be reinstalled, but system-related settings and user accounts won't be touched. If reinstalling in that fashion doesn't resolve your problem with Mac OS X, there's yet another way to accomplish this mission; it requires a clean installation, which means you must remove all vestiges of Mac OS X.

NOTE: *If you have updated Mac OS X to a later revision since the original installation, doing a simple installation is no longer possible. Such an attempt will either fail or result in a possible failure to run properly even if the installation "takes." Your option is to either erase the partition or follow the steps I'm going to outline to perform a clean installation without taking such a drastic step.*

Unfortunately, some of the files included with the operating system are hidden or "invisible," meaning they are present but not visible under Mac OS 9.

WARNING!   The installation method I'm describing here will remove all of your Mac OS X applications and settings. In effect, you're starting from scratch, so you'll need to follow the steps in Chapters 2 and 3 to install and set up Mac OS X all over again.

NOTE: *You will need a program that can view invisible files. Although you can do that in Sherlock, you have to know which files to search for, and find the files one at a time. It's much faster to have all the files displayed at once. One promising option is File Buddy, which you can use to view and edit invisible files. You can get a copy from the publisher's Web site at* **www.skytag.com**. *Another program, not easily obtainable, is DeskZap, a shareware application from the early 1990s that remains compatible with Mac OS 9.2.2.*

Here's how to accomplish this "impossible" task:

1. Assuming you're using File Buddy, launch the application after rebooting under Mac OS 9.x.

WARNING!   Do not try doing any of this while booted under Mac OS X. At the least, you won't be able to trash the files. At worst, you risk a nasty system crash if you attempt to remove files that Mac OS X needs to run.

2. Choose Find Invisible Files from the program's Cleaning menu. A screen like the one shown in Figure 19.4 appears.

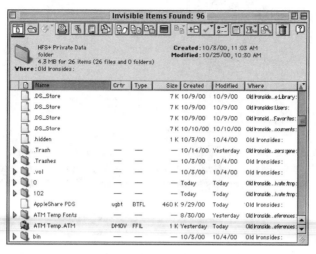

Figure 19.4   File Buddy can display invisible files on your Mac. Use it
with care.

WARNING!   *Make sure you remove only the folders I've listed in this chapter. Removing
the wrong item may affect other aspects of the way your Mac functions. Depending on
the revision level of Mac OS X, some of these items may no longer be present.*

3. Select the following items, and click the Trash icon in the File
   Buddy window:

   - .DS_Store

   - .hidden

   - .Trashies

   - .vol

   - bin

   - cores

   - dev

   - Developer

   - etc

   - Network

   - private

   - sbin

   - usr

   - vmr

   - Volumes

4. With the files removed, quit File Buddy. Then, trash the following items on the top or root level of your hard drive:

NOTE: *If you have installed any Unix services that weren't part of the original installation, they will also have to be reinstalled after your new installation of Mac OS X.*

- Applications

WARNING! *When you trash this folder, all of your installed applications go with it, unless they are located in a Classic Mac OS folder. That means you'll have to reinstall these programs. The safest approach is to place this folder on your Classic Mac OS's desktop.*

- Library
- mach
- mach.sym
- mach_kernel

NOTE: *In some installations of Mac OS X, the previous file might be hidden. Regardless, it needs to be deleted.*

- System

WARNING! *To preserve your personal user settings and files, you should place the Users folder on the desktop so that you can retrieve information from it after the new system is installed. Otherwise, delete it.*

5. Empty the trash. This process may take a little time, because lots of files are being removed.

6. Restart with your Mac OS X CD and follow the instructions in Chapters 2 and 3 to install and configure the new operating system.

Related solutions:	Found on page:
Installing Mac OS X	30
Setting System preferences Under Mac OS X	44

Solving Other Common Mac OS X Problems

Here are other problems you might encounter with Mac OS X. They usually have solutions, but some may not be as easy as you'd prefer:

- *Your Mac experiences kernel panic.* White-on-black text splashes on the top left of your Mac's desktop. What's wrong? This is due to a system-level crash of some sort, and you've been exposed to the command line. Press the R key to restart; you may need to do it a second time. Usually things will be all right after restart. If not, you'll need to force a restart, using the appropriate reset key on your Mac (signified by a back arrow icon).

- *The screen remains dark when booting from the Installer CD.* Mac OS X only supports graphics cards and chips from ATI Technologies, IX Micro, and NVIDIA. If you're using a graphics card from a company such as Formac, contact the manufacturer directly about a Mac OS X–compatible version.

NOTE: *If you are using a Voodoo graphic card from 3dfx Interactive, you may be out of luck. With the departure of the company after selling its assets to rival NVIDIA, the likelihood that driver updates will be produced are very slim, although several independent developers were working on drivers when this book was written. Fortunately, Mac OS X–compatible graphics cards are not terribly expensive. The ATI Radeon 7000, which outdoes the fastest Voodoo card in virtually all respects, was selling for less than $129 when this book was written.*

- *The printer isn't recognized.* Mac OS X should recognize most laser printers. However, ink jet printers and some USB-based laser printers require special drivers to work. Drivers for some Canon, Epson, HP, and Lexmark ink jets are provided with Mac OS X. You'll need to contact the manufacturer about the availability of driver updates for unsupported models. If none are available, the devices will work only for Classic applications.

- *The scanner doesn't scan.* This issue is the same as the printer not being recognized. It is up to the manufacturer to deliver a device driver that will function. If you cannot locate a Mac OS X–compatible version for a specific make and model, you should see if the software for a similar product in the manufacturer's line runs. Quite often, scanner drivers recognize a number of different models.

> **TIP:** *One possible solution if your scanner maker doesn't have a Mac OS X driver is a shareware program, VueScan, from Hamrick Software (**www.hamrick.com**). This nifty application comes in versions for the Classic Mac OS, Mac OS X, Windows, and even Linux, and supports dozens of flatbed and slide scanners from all the major makers, such as Agfa, Epson, HP, Microtek, and Umax.*

- *You cannot burn a CD.* Mac OS X supports a number of third-party FireWire and USB CD burners in addition to Apple's own drives. This support allows you to use the Finder-level CD burning feature with a number of mechanisms. But a number of drives aren't supported (and this is especially true for SCSI-based CD burners), in which case, you'll have to ask the manufacturer of the product about Mac OS X–savvy software. Or, just reboot under your Classic Mac OS.

> **TIP:** *As of the time this book was written, Roxio, publisher of Toast, had released Toast 5.1 for Mac OS X. This product will recognize most any CD or DVD burner, including Apple's.*

- *You can't use a digital camera.* Apple's Image Capture application supports a wide variety of cameras from most major makers. If your device isn't supported, check with the manufacturer about what options you might have with regard to image capture software.

- *Input device features are not recognized.* Mac OS X has built-in support for the second button and the scroll wheel on some input devices, but others require special software. You'll need to contact the publisher about compatibility issues.

- *Not all drives are recognized.* Mac OS X provides standard support for many popular removable and fixed storage devices, such as Imation and Iomega drives and devices from LaCie, Maxtor, and SmartDisk. If the product you want to use won't run, the manufacturer is your best resource for assistance.

> **NOTE:** *If your storage device is connected courtesy of a SCSI adapter card, contact the maker of the card about Mac OS X support. Not all products will run, and some may require the installation of a new ROM chip to function properly.*

- *You can't install Classic applications.* If you get a message that you don't have the proper access privileges for such an installation, you will need to log in as administrator of your Mac to perform such an installation. Another route is to restart under your Classic Mac OS.

- *The Dock freezes.* On occasion, the Dock may fail to work, or open applications will not have the telltale arrow beneath their icon. Unfortunately, the Dock isn't recognized in the Force Quit window, so you can't quit it that way. The solution is to locate the ProcessViewer application in the Utilities folder. With ProcessViewer launched (see Figure 19.5), locate and select Dock. Now choose Quit Process from the Processes menu, and then choose Quit in the Quit Process dialog box. Within seconds, the Dock will disappear and relaunch itself, after which it should run normally. If it doesn't, restart your Mac.

- *You can't delete a file.* When you try to empty the trash, you get a message that the trash is in use, or that you don't have permission to zap a file. If this happens, locate the Terminal application in the Utilities folder and launch it. With Terminal open, type "sudo rm –rf .Trash" and press Return. Enter your administrator's password and press Return again. All the files in the Trash will be discarded (although you may have to open and close a Trash window to see the empty icon).

WARNING! *As with any Terminal action, there's no opting out. When you engage a command, the Unix core of Mac OS X will do the deed—and that, as they say, is that. Also, be sure to allow a short time for all files to be deleted before quitting Terminal; otherwise some files may still be there when you recheck the Trash.*

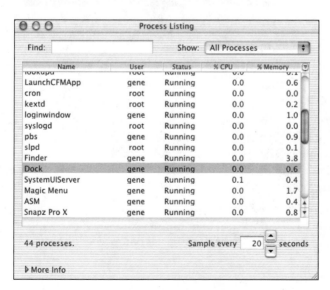

Figure 19.5   Use ProcessViewer to quit a system process that isn't recognized by the Force Quit function, such as the Dock.

Performing System-Level Disk Diagnostics

The arrival of Mac OS X brings with it a tremendous number of changes in the way your Mac runs. Although some functionality will no doubt change further as Mac OS X continues to be developed, there will be some constants, such as the underlying Unix core, which are just waiting to be explored by power users who want to see what makes the new system tick.

Hard-disk management is done with a new, combined application called Disk Utility, found in the Utilities folder. It combines Disk First Aid and Drive Setup. Unfortunately, the version offered with Mac OS X cannot examine or repair damage to your startup drive. Although your drives are checked every time you boot your Mac, as an ounce of prevention, you can also perform a disk diagnostic by rebooting with your Mac OS X CD and accessing Disk Utility from the Installer's application menu. If you don't have your system CD readily at hand, here's another alternative—a disk-checking process that allows you to explore the depths of Mac OS X and have your Mac run in a fashion you never expected.

Here's what to do:

NOTE: *There's no way to provide illustrations of this process with the standard screen shot. The information provided, however, should be clear enough. Don't be alarmed by what you see; this is the way Mac OS X is designed. Just bear in mind that doing a disk repair from the command line is no more effective than running Disk Utility on a drive. However, it is a useful exercise if you want to explore the depths of Mac OS X.*

---

1. Restart your Mac.

2. As soon as the restart process begins, press Command+S. What you see is only vaguely reminiscent of the DOS prompt accessed under Microsoft Windows. You see a true Unix command line, and if you thought DOS looked different, it doesn't hold a candle to what you see here.

3. With the command line displayed, a mélange of text appears. At the bottom of the text is a **localhost#** prompt. Type the following command (and don't forget the space before the hyphen [-]):

   ```
   fsck -y
   ```

4. Press Return. Over the next minute or two, a series of status messages appear that are not dissimilar from those you'd see in

Disk First Aid. These messages indicate the progress of the disk check. You'll also see an indication that the disk is being repaired, if this is necessary. When the disk check is finished, the **localhost#** prompt returns.

5. It's time to restart and return to the comfort of the familiar Aqua interface. Type the following:

```
reboot
```

6. Press Return. The screen darkens, and the Mac's startup chord sounds. Then the familiar Mac OS X startup screen appears.

NOTE: *I remember a line that Sean Connery uttered in one of the early James Bond movies when he was shown something unexpected during one of his save-the-world trips: "Shocking."*

Setting Root Access

Some Mac OS X installations require that you access the root or top level of your system under the Terminal application. Usually the administrator's password is sufficient to gain this access, but the password will be rejected unless you enable this feature.

To solve this problem, follow these steps:

1. Go to the Utilities folder and launch the NetInfo Manager application (see Figure 19.6).

2. Go to the Domain menu, choose Security, and select Authenticate from the submenu.

3. In the password prompt, enter the administrator's username and password and then click OK.

4. With access gained, return to the Security command in the Domain menu and choose Enable Root User from the submenu.

5. Enter the password for the root user in the password prompt and then reenter it when requested. When it's entered, root access will be enabled or reset for your Mac, and you'll be able to use the full scope of available administration tools.

WARNING! *Some Unix mavens say enabling root access presents a security risk, so use this process only as a last resort.*

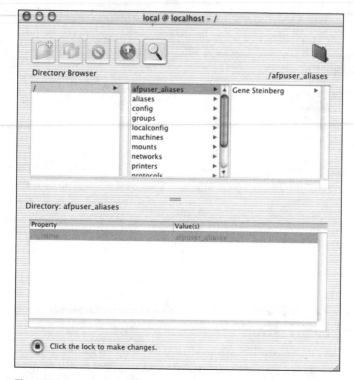

Figure 19.6   The NetInfo Manager is a useful network administrator's tool.

Monitoring System Use to Check for Conflicts

Although Mac OS X may is an extremely robust operating system, it isn't perfect, and many applications are less so. From time to time you'll need to examine how your Mac is running to help a software publisher find the source of a conflict.

Here's a way to see how programs are using system and memory resources, using the Terminal application:

1. Go to the Utilities folder and launch Terminal.

2. With Terminal open, type the command "top" and press the Return key. You'll see an interactive display showing how

resources may be using CPU or RAM on your Mac (see Figure 19.7). This information can help a software publisher see if there's the potential for trouble.

3. Launch Console, also located in the Utilities folder. This program will display a log of system activities (see Figure 19.8) that a publisher can use to trace the possible cause of a crash or other performance problem. The log can be saved or printed for later review.

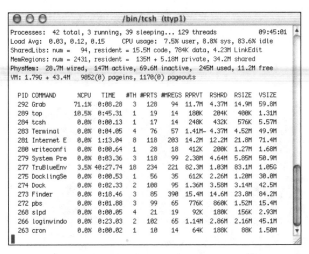

Figure 19.7   Terminal is used to access Mac OS X's Unix core directly.

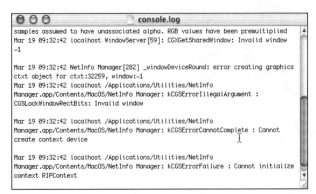

Figure 19.8   Console logs system operations and is a useful tool to diagnose software conflicts.

TIP: Like other Unix-based operating systems, Mac OS X is designed to perform system maintenance and update processes between 3:00 A.M. and 5:00 A.M. each day. The process includes updating and cleaning out system database and log files. If your Mac isn't running at that hour, you may find that performance dips over time, or the logs become huge. One solution to this dilemma is a freeware application, MacJanitor, which can manually run all those maintenance processes. You can download a copy from the author's Web site at **http:/ /personalpages.tds.net/~brian_hill**. The author assures us that Mac OS X, through version 10.1.1, still performs these basic maintenance operations.

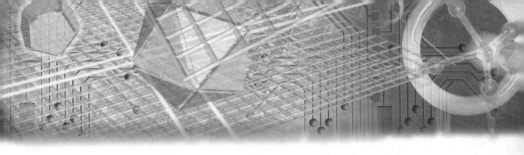

Part IV

Taking Mac OS X Online

Chapter 20

A Fast Introduction to Mac OS X's Unix Environment

In Brief

Deep within the bowels of Mac OS X exists what some might regard as another universe. To enter this Twilight Zone of the operating system, you need only launch a simple application and enter a few text-based commands.

NOTE: *I'd like to give special thanks to my friend, colleague, and spirited technical editor, Pieter Paulson, for his immense help in writing this chapter.*

So far in this book, you've seen a glimmer of this strange new world, as I've shown you command line solutions to a few vexing problems with Mac OS X. For the most part, however, access to Darwin, the Unix core of Mac OS X, is optional. Apple includes a rich set of graphical tools that you can use to access many of the features you need to configure and manage your Mac. In addition, Unix mavens the world over have been toiling day and night to provide pretty Aqua front ends to hidden features, such as BrickHouse and Firewalk X, two utilities that can harness the power of Unix's built-in firewall.

Although previous versions of the Mac OS have limited command line excursions to such utilities as ResEdit, the Terminal application (see Figure 20.1) located in the Utilities folder is far more powerful and encompassing. Terminal gives anyone with administrative access to a Mac direct control of the command line interface and the ability to harness the power of Unix to move files, manage services, and tell the computer how to function.

NOTE: *Even if you don't have administrator's access, you'll be able to do some things in Terminal, but you will be limited to commands that encompass your limited access level.*

When you first launch Terminal, you may think for a moment that you've entered the world of that other command-line operating system, DOS. No, you are seeing Unix in all its glory. With Terminal open, you'll see your username followed by a percent sign (%). This is the first stop on your voyage into the world of the command-line interface (CLI). If you've lived your life in the graphical user interface world, a CLI takes some getting used to. More to the point, it is far less forgiving than the safe, graphical world Aqua provides. When you engage a command, there will be no turning back—no prompt giving

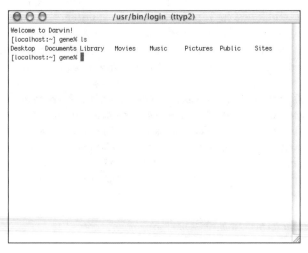

Figure 20.1   Apple's Terminal application is your gateway to the world of Unix.

you the chance to opt out. So, until you learn the lay of the land, proceed with caution.

When you get used to typing a command rather than pointing and clicking, you may find that the using the CLI is far faster for some functions. However, it requires a lot more attention to detail, because every keystroke you type is a literal request to do something.

Looking at the Nuts and Bolts of Darwin

Terminal is a shell interface. A shell program offers a set of utilities and commands that let you write executable scripts to automate certain tasks, much like AppleScript. Shells also act as the buffer between you and the bare operating system, making your life a bit easier.

When you launch Terminal, you access the tcsh shell program. This is one of the more popular shell programs and is a good choice for most users. If you're experienced in the Unix environment, you'll be pleased to know that such shells as zsh, csh, bash, and plain old sh are also available in Mac OS X. Each of these shells has its fans and detractors, but a description of the plusses and minuses of these programs is way beyond the scope of this book. If you are interested in exploring the Unix environment in more detail, you should read a library reference work on Unix.

The first thing you'll see in Terminal is the ubiquitous % that indicates you are running tcsh. From this prompt, you can type in the first command. We'll start with a command that lets you examine the contents your personal Users file and folder directory: **ls**.

WARNING!   *When I say that Unix is literal minded, I'm very serious. You need to be careful when you type commands and filenames, because every character must be accurate. Unix is also case sensitive. An extreme example of the consequences of a mistake was Apple's original release of iTunes 2. A basic syntax error resulted in the loss of data from a small number of hard drives belonging to folks who installed the software. Fortunately, Apple realized its mistake and released a fixed installer, and also provided help (and sometimes reimbursement for drive recovery) to folks who lost data. However, it's just as easy for you to wipe out the contents of your drive if you do the wrong thing, so the watchwords are "be careful."*

When you have typed "ls-", press the Return key to execute the command. Looking at the results, you should see a list of all the files and folders in the current directory.

OK, that's a good start. Now, to take things a bit further, perhaps you'd like to see a list of all the files, their security settings, and such interesting data as file size and commercial and modification dates. To do so, add the **–l** switch or modifier to the **ls** command, just as we did in Figure 20.2.

Just type "ls –l" and press Return. You should now see an expanded list showing the number of files in each folder.

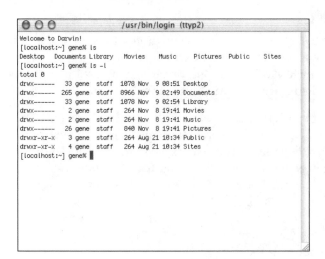

Figure 20.2   A simple Unix command, in this case **ls -l**, delivers this long folder listing.

TIP: To repeat the command you just activated, press the up arrow so that **ls –l** appears once again at the command prompt, and press Return. The tcsh shell is smart, and it retains a history of most or all of the commands you've entered since you began your Terminal session (the number depends on its configuration). In addition, you can save the session as a text file for later access if you want to review what you did.

By using the up and down arrows, you can scroll back and forth through all the commands you've used. This is a very useful feature if you've entered a particularly long and complex command and you'd like to use it again. It's also helpful in the event you made a mistake and want to fix the error rather than repeat the command. With all the modifications, some Unix commands can be long and complex; an easy fix is often the best way to proceed.

Introducing the Autocomplete Feature

In addition, the tcsh shell offers a really nice feature (also present in some of the other Unix shells) known as *Autocomplete*. This feature—reminiscent of the one you find in such applications as Microsoft Entourage, Internet Explorer, and Apple's Mail—lets you simply type in the first few letters of a filename or folder name or directory path and press Tab; Autocomplete then attempts to fill in the rest of the name. If two or more names match the letters you've typed, Autocomplete fills in the remaining letters to the point where the different versions diverge; then it beeps.

Here's an example: Suppose I want to go to a directory that contains the files for my latest book. I type something like "cd /Users/gene/Ro" and then press the Tab key. The tcsh shell fills in the remaining characters so that I see **cd /Users/gene/Rockoids**. As soon as I press Return, I'm taken to the proper directory. On the other hand, if more than one file or folder name begins with *Ro* in my home directory (such as Rockoids and Rockoids2_the_coming_of_the_protectors), pressing Tab makes Autocomplete fill in everything up to *Rockoids* and then beep to let me know it has found two or more files or folders that match my criteria.

NOTE: See anything strange here? Unix doesn't believe in word spaces. If you need one in a file or directory name, use an underscore instead, just as I've done here.

What do I do next? To go to the Rockoids2_the_coming_of_the_ protectors directory, I type "2" so that the names are no longer ambiguous, and then press Tab again. Autocomplete shows **cd /Users/ gene/Rockoids2_the_coming_of_the_protectors**, and I can press Return to jump to that directory.

Running Software from the Command Line

You are no doubt accustomed to simply double-clicking on a document or application to launch it. In contrast, running programs from the command line can be a bit of a trick if you've never used a CLI before. When you type a command name and press Return, Unix searches the directories specified in its path to see if they contain a file whose name matches what you typed in. If it finds such a file, it will launch the application.

However, Unix doesn't search the directory you are currently in, and thus it is common for users to mistakenly launch or execute the wrong application. To launch a file in the directory you are currently in, you can preface the command with a period followed by a slash (*./*) to force Unix to execute only files in the local directory; or, you can preface the filename with the whole path. For example, to launch the setup or installation program for a game you downloaded, you would switch to the directory that holds the file using a command similar to **cd /Users/gene/downloads/reallycoolgame**.

NOTE: *Don't forget to press Return each time you want to engage a command. Also, don't use the period at the end of the sentence. It's just there in the interests of good grammar (otherwise my publisher's copy editors would object).*

Once you're in that directory, you could use the command **.*/setup*** or **/Users/gene/downloads/reallycoolgame/setup** to execute the setup utility.

WARNING!   Most experienced Unix users prefer to use the full path when executing applications rather than the ./ shortcut, because doing so is more reliable and less prone to error. In addition, you will sometimes find that you cannot execute a file even if you are the owner and have full control of it. The problem is that you have not set the permissions on the file to allow execution. To fix this situation, use the chmod command to set the execute rights. The full command is chmod +x followed by the filename.

Backing Up Files and Folders

It is possible to back up files via the Unix command line, using the copy and move commands mentioned in the "Immediate Solutions" portion of this chapter. But this process has limitations. For one thing, many Mac files have two parts—a data fork and a resource—but Unix doesn't recognize the latter. So, if you copy a file via the command line using the **cp** (Copy) or **mv** (Move) command, you'll end up with a file that is not quite the sum of its parts.

This result presents no problem if you're just copying regular document files or Mac OS X native applications. However, if you need to copy a Classic application or file related to your Classic system software, you are best advised to use the Finder and let it do its thing.

Suggested Reading

If you're curious about learning more details of Mac OS X's Unix environment, you'll want to check this material for further information:

- To learn more about the tcsh shell, point your browser to **www.cnr.berkeley.edu/~casterln/tcsh/The_commandline_editor.html**.

- If you enjoyed trying the Terminal tips listed here, you'll find additional information at **http://homepage.mac.com/x_freedom/tips/terminal.html**.

Immediate Solutions

A Short List of Popular Command-Line Features

To further acclimate you to Mac OS X's Unix environment, here are some common and very useful commands and the functions they perform. To make them easier to use, I've grouped similar commands together, even though they are not in alphabetical order:

NOTE: *A number of the commands I use here require that you first enter your administrator password in the Terminal command line. After you do that and press Return, you'll be able to activate these functions.*

- **cd** *(change directory)*—The **cd** command lets you switch directories, provided of course that you have the rights needed to access that directory. For example, **cd /Users/gene/Rockoids** will take you to the Rockoids directory located inside the my home directory (to use an example on my own Mac). Likewise, **cd ..** will move you to the directory one level above the one you're currently in.

- **cp** *(copy)*—This command allows you to copy a file or directory from one location to another. You can also use the **cp** command with wildcards (an asterisk) to move only those file(s) that match certain criteria. For example, the command **cp cd /Users/gene/Rockoids/Chap* /Users/gene/Rockoids_backup** will copy (not move) all files that start with *Chap* from my Rockoids directory to my backup folder.

- **mv** *(move)*—This command is used to move (not just copy) files from one location to another. The command **mv /Users/gene/Rockoids/Chap* /Users/gene/Rockoids_backup** will transfer and not copy files that begin with the word *Chap* to the target directory.

TIP: *The **mv** command is also used to rename files. For example, to rename a file named Chapter40 to Chapter41, use the command **mv Chapter40 Chapter41**.*

WARNING! *A good caution is worth repeating. Don't forget that Unix doesn't recognize the resource fork of a Mac file. So, restrict your copying and moving efforts to document files or Mac OS X applications. Stay away from Classic applications or system files, and you'll stay out of trouble.*

- **chgrp**—This command changes the group associated with a file. For example, as administrator, you can change the group listed for a file or directory from one user to another. To change a file's group to authors, if the file is currently assigned to a different group, use **chgrp authors [*file or directory in question*]**.

- **chmod** *(change file permissions)*—This is an extremely powerful command that you use to set the access rights for your files and directories. Although this is easy to do in the Finder's Show Info window, in the Privileges category, **chmod** is far more encompassing. What's more, it can be a saving grace in the event you encounter problems with permissions on a file or folder—a dreaded warning that you don't have the right to access, change, or copy a file (a not-uncommon event in Mac OS X). You can also use **chmod** to change the permissions on a large number of files and directories quickly, using wildcards.

  For example, you can limit the ability of others in the authors group to change certain files, but still let them read the files. Here's the command I would use to modify those file permissions: **chmod o=r / Users/gene/Rockoids/Chap***. The end result? This command sets the file permissions for all files that start with "Chap" in the directory **/Users/gene/Rockoids** to read-only status, for everyone but me as owner of the file and those in the group associated with the file or directory. You can use this command in the same fashion to let others read but not executive or modify your files.

- **chown**—This command changes the ownership of a file. As administrator of your Mac, you can use this command to switch ownership of a file or folder from one user to another. Say you wanted to switch ownership of a file created by another user. Just type the command **chown [*username*] [*name of file*]**. A press of the Return key makes you, or the person named in the command, the owner of that file or folder.

- **ln** *(link)*—The Unix variant of an alias is known as a *symbolic link*. This command, when used with the name of a file, creates a symbolic link to that file. You can use it in much the same fashion as an alias to access that particular file. For example, suppose I want to create a symbolic link to a file named Rockoids in my root or top directory. To begin with, I use the command **cd /** to switch to the root directory. Now, I type "ln /Users/gene/Rockoids Rockoids". The result is a symbolic link named Rockoids that will access the folder named Rockoids on the root directory of my Mac's hard drive.

- **ls** *(list directory)*—In combination with the **ln** command, you can use this function to create a link to a specific directory.

- **less**—Enter this command plus the file name, and you'll be able to browse the contents of a file without modifying it.

NOTE: *If the file isn't a text file, you will be informed that the file may be binary and asked if you want to view it anyway.*

- **pwd**—This simple command displays the directory you are currently in.

- **mkdir**—This is the command line equivalent of the New Folder command in the Finder and in Open and Save dialog boxes. To create a folder called Rockoids2 in my home directory, I enter this command: **mkdir /Users/gene/Rockoids2**. When I open a Finder window, a folder appears in the location in which I established it via this command.

NOTE: *To use a word space for your new folder, you would, for example, specify the name* **Rockoids_2** *in your* **mkdir** *command line. When you view the new folder in the Folder, it will have a normal word space.*

- **rmdir** *(remove directory)*—This command is rather destructive, because it removes whole directories. Fortunately, it can delete a directory only if it has no files in it; Unix does offer some protection against deleting the wrong files.

- **rm** *(remove)*—Use this command with extreme care, because, as I said before, there's no turning back in Unix, no "Are you sure you want to erase your hard drive?" prompt if you go to far. The **rm** command deletes files. There is no corresponding undelete command. For example, to remove a file named ooops from my home directory, I'd use the command **rm /Users/gene/ooops**.

- **more**—This is a command similar to **less** that allows you to look at the contents of a file without changing it. You will not be warned, however, if you're trying to view a binary file. The command **q** can be used to exit the file.

- **passwd**—Want to change your password? Type this command, and you'll be prompted for your current password. Once you've entered that, you can enter your new password (but type it carefully, because you won't even see the number of characters displayed in the Terminal prompt).

Using Mac OS X's Command-Line FTP Software

Several flexible Aqua-based FTP applications are available, such as Fetch and Interarchy, but you do not need any extra software to send and receive files via FTP. The tools are already present and available via Mac OS X's command line.

TIP: *For a comprehensive list of available Mac OS X FTP software, check out www.versiontracker.com.*

In this exercise, you will have a chance to check Apple's FTP site for available updates. Here's how it's done:

1. Launch Terminal from the Applications folder.

2. When you download files from the FTP site, no doubt you'll want them on your desktop for easy access (otherwise they go to the root level of your Users or Home directory). Type "cd desktop" in the Terminal window to change the location.

3. To connect to the remote site, enter the command **ftp** followed by the name of the site, in this case **ftp.apple.com**. The result, shown in Figure 20.3, will be a request for you to enter your name.

4. Enter "anonymous" to gain guest access. In the password prompt, enter your email address.

NOTE: *Not all sites allow anonymous or guest access. If you cannot enter a site in this fashion, you will need to contact the company or administrator for the proper access credentials.*

---

5. To see a list of available files, enter the command **ls** or **dir**. Use the **cd** command, as needed, to burrow through the file directory.

NOTE: *If you know the entire path to get to the directory you want, you can type it instead, separating each directory in the hierarchy with a slash—for example, **pub/software**.*

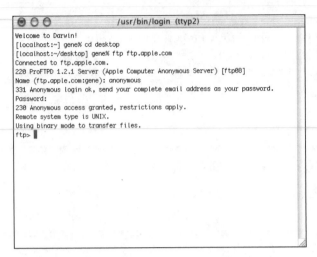

Figure 20.3   Access an FTP site via Mac OS X's command-line interface.

TIP: *Because the name of the file or directory must be entered exactly, using upper- and lowercase as needed, you can copy the name from the Terminal window and paste it when needed to be sure it's accurate.*

---

6. When you've located the file you want to retrieve, enter the command **get** followed by the name of the file. In the example shown in Figure 20.4, I wanted to retrieve a firmware revision for my Power Mac G4. Thus, I entered the command **get G4_FW-Update_4.2.8.smi.bin.** After the command has been given, file retrieval will take a few seconds to begin. When it's finished, a Transfer Complete message will appear, including both the time it took to retrieve the file and the speed (bytes per second).

TIP: *Sending and receiving files to a remote FTP site is one way to test the speed of your Internet connection, free of the constraints of the Web. However, if a site becomes busy, the speed ratings may not reflect the potential. If you can access a site that allows both file uploads and downloads, it's best to test performance during the wee hours of the morning.*

---

7. To send a file, you use the command **put** followed by the location and name of the file. Bear in mind, though, that commercial FTP sites usually do not allow uploads without permission, except where special folders are set up for those files.

```
 ● ● ●                    /usr/bin/login  (ttyp2)
drwxrwxr-x   6 ftp    ftp         512 Mar 18  2001 Printing
drwxrwxr-x  24 ftp    ftp        1024 Aug 23 19:30 System
drwxrwxr-x   2 ftp    ftp         512 May 31 14:57 USB_Updates
drwxrwxr-x  10 ftp    ftp        2048 Mar 18  2001 Utilities
drwxrwxr-x   2 ftp    ftp         512 May 31 07:53 iBook
drwxrwxr-x   2 ftp    ftp         512 Sep 28 21:31 iMac
226 Transfer complete.
ftp> cd Power_Mac_G4
250 CWD command successful.
ftp> ls
200 PORT command successful.
150 Opening ASCII mode data connection for file list.
-rwxrwxr-x   1 ftp    ftp         737 Jun 30  2000 About_This_Software.txt
-rwxrwxr-x   1 ftp    ftp      469248 Dec 19  2000 Apple_CPU_Plugin.smi.bin
-r--r--r--   1 ftp    ftp     1293312 Oct 19 05:12 G4_FW_Update_4.2.8.smi.bi
n
-rwxrwxr-x   1 ftp    ftp      712064 Jun 30  2000 G4_FirmwareUpdate_2.4.smi
.bin
-rwxrwxr-x   1 ftp    ftp      452864 Jan  9  2001 PowerMacG4_AGP_Update.smi
.bin
-rwxrwxr-x   1 ftp    ftp     2600320 Jun 30  2000 Power_Mac_G4_ROM_1.8.1.sm
i.bin
226 Transfer complete.
ftp> get G4_FW_Update_4.2.8.smi.bin▊
```

Figure 20.4   I retrieved a firmware update for my Mac.

8. When you're finished checking and retrieving files, you can quit
   Terminal or run a different FTP session.

Chapter 21

Surfing the Net

In Brief

A survey of iMac users in the months following its introduction in 1998 showed that more than 90% of them used the pear-shaped consumer computer for Internet access. Sure enough, since Apple began coming back from the brink in 1997, it has focused more and more on the Internet, to reflect the growing number of personal computer users who need to get online. In fact, the *i* in the names iMac and iBook (but not, of course, the iPod music player) is designed to reflect the idea that these consumer computers can get you hooked up to the Internet within minutes after you install them for the very first time.

In short, the ability to surf the Net easily and efficiently is a prime need for any personal computer, including the Mac. In this chapter, I focus on maximizing your Internet experience.

The Coming of Broadband Access

You hear it in the newspapers, on radio and TV, and when you're online: Despite some bumps along the road, due to the technology industry's woes, broadband Internet access is coming to your neighborhood, and your online experience will never be the same. You've no doubt seen offer after offer filled with promises of huge speed increases over the conventional modem. Claims such as, "Experience full-motion video and high-quality stereo sound" and "Retrieve files in seconds" abound.

But when you try to have those new features installed in your home, something… well… doesn't quite jibe with the promises. For one thing, there is the fine print; perhaps such high-speed services aren't available everywhere. In fact, they may not be available at your home or office because you are too far from the telephone switching center or the upgraded cable TV lines that allow you to get onto the supercharged Internet highway.

I can't promise that I can help you get broadband any faster, but in this section, I'll cover the various technologies you'll be able to access on your Mac with Mac OS X.

NOTE: *Getting online at high speed is only part of the equation. If you already have an ISP, you may or may not be able to continue to use the service when you switch to high speed. Some of these ISPs don't offer faster access, and others are still fighting with cable TV companies for open access (this was a big issue in the government's review of the merger between AOL and Time Warner that was concluded in January 2001). You may have to use another ISP, and end up changing your email addresses, when you move to broadband.*

Following are the technologies currently available, as well as those that may become available in the future:

- *DSL*—Short for Digital Subscriber Line, this service allows your phone line to do double duty. First, it handles phone calls and faxes just as it does now. But it can also carry high-speed digital data to and from your Mac, without affecting the use of your phone in any way. Compared to what you get with a 56Kbps modem (which actually connects at speeds from as low as 9600bps all the way up to 53Kbps—and the latter very seldom), DSL starts at around 256Kbps and generally delivers up to 1Mbps (megabits per second); speeds are higher with business-oriented services. One consumer-oriented variant, ADSL (the *A* is for *asymmetric*), throttles the upload speed to something far less— usually around 256Kbps. The reasoning is that most folks, except those who need to send large files all the time, perform far fewer upstream tasks than downstream tasks, and hence, they won't suffer much from the speed sacrifice. DSL service hooks up to a standard Mac Ethernet network, using a special device that acts like a modem to send and retrieve digital data from your phone line.

- *Cable modem*—Via the same cable from which you receive cable TV broadcasts, you can get high-speed Internet access. Speeds are potentially even higher than DSL, up to 3Mbps and more in some situations. However, access to the cable is shared among a group of several hundred users on a single node or segment. If a lot of folks are accessing the Internet at the same time you are, expect performance to nosedive to speeds that may not be much greater than regular DSL. Upload speeds are usually throttled to 128 or 256Kbps. An interface device, the cable modem, is used to bring the signal from the cable line to your Ethernet network.

NOTE: *Some cable modem services offer a hybrid or telco service. This system uses an analog modem built into the cable modem that offers 33.6Kbps maximum uploads via a regular phone line. Although this may be the only way the service is available, other services offer the hybrid*

21. Surfing the Net

service as an intermediary step to sign up customers while they finish rewiring a neighborhood. Once the wiring is done (assuming it ever is), customers are moved to the higher-cost full service, and the preliminary service is discontinued.

- *Wireless Internet*—Do you live in a city or small town where broadband seems years away, or may never come, because the work required is too great or the population density just isn't enough to support cable modems or DSL? There's yet a third choice: wireless. Whether by satellite disk or land-based transmitters, these services offer options that are otherwise unavailable. They may cost more, and they may not give the same level of performance as a cable modem, but in some situations, they may be the only choice.

NOTE: *One wireless service, Sprint Broadband Direct, does promise (and usually delivers, as far as my experience with the service is concerned) speeds that are close to what a cable modem or the fastest DSL services provide, at least for downloads. Upload speeds tend to vary much more than with a cable modem and are sometimes slower than with an analog modem. At press time, only few cities offered the service. According to information at the company's Web site,* **www.sprintbroadband.com***, the company is no longer accepting new subscribers (at least as of the time this book was written). This and the fact that AT&T is apparently giving up on its wireless network may spell an end, for now, for growth of this fascinating broadband technology.*

- *Future technologies*—Of course, determining the technologies of the future is a highly speculative matter, but many are betting that even faster services will emerge, using all fiber-optic cabling or other new technologies. Rewiring a city may cost billions upon billions of dollars, but if it all comes to pass, speeds on the Internet will rival those of a standard high-performance Ethernet network. If this technology is realized, you'll be able to view full-screen, full-frame video presentations via the Internet as easily as you can via cable TV and satellite. What's more, you'll be able to transfer files across the Internet at the speed of a local network. The ultimate vision of a wired generation may truly come far sooner than we expect, in keeping with the vision of a digital lifestyle espoused by Apple CEO Steve Jobs.

Mac OS X Web Browsers Profiled

The advent of Mac OS X has brought two kinds of software to surf the Net. The first is simply the Carbonized version of an existing Mac browser, as typified by Microsoft's Internet Explorer (which has been standard issue on Mac OS installations for quite some time) and such contenders as iCab, Netscape, and Opera. The second is unique to the new operating system on which Mac OS X is based, often from publishers with experience designing programs for the NeXTSTEP operating system.

In the following pages, I'll describe five Web browsers that come from both environments. You'll learn the basic features, and then, in the "Immediate Solutions" section, you'll discover ways to maximize your online performance with these programs and others offering similar capabilities.

NOTE: *The client software for AOL and CompuServe 2000 uses Internet Explorer 5.1x as their embedded browser, and performance levels and the quality of Web page display should be similar to the standalone version.*

Microsoft Internet Explorer

Since becoming the default browser on the Mac as a result of Microsoft's $150 million investment in Apple in 1997, this application has taken over from rival Netscape as the number-one Mac browser (see Figure 21.1).

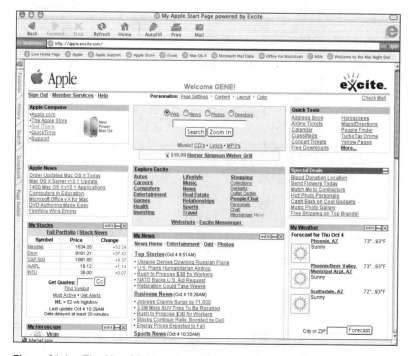

Figure 21.1   The Mac OS X version of Internet Explorer bears more than a striking resemblance to its Classic version.

Here are the basic features of the current version of Internet Explorer:

- *Tasman browser engine*—Beginning with Internet Explorer 5, Microsoft presented a new rendering engine designed for speedier display, particularly of graphics. The Tasman engine is designed to offer full support of the Internet standards in effect when the program was created.

- *Search Assistant*—This feature (see Figure 21.2) takes a task-based approach to locating information on the Internet. You click the Search button, select the category of the search, and then enter the search request in the text field. You can easily switch among search engines if the first doesn't deliver the results you want.

- *Improved address auto-complete*—When you enter a site's address, a pop-up menu appears (when available) with additional choices that begin with the information you entered. Select the one you want, and you can revisit sites with the most complex addresses in minutes. Of course, adding a site to your Favorites list is the best approach.

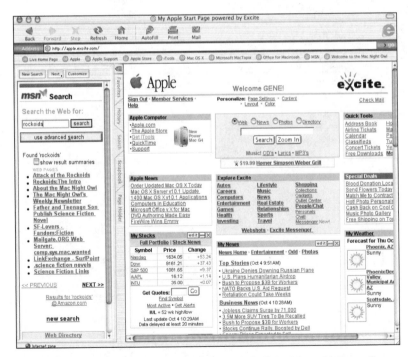

Figure 21.2   Use the Internet Explorer Search Assistant to get information from the Net more quickly.

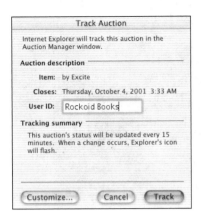

Figure 21.3 Don't let anyone outbid you. Internet Explorer's auction tracker makes it possible to know when you need to increase your bid.

- *Auction tracker*—If the online auctions from such services as eBay and Yahoo! interest you, this new feature (see Figure 21.3) lets you enter the information about the auctions in which you participate. If someone exceeds your bid for a particular item, you're notified via a browser display (or even by email), so you can decide whether to return and change your bid.

- *Multiple themes*—You can easily customize the browser's color scheme with your favorite Mac colors or move and replace items in the toolbar, as you prefer. This is part of the increasing concession on Microsoft's part to make its software more Mac-like.

iCab

The subject of an extended public preview program (one that was still in progress when this book was written), iCab (see Figure 21.4), the slim Web browser from a German-based software publisher, is designed to be competition for the big entrants in this product category.

TIP: You can download a copy of the latest version of iCab from ***www.icab.de***.

Following is a list of major iCab features that are designed to differentiate this program from the pack:

- *Support for current Web standards*—The publisher of iCab promises support for current Web standards, including HTML 4.0 and Cascading Style Sheets Level 2 (CSS2). In addition, iCab provides extra support for specific Internet Explorer and Netscape extras, such as the Netscape **<BLINK>** command.

Figure 21.4   iCab is a worthy alternative to the big guys.

- *Support for older Macs*—In addition to the Mac OS X edition of iCab, another edition runs with Mac OS 7.0.1 or later with 4MB free RAM; even Macs with a 68020 processor are supported. Only Opera can match this application's support for older Macs. Such support may make it possible for you to deploy this browser on an entire network consisting of Macs with widely varying hardware and system setups.

- *Cookie filters*—Most Web-based cookies serve a useful purpose, such as letting you track your visits to a Web site to ease navigation. However, if you want to selectively or completely disable the cookies, you can do so in this program.

Netscape

Some time in the distant past, Netscape ruled the roost among Web browsers. Although Microsoft's Internet Explorer has long since taken over on both the Mac OS and Windows platforms, AOL Time Warner's

Netscape subsidiary has been busy creating new, more feature-laden versions of the program. Netscape 6.2 for Mac OS X (see Figure 21.5) loses some of the interface oddities of the original 6.0 release while retaining its huge range of features.

Here are a few examples from the huge feature set of Netscape 6.2:

- *Gecko rendering engine*—Part of its open-source Mozilla project, Gecko is the counterpart to Internet Explorer's Tasman feature. It is supposed to provide speedier, accurate display of Web pages.

- *User-customizable sidebar*—The busy sidebar puts your favorite sites and features front and center for easy access. Additional default tabs can be added, and Netscape offers extra options at its Web site.

- *Built-in email client*—Unique among the browsers described in this chapter, Netscape includes a full-featured email client (see Figure 21.6) that can manage multiple accounts and (no surprise) even AOL email (with full support for your AOL address book).

- *Built-in Instant Messaging*—AOL's popular AIM client is also part of Netscape, so you can stay in touch with your online buddies.

21. Surfing the Net

Figure 21.5   Netscape 6.2 remains the most feature-complete Web browser.

21. Surfing the Net

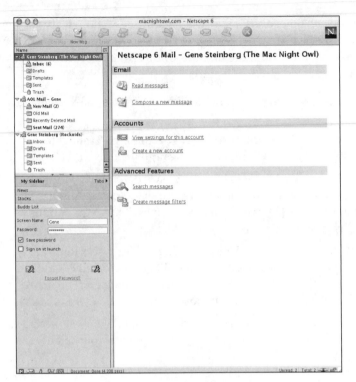

Figure 21.6   Manage your email with Netscape without the need for any other application.

- *Automatic importing of MSIE bookmarks*—Part of the setup process includes automatic importing of your Microsoft Internet Explorer Favorites, so you don't have to rebuild the list if you decide to continue using Netscape.

OmniWeb

The major independent contender in the Mac browser wars comes from a long-time NeXTSTEP developer, The Omni Group. OmniWeb is distinguished by being developed in Apple's Cocoa programming language and featuring a decidedly different interface (see Figure 21.7).

TIP: *You can easily get the latest versions of iCab, Netscape, OmniWeb, and Opera from a popular Web site that tracks and links to the latest software updates. Just point your browser to **www.versiontracker.com**. In addition to these programs, you'll find a healthy collection of software for both the Mac OS 9 and Mac OS X user environments.*

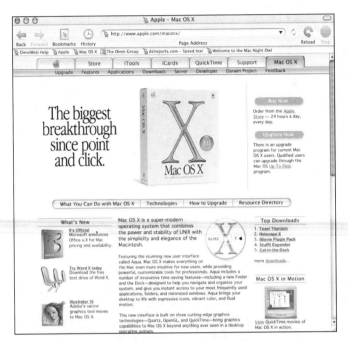

Figure 21.7   OmniWeb was created by an experienced developer of
NeXTSTEP software.

Although most features simply match the other browsers, OmniWeb offers a few variations on the theme:

- *Full support of Web standards*—As with the other programs, and despite the fact that pages render differently from program to program, OmniWeb promises to deliver support for all or most current HTML standards and CSS2.

- *Slide-out drawers*—Rather than access menus, OmniWeb's bookmark and history lists are available as drawers that simply slide out from the main application window (see Figure 21.8). This is both an advantage and a disadvantage, because the drawers can intrude on screen space.

- *Drag-and-drop bookmarks*—You can drag and drop pages to and from the bookmarks, and they'll be automatically checked for new material.

- *Easy importing of bookmarks*—Just copy the bookmarks file from either Internet Explorer or Netscape onto the bookmarks file used by OmniWeb and launch the program. The bookmarks will be automatically converted to the application's native format, so you can continue to use your existing repository of bookmarks.

Figure 21.8   OmniWeb has a unique way to access your favorite Web sites.

NOTE: *Where's that folder? With OmniWeb 4.1, it's located inside the Application Support folder within the Library folder that's placed within your personal Users folder.*

Opera

From Norway comes the last and certainly not the least contender in the race to gain a foothold in the Mac Web browser marketplace. Opera for Mac OS X (see Figure 21.9) promises superior support for emerging Web standards, and speedier browser display.

The version of Opera I examined for this book wasn't complete, but it was sufficiently populated with features to get a good idea of what it does:

- *Superior Web standard support*—All Web browsers tout their support for the various World Wide Web Consortium (W3C) standards. Opera's publishers list a full range, including CSS1, CSS2, XML, HTML 4.01, and more.

- *Super-fast rendering engine*—All right, everyone claims to do it better. Opera displays the time it takes to retrieve a Web site, so you can easily do comparisons.

- *Zooming*—This feature is unique to Opera. A pull-down menu lets you select a zoom factor for a Web page (see Figure 21.10), as you

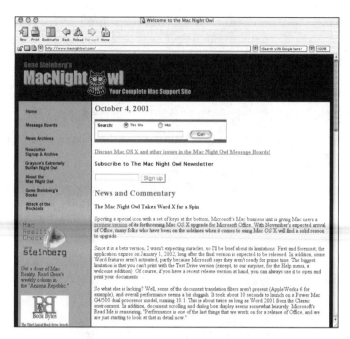

Figure 21.9   Available for a number of operating systems, Opera claims to
be the fastest browser on the planet.

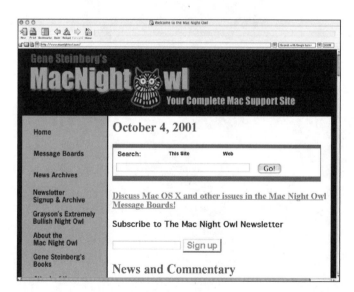

Figure 21.10   This is the author's Web site, blown up 200% courtesy of
Opera.

would in a word processor. The settings range from 20% to 1000%. Mac OS X's smooth font rendering makes text look great, but graphics will, naturally, suffer as their size increases.

- *Direct access to search engines*—Click on a down arrow and get a list of popular search engines (which you can customize) for convenient searches for the Web-based information you want.

Mac Internet access is a highly simplified process: You launch your browser and you connect. But behind those simple actions are many more considerations to get the maximum value from your online experience and steps you can take to get the maximum stability from your surfing experience. We'll look at these issues in the next section.

Immediate Solutions

Deleting Browser Caches

A Web browser uses a *cache*, consisting of a single file or several files, to store the artwork accessed from a Web site. Whenever you call up the site, the contents of the cache are compared with the site, and only new artwork is downloaded. This process can speed up Net performance, sometimes dramatically. But if performance bogs down or you find that your browser is crashing, the next step is to delete the cache.

WARNING! *A separate set of cache files is stored in each user's Preferences folder, inside his or her Library folder. If you remove the cache files while logged in under one user account, those files won't be removed for all others. However, the administrator can do a search of all user folders with Sherlock to find and remove all the caches.*

The following sections describe how to delete the caches in the five browsers described in this chapter.

TIP: *When you empty a Web cache, all the artwork is gone. As a result, the browser must retrieve it again. You won't see a performance gain until the browser retrieves the site for a second time. And don't forget, the steps described here must be repeated for all users of your Mac unless the administrator performs them manually via a file search.*

Killing the Cache in Internet Explorer

The user interface of the Carbon version of Internet Explorer is close enough to the Mac OS 9 version that the Preferences panels seem nearly identical. Here's how to clear the cache:

1. With Internet Explorer running, go to the Application menu and choose Preferences.

2. In the Preferences panel, scroll to Web Browser and click on the disclosure triangle to expose the settings under this category.

3. Click on the Advanced category, which produces the dialog box shown in Figure 21.11.

4. Click Empty Now to delete the contents of the cache file. Because Internet Explorer stores its entire cache in a single file, IE Cache.waf, this process should take only a second.

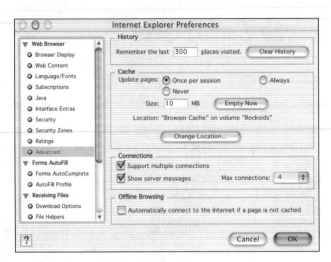

Figure 21.11   Empty the cache and perform some additional operations in this dialog box.

NOTE: *As with the traditional Mac OS version, AOL and CompuServe 2000 share the same Web cache as Internet Explorer. Even if you delete the cache and have Internet Explorer build a fresh one, it will switch to the cache file it shares with AOL or CompuServe 2000 the next time either program launches and retrieves a Web page. Should this happen, you'll find the cache file located in a folder called America Online or CompuServe, either or both of which will be located in your Preferences folder (inside your personal Library folder). If you are a subscriber to either service, you'll find an Empty Cache Now button in the Preferences dialog box for either service's client software under WWW.*

---

5. Visit your favorite sites and see if the appearance or performance improves after the site is visited for the second time.

6. If performance doesn't improve, delete the actual cache file. You'll find it in the Preferences folder inside the Library folder, which is, in turn, located in the Users folder bearing your login name. Look for a folder labeled MS Internet Cache or Explorer for this file.

Killing the Cache in iCab

The process of emptying iCab's Web cache under Mac OS X is the same as in the Classic versions. Just follow these steps:

1. With iCab running, go to the Application menu and choose Preferences.

2. Locate the category labeled Caches, and click on the disclosure triangle to show all the subcategories.

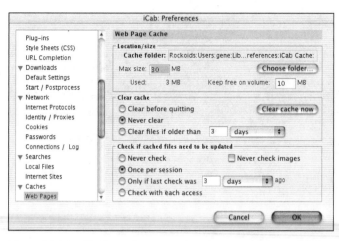

Figure 21.12   iCab's cache removal options are fairly straightforward.

3. Locate and click Web Pages. You'll see iCab's various cache options, as shown in Figure 21.12.

4. To delete the cache, click the Clear Cache Now button. Because the cache is stored in a number of separate files, it may take a little while to remove a large cache.

5. When the cache has been removed, click OK. The Preferences dialog box closes.

6. Visit your favorite sites and see if the appearance or performance improves.

Killing the Cache in Netscape

Netscape's cache-killing process is, like the others mentioned so far, pretty straightforward:

1. Launch Netscape for Mac OS X, go to the Edit menu, and choose Preferences.

NOTE: *The presence of Netscape's Preferences dialog box on the Edit menu is limited to the early versions, even though they are supposedly full release products. Expect it to move to the Application menu as Netscape for Mac OS X is revised.*

2. Click the arrow next to Advanced so it points downward (or leave it alone if it's already that way).

3. Click Cache to bring up the dialog box shown in Figure 21.13.

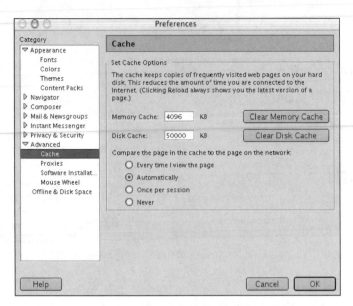

Figure 21.13   Clear Netscape's cache from here.

4. Click Clear Disk Cache to zap the cache files. As an extra ounce of prevention, you may also want to click Clear Memory Cache, which also removes the artwork cached in memory.

5. Click OK to close the Preferences dialog box.

Killing the Cache in OmniWeb

It's not just the interface that's different. There are two ways to handle the cache in OmniWeb. To actually clear the cache, simply choose Flush Cache from the Tools menu. The other cache management tool is the Cache Timeout feature, which sets the time when a cache is considered out-of-date and when a new version of the site is available. That one is in the Preferences dialog box. Talk about different!

Killing the Cache in Opera

This is an early release version, so don't be surprised to see Opera's Preferences dialog box on the Edit menu. Here's how to empty the cache:

1. With Opera open, bring up the Preferences dialog box from the Edit menu.

2. Click History And Cache to bring up the dialog box shown in Figure 21.14.

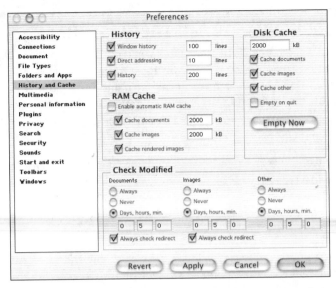

Figure 21.14   You can clear Opera's cache from this rather busy window.

3. Under Disk Cache, click Empty Now to remove Opera's cache files.

4. Click OK to dismiss Opera's Preferences dialog box.

Determining Whether a Larger Cache Is Necessary

The standard Web cache is usually 5MB to 10MB (it was 2MB in the version of Opera examined for this book), but you can easily increase it to a higher figure if you prefer by accessing a browser's Preferences as described previously. Before you do so, however, consider that having a Web cache that's too large may be counterproductive. For one thing, if the browser spends additional time checking the contents of the cache before accessing an updated site from the Web, performance may actually be slower.

However, if you frequently access a large number of Web sites with plenty of artwork, a setting of 15MB or even 20MB may be useful; iCab sets its cache at a maximum of 30MB, and no appreciable slowdown results. Your mileage may vary. If you choose to reduce the size of a cache, however, empty it first.

Using Bookmarks to Get There Faster

Over time, you'll come across Web sites you'd like to visit on a regular basis. The best way to keep track of these sites is to save them as bookmarks. Each browser has a different name for its bookmarks feature. For Internet Explorer, it's called Favorites; for iCab, it's the Hotlist; and OmniWeb uses the traditional name Bookmarks (as do Netscape and Opera).

In each case, there is a menu with the name of the bookmarks feature. To add a page to your bookmarks, access that menu and use the command to add the current page. You may see a confirmation message that you must OK in order for the page to appear on the list.

Removing a bookmark involves opening the list, selecting the bookmark, and then pressing the Delete key or choosing Delete from the Contextual menu or Edit menu (it varies from browser to browser). Again, you'll usually need to OK a prompt to delete the entry.

Solving Internet Connection Problems

On the surface, getting on the Net with Mac OS X should be no more complicated than doing so under Mac OS 9. However, the new networking architecture may create problems from time to time, especially with programs that have only recently made the migration to the new operating system. Here's a list of some of the most frequent problems and what you can do to resolve them:

* *You cannot get online with a cable modem or DSL.* Some ISPs require special software to connect. You'll have to contact the service to see when a Mac OS X–compatible version is available, or whether other connection options can be found. In the meantime, check whether your service will give you a static set of IP access numbers, which might get you connected when you enter them via the Network pane of the System Preferences application.

TIP: *Some cable providers require entering a dedicated modem ID address in your network settings to allow you to access their network. You will need to enter that information correctly in order for you to connect to that service; the Mac OS X Setup Assistant and the Network preference panels both include a place for you to put this information. Others may even require use of a special application to log in; you will have to contact the ISP directly as to what's needed to access its networks if the usual steps don't succeed.*

- *Classic applications may not run with dial-up connections.* The watchword is to try first. Aside from proprietary services, specifically AOL and CompuServe, you may not need to be concerned about this issue. There is enough Mac OS X–savvy software around to provide a satisfactory Internet experience until your favorite is updated.

NOTE: *One possible solution for this problem is a shareware utility, PortReflector, which reflects the TCP/IP connections from Mac OS 9 to Mac OS X so you can continue to use your Classic dial-up program.*

TIP: *It's a good idea to retain a backup of your TCP/IP Preferences file before installing Mac OS X to avoid problems in case you need to use your ISP when going back to Mac OS 9.2.1.*

- *Artwork changes from browser to browser.* This issue is due to the inexact nature of the way a browser interprets a page and is a chronic problem (and the source of endless headaches) for Web authors. Despite claims from each publisher that its browser supports standards better than the competition, expect differences. If you want to view a site in a particular way, you may want to stick with the browser that presents it the way you like. Another possibility is to report a display problem to the publisher of the browser application, so it can examine the situation and see if it can do anything to update the program for better display.

- *A site is not accessible.* This may be the fault of the site itself or of Internet congestion and not your browser or connection. The first possible solution is to click the Refresh or Reload button on the browser, so that the site is retrieved again from scratch. Another possible solution is to log off from your ISP and then reconnect. If neither step resolves the problem, try to access the site again at a different time.

- *A site's artwork is distorted.* One possible solution is to just refresh or reload the page, which delivers the site from scratch. If that fails to resolve the problem, follow the steps in the earlier section "Deleting Browser Caches" to empty the Web cache. If doing so doesn't resolve the issue, it may be the fault of the Web site itself, so there's nothing you can do but complain to the Webmaster.

21. Surfing the Net

437

TIP: *If you use the embedded version of Internet Explorer supplied with AOL or CompuServe 2000, go to the Preferences dialog box of either application. Scroll to the WWW category and uncheck the Use Compressed Images option. This setting keeps AOL from converting the Web artwork to a proprietary format and delivers a more accurate rendering of Web artwork and photos.*

- *Download speeds vary.* It is normal for the speed of a file download to vary somewhat, whether you have a dial-up connection or broadband. This is a normal part of the process; sometimes, it's a problem with your connection or with congestion on the part of the Web server hosting the site. However, if download speed bogs down, you may want to stop the download and try again. If you have a dial-up connection, you may also want to log off and then reconnect; however, if all other services run at normal speed, there may be nothing you can do to resolve the problem.

- *Internet Connect doesn't support your modem.* As with the Classic Mac OS, only a fixed number of popular modem makes and models are supported (although the list is quite large in Mac OS X 10.1). Most Macs that can run Mac OS X already come with an Apple internal modem, so this may not be a serious issue for you. But, if you have a different modem, feel free to experiment with a similar make or model, or just use Hayes Compatible. Most modems that support standard setups will probably function in a satisfactory manner. If you still do not get acceptable performance, contact the manufacturer of the modem directly for suggestions.

- *Dial-up connection fails.* You try to log in and don't succeed. Should this happen, verify the information you placed in the Internet Connect application. Review Chapter 8 for information on how to set up this program to work with your ISP. If the information is all right, try to connect once again. If the connection still fails, contact your ISP and see if it is doing system maintenance or can offer you alternate connection numbers.

- *The browser crashes.* With Mac OS X, you do not need to restart your Mac whenever a program freezes or suddenly quits. You can continue to work, and even try running the application again. Because some of the applications for Mac OS X are beta versions, check with the publisher's Web site for newer versions. You should also read Chapter 19, which covers a number of ways to troubleshoot Mac OS X.

- *Java applets don't run.* Although Mac OS X incorporates the very latest Java technology from Sun Microsystems, not all Web browsers were working properly with Java applets when this book was written. This was particularly true of iCab and Opera, both of which were in public beta form. In addition, Netscape 6.2, though a release version, also had problems resolving some of the applets I tried (including the ISP bandwidth tests from DSLReports.com). If you run into a problem, first try the site in Microsoft's Internet Explorer and if it works there, check the Web site run by the publisher of your preferred browser (or VersionTracker.com) for information about an updated version that might fix the problem.

Related solutions:	Found on page:
Using Internet Connect for Dial-Up Networking	182
Solving System Crashes and Freezes	384

21. Surfing the Net

Chapter 22

Exploring Apple's Email Software

In Brief

When it comes to sending messages, email rules. In fact, where would we be without it? Each day, hundreds of millions of messages cross the Internet on their way to folks across the world, and email has long since supplanted postal mail in the eyes of many people for sending messages to family and business contacts.

In addition, offices use email for exchanging messages within their companies. This is becoming increasingly common, even if the recipient sits in an adjacent office or cubicle. In fact, email has sometimes replaced the practice of actually speaking with a nearby coworker.

NOTE: *Just as an example of what might be considered using email to the extreme, I have observed two coworkers seated next to each other exchanging lengthy email messages rather than simply talking it over.*

All recent versions of the Mac OS have shipped with email software, usually Microsoft's Outlook Express and Netscape Communicator, both of which operate in the Classic environment. With the arrival of Mac OS X, there's a new kid on the block named, simply enough, Mail (see Figure 22.1).

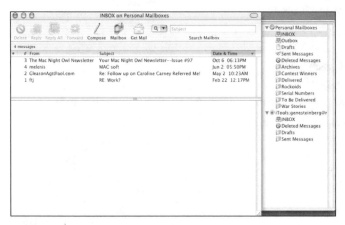

Figure 22.1   Apple's email client is clean, uncluttered, and lightning-quick.

Introducing Mail

Apple's new email program, based in part on the email software shipped with the NeXTSTEP operating system, the precursor to Mac OS X, isn't quite as full-featured as the other programs in this arena. However, Mail provides the essentials needed to manage one or more email accounts, and it is at least worth serious consideration.

Here's a brief list of its important features:

- *Multiple user accounts*—Do you have home and office user accounts, or different email addresses for business and personal use? Mail lets you configure the program to handle all of them. You can set it to log in at specified time intervals so you're never out of touch. In addition, other users who work on your Mac can configure their own settings and store their own collections of email without having access to anyone else's mail.

- *Ability to Import Mailboxes*—No doubt, you have an email account set up with another program. With a reasonable degree of fidelity, you can import your mailboxes from Entourage, Netscape 4, Eudora, Outlook Express, and Claris Emailer.

NOTE: *Neither AOL nor CompuServe 2000 mailboxes are supported, and that is not expected to change. Check Apple's Web site for the latest updates.*

- *HTML formatting supported*—You can send and receive messages with Web links and full text formatting, depending on the limits of the recipient's service. Additionally, you can place pictures within your messages, such as family photos to go with your descriptions of a family vacation.

- *Management of stored email*—With this feature, you can set up extra folders in your personal mailbox to store the messages you receive in different categories. You can also use email rules to make sure that messages from specific sources are placed automatically in a particular folder. Rules are useful if you want to store mail for later retrieval, or if you receive lots of junk mail from a particular source and want to gather it for later disposal.

NOTE: *The ability to set rules for the Mail application isn't quite the same, nor is it as flexible as an email filter, which can be used to flag messages as "junk" for removal. For regular message handling, it's a fairly flexible feature, because it lets you automate a series of specific steps.*

- *Automatic signatures*—You can create and store multiple signatures for personal and business messages. There's also a "rich text" option that lets you include automatic email and Web links in a signature.

- *Spellchecker*—As you write a message, if you leave on the option for interactive checking, words with potential spelling problems are flagged in red. Otherwise, you can spell-check manually before you send a message.

- *Message searching*—Messages can be searched by sender, recipient, subject, or content. This is a powerful tool that you can use to find information quickly in the messages you've stored.

NOTE: Whenever email awaits you in the Mail application, the icon for the program in the Dock will include a number specifying how many messages are unread.

Reviewing Other Mac OS X Email Choices

Don't get me wrong. I don't want to create the impression that Mail is your only choice in Mac OS X email software. The fact that it comes free with your installation, however, and is configured when you set up Mac OS X in the System Preferences application, gets you through the initial hurdles of configuration.

But it is by no means your only choice. Here's a brief look at other options you may want to explore before you make a final decision. In each case, I'll ignore the basic email features that they all share, such as multiple user accounts, the ability to import messages from other programs, and message filtering, and move on to some of the unique attributes that are worth considering if you're looking for alternatives.

Entourage X

Part of Microsoft's Office v. X for Mac business application suite, Entourage X (see Figure 22.2) is descended from the free Outlook Express application. But it's not just restricted to email and newsgroup messages. This is a fully featured personal information manager that includes a calendar and task and event reminders and organization. The major features of Entourage include:

- *Rich content*—Similar to a feature that is supported in Mail and AOL's email, you are able to insert graphics and photos within the

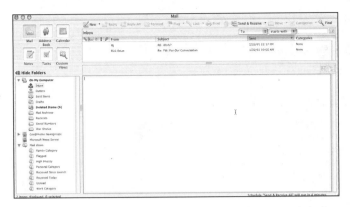

Figure 22.2   Entourage X inherits Mac OS X's Aqua user interface, plus plenty of powerful contact management features.

body of your message. Going further, Entourage X also works with sounds and video clips.

- *Junk mail filter*—If you're bothered and bewildered by a constant flurry of offensive or annoying sales pitches, you can set Entourage X's filter to check and flag spam. The sensitivity of the junk mail filter can be adjusted to lessen flagging of messages you do want to retrieve. In addition, you can set up exceptions, so that certain messages are not labeled as "junk."

- *Address Book with international support*—Entourage X's Address Book feature includes all the basic contact information, such as name, address, email address, and so forth, plus personal information, including birthdays and anniversaries. In addition, it provides automatic support for the unique mailing address formatting used in a number of places around the world, such as Europe and Japan.

- *Tri-pane calendar*—You can view your appointment and event calendar by month, week, or even workweek. You are also able to put tasks that are due or overdue in a separate pane for easy organization.

Eudora Pro

You can download and install the current version of Eudora Pro (see Figure 22.3) from the publisher's Web site (**www.qualcomm.com**) without paying a license fee, but the program has three modes of operation depending on whether you want to upgrade to a paid version. The first, Lite, is roughly equivalent to the Eudora Lite software used on Macs for years. You get full use of the software, but three key

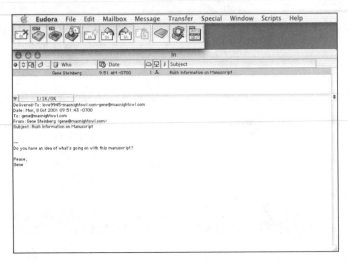

Figure 22.3   This is the Paid version of Eudora Pro, fully featured without ad banners.

features, such as the ability to use Secure Sockets Layer (SSL) in logging on to an email server, placing photos in the address book, or using the MoodWatch feature (more about this feature shortly) are not available. The second free mode is called Sponsored, in which you see little ad banners on your email screen; and the final is Paid, when you pay a license fee to get full use of the software without being presented with any advertising.

Here's a brief look at some of the distinctive features of Eudora Pro:

- *SSL support*—This feature lets you gain access to email services (usually corporate and educational) that require encrypted authentication. It also lets you encrypt your email for maximum security. Apple's Mail doesn't offer this feature (although I understand it's being considered for a future version).

- *MoodWatch*—Did you ever write a message in which you expressed anger over a person or situation, and then regret what you wrote after it had been sent? The MoodWatch feature can be set to flag language that may be offensive or inflammatory, and delay sending the message to allow a cooling-off period. That way, if you decide that maybe you were just a little too over-the-top in your message, you can revise it before it's sent. It's a great way to keep friends and business contacts when the going gets tough.

- *Photos in Address Book*—AOL users have enjoyed this feature for a while: the ability to insert someone's photo in your personal address book.

Netscape

Once upon a time, Netscape was the market leader in Web browsers, and it remains unique among the programs discussed here because it integrates the browser and the email client (see Figure 22.4) in a single application (an instant messaging client is also included).

Here are the basic features of the email component of Netscape 6.2 for Mac OS X:

- *AOL support*—Here's a feature that is not likely to be found in any other Mac OS X application, other than AOL's own client software. It allows you to retrieve your AOL email in the same fashion as you can retrieve email from any other online account.

- *Separate mailbox for each account*—This feature lets you easily sort messages from your various Internet accounts without having to configure an all-new mailbox for each address.

How Does Mail Rate?

Considering that some pretty powerful email programs are available for the Mac OS, just where does Mail stand when compared to Microsoft's Outlook Express and Entourage, Netscape Communicator, Qualcomm's Eudora, or even the defunct mail client, Claris Emailer? Here's a brief list of features that are lacking or only partly implemented in Mail:

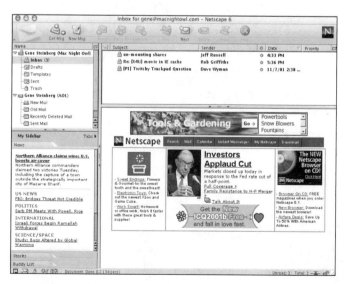

Figure 22.4   Netscape 6.2's email window is similar to the one available in prior versions of the program.

NOTE: Claris Emailer, which was discontinued several years ago, works well from the Classic environment. Aside from Netscape 6.2 for Mac OS X, it is the only program that can handle mail from standard Internet accounts and AOL, which is one of the reasons (aside from its simple, uncluttered interface) that I continue to use it.

- *Separate address book*—Apple has provided a different program, Address Book (see Figure 22.5), for managing your address list. It should suit most purposes. It is linked directly with Mail and provides limited options to import the address lists from other programs.

- *Limited message filtering*—You can establish rules for messages, but you cannot have Mail flag possible spam email and have the messages automatically deleted, as you can in the competing programs.

- *No newsgroup support*—Microsoft's Entourage and Outlook Express and Netscape can retrieve Usenet newsgroup messages. Mail doesn't support this feature. If you are interested in this option, look for a Mac OS X—savvy news-reading program to support your needs.

Figure 22.5   Use this program to configure an address book for messages.

TIP: *Two very useful options for reading newsgroup messages are NewsWatcher-X, the Carbon update to the popular free newsgroup application; and Thoth, from Brian Clark, author of YA-NewsWatcher. The latter, however, is demoware, and the downloadable version is crippled in key functions, such as saving updates to subscribed newsgroups, unless you buy a user license. However, Thoth is worth the modest fee and is my favorite.*

- *No automatic connections*—Microsoft's Outlook Express and Entourage can both be configured to check email at regular intervals, even if the program isn't open, by launching and establishing your Net connection. Mail can recheck for messages on a regular basis only when it's running.

- *No support for AOL email*—As mentioned earlier, only Netscape 6 and Claris Emailer can retrieve AOL email. If you wish to access your AOL messages otherwise, you have to log on to the AOL Web site (**www.aol.com**) with your browser and access its NetMail feature.

NOTE: *As this book was written, Mail also didn't support Microsoft's Hotmail service. You can set that up courtesy of Microsoft's own email clients, or via your Web browser.*

If you've worked with other email programs, you'll find that setting up and using Mail is pretty straightforward, and the differences aren't all that significant. The "Immediate Solutions" section covers the basics of using this application.

22. Exploring Apple's Email Software

Immediate Solutions

Setting Up Your User Account

When I described how to work with the Mac OS X Setup Assistant in Chapter 3, I explained how to enter your email settings during the initial setup of the new operating system. However, if you need to change those settings or add an extra user account, just follow these steps:

NOTE: *If you gave your email account information when you ran the Mac OS X Setup Assistant, it will all be here. You can edit it as needed, or add any additional ISP accounts you want.*

1. Launch the Mail application.
2. Go to Mail's Application menu and choose Preferences. The screen shown in Figure 22.6 appears.
3. Click the Accounts icon, and then the Create Account button, shown in Figure 22.6, to bring up the Account Information dialog box (see Figure 22.7).

NOTE: *If your Mac is set up with multiple user accounts, each user will be able to configure Mail separately to handle his or her accounts and email from that user account. The information isn't available to any other users, unless they log in to the same account.*

Figure 22.6   Set up and manage Mail's settings from this screen.

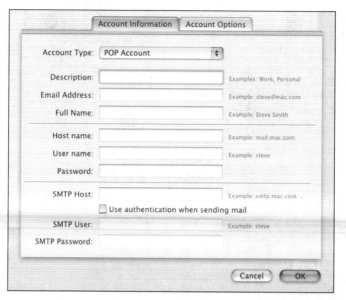

Figure 22.7   Enter your basic email user settings in the Account Information dialog box.

4. Under the Account Type category, choose the type of email account you're establishing (usually a POP account, although some ISPs support IMAP instead) and give a description, such as "Work", "Personal", or the name of the ISP (a default will be entered by the program otherwise).

NOTE: *Not sure what account settings to use? Check with your ISP. While it may be possible to predict some settings, such as the name of a POP server (such as **pop.[ISPname].com**), even a single wrong entry will make it impossible to send or retrieve your messages.*

---

5. Enter your email address and full name in the first section of the dialog box.

6. Under Host Name, enter the name of your ISP's mail server. Insert your username and password as needed to connect to your ISP.

7. In the final category, enter the name of the outgoing mail server of your ISP and, if necessary, authentication or password account information.

8. When your settings are complete, click OK to store them. Or, if you prefer, click the Account Options tab (see Figure 22.8) to further customize your settings.

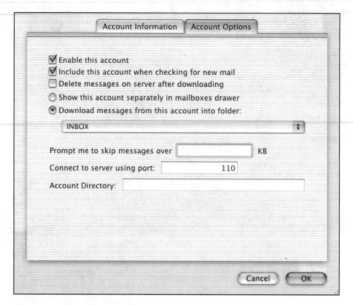

Figure 22.8   Customize your email sessions from the Account Options
dialog box.

9. Choose your optional account information under the various
   setup categories:

   - *Enable This Account*—Normally checked by default. You can
     disable a user account if you don't want to retrieve messages
     from it for a while.

   - *Include This Account When Checking For New Mail*—For
     whatever reason (perhaps the account is only used rarely),
     you may choose not to check for a specific email account
     when new mail is automatically accessed.

   - *Delete Messages On Server After Downloading*—Normally,
     messages are left on your ISP's mail server. But if you get a
     lot of email, you may find it convenient to check this option
     so that the messages will be removed (at the expense of
     making them unavailable if you want to check for them on
     another computer).

   - *Show This Account Separately In Mailboxes Drawer*—
     Having a separate entry means separate mailboxes to check
     for different accounts. This may be a blessing or a curse,
     depending on your situation.

   - *Download Messages From This Account Into Folder*—
     Normally the Inbox applies to an account, but you can

specify a separate folder if you want to organize messages by account to check specific items more easily.

- *Prompt Me To Skip Messages Over*—Specify a size if you don't want to look at large messages or those with large attachments right away.

- *Connect To Server Using Port*—This setting is entirely based on the requirements of your ISP or network system. Normally it's best to leave the default entry.

NOTE: *If you're not sure what settings to enter for your email options, contact your ISP for the proper access information. It will vary considerably, depending on an individual service's setup.*

---

10. When your settings are complete, click OK to store them.

TIP: *Another useful email preference is available in the Viewing pane of the Mail Preferences dialog box. Just choose an account, click Edit and then the Account Options tab. You can use these settings to determine when messages are automatically purged from your mailbox and whether to download email images, animations, or other HTML attachments. If you don't want to view lots of clutter in your messages, particularly if most such messages are really junk mail, you'll want to turn off that option.*

Related solution:	Found on page:
Setting System Preferences Under Mac OS X	44

Importing Your Email Messages

Once you've given Mail a test run, perhaps you'll decide to keep using the program. What do you do about the messages already stored in other software? Fortunately, Mail can import the contents of those mailboxes with a reasonable degree of fidelity.

Here's how to use that option:

1. With Mail open, choose Import Mailboxes from the File menu to bring up the import assistant shown in Figure 22.9. Click the right arrow to proceed or (when not grayed out) the left arrow to recheck your settings.

2. Choose the email client from which you want to import messages. Mail isn't able to translate mailboxes for programs other than the ones listed. As you progress through the dialog boxes,

Figure 22.9   Begin the email import process in the Import Mailboxes
dialog box.

click the right or "next" arrow to proceed. When you select an
email client, you'll see an acknowledgment such as the one
shown in Figure 22.10.

NOTE: *This process must be done separately for each email program you're using. In addition,
the mailboxes will all be placed in separate message folders; there's no way to put them together
except by manually dragging and dropping them into the proper location.*

3. After you've selected the mailboxes that apply to the email application (see Figure 22.11), select the ones you want to convert and
click the right arrow to proceed. By default, all of the folders in
the email application that you're importing will be checked.

Figure 22.10   Mail notifies you that the selected email client—Entourage, in
this case—will be launched as part of the import process.

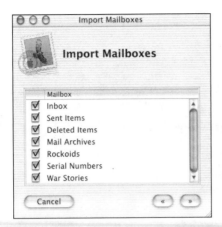

Figure 22.11   After you've selected mailboxes, a click of the right arrow will begin the import process.

4. You'll see a progress bar showing the number of messages being retrieved. When the import process is complete, click Done to wrap up the process and dismiss the dialog box.

5. If the list of mailboxes isn't displayed, choose Show Mailboxes from the View menu. You'll see additional folders in your Mail drawer that match the ones in your email program. Click on any of them to finish the process: Mail will update its database to incorporate the messages you've imported.

*TIP: If you have an email application not supported in Mail's Import feature, or if the import process goes badly, you may want to try AppleScript import tools that promise better-quality imports. The files are available at Apple's Support Web site: **www.apple.com/downloads/macosx/apple/mailimportscripts.html**.*

Customizing Mail's Toolbar

Extending the Finder-like display of Mail, you can easily customize the toolbar in the same fashion as the Mac OS X Finder. To make these changes, follow these steps:

1. With Mail open, choose Customize Toolbar from the View menu. The display shown in Figure 22.12 will appear.

2. To add icons to the toolbar, click and drag them to the desired location in the toolbar.

Figure 22.12   Click and drag the items you want to the toolbar.

3. To remove an icon, just drag it off the toolbar, and it will disappear.

4. To restore the default set of icons, click and drag the Default Set icons to the toolbar.

5. Click Done to store your settings.

Composing a New Message

To write a brand-new message in Mail, just follow these steps:

1. Click on the Compose button, which brings up a blank email screen, shown in Figure 22.13.

2. Type the recipient's email address in the To field (such as mine, **gene@macnightowl.com**). If you enter the name of more than one recipient, separate the names with a comma. If the email address you're looking for is in your Address Book, click the Address button to bring up that program so you can add the names you want.

Figure 22.13   Begin writing your message here.

NOTE: *As you type the address, Mail will consult your Address Book and the messages you've sent and received, and attempt to auto-complete the address for you. If the correct name is selected, click Tab or Enter to move to the next field.*

---

3. To send courtesy or carbon copies to other recipients, place their addresses in the CC field, separated by commas.

NOTE: *A third addressing option, BCC, sends a blind carbon copy to recipients. None of the recipients will see the names of those in the BCC field. By default, this option is turned off, but you can activate it by going to the Message menu and choosing Add BCC Header. Unfortunately, the BCC field can only be added on an individual message basis. There is no global setting to include this option.*

---

4. Enter a topic for your message in the Subject field. You can move through fields with the Tab key, or reverse the motion with Shift+Tab. This is the same behavior you find in any email program.

5. Type the text of your message. If the spellcheck feature is turned on (and it is by default), you'll see spelling errors flagged in red.

6. When you've completed your message, click the Send button to speed it on its way.

7. To work on the message again at a later time, go to the File menu and choose Save As Draft. The message will be stored in your Drafts mailbox for later updating.

NOTE: *By default, the messages you send are saved in the Sent folder in your personal mailbox. This and other settings for the messages you write are saved under Mail Preferences, when you click the Compose button. In this settings panel, you can also specify a different location for sent messages.*

Responding to a Message

When you receive messages, they'll show up in your Inbox, and just clicking on a title is sufficient to see the contents in the bottom pane of the Mail application window. New messages are signified by a blue button at the left of the message's title.

Once you've finished reading a message, you might want to write a reply. To do so, click the Reply button to bring up a response window, shown in Figure 22.14.

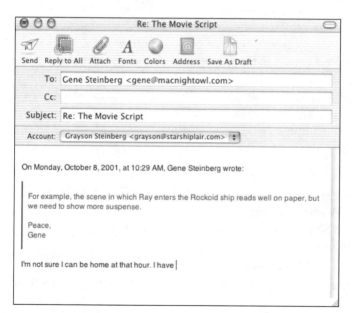

Figure 22.14 Write your answer in the response window.

NOTE: *If the message went to more than one recipient, you have the option to reply to the original sender or, by clicking Reply All, to everyone who received the message, including those listed in the CC field.*

When you've finished writing your message, click Send to whisk it on its way (you have to be connected to your ISP for this to work, of course).

Quoting Messages

When you respond to a message, it's customary to quote relevant portions of the message to which you're responding. The normal way to do this is to first select the material that you wish to quote, and then click Reply. The quoted portion will show up in your response window.

WARNING! *By default, if you don't select the portions of a message to be quoted, the entire message will appear in the response window. If you're responding to a long message, seeing so much material can be irritating for the recipient. It's better to quote just enough of the message so the recipient knows precisely what your response is about.*

Spellchecking Your Messages

Mail excels in its ability to automatically check your spelling as you type, marking words with questionable spelling in red (see Figure 22.15).

Here's how you can handle Mail's powerful spellcheck features:

1. When Mail flags a word whose spelling is in question, you can either make your correction as you proceed, or Control+click the word to see a contextual menu with your spellcheck options (see Figure 22.16).

2. From the contextual menu, you can choose a different spelling from the list of suggestions, or have the spellchecker ignore or learn the word as it's spelled. When you specify a different spelling for the word, it will be replaced automatically.

22. Exploring Apple's Email Software

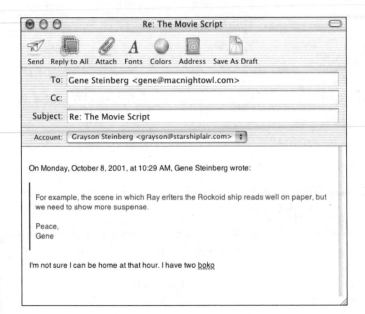

Figure 22.15   Where would your long-suffering author be without the ability to fix his spelling errors?

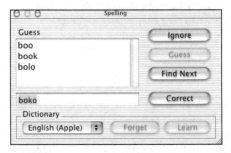

Figure 22.16   Correct the word or leave it as is.

3. To perform a batch spellcheck, simply choose Spelling from the Edit menu, and then Spelling from the submenu. Or, press Command+:.

Sending Email Attachments

To send one or more files with your email, you'll find the process is at once simple and complex. To attach a file to your email, follow these steps:

1. Open a New Message window.

2. Click the Attach button to produce an Open dialog box, shown in Figure 22.17.

3. Select one or more files to send, and click the Open button.

4. Continue to prepare to send your message, and then click Send. If the Activity Viewer window is displayed (it's a command in the Window menu), you'll see a progress indicator showing how much of your message has been sent. The time it takes to transfer depends on the size of the file you wish to send and the speed of your Net connection.

When sending attachments, you'll need to consider a few items to make sure your files reach their destination intact:

- *Make sure your recipient can open it.* If your attachment was created in a particular application, you should check whether the recipient has the same program, or a program that can handle that type of document. For example, if you're using Microsoft Word, a Windows user with a recent version of the program can read the document. In addition, many other programs can read Word documents. However, more specialized software, such as QuarkXPress, requires that the recipient have the same program on hand.

Figure 22.17   Select a file to accompany your email.

- *Name Windows files properly.* Whereas the Mac OS, both old and new, doesn't need a file extension to identify the type of file, Windows does. The file types are entered as three-letter extensions. Common names include .doc for a Word document, .jpg for a JPEG file, and .gif for a GIF picture.

TIP: *Some programs, such as Word and recent versions of Adobe Photoshop, can be set to automatically append the proper extension for a file. The Mac OS X Finder and native programs are savvy about proper file extensions, but it never hurts to double-check.*

- *Be careful about compressing files.* Whereas Mac users can handle files compressed in the industry-standard StuffIt format, users of Microsoft Windows generally use Zip files (although there is a StuffIt version for Windows, as well). If you know your files will be read by both Mac and Windows users, consider the DropZip utility that comes with the latest versions of Aladdin Systems' StuffIt Deluxe. That's what I used to handle the cross-platform needs of my publisher while writing this book.

- *Don't send multiple attachments to AOL users.* AOL's email servers have problems decoding email with more than a single attachment. Just send one attachment with each message. Or, for convenience, consider using a compression program to combine the attachments into a single file. You'll also get the added benefit of being able to send a smaller file.

- *Watch out for file-size limits.* You may run into problems with large attachments. As mentioned, some services, such as AOL, limit attachments to 2MB from sources outside the service. Others can be as high as 10MB (EarthLink) or 5MB.

Forwarding Email

Have you ever received a message that you really wanted to send to a third party, whether a friend or business contact? To send that message intact, or with some annotations of your own, just follow these steps:

1. With your new message open, click Forward.
2. Address the message in the appropriate field.

3. Add text before or after the message you're forwarding, if necessary.

4. Click Send.

WARNING! *It's bad form to forward to a third party a message that the original sender might not want to disseminate. If you have any concerns about doing so, contact the original sender and ask if it's all right to send it elsewhere; if need be, specify the names of the intended recipients.*

Adding Email Signatures

Just as you put a signature on a regular letter, it's a good idea to use a signature on email as well. Although you can easily enter a signature manually, if you want to use it regularly, you can store it in Mail.

Here is how to set up a list of stored signatures:

1. With the Mail application open, go to the Application menu and choose Preferences.

2. Click the Signatures button.

3. In the Signatures dialog box, click Create Signature and type the text for the signature you want to use.

4. Enter the signature's description in the Description box (see Figure 22.18).

5. Follow the preceding steps to add extra signatures as needed.

6. With all your new signatures set up, click OK. Then, click the Active column next to the name of the signature to make it

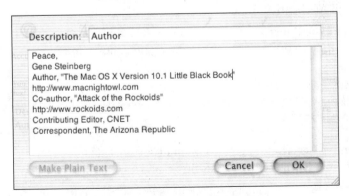

Figure 22.18   This is the author's actual signature.

active. From here on, you can specify the signature to use from the Signature pop-up menu.

TIP: *If you are sending a message to a recipient who might not be able to see email formatted with rich text, which will show Web links and formatted text, click the Composing icon and select Plain Text from the Default Message Format pop-up menu. Doing so will affect not just your signatures, but your entire message until the setting is changed.*

Formatting Email

Mail gives you a fairly decent set of formatting controls to handle the style of your messages. With a message window open, click the Format menu to choose font style and size, and text orientation, such as left or centered. If the recipient may not be able to see a styled message, choose Make Plain Text from the Format menu.

Setting Mail Rules

Within a limited range, you can specify custom rules to store and sort email messages. Such rules will help you organize messages for later review or disposal. Although this feature isn't as powerful as the filtering options provided by other programs mentioned in the "In Brief" section of this chapter, it's nonetheless quite useful.

Here's how to establish a mail rule:

1. With the Mail application open, choose Preferences from the Mail Application menu.

2. Click the Rules button. In the setup pane that appears, click Create Rule to bring up the setup dialog box shown in Figure 22.19.

NOTE: *By default, email rules are created for Apple's own information services. You can click the Remove buttons in the Mail preference box to dispose of them, or just uncheck the Active buttons to make them hibernate until you need them.*

---

3. Under Description, give your email-sorting rule a name. By default, it will be Rule #1, Rule #2, and so on.

4. In the first Criteria pop-up menu, select the field that applies to that specific rule, such as To, From, Subject, and so on.

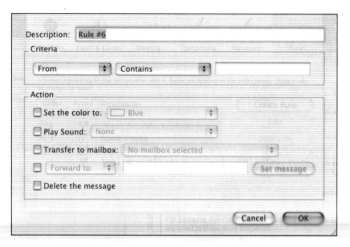

Figure 22.19   Create an email rule here.

5. In the second pop-up menu, choose the criteria that triggers the rule, such as whether the message Contains, Does Not Contain, Includes, and so on.

6. Type the word or phrase that field must contain to trigger the rule. For example, if all messages from someone named **grayson@rockoids.com** are to be stored, you'll enter that information for this particular rule.

7. Under Action, check the items that determine how your rule will be applied. The first two, Set The Color To and Play Sound, are simply appearance and notification options that don't change the message.

8. In the Transfer To Mailbox field's pop-up menu, you can select the mailbox to which the message is to be moved. If an appropriate mailbox isn't available, choose New Mailbox from the application's Mailbox menu and produce a new mailbox that does meet your needs.

9. To forward all messages that meet the criteria to another address, select the Forward To checkbox and specify the address.

10. You can also delete a message that meets the criteria, by selecting the Delete The Message checkbox. This option is a good way to dispose of known email offenders, although there are plenty of unknown ones who can keep you working overtime to create new rules.

11. When you're finished, click OK to close the Mail Preferences window. From here on, any email that matches the rule criteria will be stored as you've selected. You can create different rules for different messages to provide a full range of options for storing your messages.

Getting Your Email Automatically

When you first use Mail, it automatically checks for your email on all active accounts at regular intervals. You can change this option if you want only to retrieve email manually.

Here's how to adjust the option:

1. With Mail open, go to the Application menu and choose Preferences.

2. Click Accounts and select the account for which you want to change the setting.

3. In the resulting setup window, click Show Advanced Options, and then check or uncheck the Include This Account When Checking For New Mail option (it's checked by default).

4. Click OK to store the settings. You'll be returned to the main Accounts setup window. From here, you can choose the Check Accounts For New Mail pop-up menu to look for new messages in your active accounts at a given interval (normal is five minutes) or manually.

5. The last setting allows you to select a sound from the pop-up menu that will notify you when a new message is received (I like Temple, but you can select None if you don't want to be disturbed). Click the close box after you've made your changes to complete the process.

Using the Address Book

No doubt you have regular contacts you'd like to send messages to without having to enter the names manually in an email message window. Mac OS X includes a simple Address Book application (see Figure 22.20) that you can use to store your commonly used email addresses, or just to keep a record of your regular contacts. In

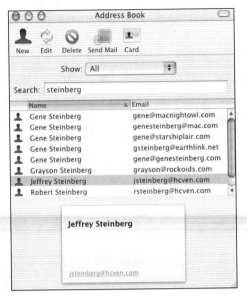

Figure 22.20   The Address Book application provides no-frills handling of your regular contacts.

addition, you can import your contacts from other email programs, although the range of information is not as extensive as, say, Microsoft's Outlook Express or Entourage X.

To use this program, perform the following steps:

1. Choose Addresses from Mail's Window menu. If Mail isn't open, you'll find the Address Book application in the Applications folder.

2. In the Show menu, click on the category that describes your contact: All, Buddy, Home, Favorite, or Work.

3. To create a new contact, click New. Enter the information in the appropriate contact fields in the Address Card window (See Figure 22.21). Pop-up menus give you different categories for the information fields.

NOTE: The four Custom fields let you create custom labeled fields for different types of information, such as birthdays, anniversaries, and so on.

4. When the address card is filled in, click the Categories button to produce the Choose Categories dialog box (see Figure 22.22), and specify the appropriate categories.

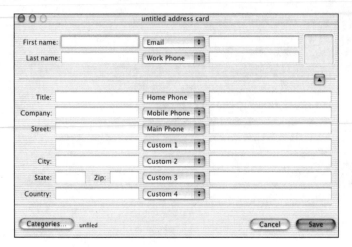

Figure 22.21   Fill in the blanks to set up a new contact.

Figure 22.22   Select one or more categories.

NOTE: *You can attach one address card to multiple categories, or even create new categories as needed.*

---

5. Click OK, and click Save to store the settings.

6. Repeat the preceding steps for each individual or group you wish to store.

NOTE: *To delete an address book entry, just click on it and press Delete. Zap, it's gone. But be careful, because there's no way to restore it without re-importing it or typing it all over again.*

---

7. Once you've completed an address card for a contact, you can click on the name and see the basic contents in the Preview window at the bottom of the Address Book window.

Importing an Address Book

You do not have to redo your entire address book once you've moved on to Mail. A reasonably adept Import feature will let you import basic information from other email programs. To use the feature, follow these steps:

1. Go to your email program and use the options available (if any) to export your address book as a separate tab-delimited file (one in which each field is separated by a tab, and each record is separated by a return). Original email databases for the various programs are not likely to be recognized unless imported.

> **NOTE:** Address Book only works in one direction as far as getting address information from other programs is concerned. It cannot export the address book you create in the program so you can use it in another program. I wanted to bring them into Microsoft's Entourage X, but neither Apple nor Microsoft had a way to do it beyond the standard cut and paste routine.

2. With Address Book open, choose Import from the File menu to bring up an Open dialog box shown in Figure 22.23.

3. Select the file you want and click Open. The list you selected will be added to your Address Book, using nearly the same fields as the original.

Figure 22.23   Choose the address book file from the Open dialog box.

NOTE: *If Address Book can't parse the fields, a dialog box will open in which you can select the proper destination fields for your data from a pop-up menu. If the address book entries don't come through accurately, you will need to select them in Address Book, click the Edit button, and adjust them as necessary.*

Finding a Message

Did you ever wonder what you said in that message you sent to a client a week earlier? Or, perhaps you want to find out if you sent your aunt a birthday gift, or you just need to recheck the acknowledgment letter you got from a dealer so you can track the progress of an order. Mail provides a decent set of search options so you can easily locate the message you want.

You can search by the message's header, such as the From and To information; by its subject; or by content. Here's how to run a search:

1. With Mail running, locate the mailbox you want to search, and click on its name in the Mailboxes drawer.

NOTE: *Mail indexes the contents of text messages, but you cannot search for text within an image or a file attachment of any kind.*

---

2. Enter the word or phrase that describes your search in the Search field of Mail's Edit menu.

3. If a match is found, you'll see it displayed in a results window.

4. If your search ends up with the wrong result or no result, consider these options to refine your search request:

   - *Include All Words*—A search request that reads "Cars and Ford", for example, will look for email that contains these words. Use the word "and" between each word in your search.

   - *Include One Word Or The Other*—If you enter "Cars and Ford", Mail will look for matches that contain either word.

   - *Use Either Or*—If you enter "Cars and (Ford or Cadillac)", material in the first category will be located, as well as either of the items entered within the parentheses.

Why Can't I Send My Email?

Although Mail is a fairly robust application, at times it simply won't work properly. If you encounter any difficulties getting your email to go out to its recipient, consider these remedies:

- *Are you connected?* Make sure that you are actually connected to your ISP. If you're using Internet Connect for a dial-up connection, open that application and look at the status screen to make sure a connection has been made. If you've activated a system status icon for Internet Connect on your menu bar, the connection bar above the phone icon should remain solid. If it flashes, a connection hasn't been achieved. If you're connected but your email still won't work, click Disconnect to log off. Then, when the button changes to Connect, click it again to log in. If you're using a broadband connection to the Internet, such as a cable modem or DSL, you may want to try accessing a Web site to see if you have a connection. If you are connected via dial-up, or see no indication that your broadband connection is offline, contact the ISP directly for further help.

- *Message saved as a draft?* Maybe you clicked the wrong button when you wrote your message. To handle this problem, look at the folder where you put your draft email messages and select the message you want to send. Then, go to the File menu, choose Restore From Draft, and try sending your message again.

- *POP server's port number is incorrect.* Open Mail's Preferences window and click the Account button. Click on the name of the account you're using, and click Edit Account. With the account information displayed, click the Show Advanced Options button. Then, remove the entry at the bottom of the dialog box next to Connect To Server Using Port. Once you OK all the settings, Mail sets the proper number automatically when you again make your connection (assuming your ISP follows standard email protocols).

- *It's your ISP's fault.* Sometimes the fault lies with the service that provides your Internet connection. Check its Web site or call the ISP for information about maintenance or system-related problems.

NOTE: *On one occasion, I was unable to access the mail servers for my Excite@Home account. The technical support people gave me a different setting for its mail servers, and, once the changes were made, I was able to retrieve my email without further trouble. In addition, sometimes an ISP will change its server settings without proper notice to its subscribers (that is, in fact, what happened to me).*

22. Exploring Apple's Email Software

Why Are Messages Scrambled?

With your regular setup, Mail formats all your messages in Multipurpose Internet Mail Extensions (MIME) or Rich Text Format. That way, you can use text styles, color, embedded graphics, and Web links in your messages. Keep in mind, however, that not all email programs can read these added frills.

To remove the formatting option, just open a new message window, and then go to the Format menu and select Make Plain Text. That should take care of this problem.

NOTE: *Although Claris Emailer won't interpret Rich Text in messages, it usually provides the text along with the core HTML code (the latter sometimes as an attached file). As a result the messages are, at least, readable.*

Why Doesn't Mail Check All My Accounts?

If you want Mail to automatically check for email from a specific email account, you must make sure the account is active and that it is accessed when you check for email. Here's how to confirm these settings:

1. Open Mail's Preferences window by choosing that option from the Application menu.

2. Click on the Accounts icon, select the email account, click Edit, and then click the Account Options tab.

3. Make sure the Enable This Account option is checked. It is that way by default, but you might have unchecked it to test a preference or to temporarily disable the account.

4. Click OK to store the account changes, and then close the Mail Preferences window.

With the settings configured properly, Mail should be able to retrieve your messages automatically from all active accounts.

Related solution:	Found on page:
Using Internet Connect for Dial-Up Networking	182

Chapter 23

Exploring Apple's iTools

In Brief

A Mac is not just the hardware and the operating system. Beginning a trend that was later echoed by other companies in the PC industry, Apple CEO Steve Jobs offered a visionary look at taking the company beyond the box during his Macworld Expo keynote in January 2000 in San Francisco. Instead of just selling computers, displays, peripherals, and the Mac OS, Apple wants to deliver additional user experiences that make the platform more compelling.

The first new feature announced was iTools (see Figure 23.1), a collection of exclusive features that only Mac users with Mac OS 9 or later installed could set up (although some features can be used by

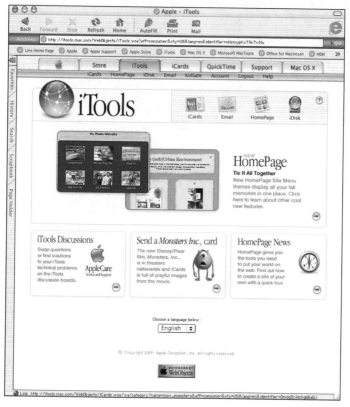

Figure 23.1   iTools is a collection of features that are only available to
Mac users.

folks who have older versions of the Mac OS or computers with other operating systems installed).

NOTE: *Another of Apple's "beyond the box" is a different sort of box, the iPod. Introduced in November 2001, the iPod is a miniature jukebox player that mates with iTunes to help you take your tunes on the road. This clever little device also serves duty as a small FireWire backup drive for your Mac.*

Some of the features of iTools are fluff, such as a Mac.com email address and the ability to review Web sites and have the reviews appear online; the latter feature, in fact, was later dismantled. But some of the other tools are downright useful, particularly the free storage space and the ability to create a simple Web site for your friends and family. Both areas will be covered in this chapter.

NOTE: *During his keynote announcing iTools, Jobs said that additional features would be added periodically. However, the reverse has been the case. First the Web site review area was dismantled, and then the KidSafe feature, which allowed parents to provide a safer Web surfing experience, was discontinued due to lack of interest.*

Reviewing iTools Features

iTools is designed to be a set of Internet-based services that, for the most part, are free and that help Mac users expand their surfing experience. Here's a list of the four features available to iTools members at the time this book went to press:

- *Email*—Create an email address with a Mac.com domain (see Figure 23.2). The feature can be set up with any email application, other than AOL and CompuServe 2000, and it gives you an email address that can be considered prestigious, or just a reflection of your commitment to your favorite computing platform.

NOTE: *Apple's iTools are not meant to replace your ISP. You need an Internet account to access these services. In addition, AOL's proprietary email system makes it impossible to send email via the Mac.com address. If you join EarthLink through your Mac OS X Setup Assistant, Apple will automatically configure a Mac.com email address as part of the package.*

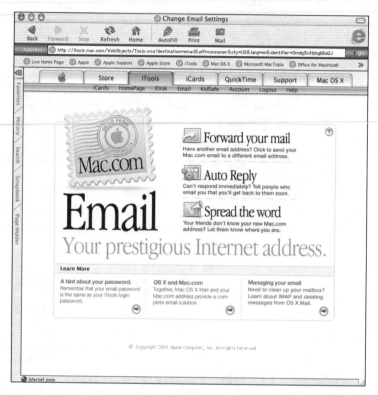

Figure 23.2   A Mac.com email address is one of the popular features
of iTools.

- *iDisk*—Apple gives you 20MB of free storage space at its Web
  site, free of charge. You can use iDisk, shown in Figure 23.3, for
  backups, your personal Web sites, or to make files available to
  friends, family, and business contacts. Apple also lets you purchase extra storage space of up to 1GB for an annual fee.

- *HomePage*—Would you like to build a Web site, but you don't
  want to learn a new application or hassle with HTML coding? No
  problem. Apple's HomePage feature lets you put up your personal
  Web site with a photo album, iMovie home videos, résumés, and
  more in just three convenient steps, all in a matter of minutes.
  Once your site is set up, it is handled by Apple's Web site, free of
  charge. The feature is similar to those offered by such services as
  AOL and EarthLink. And, like the other free Web sites, the site

476

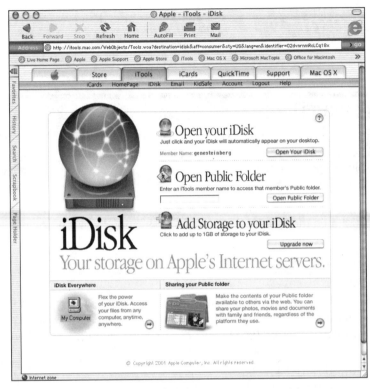

Figure 23.3   Use iDisk for online backups and other storage purposes.

can be accessed by anyone with Internet access; it's not restricted
to iTools users or even to
Mac users.

NOTE: *Such free no-hassle Web builders as HomePage aren't designed for a full-fledged
business site. They are fine for a personal page or a family photo album or even for posting your
own résumé. But if you wish to do business on the Web, the best way is to use a professional
Web-authoring program for your site (such as Adobe's GoLive or Macromedia's Dreamweaver)
and then get a regular "dot.com"-style custom domain name via a commercial Web hosting
service.*

- *iCards*—Send personal greeting cards or business announcements using a convenient array of photos and artwork. iCards
  also features a fairly decent selection of fonts and color styles.

Immediate Solutions

Installing iTools

The first stage of the setup process is to register your iTools account at Apple's Web site. This step was part of the initial Mac OS X Setup Assistant process, which means you may have already set up such an account. However, if you didn't set up your account at that time, here's what to do:

1. Launch the System Preferences application from the Dock or its normal place in the Applications folder.

2. Click on the Internet pane and make sure the iTools tab is selected.

3. Click the Free Sign Up button. This action will take you directly to the iTools sign-up page, where you can enter your registration information (see Figure 23.4). Click Continue to proceed.

NOTE: *The iTools interface at Apple's Web site undergoes constant updating. If what you see online differs from what you see in this book, don't be concerned. Simply follow the instructions listed, using the following material as a guideline.*

4. As with a regular ISP, user names can't be duplicated. If the name you selected is already in use (don't even try **steve@ mac.com**, for obvious reasons), you'll see a Select Another Name prompt that provides a list of alternate names. You can either select one or enter another name in the information field and then click Continue.

NOTE: *Don't be surprised if you have to continue to experiment with alternative names until one is accepted, in the event you don't pick the ones offered.*

5. After you've set up your account, you'll see a Save For Your Records page, which you can print out to have a hard copy record of your user name, password, and the required email settings (Apple's Mail application sorts out most of this information for you in its setup box). A copy will also be emailed to you at your new Mac.com address. Click Continue to move on.

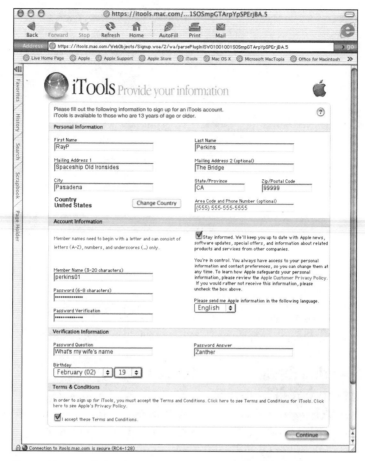

Figure 23.4   This is, of course, not a real registration.

6. Once your account is set up, you'll see a welcome screen. Click Start Using iTools to go to a page where you can send an iCard to your online contacts, notifying them about your new address (see Figure 23.5). You can, of course, bypass this process if you don't want to send the notice.

7. You can continue to use iTools or return later to sample the features.

TIP: *If you plan to revisit the iTools Web site frequently, you'll want to bookmark the site in your Web browser. It's already available under Favorites in Internet Explorer (as a submenu among the Apple bookmarks).*

Figure 23.5   Send an email announcement about your new address.

Configuring Email Software to Access Your Mac.com Email Address

Once you've registered your new email address, you'll want to configure your email program to access the mail. For this chapter, I'll use Apple's Mail application to show you the process, but you can also configure any other email client in pretty much the same way. Just follow these steps:

NOTE: By default, Mail is configured with your iTools email account, but I'm discussing configuration separately in case the settings need to be redone for a new user or made at a later time. For more information about using Mail, please read Chapter 22.

1. Go to the Dock and click the Mail icon; if it's not in the Dock, launch it directly from the Applications folder by double-clicking its icon.

2. With the program running, go to Mail's Application menu and choose Preferences. The window shown in Figure 23.6 appears.

3. Click the Accounts icon, and click the Create Account button to bring up the Account Information dialog box.

Figure 23.6 Switch to your Mac.com email account in the Mail Preferences dialog box.

TIP: *You can create separate Mac.com user accounts for each user of your Macs to give them maximum flexibility to use iTools on a single Mac; or, better, just set up individual user accounts for each, using Mac OS X's multiple users feature, as described in Chapter 6.*

---

4. Choose Mac.com Account from the Account Type pop-up menu. Doing so will automatically insert the default mail server settings needed.

5. Give your account a description (it's optional, but helpful if you want to recheck the settings later). I call mine iTools Account for obvious reasons.

6. Enter your full name, user name, and iTools password. You can't put in the email address (it will be added automatically later).

7. When your settings are complete (see Figure 23.7), click OK to store them.

NOTE: *As soon as you establish your iTools user account, Apple's mail server will be checked and your mail database will be synchronized to make it up to date. This is also done to verify that your account settings are correct and to track your mailbox on the server as mail is received, sent, and deleted. If there's a problem, you'll see an error prompt indicating that the account couldn't be synchronized or located. If that happens, just recheck your account setup and make sure all information is correct.*

Related solutions:	Found on page:
Setting Up Multiple-User Access	133
Setting Up Your User Account	450

23. Exploring Apple's iTools

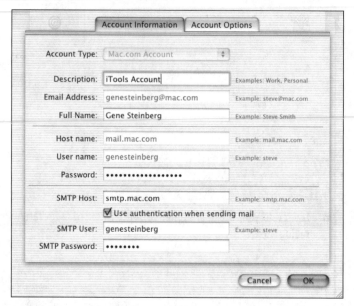

Figure 23.7   The author's account, already established.

Forwarding Mac.com Email

If you prefer to keep using your existing email account to handle messages, you can arrange to have your Mac.com email forwarded to that address. Just follow this setup procedure:

NOTE: *In addition to being able to forward email, you can use your email software to create custom signatures, automatic message retrieval, and so on.*

---

1. Access Apple's iTools Web site at **www.apple.com/itools**.

2. Log on to iTools by typing your username and password at the Sign In prompt.

3. With the iTools page on your browser, click the Email button at the iTools Web site to access the page shown in Figure 23.8.

4. Click the Forward Email button. The window shown in Figure 23.9 appears.

5. Change the Email Forwarding Is radio button to On.

6. Enter the complete email address where you want your Mac.com email forwarded.

Figure 23.8   Configure Mac.com email features here.

Figure 23.9   Enter an address to forward your email to.

23. Exploring
Apple's iTools

WARNING!   When you opt to forward email, the messages are not stored on Apple's email server. The only way to retrieve those messages is from the address to which they were sent until the setting is changed.

7. Click the Submit button to store your changes. You'll be returned to the Mac.com setup page, and all your subsequent email will be forwarded to the email address you specified.

NOTE: *The address you specify isn't set in stone. You can change it to another address at any time, or just click the Off button in the Email Forwarding page to deactivate the feature.*

Telling Your Friends About Your New Address

Now that you have a new email address, you'll want to let your friends know. Just follow these steps to have an iCard sent to your mailing list:

1. Bring up Apple's iTools Web site at **www.apple.com/itools**.

2. Log on to iTools by typing your username and password in the Sign In prompt.

3. On the main iTools screen, click the Email button.

4. Click the Spread the Word button to bring up a page where you can address your iCards (see Figure 23.10).

Figure 23.10   Send iCards to your regular contacts.

5. In the Recipient's Email text field, enter the address of someone to whom you want to send the announcement.

6. Click Add To List.

7. Repeat Steps 5 and 6 for each additional recipient. As they are added to the list, they'll appear in the Recipient List category.

8. If you want a copy of the iCard for confirmation, select the Send A Copy Of This iCard To Myself checkbox (it's set that way by default).

9. When you're finished, click the Send iCard button to speed announcements on their way.

Sending Vacation Notices

While you're away on vacation or on a business trip, wouldn't it be nice if folks who wrote to you knew that you were away and you were not being rude because you didn't respond to their messages? The iTools Email tool lets you send an automatic reply, so they'll know you're not around to give a personal response.

Here's how to use the feature:

1. Connect to Apple's iTools Web site at **www.apple.com/itools**.

2. Log on to iTools by typing your username and password at the Sign In prompt.

3. With the iTools page displayed, click the Email button.

4. Click the Auto Reply button. The window shown in Figure 23.11 appears.

5. Change the Auto Reply Setting radio button to On to activate the feature.

6. In the Auto Reply Message field, change the sample text if you want something with more details about when you'll be able to check and respond to messages. Or, if you prefer to use the existing message, just leave it as it is.

7. Click the Submit button.

8. To turn off the Auto Reply function, just return to the Email Auto Reply page and select the Off radio button.

9. Click Submit to store your changes.

Figure 23.11   Tell your contacts you're not around to answer.

Using the iDisk Feature

One of the more useful functions of iTools is iDisk, which, by default, gives you 20MB of free storage space to use as you wish. Here's how to use the feature.

From the Mac OS X Finder, choose iDisk from the Go menu or press Command+Option+I. Within a few seconds, the icon for your personal iDisk will appear on the desktop and be listed under Computer in the Finder. You can now access this disk in the same fashion as any other available share, viewing files, sending and retrieving files, and so on.

NOTE: *The speed of iDisk access depends on several factors, not the least of which is the speed of your connection to your ISP. It will be slow going with a dial-up connection, but reasonably swift with a broadband hookup. In addition, network congestion at Apple's Web site may contribute to performance slowdowns.*

TIP: *You can also add the iDisk icon to the Finder's toolbar. Choose Customize Toolbar from the View menu, and when the list of icons appears, drag the iTools icon to the position you want in the toolbar. Click Done to make it so.*

However, your iDisk isn't exclusive to your Mac running Mac OS 9 or X. You can access your files from any PC running the Linux or Windows operating system if it uses a WebDAV client application.

Here's how it's done:

1. From the PC, launch your Web browser and enter the following URL: **http://idisk.mac.com/*username*** (where you enter your iTools account name).

2. Enter the password from the login prompt.

Alternately, you can access your iDisk right from the iTools Web site, so you can easily get to it should you be using a Mac other than the one you normally work on. Just follow these instructions:

1. Access Apple's iTools Web site at **www.apple.com/itools**.

2. Log on to iTools by typing your username and password at the Sign In prompt.

3. On the main iTools page, click the Go button in the iDisk category to bring up the setup page, shown in Figure 23.12.

4. To open your iDisk, simply click the Open Your iDisk button. Within a few seconds, the icon for your disk will show up on your Mac's desktop.

5. Among the features of iDisk is the ability to set aside a Public folder, where other users of the feature can send and retrieve files. To open someone else's Public folder, enter his or her member name in the text field, and then click the Open Public Folder button. That folder will appear on your Mac's desktop.

NOTE: *Other users can access your Public folder on your iDisk without having to know your password. Have them point their browsers to **http://idisk.mac.com/username/Public**. Any file placed in your Public folder can be retrieved in this fashion by anyone with Internet access, so be careful what you put there.*

6. The remaining option costs extra: To increase storage space beyond the standard 20MB, you can purchase up to 1GB of storage space, at an annual fee. Click the Add Storage To Your iDisk button to access the information page where you'll see the latest price list and how to place your order.

NOTE: *You could, of course, create separate iTools accounts for yourself and get 20MB for each, but that would be a rather convoluted way to manage the various free disk space features.*

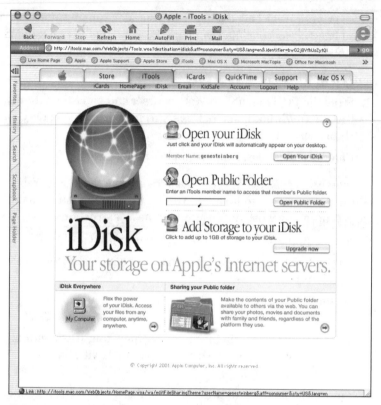

Figure 23.12   Configure your iDisk options here.

Creating a Web Site with HomePage

Some of the popular ISPs offer a convenient feature for budding Web authors: a free Web space where you can post a personal page. Depending on the service, you may even get a free setup program that uses templates and step-by-step wizards to set you up in minutes.

Here's how to set up your Web site on Apple's Web servers using Apple's HomePage Web authoring tool:

1. Connect to Apple's iTools Web site at **www.apple.com/itools**.

2. Log on to iTools by typing your username and password at the Sign In prompt.

3. When you see the main iTools page, click the Go button under HomePage to call up the window shown in Figure 23.13.

Figure 23.13   Apple makes it super easy to build your personal page at its
Web site.

4. At the left of the HomePage site are buttons that specify the type of page you can make. To get started, just click a page category. As a sample, I'll use Personal, which produces the page shown in Figure 23.14.

5. On the next page, choose a theme for your page from those offered. I'm deliberately not showing you the choices here because they change on a regular basis.

6. To add your text, click the Edit Text button, and make your entries in the text fields provided. You have several options with which to edit and style text to your taste.

7. Click Apply to store your text.

8. To add images to your site, click the Choose button in the image area, and then pick an image from those shown in the iTools Image Library. You can also choose any image that's stored on your personal iDisk.

Figure 23.14   From here to a home page on the World Wide Web takes just a few minutes.

TIP: When using your own pictures, stick with the tried-and-true Web picture formats, such as GIF, JPEG, or PNG. If you try to use pictures of other formats, at best, they just won't display; and at worst, you'll cause those accessing your site to download unknown files.

---

9. To add Web links pointing to your favorite sites, click again on the Edit Text button and enter the URLs of your favorite links.

10. Click Publish to store the settings.

11. At any time, you can look at your work in progress by clicking the Preview button; Figure 23.15 shows an example. You can perform this step over and over again to double-check your work.

NOTE: As explained in the next section, you can easily edit your pages even after they're published on the Web.

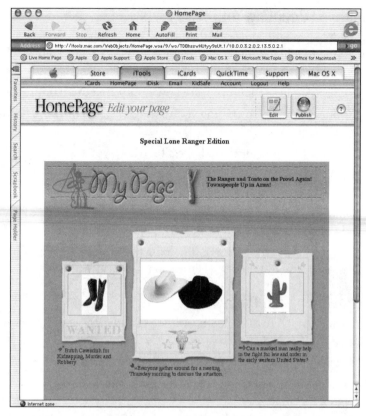

Figure 23.15 All right, it's not finished, but here's how the work I have done looks so far.

12. All done? Just click Publish to make your site available to anyone with Web access. You get an acknowledgment indicating the URL of your new Web site. Now you can send an iCard to your online contacts so they can pay a visit.

TIP: You can follow the preceding steps to create additional pages at your Web site and then use links on a page to access the next one. Doing so can greatly expand the features of your site. You can also keep the pages separate and give visitors the various URLs to access the pages you want them to see.

NOTE: The first page you create with HomePage is your site's home (or start) page as well. When you access the HomePage area, this page will be marked with an asterisk in the list. To change the home page that visitors access when they call up your set, connect to the HomePage site, select the name of the page you want to make your site's home page, and click Set Start Page.

491

Editing or Updating Your Web Page

Once you've created and published your Web site, it's easy to change it any time to add text and pictures or adjust Web links. Here's what to do:

1. Access Apple's iTools Web site at **www.apple.com/itools**.

2. Connect to iTools by typing your username and password at the Sign In prompt.

3. Go right to the main HomePage site, where you'll see a list of the pages you've created with HomePage.

4. Select the page you want to alter, and click Edit.

5. On the next page, make your text changes and, as necessary, add or remove pictures from your page.

6. When you're through, click the Publish button to make the updated site available to visitors on the World Wide Web.

Removing a Web Page

Have you decided to take down your site, or do you want to remove some of the pages you've created? Here's what to do:

1. Access Apple's iTools Web site at **www.apple.com/itools**.

2. Connect to iTools by typing your username and password at the Sign In prompt.

3. Go right to the main HomePage site, where you'll see a list of the pages you've created with HomePage.

4. Select the page and click the minus sign located adjacent to the Edit button. You will go to a page where you must OK removal of the page before it's done (this way you can go back if you have second thoughts).

NOTE: Even though you are deleting your Web page, any images on that page will remain on your iDisk for storage or to use for another purpose.

Solving HomePage Problems

When your site's URL is accessed, it should show the exact site that you created. However, sometimes it may not look right. Here are some possible problems and solutions:

- *The site isn't available.* Are you sure you published your site in HomePage? Just to be sure, go back to HomePage, edit your Web page, and publish it again. If you can't access Apple's site, the problem may be due to maintenance at Apple's Web servers. Of course, you should also double-check that you can access other sites. If not, you may need to log off your ISP and then reconnect.

- *The wrong version of the site appears.* First, click the Refresh (or Reload) button on your browser to load the page from scratch. If that doesn't work, go back and edit and publish your site again. Perhaps you missed a step, but this way, you'll be sure that the correct version of the site is available.

NOTE: *AOL, CompuServe 2000, and some ISPs may cache sites frequently accessed by their members. As a result, the update may not be available immediately.*

- *The site looks different on other browsers.* You probably can't do much about this problem. Different Web browsers interpret the HTML code that makes up a Web page differently. Text may be larger or smaller; and tables, pictures, and other elements may appear somewhat different. You might want to examine your site in both Microsoft Internet Explorer and Netscape, and perhaps even OmniWeb, to be assured that the look is acceptable (even if different) from browser to browser.

- *The artwork looks fuzzy on AOL.* AOL has a program preference called Use Compressed Images in its Web settings. The primary purpose of this setting is to increase the speed of retrieving a Web site, by compressing images on the fly at AOL using a proprietary format called .ART. But sometimes it will hurt quality and may prevent Web animations from appearing. The best approach is usually to turn it off. You can access your Web settings under Preferences from your AOL software.

23. Exploring Apple's iTools

Glossary

10BaseT—The designation for standard 10Mbps Ethernet run over twisted-pair network cable. 10BaseT is the most common form of Ethernet available today and has largely supplanted the other forms of Ethernet: ThickNet and ThinNet (which use coaxial cable). 10BaseT utilizes either Category 3 or Category 5 four-pair twisted-pair wire to send data up to 100 meters without the need for a repeater. The follow-up to 10BaseT is the newer 100BaseTX, which sends data at 100Mbps over Category 5 twisted-pair cable. As the cost of 100BaseT network adapters and the associated hubs and switches continues to drop, expect that 100BaseTX will replace 10BaseT. Other variations include 100BaseFx and 100BaseVG. The latest generation, supported by Apple's current line of desktop Power Macs and the revised version of the PowerBook G4, is 1000BaseT, also known as Gigabit Ethernet.

active window—The Finder or document window that you are presently using. The Finder lets you work in single-window mode, where the nonactive Finder and document windows are collapsed and moved to the Dock.

alias—A pointer or reference to an original file that is accessed in the same fashion as the original. An alias allows you to more easily access a file, regardless of whether it is located on your Mac's drive, on a networked drive, or on the Internet; the Unix version is the Symbolic Link.

America Online (AOL)—The largest Internet Service Provider (ISP) in the world, with more than 33 million members and increasing as fast as we speak. Headquartered in Vienna, Virginia, AOL (part of the AOL Time Warner conglomerate) provides Internet access to users worldwide.

Apache—The world-famous Web hosting software is built into Mac OS X, and is activated simply by starting Web Sharing in the Sharing preference panel. Once activated, you can host your own Web site on your Mac.

Apple menu—The menu that sits in its accustomed spot at the left side of the menu bar. Apple has revised the Apple menu to include system-wide commands formerly reserved for the Special menu. These include the ability to restart and shut down the computer.

AppleScript—Apple's scripting language, a natural language programming feature that lets you automate repetitive or complex routines by running a small application (or applet).

AppleTalk—A network protocol developed by Apple Computer in the mid-1980s to provide networking services for Macintosh operating system (OS) computers. AppleTalk is available in two forms: AppleTalk Phase 1, which was developed in 1984, and AppleTalk Phase 2, which was released in 1988 to address many of the issues that plagued AppleTalk Phase 1. AppleTalk is available on all Macintosh-based computers and provides a quick and simple workgroup networking solution that can be set up in minutes.

AppleTalk Phase 1—Introduced in 1984, a protocol that provided a quick and easy way to network Macintosh computers together. Unfortunately, AppleTalk Phase 1 networks are limited to only 127 computers per network.

AppleTalk Phase 2—Introduced in 1988, a protocol designed to address the limitations of AppleTalk Phase 1. Unlike AppleTalk Phase 1, AppleTalk Phase 2 networks can have up to 65,298 network segments, known as zones, and can have up to 254 AppleTalk devices per zone.

AppleTalk zones—The segments into which a network is divided. This method allows more AppleTalk devices on the same network segment than would normally be permitted by the limit of 254 AppleTalk devices per network. AppleTalk zones are also used in a manner somewhat like an office workgroup or department, in which all the computers in a specific AppleTalk zone have access to all the resources that are available on that zone.

AppleWorks—Apple's business application suite, supplied free on consumer models, such as the iBook and iMac. AppleWorks 6 was one of the first programs Carbonized to run native under Mac OS X.

application—The program that actually lets you do work on a Mac. An application may handle word processing or page layout chores, allow you to access the Internet, or perform preventive maintenance on your Mac by checking your hard drive.

Application menu—Represented by the application icon or name at the left side of Mac OS X's menu bar, the Application menu lets you access additional features, such as quitting an application or accessing its preferences. In some programs, particularly ones not fully ported to the new operating system, the File menu provides some of these features.

Glossary

application programming interface (API)—The set of tools programmers use to develop software for a specific operating system. See also *Carbon* and *Cocoa*.

assistants—Special programs, such as the Setup Assistant, that are used to configure settings for your Mac operating system or to perform a complex function in software. Examples of the latter include the assistants provided with programs such as AppleWorks to set up a template for a specific type of document.

attachment—One or more files that are connected to your email message, in effect going along for the ride. You can attach a document, graphics, or program file, but your ISP may restrict the maximum size of the file.

back up—The process of making one or more extra copies of your files as a protective measure to guard against the possibility that your original file may become lost or damaged.

binary numbers—The 1s and 0s that make up computer language.

Blind carbon copy (BCC)—This is a copy of an email message sent to recipients without displaying the names of others who might receive the message.

bookmarks—See *Favorites*.

boot—Short for *bootstrap*, the process of starting a computer. During the boot process, your Mac's hardware is checked, and then the operating system components load.

browser—A program that's used to view files. This term is generally used for a Web browser, a program that accesses and interprets documents on the World Wide Web and converts them to a form that reflects their original content.

byte—The basic object of data that a computer uses. In a modern computer, a byte consists of 8 bits—that is, 1s or 0s that represent a binary number. See also *binary numbers*.

cable modem—A device that works with a standard cable television connection to provide high-speed Internet access.

cache—Usually, a small amount of memory allocated for frequently used data. You'll find a cache in such places as a hard drive, a CPU, and a logic (or mother) board.

Glossary

Carbon—A set of application programming interfaces that allows a software publisher to update its existing programs to support the Aqua interface and most other features of Mac OS X. See also *application programming interface (API)*.

carbon copy (CC)—The process of sending one or more extra copies of email messages to other recipients.

CD-ROM—Stands for compact disc read-only memory; a variant of the music CD that stores computer data. CD-ROMs are also used for software installations. The departure of floppy drives from Macs, the lower cost of pressing CDs, and the larger space taken up by software have all contributed to the switchover.

checkbox—A small, square box that's used to toggle a specific program function. You may, for example, click on a checkbox to insert a checkmark that activates a feature; then you click again to remove the checkmark and turn off the feature.

checksum—A number that is calculated based upon the data in a packet or file. Checksums are reviewed as the data is being examined after transmission to see if the checksum calculated before transmission and the checksum calculated after transmission are identical, indicating that the data was not corrupted.

Chooser—In Mac operating systems prior to Mac OS X, a program that controls the Macintosh's networking and printer connections.

click—The process of moving your pointing device (mouse, trackball, and so on) over an item, and then pressing the mouse button one time.

clipboard—A memory-resident area onto which you copy or cut data from a document. The present iteration of the Mac OS clipboard stores just one item, so when you copy a second, it replaces the first. However, some programs (such as recent versions of Microsoft Word) have their own clipboard-handling features, which give you additional storage areas.

Clock—A Mac OS X application that displays an analog or digital clock on the Dock or, optionally, as a floating window.

close button—The small red button with an *X* in its center when the mouse moves over it, located at the top of a Finder or document window (it's gray when you access the optional Graphite interface). Clicking on the box closes the window but may not necessarily result in quitting the application.

Cocoa—An application programming interface for Mac OS X applications. Cocoa is descended from the NeXTSTEP programming environment, called Objective C, which is designed to make it easier to build complete applications using a set of predefined components called objects.

collapse button—The yellow Finder button (with a – in it when the mouse passes over it) that is used to minimize a window and move it to the Dock (under the optional Graphite interface, it's just gray).

ColorSync—A settings pane in the System Preferences application that allows you to configure color-matching options. ColorSync is a component of the Mac OS that allows input devices, computer monitors, and output devices, such as printers, to be more accurately calibrated.

command—A means of telling your computer how to perform a function. Commands may be entered by text or by selecting a menu item.

command-line interface (CLI)—A way of interacting with a computer or other intelligent devices using commands that you type in via a keyboard. Mac OS X includes an application known as Terminal that allows you to interact with the operating system the same as you do with any Unix-based system.

compression—A means of reducing the size of a file using mathematical algorithms that check for redundant data. Compression programs include such products as the StuffIt family from Aladdin Systems.

computer name—A name assigned to your Mac when you install Mac OS X, allowing it to be properly located and identified on your network. The name can also be modified in the Sharing panel of the System Preferences application.

contextual menu—A pop-up menu accessed by a Control+click. It displays a set of commands that relate specifically to the selected item, such as file management functions. For example, Control+clicking on a folder or disk icon will bring up a contextual menu of file management functions.

cooperative multitasking—The inefficient multitasking scheme of the Classic version of the Mac operating system in which programs are designed to work together to share CPU time. See also *preemptive multitasking*.

Glossary

creator type—A 4-byte code assigned to a Macintosh file that tells the Finder the application program that created it. The traditional Macintosh operating system (OS) uses creator codes to determine which application should be launched when a user attempts to open a specific file. In addition, Mac OS X can interpret file extensions, such as .doc for a Word document, to determine which application may be used to open a document (this is also done under the Classic Mac OS by way of the File Exchange Control Panel).

Darwin—The core of Mac OS X, incorporating a Unix microkernel that consists of Mach 3.0 and FreeBSD. Making this element of the operating system open source (meaning the programming code is available for use by anyone signing Apple's legal document) allows third-party programmers to develop updates and improvements that can then be shared. These changes may be used by Apple for updates and improvements to Mac OS X.

Date & Time—A settings panel in the System Preferences application that lets you set the time and date and whether your Mac's clock is automatically synchronized to a network or Internet-based time server.

DAVE—A tool from Thursby Software Systems, Inc., which allows the Macintosh to communicate using the Network Basic Input Output System (NetBIOS) protocol used on Windows-based networks. DAVE also provides Macintosh users with a variety of tools to access resources on the Windows-based network. See also *NetBIOS*.

desktop—The backdrop or background artwork that appears behind your Finder or file windows on your Mac. Icons representing files or disks may be placed upon the desktop for convenient access.

DHCP—Stands for Dynamic Host Configuration Protocol. A network protocol that automates the process of assigning an Internet Protocol (IP) address and other network-specific information to computers that request it on the network. A DHCP server on the network responds to requests from a computer on the network and then assigns an IP address to computers for a specified time. By only leasing the IP address to each computer, DHCP allows the IP addresses of computers that are no longer using them to be reclaimed and redistributed to other computers on the network. See also *IP*.

dialog box—A window that contains items you must click or enter data into to activate a particular function.

directory—See *folder*.

Dock—Mac OS X's taskbar, consisting of a row of colorful icons at the bottom of the screen (or, optionally, at the sides) that are used for one-click access to applications, files, and folders. It's meant as a replacement for the application switcher and Control Strip features of previous versions of the Mac OS.

domain—The organization to which servers and computers belong. For example, **www.apple.com** is a computer in the **apple.com** domain. Like the Domain Name Service (DNS), which controls domain information on the Internet and your local network, Microsoft Active Directory is based on the domain structure. See also *Domain Name Service (DNS)*.

Domain Name Service (DNS)—The service on the network that matches up a computer's host name with its Internet Protocol (IP) address. DNS servers receive requests from computers on the network that request the IP address of a server using a specific Internet domain name. For example, when you type in **www.apple.com**, your computer contacts a DNS server to get the IP address assigned to the computer named **www.apple.com**. It then takes the IP address it receives from the DNS server and uses it to connect to the remote computer. See also *IP* and *computer name*.

double-click—An action whereby you point at an item, and then press the mouse button twice in rapid succession to open or activate the item.

double-click speed—The rate or rhythm of a double-click required to activate a function. This setting is user-dependent and can be configured as a mouse setting in the Preferences application.

download—Receiving a file from another computer, whether on your network or via the Internet.

drag—Moving a selected item from one place to another. You can drag such things as picture objects, text, disk, and file icons.

drag-and-drop—Clicking on an item to select it, and then dragging it to a new location and releasing the mouse button, thereby dropping it into its new locale.

driver—A program that allows your Mac to work with a peripheral device, such as a printer, removable hard drive, scanner, or digital camera.

DSL—Short for Digital Subscriber Line. A method designed to deliver high-speed Internet connections to a home or office using standard telephone lines. A variation, ADSL, will throttle upload speeds to a fraction of download speeds, and is usually available at a lower monthly charge.

Glossary

501

duplex—The way a computer transmits and receives traffic on the network. Half-duplex mode means a computer must wait for all transmissions to it to cease before it begins sending out data. Full-duplex means a computer can send and receive data at the same time. 10Mbps Ethernet is normally half-duplex (full-duplex mode is not often implemented). 100Mbps Ethernet, also called Fast Ethernet, supports full-duplex mode; it allows a computer to send and receive data at 100Mbps each way, bringing the actual throughput up to 200Mbps. See also *Ethernet* and *Fast Ethernet.*

duplexing—A feature offered by some printers that allows you to automatically print on both sides of the page. If the option is available, you can configure it in Mac OS X's Print Center application and then the Print dialog box. Where the feature is offered, the printed page goes through a special paper path in which the paper is reversed so that the back side is printed after the front side.

DVD drive—A device using an updated version of CD technology that allows it to store a much greater amount of data. DVD-ROM drives can read regular CDs, plus those based on DVD technology (including videos). A DVD-R drive, such as the Apple SuperDrive, can burn both CDs and DVDs. DVD stands for Digital Versatile Disc (not Video, as commonly believed) because of the variety of formats it supports.

Edit menu—A menu used for text and picture editing functions, such as copying and pasting.

Eject—A Finder command that has two functions, depending on the kind of drive selected when it's accessed. It either dismounts a drive from your Mac or, if the drive is removable, ejects the disk media from the drive.

email—Short for electronic mail. One of the most popular forms of online communication. It's the process of sending messages across a network within an online service or across the Internet. See also *attachment.*

email address—The identity of the person you're contacting. The email address consists of two parts: the username, followed by an @ symbol, and then the location or domain that hosts the user's account. AOL and CompuServe members, on the other hand, use just their username (called a screen name) without a domain to communicate to other members of the service.

Empty Trash—A Finder command that removes any items placed in the Trash.

Glossary

Energy Saver—A settings pane in the System Preferences application that lets you set an idle time interval for a Mac system to shut down or sleep.

Erase—A function in Mac OS X's Disk Utility application that deletes the contents of a selected disk and creates a new directory (the same as the Initialize function in a disk formatting program). This function is disabled on the startup disk.

Ethernet—A network standard developed in the 1970s by Bob Metcalfe at Xerox PARC as a way to provide a high-speed connection between computers and printers. Over the years, Ethernet has become the principal network technology that links computers and other network-based devices on a local area network (LAN). Ethernet is most commonly seen in two varieties these days: standard Ethernet, which moves data at 10Mbps, and Fast Ethernet, which moves data at 100Mbps. Gigabit Ethernet, which moves data at 1 billion bits of data a second, is starting to become more widespread since its introduction in the desktop Power Macintosh line in the summer of 2000. See also *Fast Ethernet*.

Fast Ethernet—The version of Ethernet that transfers data at 100Mbps in half-duplex mode. Fast Ethernet can operate in full-duplex mode as well, so actual throughput using Fast Ethernet can reach 200Mbps.

Favorites—A feature of Mac OS X that lets you store aliases to items you wish to revisit on a regular basis. A similar feature is provided with a Web browser, where links are stored in a menu for quick access to the sites to which you want to return. However, the names of this feature vary. Although it's Favorites with Internet Explorer, Netscape calls it Bookmarks instead. See also *history*.

file extensions—The three-character suffixes on MS-DOS, Unix, and Windows files that tell the operating system what type of data the file contains. For example, a .doc file extension tells Windows that the file in question is a Microsoft Word document. Mac OS X recognizes a file either by its creator and type information (as with previous Mac OS versions) or by its file extension.

File menu—The menu that accesses file-related functions, such as opening and saving documents.

File Sharing—A feature of the Mac OS that allows you to easily share your Mac's files with other computers on a network or over the Internet.

Glossary

file system—The fashion in which files are stored on your Mac.

file type—The 4-byte code that tells the Macintosh operating system (OS) what type of data is contained in the file. For example, a file type of TEXT indicates that the file contains text.

Finder—An application that manages the file viewing and transfer process for the items available to your Mac, either locally or via a network. The Finder displays the list of available files, allowing you to open or transfer them to another location (such as a different drive volume or a networked volume).

firewall—A computer or router configured to act as a gateway between your local area network (LAN) and the Internet. Firewalls can be anything from a Cisco router with some access lists applied to the interface that is connected to the Internet, to special software you set up on your Mac. By limiting the access that computers on the Internet have to your LAN, the firewall protects you from attack and intrusion by hackers and other unfriendly elements. Mac OS X has a built-in command line firewall that can be enabled via the Terminal or via a shareware utility, such as FireWalk X.

FireWire—A high-speed peripheral bus that is now featured on all Macs but the entry-level iMac. It provides plug-and-play capability, a potential throughput of 400Mbps, and support for up to 63 daisy-chained devices for each FireWire port. See also *USB*.

floppy disk—An older magnetic storage medium consisting of a small square object, inside of which is a flexible sheet of magnetic material. Because of the limitations of this storage medium, newer Macs have dispensed with such drives. However, a later generation of storage devices called SuperDisk uses floppy-based media with up to 240MB of storage capacity. The Iomega Zip drive, with 100MB and 250MB capacities, also uses some floppy disk–based technology.

folder—A container-like item on your Mac identified by a folder-like icon that holds other folders and files; also referred to as a directory.

formatting—(1) The process of erasing the contents of a drive and preparing it for use or reuse. (2) The characteristics of the text in your document, which include font, size, style, and color, along with the layout of the document.

fragmentation—In terms of disk storage, the separation of the various segments of files, which are placed on different parts of a drive. Fragmentation happens when larger files are frequently copied and removed from a drive. Computer memory may also become fragmented, but Mac OS X is designed to control the situation by allocating memory dynamically as needed by an application.

FTP—Stands for File Transfer Protocol. A protocol used to move files across the Internet, usually from a remote server to your desktop computer. FTP is commonly used to move files larger than 1MB because it is a more efficient protocol for moving data than Hypertext Transfer Protocol (HTTP). FTP uses Transmission Control Protocol (TCP) port 21 to send FTP commands between the sending and receiving computers, and a randomly assigned TCP port above 1024 to transfer the data. The most common FTP application on the Macintosh is known as Fetch. See also *HTTP* and *TCP.*

gateway—A computer or router that directs traffic off the current network segment and out to the rest of the network.

General—A settings pane in the System Preferences application. It's a throwback to the General Control Panel of Mac System 6 and earlier, where appearance options for titles, highlighting, and such options as text smoothing thresholds are set. By default, you can choose the Blue Aqua interface or a more subtle Graphite (Gray) option.

gigabyte (GB)—A term that refers to 1,024 megabytes.

Go menu—A menu, new for Mac OS X, that offers access to frequently used document folders, networked computers, and the Finder's toolbar buttons.

Grab—An application that performs screen captures. Mac OS X 10.1 also supports the traditional Mac method, Command+Shift+3, to capture a picture of your screen.

hard disk—A storage mechanism that consists of an assembly of rapidly spinning disks placed inside a sealed, rectangular enclosure. Data is read and written by one or more heads that access the data stored on the spinning disks. Also known as a fixed hard drive or just as a hard drive or fixed disk.

Help menu—A menu that, when accessed from the Finder or desktop, provides immediate access to the Mac OS Help menu. Most other applications also offer a Help menu of one sort or another.

hexadecimal numbers—Another method of describing the numeric value of a byte. Hexadecimal values are based upon base 16 math, where numbers range from 0 through F. To display the full value of a byte, you use two hexadecimal numbers. For example, to represent a byte with the value of 255, type "FF". See also *binary numbers.*

Glossary

HFS+—A version of the Macintosh file system that increases the number of files that can be supported on a Mac drive, thus reducing the minimum file size on larger devices. Similar to FAT32 under Windows. Sometimes known as Mac OS Extended.

Hierarchical File System (HFS)—The standard system for organizing files on the Macintosh operating system (OS). Similar to FAT16 on the Windows platform. Sometimes known as Mac OS Standard.

history—A feature of a Web browser that displays a list of recently visited sites. In contrast to a Bookmarks or Favorites feature (which includes the links you actually store), the history constantly updates as newer sites are accessed. The history list is normally cleared when you quit the application. See also *Favorites*.

home page—The introductory or index page of a Web site. A home page usually contains information about the site's purpose, along with links to its popular features. You can specify a default home page in your Web browser so that you always visit that site upon launching the browser.

HTML—Stands for Hypertext Markup Language. A text-based formatting language used to describe the elements of a Web page.

HTTP—Stands for Hypertext Transfer Protocol, the Internet Protocol (IP) network protocol that is used to move data from Web servers to your Web browser. HTTP utilizes Transmission Control Protocol (TCP) to send and receive information from a Web server and then to send back information to the Web server, allowing you to interact with it. It is a connectionless protocol, meaning that it sends or receives one piece of information and then closes down the connection. Although this approach made sense with small amounts of data, as on early Web pages, as Web pages grew, performance was apt to suffer. To improve HTTP's performance, HTTP version 1.1, which allows whole Web pages to be downloaded without breaking the connection, was developed. See also *HTTPS, IP,* and *TCP.*

HTTPS—The version of Hypertext Transfer Protocol (HTTP) that uses Secure Sockets Layer (SSL) encryption when you are sending and receiving data from secure Web servers. HTTPS normally uses Transmission Control Protocol (TCP) port 443 to send and receive information. HTTPS can use either 40- or 128-bit encryption, depending on where the browser or the server is located. See also *HTTP* and *TCP.*

hub—A connection device that forms the center of an Ethernet network; also used to extend the ports available via FireWire or USB.

hyperlink—An item in a document or on a Web page that, when you click it once, takes you to another page or site.

icons—One of the key features of a graphical computer operating system, such as Mac OS X. Icons are pictures used as metaphors for real-world items, such as folders, files, documents, or disks.

ICQ—The original instant-message protocol that is used to send instant messages across the Internet. ICQ is now owned by AOL Time Warner (see *Instant Messenger*). A related protocol, ICQW, also allows users to see when others are connected to the Internet and to set up multiperson conversations across the Internet.

iMovie—A desktop video editing program from Apple that is included with Mac OS X. It allows for simple drag-and-drop editing from a digital or DV camcorder, or from a multimedia file.

insertion point—A thin vertical bar in a text box that indicates where text is being entered.

Instant Messenger—A program from America Online (AOL) that sends instant messages across the Internet. This program also allows users to see when others are connected to the Internet and to set up one-on-one conversations with them. Special "branded" versions of Instant Messenger are provided by such companies as EarthLink and Netscape (a subsidiary of AOL). Microsoft's variation on the instant messaging theme is called MSN Messenger. See also *MSN Messenger* and *ICQ*.

International—A settings pane in the System Preferences application where you can specify system languages and currency conversion options, in addition to date and time formats unique to a specific part of the world.

Internet—(1) A worldwide computer network consisting of hundreds of millions of computers, used to spread data from computer to computer. The Internet has become the focal point for such enterprises as email, shopping, and mass communication. (2) A settings pane in the System Preferences application that lets you enter settings for hooking up to your ISP.

Internet Connect—An application used to make dial-up connections to your ISP. It combines functions from both the Remote Access and TCP/IP control panels of previous versions of the Mac OS.

Glossary

Internet Relay Chat (IRC)—A set of client software and servers that allows groups of users from all across the world to have interactive conversations in real-time. Users who want to join an IRC use an IRC client to connect to server networks on the Internet. Once connected to one of the many IRC networks, users can create or join conversations on just about every subject known to humans.

Internet Service Provider (ISP)—A company that provides users with a connection to the Internet. From huge ISPs such as America Online (AOL) and EarthLink to small local operations such as FastQ and Aracnets.com, an ISP allows users to dial up and connect to the Internet from their home or office.

IP—Stands for Internet Protocol. The network protocol that is used to send information over the Internet. IP was developed in the 1970s by Vincent Cerf and others to provide a reliable method of transferring data over the Internet. IP can send network traffic over many network media, from low-speed serial connections to multigigabit fiber connections.

iPod—A tiny jukebox player from Apple Computer that mates with iTunes and uses a Mac's FireWire port to synchronize your playlists, run as a backup storage device, and to receive electrical power.

iTunes—A jukebox program from Apple Computer, descended from Casady & Greene's SoundJam. It comes with Mac OS X and allows you to encode (rip) music from an audio CD, create playlists, play music and Internet radio, and burn music CDs.

Java—A cross-platform programming language that allows applications (or mini applications called applets) to execute or run on computers running a variety of operating systems. Mac OS X's Cocoa component includes native support for Java. Java is the brainchild of Sun Microsystems.

Jaz drive—A removable storage product from Iomega that uses standard hard drive technology and supports storage of 1GB or 2GB, depending on the drive and media used.

JetDirect—The trade name of a series of network interface cards and their associated software created by Hewlett-Packard for use with its DeskJet and LaserJet printers. JetDirect cards provide the printer with an Ethernet port and allow it to send and receive data from a server or workstation that is configured to host the printer.

Keyboard—A settings pane in the System Preferences application that is used for keyboard speed and repeat rates.

kilobyte (KB)—The equivalent of 1,024 bytes of data.

kbps—Short for kilobits (thousands of bits) per second; typically a measurement of data transfer rate.

link—(1) See *hyperlink*. (2) The Unix equivalent of an alias. See *alias*.

local area network (LAN)—A high-speed network, either in a single building or multiple buildings at a single site. LANs are almost always connected by some sort of high-speed networking infrastructure such as Ethernet.

LocalTalk—The Mac's original networking method, a slow but usable way to transfer data. Over time, Ethernet support was added; native LocalTalk was removed from new Macs beginning in 1998, with the introduction of the iMac. See also *network adapter*.

log in—The process of entering your username and password to access a specific computer or network service.

Login—A settings pane in the System Preferences application where you can also specify whether a login prompt appears at startup and which applications are turned on with your system. In that way, it provides a function similar to the Startup Items folder in previous versions of the Mac OS.

log off—The process of ending your session with a computer or network service.

Macintosh HD—The common name Apple gives to the hard drive on your new computer. This name can be easily changed, as long as the drive itself is not being shared over a network.

Mail—The email application that Apple provides with Mac OS X. It provides simple management of user accounts and also offers timed retrieval of messages.

mailbox—In email programs, a folder that contains the email messages you've stored or received.

maximize—The act of expanding a Finder or application window to its largest possible size. The maximize function under Mac OS X is controlled by a green button (with a plus sign inside when a mouse passes over it) at the left side of a window's title bar (it stays gray in the optional Graphite view).

Glossary

Mbps—Short for megabits (millions of bits) per second; typically a measurement of data transfer rate.

megabyte (MB)—The name for 1,024 kilobytes of computer data.

menu—A small window without title or control bars or buttons that contains a list of commands you can access to perform a function on your computer.

menu bar—A horizontal bar that extends across the top of your Mac's display, containing a list of labels of functions relevant to the Mac OS or the program you're using. Clicking any of those labels produces a menu with commands that relate to that label.

minimize—The act of reducing a Finder or application window to an icon that appears on the Dock. The minimize function under Mac OS X is activated by a yellow button (with a minus symbol within as the mouse passes over it) at the left of a window's title bar. See also *collapse button* and *Dock*.

modem—A device that is used to transfer digital computer data across analog telephone lines.

Monitors—Similar to the Control Panel under Mac OS 9; the settings pane available from the System Preferences application that lets you change screen depth and resolution. For some Apple-brand displays, geometry adjustments are also present.

Mouse—Part of the System Preferences application; the settings pane used to set mouse clicking and tracking rates.

MSN Messenger—Microsoft's version of an instant messaging program. See also *Instant Messenger*.

multitasking—A computer's performing more than a single function or running more than a single program at the same time. See also *cooperative multitasking* and *preemptive multitasking*.

NetBIOS—A networking scheme that allows applications and network services to communicate in a more or less transparent way. It is used by such programs as Thursby Software's DAVE and Connectix's DoubleTalk to provide networking between Mac and Windows-based personal computers. SAMBA, a NetBIOS client for Linux and Unix, became part of Mac OS X beginning with version 10.1.

network—A system consisting of two or more computers or a computer with shared printers. A network may be connected by wires or by such wireless features as Apple Computer's AirPort products.

Glossary

Network—A settings pane in the System Preferences application used for your network options.

network adapter—The piece of electronics that connects a computer to the local area network (LAN). One example of a network adapter is the Ethernet port that is included on all current Apple computers (such as the iBook, iMac, PowerBook, and Power Macintosh) and many modern Windows-based PCs. Other types of network adapters include Token Ring, an older IBM network system; and LocalTalk, the original network solution that Apple developed for inclusion with the Macintosh. See also *LocalTalk*.

network hub—A small electrical device that connects several network connections. To prevent signal loss, Ethernet hubs, for example, amplify the network signal so that it does not become degraded as it goes through the hub to its destination. The downside to hubs is that they connect all the computers on the network together and thus frequently cause performance degradation because of packet collisions. See also *hub*, *network switch*, and *packets*.

network segment—The portion of the network that is connected to a router. Network segments can range from a small two- or three-host network connected to an interface on a router to a large switched network with hundreds of computers all connected to a series of switches and then a router.

network switch—A small network device that connects several network connections together. To prevent signal loss, network switches amplify the network signal so that it does not become degraded as it goes through the switch to its destination. Switches, unlike hubs, do not connect all the computers on the network together, except as a virtual circuit. Thus they avoid performance degradation caused by packet collisions, because they create a connection directly between the source and the destination. See also *network hub*.

newsgroups—Internet-based bulletin boards where users from all over the world can converse and share information regarding a variety of topics. For instance, if you are looking for technical information about a problem you are having with a computer or your network, checking the appropriate newsgroups or posting a message may well get you an answer. Also called Usenet. You can use such programs as Microsoft's Entourage X, NewsWatcher X (a freeware application), or Thoth (shareware) to access newsgroup messages.

online service—The outgrowth of the original bulletin board systems (BBS) in the early days of personal computing. An online service consists of such features as message boards, email service, information centers, files for download, and chat rooms. The popular online services of the present day, including AOL, CompuServe, and Prodigy Internet, also include Internet access.

Open dialog box—A dialog box used to select a document to open from within an open application.

Open GL—An industry standard 3D technology commonly used for games, such as Quake 3 Arena from id Software. It is also used for 3D rendering programs, such as Maya, an animation program from Alias/Wavefront widely used in the motion picture industry.

packets—Little pieces of data formed when larger data is divided for efficient transfer over a network.

password—A set of characters (consisting of letters and/or numbers) that is used to gain access to a protected feature. You use a password for such functions as logging in to your Mac, to a network, or to your ISP.

point—The act of directing the mouse cursor above a specific item.

pop-up window—A menu listing various commands that is accessed by a Control+click (Apple's contextual menus feature) or from a dialog box.

port—(1) A connection jack used to attach peripherals to your Mac. These include such staples as your keyboard and mouse, as well as printers, removable drives, digital cameras, and other items. Current-model Macs include Ethernet and USB ports, and some include FireWire. (2) A reference to the connection points used for Internet access.

Post Office Protocol (POP)—The primary network protocol that mail servers use to distribute email to users across the network. Programs such as Eudora, Microsoft Outlook Express, Microsoft Entourage X, and Apple's Mail connect to the central email server using POP. Once they have logged on to the mail server, they can receive email that has been stored on the server waiting for the user to retrieve it.

PostScript—A page-description language developed by Adobe Systems in the early 1980s to improve the print quality of documents. In PostScript, the contents of a page are reduced to mathematical calculations, and as such, PostScript is commonly regarded as being device-independent. This means the quality of the printed document depends on the capabilities of the output device. Over the last 15 years, PostScript has evolved into the primary printer description language. Portable Document Format (PDF), which is the basis of Mac OS X's imaging technology, is based on PostScript. See also *TrueType*.

PostScript Printer Description (PPD) file—A file that tells your computer how to communicate with a specific PostScript printer to support its special features. For example, a PPD may tell your computer that the printer has multiple paper trays and allow you to select among them.

preemptive multitasking—A feature of Mac OS X and other operating systems in which the operating system serves as the task manager or traffic cop, parceling out CPU time to the various programs you are running. Compare with *cooperative multitasking*, a feature of older versions of the Mac OS in which the programs themselves shared CPU time.

preferences—A Mac OS X application or dialog box in which you make a set of configuration settings.

Print Center—An application used to select printers, manage printer options, and track and control printer job queues.

printer driver—A program that tells your computer how to communicate with the printers on your network. A LaserWriter printer drive ships with Mac OS X. Some laser printers require special, custom drivers to deliver specific features. Other kinds of printers, such as ink jet models, come with their own software that must be installed for them to work with your Mac.

print queue—The service on the computer or server hosting the printer that stores print jobs as they are getting ready for the printer. Setting access rights on the print queue is very important so that you do not allow inappropriate users to delete another user's print jobs.

Process Viewer—An application that lets you see how much RAM and processor power the system and opened applications are using. It can also be accessed via the Terminal when you do an ADMIN login and type the command "TOP".

protected memory—A feature of Mac OS X and other operating systems in which the programs you run each have a separate memory space. If the program crashes for any reason, it will be shut down and the memory address space cleared. This approach prevents that program from affecting other functions on your Mac and helps prevent a system-wide crash.

Glossary

pull-down menu—A list of commands that appears when you click on an item in the menu bar.

Quartz—The new imaging technology used for Mac OS X. It combines several standards, such as Open GL, PDF, and QuickTime, to provide the stunning visual effects that are part of the Aqua user interface.

QuickTime—Apple Computer's multimedia protocol, which supports a variety of audio and video compression methods to create and play back such productions. QuickTime is available in both Macintosh operating system (OS), Linux, and Windows versions. Preferences for Apple's QuickTime software can be set with the panel available from the System Preferences application.

QuickTime TV—A service of QuickTime, similar to RealAudio and its competitor, in which streaming audio and video presentations can be viewed from the Internet.

radio button—A small button, usually in a dialog box, that functions similarly to a checkbox. However, whereas more than one checkbox may sometimes be selected, a radio button toggles a function when clicked.

RAM—Stands for Random Access Memory. A computer chip designed to hold temporary memory, used by your Mac OS software and the application software you are running.

RAM Disk—A portion of RAM allocated to simulate a hard drive.

RealAudio—A popular Internet-based multimedia streaming protocol that allows users with a RealAudio or RealVideo player to hear audio and video productions direct from a Web site. It competes with QuickTime TV, which offers a similar capability.

reset switch—A small button (sometimes recessed) with a triangular-shaped icon above it or inside it. This button is used to force your Mac to restart in the event of a system crash. Mac OS X is designed to minimize the prospects of such problems.

router—A specialized computer whose sole purpose is to move network traffic from one network segment to another.

Save—The command you access to continue saving the contents of a document that has already been named and stored via the Save As dialog box.

Glossary

Save As—A dialog box that drops down as a sheet in the appropriate document window. It's used to name your file and to specify such items as file format and the location where the file is to be stored.

scalable font—A font that can be viewed or printed in any available point size. Both PostScript and TrueType fonts are scalable font formats.

Screen Saver—A pane available via the System Preferences application. It lets you activate Apple's new screen saver and set the idle time interval. This is a feature that more or less mimics the one previously available under Windows.

scrollbar—A vertical or horizontal bar that you drag to navigate a Finder or document window.

seed routing—The seeding of an AppleTalk network with a network number, also known as a cable range. By seeding the AppleTalk network's cable range, you can create zones on AppleTalk Phase 2 networks.

serial port—A connection jack used for such devices as modems, some printers, and digital cameras. Serial ports send data 1 bit at a time to the printer. Until Apple switched to USB for low-speed serial devices, all Macs had separate modem and printer ports for these functions (although they were combined in some PowerBooks).

Services—A feature of the application menu that displays links to programs that work with the one you have open to provide additional features.

Sharing—A pane under the System Preferences application where you can activate file sharing. The Mac OS X version also allows you to log into your Mac via Telnet and FTP.

Sheet—Mac OS X's revised Open and Save dialog box, which drops down from the window of the document to which the operation applies.

Sherlock—Apple's search program, which is used to locate items on your Mac's drive, on a networked volume, or on the Internet.

SMTP—Stands for Simple Mail Transfer Protocol. The network protocol that transfers mail between mail servers over the Internet. SMTP is a text-based protocol that runs over Transmission Control Protocol/Internet Protocol (TCP/IP) on port 25.

Sound—The settings pane in the System Preferences application that lets you set system and alert volumes, and choose from the repository of alert sounds.

Glossary

Special menu—No longer included with Mac OS X. This menu's functions have been moved to the Apple menu.

Speech—The settings pane in the System Preferences application that is used to select alert voices and speech rates for applications that support text-to-speech translation.

spooler—A program on a printer or on a server controlling the printer that stores print jobs until the printer is ready to print them. A printer spooler allows multiple people to print to the printer at the same time and then have each printer job stored and printed in the order that it came in. Some spooler programs prioritize the order in which print jobs are printed, based on who sent them and the priority assigned to them. The Mac OS X print spooler is the Print Center application. See *print queue.*

Startup Disk—The settings pane in the System Preferences application used to choose the disk from which your Mac starts. It can also be used to select between Mac OS X and older Mac OS environments.

StuffIt—A data-compression program from Aladdin Systems commonly used on Macintosh-based computers. Stuffed files are compressed using mathematical algorithms to reduce the space that the files take up on the computer. Stuffed files are commonly sent over the Internet because they can check themselves for consistency when the file is being unstuffed. Similar to the Zip protocol on the DOS and Windows platforms. See also *ZIP.*

SuperDisk—A removable device format that reads both regular HD (1.4MB) floppy disks and special 120MB and 240MB floppy-disk media.

surf—The act of browsing through Web sites in search of the ones that interest you.

System Menu—A type of application that puts up a display on the menu bar showing the status of a system setting. Mac OS X's System Preferences application lets you turn on a system menu for such functions as display resolution and color depth, volume, modem connection status, and AirPort networking.

System Preferences—An application that, in part, replaces the Control Panels folder. It offers direct access to Mac OS X system preferences, such as date and time, monitor resolution, and network configuration.

Glossary

TCP—Stands for Transmission Control Protocol. A connection-oriented network protocol that moves data over the local area network (LAN) or the Internet safely and reliably using Internet Protocol (IP). TCP relies on a built-in error-correction system to identify problems in the transmission of data and then retransmit them, ensuring that the data is transferred properly. TCP can also dynamically alter the speed of transmission to reflect changing network conditions or the load on either the sending or receiving computer. See also *IP*.

Telnet—A text-based network protocol that operates on Transmission Control Protocol (TCP) port 23. Telnet is frequently used when you want to communicate with a computer or router on the network that uses a command-line interface (CLI). Telnet is a popular tool used when you are connecting to routers on the network because it allows you to connect to any router on the network from one workstation. You can also use Telnet programs to connect to other TCP ports, such as port 25—Simple Mail Transfer Protocol (SMTP)—to probe them, and see whether the programs that use these ports are functioning as expected. See also *command-line interface (CLI)*, *SMTP*, and *TCP*.

Terminal—A Mac OS X application used to access the Unix command-line interface.

title bar—A rectangular area at the top of a Finder or document window that contains its name and navigation buttons.

toolbar—A row of icons or buttons that, when clicked once, activate a specific command in a program.

TrueType—A printer technology developed in the 1980s and 1990s, first by Apple Computer and later with the help of Microsoft, as an alternative to Adobe's PostScript fonts. Like PostScript, TrueType describes fonts as mathematical expressions so that they can be scaled or manipulated without destroying the original font's proportions. Although originally designed for the Macintosh operating system (OS), TrueType has become more popular on the Windows platform. See also *PostScript*.

typeface—A specific design for a set of printed letters and other characters. An example of a typeface is Helvetica Bold.

type size—The size of letters and numbers, measured in points (approximately 1/72 of an inch). The point size is measured from the top of a capital letter to the bottom of a descender, such as appears in the letter *y*, plus a little space for air.

type style—The altered look of a typeface in various forms, such as italic, bold, bold italic, and underlined.

UFS—Stands for Unix File System. A file system available under Mac OS X. A UFS-formatted disk is free of disk fragmentation problems and is a good environment for developing Unix and Mac OS X applications, but isn't compatible with the Classic Mac OS.

Unix—A popular industrial-strength multitasking operating system that was developed at AT&T Bell Laboratories. Originally intended for minicomputers, it has been modified for use on personal computers. Various flavors of Unix are available. Popular variations include Linux and Mac OS X.

upload—The process of transferring a file from your Mac to another computer on a network or via the Internet.

URL—Stands for Uniform Resource Locator. The information used to locate and access a site on the Internet or on your local network.

USB—Stands for universal serial bus. A low- to moderate-speed plug-and-play peripheral standard developed by Intel that is used on Macs for the keyboard, mouse, digital cameras, drives, and printers. A high-speed variation, USB 2.0, debuted early in 2001 but had not been supported by Apple at the time this book was written. Compare with *FireWire*, which handles high-speed peripheral devices.

View menu—A menu available from the desktop or Finder that sets Finder viewing options, such as icon or column view, and whether the toolbar buttons should appear.

virtual memory—A method used to extend the memory available to your Mac by allocating a portion of your hard drive as a swap file. When built-in memory is not sufficient to meet operating system or program needs, Mac OS X uses the file to swap unneeded data. Beginning with Mac OS X, the memory needs of an application are established dynamically as needed.

virus—Computer code that attaches itself to a program or document and causes an unsavory side effect (a silly message or, at worst, damage to the file or drive) or that just replicates itself and passes itself on to another program or document. All personal computers are vulnerable to viruses, and it's a good idea to purchase up-to-date software to protect your Mac.

Glossary

Web (World Wide Web)—The preeminent Internet feature that provides animation and graphical and text displays of information. The Web is read by using a program called a browser. See also *Web browser*.

Web browser—A program designed to view documents created for display on the Web. The most popular Web browsers are Microsoft Internet Explorer and Netscape Navigator (or Communicator). A third Web program, OmniWeb, supports only Mac OS X.

Web page—A single document designed for display on the Web.

Web site—A location on the Web that contains one or more Web pages and is designed for business or personal use (or both).

window—A rectangular (or square) object that displays the contents of a document or directory.

Window menu—The window used to select from open document or folder windows.

Wireless Internet—Technologies that use either satellite transmissions or fixed wireless transmission systems to deliver high-speed Internet to a home or office without the need for a wired connection. An example of such a service is Sprint Broadband Direct (a service being phased out due to high costs and network bottlenecks).

ZIP—A compression format that works on PCs, Macintoshes, and Unix-based computers (although it's primarily oriented towards the DOS/Windows markets). The ZIP file format employs mathematical algorithms to reduce the space that the files take up on the computer. Zipped files are also frequently sent over the Internet because they can check themselves for consistency when the file is being expanded. See also *StuffIt*.

Zip drive—A removable storage device from Iomega Corporation. This drive uses media that look like thick floppy disks and store either 100MB or 250MB of data (depending on the kind of drive and media type you use).

Glossary

Index